THE
Second Battle
of New Orleans

THE
Second Battle of New Orleans

THE HUNDRED-YEAR STRUGGLE TO INTEGRATE THE SCHOOLS

Liva Baker

HarperCollins*Publishers*

HarperCollins books may be purchased for educational, business, or sales promotional use. For information please write: Special Markets Department, Harper-Collins Publishers, Inc., 10 East 53rd Street, New York, NY 10022.

FIRST EDITION

Designed by Alma Hochhauser Orenstein

Library of Congress Cataloging-in-Publication Data

Baker, Liva.
    The second battle of New Orleans : the hundred-year struggle to integrate the schools / by Liva Baker. — 1st ed.
        p.   cm.
    Includes bibliographical references and index.
    ISBN 0-06-016808-0
    1. School integration—Louisiana—New Orleans—History—20th century.
2. Afro-Americans—Education—Louisiana—New Orleans—History—20th century.   I. Title.
LC214.23.N46B35   1996
370.19'342—dc20   96-4158

96 97 98 99 00 ❖/RRD 10 9 8 7 6 5 4 3 2 1

To Sylvia Frey
with thanks

Contents

Illustrations follow page 244.

Acknowledgments

My first and largest debt is, as always, to the Library of Congress: all those men and women in the general reading rooms, the manuscript room, the law library and the periodicals reading room who eased the burdens of research, plus the study facilities staff who provided me with a cubbyhole in which to do it.

I also want to thank

The staff at the Amistad Research Center in New Orleans. Former archivist Andy Simons's winning ways with audiotapes deserve special mention, as does Elise Dunn Cain's vast knowledge of New Orleans's black community; those few members she doesn't know personally, she can usually track down;

The staff of the Earl K. Long Library at the University of New Orleans, especially Beatrice Owsley and Clive Hardy;

Esme Bahn, formerly of the Moorland-Spingarn Research Center at Howard University. Her unique archival knowledge is missed;

Molly and Leonard Curry for their continued interest and hospitality;

Jean Danielson, a transplanted Chicagoan whose knack with etouffe would make you think she was a native New Orleanian;

John Lovett, who made invaluable suggestions;

The Honorable Eleanor Holmes Norton, whose staff helped to pry loose material from a sluggish Federal Bureau of Investigation;

Adell Wade, who kept the home fires burning;

Irene Wainwright, Louisiana room, New Orleans Public Library;

The Honorable John Minor Wisdom, who kindly tracked down a judicial obscurity for me;

All those who trudged through all or part of the manuscript at early stages and generously offered comments: David Baker, Sylvia Frey, Sheila Gellman, Andrea Kerr, Mort Lebow (who, unbelievably, read the whole thing twice—something far above and beyond the call of friendship), Joseph Logsdon and Jane Ann Spellman;

All those who shared their memories of the struggle for the schools in New Orleans;

My fellow writers and scholars on the fifth floor of the Adams Building at the Library of Congress who tolerated my teeth-gnashing and bad jokes with good humor;

My agent, David Black, who believed in the project when few others did—except my children and they didn't have a choice;

And at HarperCollins, M. S. Wyeth, Jr. His nickname is "Buz," and it was an easy step of transference to think of him as the "buzz saw." But in retrospect, it was he who kept the book within reasonable bounds.

Foreword

When this book, which tells the story of the hundred years' war for the New Orleans schools, first took shape in my head, it was to be an essay on courage, specifically the courage shown by J. Skelly Wright, the white federal district judge for the Eastern District of Louisiana during the time of the main action. His development from "just another southern 'boy'" to a passionate advocate of civil rights who years later wept over the "dream" of Dr. Martin Luther King, Jr., his square-jawed defiance of Louisiana's entire government, his endurance of vilification and ostracism were the stuff of which American legends are made.

As I dug deeper into the material and talked with participants in the desegregation of the city's schools, I became increasingly aware of the courage of others: of A. P. Tureaud, the black Creole lawyer whose vision of a better world built by black and white together drove him, day after humiliating day for forty years, into Louisiana's courtrooms dominated in the early days by white judges, white lawyers and white staff, most of whom had only contempt for the man they considered an intruder; of young Joe McKelpin, a black teacher in a black public school who was on the verge of promotion but was fired instead because he had the nerve to sue the school board to bring his salary into line with that of his white counterparts; of Ruby Bridges, a six-year-old black girl who single-handedly desegregated the William Frantz school, although for the first year she had to make her way through a mob of booing, spitting, egg-throwing white women.

Gradually, the focus of the book changed. The story of courage in one man broadened into the story of courage in many along with the lack of it in others, the New Orleanians who kept silent, rode out the crisis as if it were just another hurricane off the Gulf and not a moral issue, leaving a void for the demagogues to fill.

I began, too, to ask myself what I would have done in similar circumstances. I asked the question every time I read one of Skelly Wright's unflinching orders, every time A. P. Tureaud confronted the white legal establishment, every time Ruby Bridges marched straightbacked into the Frantz school. And every time I came up with the same answer:

I don't know.

What follows is not a pretty story. I think, though, that if we are ever going to live together amicably, races, ethnic groups, the religious and the doubters, men and women in *all* their various and splendid guises, it behooves all of us who have been thrown together on this wayward planet to look deeply into ourselves, and to look back, to try to understand the directional signals the past has given for the future, to learn from our experience, especially, perhaps, when it isn't pretty.

CHAPTER I

"Two, Four, Six, Eight, We Don't Want to Integrate"

D uring the time of the troubles, as white southerners, their way of life threatened as it had not been for a hundred years, their collective psyche simultaneously pulled by their oldest traditions and pushed by contemporary realities, groped for answers to questions that had gone largely unasked before, a friend was instructing the future Nobel laureate for literature, John Steinbeck, in the complexities of southern racial mores. He particularly wanted to convey the notion that "separate but equal," the white South's* formula for successful relations between the races in public places, especially schools, which were the fortresses of intellectual and emotional Jim Crow, was by far the most effective route to compatibility between black and white.

"It just happens," the fellow argued, "that in my own town there are three new Negro schools not equal but superior to the white schools. Now wouldn't you think they would be satisfied with that? And in the bus stations the washrooms are exactly the same. What's your answer to that?"

Steinbeck suggested that perhaps the blacks in his friend's community had been misinformed and that switching schools and toilets might clear up the confusion. "The moment," Steinbeck explained, "they realized that your schools weren't as good as theirs, they would realize their error."

---

*South is a sprawling term. Unless otherwise noted, my South is limited to the eleven states of the former Confederacy—Alabama, Arkansas, Florida, Georgia, Louisiana, Mississippi, North Carolina, South Carolina, Tennessee, Texas, Virginia—a discrete emotional as well as geographical and political entity.

The smile on his friend's face could not entirely mask the sharpness of the fellow's reply:

"You troublemaking son of a bitch."

Two, four, six, eight,
We don't want to integrate

rose in a descant above the cacophony of insults and obscenities shrieked by a crowd of angry white women in pincurlers and toreador pants lining the sidewalks leading to the William Frantz Elementary School in a blue-collar section of New Orleans. Their chanting set the pace for a six-year-old black girl, who thought it sounded like a nursery rhyme, to march toward the redbrick building on the sultry, sullen morning of Monday, November 14, 1960. Until that moment, the student body of the William Frantz Elementary School had been entirely white.

The little girl's name was Ruby Bridges, but that wasn't generally known at the time. Her identity had been kept secret in order to avoid harassment of her or her family. She was braving the crowd's hostility because her mother, the daughter of Mississippi sharecroppers, who could read a little and write a very little, "wanted it better for [her] kids."

Steinbeck, who visited New Orleans a few weeks later and watched as the disturbances continued, described Ruby in his best-selling *Travels with Charley* as "the littlest Negro girl you ever saw, dressed in starchy white, with new white shoes on feet so little they were almost round." As tomatoes, rotten eggs, and spittle whizzed over her head, barely missing her, she looked, said Steinbeck, like a "frightened fawn." The hair ribbon on her pigtail bobbed up and down exuding a perkiness nobody felt.

A few blocks away, at McDonogh 19 Elementary School, three other little black girls—Tessie Prevost, Gail Etienne, and Leona Tate—were the targets of similar attacks. Together, the four girls were the first black children to enter an all-white school in New Orleans since Reconstruction.

Grim-faced federal marshals, the bulge of their guns barely visible under their coats, flanked the children at both schools. The men could protect them from physical harm, but not from the sting of the verbal assaults.

The law suit responsible for the children's admission to the white schools in the fall of 1960, *Bush* v. *Orleans Parish* School Board,* was already eight years old—older than Ruby Bridges and the other three

---

*In Louisiana, the term *parish*, derived from the ecclesiastical term for the original subdivisions of Roman Catholic church jurisdiction, today denotes the political subdivision other states call counties.

black girls entering white schools. Earl Benjamin Bush, the youth whose name it carried, had been sixteen when the suit was filed in federal court in 1952, two years before the United States Supreme Court had announced in *Brown* v. *Board of Education of Topeka* that racial segregation in public schools violated the federal Constitution. A man now, Earl Bush was long gone from the New Orleans school system.

Bush seemed old for a law suit, but the local school board, pushed by state officialdom, all of them claiming to represent the will of white New Orleans, had obstructed school desegregation all that time. Frank T. Read and Lucy McGough in their book *Let Them Be Judged* described New Orleans's eight-year struggle over desegregation, which sorely tried the concept of federal supremacy hard-won on the battlefield a century ago, as an "encyclopedia of every tactic of resistance employed by all the other states combined."

Until November 14, 1960, however, a day that became known in New Orleans annals as D-Day, the generals had played out their aggressions in the courtroom and on the floor of the legislature, their weapons limited to words and legal and political maneuvering. Now with the reality of the dreaded school desegregation descending on the city, long pent-up emotions had erupted.

Between the summer of 1954 when the Supreme Court had ruled school segregation unlawful and the fall of 1960 when New Orleanians faced the unmwelcome difficulties of school desegregation, a few cities in border states had obeyed the Court's orders and allowed blacks to enter all-white public schools: some, like Little Rock, Arkansas, under duress; others, like Baltimore, Maryland, voluntarily. But no large city in the deep South in 1960 had complied with the Court's directives.

New Orleans, with a public school population of 90, 693–52, 581 of whom were nonwhite—was the first, the test case. Atlanta, scheduled to begin the process the following fall, was watching anxiously, as were Savannah, Charleston, Birmingham, and Dallas, for which it would be only a matter of time. Writing in the *New Republic* in February, 1959, Helen Fuller had described New Orleans as potentially "the chink in the wall of 'states' rights' defiance of the Supreme Court," the deep South city programmed by its past and present to lead its sister cities in peaceful public school desegregation.

Rising at the mouth of the Mississippi River, 125 navigable miles from the Gulf of Mexico, New Orleans was no backwater bayou town. Having put twentieth-century technology to work for it to keep the river, which was fed, sometimes overfed, by the Ohio, Missouri, Arkansas, and others, within its banks, it was the nation's third (after New York and Houston) busiest port in 1960, an outpost of unsouthern hustle. With its population of 627,525, it was the South's second (to Houston) largest city. In appearance its business section was indistinguishable from Detroit's or Omaha's.

Its family tree looked like no other in America. Following subjugation of the native Choctaw, Chickasaw, and Natchez tribes, the city had been governed successively by French cavaliers, who gave the city its permanent aroma of French roast, Spanish conquistadors, American bureaucrats, Yankee General Benjamin F. "Beast" Butler, and northern carpetbaggers. When the modern city emerged in the late nineteenth century, its population had been further leavened by waves of Irish, German, and Italian immigrants. Blacks—233,514 in 1960—whose music, folklore, and literature had etched such deep lines on New Orleans's face that historian Gwendolyn Midlo Hall called the city "in spirit the most African city in the United States," were the constant in the colorful entrepôt.

Known in 1960 for its good food, good music, and annual madcap revel, Mardi Gras, New Orleans was seen as an intoxicating, sensual Latin-flavored Mediterranean metropolis, a Marseilles transplanted to the jasmine-scented American South. Neither its weather, which was perfect for the breeding of mosquitoes, nor its unusual open tolerance for vice and political corruption detracted from its reputation as a thoroughly charming, colorful, cultured, and cosmopolitan place, truly a "City That Care Forgot," as the travel guides put it.

As a testing ground for school desegregation, it seemed about right. It appeared to lack the rigidity of Montgomery or Memphis, to have, on the surface, the least southern mindset of any deep South city, its mixed cultural heritage offering the best conditions for social change, even change involving so long settled a matter as relations between the races.

New Orleans, however, was less a place apart than it looked. As the scenes at Frantz and McDonogh 19 that day demonstrated, white New Orleanians had their share of bigotry. Over the years they had devised segregation codes every bit as harsh as Birmingham's.

Black resentment had been building over the two and a half centuries since the first slave ship arrived in 1719, a year after the city's founding, and in 1960 had come to focus on the physical deterioration and overcrowding of the blatantly inferior schools provided by white officials for blacks. The reservoir of racial bitterness that overflowed during the desegregation of New Orleans's schools, manifesting itself most prominently in near riots at the chosen schools, could hardly have been reassuring to her sister cities.

*   *   *

That same day in Baton Rouge, the state capital some eighty miles upriver, Louisiana's white lawmakers, who had been quick to smell political profit in the race issue the minute the U.S. Supreme Court ruled out school segregation, were responding to the crisis in New Orleans by turning the special session of the legislature, called ten days before, into a political wilding. It was an unusual development in Louisiana, which was not in the habit of producing racial demagogues. In general the Negro-baiting "Pitchfork" Ben Tillmans and Theodore Bilbos fared better in the richer racist soil of South Carolina and Mississippi.

But in the fall of 1960, a majority of the legislators came from the rolling red clay hills of rural north Louisiana where segregationist sentiment was running high. Believing that if they couldn't stop racial mixing in the New Orleans schools, the rest of the state would soon be engulfed, they had decided to make their stand there. Their employment of every available means short of violence to stop school desegregation marked the climax in the century-old blood feud between state and federal governments.

In six hundred well-chosen words, polite but firm, United States Attorney General William P. Rogers had warned the Louisiana governor not to interfere with the federal court's order to desegregate the New Orleans schools. Nonetheless James Houston ("You Are My Sunshine") Davis, who had invited members of the National Association for the Advancement of Colored People—colloquially, the N-double A-C-P—*not* to vote for him in the recent gubernatorial election, which he had then won handily largely on the strength of his stand for preserving racial segregation, was still committed to maintaining the tradition despite the federal official's warning.

But Davis talked a better war than he wanted to wage, and for all his talk, he preferred to avoid the kind of confrontation the New Orleans crisis foreshadowed. It was he who had called the special legislative session, and as the head of state, he remained nominally in charge, but he was a front man, really. It was Leander H. Perez, legendary political boss of Plaquemines Parish, local pit bull of segregation, and segregationist czar of the South, who was driving the state during the 1960 school crisis.

It was Perez who was devising the legislative strategy, Perez who was powering the virulently segregationist White Citizens' Council, Perez who was behind the growing interest in private schools as alternatives to desegregation, and Perez, it was widely believed, who was having outsiders bused into New Orleans to fill out the ranks of the neighborhood women who were so stridently protesting the desegregation of the Frantz and McDonogh 19 schools.

His pompadour had turned to a delicate shade of pewter since he'd been an architect of the Dixiecrats' angry secession from the Democratic Party in 1948. At five feet nine inches and 188 pounds, his sixty-nine-year-old body was still compact, hard, and his posture was erect. Speaking to friendly audiences, his charm, impeccable manners, and native dignity prevailed, but serious debate could send him spinning out of control, revealing the tempests within and bringing out all the ruthlessness and bigotry of which he was capable.

Perez hated blacks and Jews about equally. He professed to believe that both groups were connected to a Communist conspiracy to destroy the United States by "mongrelization," and he liked to quote from the 1902 edition of the *Encyclopaedia Britannica* to support his own theory that blacks were inferior because of inadequate brain cavities.

He had only contempt for the United States Supreme Court, which over the last two decades had applied the federal scalpel to southern tradition through its decisions empowering blacks, particularly its decisions of 1954 and 1955 ordering the racial desegregation of public schools. The Court, he would thunder, had "plainly usurped powers it does not have under the Constitution."

He hadn't missed a session of the state legislature in fifty years. They called him the "third house of the legislature" and they were only half joking. He'd swagger around the floor, laze in the lawmakers' chairs, even address the Speaker, though he'd never been a member of either house. Governor Davis had given him a certificate entitling him to exceed the speed limit on his frequent drives between Plaquemines Parish, where he lived, and Baton Rouge, where he spent an inordinate amount of time.

His devotion and dedication to the cause of segregation combined with his brilliance as a constitutional lawyer made Perez a formidable player in the political game Louisianans were playing in 1960. He did not, however, rely entirely on his zeal or intellectual inspiration. He also did his homework. Prodigious amounts of it. He had familiarized himself thoroughly with segregation cases currently before the courts throughout the South. He kept files on legal arguments for use in future cases. And he maintained close and constant contact with segregation leaders in neighboring states. He sucked up information with the efficiency of a vacuum cleaner, digested it, and used it to draft the legislation he fed in a steady flow to his allies in the state senate and house. It was commonchange knowledge around the capitol that Perez could write a bill any way a lawmaker wanted it.

Down at the federal courthouse in New Orleans—officially the Federal District Court for the Eastern District of Louisiana, that repository of majesty and power known to New Orleanians, not particularly affectionately, as the Yankee Court—J. (for James) Skelly (which everyone called him) Wright, "Judas Scalawag" Wright as local segregationists were referring to him now, was issuing order after order nullifying the enactments of one of the most rambunctious legislatures in the history of a politically rambunctious state. Before the crisis ended, he would slap down nearly one hundred such measures.

New Orleans born, bred, and educated, Wright was forty-nine years old in 1960, a veteran of a decade on the federal bench. His uncomplicated face was still wrinkle-free. Horn-rimmed glasses, roughly the color of his thinning brown hair, framed his sharp blue eyes, which had both austerity and gentleness in them. He had the complexion of a brunette with redheads in his background.

The built-in theatrical quality of the courtroom—the black robe clothing power contained, the elevation of the bench adding height to its occupant—created an image of strength and resolve. Some years later, the plaintiff in one of his cases was astonished when, meeting Wright outside the courtroom for the first time, he realized that he himself actually towered over the judge.

Wright was known as a low-key judge who wielded his authority quietly but nonetheless firmly. It was his handling of the various parties to New Orleans's school crisis that demonstrated just how formidable the determination of this reserved, soft-spoken man could be.

Before he became a judge, Wright had been, as he himself confessed, just "another southern 'boy,'" silently acquiescing in the traditional local arrangements for the coexistence of the races. After he became a judge and confronted the judicial precedents of the recent past, especially the voting rights and university segregation suits, he became a vigorous supporter of blacks' civil rights, some inner moral compass seeming to reinforce the newly acquired legal certainties.

There had been opposition a couple of years before to his order to desegregate the city's public transportation system, but that had amounted to no more than a nip at the heels compared with the angry snarls and ever closer snapping he was enduring since he ordered the local schools to desegregate. The first federal district judge to issue such an order, he stood alone now with no precedent or pattern to guide him, vulnerable to incessant attacks on his character and his judging. Because some of this recent opposition came from friends, people in positions of leadership whom he had respected, he had occasional twinges of doubt about the course he now set for himself.

There was, however, no retreat. Fighter-pilot cool, and keeping to himself his concern for the safety of his wife and son as the ugliness of

the mood in the city intensified, he stood firm, his principles not nego-
tiable. "May his name go down in the annals of heroic Irishmen," prayed
W. J. Weatherby, a reporter for the *Manchester Guardian Weekly.*

A. P. Tureaud's full name was Alexander Pierre Tureaud, but like
many black lawyers of his time and place, he used only initials, hoping to
escape the humiliation of white judges and lawyers reminding him of his
inferior status by using his given name as if he were a ten-year-old.
Although he frequently had to look hate in the eye, he brought his natural dignity and soft-spokenness to his role as a courtroom gladiator,
which he had been for twenty-five years when in 1952 he marched on the
federal court in New Orleans brandishing the suit to desegregate the
local schools.

Over the years since his admission to the state bar in 1927, there had
been periods when he was the only black lawyer in Louisiana, and he'd
had to leapfrog from court to court, parish to parish, filing petitions in St.
Helena Parish to force white registrars to enroll blacks on the voting
lists, in Ouachita Parish to demand equalization of white and black
school facilities, in New Orleans to equalize the salaries of white and
black teachers, in Baton Rouge to desegregate the state university. He'd
testified before the state board of pardons on behalf of criminal defendants; investigated reports of lynchings at Minden and rape charges at
the state hospital in Jackson; looked into police brutality in New Iberia,
racial disturbances at the state penitentiary in Angola, and beatings of
Negro voting registrants by the St. Landry sheriff at Opelousas; and listened to horror stories of racial discrimination whenever he stood still
long enough.

He hadn't time to answer all the letters, no matter how indignant,
outraged, or sad they were. People said he always seemed to be in a
hurry, and he gave off an impression of flying shirttails. He appeared to
gain rather than lose momentum as he approached his middle years, and
he proposed to fight as long as "there's breath in me."

He was bucking two and a half centuries of custom and tradition. His
race subjected him to constant humiliation. He never knew when violence lurked in the shadows. So far the worst that had happened to him
personally was being run off a country road in his car into a ditch. The
worst public confrontation in which he'd been involved was D-Day in
New Orleans. But he could not and did not allow the insults, inevitable
defeats, the fears and apprehensions to distract him from his purpose,
which was to use the law to treat the pathology of race and thereby alter
the course of the society in which he lived.

On D-Day, Tureaud and Dan Byrd, the NAACP field secretary who'd recruited the plaintiffs for the school suit, along with Thurgood Marshall, the NAACP-affiliated Legal Defense Fund's chief counsel who'd come south to watch firsthand the first court-ordered school desegregation, plus a posse of other NAACP officials, were spending the long and disheartening hours glued to the radio in Byrd's home a few blocks from McDonogh 19. As fast as the legislators passed obstructionist measures, the lawyers at the Byrd house prepared petitions for restraining orders, then rushed them to the federal courthouse for Skelly Wright to sign. Although Wright was doing his best to keep up and was backed by the full force of the federal government, Tureaud was worried, afraid New Orleans would become another Virginia, where militant segregationists had forced the closing of the public schools.

The serene mood along New Orleans's grandest boulevard, St. Charles Avenue, which bisects the fashionable uptown section of the city, contrasted sharply with that in the blue collar section of downtown where the two desegregating schools were located. Genteel St. Charles, with its Victorian mansions interspersed with Greek Revival and Georgian plantationlike structures, all surrounded by luxuriant Spanish moss, oleanders, and bougainvillea kept manicured by black groundsmen, was home to the white men—and in the New Orleans of the 1950s and 1960s, they were practically all men—who set the community's tone: the leading bankers, lawyers, clergymen, real estate titans, and corporate executives. It was a place not only geographically but also psychologically remote from the disturbances across town.

For more than four years after Skelly Wright first ordered the local schools to desegregate, these mandarins had demonstrated vividly just how remote they were. With a few notable exceptions, they had said and done nothing to ease the tensions the racial conflict was bringing, and nothing to encourage New Orleanians to obey or to honor the federal Constitution, leaving a vacuum for the rabble-rousers to fill. They waited to speak out until the very last minute, and then it was too little and too late.

They were a homogeneous group, a small hereditary clique of white elite connected by family, tradition, religion (largely Protestant), and money, although it was far more important to have an ancestor who'd settled in the city 100 or 150 years before, or a grandfather who'd fought in the Confederate army than any amount of wealth. Upper-class New Orleanians in fact prided themselves on their dissimilarity to those they considered the money-grubbers of Atlanta and Houston. A former king of Mardi Gras, the very peak of social prominence, could descend to running a boardinghouse, if it was financially necessary, without losing his social standing. A newcomer on the other hand had about the same chance of buying his way into New Orleans society as had the biblical rich man of buying his way into heaven.

These weren't Negro haters or baiters. They assumed blacks' contentment with the quasi-feudalistic social system—a remnant of slavery—and they were quick to demonstrate their racial tolerance with stories of maids, cooks, and nurses with whom they'd grown up in affectionate familylike relationships.

Most wouldn't have joined a White Citizens' Council for all the tea in China. But they had been painfully slow to publicly support the local school board in its hour of crisis, and when they finally did, they hid behind euphemisms and ignored the real issues. Now, while racial turmoil unhinged the neighborhoods around the Frantz and McDonogh schools, they were going ahead with the preparations for the approaching Carnival season as if nothing more momentous than the timeless measured lapping of the Mississippi against the levees had occurred since last year's bacchanal.

The parades and balls of Carnival always began on January 6, Epiphany, and climaxed on Mardi Gras, or Shrove Tuesday, the final feast before Lenten fasting. This year it would fall on February 14, 1961.

Mardi Gras was New Orleans and New Orleans was Mardi Gras. On this one day the city revealed its French spontaneity, Spanish piquancy, and American commercialism, its Christian affinities and its pagan soul. This year, as the jaybirds jeered in the camphor trees, there were subterranean rumblings and a fear that all might not be well for the holiday.

Black resentment of the vicious white opposition to school desegregation, the latest in the series of local racial encounters over black access to white facilities—whites had given up nothing voluntarily, not the public library, not the city-operated recreation facilities, not public transportation, not their monopoly on the franchise—had blacks, including the famous Zulu maskers, now talking about boycotting Mardi Gras. The Zulu parade, which traditionally opened the festivities on Mardi Gras morning, was one of the most popular attractions of the day. It began with the landing of King Zulu and his zany entourage—a band of African-Americans made up in blackface and wearing grass skirts—at the Poydras Street Wharf, then parading joyfully through the black sections of the city aboard tinseled floats, clowning, tossing painted coconuts to the shouting crowds, and stopping frequently for liquid refreshment. But it was beginning to look and feel like the old minstrel show, too undignified, and blacks had wearied of playing what they had come to believe was a collective modern-day version of Sambo at a time when they were embroiled in a fight for human rights. They didn't want to be entertainers anymore. They wanted respect, not laughter, and as night fell on New Orleans, and the city was quiet following the first day of demonstrations protesting school desegregation, they were having second thoughts about their role in the upcoming holiday fun.

The advanced state of communications in November 1960 made certain that the pain in one part of America could nevermore be localized, and as events spun out in New Orleans, the entire nation, along with much of the western world, watched—and wondered. The photos that flashed across television screens during that evening's newscasts—four defenseless six-year-old black girls entering two all-white elementary schools under a barrage of threats, curses, and garbage—revealed a dark side of the city that was not always visible beneath its otherwise mellow veneer.

CHAPTER 2

The "Stubborn" Creoles

D uring one of the "trying periods" of racial upheaval preceding D-Day, one of his friends had told A. P. Tureaud, the lawyer who'd nursed the school segregation case that climaxed in the disturbances of November 1960 through its eight years of courtroom contention, that he was a "stubborn creole." The description had been intended as a compliment, and although Tureaud, a genteel and dignified man for all his mulishness, might have preferred a more decorous *persevering* or *resolute* to characterize him, he probably was pleased with his friend's choice of words. He *was* stubborn. A knight-errant had to be.

Activism, protest, and not a little of his stubbornness had come in Tureaud's genes. He came from a local society called black Creoles whose golden age spanned the middle to late nineteenth century. An intellectually vigorous and politically aggressive group with a tradition of organized resistance to racial injustice unmatched in the South at the time, particularly, but not limited to, the injustice they perceived in school segregation, they were the subversives of their time and place.

Resistance. But not rabble-rousing or rebellion or riot. In general, these protesters were educated, politically astute men of some means, professional men with substantial financial and deep emotional investment in their community, and, like Tureaud later, who was familiar with their history and had caught his own activism from them, preferred discussion to disturbance, court suit to street confrontation, assimilation to alienation. But let no man mistake their good manners for weakness of will.

The name *black Creole* evokes romantic images of liaisons between wealthy white men and handsome, cultivated light-skinned Negro women meeting at antebellum New Orleans's famous quadroon balls to contract alliances known as *plaçage*. The women were usually settled in comfortable little houses at the edge of town; offspring generally took their father's name. Daughters were brought up to carry on the tradition into which they'd been born; sons were usually educated and placed on plantations or in local offices. *Plaçage* arrangements lasted anywhere from a few months to life. Some historians regarded the system as institutionalized common-law marriage; others viewed it as outright prostitution.

An important fact of social life in New Orleans at the time, *plaçage* was, however, peripheral to the main currents of black Creole culture. A flavorful blend of Europe and Africa, the black Creole society had been a dynamic of the multicolored and multicultural city for a century and a half.

An exact meaning of the word *Creole* is elusive. It has been redefined over and over during its long life. Originally from the Portuguese *crioulo*, meaning a slave of African ancestry born in America, it came to include Europeans born in the New World. The nineteenth-century activists to whom A. P. Tureaud felt strong kinship mostly traced their origins to eighteenth-century unions of French and Spanish settlers with indigenous Indian women, African slaves, and black refugees from later political upheavals in the Caribbean. They were also called *gens de couleur,* people of color, and many carried French and Spanish names.

Their color ranged from very dark to very light, and there were always some who disappeared into white society. In the local patois, the passage was called *passe en blanc.* Lest they suffer embarrassment in their new lives, their black Creole brothers and sisters often omitted their names from newspaper announcements of deaths in the family.

The Tureauds were light skinned, as one of them put it, "caught between the devil and the deep blue sea. They looked white, and they felt like they were black." A. P. himself, with his pale complexion, straight hair, and no hint of Africa in his face, could easily have passed for white. Two of his sisters did. The Tureauds didn't talk much about them. They might as well have been dead.

White New Orleans boxed black Creoles with the rest of the city's blacks, but in fact they were a culture apart. The black Creole historian Rodolphe Desdunes later characterized his people as "Latin Negroes" as opposed to the "Anglo-Saxon" or "American" Negroes. They lived apart; Latin Negroes concentrated largely downtown among the immigrants of all colors and hues near the river, and American Negroes clustered upriver above Canal Street. They worshipped different gods, black Creoles being largely Catholic, American Negroes largely Protestant. Language further separated them, many black Creoles speaking more French than English, American Negroes speaking largely English.

But most important perhaps, black Creoles thought French. American blacks thought Anglo-Saxon, particularly where politics was involved. Their vision of what to expect from life differed sharply, and neither of the two groups fully trusted the other politically.

The Latin Negro, heir to the French tradition of *liberté, égalité, fraternité,* worked for a future in which all color lines would disappear entirely, when all children would be welcomed to all schools, and people would ask, "What was segregation, anyway?" The American Negro at the time tended to shield himself from race discrimination by living apart in black institutions he had erected for the purpose. The American Negro craved education, too, but made his stand for *liberté* and *égalité* and didn't concern himself much with the *fraternité.* As a result the two often worked at cross purposes, each resenting the other's unwillingness to work together, to present a united front to the white world.

Eighteenth-century French and Spanish rule, relatively if not entirely relaxed in matters of race, had black Creoles living proudly if often precariously outside both the American black and the American white social orders, enjoying most economic and legal rights afforded white New Orleanians. But they were largely excluded from white political and social spheres, and they had developed a certain outspokenness along with the confidence to have their say and the determination to back it up. Following President Jefferson's purchase of Louisiana in 1803 and the transfer of political power to the less relaxed Anglo-Americans from the North and East whose social vision did not include assimilation of black cultures, Louisiana's black Creoles were gradually penned with the Negroes and their traditional rights curtailed.

After 1803, they were subjected to the same indignities in the law books and on the city's streets as were all blacks. The state constitution of 1812 kept them off the voting rolls. City ordinances separated them from white New Orleanians on public transportation and, until Reconstruction, in theaters and the opera house. Restaurants and saloons were segregated. Neither fraternal orders nor private clubs admitted blacks, and hotels were entirely off-limits—though the black personal servants of whites were readily admitted. Charity Hospital segregated its wards. In 1835 the city council passed a measure zoning cemeteries into separate sections for whites (half), free Negroes (a quarter), and slaves (a quarter). Whites and blacks were not only segregated in the city jail but were issued uniforms of different colors.

The black Creole culture, concentrated in downtown New Orleans near the river, nonetheless flourished throughout the nineteenth century. Economic status ranged from a few planters rich enough to own slaves themselves, to poor menial laborers who were treated almost like slaves. Most fell somewhere in between. A professional corps of physicians, lawyers, teachers, and the like developed. Black creole merchants found profit in the booming port business. A cadre of skilled artisans sprang up; much of the trademark ironwork that outlines the balconies and stairwells of the old city was wrought by black Creoles. An artistic community of musicians, sculptors, playwrights, and poets immortalized their culture. Gentility was important to black Creole life at all economic levels. They took pride in "good things," a fine clock or a vase; those who could afford it patronized the opera and read widely. School Superintendent Mortimer A. Warren bragged in 1866: "We have in our city the colored intelligence of the whole South."

For black Creoles, education was where ideals and reality, principles and practicalities intersected, an article of the democratic faith and one of the most important. But access to it in antebellum New Orleans had been fraught with barriers and obstacles since 1724 when the Code Noir strictly limited slave learning to the reading and writing necessary to religious life. The way black Creoles saw it, the century and a half that followed was a bitter struggle against white institutions, white law, and white government supported by a white majority population intent on frustrating black aspirations for social, economic, and political progress by denying education.

To the white ruling class, on the other hand, the education of the blacks among them was dynamite. Knowledge was power and not to be shared. Black education threatened the very foundation of the fiction of white cultural and intellectual superiority, injected another element of competition into the labor market, and fomented rebellion among slaves, for which they had plentiful evidence, pointing to a spate of insurrections across the South—Gabriel Prosser's and Nat Turner's in Virginia, Denmark Vesey's in South Carolina, and closer to home, uprisings in St. John the Baptist and St. Bernard parishes in Louisiana. By 1830, anyone in New Orleans caught teaching a slave to read or write at all risked a month to a year in prison. When the city's public school system was finally organized in 1841, state statutes prohibited even free blacks from attending.

When John McDonogh, an eccentric local millionaire with a social conscience and the patron saint of public education in New Orleans, died in 1850, he left the bulk of his estate for the education of poor children— all poor children: "Both sexes and all classes and all castes of color"—in

New Orleans where he'd made his fortune and in his hometown of Baltimore. McDonogh's wishes notwithstanding, New Orleans's share of the money went into the new public school system, which was off-limits to blacks. At the end of the Civil War, white illiteracy stood at 6.5 percent, black at 61 percent.

Black Creoles, however, were not without resources. What they couldn't get legally, they bootlegged. Many of the light-skinned among them "passed" into white schools without discovery. A few free blacks risked establishing their own schools, and while the law winked at their parochial institutions, the secular had to be kept secret, their classes held in private homes of undistinguished appearance. Not all disguised their purposes successfully, and one John F. Cook, a white man from St. Louis intending to open a school for free blacks, barely escaped ahead of the law after his barber warned him he was about to be arrested. In 1850, a thousand free blacks attended private schools. Black Creoles who could afford it, and many could, sent their sons and daughters out of the city to be educated. The North and West attracted some. Paris was particularly popular. Finding the foreign political climate less oppressive than that of New Orleans, some of the most talented remained abroad for years, even permanently.

All of which accommodated the well-to-do. The city's poor blacks, however, had nowhere to go until Marie Couvent died.

A free black African-born widow, Madame Couvent was herself unlettered, but, as the black Creole historian Rodolphe Desdunes described her in *Nos Hommes et Notre Histoire* (*Our People and Our History*), she was a pious and charitable woman "blessed with a wealth of common sense" and a "deep compassion for children condemned to live without the advantages of education in the midst of so much indifference and even hostility toward a class of people sorely tried." When she died in 1837, she left her fortune in real estate for the establishment of a school for needy black Catholic orphans. Implementation of her stated wishes required more than a decade, the delay due in part to fear of offending the white establishment. But when it opened in 1848, the Institution Catholique des Orphelins Indigents admitted not only black orphans but also a large number of boys and girls who were neither Catholic nor orphaned but only black and poor. The pretense was, however, maintained, less to honor Madame Couvent's wishes than to conceal from the authorities the school's larger purpose of producing a class of educated blacks and black Creoles.

Continuing support came from philanthropic black Creoles who understood the value of educating the young of their community. Appearing to fall for the cover story that the school was only an orphanage, the state legislature actually appropriated small sums for its maintenance. The Institution Catholique was the first free school for children of color opened not only in New Orleans but in the United States. At its high point, 250 children were taught in both French and English by a black faculty.

Having to bootleg their education, in addition to the other humiliations of race in New Orleans, further fueled black Creole resentment. In war, they'd given freely of their blood beginning in 1727 in the battles against the Choctaw. Upward of 400 free blacks had fought with distinction alongside General Andrew Jackson's 3,000 white troops at the Battle of New Orleans in 1814 while their nurses tended the wounded. In peace, they'd contributed handsomely to the cultural life of the city, its political life whenever they'd been allowed, and they were expected to pay their taxes like everybody else. They felt they deserved better.

Their literature, their art, their music—all of it is suffused with themes of grievance against the injustices black Creoles suffered because of their race. Their most famous publication, *Les Cenelles,* an anthology of black Creole poetry that appeared in 1845, contains the usual assortment of love poems, historical epics, and hymns to nature, but the thread that binds the collection together is the authors' protests against racial prejudice and persecution, and the overall feelings the work transmits are despair and disenchantment.

Only political activism could be the next step. Their education and their willingness to protest injustice assuring them of local prominence, black Creoles naturally assumed the leadership of the black community in New Orleans after the Civil War and well into the twentieth century. Although in the end they were unable to arrest Louisiana's relentless late nineteenth-century march toward racial separation and all that it implied, they resisted it stubbornly, crying out against it in their newspapers and fighting it in the courts.

The decade and a half following the Yankee military occupation of 1862 had been a living hell for all black New Orleanians: fifteen years of violence, lawlessness, economic nightmare, and political corruption during which despair had alternated with shorter periods of optimism. On the one side stood the winners of the war, many of them carpetbagging Republicans down from the North, some well intentioned, others there for personal or political plunder, all of them representative of the people and principles—Abraham Lincoln, Charles Sumner, abolition, union—on which southerners had turned their backs. On the other side stood native Democrats, the party of slavery, states' rights, and secession. They were still unable to forgive or forget war-ravaged cane fields, torched cotton bales, the razed corncribs still evident in the countryside, or the arrogant heel of the conqueror grinding down the conquered in the cities—the Union general whose forces had occupied New Orleans, Benjamin F. Butler, was better known to New Orleanians as "Beast"—they were perverse in defeat, unwilling to abandon old attitudes of race or politics. And in the middle, at the vortex of the conflict, the object of all the controversy and pawn of all the politics, the Negro stood, his aspirations now cultivated, now thwarted, his hopes now raised, now dashed.

Spirits soared when federal occupation forces established schools for blacks. Booker T. Washington described his people's craving for learning during those heady moments of first freedom following the war, reporting in his autobiography *Up From Slavery* that the freedman "was a whole race trying to go to school. Few were too young, and none too old, to make the attempt to learn."

The young who saw their new freedom as opportunity; fifty- and seventy-five-year-olds who only wanted to read the Bible before they died. As fast as teachers and classroom space could be found, the human waves of eager learners washed in: "Day-school, night school, and Sunday school were always crowded, and often many had to be turned away for want of room."

The euphoria was short-lived. Black Louisianans could only look on with dismay when, following Lincoln's assassination, the new President Andrew Johnson, no friend of blacks' civil rights, dismantled the school system the army had set up, kicking away the fragilely constructed ladder on which blacks had begun to climb to literacy. Even worse for blacks' postwar prospects, ex-Confederate leaders and sympathizers began to drift back into public office in New Orleans as well as in other sections of the state. It soon became apparent that the old guard was taking charge in Louisiana and that it had the enthusiastic support of the white majority.

Again, help seemed to be on its way when Congress passed and the required three-quarters of the states ratified the trio of so-called Civil War amendments to the federal Constitution almost before the dead had been removed from the battlefields. America's first civil rights measures, they seemed to promise the earth.

Sandwiched between the Thirteenth, which outlawed slavery wherever the United States had jurisdiction, and the Fifteenth, which prohibited denial of suffrage on account of "race, color, or previous condition of servitude," the Fourteenth, the biggest blockbuster of them all, should have been the Negro Magna Carta. It was meant to be, to make blacks first-class citizens at last by ordering the states to keep their hands off constitutional rights. The states were not to make laws denying any American his constitutionally guaranteed "privileges and immunities," his "life, liberty, or property without due process of law," or, what was to become most significant for the twentieth-century civil rights movement, the "equal protection of the laws." Their political sensitivities notwithstanding, the states had been thrust into the individual rights business.*

It's been said that the Civil War amendments, particularly the Fourteenth, signified the completion of the American Revolution at last. But the dream and the reality did not coincide. A century of intense struggle followed the Fourteenth Amendment's ratification in 1868, the first three-fourths of it marked by clear victories for the white majority. That bloc stoutly maintained that this upstart amendment conflicted with the older Tenth Amendment (ratified 1791), which reserved certain powers, including the power to operate public schools, to the States and had been intended to protect the states from the very kind of incursion the Fourteenth Amendment threatened. Beginning with the initial refusal of ten of the eleven former Confederate state legislatures, including Louisiana's—Tennessee's was the single exception—to ratify it, it required every minute of every day of the next century to install the Fourteenth Amendment as the sentinel of racial justice in America, a century throughout which Louisianans, among others, did their political best to ignore it. And in late 1960, even as little Ruby Bridges trudged resolutely into New Orleans's formerly all-white William Frantz School, the state's lawmakers were at that very moment still vigorously denying their responsibilities under it.

The Reconstruction roller coaster carrying blacks' hopes rattled on. Of the ninety-eight delegates to the convention that produced the new state constitution in 1868, half, by previous agreement, were black, half, white. Within this group of forty-nine black delegates, black Creoles were in the majority, and it was largely their efforts that shaped the controversial article 135. Over the objections of white delegates from rural areas of the state, who predicted a violent reaction by white supremacists in their districts, a coalition of blacks and white Republicans, many of them carpetbaggers, handily won approval of the blacks' primary objective: an arti-

---

*The other sections of the Fourteenth Amendment had more limited application. The second section removed the designation of slaves as "three-fifths of . . . persons," which the framers had written into Article 1, section 1, of the Constitution's main body, the compromise arrived at to mollify the North, which wanted slaves counted low for tax purposes, and the South, which wanted them counted high for representation purposes—the new Thirteenth Amendment had obviated the need for definition.

The third and fourth sections were punitive. The third barred government officials, federal and state, who'd participated in the rebellion, from holding public office again unless and until Congress removed such "disability." The fourth absolved federal and state governments from all debts incurred in aid of rebellion.

cle ordering the end of white-only schools. "All children of this State between the years of six and twenty-one shall be admitted to the public schools . . . without distinction of race, color, or previous condition."

The lawmakers were directed to establish "at least one free, tax-supported school" in every parish in the state. Its companion, article 136, prohibited any "municipal corporation"—i.e., school board—from making "any rules or regulations contrary to the spirit and intention" of article 135.

It was a historic moment: two tradition-busting firsts—recognition in a state constitution not only of blacks' right to education but also their right to the same schools as their white neighbors. "Great God," groaned one white old-timer a little later when the reality bore down on him, "I wonder that the spirits of our dead do not rise up to jeer and scoff us when such degradation of soul is witnessed." He continued.

> Methinks I see Lee, Jackson, and a host of their compeers standing
> upon the eternal shore with faces veiled in shame and sad tears rising
> at the sight of people so fallen.

Despite some protests, the new constitution was approved by the voters, a majority of them newly registered blacks rounded up by the federal military commandant, in April, 1868, satisfying at last the federal requirements for readmission to the Union. Louisiana regained statehood the same month. Federal troops, however, were kept in place and at the ready.

The new constitution looked promising on paper. Forcing it, however, on white Louisianans resentful of a document they never made and an alliance with an overbearing Union they never wanted required the strength and determination to roll back the currents of the mighty Mississippi. For black New Orleanians, disappointment and disillusion returned in their customary roles.

Rural Louisiana's initial response was uncomplicated and rigid noncompliance. The predicted violence did not materialize—yet. Opposition focused on evasion: outright disobedience, circumvention, tacit agreements between blacks willing to sacrifice integration for whatever crumbs of schooling they could salvage and whites who wanted no part of them, the sudden popularity of alternative segregated institutions for white youngsters, particularly Roman Catholic schools. All these combined to assure the overwhelming white population that black youngsters would not desecrate the altars of white supremacy.

In New Orleans, graduates of the Institution Catholique had come of age by the late 1860s and were taking their place among the city's black intellectual elite. It was only natural that they should lead the movement to integrate the public school system the first chance they got. The black Creole newspaper editor Paul Trévigne was thundering:

> The objection "too soon" is but laughable. It is repeated at each and every reform to be accomplished. . . .
>
> When will the right time come? Is it, per chance, after we have separated for 10 or 20 years the two races in different schools, and when we shall have realized the separation of this nation into two peoples?

But the white majority was not in a mood to listen. Trévigne might as well have spoken to the statue of Henry Clay that was obstructing the increasingly heavy horse-drawn traffic on Canal Street. In the end, it required nearly three years of intense, concentrated effort and a court order to break the color line in New Orleans's public schools. In retrospect, the drama looks like the dress rehearsal for D-Day, 1960.

Protests by the white ruling class were unrestrained. The opposition lashed out immediately, making words do the jobs whips did before the war. The *Daily Picayune,* whose editors believed the "Negro has a long stride to make before he reaches the degree of intelligence of even the most ignorant class of whites," labeled article 135 "the most thoroughly infamous provision in the constitution of 1868," and urged opponents of integration to abandon the public schools for private institutions. Readers wrote in, reminding New Orleanians just who it was that paid for the schools—a canard that proved useful to segregationists a century later. "Pacificus" warned in the *New Orleans Times* that as tensions mounted, it would require "but little combustible material to kindle a flame."

The local school board exploited every legal loophole. At one point no fewer than five suits were before the courts. Every stratagem was explored until a dead end was reached.

In late November, 1870, two and a half years since the constitution of 1868 was ratified, the Yankee-born carpetbagger judge Henry C. Dibble of the local state district court removed the last obstacle to ending racial segregation in the city's schools. It could no longer be avoided or evaded.

The three adopted daughters of Oscar J. Dunn, a former runaway slave who'd bought his freedom and risen through Republican ranks to become the first black lieutenant governor of Louisiana, led off the school desegregation effort. Following the Christmas holidays of 1870, they enrolled in the fashionable Madison Girls' School, the first known black girls ever admitted. The principal regretted the subsequent withdrawal of her two best white pupils. She fully expected the withdrawal of others.

Racial labels were dropped from school records during this period, and figures for the total school desegregation can only be estimated. The best estimates indicate that probably a third of the city's schools desegregated, a third remained all white, and a third all black.

Blacks, however, had little cause for optimism.

The hard-core opponents resorted to boycotts. The parents of about five thousand white pupils immediately removed their youngsters as the dreaded black invasion approached, shrinking public school enrollment in the first year of desegregation from 24,892 to 19,091. The number of nonpublic schools multiplied apace, though most of these were academically uninspired, physically inadequate, and sparsely funded. Nonetheless, enrollment in them surged from about ten thousand in 1869 to seventeen thousand in 1873.

Initially enthusiastic, white parents, especially those with several children to educate, soon found the tuition at both parochial schools— one to two dollars a month—and the new unaffiliated private schools— two to four dollars a month—onerous. By 1875, so many white students had returned to the public schools that enrollment reached its nineteenth-century peak of 26,251.

Despite widespread opposition among whites, public school desegregation proceeded surprisingly peacefully for three years. A local journalist, assigned by his editors at the *Picayune* to expose the evils of desegregation, reported, instead, instances of "white ladies teaching negro boys; colored women showing the graces and dignity of mental and moral refinement . . . ; children and youth of both races standing in the same classes, with black teachers pushing intelligently up into the intricacies of high school mathematics."

Neither the predicted violence nor whites' en masse refusal to pay their taxes materialized as they recognized the desirability of accommodating some black demands if they were going to be able to engage black help in voting out the despised carpetbaggers and sending the federal troops packing. Except for a fracas at Central Boys' High School when a mulatto graduate of École Polytechnique, Paris, was hired to teach mathematics, and the boys, applauded by the newspapers, mutinied until the appointment was withdrawn, a superficial tolerance of mixed schools kept the New Orleans system together for a time. When in 1872 William G. Brown, a black man, was elected state education superintendent, it caused little commotion. The city was being talked about as a model system. Then the bubble burst and violence shattered the veneer of calm.

The declaration of race war came from the three former Confederate officers who published the *Alexandria Caucasian*. They predicted in the spring of 1874 that

> There will be no security, no peace, and no prosperity for Louisiana until the government of the state is restored to the hands of the honest, intelligent, and taxpaying masses; until the superiority of the Caucasian over the African in all affairs pertaining to government is acknowledged and established.

Blacks could only watch helplessly as white Louisianans translated that and subsequent editorials into action, and the new fraternities of terror, the paramilitary White Leagues, sprang up throughout the state. By midsummer of that year, most Louisiana parishes, including Orleans Parish, had resident White Leagues sworn to return state government to its "rightful [white] heirs" and to "unite as a race to protect ourselves against . . . the other race."

Early on, the leagues put pressure, often successfully, on Republican office holders—formerly blacks' best friends—to resign. As their patience expired and their confidence increased more or less in proportion to the growth in their numbers and influence, the militant groups resorted to violence. Lynchings and massacres of blacks were reported throughout the state that summer.

In New Orleans, the local chapter of the White League, supported by local business leaders, managed to unseat the state government on the afternoon of September 14, 1874, in a fierce battle with metropolitan police on Canal Street. By evening the insurgents had won control, and only after President Ulysses S. Grant sent federal reinforcements was government restored. The confrontation, known as the Battle of Liberty Place, demonstrated to all New Orleanians, black and white alike, the tenuousness of the state's hold on stability without the backing of federal bayonets.

The incident also enhanced the climate, already heavy with bitterness, for further violence. The city had barely recovered when, three months later—in late December, 1874—it was prostrated again by a three-day riot incited by the White League. The ruffians rampaged through all the desegregated schools breaking windows, intimidating teachers, and evicting black pupils. Black youths responded in kind. The White League was ultimately persuaded to rein in the troublemakers, although not before two lives were lost and 350 windows broken.

When it was all over and routine had returned to normal following the Christmas holidays of 1874, blacks feared and whites hoped the experiment in mixed schooling had ended. In fact, public schools reopened in January, 1875, and continued to operate for two more years on an unsegregated basis.

Tension, heightened by passage in Congress of the Civil Rights Act of 1875, intended to implement the Fourteenth Amendment, which was drawing little respect in the South, filled those final years of school desegregation. Then, suddenly, Reconstruction ended, a period aptly called Redemption began, and black fortunes plummeted, not to be recovered for the better part of a century.

Following the close presidential election of 1876 between Republican Rutherford B. Hayes and Democrat Samuel J. Tilden, the Republicans, for whom the southern black had by now become an albatross, promised boatloads of federal money for southern public works plus the withdrawal of federal troops from Louisiana, Florida, and South Carolina in exchange for the disputed electoral votes of these states, which Hayes needed to win. For southern whites, the deal was irresistible economically, politically, and psychologically.

Both sides kept the bargain, known as the Compromise of 1877. On April 24, 1877, six weeks after his inauguration, the new President Hayes ordered the removal of the last federal occupation from the South, in effect pulling out federal support of blacks' civil rights and leaving the freedman with nothing between him and the white southerner's rage. The South had lost the war, but won the peace.

In Louisiana, the compromise involved a round of hard and complex horse trading between the national Republicans and the state Democrats over the disputed gubernatorial election of 1876, the result of which was the takeover of the state government by the Democrats at last and the installation of the White League–backed Francis T. Nicholls as governor. Although they had unblushingly solicited black votes during the election campaign, the victors made haste to restore the antebellum social and political ambience to the state and city. Public school resegregation was one of the highest priorities.

The outspoken Robert M. Lusher, whose creed it was that white students should be "properly prepared to maintain the supremacy of the white race," was installed as state superintendent of education. He immediately attacked article 135 of the 1868 constitution as "offensive." In his first annual report, he urged state legislators to waste no time replacing it with "more acceptable provisions for the mental instruction and moral training of the two races, in separate schools." Assuming broad powers, he purged the twenty-member school board of known integrationists and replaced them with segregationists. Their ranks were broken only by the presence of four new black appointees, part of the price exacted by local Republicans for their support of the Compromise of 1877, but their numbers were in no way threatening. With William O. Rogers, a prewar city school superintendent, back in his old office, planning for the resegregation of the public schools began in earnest.

To lend the scheme a look of legitimacy, a committee investigated conditions at the mixed schools and reported what the authorities wanted to hear: that public education in New Orleans had "greatly deteriorated since colored and white children were admitted indiscriminately to the same schools." They had the excuse they were looking for, if any was needed, given the temper of the times. School resegregation became a certainty.

Within weeks of the new governor's inauguration, a delegation of black Creoles came forward to challenge the recent school policy decisions, marching in anger on the statehouse (federal forces had moved the capital from Baton Rouge to New Orleans in 1862; it remained there for twenty years). It was a valiant gesture, but in the end as futile as all the rest.

The block-long building to which the men were bound was the former St. Louis Hotel, purchased by the state in 1874. It stood on St. Louis Street in the oldest part of the city. The newspaper editor Paul Trévigne remembered when its rotunda, now the senate chamber, had served as the city's principal auction mart, whose wares included human chattel. New Orleans had been a major distribution point for slave traffic flowing from the East to plantations beyond the Mississippi.

The committee of protesters, thirty-one in all, wound through the statehouse corridors to the lieutenant governor's office where the meeting was to be held, the office of the chief executive himself having been previously occupied.

The chairman was Aristide Mary, one of the wealthiest men of any color in New Orleans, having inherited from his white father an entire city block on Canal Street. He had lived in the comparative freedom of France for nearly twenty years and had been continually frustrated on his return by the racial restrictions in his native city. He was refused seats at the opera house and had to take management to court to desegregate it. He'd had to wait six years—from the federal occupation to the constitution of 1868—to vote. His fellow black Creoles had proposed his candidacy for governor in 1872; although he knew he couldn't win, he ran, largely, as Rodolphe Desdunes put it in his black Creole history, for the purpose of establishing "the *right of aspiring* to the position of governor"; his name on the ballot was "like defiance thrown in the face of prejudice." Now, five years later, in the summer of 1877, Mary had not yet found any reason to abandon his discontent with the way the future of black New Orleans was shaping up. This plan to resegregate the city's schools only deepened his anxiety.

His sentiments were shared by the rest of the group, some of the most assertive and influential men of the black Creole community. Dr. Louis C. Roudanez was there. The son of a French merchant and a black woman, his baptismal records listed him as white, but he chose to live as a Negro. He took his medical education in Paris where he manned the barricades for the Socialists during the uprising of 1848. On his return to New Orleans, he launched the militant bilingual newspaper *L'Union,* and when it collapsed, followed it with the equally militant *La Tribune de la Nouvelle Orléans.* In 1877, the fifty-four-year-old Roudanez was devoting less of his time to political melees and more to his medical practice. He had, however, unhesitatingly joined his friends in their protest to the governor.

Paul Trévigne, whom Roudanez had hired as editor for both his papers, was also there. C. C. Antoine, former lieutenant governor recently defeated for reelection, lent political prestige, although he may have felt a little strange meeting in the office he'd just vacated. Octave Rey was a respected war hero and captain in the metropolitan police. Louis A. Martinet, only a year out of Straight College Law School and one of the four blacks appointed to the new school board, let the governor know right off that had he, Martinet, had any idea that separate schools had been the board's intention, he never would have accepted the appointment.

Except when Roudanez threatened to "sound the tocsin of alarm throughout the country" if the governor couldn't muster "the moral influence" to enforce blacks' constitutionally mandated right to integrated schools, the dialogue was civilized, dignified, polite, and rational, though it had that black Creole quality of adamance about it, an unwillingness to compromise. Emotion remained below the surface, but there was no question it was there.

Governor Nicholls had lost an arm at Winchester and a foot at Chancellorsville. His empty sleeve and his limp, recalling the suffering and sacrifice of the Confederate soldier, had been political assets during the recent election campaign. They were substantially less appealing at this meeting.

He listened patiently to his visitors, who made an articulate chorus but were no match for his excellency. He deftly fielded their arguments, which boiled down to protest of the governor's failure to enforce the 1868 constitution's provision for integrated public schools. Several times he told the men they were being driven by their "feelings," which they vehemently denied. His final word to them was that if they really did believe their constitutional rights had been violated, the courts were open to them.

The meeting broke up with polite handshakes all around. Nothing had been accomplished. Not one mind had changed. The governor returned to state business. The black Creoles carried their frustration away with them, took their demands to the school board a week later, and were denied again.

A few days later the *New Orleans Democrat* took the committee to task, describing its members as "a puffed-up tribe of mulattoes and quadroons who, proud of their Caucasian blood which circulates by indirection through their veins, think their children too good to go to 'nigger schools' and set up claims to an equality, the advantages of which would be altogether on their side."

The black Creoles of 1877, at least those who'd confronted the governor, recognized the resegregation of schools for what the white majority intended: the opening wedge in the movement for total black subordination and return to antebellum status. Paul Trévigne, however, did not allow their protest to die so ignominious a death. Unwilling to accept Nicholls's no for his final answer, and challenged by the governor's suggestion that the group take their complaint to the local courts, Trévigne immediately put together a test case and on September 26, 1877, sailed into state court demanding the school board and its superintendent be prohibited from reinstating racially segregated schools.

The fifty-two-year-old Trévigne, scion of an old and respected black Creole family in New Orleans, was an activist long before he joined his fellows in their angry march on the Louisiana governor's office that steamy June day in 1877. After teaching French history and literature at the Institution Catholique for some years, he had been installed as editor of Louis Roudanez's new *L'Union*. Trévigne's easy outward manner belied a reservoir of rage, which often found its way into his editorials as he pounded away at themes of racial injustice in his native city. His words had so inflamed white passions that local vigilantes threatened to kill him and burn the paper's printing plant. But they did not silence Trévigne.

He continued to write for *L'Union,* and when it collapsed, for its successor, *La Tribune de la Novelle Orléans.* When it, too, folded, he wrote *A Centennial History of the Louisiana Negro.* In 1877, he was still an angry man. This move to resegregate the city's schools could only force him to action.

Although Trévigne grounded his case for unsegregated schools firmly in the law of his time, citing the 1868 state constitution's guarantees of equality to all races as well as the nine-year-old Fourteenth Amendment's promise of "equal protection of the laws," he added a new element that gave a psychological twist to his suit.

Having been forced to eat of racism's bitter fruit for all of his fifty-two years, he knew as much about self-abasement as any man living. As a former teacher, he had watched that state of mind develop in children and shape the images of themselves they would carry in their souls all their lives.

And so he stretched the constitutional principles laid out in his brief to include psychological principles not yet articulated. The passage was brief, the prose simple, unburdened by scientific jargon, but his point was as clear as the most closely reasoned professional paper. The policy of racial segregation in the public schools, Trévigne declared,

> works an irreparable injury to the entire colored population of the city in that it tends to degrade them as citizens by discriminating against them on account of race and color.

And he demanded that hereafter "no distinction shall exist among citizens of Louisiana in any of our public schools or state institutions of education supported by the State, city or parish."

That racial segregation did "irreparable injury" to the human personality was a novel idea in 1877 and remained one for nearly three-quarters of a century. Trévigne, however, had put his finger on what became the bedrock of the arguments made in the early 1950s by black lawyers, who never heard of Paul Trévigne, attempting to desegregate public education in America.

On October 23, 1877, just short of a month after Trévigne filed his suit, the court dismissed it, largely on technical grounds. More important to later suits initiated in the name of racial justice, Trévigne's resort to psychology failed to impress the judge—as similar approaches, though better documented, failed to impress lower court judges in the next century.

Trévigne, the court said, had offered no evidence that segregation caused "irreparable injury" to blacks, and he hadn't demonstrated a "wrong inflicted upon himself or a right violated to his personal detriment." His son, after all, hadn't been denied admission to a white school; he hadn't applied. Concrete damage was a prerequisite to the successful prosecution of a court suit. General and abstract questions only wasted the court's time.

Superintendent Rogers and his board had already begun to reorganize and resegregate New Orleans's school system, reassigning the few hundred black students still attending mixed schools to all-black facilities. The policy remained in effect without interruption until D-Day, 1960, when Ruby Bridges and the other three little black girls finally broke the color line.

Less than a month after the state court dismissed Paul Trévigne's suit, the seven- and nine-year-old sons of E. Arnold Bertonneau tried to enter the all-white Fillmore public school three blocks from their home, but were turned away because of their "African Descent."

Like Trévigne, Bertonneau was a prominent black Creole, a wine merchant by trade and a political activist by preference. During the recent war he'd been a captain of black Union troops. In 1864, he'd gone with another black Creole, Jean-Baptiste Roudanez, to President Lincoln himself to ask for blacks' voting rights in Louisiana. The pair had gone on to Boston where they were feted by state officials and abolitionists, and at the dinner in their honor, Bertonneau announced a vision as radical as abolition had been at one time: the racial integration of New Orleans's schools and the dawning of a day when "caste, founded on prejudice against color, disappear[ed]." It was Bertonneau in 1868 who as a delegate to the state constitutional convention had been responsible for fashioning the articles mandating integrated education for blacks. Now, in pursuit of his dream a decade later, he followed the example of his friend Trévigne and filed a suit against the city school superintendent, the school board, and the principal of the Fillmore school. Not in state court this time but in federal court, where it was possible some remnant of the former mindset had lingered on.

Bertonneau's suit appeared to meet the court's objections to Trévigne's. Bertonneau's children had actually been rejected; Trévigne's hadn't applied. Bertonneau steered clear of Trévigne's suggestion that discrimination caused psychological damage and stuck to legal and constitutional principles, complaining, as had Trévigne, that his children's rejection by the Fillmore principal violated state and federal constitutional protections.

The case wound up on the desk of Federal Judge William B. Woods (later Justice Woods of the United States Supreme Court). On paper, he seemed right for Bertonneau's suit: a native Ohioan and former Republican politician who'd settled in Alabama after the war; a carpetbagger without question but apparently one of the better intentioned among them. Following his election to the state bench there, he'd earned a reputation for conscientious decision making divorced from political and social concerns. Appointed in 1869 to the United States Court of Appeals for the Fifth Circuit, which met in New Orleans and had jurisdiction over

Florida, Georgia, Alabama, Mississippi, Louisiana, and Texas, he hoped to create a body of law useful to the postwar southern society then in utero. In 1871, in connection with a raid by white Alabamans on a political meeting of blacks, Woods firmly upheld the blacks' right to free speech and assembly as "secured by the Constitution" and protected within the states by the Fourteenth Amendment.

With his case in the hands of a man with Woods's judicial temperament, prospects for a favorable decision in Arnold Bertonneau's suit appeared somewhat better than Paul Trévigne's in state court. Woods, however, still had some surprises in his repertoire, including, in this very case, an early articulation of the basic formula for education of the races in the South over the next century. Woods never used the phrase "separate but equal" exactly, but it was clear that was what he had in mind.

His major premise was that "equality of rights does not necessarily imply identity of rights." Arnold Bertonneau's sons had not been excluded from all the public schools of Louisiana on the basis of their race. They'd been excluded only from those schools established for white children. If the state could educate the sexes separately—and it did at the time—it could educate the races separately without violating the Constitution. Other than "conceding equal privileges and advantages to both races" and insuring that both races were treated "precisely alike," the state, Woods reasoned, was entirely free to "manage its schools in the manner which, in its judgment, will best promote the interest of all." He summarized:

> White and colored children are compelled to attend different schools.
> That is all.

The *Daily Picayune* could hardly contain its joy. The editors only wished the "learned judge" had gone further and pointed out what white southerners over the whole of the next century would rely on most steadfastly to stave off the racial integration of their schools, that "the constitution of the United States does not create schools or confer on any body any right in any school in the State." The regulation of the public schools had nothing to do with federal authority at all, they argued, but lay "exclusively within the jurisdiction of the separate States." The "learned judge," however, had done his job well when he "swept away every obstacle to the successful workings of our school system that political and social theorizers have attempted to set up."

In fact, Bertonneau's was the last of the black Creoles' formal protests against racially segregated schools in New Orleans until the middle of the next century.* When scarce public funds loosened a little in the late 1880s, and money became available to hire more teachers, raise the salaries of longtime employees, and introduce new subjects into the curriculum, it all happened in the schools for white New Orleanians. Schools for black New Orleanians deteriorated proportionately. Eighteen new schools were built with philanthropist John McDonogh's money between 1877 and 1889, but none was allocated to black children. As the historians Donald E. DeVore and Joseph Logsdon put it in their *Crescent City Schools,* local educational facilities for blacks suffered into the mid-twentieth century from "benign neglect."

The court defeats failed to silence black Creoles, and the activists among them continued to protest voting irregularities, police violence, and racial segregation in schools and public accommodations.

In 1879, Louisiana got a new constitution that essentially gutted the previous liberal document. Color lines were reinstated, although the framers were careful to avoid actually defying federal authority. They authorized, for example, "free public schools," but omitted any reference to racial composition. No one doubted what it would be, given the temper of the times; nowhere in the new constitution did the lofty "without regard to race, color or previous condition" survive.

Color was specified only once: in article 231 creating Southern University, to be operated by the state solely for black Louisianans. Replacing the previously desegregated Agricultural and Mechanical College, which was being moved from New Orleans to Baton Rouge to become part of Louisiana State University, Southern's stated mission was to provide vocational and agricultural—but not legal or medical—training for the state's blacks; its unstated mission was to take the pressure off the recently segregated LSU to admit them.

As the Compromise of 1877 and the Constitution of 1879 intended, the remaining shreds of Reconstruction unraveled. Jim Crow, a name whose unremarkable birth in the title of an antebellum minstrel-show routine belied its venomous adulthood as a tissue of beliefs defining blacks as inferior beings, became shorthand for racial separateness. The federal Civil Rights Act of 1875 prohibiting segregation in public accommodations might as well have never been passed. Color barriers reappeared. Hospitals, churches, sporting events, restaurants, theaters: they fell like dominoes. Even New Orleans's brothels began to observe the color line.

*Paul Trévigne lived out his life in his native city, later going to work for Louis Martinet's *Crusader,* which the lawyer founded in 1889. He died in 1907 at age 82. Arnold Bertonneau left New Orleans shortly after his court suit, living out his final years in California. His death certificate listed him as white.

The recreation of the prewar social ambience required time, of course: two painful decades during which the Fourteenth Amendment lay dormant and the rights of black people were about given up for dead. The Democratic majorities in the state legislatures led the movement, but they had substantial help from a consistently conservative and sympathetic U.S. Supreme Court, which, while it gave its blessing to the maintenance of blacks' political rights, to serve on juries, for example, it sternly rejected any claim with social implications.

When C. C. Antoine's daughter, Josephine De Cuir, the next black Creole to challenge racial segregation in the courts, was refused a cabin for a steamboat trip upriver from New Orleans to Hermitage, a landing on the Louisiana side of the Mississippi, she sued the captain. Basing her case on a Louisiana civil rights statute passed in the euphoria of Reconstruction that prohibited racial discrimination on vessels transporting passengers within the state's borders, she won in the state courts. In 1879, the U.S. Supreme Court, however, reversed them. Making an end run around the civil rights issue, the justices turned De Cuir's claim into an issue of federalism and ruled that Louisiana had no authority to regulate travel on the Mississippi, an interstate waterway under congressional jurisdiction. That her trip was to begin and end within Louisiana was irrelevant.

The case caused no ripples anywhere outside Louisiana. It didn't seem to be an important case, to be a useful precedent, or to possess any of the characteristics that make a case a landmark. In fact, however, it turned out to be the first stroke in the death knell of the Supreme Court's support of blacks' equality implicit in access to restaurants, steamboats, schools, and railroad cars. Four years later, the Court sent the federal Civil Rights Act of 1875, with its equal access provisions, the rest of the way to the graveyard. This case *was* a landmark, recognized as such at the time.

By 1883, suits testing the statute's constitutionality were flooding the federal courts. Lumping them together under the umbrella of the *Civil Rights Cases,* the justices of the Supreme Court chose five that were being pressed by the federal government on behalf of blacks who'd suffered discrimination in hotels, theaters, and railroad cars—one each from Kansas, California, Missouri, New York, and Tennessee. Joseph P. Bradley of New Jersey wrote the Court's opinion. Seven of his brethren joined in.

Although Bradley had once written privately to a fellow judge that constitutional rights could only be secured by federal intervention, he seemed to have changed his mind, and he had joined the Court in rejecting Josephine De Cuir's claim of racial discrimination. Now as he methodically tore apart and struck down the Civil Rights Act of 1875, his dicta laid down a firm bedrock rationale of objection to blacks' enjoyment of the equality the law had promised, an argument that was to become increasingly familiar over the next seventy-five years:

It would be running the slavery argument into the ground to make it apply to every act of discrimination which a person may see fit to make as to the guests he will entertain, or as to the people he will admit into his coach or cab, or car, or admit to his concert or theatre, or deal with in other matters.

So went the eulogy for 1875's Civil Rights Act, its demise mourned by few outside the black communities. At the same time, the Court was giving the Compromise of 1877 its seal of approval and leaving the black population of the South dependent on the caprices and whims of local legislatures and courts. It had turned the clock back almost beyond human memory.

The lone dissenter was the big bald-domed, ruddy complexioned Kentuckian John Marshall Harlan. He had been appointed to the Supreme Court by a grateful President Hayes in 1877—the agreed-upon price of his persuading the Kentucky delegation at the Republican National Convention of 1876 to throw its votes to Hayes at a critical moment. Harlan had been a slave owner himself before the war, but his dismay at the vengeful lynchings and beatings of blacks during the Reconstruction years in his native state had forced him to rethink some of his convictions.

On the Court, the conscience-stricken Harlan had become a devout supporter of blacks' civil rights, making his position clear in his writing of the Court's opinion striking down Delaware's statute that excluded blacks from jury participation. Now in 1883, he was about to make it equally clear that he didn't agree with his brethren's stand on certain other civil rights matters.

As his pen scratched across the page in dissent, Harlan's customary high emotional level was further elevated by the fact that the ink flowing from it came from the quaint, old-fashioned inkwell Chief Justice Roger B. Taney had used in writing the Supreme Court's opinion in Dred Scott's case in 1857. Aware of Harlan's interest in historical memorabilia, the marshal had given it to him not long after he was appointed to the Court, and his wife believed he found considerable satisfaction in the idea he was using it to argue, in effect, for reversal of Taney's opinion in that case. That delicious irony, she thought, helped to propel his pen that day when he wrote:

> [T]here cannot be in this republic any class of human beings in practical subjection to any other class. . . . The supreme law of the land has decreed that no authority shall be exercised, in respect of civil rights, against free men and citizens because of their race, color, or previous condition of servitude.

The sole dissent, Harlan's opinion carried no weight in law. It mattered to history, though, and it was not the last time Americans would hear from him on this subject. Next time he would turn up the volume.

The Supreme Court's failure to uphold the Civil Rights Act of 1875 sent southern state legislatures into a frenzy of creativity as they sought new ways to satisfy their craving for replacing slavery with the next best thing, segregation. Following the examples of Florida, Mississippi, and Texas, the Louisiana legislature in July of 1890 passed—and the black Creole committee's old adversary Francis Nicholls, reelected governor in 1888, signed—what these same black Creoles labeled the "abominable separate car statute" requiring white and Negro passengers to ride in separate railroad cars. It was the first of three measures approved in Louisiana during that decade that regulated by law relationships previously left to custom and tradition. The second measure extended the separate car statute to the interior of the railroad station, and the third was a constitutional provision at last replacing Arnold Bertonneau's controversial article 135 of the 1868 constitution prohibiting racially segregated public schools. From here on, school segregation would be required.

Once again New Orleans's black Creoles, many of them the same men who'd confronted the governor with their objections to school resegregation in 1877, older and wiser now, banded together in protest. Aristide Mary was old and infirm now, but he was still angry at the treatment blacks received before the law and still frustrated by the indignities he himself was subjected to daily by the society in which he lived. Lacking the energy to protest again, he suggested that Louis Martinet, who'd founded the fiery weekly *Crusader* since his unhappy term on the Orleans parish school board, hired Paul Trévigne to edit it, and during the "abominable" separate car statute's first year of life had drenched the little newspaper's pages with attacks on the new law, assemble a committee to initiate a court suit testing the measure's constitutionality.

The committee came together in the *Crusader*'s offices on the unseasonably cool night of September 1, 1891—eighteen in all when their number was complete. The *New Orleans Times-Democrat* described them as "agitators." They were, but, like the old group of 1877, they were men of substance deeply involved with their community.

Martinet was their unofficial leader. He would hold no office but would provide inspiration and momentum. He was already in touch with Albion Tourgée, an upstate New York lawyer and civil rights activist.

Dr. Roudanez was dead now. He had lived out his final days in New Orleans but had sent his seven children away from their native city. In 1890, three sons were in medical school at Dartmouth, a fourth attended medical school in France, and three daughters lived in Paris.

Former lieutenant governor C. C. Antoine, a member of the old group, was there and would be elected vice president. The broker Pierre Chevalier had come, along with Arthur Giuranovich the watchmaker, Myrthis Piron and Alcée Labat, both undertakers, Eugene Lucsy, a lawyer like Martinet, and others of similar professional status and political persuasion.

Arthur Estèves would be elected president of the group. The Haitian-born Estèves had come to New Orleans young and poor, had learned sailmaking, and had founded the city's leading firm of sailmakers. In 1891, he was prosperous and prominent in local philanthropy, had served six years as a director of the Institution Catholique, and had just been elected president of the board.

Rodolphe Lucien Desdunes's father was a political refugee from Haiti; his mother, a Cuban. In the normal course of events, young Rodolphe, who'd been a student of Paul Trévigne's at the Institution Catholique and, like Martinet, had graduated from the law school of Straight University, would no doubt have entered his family's cigar factory, but he had no head for business. In his heart of hearts, he was a poet.

In the summer of 1891, he was an angry poet. What energies he had left after a day at the U.S. Customs Service where he was employed as a clerk he was spending on writing columns for Martinet's *Crusader.* Passage of the separate car law had stung him as few racial insults during his forty-two years had. The minor irritations it imposed—the inconvenience, the indignity, the excessive authority conferred on conductors to decide racial identity on the spot—were nothing, he believed, to the offense the measure gave the blacks' sense of themselves as people, members of the human race. As his former teacher Paul Trévigne had described the effect of school segregation on black children, the "abominable" car law "tends to degrade" blacks as citizens. In Desdunes's mind, a man passionately committed to a belief in the inherent humanity of all, separate car laws practically made a Negro an untouchable.

Desdunes would have preferred to boycott the railroads than risk a court suit. Nonetheless he had helped Martinet organize this meeting.

The first meeting of what shortly became known as the Comité des Citoyens—Citizens' Committee—focused first on racial segregation. The consensus was that the despised car law represented only one small part of the statewide effort to wipe out the social and political advances made by blacks during Reconstruction. The law's capacity for mischief, its expansive implications for future oppression, were disquieting. What, these men were wondering, would the lawmakers try next? Where would they stop?

The second order of business involved finances. The men issued an immediate appeal for "moral sanction and financial aid." Within a few weeks they had collected $1,500 and had expectations of more, which encouraged the committee to elect the New Yorker Tourgée as "leading counsel in the case."

As fall merged into winter, plans for the test case unfolded. Rodolphe Desdunes's twenty-one-year-old son Daniel volunteered as plaintiff. The railroads, opposed to the separate car law because it meant added expense for them, agreed to cooperate with the committee and alerted conductors on the Louisville and Nashville line that young Desdunes, holding a first-class ticket to Mobile, Alabama, would board a car reserved for whites at Canal Street in New Orleans on February 24, 1892.

Everything went off on schedule. As instructed, the conductor approached young Desdunes immediately and ordered him into the coach provided for blacks. Desdunes politely but firmly refused to move. As arranged, the conductor had the train stopped. Two city detectives boarded and arrested Desdunes. The elaborately staged little drama, however, never reached the scripted final act. At the trial, the judge dismissed the case, holding that as the U.S. Supreme Court had ruled in Josephine De Cuir's suit against the steamship captain, Congress, not the state legislature, made the rules for *inter*state travel. Louisiana's separate car law didn't apply to passengers bound for Alabama from Louisiana.

Homer A. Plessy, shoemaker, black Creole activist, and friend of the elder Desdunes, stepped up next. On June 7, 1892, he bought a first-class ticket to Covington, near the Mississippi border but still within Louisiana. He boarded the East Louisiana Railroad as planned and took his seat in the first-class coach reserved for white passengers. Again the actors took their places and repeated their lines. Plessy was arrested. This time the law was upheld, first by Judge John H. Ferguson in the local criminal court, then by the Louisiana Supreme Court—to which former governor Nicholls had been recently appointed chief justice.

The *New Orleans Times-Democrat* fervently hoped these adverse rulings would have "some effect on the silly Negroes who are trying to fight this law." They did, of course, but not in the way the *Times-Democrat* meant. As the lawyer Tourgée and members of the committee planned, these lower court decisions gave them the legal prerequisites they needed to carry Homer Plessy's case to the United States Supreme Court.

With the assistance of a local lawyer who filled him in on the intricacies of Louisiana law, and a Washington, D.C., attorney who kept him au courant with developments within the Court, Tourgée filed an application to the Court to hear Homer Plessy's case. The question at its heart was: Had Plessy been denied the "equal protection of the laws" required by the Fourteenth Amendment, which most people thought when it was ratified in 1868 had removed blacks from just such discrimination by the state as the car law imposed?

Tourgée was summoned to present Plessy's case to the justices on April 13, 1896. All the lawyers were white in 1896, as were the nine members of the Court. The black presence consisted only of menials: the Negro messengers moving silently through the hushed courtroom, which was in the old Senate chamber in 1896, and the Negro staff in the kitchen behind the partition, whose occasional chatter could be heard as they went about preparing the justices' midday meals. No one in the courtroom was aware of either group. The justices did not tip their hands during the argument.

The committee members back in New Orleans could only cross their fingers and wait. The weeks passed slowly, each one at least a decade. Finally, on May 18, 1896, five weeks after oral argument, the Court announced its decision in Homer Plessy's case.

Henry Billings Brown wrote the opinion. He came from the former militantly abolitionist state of Massachusetts but had paid for a man to take his place in the Union army during the late war. A relative newcomer to the Court, he had taken his seat early in 1891, too late to participate in the Court's decision upholding Mississippi's separate car law. He was not, however, a blank sheet of paper. His jurisprudence as expressed thus far, developed over fifteen years as a federal district judge, clearly reflected mainstream American thought on social and economic issues, including its low estimate of the African-American who lived within its range. Brown's opinion in *Plessy* v. *Ferguson*—the case was named for the plaintiff and the New Orleans trial judge who first heard it—represented this estimate in all its dimensions.

Brown began with a brief—and dry—statement of the facts in the case and the Fourteenth Amendment issues these facts raised for the

justices. He cited the *Civil Rights* cases as one of the operative precedents and quoted the complaint of its author—who'd since passed on to
his final reward—that social mixing of the races was "running the slavery argument into the ground." Then he sailed into his major premise,
which was essentially a rephrasing of Bradley. The Fourteenth Amendment, to be sure, he explained, demanded the "absolute equality of the
two races before the law." The intent, however, had not been to "abolish
distinctions based upon color, or to enforce social, as distinguished from
political equality, or a commingling of the two races upon terms unsatisfactory to either." Brown didn't believe for a minute that racial segregation implied "the inferiority of either race to the other." Had he been the
judge deciding Paul Trévigne's suit in 1877, he could have dismissed it
with one word: "Nonsense!" In any case, in the Court's judgment, matters such as separate car laws were the responsibility of the state legislatures.

There it was: the course of American jurisprudence in racial matters
laid out for the next half century. The Fourteenth Amendment's command to the states never to deny the "equal protection of the laws"
notwithstanding, the states retained jurisdiction over many areas of their
citizens' lives, particularly in the social realm. That was what Brown had
set out to say. His gratuitous inclusion of school segregation as "valid
exercise of the legislative power," his reference to an 1849 school segregation case in Boston, Massachusetts as if it remained an authority, his
citation of Arnold Bertonneau's nearly twenty-year-old suit in New
Orleans—this was all commentary. His conclusion, however, would
never be forgotten. It nourished the hearts of segregationists for generations to come.

> If one race be inferior to the other socially, the Constitution of the
> United States cannot put them upon the same plane.

The judgment of the Louisiana courts was thus confirmed. The separate car law with all its ramifications had survived intact. America could
forget its Negro problem for now. The Homer Plessys, the Rodolphe
Desduneses, the Louis Martinets, and, later, the A. P. Tureauds were
safely locked into their separate railroad cars.

Brown had not used the phrase "separate but equal," which simply
meant that separation of the races was permissible so long as all were
provided with equal facilities. The phrase, which became the formula for
Jim Crow arrangements following the Court's decision in *Plessy,* originated in the lower courts as they struggled to interpret the higher
Court's standards. The phrase caught on not only in the law reports but

also in officialdom where the rules were made, and it became a code phrase in the popular culture. Everyone knew what it meant, and everyone had his or her opinion, usually strong, about how it applied to any given local situation.

Paradoxically, it was the southerner, the former slaveholder, John Marshall Harlan who contested the New Englander's affirmance of the separate car law. Harlan would be best remembered for two things: as the last of the tobacco-spitting justices, and the eloquence of his dissent in Homer Plessy's case. It can truly be said of Harlan that his dissents in civil rights cases, especially *Plessy,* represent what Chief Justice Charles Evans Hughes three decades later described as "an appeal to the brooding spirit of the law, to the intelligence of a future day, when a later decision may possibly correct the error into which the dissenting judge believes the court to have been betrayed."

Writing with the certitude of the convert and the passion of—he had in fact incorporated many of Tourgée's arguments—the advocate Harlan laid down his major premise:

[I]n view of the Constitution, in the eye of the law, there is in this country no superior, dominant, ruling class of citizens. There is no caste here. Our Constitution is color-blind, and neither knows nor tolerates classes among citizens. . . . The humblest is the peer of the most powerful. The law regards man as man, and takes no account of his surroundings or of his color when his civil rights as guaranteed by the supreme law of the land are involved.

The passage was a rewording of his dissent in the *Civil Rights* cases thirteen years before, but it was strengthened now by Albion Tourgée's felicitous phrasing in his brief for Homer Plessy declaring that

Justice is pictured blind and her daughter, the Law, ought at least to be color-blind.

Harlan's "our Constitution is color-blind" became one of the, if not *the,* most quoted statements in American constitutional history.

Like Desdunes and Martinet, and, later, A. P. Tureaud, Harlan believed that the Fourteenth Amendment had unequivocally "removed the race line from our governmental systems." He also understood that, as he put it, the "destinies of the two races in this country are indissolubly linked together," and he warned against the "common government of all" permitting "the seeds of race hate to be planted under the sanction of law."

How far might a state go in imposing regulations on its people? Harlan wondered, articulating the very concerns that had persuaded the Comité des Citoyens to take action. If the state could regulate who could ride in which railroad cars, he reasoned, reducing the proposition to absurdity,

> [w]hy may it not so regulate the use of the streets of its cities and towns as to compel white citizens to keep on one side of a street and black citizens to keep on the other? . . . Why may it not require sheriffs to assign whites to one side of a court-room and blacks to the other? . . . [W]hy may not the State require the separation in railroad coaches of native and naturalized citizens of the United States, or of Protestants and Roman Catholics?

Demonstrating considerable prescience, Harlan accused the Court majority of mortgaging America's future:

> [T]he judgment this day rendered will, in time, prove to be quite as pernicious as the decision made by this tribunal in the *Dred Scott* case. . . . What can more certainly arouse race hate, what more certainly create and perpetuate a feeling of distrust between these races, than state enactments which, in fact, proceed on the ground that colored citizens are so far inferior and degraded that they cannot be allowed to sit in public coaches occupied by white citizens?

Harlan's spirited dissent could hardly compensate the Comité for the pain of the majority's decision, which institutionalized racism in the United States for decades afterward and did, as Harlan had prophesied, "prove quite as pernicious" as the decision in Dred Scott's case, which crystallized the issue of slavery and helped bring on the Civil War. Indeed, *Plessy*'s ghost was still spry enough to haunt New Orleanians as late as 1960.

What protection had these men left? As Harlan said, the Supreme Court had given the state legislatures carte blanche, and, in so doing, had made it clear that blacks could not depend on the federal government. The Fourteenth Amendment was comatose now. The Fifteenth was dying as states competed to disenfranchise the blacks among them. Where else was there to go? What were blacks to do?

Press reaction divided at the Mason-Dixon line. Northern newspapers took strong issue with the Supreme Court majority. Southern newspapers made the collective southern sigh of relief palpable, gave new life to the fantasy that the war had come out differently after all, and the

Fourteenth Amendment had never passed, was only a figment of Republican political imagination.

Overcome by discouragement and fear, financial backers of the Comité withdrew their support. The committee itself was forced to disband, and shortly afterward Martinet's *Crusader* stopped its presses permanently. The men believed, Desdunes explained, that "continuation of the *Crusader* would not only be fruitless but decidedly dangerous."

Treasurer Paul Bonseigneur reported when the receipts were all counted that expenses in the case amounted to $2,762 of the $2,982 collected. Of the $220 "on hand" at the end, the committee donated $160 to various local charities and spent the remaining $60 on a testimonial to Albion Tourgée, who had prosecuted Plessy's case without compensation. (The New Orleans lawyer who assisted him and the Washington lawyer each received fees: the former, $1,073; the latter, $514.)

Four and a half years after Homer Plessy's abortive attempt to ride in a first-class passenger coach to Covington, on January 22, 1897, he reappeared in the local criminal court, pleaded guilty to violating the separate car law of 1890, and payed his fine of $25. His public life ended there, quietly, without fanfare, and he vanished without further ado into the mists of time. He died in 1925 and was buried in New Orleans's St. Louis Cemetery. His name lived on in every courtroom in America.

A year after the U.S. Supreme Court's decision in *Plessy,* President William McKinley appointed Albion Tourgée American consul at Bordeaux, where the lawyer died in 1905 at the age of sixty-seven. Louis Martinet's days as a revolutionary ended with the demise of his newspaper. He lived out his final two decades as a lawyer and physician in New Orleans where he died in 1917. C. C. Antoine disappeared from public life after the committee disbanded, at which time he was sixty years old, ready perhaps to retire to his plantation in Caddo Parish, to enjoy some serenity outside the rough-and-tumble of Louisiana politics. He died in 1921 at the age of eighty-five. Chairman Arthur Estèves continued as a sailmaker and died in New Orleans in 1906.

Aristide Mary's sponsorship of the citizens' committee had been the last political act of a disappointed old man. In the spring of 1893, he killed himself. His life of frustration was over, except for one last defeat; his suicide precluded a Catholic church funeral, and the service was held at his brother's home.

Three years after the U.S. Supreme Court's decision in *Plessy,* Rodolphe Desdunes was appointed a weigher at the customhouse in New Orleans, a position that allowed him time to write, and he continued to protest racial injustices in print, finding alternative outlets to the now-defunct *Crusader.* While supervising the unloading of a shipment of granite one day, dust was blown into his eyes, partially blinding him, and he was forced to resign. Despite his deteriorating eyesight, he was able to write his magnum opus, *Nos Hommes et Notre Histoire,* a proud history of black Creoles in nineteenth-century New Orleans, his way of telling a multicolored world, born and unborn, what racial oppression meant, and what the struggle against it cost: his plea for racial justice and the courage to fight for it. He died in 1928 at the age of seventy.

The final report of the Comité des Citoyens, made public on April 2, 1897, nobly concluded that

> In defending the cause of liberty, we met defeat, but not with ignominy.

By the time Desdunes died in 1928 the committee had a successor in the by then well-established New Orleans chapter of the National Association for the Advancement of Colored People, founded locally in 1915.

By that time, too, its members had a twentieth-century heir ready and willing to carry on the traditions. The torch had been passed to A. P. Tureaud, a modern black Creole activist combining the aggressiveness of Paul Trévigne, the determination of Aristide Mary, the crusading spirit of Louis Martinet, and the dignity and sense of human brotherhood of Rodolphe Desdunes. By 1928 Tureaud had graduated from law school and was shortly to resume the committee's work, to make the connection between the first and second reconstructions in his city and state.

CHAPTER 3

"A Credit to His Race"

B y the time A. P. Tureaud was born on February 26, 1899, just under three years after the U.S. Supreme Court had legitimized racial segregation on passenger trains via Homer Plessy's case, Jim Crow had spun a web of rigid laws and customs that raised the walls of color higher yet. The dire warnings of virulent "race hate" and "feelings of distrust" between the races which the dissenter John Marshall Harlan had issued had taken over the cities and towns of the South, and the outward structure of Tureaud's life over the next half century had been determined before he could walk or talk, not by his parents, but by external forces he and they were powerless to control.

Race discrimination touched nearly every facet of black life outside the home—all except tax assessments, the prices blacks paid for tickets in segregated theaters, or the fares they paid on segregated transportation. There were no discounts on the inferior accommodations. Not all the beauty of the southern landscape, the storied courtliness of white southern society, or legendary generosity of southern people could mask or compensate for the debasement black citizens endured during the decades that followed *Plessy.*

The century turned. In New Orleans, shouts of "Bonne Année" mingled with "Happy New Year." The end of a century and the beginning of another changed nothing, and celebrations had a traditional feeling to them. Merrymakers thronged Canal Street where businesses were closed for the day, the usual number of firecrackers accidentally singed spectators who strayed too close, largely white crowds gathered in candle-lit Catholic churches where choirs outdid themselves in the singing of the "Te Deum," blacks assembled at the Simpson Chapel for an oral reading of the Emancipation Proclamation on its thirty-seventh birthday. Following this last event, the master of ceremonies looked forward to some future time when "we will be able to work side by side with the white men for the public good."

If the recent half century was any indication, that future was still remote. During that time, blacks had acquired, though briefly, some little political leverage and enough education to stimulate a taste for more. These advances they made on the foundations of American government and society ought, they reasoned, having watched the formula work for whites, to have made eventual economic parity possible and enhanced their standing in the larger community.

Their progress had seemed, rather, to diminish their position, to make them targets of political manipulation and intellectual bullying, hostages to white resentment that had a tendency to boil over into violence. The high-flown phrases of federal law had failed to protect them, and the federal courts had made it clear that there was no refuge there.

It was to this debased condition that the simple desire for recognition of their humanity had brought them. As the twentieth century dawned, the freedman was a long way from being a free man.

He had no choice but to submit, to suppress his humanity, to hope, to pray. If past experience had a moral to it, only the submission was relevant.

During Tureaud's childhood and youth, the very air around him seemed to reverberate with racism, the fast-ripening fruit of Henry Brown's majority opinion in *Plessy*. Populists were still winning elections on the strength of their race-baiting. As shrewd, eloquent, and persuasive as they were vulgar and ruthless, they became governors and senators and influences within their party by exploiting the discontents of their white audiences.

Race-hating writers like Thomas Dixon, Jr., whose immensely successful novel *The Clansman* was published in 1905, were all the rage during the first decade of the new century. *The Clansman* is a perverted story of Reconstruction in which the southern Negro, portrayed as clown and rapist and drawn as stupid, violent, and depraved, stars as villain and the Ku Klux Klan, portrayed as brave, loyal, courtly, and kindly, stars as hero. Klaverns used *The Clansman* as recruiting material. When David W. Griffith made it into the movie *Birth of a Nation* in 1915, it debuted in New Orleans before opening in New York. Later it was hailed as an original epic, the first of its kind in the world, but that wasn't what drew the crowds in 1915. Historian John Hope Franklin credited *The*

Clansman with doing "more than any other single thing to nurture and promote the myth of black domination and debauchery during Reconstruction."

Scholars bent Charles Darwin's theory that racial characteristics result from evolution to defend social inequalities and to bolster white supremacy. Sociologist John Moffatt Mecklin focused on physiological comparisons of the races, blaming what he described as the "uniformity and monotony" of the "negro mind" on the smaller size of "negro skulls." Thomas Pearce Bailey, dean of the University of Mississippi's Department of Education, looked to the social sciences to justify such statements as "in educational policy let the negro have the crumbs that fall from the white man's table" and "let the lowest white man count for more than the highest negro."

The law both reflected and reinforced the popular mood. The U.S. Supreme Court continued on the roll that had begun in 1879 with Josephine De Cuir's suit against the steamship line that had denied her first-class accommodations on the basis of her race. In 1898 the Court supported voting restrictions recently added to Mississippi's constitution and that same year gave official sanction to Henry Brown's remarks regarding racial segregation in schools that he'd dragged into the opinion he wrote in Homer Plessy's case. What was surprising about the latter case was the author of the opinion. John Marshall Harlan, who'd gotten such a lift from dipping his pen into Chief Justice Taney's inkwell and who'd characterized the Constitution as "color-blind," shocked his admirers when he denied satisfaction to blacks suing a Georgia school board for cutting the high school planned for them out of the budget. At the same time he handed the South a powerful argument that would serve them well for many years, writing that tax-supported education was a "matter belonging to the respective States"; only in the case of a "clear and unmistakable disregard of rights secured by the supreme law of the land" could interference be justified.

In 1901, the justices made it clear that the "supreme law of the land," the sacred articles of the federal Constitution, did not apply to the large nonwhite populations of the recently acquired Philippines and Puerto Rico. Then in 1908 they ducked out of confronting civil rights issues involved in southern peonage laws and went on in that same year to tell the state of Kentucky it could go ahead and segregate students by race even in the entirely private Berea College, which had courageously admitted both black and white students since its founding in 1859 but had recently been ordered by the state legislature to educate them in separate classrooms.

Louisiana's lawmakers adapted the national mood to local conditions.

The new state constitution of 1898 emphatically retained racial segregation in Louisiana's schools and imposed voter qualifications few blacks could meet: ownership of property valued at not less than $300, a minimum standard of literacy, and the ability to calculate age by the number of years, months, and days since birth; a standard ploy was to catch blacks out on miscalculations of days in the leap years. Exceptions were made for men who'd been entitled to vote on January 1, 1867, and their sons and grandsons—a popular political ploy known as grandfathering that saved the poor and illiterate white but excluded black voters. Between the census of 1890 and that of 1900, the number of registered black voters in Louisiana fell from 126,923 to 5,320; the total number of registered white voters fell during the same period only from 126,884 to 125,437.

Laws passed the legislature forbidding marriage between whites and blacks. One law required separate ticket windows at the circus. Courts kept separate Bibles for swearing in white and black witnesses.

A. P. Tureaud was a toddler when a law requiring segregation on local streetcars went into effect in New Orleans in 1902. It ordered the street railway companies either to provide separate trolleys for black passengers or to fit all the vehicles with movable partitions to separate the races—requirements that endured until 1958. When Representative Harry Wilson of Tangipahoa Parish, which had no streetcars, introduced the law to the legislature in 1900, he described as its purpose not so much to keep the races from rubbing elbows as the demonstration of "the superiority of the white man over the Negro."

What the law couldn't accomplish, other forces did. Blacks began to sink lower and lower on the economic scale. Many of them semiliterate and unskilled, they commanded lower wages in a job market mechanization was shrinking. Labor unions wanted no part of them. Lending institutions made getting mortgages difficult, and private insurance companies demanded blacks pay higher premiums than whites. The now defunct Comité des Citoyens in New Orleans had called it right. The separate car law of 1890 had been just the beginning.

The black Creole community, tightly knit by a common language, religion, and some surviving Continental traditions, gave a growing child a strong sense of identity. One of eleven children born to Louis Tureaud, a local building contractor, and his wife Eugenie (DeJan), A. P. grew up in an integrated neighborhood on Kerlerec Street, close by the French Quarter, where European and Central American immigrants often made their first stop in the United States. Members of the Comité des Citoyens still lived and tended their businesses there. There was very little mixing with "American" blacks who lived uptown, and a black Creole who ventured onto the alien turf had better listen for footfalls behind him; he would not be the first youth to be beaten. A similar caveat applied to American blacks crossing into the downtown community.

The black poet Langston Hughes had been surprised when black Creoles welcomed him into their homes in the mid-1920s. He'd been told that "Creoles did not mix much, or show hospitality toward the English-speaking Negroes 'across Canal Street.'" More than a half century later, a black Creole might well break the glass from which a visiting "American" Negro had drunk.

But A. P.'s heritage, however rich, and his community, however warm, couldn't compensate for the pain that spoiled so many of his childhood pleasures. The self-confidence he gained, for example, on his first job—delivering bread at a salary of one dollar a week, just enough for school carfare with a few pennies left over for lunch—was soon destroyed when the shop owner discovered the boy was black and fired him. Performance on the job was not even a factor in the proprietor's decision. Only the boy's race mattered.

A. P. skated, swam in the Mississippi, and harassed the peddlers in the nearby French Market with the neighborhood Filipino, Italian, and Spanish boys. In the New Orleans tradition he dressed up for Mardi Gras and begged for trinkets as the floats passed on Canal Street. He got on the invitation list for the small, private black Creole–sponsored dances and entered his teens to the tunes of Louis Armstrong and King Oliver.

But his friends went off to white schools every day while A. P. went to the all-black Bayou Road School, which met in an old house. He considered himself "pretty well off" compared to some black New Orleanians who went to schools in old barns, abandoned churches, even a former barroom. Some had no drinking water; pupils either walked several blocks to a well or drank out of ditches.

A. P.'s playmates were welcome in city parks: "for white only" signs kept A. P. out. Even Congo Square, where slaves had congregated to dance and party on Sundays before the Civil War, had one. A. P. could walk through but he couldn't stop.

He went to catechism, made his first Holy Communion, and went regularly to mass at nearby St. Augustine's where the services were in French and where his friends went. But he soon began to think, as his father had long thought, that the priests at St. Augustine's were not particularly interested in his spiritual development. They performed their prescribed duties, baptized the neighborhood blacks, most of whom were Catholic, confirmed them, married them, and buried them. But to Tureaud, they seemed to discharge the holy offices perfunctorily. No blacks, not even black Creoles, many of them as white and educated as the priests themselves, had any role in the church organization. When the church was crowded, Tureaud and his family stood in the back. Like his father, who resented everything about segregation and finally stopped going to church, Tureaud found it "humiliating," one more affirmation that authority and power were white; perhaps God was white, too.

A. P. was discovering as a child, too young to understand the fears and perversities that underlay Jim Crow, what Desdunes and Trévigne and Martinet and the rest had always known: that being black, even if you looked white, was physically, mentally, and emotionally draining. Color, despite A. P.'s lack of it, was becoming the major constant in his life. There was no escape.

There was no high school for blacks in New Orleans when A. P. was ready to enter, and there was clearly no future for him in his native city. He took a civil service exam for a job in Washington, but got no word of his grade before a labor recruiter appeared in New Orleans in 1916 with a spiel about free transportation to the racial freedom of a "promised land" just a thousand miles away in Chicago. To the dismay of his family, Tureaud signed on. He was only seventeen and he had to lie about his age. Nevertheless he joined the other black men on the train north, becoming part of the Great Migration that would take a million and a half black men for whom sharecropping was the deadest of dead ends away from their homes, off the land, and out of the South over the next twenty-five years.

All the way to Chicago, the train didn't stop, only slowed enough to let the destitute and often desperate men leap aboard. Like black men all over the South who joined this historic trek to northern cities during and after World War I, they risked their lives with that final jump onto the moving vehicle, but they risked as much by staying at home to work the cotton fields. If the boll weevil didn't ruin the crop, the annual spring floods did.

In Chicago, Tureaud laid railroad track for a time, then made forms in an iron foundry. The work was hard and the hours, long. But Tureaud had learned about both during the summers he worked as a cement finisher in his father's business. It wasn't the hard work that disheartened him.

Chicago, as Tureaud and all the desperate men discovered, wasn't the paradise the recruiters had led them to believe. There were new sounds, new sights, new accents, a faster pace, but the same old racial discrimination, no less oppressive in Chicago than in New Orleans. Tureaud and the other black Creoles in the group met regularly for meals and shared their gumbo, but the aches subsided only temporarily.

There were no FOR WHITE ONLY signs in the parks, but the chill was there all the same. Tureaud knew from his own experience that the labor unions didn't want him. He had a black friend who couldn't move into a white residential neighborhood; he could see with his own eyes that there were no black cab drivers or bus drivers or even sales clerks in Chicago. And every black immigrant passed on his war stories of bartenders who smashed the glass from which a black customer had drunk. Chicago was New Orleans without signs, which itself added to the problem: Tureaud could never be sure of his reception unless a fellow black had preceded him. It was risky even this far from New Orleans to venture into a new place. Eden was obviously elsewhere.

Other aspects of black life in Chicago, however, contrasted sharply with those in New Orleans and in fact served to remind Tureaud how stagnant life for blacks was in his native city, in Louisiana, and in the South generally. He began to read the *Chicago Defender,* the militant black newspaper that had brazenly asked shortly before the end of World War I: "Why Fight for the Flag Whose Folds Do Not Protect?" He listened to the men around him discuss local black candidates for public office and was reminded that most Louisiana blacks couldn't meet the property and literacy requirements even to register. He noticed Chicago Negroes' awareness of a need for change and "unconsciously," as he retold it later, he began to develop a political sense as well as a similar awareness. He heard Chicago blacks talking about opportunities and the importance of education. "Go to school, go to school" had become their rallying cry. A. P. was still young, still directionless, but things were beginning to happen in his head.

But Chicago "wasn't for me," he said later, and when his brother and uncle invited him to join them in New York, feeling he was "destined" for it, he took a train to Buffalo, worked there as a dishwasher for two weeks to pay the rest of his fare, and met them in Harlem. Life there was little better than in Chicago. Jobs were scarce, race discrimination pervasive and increasing as more and more blacks, most of them poor, arrived from the South, applying extra pressure on an already-tight labor market.

Black history, however, was happening all around him. Poor and desperate as they were, the blacks fleeing north, leaving behind familiar surroundings, at the same time having imbibed the democratic ideals publicized during World War I as they urbanized, developed a new self-confidence and sense of solidarity. Long suppressed anger, bitterness, and not a little defiance surfaced North and South as they discovered that democratic doctrine still didn't apply to them despite the blood they'd spilled and the lives they'd given.

Some succumbed to the easy temptations of socialism and Communism. Postwar race riots tore East St. Louis and Chicago and Omaha apart. New York escaped the violence and became the crucible for the postwar socioliterary movement variously labeled the Harlem Renaissance, the Black Renaissance, and the New Negro Movement. Like New Orleans's black Creoles before them, black writers were packing their poetry, prose, and plays with their protests, using their art to publicize their heritage and to confront the racism they all shared. Still others took their grievances to court, bringing legal suits against the institutions that discriminated against blacks.

Tureaud failed to find a job in New York, but while he was there he got word he'd passed the civil service exam he took in New Orleans before he left, and once again he packed his belongings and headed out, this time for Washington, D.C. His grades on the civil service exam won him a job in the library of the Department of Justice where he got interested in the law. He knew a little something about it, having been one of the few on the train from New Orleans to Chicago who could read and a natural choice of his fellow travelers who couldn't to review their employment contracts. Now in Washington, the school dropout from New Orleans, politically sensitized and intellectually curious, finished his secondary education, then entered Howard University Law School.

Howard had been established in 1867—in a former beer-and-dance hall—as a theological seminary to supply clergymen who could minister to the spiritual needs of the newly freed blacks. The law school had opened two years later. Other departments followed. Over the opposition of its southern members, who objected to any higher education for blacks, Congress, beginning in 1895, began to subsidize the new university. Although regarded during its first three-quarters of a century as something of an academic backwater, it was the only real university blacks had during those years, and a diligent young man like Tureaud could get an adequate if not necessarily superior legal education there. He could also—and Tureaud did—develop a sense of black history and begin to write a role for himself in it.

When Tureaud arrived at Howard in 1922, the law school had trained more than three-quarters of the black attorneys in the United States and was just then revving up to apply for accreditation by the American Association of Law Schools, symbol of first-class citizenship within the community of American universities. While he was still there, in 1924, Charles Hamilton Houston, his copper color hinting at Native American blood, his credentials—degrees and honors from the elitest of elite white institutions, Amherst College and Harvard Law School—proclaiming his intelligence and refuting the popular notion of black inferiority, joined the faculty. It was his first academic appointment following his graduation from Harvard. He intended to change whites' perceptions of blacks and blacks' perceptions of themselves by training young blacks to work through the legal system and close the gap between American law as it was written and American law as it applied to black Americans. Thurgood Marshall was one of his finest products.

It was during these three years that Tureaud first studied *Plessy* v. *Ferguson* and the shadows of Rodolphe Desdunes, Louis Martinet, and the Comité des Citoyens fell across his life. That they were not only fellow New Orleanians but black Creoles like himself was not irrelevant.

The potential for protesting contemporary racial discrimination may have come out of his friendship with his Howard classmate Eugene Davidson, whose father, Shelby, had been the first president of the District of Columbia's NAACP branch. The younger Davidson had written editorials for a local black newspaper every bit as heated as Desdunes's *Crusader* pieces had been. Davidson called himself a "troublemaker" and went on to lead the D.C. NAACP through the segregation battles of the 1960s. Tureaud became an active member during his three years in Washington, beginning his fifty-year affiliation with the nation's most prominent civil rights organization.

By the time he graduated in 1925 and returned to New Orleans the following year after a brief and not encouraging fling at practicing law in the nation's rigidly segregated capital, the seeds of his activism had been sown. He liked to recall much later, as the race wars raged all around him, the "horsemeat" served at Miss Hatcher's boardinghouse. He supposed, he said, "it was the food we had there that really toughened us for the experience we are now having." But he'd seen the "hurt," he knew the "need," he'd acquired the tools. He was prepared now in 1926 to "right the wrongs."

The times were ripe for Tureaud as they hadn't been for the old Citizens' Committee. Martinet and Desdunes had happened along at the moment the low tide of racial oppression was about to reverse, and they had been powerless to prevent the further erosion of the American creed. Tureaud happened along just at the moment Jim Crow's high tide in which he'd floundered as a child and young man was itself about to reverse, and he would be in a position to make a difference.

First, though, immediate problems of everyday living had to be faced. Civil rights cases didn't pay much of the rent in the middle to late 1920s, and black lawyers in private practice had a particularly difficult time of it. Blacks were as welcome in the professional callings as they were in the white schools and for the same reasons. Their presence, like a high school education comparable to a white youth's, challenged the myth of white supremacy at the same time it added competition for clients.

Hostility toward black professionals was sometimes subtle, sometimes blunt. They couldn't join the bar associations. Their self-respect in the "lily white" courtroom was subject to constant harassment. Even years later, black lawyers could recite horror stories of indignities suffered there. "Nigger" was almost as common a term of address as it was on the street, and one state judge had been heard to comment in open court:

I didn't know they let you coons practice law.

Potential black clients, even within Tureaud's own social circle— physicians and other professional men, some of whom he'd known at Howard—were persuaded that white lawyers were not only more competent but carried more clout with white judges, and so it was white lawyers, the very people discriminating against blacks, who got the cases that promised the fattest fees. Tureaud and his ilk could perhaps be trusted to draft a will or handle a real estate closing, but a businessman would think twice before he hired a black lawyer to handle a big tax case or a complex corporate matter.

One tactic black lawyers employed to circumnavigate the problem of color was to team up with a white lawyer who then served as a "front." Tureaud would have nothing to do with the subterfuge, but occasionally did drag out his questioning of witnesses in court to demonstrate his competence.

Such strains on making a decent living may be why, when Tureaud was admitted to the Louisiana bar in 1927, there were only four black lawyers in the whole state—three in New Orleans, one in Shreveport, Louisiana's second largest city, and none in rural areas where the need was often greatest. It was clear to the returning native that in the beginning, at least, he would have to have a source of income besides the pennies a small legal practice would bring in.

The Compromise of 1877 and its aftermath notwithstanding, blacks in New Orleans and the South generally in the 1920s still looked at the Republican Party as that of Abraham Lincoln, Charles Sumner, and emancipation, the Democratic Party as that of segregation and white supremacy. Tureaud registered Republican on his return to his native city which not only satisfied his principles but also gave him some political leverage on the lists for federal jobs during a national Republican administration.

In New Orleans at the time, federal patronage was dispensed by the legendary Walter L. Cohen, part Negro, part Jew. He was famous locally for his remark that in him were embodied the three groups that the Ku Klux Klan hated most: Negro, Jew, and Catholic.

Born in 1860, he'd been active in local Republican Reconstruction politics. His first federal appointment was as registrar of lands in the McKinley administration. In 1922, President Warren G. Harding named him customs comptroller in New Orleans, and after a bitter fight in the Senate, during which Southerners protested Harding's nomination of a Negro to such a prestigious—and patronage-laden—position, he was confirmed in 1924. He remained comptroller, with jurisdiction over seven customs districts between Mobile, Alabama, and Port Arthur, Texas, as well as thirty-three subports, until his death in 1930. The workforce in his jurisdiction totaled seven hundred, which white southerners considered a lot more patronage than a black man from New Orleans whose formal schooling may have ended at the fourth grade ought to control.

Politically, he was an accommodationist. He was a strong promoter of blacks' interests who took pains to pacify the white establishment. Which may be why he was one of the rare black officials to survive the excesses of the Redemption era.

Cohen did offer Tureaud a job, as cashier in Cohen's office. Tureaud held the position until the Democrats swept back in 1933, earning the principal part of his living by day, practicing law at night. If it wasn't an ideal arrangement for a young man impatient to use his new law degree to reweave the social fabric of the world in which he'd grown up, Tureaud could take sustenance from the recollection that his hero, Rodolphe Desdunes, had worked there while he wrote his masterpiece; a lot of blacks with advanced and professional degrees got no further than a minor clerkship at the post office. It was the only way, Tureaud believed, to cope with the financial shortfall of his legal practice.

Difficult and discouraging as the process was, Tureaud slowly put together a legal practice. He had no retainers; it was a "day to day existence" he told a friend. He would never be wealthy, and his fee might be paid in chickens, but he would always make enough to support his habit: his poorly paid or unpaid civil rights work that for the rest of his life was to consume the larger part of his time as well as his interest and attention.

At Howard, Charlie Houston was calling for the services of the black lawyer as "social engineer" trained to work on the "economic, political and social problems of the Negro," particularly in the South where the older generation of black lawyers "has tended to avoid highly inflammable issues and stay in the less controversial fields of strictly civil work and office practice." Houston was looking to the younger generation to assume the risks attached to litigating "on the social frontier."

One of the first things Tureaud did on his return to New Orleans was to ask Louis Martinet's widow for her late husband's *Crusader* files. Mrs. Martinet regretted, however, that only days before Tureaud's appearance at her door, she had cleaned out the garage and sold them to a junk dealer.

Disappointed but no less determined, Tureaud responded to Houston's challenge, taking up where Martinet and Rodolphe Desdunes had left off on the long road to revolution, using the law to build the "bridges" that would "bring people together" in joint "humanitarian" projects, longing, like the idealistic Desdunes before him, for the time "when we shall cease to be Negroes and white men to become plain American citizens." For nearly a half century, he dedicated himself unhesitatingly to blacks' civil rights as if the cases involved nothing more "inflammable" than the defense of a petty thief or the determination of liability for an automobile fender dented in a street accident.

If his ideas seemed radical at the time, his behavior wasn't, and he had only contempt for the street-confrontation style of social change. He harbored no hate, led no demonstrations, delivered no ultimatums. Polemic was foreign to his nature. Although he sometimes felt the pressure from those who would take more extreme measures, he maintained the quiet demeanor that expressed a more patient man, one who understood the perseverance required to reshape a society whose traditions, customs, and power structures were heavily weighted against him. When critics accused his old boss Walter Cohen of "Uncle Tomism," Tureaud commonly retorted that Cohen had been "as aggressive as the times permitted." Which, he implied, was all a man could or should do.

Tureaud was a good-looking young man in the 1920s and 1930s, 5 feet 6 inches tall and broad-chested. He still had a full head of "good" hair (not nappy) and large, soulful brown eyes in which no noticeable crusader's fire burned, but it was apparent to those who knew him that he was convinced his way was the best for both races.

As he became an increasingly familiar figure in local courtrooms, white lawyers began to respect his objectivity, his fairness and decency. Judges appreciated the soundness of his preparation, his gentleness and softspokenness, his general all-round courtesy. Before they realized what he was doing to them and their way of life, they had begun to talk about him as a "credit to his race."

Blacks who knew Tureaud well, on the other hand, respected his determination and courage in moving forward into uncharted waters, almost, an old family friend recalled much later, "as if he was preordained" to do it, and she wondered whether or not he ever considered the dangers to himself and his family.

In 1931, he had married Lucille Dejoie, member of an old established local black Creole family, owners of several local pharmacies. As a girl she had had all the advantages upper-echelon black Creole society offered, including boarding school at Talladega, and she had studied for a degree in pharmacy at Howard at about the same time Tureaud was learning law there, but they hadn't met until both returned to New Orleans.

If over the years her fears for her husband's safety grew in proportion to his prominence as a civil rights lawyer, she never showed it. She supported him absolutely. If she worried when he was late returning from some isolated rural section of the state where mysterious and some not-so-mysterious accidents happened to blacks, if every passing car gave her a little start as she waited during those long and lonely nights, she did not transmit her terror to their six children. She calmly dismissed young A. P. Jr.'s fears that his father was "not going to live to see him to adulthood" with a casual wave of her hand and an "Oh, don't be silly."

On his return to New Orleans, Tureaud joined the local branch of the NAACP, established locally in 1915 after a false start four years before. It was the first branch established in the deep South.

At the time Tureaud joined, the local group was embroiled in a quarrel over whether black or white lawyers should be engaged to fight its battles in the courts. The national organization had originally used prominent white members of the national bar to represent it in the white courtrooms of the South and before the U.S. Supreme Court for the same reasons white lawyers were hired to represent blacks in their private legal transactions. After 1915, however, black leaders began to urge the hiring of black lawyers, partly as a matter of racial pride and partly as recognition of blacks' greater sensitivity to blacks' concerns. The organization shortly began to recruit black lawyers to handle the burgeoning number of cases it was attracting. By 1928, the national office had added Tureaud's name to its official directory.

However, he had to watch white lawyers bungle a couple of local cases and to do battle with the organization's old guard before he won its confidence, at one point petitioning the national office to sponsor a competing group in New Orleans. When he finally got a case, however, it wasn't one of the complaints against lesser Jim Crow regulations that didn't "generate a whole lot of hostility," as he recalled later, the hat-in-hand "supplication" which the cautious local branch was accustomed to initiating. It was no less than the biggest case of that period, the equalization of black and white teachers' salaries, a battle that consumed the better part of a decade.

By the early 1930s, it was becoming increasingly clear to the national office that education was the key to equality: the lack of it was keeping blacks down, the availability of it would give the lie to the so deeply entrenched tradition of white supremacy. As the Depression began to lift in the mid-thirties, the NAACP declared war on the school boards of America.

The organization had chosen its target carefully: a broad area over which a course of legal action could establish barrier-breaking precedents. "What you were supposed to do," Robert L. Carter, one of the lawyers prominent in the movement a little later, told an interviewer in 1979, "was to push the law to its very limits in terms of effectuating social change. . . . And the role of the lawyer was to attempt, as convincingly as you could, to articulate a . . . sound legal basis" through which the judge, however drenched in the local customs and mores, could accept the views being presented. Carter called himself and his colleagues "social engineers." Charlie Houston would have responded "Hear! Hear!"

The NAACP's first strike was aimed at the regionwide inequities in salaries paid to white and black public-school teachers. In 1931–32, black teachers in the South's public schools received approximately half the wages white teachers received. Of the fifteen southern states the NAACP surveyed in 1935–36, Louisiana ranked third from the bottom with white teachers averaging $931 a year and black teachers, $403, or about forty-three cents on every dollar paid to their white counterparts. Government payrolls, at the very least, officials of the organization reasoned, ought to be color-blind.

Starting from a different premise, southern school boards came to different conclusions and continued to cast blacks in the role assigned to them by Chief Justice Taney in Dred Scott's case: history, he'd said, had established blacks as "beings of an inferior order." According to the school boards' cyclical line of logic, the black schoolteacher could live on less money, blacks taught shorter terms, and deserved less money, and since few blacks had advanced degrees they were worth less. If all these failed to convince, white officials could always fall back on the politically convenient fiction, a southern article of faith, that whites, by paying the bulk of the taxes, in effect, owned the school system and would not be willing to pay the increases higher salaries for black teachers would require.

The NAACP established its first beachhead in 1936 in Montgomery County, Maryland, a border state adjacent to the nation's capital and one of those believed by the organization to be critical in its struggle to beat Jim Crow. The chief strategist was the big genial Baltimorean Thurgood Marshall, great-grandson of a slave and son of a head steward at local white men's clubs and an elementary schoolteacher. He'd fallen under the spell of Charlie Houston at Howard University Law School and emerged in 1933 a dedicated and accomplished courtroom fighter for blacks' civil rights. In 1936 he was fresh from persuading the courts to admit the Negro Donald Murray to the University of Maryland Law School when he appeared in suburban—and affluent—Montgomery County where white *janitors* were paid $339 a year more than Negro elementary schoolteachers and $101 more than Negro high-school teachers. Marshall convinced the local court to order equalization of all salaries within two years.

At the prodding of Marshall, who was cruising the state in his old Ford urging teachers to demand equalization and filing court papers against recalcitrant school boards, the Calvert County Board of Education agreed a year later to equalize the salaries of its black and white teachers, and in 1940, Prince George's County became the eleventh Maryland county to be either persuaded or ordered to wipe out salary differentials based on race.

By this time the NAACP had set up the Legal Defense and Educational Fund, Inc. (LDF), which became known to blacks all across the South as the Inc. Fund, as an autonomous enclave closely associated with the parent organization. Its driver was, of course, the NAACP's top legal talent Thurgood Marshall, whose forays into southern as well as Maryland courts were becoming the stuff of which legends are made. The Inc, or Legal Defense Fund's long-term mission was to make the Fourteenth Amendment to the Constitution a reality, and it would not be long before Marshall and his legal staff would reach beyond Jim Crow in schoolteachers' salaries and attack Jim Crow in the schools themselves. For now, however, its purpose was to jar southern boards of education and southern judges into bringing the salaries of white and black public-school teachers into alignment.

So vulnerable to pressure from their employers, plaintiffs were not lined up at the doors of the LDF. Aline Black's legal action against the Norfolk, Virginia, public school system got her fired. John Gilbert's suit against the Brevard County, Florida, board of education got him fired, too. A lot of black teachers weren't willing to rock the boat, and one black teachers' association begged the NAACP to stay out of the state, please; its members were

satisfied that the good white people will do the right thing.

On February 29, 1940, the District Court for the Eastern District of Virginia dismissed Melvin O. Alston's complaint, which had been drawn up and filed by Thurgood Marshall, that the Norfolk, Virginia, school board's salary scales for white and black public-school teachers discriminated on the basis of race. After five years at Booker T. Washington High School, Alston was getting $921; white teachers at his level, with identical credentials, were getting $1,200. Alston, however, declared the judge, couldn't legally complain because he had, after all, signed up to teach that year at the price fixed in his contract. It was another of those Catch-22s that constantly dogged blacks' progress. They couldn't challenge a signed contract, but they couldn't achieve legal standing as teachers unless they signed it. Let stand, the court's dismissal of Alston's suit might have stalled salary equalization for years.

Thurgood Marshall, however, hadn't finished with Melvin Alston. The Norfolk school board had refused to renew Alston's contract almost the minute his complaint was filed, and Marshall was aware that Virginia school boards in several counties were informally warning their teachers off legal action. He had to show some results.

He took Alston's case to the United States Court of Appeals for the Fourth Circuit, which, as he'd hoped, reversed the district court, although he had some uncomfortable moments while he waited to hear. The argument for Alston was Marshall's debut in a federal appellate court, and the chief judge was John J. Parker, whose nomination to the U.S. Supreme Court a decade before had been defeated largely by efforts of the NAACP.

Parker himself wrote the court's opinion. If the scar tissue from that earlier confirmation battle still ached, he did not reveal it publicly, and he left no doubt in anyone's mind about the unconstitutionality of the school board's paying less "for public services of the same kind and character to men and women equally qualified according to standards which the state itself prescribes." Parker wanted no part of it:

> This is as clear a discrimination on the grounds of race [he wrote] as could well be imagined and falls squarely within the inhibition of both the due process and equal protection clauses of the Fourteenth Amendment.

The Norfolk school board took its case to the U.S. Supreme Court but failed to persuade that Court even to hear it. Parker's opinion stood.

Alston applied only to the states within the Fourth Circuit's jurisdiction. Southern school boards, beholden to white voters and not particularly progressive themselves, were not about to alienate the electorate by abandoning so entrenched a tradition or by changing the rules as well as the social assumptions with which their fathers and grandfathers had grown up. As one South Carolina state senator observed:

> They're not going to pay the Negroes money Supreme Court or no Supreme Court. If the Supreme Court does say that we must pay the Negroes, how are they going to make us do it?

They made the LDF lawyers sweat for every one of their schoolteachers, forced them to litigate each suit separately, an expensive as well as a slow process and an effective delaying tactic if they could not, though in their hearts they hoped they could, defeat the blacks' plans.

The LDF lawyers plodded on, district by district, board by board, plaintiff by plaintiff, with only the courage of Melvin Alston, the conviction of Judge Parker, and the determination of Thurgood Marshall to hearten them. It was enough. Louisville, Kentucky, fell. Suits were promptly filed in Nashville and Chattanooga. Teachers' groups in Georgia, Oklahoma, Alabama, Texas, and South Carolina besieged the NAACP for legal advice and assistance. By 1941, eight southern states had established policies of paying equal salaries to black and white teachers.

The Democrats were in power in Washington now, the civil service had cracked down on moonlighting by government employees, and A. P. Tureaud had left the customhouse to practice law full time. He was working out of a walkup office, which was the former autopsy room of a hospital converted to an office building. It was short on books, furniture, and much of the equipment that commonly filled the typical white lawyer's place of business. The teachers' salary equalization cases would be his first big legal contest. It would require all his skills and severely test the strength of his commitment to civil rights.

In New Orleans, where the legal shock troops always attacked first in these cases, a first-year teacher with a B.A. in 1937 was paid $1,000 a year to teach small classes in freshly painted and otherwise well-maintained schools. His or her black counterpart with the same credentials, including a B.A., was paid only $909 a year to listen to students recite from out-of-date textbooks in a gloomy ramshackle school building; it was not uncommon either for the black teacher's students to number 50 percent more than the white teacher's. While facilities at the white schools improved over the years and facilities at the black schools deteriorated, the salary differential increased geometrically rather than mathematically as the teachers acquired seniority. The white teacher earning $1,000 that first year would be making $2,600 in ten years, but his or her black counterpart would be earning only $1,380.

In 1938, black teachers asked the Orleans Parish School to end the inequitable salary schedule. They were ignored, and they realized they would have to take more drastic action. In March, 1939, a group of particularly activist teachers invited Thurgood Marshall, whose court appearances—and victories—they had been watching carefully, to come to New Orleans and discuss strategy with them. Marshall, they'd seen, was a man who got results.

Marshall came. He explained to the group just what steps they should take to raise funds and find a plaintiff. He also urged them to use A. P. Tureaud as their local legal representative. Tureaud would handle the local, day-to-day aspects of their case; Marshall himself would review Tureaud's briefs, offer suggestions, and edit the final complaint to conform to Inc. Fund legal standards. This tandem style, he told them, was the usual mode of operation at the Inc. Fund. It saved money for the organization, and it tapped into local talent and support.

Before he returned to New York, Marshall gave a pep talk at the Old Baptist Church at Third and South Liberty, illustrating for his latest clients with his gestures and oratory what it was about him that gave his teams the heart to go on. His closing remarks he fairly shouted:

> I wish to plead guilty to stirring up a fight. I want to see the teachers
> of this city fight for equal salaries and better schools.

Stirred to action, the teachers organized the Citizens' Committee for Equalizing Educational Opportunities. The challengers would, of course, need money not only for expenses incurred but enough to guarantee the teacher or teachers—the plaintiffs—a year's salary in the event of their being fired. The black teachers in New Orleans were asked to contribute ten dollars each, which proved, in view of possible reprisals, more difficult than initially anticipated. Some contributed under assumed names. Others didn't contribute at all but continued to trust the school board to "do the right thing."

The plaintiff eventually found was Joseph P. McKelpin, an untenured teacher at the F. P. Ricard School who was earning $360 less than a white teacher with the same credentials. Originally from Bogalusa, Louisiana, McKelpin was scheduled to receive his B.A. from all-black Southern University in June, 1942, which, had he not taken legal action against the school board, would have guaranteed him a raise, perhaps a promotion.

He was a quiet young man, a regular at Sunday church, and he surprised all who knew him when they realized it was their easy going, though serious, friend who was taking on the Orleans Parish School Board. He understood the risks of his decision, but he had a "deep feeling," one of his friends recalled years later, that the scale was "definitely wrong," and he was young enough, resilient enough, and self-confident enough to believe he could afford to lose his job if it came to that.

On May 9, 1941, Tureaud filed a petition with the school board on McKelpin's behalf, the usual procedure, in legal jargon, for exhausting administrative remedies before taking a case to court. The lawyer demanded that the board institute a "salary schedule free of all racial discrimination or differential" and make it "applicable to the compensation of all teachers and principals" in the city. Since this was not the first petition the board had received, Tureaud urged "prompt action." Past experience, however, had taught him not to expect results.

Tureaud's petition of May, 1941, was his final shot over the bow, the teachers' last offer to negotiate. Unless they got results, Tureaud was authorized to take their grievances to court.

As it usually did, the school board promised to consider their request. Two weeks passed. No answer came from the school board. For all his quiet dignity and self-effacing manner, Tureaud's patience could be exhausted. If the matter was to be settled before school opened in September, negotiations would have to begin. Tureaud wrote the school board president urging timely action. An assistant superintendent promised consideration of Tureaud's petition at the next regular meeting.

At the same time, the state attorney general, Eugene Stanley, remarked to a group of white teachers, who feared equalization of black and white teachers' salaries would cut into their own share of the state's budget, that perhaps black teachers' demands could be met through a simple system of reclassification. He made no specific suggestions, but the little he said was enough to scare black teachers. They would not, they knew, be the first to be "reclassified" out of their jobs.

When no report, much less real action, from the school board was forthcoming—a standard pattern of nonresponse that the board would develop into high art over the next several years—Tureaud filed suit in the federal district court in New Orleans on June 14, 1941: Joseph P. McKelpin and "others similarly situated" against the Orleans Parish school board and the superintendent of schools. In "others similarly situated" he used the language of the class-action suit authorized by Rule 23(a) of the Federal Rules of Civil Procedure when the "character of the rights involved are of common and general interest to the members of the class represented by the plaintiff." It was a legal concept that would become increasingly familiar as the various school segregation cases made their way through the courts and into the morning headlines.

By 1941, the Constitution's Fourteenth Amendment had outlived the disrepute in which the courts, including the U.S. Supreme Court, had held it in Homer Plessy's day. Largely because the federal courts were finally supporting lawyers' claims that its clause guaranteeing "equal protection of the laws" meant what it said, it had become the linchpin of civil rights cases.

Tureaud put it to work once again. "By rules, regulations, practice, and usage and custom of the State of Louisiana," he argued in his formal complaint, McKelpin and "all other Negro teachers and principals in Orleans Parish are being denied the equal protection of the laws in that solely by reason of their color and race they are being denied compensation from public funds for their services as teachers equal to the compensation provided from public funds for and being paid to white teachers with equal qualifications and experience for equivalent services." He asked the court to declare the "rules, regulations, practice, and usage and custom of the State of Louisiana" unconstitutional and to prohibit the school board from setting teachers' salaries on a racial basis.

The lawyer for the school board, in what was to become the white institutional first line of defense, asked the judge—Wayne Borah in 1941—to dismiss the case for want of jurisdiction. Thurgood Marshall, who had faced dozens of similar motions for dismissal of his civil rights suits in the few years he'd been the LDF's top lawyer, assured the less experienced Tureaud that the school board's motion was "completely without foundation," that it, not Tureaud's case, was certain to be dismissed. Recognizing the significance of McKelpin's case for other parishes in the state, Marshall stood "ready," he told Tureaud, "to come down at a moment's notice."

As Marshall had predicted, Judge Borah did refuse to accede to the school board's motion to dismiss McKelpin's case. Following some further preliminary skirmishing, which included requests by the school board's lawyer for delays, another tactic white institutions frequently relied on to ward off the inevitable, Borah finally scheduled McKelpin's case for hearing in June, 1942.

The school board's lawyer didn't deny the complaint that black teachers earned less than their white counterparts. He responded with the usual vague promises to improve the salary schedules *if* the state legislature appropriated sufficient funds. Sufficiency, however, was not defined, and no specific amounts were offered. It was left unsaid, but it was common-change knowledge that the chances of the state legislature, made up largely of rural and small-town Louisianans, appropriating funds to equalize *anything* for blacks and whites were not high.

Judge Borah was no more patient a man than was A. P. Tureaud, and he clearly was not impressed by the school board's defense. He read the federal court reports. He knew what had been happening over the past five or six years in similar cases. The issue of salary inequities had been in the courts now long enough for patterns to be set. Following these examples, Borah issued the injunction Tureaud had asked for and ruled that Joseph McKelpin and "all those similarly situated" were entitled to be paid on the same salary scale as white teachers. The judge would, however, consider suggestions for a remedy from both parties to the suit.

The plaintiffs demanded full and complete equalization of salaries immediately. The school board offered a gradual equalization over a five-year period, to which Thurgood Marshall replied tersely: "It stinks." The school board backed down to three years. Marshall was completely opposed.

Tureaud finally offered a compromise: a two-step, two-year equalization. The first time around, the school board rejected it, but the judge urged acceptance, and the board not only agreed to increase black salaries 50 percent of the difference between white and black pay the first year and the other 50 percent the next year, but, undoubtedly aware of the legal realities of Norfolk's unsuccessful appeal of Melvin Alston's case two years before, promised not to appeal. Borah signed the decree on August 31, and a jubilant Tureaud prepared to carry the battle into Louisiana's outlying parishes. By Tureaud's estimate, one thousand two hundred Negro teachers would benefit from the suit. "We made," he recalled with some pride later, "quite a hit with the community."

His jubilation was short-lived. The first casualty of the suit was Joseph McKelpin, who was immediately fired and told he'd never work in New Orleans again. Then the Citizens' Committee balked at paying Tureaud's $3,500 bill for research, brief-writing, and court appearances. It was Thurgood Marshall, the committee argued, who'd carried the major burden of the case.

One of the members in fact asked Marshall what he would advise the committee to pay its local lawyer. What was national policy? Marshall replied the LDF had no policy; fees varied from city to city, case to case. Oliver Hill, who'd taken Melvin Alston's case as far as the Supreme Court, had been paid $50. Prentice Thomas got $300 for the Louisville, Kentucky, case. A Florida lawyer, on the other hand, was getting $2,000 a piece for four cases and $2,500 for a fifth one. Legal fees were local matters, to be set and settled in the community. Marshall sincerely hoped, he said, this dispute could be settled—amicably. Negroes in New Orleans, he concluded, "should now be ready to rejoice, and not be tearing at each other's throats."

The committee subsequently offered Tureaud a "donation" in appreciation of his services. The offer saddened and angered him and he answered with a display of emotion unusual for him. "I am not," he said, "seeking charity . . . it is indeed surprising to learn that those for whom I worked would now consider me an object of charity," and he refused to accept it.

> Of all the humiliations [he had] put up with in this case, this [was] the limit.

In the end, following further negotiations, Tureaud and the committee agreed on a fee of $2,000.

As it turned out, the fee negotiations were not "the limit" in personal humiliations Tureaud endured in the salary equalization case. While he and the committee were still discussing terms, a local black weekly newspaper, the *Sepia Socialite,* accused Tureaud on its editorial pages of benefiting financially from the case. Threatened with a libel suit, the paper soon backed off, but not before Tureaud swore out a complaint.

In its conclusion, the salary equalization case had exacted some unanticipated expenses, especially in the area of Tureaud's emotions. Could he continue, he must have asked himself a thousand times during those bleak months, along the road he had mapped for himself? Did he want to now?

He did. He refused to allow his personal difficulties to get in the way of the work he had set out to do, which in the fall of 1942 meant winning complete salary equalization throughout the state. If he thought the previous federal court ruling in Melvin Alston's case or the precedent he himself had set in New Orleans would make the task any easier or would make defiance futile, he was mistaken. School boards outside the city were just as insolent and stubborn as the Orleans Parish school board was. All of them hired lawyers to oppose Tureaud's suits, even though it meant incurring heavy expenses and, in the end, defeat.

For Tureaud, these years must have seemed like watching the same movie run over and over. If the characters' names and faces changed, their behavior didn't. The issues, the arguments, the tactics were replays of those in New Orleans. Jefferson Parish, Iberville, East Baton Rouge. Twelve cases altogether. Tureaud trudged on, making the arguments, resenting the evasions, savoring the victories while pitying plaintiffs who were fired. By 1948, Louisiana was helpless to resist any longer. Backed against the wall as well as confronted with increasing numbers of black voters encouraged by recent U.S. Supreme Court decisions overturning restrictions on the franchise, the state legislature appropriated the funds to equalize teachers' salaries in all the parishes, nullifying the excuses, and making the cases in progress moot. It was Tureaud's final triumph and the taste was sweet.

Consuming the better part of his forties, the time a man's hair begins to thin and his creative juices to flow at their peak, the salary equalization suits had been challenging and exciting, though not without personal cost. A lesser man nearing fifty might have yielded to resentment, frustration, perhaps abandoned the work there and settled for a comfortable if not luxurious living as an all-round practitioner of the law.

But it had also been a learning experience. Tureaud had acquired a keener understanding of his people, their strengths and weaknesses both. He had gone up against some of the state's best white lawyers and would know better what to expect when next he met them on their ground. He had developed a rudimentary legal formula based on the Fourteenth Amendment to the Constitution which promised good service in the future. Being, as Ralph Ellison put it in *Invisible Man,* a story of Tureaud's time, one of "them what knows the fire and aint forgot how it burns," he could only persevere, despite the tricks, booby traps, and barbed wire he knew were waiting for him down the road.

CHAPTER 4

"Ya Gotta Stop Pushin' That Mule Around"

ome years later, the fiery-tongued Leander Perez, district attorney-for-life (or so it seemed at the time) of Plaquemines Parish, political boss of southeastern Louisiana, and flag carrier for segregation in the South, would push his big cattleman's hat to the back of his head, clamp his cigar between his teeth, scowl his most ferocious scowl, and point to these midcentury years as the time it all started: when the "uppity" Negroes, bankrolled by the Zionist Jews, inspired by the "international Communist conspiracy," supported by the United States Supreme Court, and encouraged by the gritty American President Harry S. Truman, had plotted together to deliberately destroy the rights of the American states that had been reserved to them by the Tenth Amendment to the federal Constitution. His usual courtliness suppressed for the moment, he would impatiently explain how the federal government stole Louisiana's oil profits, meddled with the state's voting laws, and dictated how local officials were to run the schools. In effect, destroyed the "southern way of life."

Perez had seen it all coming and had warned of the consequences. But all his attempts, including his Dixiecrats' bid in 1948 to restore southern influence to national politics, had fizzled. And now four little black girls were entering New Orleans schools that had been pure white since Reconstruction. Perez's world had changed radically over the past twenty years. He didn't like it.

Perez was the autocrat of his native Plaquemines Parish where it was said there was less democracy than anywhere else in the United States.

His rule was absolute. His word was final. His supporters still affectionately called him "Judge," although he had been a minor judge only briefly longer ago than most people remembered. His detractors gave the title a little sardonic twist, but there weren't many of these.

Salvador Chiapetta, a former highway maintenance foreman, learned local etiquette the hard way. After complaining to neighbors that Perez had been using state labor to build a private road and fish pond at his plantation Promised Land, Chiapetta suddenly found himself jobless. No private or public employer would touch him. Even his seventeen-year-old son couldn't get summer work cutting grass on the levees.

Chiapetta was tireless in his efforts to register to vote, but the registrar and his deputy were conveniently away from their desks whenever Chiapetta appeared at the courthouse in Pointe a la Hache. Possibly they were chatting in the registrar's automobile somewhere, or sitting on the ferry which was taking an unscheduled trip downriver. They could always find a way to elude undesirable voters. Later, when federal civil rights legislation empowered the Department of Justice to oversee local registration and election procedures, Perez himself would appear at polling places trying to intimidate federal observers with curses and obscenities.

In the long run, it probably didn't matter that Chiapetta couldn't find the registrar. His vote would have had little influence in a parish where the vote counters based their reports on the number of votes needed to elect Perez's candidates, and the totals had been known to exceed the population of the parish. Senator Russell Long, for one, admitted that Perez had stolen seven thousand votes for him in 1948.

To those who stood with Perez, doffed their hats and bowed low, he was a benevolent, bountiful, and often charming father figure. The parish blacks were strictly segregated and kept off the voting rolls. Yet even among these, a loyalty to the local *patrón* had developed, and A. P. Tureaud later recalled his astonishment at hearing relatives in Pointe a la Hache declare their undying devotion to Perez.

To those who for any reason challenged Perez, he was a bona fide, credentialed monster. Tales of his maliciousness abound, stories of opposition candidates in parish elections issued the wrong filing forms, of flaming roadblocks made of oil-soaked oyster shells set up to keep out intruders.*

---

*Rumors of Mafia connections surface periodically, but evidence of them has not been found. Glen Jeansonne, a biographer of Perez, believed the Louisianian was too independent to tolerate any outside authority as well as unwilling to share Plaquemines's oil wealth. FBI files on Perez, obtained under the Freedom of Information Act, showed no connection between Perez and any Mafia figures.

One of Perez's biographers, Glen Jeansonne, in *Leander Perez: Boss of the Delta,* explained his subject as "an almost perfect example of what psychologists term the authoritarian personality": fearful of the slightest change that threatened his own comfort, security, or exalted position. As Jeansonne described Perez, Communism threatened the economic system that had made him rich. Racial integration threatened the racial purity of which he was an example—he hadn't a single doubt that blacks and whites learning to read together would inevitably lead to sleeping together. The federal government's advocacy of blacks' voting rights threatened his popularity at the polls. He blamed unorthodoxy, intellectuality, and liberalism for the shakiness of his position, all qualities he saw personified in Jews and "Reds." From which point it was easy for him to construct a conspiracy in which the Jews, leaders in the movement for racial equality, and Communists, the sworn enemies of the United States, had teamed up to use blacks as innocent dupes to "mongrelize" the nation, thereby weakening it and ultimately destroying the American way of life.

Perez's fears that all these forces of evil would bring his world crashing down around him so unnerved him that he hid them behind an overly aggressive and self-confident manner. He imagined himself a feudal baron crusading against the barbarians from the North bent on imposing their alien ideologies on a people committed to the old-fashioned virtues and values of an earlier, rural America. His favorite comic strip was "Prince Valiant."

According to Jeansonne, Perez's adult values had come out of a home and a Catholic religious and secular education in which conventionality and conformity had been stressed above investigation and exploration. As a boy he'd been an exemplary student but an indifferent scholar, unimaginative, uncreative, uncurious, and unreflective, content with the rote learning he was offered.

As an undergraduate at Louisiana State University, Perez decided on a career in politics, and in the manner of the authoritarian personality, relentlessly pursued the uncommon power he knew a master politician wielded. When he was not waiting tables or playing football at LSU, he could usually be found in the galleries of the state legislature, learning the maneuvers of the lawmakers. After graduating from Tulane Law School in 1914 at the age of twenty-three, he leaped almost immediately into local politics. He lost his first campaign, a race for that same legislature, but won the support of local party bigwigs for his willingness to fight hard, and when an opening on a minor local bench occurred, they thought first of the young man with the heart for a good fight. He stayed only a couple of years. He resigned in 1924 to run for district attorney of

Plaquemines and St. Bernard parishes, which comprised a single judicial district and shared a district attorney. Victorious this time, he set up shop in an office in Pointe a la Hache.

District attorney was the most powerful local official in Louisiana. His choices of what to investigate and whom to prosecute, his accumulation of information that could be a lethal weapon in settling political matters, the value of his advice to grand juries and other parish units, combined to make the parish district attorney royalty.

And Perez was. He didn't want to be governor or president. Too risky. Extravagantly rewarding his friends and vengefully annihilating his enemies, for nearly four decades he basked in the idolatry the people of Plaquemines showered on him. At the same time, and not incidentally, he got rich.

Perez's rise to prominence and power coincided with the discovery in 1928 of valuable mineral deposits, oil and sulphur, particularly oil, right there in his own Plaquemines Parish. Its soggy fields and forests lay low in the water, like an overloaded freighter, stretching along the southern tip of Louisiana, below New Orleans, to where the chocolate-colored Mississippi courses into the clear blue water of the Gulf, the area known as deep delta country.

Prior to the discovery that Plaquemines was kept afloat, literally and figuratively, by oil, its marshes and swamps had been home to water moccasins, mosquitoes, and one of the most profitable muskrat trapping industries in America. Following the discovery of oil, the face of Plaquemines changed. From Louisiana's poorest parish it became one of the richest.

To make sure he secured control of the oil under the parish, Perez, who recognized the potential early, cozied up immediately to the new governor, Huey Long, whom he would come to admire extravagantly and whose autocracy he imitated closely. Shortly afterward, Perez had a chance to earn Long's eternal gratitude by helping to save him from a threatened impeachment proceeding. It required less than three years for nearly all the oil lands to fall under the control of the local $5,000-a-year district attorney.

Getting the profits into his pockets was a little more complicated and took a little longer, but Perez was a master legal technician, setting up dummy corporations to lease the oil lands, with the advice, of course, of private lawyer Perez. The corporations in turn, also on advice of counsel, whose fees were not a negligible part of the deal, parceled out the property to interested oil producers. Although Perez was modest about his wealth, and to hear him talk an outsider might think he subscribed to the little-tin-box method of saving, he admitted to making a million dollars before he was fifty. When the state attorney general suggested Perez's public and private roles in the oil deals might indicate a conflict of interest, Perez told him to

Go to hell!

A former down-at-the-heels rural parish, Plaquemines, which remained the real owner of the oil lands, also got rich as the royalties and its share of the severance tax paid to the state by the oil companies rolled in. Proud as a Middle Eastern sheikh, Perez showed off to visitors what oil royalties had done for his native parish—at his direction and through his patronage, of course: libraries, free ferries, levees, water purification plants, drainage facilities, schools, hospitals, and a lot of other accoutrements of modern life that were changing the way even the old muskrat trappers lived back in the bayous.

The oil companies had soon found they did business with Perez or they didn't do business at all. For any reason, or for no reason, he could block the laying of a pipeline, have his safety commissioner find a fire hazard in a company's operation, or direct his highway commissioner to declare the company's semis overweight and unable to travel safely on local roads.

The trouble in this paradise of Perez's was not over the oil that was keeping Plaquemines afloat. Perez had that under control. The trouble came with the discovery of rich oil beds offshore in the Gulf on which the federal government had cast a thirsty eye. The entrepreneur in Perez disapproved of the federal government's interest in practice—all that money going north—and the states' righter in him disapproved of it in principle. But he was unable to stop or even delay what he saw as the federal juggernaut about to crunch state interests under its powerful wheels.

The potential in the offshore oil fields was too big even to guess at. Although it was also discovered that the cost of producing oil found beneath the waters was fourteen times greater than that of producing it from land-based wells, Louisiana had immediately gone on a spree of exploration and development that thirty years later would bring in millions annually in cash bonuses, rentals, and royalties.

The spires of the oil rigs would loom cathedrallike out of the Gulf, and on the banks of the Mississippi from Baton Rouge to New Orleans, eighteenth- and nineteenth-century plantations alternated with petrochemical plants, machine shops, and refineries, their tall smokestacks spitting the characteristic orange flame skyward, lighting up the night. The taxes on offshore oil would provide social services to the poor and pensions to the elderly, and oil company executives, periodically emptying the small change from their pockets into Democratic coffers, would become increasingly influential in local politics.

In the mid-1940s, the federal government began to move on the state's profitable offshore operations. Before the money began to gush in, no one in Washington had paid any attention when the coastal states and municipalities invested public money in the regulation of fisheries, building breakwaters and dredging harbors in the coastal waters.

For the century and a half between ratification of the Constitution, which said nothing about ownership of submerged lands off the nation's seacoasts, until the 1940s when title to these lands, by that time known to be oil-soaked, erupted as a public issue, it had been assumed that since the lands had not been specifically granted to the national government, they belonged to the states for three miles out from the low-water line. The mileage was an arbitrary creation of international law based on the range of a cannon.

The nation's need for oil during World War II, however, drew attention to this relatively new source, and the Roosevelt administration set out to establish federal ownership. But Franklin Roosevelt was old and tired with a war on his hands, and he hadn't the heart to start a potentially bruising argument between the states and the federal government.

Roosevelt's successor, Harry Truman, was also a firm advocate of federal ownership, arguing that the tidelands, like the White House and the Capitol, belonged to all the states, not just the fortunate few along the coasts. He ordered his attorney general, the genial Texan Tom C. Clark, to get busy on a court case and issued an executive order proclaiming federal "jurisdiction and control" over the offshore oil beds. Leander Perez didn't vote for a Democratic presidential candidate again for more than twenty years.

In the spring of 1946, Perez accompanied Louisiana's attorney general, Fred S. LeBlanc, to Washington where both men testified in behalf of a joint Senate and House resolution ceding the tidelands to the coastal states. LeBlanc dryly recited the facts and figures of contemporary Louisiana's economic interest in the submerged lands, the productivity of its oysters as well as its oil wells. But Perez, who'd spent as much time out of as in the hearing room and had plundered Washington's mustiest bookshops and map stores for early American commentaries on coastal claims, did battle on historical grounds, citing obscure as well as better known cases that supported his view. In July, 1946, both houses of Congress approved the resolution and on August 1, the President vetoed it, partly because he disagreed vigorously with the resolution's intent and partly because Attorney General Clark's case for federal ownership was then pending before the Supreme Court.

On June 23, 1947, Hugo L. Black, senior associate justice on the U.S. Supreme Court, made history when he overturned a 150-year-old pillar of American federalism telling the state of California, which Attorney General Clark had made the defendant in the government's case, that it was not the owner of the three-mile marginal belt along its coast and that the federal government rather than the state had "paramount rights" and "full dominion over the resources of the soil under that water area, including oil."

That business about "paramount rights" scared people. If the federal government could cancel states' rights to their shorelines, could it also in an emergency claim their lakes and rivers? What about their coal, iron, uranium, food, or any other commodity? Where would the monster's appetite be satisfied?

Perez and other southerners saw a pattern developing: when a conflict of state and federal interests arose, the federal interest prevailed. They also feared, in Louisiana and Texas particularly, that they would be next.

Bascom Giles, land commissioner of Texas, thundered that he would "favor seceding before giving up these valuable lands!" Texas Attorney General Price Daniel called the Supreme Court's decision the greatest "blow against property rights of the states since the Civil War." No one mentioned, at least publicly, that Democratic cash boxes would soon empty if the oil companies, now beholden to local officials for their leases, had to apply to a faceless federal bureaucracy for permission to drill.

In Congress, advocates of state ownership attempted to legislate the Supreme Court's decision off the books. Perez and LeBlanc trudged back to Washington where again they testified against federal ownership of tidelands. Perez was a little less deferential this time, calling the California case a "totalitarian tidal land grab" and the Supreme Court the "fabled wolf that ate up the helpless little lamb."

But their trip was futile. Attorney General Clark was just warming up. He boasted to the same congressional committee that his department, even as he testified, was in the process of preparing similar cases against Louisiana and "two or three of the other states in the Gulf." It was his intention, Clark added, "to file a suit against every State" that he considered "affected" by the Supreme Court's decision.

The tidelands oil dispute was only one of the matters that sent Leander Perez into a tailspin during the 1940s. Reconstituted in recent years with Franklin Roosevelt's appointees and marching in step with his and his successor's administrations, the U.S. Supreme Court was doing all the right things to alienate the Perezes throughout the South by affirming the constitutionality of New Deal programs that brought still another unwanted federal presence into daily lives and by opening up white America to its black citizens: letting them into white universities, overturning their criminal convictions, and, the bitterest pill of all, hardly calculated to lower Perez's blood pressure as he envisioned his power over Plaquemines slipping, supporting their right to vote. From Perez's point of view, the justices were undoing in the 1940s all their predecessors had accomplished in the 1880s and 1890s when they virtually ignored the Civil War amendments to the Constitution and let the states do as they pleased.

Support of blacks' voting rights held the greatest potential for undermining Perez's sacred southern traditions. As federal judge Skelly Wright in New Orleans always said, "Once you get the right to vote, you get the politicians to pay attention."

Ever since 1915, when the Court factored out the grandfather clauses from the southern states' constitutions of the 1890s, declaring them unconstitutional, the justices and these states had been in an ongoing argument over blacks' voting rights. No sooner did the Court knock over a barrier erected by a state than the state legislature invented a legal sophistry to erect another.

In 1921, to circumvent the Court's 1915 ruling, Louisianans, carefully avoiding all references to race or color, devised for their new constitution an augmentation of the literacy qualifications previously installed in their 1898 document and required a potential voter to "be able to understand and give a reasonable interpretation of any section of either the U.S. or the state Constitution when read to him by the registrar." The limits of their own imaginations were the only restrictions the white registrars faced in devising the questions they might ask. The strategy seemed an easy way to appear to comply with the Constitution without actually doing so, and most southern states enacted similar measures.

War stories of blacks' attempts to register were passed around: of their being asked how many beans in a bushel or how many bubbles in a barrel of soapsuds. A favorite concerned a young black Ph.D. holder in Mississippi who was asked to translate one of his answers to the registrar's questions into Greek.

"Yes," I can do that," he replied serenely. "It means 'niggers can't vote in Mississippi.'"

Another tactic widely employed by southerners was to declare the primary election open only to white voters. In the solidly Democratic South, the reasoning went, the only election that mattered was the primary. The general election was only a formality. Theoretically, at least, the Democratic Party, whose members bore the primary's expenses, furnished the ballots and counted the votes, was a private organization and not an instrument of the state. Since the federal Constitution nowhere prohibited private racial discrimination, the party was free to exclude any voters it chose to, including blacks. Emboldened, states actually wrote blatantly racial primary voting qualifications into the law books.

When the Supreme Court declared the device unconstitutional in 1927 for the first time, the resourceful southern politicians dutifully removed the race specification from the statute books and wrote it into the party rules. But it didn't hold up.

After a couple of detours during the intervening years, on April 3, 1944, the Supreme Court let American political parties everywhere know, via a case called *Smith* v. *Allwright,* that primary elections fell under federal jurisdiction and their subterfuges and escape hatches could not stand. Sweeping away the accumulated legal debris the states had piled sky-high to keep blacks out of the voting booth, the Court in one broad slice slaughtered the last vestige of the white primary, declaring that without any doubt whatever, this exclusionary tactic contradicted the Fifteenth Amendment to the Constitution. No more evasions would be tolerated.

Thurgood Marshall, the LDF's biggest gun, had argued the case before the Court. A. P. Tureaud, hard at work at the time on his own first voting rights case in Louisiana, had gone up to Washington to hear him.

The strengthened muscle it gave to black political involvement made *Allwright* the most significant victory for the LDF lawyers to date, and the office party at New York headquarters to celebrate became a legend. So awash, literally and figuratively, was it in high spirits that Marshall's telephone calls had to be constantly rerouted, and he missed a congratulatory call from Justice Frank Murphy. When they talked next day, Marshall recalled, he "apologized profusely" and Murphy agreed that "a guy had the right to get drunk at a time like that."

Before the decade was out, local election officials in the South were reporting black voter turnouts in unprecedented numbers, and the *New York Times* was reporting that regionwide, the number of black voters had nearly tripled between 1940 and 1947, from 211,000 to 645,000.

There were also evasions: registrars who locked their doors against black voters or sent them home with instructions to learn the Constitution. Intimidation was common, occasionally there was violence. It took A. P. Tureaud two years after *Allwright* was handed down to pry open the registration rolls in St. John the Baptist Parish via the first voting rights suit in Louisiana, and it was several years before blacks could vote with ease in all the parishes. As the state's school boards had done in the teachers' salary-equalization cases, election officials made black regis-trants sweat over every name entered on the books.

Perez and his ilk feared they were looking at the disintegration of the whole fabric of race relations in the South, and they sought solace in politics. In the spring of 1948, as the presidential election got underway, all the fears and resentments bubbled to the surface.

Harry Truman, president by succession, wanted desperately to be nominated and elected in his own right in 1948. He knew, however, the Democratic Party, which had managed to stick together through thick and thin—secession, Reconstruction, and Redemption—had begun to fly apart. Southerners who'd traditionally counted on it as the party of white supremacy were being outnumbered and outshouted by northern liber-als, big labor, and urban blacks, whose growing voter strength was being wooed and often won.

Southerners had made the party acutely aware of their displeasure at the national convention in 1944 when seven states—Louisiana, Missis-sippi, Virginia, Texas, Alabama, Florida, and South Carolina—gave a total of eighty-nine protest votes to favorite son Senator Harry F. Byrd of Virginia. Now in 1948, the mere mention of Truman and his Special Committee on Civil Rights, which the year before had suggested several measures Congress should consider to end racial discrimination, made white southern heads spin.

Governor Fielding Wright of Mississippi was so unnerved by events in Washington that he suggested in his inaugural address that year that secession of southern Democrats from the national party was a distinct possibility should southern interests continue to be ignored. In a little experiment to snatch sure victory from the candidates of the national parties in the electoral college, Wright's own state of Mississippi had put a slate of uninstructed electors on the ballot in 1944. The exercise had been futile then, but the strategy did not lack potential. Now in 1948, a solid South, united once more by the politics of race and the specter of federal domination as it had not been since Reconstruction, might well hold a handful of trumps.

Threats, blackmail, were not the way to intimidate the little bantam president from Missouri, the "show me" state, according to legend and, later, its automobile license plates. On racial matters, it was true, he had mixed emotions.

Never publicly, but often privately, Truman had been heard to use the word "nigger," and he was not the kind of man who stalked out of the room or even mildly objected to racial jokes; indeed, he laughed with the rest of the room. It didn't occur to him that a black man was his social equal.

But when it came to equality before the law, he had few peers in the 1940s. Instances of brutality that the average newspaper reader noticed only casually outraged Truman; his "very stomach turned over" when he heard about men wearing the uniform of their country being dumped off an army truck in Mississippi and beaten. The statistics of a government report could not have touched him in the same way. Discrimination by a voting registrar, an employer, a union boss, disturbed him in a way no racial joke could. He had come to truly believe that the South was "living eighty years behind the times," and he planned to remedy the anachronism of race, the protests of the southerners in his party notwithstanding.

In 1948, of course, there was more than a little self-interest mingled with the President's dedication to racial equality. He wanted and believed he needed the growing black vote.

His response to Governor Wright's not-so-veiled threat of rebellion in the Democratic ranks was typical of this tough chief executive who'd matured in the chills and spills of St. Louis machine politics to become FDR's running mate in 1944 and now, following Roosevelt's death, President of the United States. He continued along the path on which he had set out. In so doing, he further alienated the white South and in essence touched off the revolt that followed.

The white South was gone the minute his special message on civil rights, which he sent to Congress on February 2, was published south of the Potomac River. The statement was not as bold as it might have been. Truman stopped short of endorsing all the recommendations his civil rights committee had made the previous year, and there was nothing revolutionary or startling in his text, nothing he hadn't urged on the Congress before.

But it stirred up southern feelings—and fears. He wanted, the President said, to correct the

> flagrant examples ... of discrimination which are utterly contrary to our ideals,

and he limited his demands to a ten-point program urging federal protection against lynching, increased protection of voting rights, prohibition against discrimination in interstate transportation, and strengthening of existing civil rights statutes. He hoped one sunny day in the future a permanent office for civil rights would be established within the Department of Justice.

Neither the report of his special committee the year before nor the President himself even suggested an end to school segregation. But it was the first time in this century that an American president had sent Congress a legislative package dealing solely with civil rights, and white southerners were deeply offended, as much perhaps at the singular attention given the issue as with the proposals themselves. Was this the prologue to an attack on segregation itself? they wondered. What was the real target?

The New Orleans *Times-Picayune* had suggested the year before that the President's civil rights committee's recommendations might "fan a waning fire to white and furious heat, burn away the very substantial gains for race relationships, economic progress and race advancement that have been building at increasing speed by peaceful processes." Now the editors accused the President himself of "not only risking, but inviting, cleavage of his own party and bitter dissension within his own country."

Which is exactly what happened. Truman had underestimated southern reaction, which ranged in vehemence from a Ku Klux Klan parade and cross burning in Swainsboro, Georgia, to cutting comments by southern Congressmen, including the wry prediction by Louisiana's senior senator Allen Ellender that the President's civil rights policy was

sure to have considerable effect on the amount of campaign contributions.

Between February and the national Democratic convention in mid-July, the "bitter dissension" predicted by the *Times-Picayune* became public as the party was torn apart. Louisiana's Leander Perez was one of the leading fire-eaters pushing for secession from the national party and eager to contribute his considerable energy, financial resources, time, and his well-known organizational skills to the movement. He seemed to be in perpetual motion that spring, although he worked largely backstage conferring with local political figures, chasing off to regional gatherings where possible candidates and campaign strategies were being worked out, representing the extremist point of view wherever party officials gathered around a conference table.

Southerners boycotted the annual Democrats' pep rally known as the Jefferson-Jackson Day dinner in Washington that spring. Truman was the guest of honor and Senator Olin D. Johnston of South Carolina was afraid he and his wife might be seated next to a "Nigra." Congressman John Bell Williams of Mississippi explained that southerners could not

join in such a hypocritical gesture and you will find most of us having our own Jefferson-Jackson Day dinners in gatherings in which white supremacy is the order and segregation is the rule.

The momentum for splitting the Democratic Party could not be stopped now. In Louisiana that spring the legislature passed resolutions condemning the President and urging the state to "take its rightful place at the side of all sovereign states that will oppose this unconstitutional and undemocratic 'civil rights' program."

Hoping to harness the restless but disorganized unfocused energy, southern officials and prominent politicians met in Jackson, Mississippi, on May 10, one week after the U.S. Supreme Court hammered still another nail in the coffin of states' rights with its decision declaring that courts, including state courts, could no longer enforce restrictive housing covenants intended to discriminate against black renters or buyers. The Truman administration, for the first time in a post–World War II civil rights case, had intervened as amicus curiae—literally "friend of the court"—to argue for just such a conclusion.

Further infuriated by the Court's ruling, Perez and his fellow incendiaries, with their talk of Truman's betrayal and the dangers civil rights legislation and judicial decisions posed for the South, dominated the meeting in Jackson, which produced enough heated oratory to start a global warming trend, but no agreement on candidates, platform, or strategy for southern maneuvering at the approaching national convention.

The dissidents did make plans to meet again in Birmingham, Alabama, following the July convention. They would decide then what steps to take, depending upon how the national party received them. Cooler heads among them hoped the mere threat of secession might persuade the party to weaken its commitment to civil rights, perhaps even to nominate an opponent of the legislation the President had proposed. They were not, however, optimistic.

It was a bitterly contentious group of Democrats that converged on Philadelphia that July. Some, like Perez, were defiant and talked about a final bolt from the national party. Others were concerned and cautioned against this modern political equivalent of the firing on Fort Sumter the century before. As important perhaps as the symbolism was the practical consideration: cutting all connections to the party in power, the people with the patronage, was a risky business and ought to be considered very seriously. Still others were saddened at the prospect of a rupture in the party that had weathered a century of often heavy storms with minimal damage. The informal discussions among the delegates were grave, as they pondered the limits of their power to influence the national party and the alternative if they couldn't.

Galvanized by southern implacability, national Democratic leaders stood firm. Young, ambitious Mayor Hubert H. Humphrey of Minneapolis, Minnesota, in one of the more emotional outbursts recorded at an American political convention, urged his fellow Democrats

> to get out of the shadows of States' Rights and to walk forthrightly into the bright sunshine of human rights.

All earlier hopes for an innocuous civil rights plank in the party platform were dashed when the convention accepted, after considerable negotiation, and against southern opposition, a relatively strong civil rights plank that incorporated the principles of most of the President's recommendations of the previous February. The South's entire 278 votes were cast against it. Upon its adoption by the convention, the chairman of the Alabama delegation, Handy Ellis, uttered his historic last words on the proceedings through which he had sweltered for four days:

> [W]e bid you good bye.

After which Ellis and his faction of the Alabama delegation, carrying high the state flag and joined by the Mississippi delegation, marched defiantly down the center aisle of Convention Hall and into the pouring rain outside. Both boos and cheers followed them, but the cheers were lost in the noise and confusion as the rebels surged onward.

The other delegates from the old Confederacy—nine and a half delegations—kept their seats. They planned to cast their 264 votes (North Carolina was split) for Senator Richard B. Russell of Georgia, whose name had been put forward in a gesture of defiance and denial of support for Harry Truman.

The President, who'd been listening to the ruckus on the radio as his train raced through the night toward Philadelphia, couldn't help thinking of a similar split in the Democratic Party nearly a century before—in 1860—when the southern Democrats walked out and nominated John C. Breckinridge at their own convention and left the regular party's candidate Stephen A. Douglas to fight it out with Abraham Lincoln without their support. Along with the South's subsequent secession, it was a troubling recollection for an American president moments after his own nomination.

When the convention chairman, Representative Sam Rayburn of Texas, finally gaveled the rowdy delegates to order, and the voting on the national party's nominee began, President Truman easily defeated Senator Russell on the first ballot. Mississippi's Governor Wright immediately called for protesters to follow him to Birmingham and there to nominate a states' rights candidate.

On July 17, 1948, some six thousand unhappy, perspiring Democrats clad in standard midsummer southern garb of shirt-sleeves and broad-brimmed straw hats and waving Confederate flags, converged on the redbrick municipal auditorium in Birmingham and noisily took their seats behind the banners of the eleven states represented: all except North Carolina from the old Confederacy plus Oklahoma. Photographers were quick to spot Leander Perez conferring with Governor Strom Thurmond of South Carolina and others among the coterie he'd built over the years.

In one day, the dissidents, with little debate, but much oratory, put together a platform affirming the rights of the states as outlined in the Tenth Amendment to the Constitution and chastised the federal government for its encroachment of those rights. Economic issues such as regulation of business and industry by New Deal legislation and federal dominion over tidelands oil—rumors that oil money was financing the rebellion had begun to surface—were significant factors in the southern revolt, but they were obscured by issues of race, the common denominator among the rebels, the glue that would hold the movement together, and the rallying cry that could be relied on to command the votes, come November. In their final platform, the southerners specifically

> oppose[d] and condemn[ed] the action of the Democratic convention
> in sponsoring a civil rights program calling for the elimination of seg-
> regation, social equality by Federal fiat, regulation of private employ-
> ment practices, voting and local law enforcement.

Establishment of such a program, the dissidents declared, would be "utterly destructive of the social, economic and political life of the Southern people."

Explosions of enthusiasm and choruses of "Dixie" punctuated the six-hour session as the speakers blasted the rival ticket and drew frightening pictures of the threat to "our homes, our theaters, and our swimming pools" if race barriers were removed. Rebel yells and parades on the convention floor, life-size portraits of Robert E. Lee held high, followed verbal whippings of the President and his civil rights programs as "threats to make Southerners into a mongrel, inferior race by forced intermingling with Negroes."

The choice of candidates was both predictable and unanimous. The ticket was to be headed by South Carolina's governor Thurmond. He hadn't been one of the original bolters, and he had a portrait of FDR hanging in his office—next to the empty space where Harry Truman's had once hung. But race and revolt were hot issues in South Carolina that year, and if Thurmond planned to run for the U.S. Senate in 1950, it behooved him to find a prominent place on the political bandwagon.

His record was exemplary: a grandfather who'd fought with Lee and known the poverty and bitterness of a conquered people, a list of political offices he'd held that ranged from county superintendent of education to governor, bemedaled World War II hero. There were whispers even then that the governor was helping to support a young black woman studying at the all-Negro South Carolina State College who was supposed to be his daughter, the result of a liaison with a black woman in his native Edgefield, but no one held that against him. Sexual relationships between white men and black women was the one area where racial taboos fell, always had fallen.

For vice president, the southerners chose Mississippi's Wright. Not only had he instigated the bolt from the national party, but, several months before, had delivered a rousing radio address in his home state warning Mississippi's blacks that if they were thinking about equality with whites in schools and restaurants, it would be better for them to leave the state.

Following the speeches, the delegates yelled and paraded some more, then left the city, all fired up to put their scheme of political blackmail into action. They never had any hope of winning the election, but they hoped that by replacing the candidates of the national party on southern ballots with their states' rights choices, they might take the South's 127 electoral votes and thereby deny a majority to either the Republican or Democratic candidates. Should their strategy work, the election would be thrown into the House of Representatives where, each state having only one vote, the southerners would have to be listened to. If they couldn't actually win the election, they might at least recoup their former position of influence within the national Democratic Party.

They called themselves the States' Rights Democratic Party but they were better known as the Dixiecrats, and they were another part of a modern concept of political action known as "massive resistance." It was the way Yankees described the combination of regional pride and enthusiasm for combat that surfaced in southerners as a group whenever issues of race were involved.

Former Louisiana governor Jimmie H. Davis, a full-time entertainer since he'd left the governor's mansion in Baton Rouge after his first term (1944–48), added a little coda to the political events of the summer when he was invited to sing for the President at the White House even as the Dixiecrats were meeting in Birmingham. After giving the matter serious thought, Davis agreed to go to Washington and sing for the President a brand new little ditty called

  "Ya Gotta Stop Pushin' That Mule Around"

That fall, Leander Perez led the Dixiecrat revolt in Louisiana—and in his spare time lent a hand in Texas. At the September meeting of the Louisiana Democratic committee of which he was a member, he hood-winked his cronies into making Thurmond and Wright the official nomi-nees of the Democratic Party in the state, and it took the governor, the newly elected Earl Long, and a special session of the legislature to restore the names of the regular Democratic candidates. Forty-plus years later, the complete details of Perez's sleight of hand remain murky, part of Louisiana's rich political folklore known perhaps only to the par-ticipants, all dead, but one political commentator observed shortly after Perez's performance that "rumors float around about tidelands oil." Perez himself explained simply that Truman and Barkley were the candi-dates of "not the Democratic party, but the New Deal–Communist party."

Perez did manage to transfer Louisiana's traditional Democratic sym-bol—the rooster, said to be worth ten thousand votes among south Louisiana's French-speaking voters who had been taught to *tapez le coq* (pick the rooster)—from its usual space alongside the names of the reg-ular Democratic candidates to a new place alongside the names of the insurgents. His maneuver was said to have given Louisiana to Thurmond and Wright.

In November, although less than half the state's voters turned out, the Dixiecrats carried Louisiana (49 percent of the vote)—and Missis-sippi, Alabama, and South Carolina, all states with high proportions of blacks and a correspondingly high proportion of white racial conserva-tives. But thirty-eight electoral votes were hardly enough to cause even a ripple in the electoral college, much less to force the election into the House of Representatives. Despite Dixiecrat defections on the right, and Progressive Party candidate Henry Wallace's independent crusade on the left, the President carried the rest of the South and enough of the nation to defeat the favorites, Republicans Thomas E. Dewey of New York and Governor Earl Warren of California. The extremists of all per-suasions had failed, and afterward the Dixiecrats lost popular support as well as financial backing. The national Democratic Party purged its national committee of Dixiecrats from the four states that had defected, and denied patronage to disloyal Congressmen. Morale—and financial support—sagged as Dixiecrats lost local elections and regular

Democrats returned to power in their customary strongholds.

In Louisiana, Democrat Earl Long, Huey Long's brother, defeated Dixiecrat Sam H. Jones for the governorship, and Russell Long, in whose stocky build, boyish face, and crinkly brown hair Louisianans saw the "spittin' image" of his late father Huey, won a seat in the United States Senate. In New Orleans, the progressive and ambitious young mayor DeLesseps S. Morrison, who had, as he'd hoped on his return from the war, swept the city's long-entrenched political machine out of office, reported on his brief postelection meeting with President Truman:

> I told the President that I have made many political mistakes but I did not make the mistake of falling into the Dixiecrat bear trap.

Strom Thurmond's failure in 1950 to unseat South Carolina's Democratic Senator Olin Johnston appeared perhaps to put a final period to the Dixiecrat movement. What the insurgents stood for, however, lived on in the hearts and minds of white southerners for many years to come and remained a strong bond in southern politics. Two decades later, in 1968, Perez was out campaigning for third party presidential candidate George C. Wallace, governor of Alabama and sworn enemy of racial equality and federal supremacy—as devout a Dixiecrat as Perez himself. Wallace's 40 percent of the southern white vote, which included Louisiana's ten electoral votes, doubled Strom Thurmond's share in 1948, but it still wasn't enough to change the outcome of the election, and the Republican Richard M. Nixon won easily.

Former Louisiana governor Jimmie Davis's blunt though lyrical warning to President Truman notwithstanding, Truman did not "stop pushin' that mule around." In his state of the union message to Congress on January 5, 1949, he declared his intention to

> adopt a program for the planned use of the petroleum reserves under the sea, which are—and must remain—vested in the Federal Government.

Three days later, at his news conference on the budget, he confirmed that he was asking Congress to pass legislation making it "perfectly plain as to how we can develop those resources in the interest of the public."

Working quietly offstage, well out of the public eye, was Attorney General Clark, who was preparing the government's cases against Louisiana and Texas for a hearing by the Supreme Court. On the other side, Louisiana's new governor Long had appointed Leander Perez a special state assistant attorney general to mastermind Louisiana's defense against the federal government.

Once again, Perez focused his considerable energies and lively intellect on gathering all the available facts and figures until he felt adequately equipped to collaborate with the state attorney general in the writing of the briefs for Louisiana and participating in the oral argument before the nation's highest court.

Against the government's contention that since Louisiana's case presented no new constitutional questions, the California case of 1947 should serve as the operative precedent, Perez cited a century-old suit by the United States against New Orleans in which he said the issues were analogous, and the Supreme Court denied the federal claim. He asked the Court to reconsider the recent California case.

When all the technical matter and the constitutional arguments were peeled away, however, Perez's argument boiled down to the old Dixiecrat platform:

> The fundamental issue before this Court is whether the sovereignty can be taken away from Louisiana. . . . If the United States can deprive the people of their property, it can deprive them of their freedom and liberty.

On June 5, 1950, the justices announced they had not reversed their decision in California's case as the Louisianans and Texans had urged, but had in fact made it the precedent for their decision in these latest cases. They saw "no reason why Louisiana stands on a better footing than California so far as the three-mile belt is concerned." The "national interest" was the same in the one state as in the other, and they reiterated their rationale for their conclusion in California's case:

> The marginal sea is a national, not a state concern. National interests, national responsibilities, national concerns are involved. The problems of commerce, national defense, relations with other powers, war and peace focus here. National rights must therefore be paramount in that area.

There was that business of "paramount" rights again. It looked to Perez and other southerners like open season on state interests. Where next? they asked themselves again—and again.

The *Times-Picayune* called the Court's decision "a planned and deliberate drive to expand the federal powers by contracting and nullifying the powers and rights of the several states." Louisiana's Congressmen promised early action on new legislation that would annul the Court's decision and return the tidelands to the states. The recently elected senator from Louisiana, Russell Long, had already coauthored such a measure and promised he would "attempt to force the bill to a vote in the Senate before this Congress adjourns." He was in fact flying back to Washington immediately for just that purpose.

The decision not only meant a projected loss of vast wealth in Louisiana, Texas, and Florida, but it put even more strain on the fragile living arrangements devised by the state and nation. What with the federal government telling southerners how to run their elections, to whom they could sell their property, whom they could admit to their universities, and now this, it had begun to seem that the much-vaunted Tenth Amendment to the Constitution that they had thought was supposed to protect states' rights was being whittled away to just about nothing.

As the 1950s opened, there were other matters troubling ordinary Louisianans, the upstate lumbermen, Gulf fishermen, the rice farmers of the coastal marshes, the shoe salesmen in Shreveport and Alexandria. Perez's "uppity" blacks, many of them returned war veterans, had taken seriously one of their number's observations as the ship carrying him home from Okinawa neared America's West Coast: "*Our* fight for freedom begins when we get to San Francisco."

Blacks had fought with General Andrew Jackson to save New Orleans from the British in 1814, but when the weary veterans returned to their homes following congratulations and expressions of gratitude from the general himself, the words soon lost their meaning, for the men returned also to their former lowly status, "object[s] of scorn," as Hippolyte Castra, one of their poets, put it.

Like the returning veterans then, blacks who fought on the battlefields of France a century later found American democracy still had a FOR WHITES ONLY sign on it:

We got decorated, kissed on the jaw—all that. And I was proud as I could be, till I got back home. The first white man I met, the very first one . . . told me I better not wear that uniform or that medal again no matter how long I lived. He told me I was back home now, and they didn't cotton to no nigger wearing medals for killing white folks.

Blacks had returned from the battlefields of Germany and Iwo Jima thirty years later with their heads higher, a lilt in their step, and their eyes alight with the determination to claim their rightful share in America.

More politically outspoken than ever before and demonstrating a new sense of unity, blacks were challenging southern traditions and asserting rights with an unusual aggressiveness. They were demanding the right to vote and the opportunity for better education. They were successfully competing with whites for jobs in the new industries that had located in the area during and after the war, and somebody, it seemed to some white southerners, was putting ideas into their heads.

They wanted to use the golf course and tennis courts in New Orleans's segregated City Park as well as the facilities of the Municipal Auditorium, and they'd hired lawyers to win the right to do so.

After some agitation, a black man had been appointed to the Louisiana Civil Defense Advisory Council. In Baton Rouge, the Louisiana lawmakers, fearing the next demand and hoping to head it off, couldn't pour funds into the state's black colleges fast enough. "You know," Appropriations Committee Chairman John McKeithen warned, "the situation we are facing."

The speed with which white southerners' lives were being changed caught many of them off-guard, unprepared and resistant. In a letter to their senator, Mr. and Mrs. J. D. Frazier of Biloxi, Mississippi, spoke to a past that would never be again:

> We are kind to our darkies and treat them as they deserve to be treated. As far as their education they feel that they only need enough to read and write, but the Northern people seem to think that isn't enough and we have the largest percentage of darkies here so why can't they keep their hands off and their mouths shut and let us handle this problem.

CHAPTER 5

"Just Another Southern 'Boy'"

Much, much later, Federal District Judge J. Skelly Wright would remember this moment and recognize it as the turning point, when people began to look at him "a little fishy-eyed," and even his friends demanded to know "what's happening?" He had planned at one time to write his autobiography in his golden years; he'd gone so far as to scribble a rough outline on one of his yellow legal pads. This moment had fallen into chapter 6: "Race Cases Already on Docket—LSU Law School," and he'd described it tersely as "crossed the Rubicon."

No one, not even he, predicted at this moment the depth of the agonies he—and his wife and young son—would endure because of what he was setting in motion, although he was a southerner, a native Louisianan, and if he could not foresee the *full* implications of what he was doing, he knew he was not signing a simple order awarding A a few hundred dollars for damages to a boat which B had smashed into one foggy night in the Gulf. He knew he was going unarmed into the territory of people's emotions, where reason counted for much less than the strong feelings they had about race, tradition, and the meddling of the Yankee government. Had he been a less cerebral and more emotional man, the crisis into which he was steering could have torn him to pieces.

At that moment in the fall of 1950 when he signed the order forcing the board of supervisors at Louisiana State University to admit a black man to its all-white law school, Wright was thirty-nine years old and still something of a neophyte on the bench. He'd taken his seat exactly a year ago, in October, 1949. He'd had no idea then how important to his career the lifetime tenure of a federal judgeship would be. Without that protection, he'd have been dead professionally before he was forty. People afterward described him as a "monument" to lifetime tenure.

He'd had no idea then either that before he was fifty, he would be the central figure in the local segregation crisis, that he would have attracted a following of tormentors, or that he would have become the most hated man in New Orleans, perhaps in all of Louisiana and across the South, wherever people cared about what they called the "southern way of life."

Never before had Wright been a crusader. He would have scoffed if anyone had told him history had picked *him* out for more than an ordinary role in human affairs, that in the performance of that role he would become much more than he ever thought he was. Watching him over the next decade as he stared down the entire state of Louisiana—the governor, the legislature, the state courts, and 80 to 90 percent of the people in the state—was nearly enough to convince one that Harry Truman was right when he said that "men make history and not the other way."

People who knew Wright well were often surprised at his judicial performance: his burgeoning activism in civil rights matters that came before his court, his vast reserves of resolution that backed up his convictions, and the courage his course of action required. Some saw it as betrayal and they dropped him. A private sort of person, he wasn't one to advertise his evolution, but it was all there in his past, each step: in the Irish Channel, aboard the *Thetis,* at the Christmas party for the blind, at his first argument before the U.S. Supreme Court where he fought for the life of Willie Francis, a young black man denied a fair trial under Louisiana's two-tiered system of justice. Anyone who put it all together and into perspective could have predicted how Skelly Wright's story would come out.

James Skelly Wright was born January 14, 1911, in New Orleans, the second of seven surviving children born to James E. and Margaret (Skelly) Wright. He was called Skelly to distinguish him from several other Jameses in the family.

Present-day Wrights are a little vague about their antecedents. The Wright side of the family came from St. Louis. Skelly's younger brother Jim believed Skelly and he were part of a fourth generation of Skellys born in America, that it was probably their great-great grandparents who'd come from County Cork and settled in South Louisiana. Skelly liked to say he'd sprung from "potato famine Irish."

The Irish were administering affairs in several American cities just after the turn of the twentieth century. One European observer remarked that New Orleans, a port of entry for Irish immigrants second only to New York before the Civil War, was "held captive by Irishmen and their sons." It was perhaps only natural that Skelly's family should figure in the political life of their city. His mother was a ward leader for the Regular Democratic Organization (RDO), referred to affectionately by its supporters, sardonically by its detractors, as the "Old Regulars," or the "Ring." The only political party in town worth belonging to at the time, the RDO was an effective, tightly controlled urban machine whose boss for the first quarter of the twentieth century, Martin Behrman, claimed his word was worth twenty-six thousand votes to any candidate or issue. Margaret Wright's brother, Joseph P. Skelly, had begun as one of Behrman's lieutenants and was rapidly becoming a functionary in the upper echelons of the organization. It was through his influence that Skelly's father, a plumber, was appointed an inspector for the New Orleans Sewage and Water Board.

The Wrights lived in a "shotgun-camelback" house of which there were rows and rows in New Orleans. Local lore ascribed the name "shotgun" to the fact that a man could shoot unobstructed from door to door, "camelback" to the "hump," or second story added to the structure about midway between front and back walls. It was set among others of its kind on Camp Street in a downtown working-class area of the city known as the Irish Channel, which stretched for a mile or so between the river and the affluent Garden District. At one time it was home to predominantly Irish seamen and known as one of New Orleans's tough spots.

In the twentieth century, it was perhaps best known for its language peculiarities. Despite the section's proximity to the Garden District, one was not on lower Camp Street apt to hear the accents of the next neighborhood over, the "paht" of the "wuld" in which the elite of "Niew" (rhymes with "view") "Oh' le uns" lived. One was far more likely to be greeted by "Where-yat?" instead of "How are you?," to hear "boids choip" and eat "ersters berled in erl," the language legacy of Irish dock workers from Brooklyn and Hoboken who moved south to find work along the lower Mississippi during the decades before the Civil War. Known as the "niggers of the time," it was these Irish who built the levees without which the lower river valley would be in near-perpetual flood. The immigrant Irish, the reasoning went, came cheaper than native blacks for whom high prices had been paid at auction and who were needed to work the cotton fields, not to be wasted on such unskilled work.

New Orleanians still gleefully pass on the story of Mayor Robert Maestri, the uneducated (after the third grade) son of a Sicilian poultry peddler who, told to keep his mouth shut during President Franklin Roosevelt's visit to New Orleans, could endure his muzzle no longer and blurted out after lunch: "How ya like dem ersters?" All his life Skelly

Wright "remembahed" things and called his wife "Sugah," but if his speech ever was Irish Channel, he had erased most of its reminders before he became a judge.

Which was only one of the foundations of his Irish Channel heritage from which Wright had kicked away. Compared to the others, it was probably the least important.

Had he followed the generations of Irish Channel boys who'd matured before him, he might have become a plumber like his father, or perhaps a Catholic priest in the custom some Irish families had of sending a son or daughter into the Church. Neither future was ever really a possibility: he was too ambitious for the one, too skeptical for the other.

An intensely practical streak in him precluded his acceptance of anything on faith, and although he had been born into a devout Catholic family and his mother walked to 6 A.M. mass every day, rain or shine, Skelly eventually drifted away from the Church, returning only for funerals and weddings. His son later called him a "devout agnostic." Skelly described himself as a "bad Catholic" and doubted his early religious training influenced his later humanitarian and principled judicial positions.

Although he was close to Uncle Joe Skelly and his family, spent summers at their place in Long Beach, Mississippi, followed every nuance in the older man's lively talk, young Skelly decided that he himself, although politically astute, was entirely too "thin-skinned" to be a combatant, however much he loved politics, however traditional such a career was among his clan.

Following a summer at the close of his high school career when he worked as a messenger for a downtown law firm and announced to his blue-collar family that he'd decided to be a lawyer, Skelly in effect left the Irish Channel and its traditions intellectually and psychologically. Except for Uncle Joe who'd gone to Spring Hill College in Mobile, Alabama, no one in his immediate family had gone to college. His parents' education had ended in high school, and his older brother Eddie had gone to sea at fourteen, working in the engine room of a merchant ship to help support the family. There was no precedent for Skelly's choice.

Nevertheless, as soon as his application for financial assistance was approved, Skelly enrolled, not at prestigious Tulane University where young men who expected to be taken into downtown law firms went, but at Jesuit-run Loyola University, twenty-five blocks from home by streetcar where less affluent boys, many of whom aspired to political life as their route to professional prominence and financial security, traditionally matriculated. His own scanty resources required that Skelly earn his degree as quickly as possible, and he chose the combined undergraduate/law curriculum that promised B.A. and LL.B. in six years.

He'd been born into the Progressive Era, a time when utopia had seemed to be within the reach at least of white Americans, attainable on this earth through hard work, clean living, and a little legislation larded with prudent government regulation of the very rich. Antitrust laws, minimum-wage measures, food inspection statutes, Interstate Commerce and Federal Trade commissions—armed with these and more, the reformers would soon, they believed, redistribute the pots of money that had fallen into the hands of a few entrepreneurs: Rockefellers and Morgans, Fisks, Hills, and Vanderbilts. The efforts were only mildly successful, though the times gave off an aura of aspiration and dream fulfillment that contrasted sharply with the hopelessness that pervaded the nearby black community and sent A. P. Tureaud seeking Eden in Chicago. A few reforms were actually achieved, but unfettered laissez faire continued to dominate the first three decades of the twentieth century almost as successfully as it had the last two of the nineteenth.

Before Skelly got his LL.B., the stock market had crashed, and the party had ended. There were numbness, bewilderment, disillusion, and depression where optimism and vitality had so recently reigned. It was only a matter of time before he exhausted his tuition money. As resourceful as he was resolute, he took courses in practice teaching at Tulane during the summer, earned a teaching certificate, and shifted to Loyola's night school so he could teach mathematics and history at Alcée Fortier High School during the day.

Fortier High School, on Freret Street in uptown New Orleans, was the newest (dedicated April 28, 1931), largest (1,300 students), and best public high school in the city. Its student body, all white, all male—New Orlean's schools were gender-separate at the time—was made up of formerly privileged youngsters whose fathers had lost the fortunes out of which they would have paid their sons' tuitions at private schools, and its teaching staff when Skelly joined it was made up largely of unemployed young law school graduates.

Even after he got his LL.B. in June, 1934, the bottom of the Great Depression, law positions were still scarce and young unemployed lawyers still plentiful. Skelly continued on at Fortier. But at 3:00 P.M. each day, he scurried off to a little downtown law office he was sharing temporarily with a friend and practiced what law he could from three to five. Like Tureaud's at the custom house, it was not a particularly satisfactory arrangement for an ambitious young man with a new law degree. It was, however, financially necessary, at least for a time.

If there was any strong element of conformity in Skelly's youth, it was his attitude toward blacks. Until he became a judge, he had been by his own admission "just another southern 'boy'" in the matter of race relations. The subject was rarely discussed, even more rarely was the system challenged, although it was *the* dominant concern of most southerners, white and black. It was just always there. Children sometimes sensed it and asked questions, but they were quickly hushed up.

Skelly didn't need words anyway. The signs on the drinking fountains and the barriers between the white and black sections of the trolleys told him all he needed to know, these and the unwritten code of etiquette that passed intact between the generations. From the time they were five years old, southerners—white and black—knew where to sit and where not to, who used the back door, who the front, whom they called "missus" and whom "auntie," whom they invited into their living rooms and whom they couldn't. Blatant discourtesy was almost never permitted, but it was clearly understood that when the maid was driven home at the end of the day, she sat in the backseat.

White southerners knew the rules, but they generally didn't know much about individual blacks in the early years of the century when Skelly Wright was growing up in New Orleans. About the only Negroes they knew at all were the domestics they supervised in the kitchens and laundry rooms of their homes or the dock workers they saw sitting at the back of the trolleys. Of both these groups, whites were permitted only glimpses. Many—if not most—blacks, even the most cherished domestic servant whose love and loyalty were legendary, have censored the pictures they allowed white folks to see and have taken off their masks only after they returned to their homes and communities. It was one of the ways they kept their sanity.

There were occasionally exceptions—a reaching out by one race, a response by the other. Usually it involved a maid, a housekeeper, sometimes a wet nurse. In the Wrights' case, it was the young helper on the truck that delivered ice to their home on Camp Street every day. They'd nicknamed him Brother-in-Law in honor of the intimacy he'd achieved among them, first as the close friend of the oldest Wright boy, Eddie, then as "almost a member of the family," confiding in the always sympathetic Margaret, seeking her advice and assistance, and continuing to drop in even after the advent of refrigeration. Charming, intelligent, industrious, Brother-in-Law gave the Wrights a better-than-average white southerner's glimpse of a Negro as an individual with intellectual and emotional capacities not so very different from their own, but whose natural inclinations and talents could only be restrained by the professional and social rules of the society into which he'd been born. The ice truck, though Brother-in-Law eventually owned the route, was undoubtedly the end of the line for him, as high as his aspirations and hopes could carry him. Not enough by itself to make a judicial radical of Skelly later in his life, but as a memory, it could not but help to shape an evolving consciousness of race.

Margaret Wright was casually friendly with all of the black families in the neighborhood—in the New Orleans tradition, the white block on which the Wrights lived abutted a Negro block. She made a practice of visiting neighborhood families in mourning, including Negro families, often slipping them a few dollars, and it was a Negro neighbor who woke the Wrights the night the toolshed caught fire.

But the Wrights broke no new ground in race relations. They accepted segregation and its complex of rules as unquestioningly as they accepted the rising and setting of the sun, the changing of the seasons, the timeless, relentless currents of the nearby river. The laws of nature and the laws of society were equally irrefutable. The sense had been instilled in nearly all white southerners that "blacks were inferior," not in a "bitter" context then—that came later—but Negroes at the time were "believed to be not as well educated or to have the means of white people in the neighborhood." The social arbiters got no arguments from the Wrights.

His mother's casual neighborliness notwithstanding, young Skelly's contacts with blacks were as restricted as any white boy's: occasional mixed ball games in the street, but no mixed birthday parties then and no real companionship between the two races. Summers it was Skelly's white next-door neighbor, Dee-Dee Howard, with whom he teamed up to mow lawns.

Each fall, Skelly and his brothers and sisters registered at McDonogh 7, the all-white school about two blocks away. The black children in the neighborhood went to another school nearby. Skelly probably would have been genuinely surprised at the time to discover the Negro school had too many students, too few teachers, tattered geography books, and toilets that didn't always work. During his entire academic career, he never sat next to a black boy or shared a class with one. Warren Easton High School, from which he'd graduated in 1927, was, of course, for white boys only. Loyola didn't admit blacks until more than a quarter of a century afterward.

A consciousness of race grew unhurriedly in this southern boy. As a young man, Skelly was not one of those who abused blacks at Mardi Gras parades, but he did not protest when others attacked them, even though he'd been outraged at the spectacle of white teenagers systematically working the street crowds, searching out the lone Negro, assaulting him at will.

Skelly hadn't ever tossed rotten apples and other garbage out car windows into the front yards of blacks' homes, but he'd sat unprotesting alongside friends who did. Like everybody else in his time and place, he'd called Negroes "nigger." He'd lived by the unspoken but well-understood rules that the color of his skin dictated, and left the questions and discussions to the social scientists and the philosophers. As he himself confessed later:

> I was as southern as anybody else was around there. I saw the system down there. I saw what was going on down there. While I didn't embrace it, it didn't repel me.

And on another occasion:

> Blacks were something apart. The injustice was lost on me basically. I took it like everybody else took it.

It was in the United States attorney's office that Skelly Wright's future began to assume a recognizable shape, at least the federal coloration part of it. It didn't seem so important perhaps in the mid-1930s when men were still selling apples on street corners and Americans, even in the states' rights-conscious South, were grateful for any of the federal largesse directed their way. That he grew up in the federal system, however, was essential to everything Wright did later as a judge.

Nothing Skelly experienced could, of course, match the sting of the racism A. P. Tureaud had endured. There was, however, at least a distant kinship between the men from the Irish Channel and the Seventh Ward. Wright, for example, had no illusions about his own eligibility for employment in a downtown law firm. He was acutely aware that there were varying degrees of white equality in old, clannish New Orleans. However high his aspirations, however solid his academic credentials, however sound his ability, he knew the odds against a boy from the Irish Channel being taken on by a good private law firm in those days. He realized that in New Orleans the "law business" was "rather closely held," and that even if he did beat the odds, "promotion depended to a large degree on paternal relationships with the senior partners."

Wright thought the U.S. attorney's office would be a better place to start. A lot of young lawyers, especially those who hadn't attracted many clients, started there. From all he'd heard, it was interesting work, far from monotonous, even exciting at times. It would make a good training ground, he reasoned, particularly the trial work.

In 1936, he went to Uncle Joe Skelly, who'd become a prominent figure in New Orleans as well as in the Regular Democratic Organization. After serving apprenticeships as a political lieutenant of the late boss Behrman, as registrar of voters for Orleans Parish, and state senator, Joe Skelly had been elected a city commissioner in 1930, one of the ruling quintet (the mayor and four commissioners). Uncle Joe's sponsorship of a job seeker was as good as fifty extra points on a civil service examination.

Skelly's hirability owed something to the political times, too. First under Mayor Behrman, a typical big city politician at the turn of the century, and now under Mayor Maestri, Behrman's clone, the Old Regular machine had ruled New Orleans for the first three decades of the century unchallenged. By the mid-thirties, after years of political warfare, the Long machine, which controlled the rest of the state, had at last succeeded in humbling the city organization, and the two machines were enjoying a period of wary rapprochement. All of which boded well for young Skelly Wright's finding a job.

Taking advantage of the temporary good feeling between his Old Regulars and the Long-run state machine, Uncle Joe went straight to the new U.S. senator from Louisiana, Allen J. Ellender, the bayou-born peppery little Longite whose recent election to the late senator Huey Long's seat had been supported by the Old Regulars. It would have been difficult to turn Uncle Joe down, and as quick as you could say "Atchafalaya," young Skelly Wright was an assistant United States attorney for the Eastern District of Louisiana, with a regular salary and an office in the Post Office Building, which held, in addition to the Post Office, the Immigration and Naturalization Service, the U.S. attorney's office, the federal district court, and the U.S. Court of Appeals for the Fifth Circuit—just about all the local branch offices of the federal government, immersing the new young prosecutor in the federal atmosphere.

Because of his relationship with Uncle Joe and Uncle Joe's with Mayor Maestri, Wright had begun to acquire a reputation as a crony of Maestri's. Skelly stood only on the outer fringes of Maestri's crowd, didn't even know Maestri personally, but it was the way he was beginning to be identified by uptown New Orleanians, and it was, perhaps, time to cut that particular tie to the past. A federal appointment, unconnected to and invulnerable to either city or state political pressures, was just the ticket.

The boss, the U.S. attorney, in 1936 was Rene A. Viosca, forty-six-year-old FDR appointee to the position. He assigned Wright to the narcotics division, the bottom rung in the prosecutor's office. The work was fairly routine, consisting largely of taking the guilty pleas of local offenders. Except for Carlos Marcello, the future "Mafia boss of the South," none was particularly notable in the annals of crime. In 1938, even Marcello was just another young punk caught trying to peddle twenty-three pounds of marijuana and hustled off to the federal penitentiary in Atlanta for a year's rustication.

It was said of Wright later that as a prosecutor he was less solicitous of defendants' rights than he was afterward as a judge. Within eighteen months in the U.S. attorney's office, he had disposed of 271 cases, of which 268 were convictions, a record that could do no harm, should he decide to continue on in the federal service. He would not have been the first man to march to a judgeship along the conviction route.

As the mid-thirties became the late thirties, the U.S. attorney's office in New Orleans became the vortex of the action as Viosca and his staff began digging into the scandalous behavior of Louisiana officialdom. The corruption involved the political successors to the late Huey Long who, the minute the power was theirs, had gone on an orgy of embezzling, kickbacks, influence peddling, vote stealing, and fifty-seven varieties of graft—everything but sex. Otherwise honest merchants, lawyers, newspapermen, bankers, and industrialists, many of them among New Orleans's elite, had been caught in it and feared to refuse to cooperate; they knew their coffee would rot on the docks, property assessments would rise, their clients would lose in state courts. The scale of operations was grander than most people had seen before, even in Louisiana where political corruption was a popular folk art, amusing to Yankees and other foreigners. Before his assassination in 1935, Huey Long himself, aware of his successors' intellectual capacity—having people around him as smart as he was, after all, would have made Huey nervous—and aware of their avarice, was also aware of what would happen to them:

> If anything happens to me [he'd predicted], the people who try to wield the powers that I have created will all land in jail.

The state was virtually impotent, however. Parish grand juries feared to indict; summoned to serve, potential jurymen pleaded sickness, important business, any obstacle to attendance. Records of state agencies were padlocked, sealed against the prying eyes of the public. State judges served subject to machine approval. Necessity humbled them not only to the governor but also to the local bosses and patronage dispensers. It was clear that if matters were left to the state, none of the offenders would ever see the inside of a jail.

The cleanup thus fell to the federal government. O. John Rogge, an assistant attorney general from the criminal division known as a whiz-bang untangler of complex legal matters, was dispatched by the Department of Justice in Washington to take personal charge of the investigation. He'd never before actually tried a criminal case—he'd earned his reputation winning civil suits—and Viosca had to give him lessons in elementary criminal procedure.

The usual approach to such cases was to look for income tax evasion, and a few of the malefactors *were* caught cheating on their federal taxes. But others, men who wouldn't have been caught dead revealing the details of the shell games they had been playing with the state's money, had been candid about declaring their ill-gotten financial gains on their tax forms.

Rogge finally hit on the postal laws. To some it seemed a little farfetched, almost too simple. No one had even to write a letter. He need only to cash his kickback check, which in the ordinary course of business would be mailed out to the local bank. Rogge declared it use of the mails to defraud and the courts upheld him. By the fall of 1939, Rogge, Viosca, and the staff, which had virtually moved into the office, often sleeping there when a big case demanded long hours, had dug out evidence to indict upward of twenty-five top state officials, to convict five of the ruling hierarchy, and to force the resignations of several others.

Skelly Wright always said this period was the "high point" of his time in the U.S. attorney's office. He'd been on the brink of leaving when the investigation started, but stayed on, expecting to "get a kind of experience," he said later, "that I would regret the rest of my life if I turned my back on it."

The months ahead confirmed that he had used "good judgment." He was "exhilarated" by the legal problems, the trails of evidence, the prosecution of the cases. There he was, a young man in his late twenties, shepherding the politically powerful—the governor, members of his cabinet, the president of the state university, people he knew only from the newspapers or Uncle Joe's casual conversation—through the halls of justice on their way to the penitentiary. Years later, Wright regaled dinner-party guests, lunch companions, and anyone else who was interested with his tales of the Louisiana scandals.

Prosecuting the scandals had added some zest to a job that was becoming routine, and there'd been the added prestige that attached locally to the heroes of the well-publicized dramas. But the work Wright was proudest of was his prosecution of Patrick Classic. The case went all the way to the U.S. Supreme Court and became an important precedent for the biggest black-voting rights suit of them all, *Smith* v. *Allwright.*

Classic's case, called *United States* v. *Classic,* carried no obvious implications for the races. All the actors were white. But the principle involved mattered to every southerner in America, white or black.

Patrick Classic and four of his fellow election commissioners, all Old Regulars, had been caught with their hands in the ballot box following the 1940 Louisiana primary, which included candidates for the federal Congress. The unusual thing about it was not that they'd falsified election returns, but that they'd been caught. Vote stealing by overly zealous Old Regulars, Longites, or any local sheriff with access to a ballot box was one of the most popular perversions of the political process in Louisiana, carried out with the utmost impunity.

Classic's case arose toward the end of the U.S. Supreme Court's long period of indecisiveness about federal and state jurisdiction over primary elections, its off-again on-again flirtation with the two constitutional rivals. U.S. Attorney Rene Viosca filed charges against Classic and his accomplices, explaining to his chief back at the Justice Department in Washington that he wanted to make this a test case:

> In view of the recurring demands in this state that the Federal Government do something about these election matters, I believe that this test case should be brought to a conclusion in order that we may definitely know the extent of Federal jurisdiction.

Given the South's political peculiarities, Viosca wanted to know, could federal authority be imposed at the primary stage to help eliminate the voting frauds that had long plagued Louisiana? And he put his "fledgling junior" assistant U.S. attorney to work on it.

Wright's draft of the indictment was double-barreled. Two charges relied on John Rogge's development of mail fraud law in connection with the Louisiana scandals. Recalling that, he had only to prove that Classic and the other commissioners had mailed falsified ballots and tally sheets to the secretary of state in Baton Rouge.

Defense attorneys filed a demurrer—the legal way of saying they didn't agree. They argued that state law making it mandatory for election returns to go through the mails was an open invitation to Congress to begin regulation of local elections—which was exactly what the local federal attorneys had in mind. Management of local elections, however, Classic's lawyer declared, had been left to the states by the Constitution.

The judge in the case was fifty-seven-year-old, Thibodaux-born-and-bred Adrian J. Caillouet. He had been appointed to the federal district court only five months before but was a former governor of the state bar and known to be one of the most capable members of it. He saw this part of the indictment Wright's way and dismissed the defendants' demurrer.

The other parts of the indictment, involving delicate points of federal-state relationships, were more elusive. Putting a constitutional spin on his arguments, Wright charged that Classic and his cronies had conspired to deny Louisiana voters "enjoyment of rights and privileges secured to them by the Constitution and laws of the United States." That is, voters in the Second Precinct of the Eleventh Ward of New Orleans, where Classic was stationed, had been denied exercise of the franchise in the September, 1940, primary. The defense lawyers demurred to that charge, too, replying that federal protection did not extend to state primary elections.

Anxious, too, perhaps to clarify a prickly and recurring question regarding federal jurisdiction, Judge Caillouet, explaining that he felt bound by a 1921 federal precedent, *Newberry* v. *United States,* in which the U.S. Supreme Court supported state jurisdiction, sustained the defense this time and dismissed these counts of the indictment. In so doing, he opened the way for prosecutors to take their case to the Court.

The usual route of a case from the district court, the lowest federal court, to the U.S. Supreme Court, the highest, is through a federal appellate court. The federal judicial code, however, authorized the government to appeal directly to the Supreme Court from a district court ruling under a variety of legal circumstances, including cases involving constitutional issues.

At this stage, the pros in Washington took control of the suit. Attorney General Robert H. Jackson studied Viosca's plan to make Classic's a test case and decided it might indeed be the very vehicle for overruling the twenty-year-old *Newberry.* Solicitor General Francis Biddle agreed that he and other justice department lawyers were looking for a way to abolish the southern white primary and saw in Classic's a case to begin with.

Writing the government's brief—the printed argument each party submits to the Supreme Court prior to oral argument—was taken over by Department of Justice lawyers. The New Orleanians, Wright and Viosca, were downgraded to contributors.

On May 26, 1941, the Court announced its decision. The U.S. attorney's office in New Orleans, which had asked the extent of federal jurisdiction over state elections, had its answer:

> Interference with the right to vote in the Congressional primary in the Second Congressional District for the choice of Democratic candidate for Congress is thus, as a matter of law and in fact, an interference with the effective choice of the voters at the only stage of the election procedure when their choice is of significance, since it is the

only stage when such interference could have any practical effect on the ultimate result, the choice of the Congressman to represent the district.

It was a narrow ruling, limited on its face to elections of federal officials, but Viosca immediately saw the principle and its implications. As he told the *Times-Picayune* afterward, the decision gave the federal government permission to intervene in state elections whenever federal civil rights statutes were violated.*

Classic had brought the Court to one of those junctures whose importance becomes obvious in retrospect. One road led to time past, to the indecisiveness of the past half century; the other road led to the full realization of Rene Viosca's analysis of *Classic*'s promise.

Three years later, in April, 1944, and building on *Classic* at each point of its opinion, the Court made its choice in *Smith* v. *Allwright,* imposing federal rules on primary as well as general elections. It was the farthest-reaching Court decision on the scope of the Constitution in the civil rights field thus far.

The Court, however, could hardly have done anything else. By 1944, America had been plunged into a life-or-death struggle for democracy. The justices couldn't very well have denied it with straight faces at home.

Skelly Wright, on whose notepads the major precedent for it had begun, was out of the country when the Court made its momentous announcement. He was in London, on duty with the Coast Guard, attending to other matters.

---

*The Court had also, of course, to deal with the immediate problem of the offenses committed by Classic and his fellow commissioners. The justices disposed of it by sending the case back to New Orleans for a new trial. The government dillydallied for more than a year. Finally, toward the end of 1942, the defendants plea-bargained their way out. The government agreed to settle for a $940 fine (distributed among the five men), suspended jail sentences, and five-year probations.

CHAPTER 6

The War, a Love Story

O f course, it wasn't all a love story. It was also long monotonous days patrolling the gray-green Atlantic aboard a rolling, heaving Coast Guard vessel and nights of terror as German buzz bombs rained on London, but even the buzz bombs were in a way part of the love story.

Wright had been on the verge of leaving the U.S. attorney's office when the war came. He had finally had an offer from an uptown law firm and was about to clean out his desk when the Japanese attacked Pearl Harbor. Instead, he joined the Coast Guard, the move, he himself admitted, calculated to keep one step ahead of the draft. At the time, he "didn't know the stem of the vessel from the stern."

A quick training course at New London filled in the gaps in his knowledge of seamanship, but there were no courses that could relieve the seasickness that plagued him on and off duty during the time he spent at sea. He was commissioned a lieutenant (j.g.) and assigned to the subchaser *Thetis* as executive officer. On his first day aboard, an oil slick encouraged the crew to believe it had sunk a German submarine, though Wright was aware it could have been the standard U-boat ruse.

Every time his ship left port, Wright left his old familiar world behind him, and his perspective on it began to subtly change. One of the things he noticed was the absence of Negroes among the officers, even among the seamen. All the blacks he saw were in the galleys: cooks, mess stewards, the servants. Back in New Orleans, his observation might not have registered on his consciousness. Now, he noted it, stored it away, and four decades later, he wouldn't forget it.

In 1942, Wright was reassigned to New York City where his legal talents were put to work designing a disciplinary system for the Merchant Marine. It was there that Helen Patton walked unannounced into his life.

Their love story began casually, neither of them particularly prepared for it. They met in New York one weekend when Helen, a Washingtonian and secretary to one of President Roosevelt's aides, had a date with Skelly's roommate. No neon lights yet, although Helen noticed even then on the Saturday-afternoon trip to the Statue of Liberty that Skelly had "a wonderful smile" and a "low-key, quiet" manner. A sense of humor, too. She thought he was probably bright. And, of course, he was "extremely handsome." There was, however, no immediate follow-up.

In June, 1943, Wright was transferred to London where he stayed until the war ended, adapting the disciplinary system he'd worked on in New York for overseas use and participating in court-martials of American military. Suddenly he heard that Helen Patton had been transferred to the American embassy in London.

He tracked her down there, and they began to play out their own romance. He was thirty-two; she, twenty-four. They made a handsome couple. Her reddish hair, lively blue eyes, and delicate features, so finely wrought that the sculptor Jacob Epstein, on meeting her casually one day, insisted on doing a study of her head, contrasted amiably with his rough-hewn ruddy Irish good looks.

They began a conventional courtship in an unconventional setting. The big blitz that had razed much of London in 1940 was over now, but firebombs lit up the sky every night, and the fire warden had visited Helen's flat in Blackburnes Mews to check the exits and stairwells. Just in case.

He invited her out to dinner, and she discovered what an "absolute charmer" he was. He discovered she was at home with the social customs and good manners of those who had grown up in the highest echelons of Washington's military society. Her father, Raymond S. Patton, had been an admiral, chief of the United States Coast and Geodetic Survey. She had enhanced her home training with preparatory school at Gunston Hall and two years at Sweet Briar College where Virginia's elite traditionally matriculated. She probably wouldn't understand what "ersters berled in erl" were.

He took her to the theater. She enjoyed it, though she found a little disconcerting the indifference of Londoners to "alert" signs that went up periodically on the stage. Hardly anyone fled to the shelters. The actors scarcely missed a line.

They went to little after-hours clubs where she discovered he didn't need much diversion in his life and was apt to fall asleep during the floor show—until one night the lead dancer "bopped him on the head" with a newspaper to wake him. He got her to play bridge with his friends, and each discovered the other's sociability.

It was only later that she discovered all his surface charm and conviviality hid the heart of a real loner, one who was "content" to be so. Sometimes she worried about it. Like a song they heard together later, she would remind him that "People Who Need People are the Luckiest People in the World." He would try to reassure her:

I don't need people. I need you, Sugah, but I don't need people.

Some folks were making long-term commitments during those days of nearly constant bombing. People Helen and Skelly knew weren't. Life was too precarious when walking home at night the sky was apt to burst into flames and you had to flatten yourself out right there on the sidewalk. Although the Allies seemed at last to be gradually gaining territory, the war had nearly two years to run and could go either way. No one wanted to plan too far ahead.

The Germans were in fact still hoping to regain their former position of superiority. In the summer and fall of 1944, as Allied troops were inching up through France and Italy, slowly and at a terrible price, tightening the noose around the throat of the Axis, the Germans were terrorizing the people of London and rural England with the first unmanned rockets. Hitler's long-awaited "secret weapon" zoomed through the sky and plunged first into the schools, homes, and docks of southern England, then shortly afterward into the apartment blocks, markets, and busy commercial centers of war-torn, bleeding London, killing indiscriminately. The V-1—short for *Vergeltungswaffen,* "weapon of retaliation"— came first, sending shards of flying glass and debris in all directions, collapsing walls over whole blocks of homes, killing families, shoppers at Woolworths, classrooms full of children. A near miss one weekend covered Helen's desk at the embassy with a blanket of glass splinters. Next time, it seemed to say . . .

Damage by V-1s spread over a broad surface. Their successors, the V-2s, dug deep, tearing up electric conduits and telephone cables, sewer pipes, gas mains, and power lines.

People called these mechanical terrorists buzz bombs, doodle bugs, and other, less printable, names. Pilotless, they were dispatched to their targets from mobile launches on the Continent. Military experts called them a portent of weapons to come.

Caught in the beam of a searchlight as they flew only a thousand feet off the ground toward their targets, they looked like toy airplanes whose cockpits had been sliced away. It was eerie and unnerving to think about a ton of TNT whizzing around in the sky directly overhead with no human in direct control.

Deeper shelters opened in London. At the same time women and children were evacuated as fast as the trains could move them. Craters gaped open on Oxford Street only steps from Selfridge's, the Macy's of London. During those final phases of the war the desperate Germans sent upward of a thousand rockets over England, killed nearly 3,000 people and seriously injured more than 6,000. Property damage was incalculable.

It was not a pretty time to be in love. Helen and Skelly wondered not only *whether* they'd survive, but *how,* what the war might do to them psychologically as well as physically, what they would be like after the war. It made two cautious people more cautious than ever. But they remained together through the terror, which, conceived in frustration and futility, failed to tip the balance in the Germans' favor.

At last the smoke began to clear as spring came to western Europe in 1945, and the Allies marched victorious toward Berlin. Their old confidence returned to people's voices as they began to talk about "after the war, we'll . . . "

Hollywood would have ended this little love story on February 1, 1945, when Helen Patton and Skelly Wright were married in London, then slipped away for a quiet week on the rural—and unwar-torn—Isle of Wight. But to end it there would leave out the best parts: the molding of Skelly's mind and emotions for his challenge of implacable southern racial traditions, how he came to make a complete U-turn, take on the caste system and metaphorically retaliate against the white teenagers who'd assaulted blacks at Mardi Gras parades and tossed garbage into blacks' front yards, all the while supported—unhesitatingly, resolutely, and completely—by Helen, who shared the vilification and whatever else the bad times dished out, never once flinching.

The end of the war left people suspended in time. All those years of constant exposure to mortal danger that simplified life, heightened its focus, and enlarged its purpose were over, and all the relief and joy couldn't untangle the complexities of peacetime pursuits or suppress the fact that people had to find themselves once again, would have to travel roads of self-discovery now cluttered, perhaps even confused, by the debris of wartime memories. Some people were psychologically disfigured permanently. Nobody was unaffected.

Skelly Wright himself bounced around some after his return in 1945. He and Helen settled first in Washington, D.C., where she still had family and friends. Skelly, however, was not optimistic about his professional prospects there. He knew no one in Washington, and he knew enough about legal practice to understand that its success often depended upon contacts. He decided to leave Helen in Washington while he returned temporarily to the U.S. attorney's office in New Orleans where he would have "a perch from which to look around," to assess the prospects of a thirty-four-year-old veteran with more than the usual amount of ambition and less than the usual amount of self-confidence.

When Skelly got there, he found that his old boss, Rene Viosca, was now a local judge, and Herbert Christenberry, one of the former assistants, was U.S. attorney. Christenberry had a reputation for integrity; he also had a working-class background with which Wright could readily identify. Christenberry put him to work on war frauds cases. At the same time, Wright was to keep an eye cocked for local clients whose interests he might represent in Washington, should he find it possible to join Helen there.

Wright stayed only about five months in New Orleans, not really long enough to fully digest the changes the war had wrought on the city. In addition to the economic boom induced by the war industries—New Orleans's port business had more than trebled—there was a palpable restlessness in people, a resistance to resuming old ways.

In city politics, Robert Maestri was still comfortably ensconced in the mayor's office, but after a century of political oligarchy, the spirit of reform was in the air, and he would not be there long. The personable young DeLesseps S. Morrison, better known as "Chep," who had run for and won a seat in the state legislature in 1940, then gone off to the war, had returned an army colonel and a hero, and was hell-bent to take Maestri's job away from him. Old-time New Orleanians always said independent Democrats wouldn't elect a mayor until it snowed on election day.

War veterans, many of whom, like Skelly Wright, had perhaps never lived outside New Orleans before the war, were drifting back from the Pacific, France, Germany, and Great Britain, their memories of foreign parts and customs still sharp. There was more to their restlessness than the anticlimax of returning to the farm after they'd seen Berlin—or Paris or London or wherever. To the thoughtful among them, blacks especially, who hadn't fought a war to make the world safe for Jim Crow, but some whites also, it was apparent that the democratic principles for which they'd fought fascism, Nazism, and Japanese imperialism did not always square with the realities of life back home, particularly in the

South where the paradoxes of race mocked the words of the United States Constitution and the Declaration of Independence. Many people had begun to recognize a relationship between racism and fascism, and a new consciousness was emerging among them. Perhaps this time, at last, the heroes of 1945 would not follow those of 1815 and 1918 into disrepute and dishonor. Wright caught the general sense of the new order:

> I think [he said] the war had a very great effect on this whole race problem. The Negro went to war like the white person did. He fought like the white person. We saw this, those of us who were in the service—we saw this.

Then one night shortly after he returned to New Orleans, the lesson of race came home to him with a poignance to which he was not accustomed.

It was Christmas Eve, 1945. The U.S. attorney's office was in the midst of its annual Christmas party. Distracted from the gaiety perhaps by lights dancing in the windows across the narrow New Orleans street, he began to watch a disturbing little drama unfold there. What he saw was to stay with him for the rest of his life—what he saw happening and what he may have seen in himself, a part of himself he hadn't recognized before.

What he saw across the street, although he'd had to look twice before he realized what was going on, was a Christmas party given by the local branch of the Lighthouse for the Blind. He watched fascinated as the sightless participants climbed to the second floor, where they were met by their hosts and immediately separated into white and black groups. Blind Negroes were led to a party at the rear of the building. Whites were led to a separate party. At last he realized that even the blind, although unable to see or be seen by the other partygoers, were being segregated by race on this, of all nights, Christmas Eve.

If the absurdity and inhumanity of the situation did not strike the participants or their hosts, they struck Skelly Wright that night. Aboard the *Thetis*, he had begun to wonder about the relegation of Negroes to the galley. His wonder then was nothing compared to this sudden and unexpected sense of outrage now. It was one of the rare instances in his life when his emotions matched his intellectual reaction. His response was as glandular as it was intellectual:

> It didn't shock me. . . . It just began to eat at me. And it eats at me now [1979]. It began to make me think more of the injustice of it, of the whole system that I had taken for granted. I was getting mature,

too. . . . And you begin to think of things. When you go to bed at night you think of it. That was the beginning really.

Fortified with retainers from Standard Fruit and a local shipbuilder, Skelly left the U.S. attorney's office in New Orleans in the spring of 1946 and headed back to Washington, D.C., where he found office space in a building with an old friend he'd known in the Coast Guard and a couple of other young lawyers.

The others specialized in the handling of shipping business before the Maritime Commission. Wright, who knew something about the law of the sea from his occasional handling of admiralty cases in the U.S. attorney's office, often joined his partners in these matters, but he also continued to represent the assorted legal interests of Louisianans in the nation's capital. It was the Louisiana connection that brought him the first case he argued in the United States Supreme Court. Called *Louisiana ex rel. Francis* v. *Resweber,* it had little significance in the annals of American constitutional law. It's not a landmark case, and Wright's argument before the Supreme Court was soon forgotten. But it told him, a man just then learning the calculus of race, a lot of things he needed to know about southern mores.

In June, 1946, Skelly had barely settled into the routine of a private lawyer when he was contacted by a young attorney, Bertrand DeBlanc, from Lafayette, Louisiana. At the time, DeBlanc was trying frantically to save the life of one Willie Francis, a black teenager convicted of murder whom the state of Louisiana had failed to put to death in its first attempt and now wanted to strap into the electric chair a second time. The questions in DeBlanc's mind on which he wanted Skelly's help was: Could the state do that? Or did the Constitution prohibit it? In ancient times, King Nebuchadnezzar had set a precedent when he pardoned Shadrack, Meshach, and Abednego after his fiery furnace had failed to consume them. But the question hadn't really been settled in modern times, and King Nebuchadnezzar didn't carry a lot of weight with judges and justices in 1947.

DeBlanc hoped to persuade the U.S. Supreme Court to hear Francis's case. But he'd never taken a case there before, and his background in constitutional law wasn't strong. Would Skelly take it for him? There wasn't a fee in it. Willie's father was a laborer in the local sugarcane fields and an odd-jobs man struggling to support a family of fifteen on nine dollars a week. DeBlanc got a sack of onions out of it; Wright, nothing.

Wright agreed to take Francis's case, although appellate work wasn't *his* long suit, either. He himself never had argued in the U.S. Supreme

Court, an awesome experience. DeBlanc immediately sent him the young man's records.

Race was irrelevant to the central issue in Francis's case. The trial records, however, told Skelly two stories: the first, the straightforward, unemotional narrative of fifteen-year-old Willie's conviction for the murder in November, 1944, of Andrew Thomas, a popular pharmacist in St. Martinville, Louisiana; the second, an account of one young black's experience under rural Louisiana's two-tiered system of criminal justice.

The trial in the St. Martinville courthouse, less than two miles from the scene of the crime, had been a farce. The jury, which was to decide the fate of a young black charged with the murder of a white man—a crime second in emotional content only to that of a black man's killing or raping a white woman—was composed of twelve white males and one alternate. Racial bias in jury selection had not become the issue in 1945 that it later became. In 1945, white juries were simply another fact of southern life. Nobody, except blacks, of course, and they didn't count, even thought about it.

Francis's case was assigned to two local lawyers, both white. Their efforts to defend him against the murder charge were perfunctory at best. There was, after all, no money in it, only bad publicity. They spent little time preparing the case and offered Willie none of the protections white defendants took for granted. Despite aroused public passions following Andrew Thomas's murder—for his own safety Francis had had to be transferred to the New Iberia jail ten miles away after his arrest—Francis's lawyers didn't ask for a change of venue. They offered no evidence on his behalf, called no witnesses, and conducted no cross-examinations of the prosecution's witnesses. In fact, they offered no rebuttal of the prosecution's case at all which had been based solely on Willie's confessions.

The murder weapon as well as the bullets discovered in Thomas's body during the autopsy had been lost on the way to the FBI laboratory in Washington where they were sent for ballistic tests. No one really knew whether it had been Francis's gun or someone else's that killed Thomas. There were inconsistencies in what Francis had told police after his arrest, but his lawyers failed to point these out. A witness had seen a car parked in front of Thomas's house on the night of the murder, but she was never produced. No stenographic record was made of the trial, indicating Francis's attorneys planned no appeal, should Willie be found guilty, as he surely would be. And no appeal was made. Willie's trial bore little resemblance to the rule-conscious proceedings Skelly was accustomed to in the federal courts of New Orleans. It was evident that race was a large factor here and that a white defendant would have fared differently.

It was all over in two days. Francis was found guilty and sentenced to death in the electric chair. The date set was May 3, 1946.

The transcript of the board of pardons proceedings, out of which Wright had to make his case, begins where the trial transcript stopped. On May 3, as scheduled, Francis was shaved—hair impeded the flow of electricity, and burning hair gave off an unpleasant odor. He was driven to the St. Martinville jail where Louisiana's portable electric chair awaited him. The state had no central place for executions at the time; the electric chair was kept at the state penitentiary in Angola and taken by pickup truck wherever it was needed. Francis was given the last rites of the Church, the wires were attached to his body, and he was strapped unceremoniously into the chair.

The chair had been installed and checked before Francis arrived. Everything had seemed to be in order. But they couldn't even kill him like a white man; they had to botch it. When the switch was thrown, the chair failed to function properly. As Captain Foster, who'd prepared it, plugged it in, and thrown the switch, said:

> A little wire was loose and the current went back into the ground instead of going into the nigger.

Francis didn't die.

> He squirmed around a little bit and rocked the chair and asked to "take it off" and, in a minute or two interval, "take it off" and said "I cannot breathe."

Someone tore the hood from Francis's face; the electrodes were taken off, and the straps unbuckled. With the help of a police officer, Francis stood up and walked—a little unsteadily—away from the grim symbol of death. The coroner examined him, found "nothing wrong with him" except for a slightly accelerated heartbeat, which was, he thought, easily attributable to "apprehension or being excited." Francis only commented: "The Lord was with me."

His guards hustled him back to his old prison cell in the New Iberia jail. As the condemned man left, Captain Foster shook his fist and called after him:

> I missed you this time, but I'll get you next week if I have to use a rock.

A new death warrant was issued, and the execution rescheduled for May 6, but a stay was obtained while this bizarre case, which was attracting national attention, was argued in the courts.

This time Fred Francis decided not to leave his son's life to the mercy of court-appointed counsel. He actively sought a lawyer. Through a man in St. Martinville for whom he occasionally did odd jobs, he found Bertrand DeBlanc, and "with tears in his eyes" begged DeBlanc to take the case. DeBlanc was the slain druggist's best friend with more than an observer's interest in punishing Thomas's murderer, but he believed that

> [e]very man is entitled to his day in Court whether he is rich or poor, black or white. It's not what the Courts decide in this case that is of greatest importance but the fact that a man is entitled to be heard. Otherwise, we might as well junk our system of law.

In addition to his convictions and the courage to act on them, DeBlanc believed his most valuable asset was his genealogy. He came from an old Cajun family with roots deep in Louisiana—his grandfather had signed the Louisiana Ordinance of Secession in 1861—and he may have thought such impeccable credentials would protect him from the stigma of defending a Negro. Ultimately, he *was* vilified for his defense of Willie Francis. DeBlanc, however, refused to "apologize" for taking Willie's case. He was, he said, "proud" of his decision:

> [M]y critics will soon be dead and buried but the principles involved in this case . . . will live as long as the American flag waves on this continent.

In the petition he filed with the state Supreme Court asking for a permanent stay of Franci's execution, DeBlanc ignored entirely the racial implications of the trial and concentrated on the failure of the electric chair. The court denied his request, explaining it had no authority to pardon Francis, to otherwise commute or in any way set aside his death sentence. That's what the state had a board of pardons for. But all DeBlanc's eloquence failed to move that body. If Francis's life was to be saved, it was up to the U.S. Supreme Court.

Wright set to work on the case. Five months later, on November 18, 1946, having persuaded enough justices that the case raised questions of constitutional stature, Skelly was standing at the lectern just below the bench of the Supreme Court, ready to begin his recitation. Swallowing hard, he opened his argument in the traditional manner: "May it please the Court. . . ."

DeBlanc had flown to Washington to hear him, and Helen, who knew Skelly was "scared to death," was sitting there somewhere among the spectators. His back was to her as he faced the formidable array of black robes and solemn faces above him.

Tradition prescribed the order in which the justices sat. The chief justice, Fred M. Vinson, former secretary of the treasury and one of President Truman's poker-playing cronies who'd taken his seat only the month before, sat in the center. The associate justices spread like wings on either side in order of seniority.

Though he wouldn't dare acknowledge it, Skelly recognized Hugo L. Black, FDR's first Supreme Court appointment and in 1946 the senior associate justice sitting at the chief justice's immediate left. Skelly had met him at a dinner party in Washington, but even before that he'd been an admirer of Black's work. Indeed, forty years later he could quote from one of Black's decisions:

> Under our constitutional system, courts stand against any winds that blow as havens of refuge for those who might otherwise suffer because they are helpless, weak, outnumbered, or because they are nonconforming victims of prejudice and public excitement.

Could the man who wrote that be unmoved by Willie Francis's plight?

Oral argument remained at the heart of the appellate process, an opportunity for the justices, through a question-and-answer format, to test the hypotheses put forward in the lawyers' briefs and for the lawyers to correct any judicial misconceptions that might have arisen out of the printed matter. It was often grueling for a lawyer. Prepared texts were discouraged—the justices had, after all, read the prepared texts, the briefs—and it was impossible to anticipate every question.

Justice Jackson, the former attorney general who'd put the weight of his justice department behind Rene Viosca's plan to make *Classic* the test case it became, used to say that as solicitor general, the official in charge of the government's cases before the Supreme Court, he always made three arguments in each of the cases he presented. First, there was the one he'd planned—"logical, coherent, complete." Then there was the one he actually gave—"interrupted, incoherent, disjointed, disappointing." The third was the "utterly devastating argument that he thought of after going to bed that night."

Wright made the most of the facts in the case, including the inadequacies of Francis's trial, although the justices showed no interest in what was essentially a peripheral issue here, not the reason they'd accepted the case. But he hammered hardest on the horrors of Francis's ordeal up to the minute of the failed execution, reiterated the constitutional arguments he'd made in his brief, and concluded that to go through a second execution imposed more punishment than Francis's sentence required.

Justice Felix Frankfurter busily took notes. The other justices enlivened Wright's argument with frequent questions. They seemed to be trying to explore every contingency, to discover where the line should be drawn between what punishment was allowed and what was not. Wright fielded them skillfully.

The justices imagined hypothetical situations, pushing Wright to draw a line where double jeopardy began: at the shaving of the convicted man's head? (Justice Harold H. Burton); as he started toward the execution chamber? (Justice Frankfurter). Where? Skelly reiterated what he had written in his brief: By Louisiana's failure to make Francis's death "as instant and painless as possible," the state had "forfeited her right to his life."

When the justices pressed him for an alternative to a second execution, Wright suggested not that Francis should go free—he'd never entertained that notion—but that the state of Louisiana, in its discretion, could impose any penalty it liked short of death.

The state barely touched the details of Francis's suit in its case for going through with a second execution attempt. The Louisiana officials simply dusted off the old states' rights arguments and told the highest federal court that Francis was none of its business. The Louisiana courts had made their rulings. The federal Court was powerless. Should the Supreme Court interfere, it would mean utter confusion for lawyers, local courts, and the state criminal justice system in general.

A few more questions, including Justice Black's interest in whether a state could legally install a man in the electric chair for twenty days, then singe him periodically before applying enough current to kill him, and the day ended. Later that night, Justice Burton scribbled in his diary that the arguments by both Skelly and the state had been "good," and Skelly himself was confident that he'd won.

Only a week after oral argument, he began phoning the clerk of the Court on Mondays, when decisions were customarily handed down, then wiring the dearth of news to DeBlanc back in Louisiana. His confidence didn't flag, but the suspense, which lasted no less than two months, tormented him.

Finally, on January 13, 1947 the day before Skelly's thirty-sixth birthday, the Court opinion was announced. Stanley Reed had written it for the five members of the majority, which included Skelly's new friend and old hero, Hugo Black. Reed began by reiterating the facts and judicial history of Francis's case. The state and Skelly were in substantial agreement here. Reed then demolished Skelly's contentions that the prohibitions against double jeopardy and cruel and unusual punishment applied to Francis's case:

> We cannot agree that the hardship imposed upon the petitioner rises to that level of hardship denounced as denial of due process because of cruelty.

And in conclusion, he dismissed Skelly's contention that Francis's original trial violated the black's constitutional rights.

Reed didn't really come to grips with the state's contention at oral argument that the U.S. Supreme Court lacked jurisdiction in Francis's case. By citing the Fourteenth Amendment, he implied that it did. But he largely managed to sidestep that particular irritant to the South.

Frankfurter had "to hold on to" himself not to reverse Francis's conviction. He was revolted by capital punishment, particularly the sensationalism that accompanied any capital case—the uncivilized atmosphere of the gladitorial arena had, he believed, a demoralizing effect on juries, the bar, the public, even the judiciary. Francis's case deeply offended his personal sense of decency: "Something inside of [him] was very unhappy."

He joined, however, the majority result and wrote his own concurrence:

> The Due Process Clause of the Fourteenth Amendment did not withdraw the freedom of a state to enforce its own notions of fairness in the administration of criminal justice unless, as it was put for the Court by Mr. Justice Cardozo, "in so doing it offends some principle of justice so rooted in the traditions and conscience of our people" as to be ranked as fundamental.

He did not believe in this instance that the state of Louisiana had overstepped its limits. He could not vote to stay the executioner's hand.

Following the Court's conference in June, 1946, at which the justices decided to hear Francis's case, Harold Burton had pulled Frankfurter aside as they strolled back to their chambers. "Felix," he'd said, "as you know, most of the time I agree with you and certainly I can always understand why you take the position that you take,"

> but for the life of me I can't see why a man of your intelligence should think that simply because something went wrong with an electric

wire, for which nobody was responsible, the State of Louisiana cannot carry out a death sentence imposed after a fair trial.

Now that he'd read the briefs, however, listened to Wright's argument as well as the discussion of his senior brethren at the final conference where Francis's fate had been decided, Burton had changed his mind. His dissent, which was joined by William O. Douglas, Wiley Rutledge, and Frank Murphy—one more and they would have saved Francis— spoke less to the jurisprudence and more to the consciences of the nine justices:

> Taking human life by unnecessarily cruel means shocks the most fundamental instincts of civilized man. It should not be possible under the constitutional procedure of a self-governing people.

The passion of the dissenters notwithstanding, Francis's death sentence, in limbo for the past eight months, was reinstated. Said Francis: "I guess a man's got to die sometime . . . Ain't going to wear no beat-up pants to see the Lord. . . . Them folks expecting me to come in style. I'm going to wear my Sunday pants and my Sunday heart." On May 9, 1947, Francis, a steel crucifix around his neck, was escorted to the same portable electric chair from which he had walked away a year before and was electrocuted.

For years Skelly Wright talked about his "disappointment" in both the outcome of his first case in the Supreme Court and in the behavior of his hero, Hugo Black, and Felix Frankfurter, whose work he also admired. His admiration of them never died, but this time around, at least, with their support—either one could have changed the outcome— the Court had not stood as a "refuge" for one who was "helpless" and "weak." Black's words, announced appropriately on Lincoln's birthday, 1940, nonetheless remained Wright's lodestar. He himself was often criticized later for his activism as a judge, for his own sense of justice owed the Willie Francises of the world.

CHAPTER 7

Rubicon

B y early 1948, nearly three years after Skelly Wright's return from the war, he had a wife, an infant son (James Skelly Wright, Jr., born in 1947 in Washington), and, despite a respectable record of government service and a brief encounter with private practice that included arguing before the U.S. Supreme Court, no clear idea of where he wanted to settle permanently. His diligence was overshadowed by his lack of the self-confidence he needed to solicit the clients and contacts necessary for carrying on a private legal practice profitably. His need for security often inhibited his ambitions, just as his father's similar need some years back had kept the older man from joining a friend's new business venture, even as a partner, from risking a small but steady income for the vague promises of future success. It seemed to run in the family. Helen accused him of "waffling."

So when sixty-three-year-old Federal District Judge Adrian Caillouet, the judge in *Classic,* died suddenly in December, 1946, and the U.S. attorney in New Orleans, Herbert Christenberry, who was tall and dignified and looked like a judge, succeeded Caillouet on the federal bench in early 1948, Wright decided to explore the possibility of his own succession to Christenberry's position.

It is probably safe to say that in early 1948, not a single soul in Louisiana had any ambition whatsoever to succeed Christenberry as U.S. attorney. Although the officeholder was decided locally, it was officially a presidential appointment, and Harry Truman was thought to have the bleakest of political futures after that year's election. It was assumed that the office of U.S. attorney, like all the other patronage positions from local postmaster to cabinet secretary, would fall into Republican hands and Truman's appointee would last about six months. Nevertheless, Wright decided to go after it, if for no other reason than to impress future clients with the title "former U.S. attorney" on his letterhead, should he later return to the private practice of law.

In January 1946, during an unusual light dusting of snow, New Orleanians had gone to the polls and elected the independent Democrat Chep Morrison mayor, sweeping the Old Regulars, including Uncle Joe Skelly, out of city hall. Wright went directly to Senator Ellender, who'd also helped him into the assistant U.S. attorney's slot a decade before. There being no competition for the position, it was Wright's practically for the asking.

He moved back to New Orleans, temporarily, he thought, not past the presidential election. Helen stayed in Washington, wishing he'd settle down, and Skelly flew back for visits a couple of times a month.

No one had been more surprised than Skelly Wright when Truman was elected in 1948. Wright had been one of the few Louisianans who'd stuck by the President all the way through the Dixiecrat challenge. He was "partial" to Truman, he said, and grateful to the national party for past patronage. The Hatch Act kept him, as a federal officeholder, out of the actual campaign, but his hands were loosely enough tied that he could keep contacts in the Justice Department advised about Louisiana's political ups and downs that election season as well as help in restoring the names of Truman and his running mate Alben Barkley to the local ballot after Leander Perez's Dixiecrats removed them. Truman lost Louisiana to the Dixiecrats that year, but after the rest of the country elected him, he knew who his friends were and extended Wright's appointment as U.S. attorney indefinitely.

He was a conventional chief prosecutor: nothing flamboyant, no cops-and-robbers chases, no really big busts. A conscientious public servant, he seemed content to follow Department of Justice policy. He did investigate the occasional claim that blacks had been denied their right to vote, though he did it more as a matter of public education than with any expectation that the law would run its course. Grand juries refused to indict white election officials, petit juries refused to convict. Challenging the white establishment was an exercise in futility. It was much too early.

Wright's stay in the chief prosecutor's office, however, was too short for him to develop an effective strategy for enforcing blacks' voting rights. Just over a year after his appointment, Elmo P. Lee, youngest (in terms of service) member of the United States Court of Appeals for the Fifth Circuit, died. Skelly looked longingly at the vacancy.

The Fifth Circuit, which heard appeals from the lower courts in Alabama, Florida, Georgia, Louisiana, Mississippi, and Texas—six of the eleven former Confederate states, all in the very heart of the segregated deep South—was one of the busiest appellate courts in the federal judicial system. As appeals in the mounting number of suits challenging the way southern whites were operating their election campaigns and schools accelerated, the Fifth Circuit court would become one of the most significant. For an ambitious young federal prosecutor, it was the Promised Land, and he later told his friend John Minor Wisdom on the latter's appointment to it:

> Speaking frankly, other than myself, there is no one that I would prefer to see on the Fifth Circuit.

"Why the hell shouldn't I be a judge?" Wright asked himself in the summer of 1949 as the speculation on Judge Lee's successor made the rounds of the local rumor mills. One of the position's major attractions was its lifetime tenure, the best security a man in Skelly's profession could expect. He believed his temperament and training were suited to appellate work, and he knew he had the political credentials after his display of party loyalty during the recent election.

He telephoned the United States attorney general, Tom Clark, whose backing he would need, especially in view of the President's anger at the Louisiana senators after the Dixiecrat victory in their state. Wright was on a first-name basis with Clark, whom he'd helped prosecute local antitrust violations when Clark was still a young lawyer in the Justice Department's lower echelons. If Clark wasn't on a first-name basis with the President, he was a close political associate, having insured his future when he did battle for the former Missouri senator's vice presidential candidacy at the Democratic National Convention in 1944, his reward the high office he now held.

Wright repeated to Clark the question he'd asked himself: "Why shouldn't I be a judge?"

"I don't know why," the big Texan answered, and as he considered Wright's "splendid" record as U.S. attorney, perhaps recalled Skelly's helpfulness to him nearly a decade before, as well as the Louisianan's loyalty during the 1948 presidential campaign, he added: "There's nobody else down there."

Indeed, the President had only contempt now for those Louisianans who had betrayed him to support the Dixiecrat candidates the year before, and few were the local Democrats who could apply for a federal judgeship with straight faces.

Clark put forward Wright's candidacy right away. So piqued was Truman over Louisiana's intransigence in the recent election that he didn't bother to inform the Louisiana congressional delegation, and Skelly's elevation to the federal appellate court was nearly a fait accompli when the outspoken, Bible-quoting, and occasionally crochety chief judge of the Fifth Circuit, Joseph C. Hutcheson, Jr., protested. Wright, he said, was too young (he was thirty-eight), too inexperienced.

Hutcheson had, however, an alternative suggestion. Why not promote Wayne Borah, a veteran of two decades on the federal district bench, to the court of appeals and appoint Wright to succeed Borah on the lower court? Borah had the added advantage of being a registered Republican—appointed by Calvin Coolidge—a reply to accusations that the Truman administration was politicizing the federal judiciary.

Hutcheson's suggestion appealed to nearly all concerned.*

The nominations of Borah to the appellate court and Wright to the trial court went forward. Helen Wright was the only dissenter. Her father had been in government, and she was reluctant to see her husband there permanently. Skelly, she firmly believed, could make his $15,000 district judge's annual salary many times over if he went into private practice. Skelly himself was aware of the financial sacrifices that went with government service, and there was a wistfulness in his tone when not long afterward he congratulated a friend who was leaving it, bound for a law firm: "Here's wishing you make a million."

But it wasn't only the money that disturbed Helen. It was also the "heartache and frustration" of the public servant's circumscribed life, which she'd had to endure as a young girl, that repelled her. However, she "kept [her] mouth shut" and ultimately joined the majority:

> If that was what he wanted to do, he was the one who was going to do it. That was it. Just sort of deep down inside, I thought, "Oh, here we go again."

One quiet Saturday afternoon in October, 1949, while Skelly, in Washington for one of his regular visits with his family, watched a football game on television, President Truman announced the Louisianan's nomination to the federal district bench, along with the nominations of eighteen other judges, including William H. Hastie's to the Third Circuit court of appeals (New York, New Jersey, Pennsylvania, Delaware, the

---

*Hutcheson later confessed on several occasions that his solution to the problem of Skelly was the biggest mistake he ever made. Borah came down with "writer's cramp" soon after his appointment. Skelly became a skilled writer and during his decade as a federal district judge wrote more opinions than most trial judges ever write.

Virgin Islands). Hastie was the first black to be appointed to a federal appellate court. It was a sign, if anybody was paying attention, that the times, they were a-changing.

On October 25, Wright's old boss in the U.S. attorney's office and now the other half of the federal trial court for the Eastern District of Louisiana, Herbert Christenberry, swore the new judge to "administer justice without respect to persons and to do equal right to the poor and to the rich . . . " Because Congress was not in session at the time, his had to be an interim appointment, subject to Senate confirmation later.

To which the Senate duly attended the following March. Although the President had deliberately snubbed them and had entirely ignored their recommendations, both Louisiana's senators—Ellender and the newest one, Russell Long, who'd been Skelly's student at Fortier High Schools those many years ago—attended his confirmation hearings, competing to sing their fellow Louisianan's highest praises, and Long, who had his father's gift for stump oratory in addition to Huey's physical structure and boyish good looks, jovially reminisced about his alma mater. Skelly had every reason at the time to believe he could look forward to a challenging, secure, and essentially untroubled future.

And so he *was* untroubled during the early months. Helen and their young son Jimmy finally had been able to join him in New Orleans, and the little family, together at last, bought a modest but pleasant house on Newcomb Boulevard, a quiet, tree-shaded street about two blocks from Tulane University in the Uptown section of the city. Harriet Johnson, a black woman whose sister had kept house for Skelly's mother for some years, had been installed as full-time housekeeper and nursemaid for Jimmy. And life had begun in earnest—again—for the Honorable J. Skelly Wright and his wife after years of separation and quick visits.

To get reacquainted, Skelly took Helen on their first vacation since their wedding trip to the Isle of Wight five years earlier: a cruise to Havana and Honduras on a Standard Fruit boat—"absolutely no work, all play, a real, honest-to-goodness vacation." After that, she discovered what a workaholic she'd married and "adapted herself to the role of watching over him."

Helen did, however, develop a life of her own. After the welcoming cocktail parties, many of whose hosts and hostesses were no longer friends when the Wrights left New Orleans a decade later; after she'd put the house on Newcomb Boulevard in order and settled her little brood into it, she resumed a career of volunteer civic work she'd begun as a young woman in Washington during the War. Until the name became a liability later, having "Mrs. J. Skelly Wright" on a letterhead was good public relations for local organizations, and Helen was invited to join groups ranging from the Altar Guild at Christ Church Cathedral, which she attended regularly, to the board of directors of the New Orleans branch of the National Association of Mental Health. Later she held high executive positions in both the state and national mental health bodies.

Many of the people she met in her volunteer groups came from the ranks of the city's elite, people like those among whom she'd grown up in Washington, and it was later said that it had been Helen's charm and intelligence that won a reluctant acceptance for the plumber's son from the Irish Channel, considered as much an outsider as if he'd come from Brooklyn, to one of the most closed societies in America. Not the Boston or Louisiana clubs, of course; these remained out of reach to all but the truly anointed. But there were informal friendships with some of the members of that group as well as other leading local citizens, and invitations to Mardi Gras balls and debutante parties that didn't automatically accompany a judgeship, particularly when the judge had been born outside the ruling class.

It was also said later by people who knew him well that Skelly's sensitivity to those very Irish Channel origins may have colored his later judicial behavior, that he sometimes seemed to be the Irish Channel against the world. Which may account, at least in part, for the feistiness he later displayed when elite New Orleans failed to fall in with his orders to desegregate the city's schools.

The early months of Skelly's judgeship were a relatively calm period. He settled into a daily routine: an unvarying 9 A.M. to 5 P.M. day at the courthouse, dinner, a glance at the television news, a look at the day's newspapers or a newsmagazine, then early to bed. He disliked expensive clothes, avoided fancy restaurants, and leavened his simple if austere routine with Saturday afternoon golf and occasional dinner parties for friends, after which he had been known to lead the guests down to the French Quarter for an hour or so of the jazz for which the city was so famous.

His court docket matched his personal life in serenity. The scandals, the war frauds, the national security cases—the kind that tend to generate publicity and occasionally passions—had receded into memory for the time being, and he was sitting in judgment of more mundane matters: insurance claims, minimum wages for oyster shuckers, antitrust suits, oil and gas leases, admiralty law, eminent domain, the outcome of which mattered largely to the litigants involved.

His first published opinion was typical of those early days: a dispute over the cost of salvaging a vessel that had broken loose from its moorings during high water on the river. No human life had been lost or even damaged, no broad principle of law was involved, and the total amount of money awarded was $500. Run-of-the-mill fare for a port city.

His prose, which picked up electricity over the years, was direct, lucid, low in fat, high in protein, as austere as the dark suits he customarily wore when he shed his judicial robes. Heeding English teachers' instructions to their students, he avoided adjectives and adverbs and made the verbs do all the work. He was not above a little sarcasm when he felt it was called for and once congratulated a lawyer for "making a molehill out of nothing."

His quick mind, said one man who appeared frequently in Wright's court, made him impatient, even lose his temper or get up and walk out if a lawyer used dilatory tactics on him. A juvenile in trouble, on the other hand, could move him to tears.

His integrity became legendary. As a prosecutor of the Louisiana scandals, he knew all about the temptations of public life, how little it took for a man to go wrong, how difficult it was to stop once a man had succumbed. He'd become so sensitive to the dangers of corruption that he once refused to greet a lawyer who'd come to pay his respects to the Wright family on the death of Skelly's younger brother. The man had a case pending in Skelly's court.

His colleague, Herbert Christenberry, was the more popular of the two. Christenberry fraternized with local lawyers, often lunched with them. Wright dined alone and shut himself off from lawyer friends whenever they were involved in cases before his court. A lower court judge in New Jersey once observed that during his early days on the bench, he

felt like a quarantined child looking wistfully out the window at playing friends.

This particular occupational reality gave off both positive and negative sparks in Wright's case. His being a natural loner was undoubtedly an advantage, and he seemed content to experience the drama of life through the cases that came before him: "Real novels in themselves," one of his law clerks once commented and went on to describe Skelly's nearly forty years on the bench as a "whole library of different people." A plot from Dickens here, a character from Dostoyevsky there. His ability to remain emotionally uninvolved in most of the tragedies staged in his courtroom would prove extremely useful to him when the storm finally broke.

On the other hand, the built-in isolation of the judicial life may have intensified his aloofness and his natural tendency toward solitude:

> If I have a fault [he once said] it's my inability to react to people at a personal warm level. I can be very friendly, but it's a kind of surface. The result is that I have even yet [1979] to have warm personal friends. . . . I can't explain it.

While Wright was learning the routine of judicial life, the storm was gathering virtually unnoticed by all but the people involved and readers of the law reports. Federal district courts had been authorized to "redress the deprivation, under color of any State law, statute, ordinance, regulation, custom, or usage, of any right, privilege or immunity secured by the Constitution of the United States or by any Act of Congress providing for equal rights of citizens . . ." As the 1950s opened, the postwar restlessness of black Americans, who had geared up to fight for civil rights with all the determination and vigor they had shown in their war against the Axis powers, was showing in their challenges to state laws whites believed had been permanently fixed by *Plessy* and its progeny, and the authority of the federal courts was taking on new meaning. The Reverend Martin Luther King, Jr., was to write later:

> No one can understand the feeling that comes to a Southern Negro on entering a federal court unless he sees with his own eyes and feels with his own soul the tragic sabotage of justice in the city and state courts of the South. The Negro goes into those courts knowing that the cards are stacked against him. But the Southern Negro goes into the federal court feeling that he has an honest chance of justice before the law.

Less than six months after he was confirmed by the Senate, Skelly Wright was assigned the first of many race cases he would decide as the spokesman for the federal Constitution in his corner of the world.

Every court employs some objective system for allocating incoming cases among its judges, partly in the interests of distributing the workload evenly, mostly to allay the slightest suspicion of backroom maneuvers by lawyers to land their favorite judges in particular cases and efforts of the judges themselves to decide particular cases. Some use a lottery system. At the federal district court for the Eastern District of Louisiana, it was court clerk A. Dallam O'Brien's unwavering policy to divide the cases by number: odd-numbered cases to Christenberry, even-numbered to Wright. *Dean* v. *Thomas,* number 2790, went to Wright. Had it been filed ten minutes earlier or later, it might have been Christenberry's.

This first race case of Skelly's involved voting rights, an issue com-

ing with increasing frequency to federal judicial attention as local registrars still sought new ways to thwart black voters six years after the U.S.
Supreme Court's invalidation of the white primary. One Joe Dean and
several other blacks had tried repeatedly and always unsuccessfully to
register in Washington Parish. Curtis M. Thomas, the white registrar,
had refused them every time. Dean and the others took Thomas into federal court, charging that Thomas's refusals were racially motivated and
thus violated the Fourteenth and Fifteenth Amendments to the federal
Constitution.

Wright readily agreed. This first time he endured no mental anguish.
He thought, during these early days of contention, before the races
polarized, that Curtis Thomas probably agreed, too, that what Thomas
and other resistant registrars wanted was a federal order so they could
say, "I've been required to do this." The court proceedings were almost
pro forma then. In a brief, to-the-point decision that leaned heavily on
Smith v. *Allwright,* Wright gave the registrar the excuse he wanted. He
"forever" prohibited Thomas "from denying and refusing to register eligible Negroes as electors in Washington Parish, Louisiana, simply and
solely on account of race or color."

Not many people laid down the law to white Louisianans like that.
The politically popular said just the opposite. Senator Ellender knew he
could always pick up votes with some variation on his warning that letting the Negro vote would give the race "new hope for political equality."

> You give him political equality and he will get social equality and
> social equality will lead to the degradation of the white race.

His next racial discrimination case forced Wright past the biggest,
most daunting obstacle in the course of his career to date: his choice of
judicial direction. He could sit out his life on the bench passively, continuing quietly along the well-trod paths he'd been accustomed to travel,
taking pains to stay within the limits of conventional judicial behavior. He
could follow the George Timmermans in South Carolina or the William
Atwells in Texas and defy the Supreme Court rulings that offended the
white majority in their districts. Or he could do the unexpected, take the
road less traveled, jettison the traditions he'd grown up with, and aggressively promote so far as he legitimately could the constitutional momentum toward full racial equality that the Supreme Court had just begun.

There would be no testimonial dinners, no flattering newspaper editorials, perhaps no promotion when his time came, only calumny and
abuse. Nevertheless he set out on his lonely trek down that last, least
popular, and uncharted road. *Dean* v. *Thomas* had taken him to the

banks of his Rubicon while there was still time to turn back. His next case took him across. Turning back was out of the question then.

On September 13, 1950, less than three months after Wright had handed down his decision in *Dean* v. *Thomas,* Inc. Fund lawyers opened their attack on the segregated law school of Louisiana State University. They filed their suit in the federal courthouse in Baton Rouge, which was also, along with New Orleans, a seat of the eastern judicial district of Louisiana. Even a cursory reading of the complaint pointed up the case's potential for rubbing off some of the veneer from the proverbial southern gentility and laying bare the raw emotions beneath.

One year short of its seventy-fifth birthday in 1950, LSU was one of about sixty public institutions of higher education in the South. As returning education-hungry black GIs, armed with their GI-Bill benefits, flooded the admissions departments, all of them were feeling the pressure.

In a normal year, the Louisiana school attracted a few out-of-state and foreign students, young people from the small towns and rural areas in the northern and western parts of the state, and a healthy share of the state's politically ambitious. U.S. Senator Long, whose daddy the governor had adopted LSU as one of his projects and transformed the institution from one of mediocrity to a modern university, had learned the theories if not all the practices of government there. Four of the state's governors in this century had gone to LSU, and legions of state legislators had made their early contacts there.

While at LSU, they constituted a tight little society bound together by the camaraderie of Deke dinner dances, rush parties, the comely virtues of homecoming queens, and sports, particularly football. One young man captured the institutional mindset when he wrote in the *Daily Reveille:*

> *Had Madame Curie attended LSU*
> *She'd of never discovered radium*
> *They'd have sat her down at a drawing board*
> *And made her plan a stadium.*

The alumni tended to herd together long after graduation, doing business in the happy hereafter with each other in the law offices, banks, state legislature, and country clubs of Shreveport and Alexandria, returning regularly for homecomings and football games. The Saturday afternoons spent cheering in Tiger Stadium had cemented the already strong bonds forged in daily campus contacts, and neither the old-timers nor the current students were going to readily accept the disturbance in their emotional equilibrium that the presence of black students on their campus threatened to cause.

The university, which sprawled across the south end of town, had been chartered in 1876 while the state was still operating under the old racially neutral constitution of 1868. The statute that created it had made no reference to race. Race didn't enter the picture officially until the state legislature created Southern University (1880) and Grambling College (1901) specifically for blacks, although it had already become the "custom, usage and practice" of the institution to admit only whites.

Beginning in the mid-thirties, the NAACP opened its campaign to break down the color bar in public education with an attack on segregation at the graduate and professional levels. Until 1950, there was no public institution in the South where a black student could pursue a Ph.D. (there was at least one in every state for whites), no accredited school of engineering (thirty-six for whites); there were only two schools of medicine (twenty-nine for whites), two schools of law (forty for whites), and two schools of pharmacy (twenty for whites).

The ceilings imposed on education for blacks resulted in a lopsided distribution of professional people among the black and white populations: one white physician to every 843 of the white population, one black physician to every 4,409 of the black population; one white dentist to every 2,795 of the white population, one black dentist to every 12,101 of the black population; one white lawyer to every 702 of the white population, one black lawyer to every 24,997 of the black population.

Thurgood Marshall and his legal infantry decided this was the place to start. Demands for equal facilities for black graduate students, they believed, would be financially impossible for the states to meet, and racial segregation would fall of its own weight. They also predicted judges might be more inclined to decide in favor of desegregation at that level than at the elementary, secondary, or even undergraduate stages. In addition, they guessed educated white graduate students themselves would be more amenable to accepting white blacks in their midst. The beliefs and predictions were little more than hopes as the campaign opened, but if blacks were ever to have the physicians and dentists they and their children needed, a cadre of educated men and women to lead them out of the morass in which they were languishing, not to mention the lawyers to channel their complaints into the courts, Marshall and his men would have to get busy.

The strategy proved sound. First, in 1936, Marshall and his old dean from Howard, Charlie Houston, persuaded a Baltimore judge to order the admission of Donald Murray to the law school at the University of Maryland, which had rejected the applications of every black who'd applied during the thirties, including that of Marshall himself, who swore he'd "make them pay for it." Then in 1938, Houston persuaded the U.S. Supreme Court to order the University of Missouri at Columbia to open its law school doors to Lloyd Gaines. Both victories involved universities in border states where resistance was softest, but the taste was no less sweet.

LSU had no problem with either the Gaines or Murray suits. When young Hurchail Jackson, a graduate of the all-black Xavier University in New Orleans, applied to its law school in 1938, he was simply informed that the institution did not admit blacks. He didn't protest.

When Charles Hatfield received the same treatment eight years later, he went to the NAACP. But the university was way ahead of him. Before A. P. Tureaud could even assemble the material for a suit, he got word that the Louisiana State Board of Education, in conjunction with the LSU Board of Supervisors—the governing body of the institution—in their eagerness to keep the university white, had voted to add, at considerable expense, a separate law school for blacks at Southern University. In the meantime, the educators told Tureaud, his client could attend, at state expense, a law school outside the state. The university proved to be equally adroit at deflecting blacks' applications for admissions all through the forties, even though Thurgood Marshall himself had complained to the state Department of Education and for good measure had boldly sent the department a copy of the U.S. Supreme Court's decision in Lloyd Gaines's case.

On June 5, 1950, the bottom fell out of the market for racial segregation in graduate education. Having left, as it often did, the most controversial decisions until the end of the term, the U.S. Supreme Court on that day launched its heaviest attack to date on racial discrimination at the graduate level. It behooved every public university in the South to note carefully the two landmark cases.

Heman Marion Sweatt was a mailman, but he didn't want to be one all his life; he wanted to be a lawyer. In Texas the place to get the best legal training was the Jim Crow state university in Austin, which boasted an eminent faculty, comprehensive library, and all the accoutrements of a modern law school including the next generation of the state's lawyers, the contacts that were invaluable to every practicing attorney. Sweatt's application, however, was rejected out of hand. The University of Texas did not admit blacks.

The local courts tried to pacify Sweatt by ordering the state to establish a law school for blacks. The state complied by hastily throwing up a blatantly inferior institution: a three-room basement facility, a hastily recruited faculty, and the bare bones of a library across the street from the state capitol in downtown Austin. Thurgood Marshall, who was smoking two packs of cigarettes a day by that time, convinced the U.S. Supreme Court to consider Sweatt's case.

At about the time Marshall was shepherding Sweatt through the Texas courts, George McLaurin, who had a master's degree and wanted a doctorate in education, applied to the public university in the neighboring state of Oklahoma, where it was a misdemeanor to "maintain or operate, teach or attend a school at which both whites and Negroes are enrolled or taught." McLaurin's application was denied, and Inc. Fund lawyers prepared for another costly and exhausting series of legal actions. Marshall explained later that McLaurin had been chosen from among eight potential plaintiffs because at sixty-eight, he seemed to be a living refutation of the accusation that blacks were clamoring for higher education so they could more easily marry whites.

Following a federal district court's invalidation of Oklahoma's statutes that kept blacks out of whites' public institutions, the state legislature amended them to require only that blacks could attend whites' schools wherever courses unavailable in blacks' schools were offered; the catch was that all such programs of instruction be given "upon a segregated basis." McLaurin was thereupon admitted to the University of Oklahoma where the administration solved the problem of his presence by requiring him to sit apart at a designated desk in an anteroom adjoining the classroom, to sit at a designated desk on the mezzanine floor of the library, and to sit at a designated table and to eat at a different time from the other students in the school cafeteria. Soon after, the rules were modified slightly, but not enough to effectively integrate McLaurin into the normal life of the institution. He remained essentially caged, like an exhibit at the zoo, a subhuman species presumed to be unaffected emotionally or intellectually by the humiliation.

The U.S. Supreme Court heard oral arguments for and against Sweatt and McLaurin in tandem on April 3 and 4, 1950, after which the justices retired to their chambers to consider what they'd heard in the courtroom and what they'd read in the briefs, which were voluminous. Not only had the attorneys for the plaintiffs and defendant universities submitted briefs, but both parties were supported by several amicus curiae submissions. For the plaintiffs they'd come from the American Civil Liberties Union, a group of leading constitutional scholars that called itself the Committee of Law Teachers Against Segregation in Legal Education, the American Federation of Teachers, the Congress of Industrial Organizations (CIO), the American Jewish Committee, and the United States solicitor general's office. The consensus was that the half-century–old *Plessy* should be struck down.

The old Confederacy stood firm against this impressive array. Ten of its states, their strength augmented by Kentucky and Oklahoma, lent their support to the eleventh, Texas, defendant in Heman Sweatt's suit, and submitted a joint brief invoking the mantra of states' rights and threatening to close their schools should the Court decide for the plaintiffs, explaining that

> there exists no desire to discriminate and no prejudice or hatred against Negroes in the minds of a large majority of white people in the South.

There did exist, however,

> an abiding prejudice against intimate social intermingling of the two races . . .

At the last session of the 1949 term* on June 5, 1950, the justices handed down no fewer than sixteen opinions—almost half a volume, more than two hundred pages in the *United States Reports*. The bundle included four calculated to offend southern pride, beginning with the nationalization of the oil fields off the coasts of Louisiana and Texas.

Compounding the fracture they'd made in the structure of federalism in that case, the justices told railroad companies operating in the segregated South that the traditional separation of blacks and whites in dining cars would no longer be tolerated. The room dividers, the curtains, the glass panels—the purdah—behind which the railroads for years had virtually hidden blacks would have to come down.

Chief Justice Fred Vinson never had been a revolutionary. His highest values centered around governmental stability. He was, however, chief justice and as such unofficially obligated to act as a lightning rod for the public passions aroused over controversial Court decisions, the category to which the decisions in the cases of the two Jim Crow universities belonged. He wrote carefully, as if an editor would scrutinize every word for its constitutional validity.

In Heman Sweatt's case, the Court explicitly declined to overrule *Plessy* v. *Ferguson* as Marshall had asked, but, finding no "substantial equality in the educational opportunities offered white and Negro law students by the State," ordered the University of Texas to admit Sweatt.

---

*The Supreme Court's annual term traditionally begins the first Monday in October and ends when the cases on its docket have been decided, generally June or July of the following year. The term is named for the year in which it opened. Hence, June 1950 belonged to October Term, or OT as it's abbreviated, 1949.

The chief justice waxed a little more eloquent in George McLaurin's case, although he maintained his distance from *Plessy:*

> Our society grows increasingly complex, and our need for trained leaders increases correspondingly. [McLaurin's] case represents, perhaps, the epitome of that need, for he is attempting to obtain an advanced degree in education, to become, by definition, a leader and trainer of others. Those who still come under his guidance and influence must be directly affected by the education he receives. Their own education and development will necessarily suffer to the extent that his training is unequal to that of his classmates. State-imposed restrictions that produce such inequalities cannot be sustained.

And he concluded that Oklahoma, like Texas, must afford McLaurin "the same treatment . . . as students of other races."

Both decisions were unanimous—a tradition the justices were taking some pains to establish in order to downplay any diviseiveness that otherwise could be exploited in these civil rights cases. However insulted southerners felt when they read their newspapers next day, the scope of the two decisions had been sharply limited—not all the NAACP had asked for by any means. The Court had carefully applied its rulings to the specific cases before it and steered clear of making any broad statements regarding segregation itself in public institutions. *Plessy* remained alive and well at the end of the day.

It was clear from the reaction to *Sweatt* and *McLaurin* that the Court had struck at the very heart of white supremacy. The politically powerful paraded their pain publicly. Not everyone was as crude as Representative James C. Davis of Georgia, who swore that

> The white people of Georgia, and, I believe, of the entire South, are not going to school with blacks, eat with them, or live with them.

Estes Kefauver, the junior senator from Tennessee almost ready to plunge into national politics, sounded more disappointed than irate; he thought the rulings "unfortunate," having always considered the "separate but equal" formula the "best basis for working out the problem." Texas Attorney General Price Daniel, who'd masterminded the university's case against Heman Sweatt from the beginning, focused on finding an alternative to the Court-ordered desegregation:

> Time is the essential factor. The states must be prepared to build separate colleges for Negroes immediately or else the U.S. Supreme

Court will do away with segregation in the South.

And in Atlanta, Roy V. Harris, a trusted aide to Governor Herman E. Talmadge in 1950 and later an architect of southern resistance to school desegregation, predicted it wouldn't be long before the Supreme Court would

go all the way and say there can be no such thing as separate and equal facilities.

Ironically, Thurgood Marshall and his fellow LDF lawyers viewed *Sweatt* and *McLaurin* similarly. Not only had the Court provided them with valuable precedents on which to build their next cases, but also, Marshall believed, the justices had offered directional signals. He would be a fool not to follow them.

So that when LSU, which had no more difficulty ignoring *Sweatt* and *McLaurin* than it had had ignoring *Murray* and *Gaines* a dozen years earlier, rejected a group of black applications to its law and graduate departments, Thurgood Marshall was already in touch with A. P. Tureaud, who was assembling a legal challenge in Louisiana. The Inc. Fund, Marshall declared, wanted to

be in on it from go because ... we have agreed to push all of these cases as hard as possible.

By September 13, 1950, three months after the Supreme Court announced *Sweatt* and *McLaurin,* Marshall and Tureaud were to give the justices another little shove in the direction they thought the Court had headed, and they filed a complaint against LSU for rejecting their client, Roy Wilson's, application to the university's law school. Wilson's credentials looked good: army veteran, Grambling College graduate, former schoolteacher who planned to return after law school to his native Ruston where there were no black lawyers. The case number was 816, and with Dallam O'Brien's assignment system still in place, it landed in Skelly Wright's chambers. He proceeded with his usual caution.

The lawyers had asked his court to issue an injunction prohibiting LSU from denying Roy Wilson admission on the basis of the young man's race. An injunction is simply a court order prohibiting someone from taking a specified action or commanding someone to undo some wrong or injury. It was held in disrepute during the late nineteenth and early twentieth centuries when it was used by industry to prevent labor from organizing. Civil rights lawyers revived it in the 1950s. Because issuance was solely a matter between the parties and the judge and did not involve a jury trial, it was an ideal instrument for civil rights suits.

In Roy Wilson's case, the injunction Tureaud and Marshall were asking for challenged the constitutionality of a state directive—Wilson's rejection by state officials. It was Skelly Wright's first experience as a judge with that particular problem which required three-judge court. This special panel—by law a circuit court judge plus two district court judges—condensed two judicial steps into one, expediting constitutional challenges and saving the court time and money. It also built a safeguard against arbitrary rulings by a single district judge. Tureaud and Marshall preferred the three-judge lower court and frequently asked for one. They got the combined judgment of three judges rather than one, and appeal was directly to the Supreme Court, skipping the expensive and time-consuming appellate process.

The first thing Wright did when he received the request for the injunction was to telephone the chief judge of the Fifth Circuit, still Joseph Hutcheson, in Houston. The Wilson case, he told the chief, would require a three-judge court. Hutcheson immediately appointed the new circuit judge, Wayne Borah, who'd sat as a district judge on the first of Louisiana's teachers' salary-equalization suits, plus the other half of the Eastern District's court, Herbert Christenberry, to sit with Wright. Together they set a date for a hearing at the end of September.

By the time the hearings opened on September 29, *Sweatt* and *McLaurin* had begun to ferment. It was a slow process, this institution-by-institution litigation, and an expensive one. *Sweatt* and *McLaurin* had cost the NAACP $50,000, and just days after the Supreme Court had spoken, the organization was soliciting contributions to keep the drive going. However, the money had been well spent.

A federal court had ordered the admission of Gregory Swanson, a Negro from Martinsville, Virginia, to the state university law school; Attorney General J. Lindsay Almond, who'd signed the southern states' brief in *Sweatt* and before long would become one of the leaders of the hard-core segregationists, conceded that in the light of recent U.S. Supreme Court rulings, the state had had no alternative this time. Over objections that "strife and turmoil" would follow the "letting down of the bars," the attorney general of Tennessee approved the admission of three blacks to the state university's law and graduate schools. And thirteen blacks had followed Heman Sweatt to the University of Texas, although a spokesman for the institution described the attitude of the community and parents as unfavorable; the administration expected some white parents to withdraw students.

One of the most determined holdouts was Alabama, where the state superintendent of education predicted that racial desegregation would set back education twenty years, a sentiment vigorously echoed by Mississippi's state education chief as well as Georgia's, whose governor Talmadge was bellowing that the United States hadn't enough troops or police to enforce a court order requiring blacks and whites to sit in the same classrooms, not in *his* Georgia.

Louisiana held a prominent place on the list of resisters. Aware of the stakes in Roy Wilson's case, LSU recruited some of the biggest guns in state legal circles to fight it. When the hearing opened, an impressive array of talent sat poised for combat.

The state attorney general, Bolivar E. Kemp, who'd signed the southern states' amicus curiae brief in Sweatt's suit, lent the prestige of his office to the defense table. Laurence W. Brooks, the university's own chief counsel, was to actually argue his institution's side of the suit. A half-dozen lesser lights crowded around.

It was the first time Skelly Wright had seen Thurgood Marshall, who'd come down from New York to stage-manage Wilson's case, in action, and he right then and there learned to admire the burly black lawyer for his "straight-forward, good-humored, and incisive" performances in the courtroom. Wright later credited Marshall with introducing him to "the harsh realities of racism" and persuading him "that if the law did not prohibit racial discrimination, then the law was wrong."

A. P. Tureaud, whose local reputation as a civil rights lawyer had no equals now, was sitting beside Marshall. U. Simpson Tate, NAACP counsel for the southwest region, had come over from Dallas, Texas, bringing the number at the plaintiff's table to three, none with the legal cachet of the men at the defense table.

Brooks immediately tried to cancel the whole case. Relying on the standard institutional tactic, he asked the judges to dismiss it. They didn't say yes, they didn't say no; they said they'd consider it, then went on with the discussion over whether or not they should issue the injunction the black lawyers had requested.

When Marshall's turn came, the first thing he did was reassure Brooks that his side would adhere to the pretrial agreements limiting the scope of the case to the law school. He had no intention of prying open any other of the university's departments—yet. This case, however, Marshall added, could hardly avoid the broader implications of "race disqualification." He hoped in fact to abolish race as a general ground for turning down students attempting to study at LSU.

Brooks countered that admission of any applicant depended on his or her prelegal qualifications, moral character, and whatever standards the institution established. The decision, he declared, was both the right and responsibility of the university.

Agreed, said Marshall. However,

> It is not our object to deprive the LSU Board of the right to consider who shall be admitted but this suit is aimed at removing from that consideration the question of race.

Brooks cited Louisiana's munificent ($1.5 million in 1950) support of separate black education at Southern University. He offered depositions from officials at both LSU and Southern confirming the high quality of the law school at the latter. Southern, he insisted, was entirely adequate for the practice of law in Louisiana.

Marshall immediately challenged Brooks's assessments. The library at Southern was inferior to that at LSU. Equally, if not more, important, faculty at Southern lacked the advanced degrees and teaching experience of which LSU's faculty members were justifiably proud. Even the physical plant at Southern was inferior to LSU's, and Marshall at one point trapped Southern's dean into admitting that the law school was actually housed in an attic, like the afterthought it had been.

The three black robes reeking of authority maintained strict neutrality, coming to no conclusion that day. They neither issued the injunction Marshall had asked for nor dismissed the case as Brooks had requested. They wanted to think it over and discuss it.

What the court did and how the court did it would have an impact not only on the current LSU administration, faculty, and students, but on the thousands of alumni scattered over the state, many of them influential in their communities as well as financial supporters of the institution. For Roy Wilson and the education-starved blacks he represented, waiting in the hamlets and on the dirt farms of the state, it meant professional life or death.

For the judges themselves there on the firing line, accountable to the Constitution and to their communities, it was a dilemma. Wilson's case exposed the pressure points of federalism where national policy—equal protection of the laws without regard to race—clashed with local interests: racial segregation. It was up to the federal judge to bring the two into line, however unpopular his orders and decisions might be. They were federal judges, not competitors in a popularity contest.

Sweatt and *McLaurin* stared up at them from the pages of the Supreme Court reports. Precedents, strong ones, not to be ignored, but troubling, too, in the boldness with which they attacked local tradition. Supreme Court justices could afford to be bold. They enjoyed an insulation not available to district judges, many of whom were products of the local communities in which they lived and worked. Lifetime tenure protected judicial independence, but it didn't protect the judge from his natural desire for approval among the people with whom he'd fished in the bayous, played golf, shared confidences.

Judge Borah came from a wealthy Louisiana family, had been king of Carnival in 1946, and was himself an alumnus of LSU. He seemed more socially akin to the lawyers for LSU than those for the plaintiff. Like Skelly Wright, Herbert Christenberry came from a blue-collar family, had taken his legal education at Loyola, and risen from bookkeeper to federal judge. All three men had strong family ties, friendships, and community loyalties.

Federal judges first, however, and southerners second, they proved to be bound more tightly to the commands of the Constitution than to the southern way of life, and in Roy Wilson's case, they chose to follow the path of highest resistance. Although Wright was the junior member of the trio, he wrote the opinion. District court judges in Louisiana had no law clerks in those days, and he did his own research and writing.

He was quick, though. On October 7, one week after the hearing, *Wilson* v. *Board of Supervisors of Louisiana State University* hit the streets. If Borah and Christenberry had any hesitation in joining Wright's opinion, their strong, confident handwriting—"I concur"— scrawled on his draft opinion belied it.

The major precedents were, of course, *Sweatt* and *McLaurin,* which Wright believed had brought the Supreme Court to an important intersection: it could either retreat from its forward movement toward racial equality, or it could finally reject *Plessy* and the notion of separateness, but it could not stand still.

A lower court judge, however, was obliged to stand still, and Wright did. He did not reexamine *Plessy* or move in any direction beyond the Supreme Court. That was not his job. His court's firm support of *Sweatt* and *McLaurin,* however, undoubtedly would count, as the decisions of the lower federal courts usually did, in the justices' future deliberations of segregation cases.

As briefly and as dispassionately as he could, he reiterated the facts of Wilson's case and summarily denied Laurence Brooks's motion to dismiss it, then put Louisiana on notice that federal courts meant to enforce the law. He agreed with Thurgood Marshall's assessment of Southern University's law school as vastly inferior, and in conclusion granted the injunction for which Marshall and Turead had asked. The law school at LSU, like the law school in Texas, traditional tutor to the state's white legal establishment, would have to exorcize race from its admissions criteria.

The editors of the *New Orleans Times-Picayune* recognized Wright's opinion as the opening wedge it turned out to be. They clearly foresaw that

> attacks upon the other departments [might well] prove as successful as that upon the law school. Even more disturbing is the possible application of the high court's recent rulings (*Sweatt* and *McLaurin*) to the public school systems.

LSU officials were to be congratulated for their defense of state prerogatives. But the federal courts, the editors fumed, packed with Roosevelt and Truman appointees, seemed "to be recasting our national charter to effect fundamental and revolutionary changes in our governmental system."

As for Skelly Wright, at the same time he had opened doors of opportunity to Louisiana's blacks, as well as doors to some deeply held racial feelings of his fellow white Louisianans, he had opened one to himself that over the next few years would reveal qualities within that he perhaps had never known existed. As he looked back after the disturbances had subsided, the headlines had stopped their screaming, and the politicians had turned their attention to other matters, Wright recognized Roy Wilson's case as the turning point in his life, or as he put it:

> the first making of me as a person who was not going to accept the status quo when called upon to follow the [Supreme] Court.

As events spun out over the next decade, it would become increasingly apparent that for Louisiana as well as for Skelly Wright, Roy Wilson's case marked the beginning of the end of complacency and the end of the beginning of conscience.

Then not long afterward, an incident in his chambers involving a member of his judicial "family," a messenger, gave him another shove toward righting wrongs he was only now sharpening his awareness of. The fellow was a retired New Orleans police officer. Recognizing Wright's developing racial consciousness, he approached the judge one day. He wanted Wright to know, he said, that when he was a policeman, he had never participated in beating black prisoners. He then went on to describe what he considered a minor sin, in which he *had* participated.

Over the gallery of his station house, which overlooked one of the canals that thread through of the city, a large A-frame had been erected and fitted with a heavy belt. The police interrogators would secure their black suspect with the belt, then lower him into the water and ask him if he'd committed the crime in question. If he said yes, he was unbelted. If he said no, he was returned to the water.

"This is all I ever did," the ex-policeman told Wright. "I never beat anybody."

Wright was horrified. "When a person I felt was a very decent human being himself could not see how bad this was and . . . would try to distinguish this from the other, I felt that things were possibly a lot worse than I'd thought they were."

Following a daylong secret meeting at which LSU's Board of supervisors first approved a plan for adding $5,700,000 worth of seating to Tiger Stadium, Tom W. D. Dutton of New Orleans, board chairman, announced that Roy Wilson's case, still in the hands of university attorneys, would be appealed. The good news was that appeals from a three-judge court bypassed the circuit court of appeals and went straight to the U.S. Supreme Court. The bad news was that the 30,000 seats that would bring the stadium's capacity to 70,000 wouldn't be ready for the homecoming game with Georgia Tech the following week.

Accompanied by A. P. Tureaud, Roy Wilson, the first black student admitted to LSU in its three-quarter-century history, registered for law school courses on November 1. He was assigned to a single dormitory room in Hatcher Hall, and a class schedule that began next day. He planned to audit for the remainder of the first semester and begin courses for credit on February 1.

As he made his way to his dormitory room, students gathered in the corridors and stared at him curiously. He realized, he said, "there may be some who will be reluctant to see this change." He did not, however, "anticipate any difficulty."

The university carried out its threat to appeal Wilson's case, again relying heavily on the argument that LSU and Southern offered "equal facilities for a legal education and admission to the bar" in Louisiana. Wilson "and all others similarly situated"—i.e., blacks—were not, the lawyers declared, "eligible for admission" to LSU's law school.

The justices were not persuaded. On January 2, 1951, in a per curiam—literally "by the court"; a brief statement of the court's position without written opinion—the U.S. Supreme Court, citing *Sweatt* and *McLaurin,* upheld the lower court.

"It is what we expected," crowed A. P. Tureaud.

Roy Wilson's story didn't end there neatly and happily, however. He didn't finish the course at LSU. He didn't even finish the first term, a source of substantial embarrassment for the Inc. Fund lawyers who'd sponsored him.

Unwilling to rely entirely on the federal courts for relief in Wilson's case, university officials had dug deeply into his background while their appeal was pending. Their investigators found Wilson had a police record, a "blue" army discharge (neither honorable nor dishonorable), had been a psychiatric patient, and had been expelled from Grambling for attacking a fellow student with a softball bat. In view of what he tersely called "certain situations," Wilson left LSU hurriedly, taking time out only to write Tureaud a letter in which he conveyed his "sincere and respectful appreciation" for all the lawyer and his associates had done. He was leaving, he said, "without bitterness toward anyone or [any] group."

The dignified Tureaud came about as close to losing his cool as he ever did:

It is easy to stand on the sidelines and criticize players in a game. . . . We should not be ready to censure or condemn Wilson. He made it possible for others of his race who have all the necessary qualifications to be admitted to . . . LSU. . . . It is now left to his critics to take up where he left off.

Next semester, the fall of 1951, three black students entered LSU's law school under the court order Skelly Wright had written in Roy Wilson's case. One was the black Creole Ernest N. Morial, later one of Tureaud's law partners and still later the first black mayor of New Orleans. Court orders that year also opened the nursing school, the journalism department, the business school, and the department of education to black applicants. Which meant that all major divisions of the university had been penetrated except the undergraduate college. It was only a matter of time before the whole gang—Inc. Fund lawyers, black plaintiffs, the university legal team and Skelly Wright—would meet again in the federal courtroom.

CHAPTER 8

Throwing the Bandanas on the Bonfire

When A. P. Tureaud's six children, who ranged in color from the soft caramel of A. P., Jr., to the white-like-her-father of Elise, were growing up in New Orleans during the 1940s and early 1950s, the reality of race dominated as large a part of their lives as it had their father's a generation earlier. In 1944, Gunnar Myrdal, Swedish social economist who had studied the American Negro's singular plight under his scholarly microscope for six years, reported in his seminal work *An American Dilemma* that white Americans had made very little headway toward resolving the nagging questions raised by the presence of the Negro among them. Their hearts were still torn in two by their native morality as expressed in the high-sounding phrases of the Declaration of Independence and the Constitution, and their personal feelings, influenced by economic, social and political factors, toward the black man who'd been brought to their shores in chains solely for the white man's profit. However confused, embarrassed, angry, or guilty they felt when confronted with the inconsistencies in their behavior, many managed to rationalize the perpetuation of the customs and mores that had grown up around the black man over two centuries.

Old habits of racial relationships were not dying off, and Rodolphe Desdunes and Louis Martinet would have had little trouble reacclimating themselves to the ways of their native city at mid-twentieth century. Like the elder Tureaud in 1916, younger generations of blacks were still responding to the siren songs of northern cities, many with the same feeling of desperation.

On the whole, young A. P. and his five sisters led more materially comfortable lives than had their father, a part-time cement finisher for his contractor-father at a comparable age. The family was as middle class in its values as any white professional man's. The elder Tureaud was a respected lawyer. His wife, Lucille, was a pharmacist whose social conscience, like Helen Wright's, took her into community projects: women's auxiliary of Flint-Goodridge Hospital, the local branch of the Young Women's Christian Association—one of the few racially mixed organizations in town—the PTAs of her children's schools.

They were a hard-working, law-abiding, church-going family. No one need be ashamed of his or her clothes, which were of good quality if inexpensive, and A. P. made sure that all six pairs of Buster Brown shoes were shined to a fare-the-well before his brood set out for school each morning. A. P., Jr., spent several summers at a biracial boys' camp near Philadelphia, Pennsylvania, and the youngsters could look forward to spending their teens at Xavier Prep, a parochial institution established in 1915 to make up for the city's failure to build a black public high school. The house they lived in on Pauger Street in the Seventh Ward, still the major residential area for black Creole families, was spacious and comfortable if not luxurious.

Social life was typically middle class. The younger generation was kept busy with the debutante parties and balls the black Creole community held in honor of its own. The elder Tureaud belonged to a Catholic civic organization honoring the memory of St. Peter Claver, who had dedicated his life to helping slaves in seventeenth-century South America, and to the Prince Hall Masons, the local branch of a national group named for an early champion of blacks' civil rights.

Then there were the monthly meetings of the Eat Mores—formally referred to in the dignified social pages of the black newspaper, the *Louisiana Weekly,* as the EM Club—a close-knit clique of professional black Creole men and their wives who gathered for cards and serious eating and drinking in the New Orleans tradition, all overlaid with the kind of laughter that defines old friends who've become family over the years.

The psychologically toxic burdens imposed on even comparatively well-to-do blacks like the Tureauds, however, held the potential to disfigure the emerging personalities of the younger generation. If it was too early for them to be affected by the discrimination of money-lending agencies against black homebuyers or to notice the way local white-owned newspapers featured black crime and downplayed black achievement, it was not too early for them to notice the daily hurts, what one New Orleans writer, Brenda Thompson, a generation later called "the little murders":

[E]very one of them kills a little piece of you.

Like all public-school children in New Orleans, for example, the Tureaud children dutifully recited the Pledge of Allegiance in the morning, concluding with "liberty and justice for all," then were ordered to ride at the back of the city's streetcars and buses. Forty years later, Tureaud's offspring recalled with the clarity and stridence of a siren in the night the realities of the racial discrimination they endured.

They remembered that vacation trips always started before dawn so they could drive out of the South before they had to find a place to sleep. They related instances when for one reason or another they did have to book a motel room south of the Mason-Dixon line for a night, and they could still hear their father shouting from the driver's seat, "Hide the brown kids!" as they rolled up to the motel entrance in their old car. They still shivered at remembered glimpses of robed Ku Klux Klansmen at Pass Christian in neighboring Mississippi where the family had a summer home and where the beach provided for black bathers was substantially shorter than that reserved for whites.

Elise remembered the summers the local Girl Scout camp was used exclusively by white troops most of the time; she and the other black Girl Scouts were allowed to use it for only a brief period in late August. She remembered as a teenager competing against a white girl for a trip to an international encampment in Europe and how her lifelong consignment to the fringes of New Orleans life had sapped her self-confidence and her ability to compete effectively. She was convinced all along, she said—or had convinced herself, having internalized white notions of black inferiority—that she couldn't win. And she didn't.

She remembered, too, the humiliations that lay waiting in ambush for blacks in downtown New Orleans. A lot of blacks solved the problem of downtown lunch counters being closed to them by eating before they left home. Elise had to wait until all the white customers were waited on before it was her turn to buy her box of stationery. She wasn't allowed to try on dresses in any of the white-owned local department stores, and her hair was believed to be too greasy to try on hats. If she was lucky, she might persuade a friendly clerk, all of whom were white in those days, to model a hat for her; it was her only chance to see it in action before she bought it.

A. P., Jr., remembered that as a teenager, already riddled with self-doubt, he woke up every morning wondering what's going to happen to [me] today? Who's going to say "no" to [me]? Who's going to tell [me I] can't go somewhere?

He hated the insecurities that went with his color. He hated having to spend "so much of [his] time worrying." And yet he felt he "had to deal with it." And he had to reassure himself constantly that the ever-present reminders of his color, the little voices whispering in his ear that "you're not able, you don't have what it takes," were entirely without substance.

Blacks could go to the symphony, but they had to ride the freight elevator to get to the seats provided for them at the top of the house. All the movie theaters had side and back entrances for blacks, who then had to climb steep staircases to the designated balconies. When white parents objected to the presence of black students from Xavier Prep at a showing of Shakespeare's *Macbeth* for the city's parochial schools, the blacks were hustled out of the theater.

There wasn't a single first-class restaurant in the city where Tureaud could take his wife and family. White swimming pools, bowling alleys, dance halls, and even the French Quarter places where New Orleans's famous jazz had first wailed from the throats and instruments of local black artists were off-limits to black customers.

So were tax-supported city-operated facilities. Blacks were forbidden to use the tennis courts and golf links of City Park, and black lecturers and musicians couldn't use Municipal Auditorium at all. Signs marking the "white" and "colored" sections told them where they could sit on the free ferries plying the river between downtown New Orleans and Algiers on the so-called West Bank.

White entertainers monopolized the airwaves: comedians Bob Hope and Milton Berle, soap opera characters Stella Dallas and Lorenzo Jones, news commentators Edward R. Murrow and Walter Winchell. Black roles in dramatic presentations were largely limited to maids and janitors.

The single exception was the popular radio sitcom *Amos 'n Andy,* reputed to be a favorite of former first lady Eleanor Roosevelt as well as the late Senator Huey Long, who, legend has it, was first dubbed Kingfish by one of his cronies in honor of the character of the same name on *Amos 'n Andy.* Al Smith was said to have scheduled radio spots during his 1928 presidential campaign so they wouldn't compete with the program.

Neither the show's portrayal of the leading characters' responses to universal human dilemmas—financial problems, romantic difficulties, the drawbacks in of leaving the farm for the big city, for example—nor its frequent illustrations of universal human characteristics—pathos, humor, ambition, kindness—could, however, compensate for its exploitation of the hackneyed images of blacks as stupid, uneducated, and lazy. NAACP members were so offended at the use of the "de's" and "dats," the "I'se regusted," the "'splain dat to me"—"making fun of themselves," as one black listener put it—that following the program's television (a new medium) debut in 1951, the organization officially condemned it and urged blacks to protest to the CBS network and to boycott the show's sponsors.

Writing in *Plessy* v. *Ferguson* for the United States Supreme Court's majority in 1896, Henry Billings Brown had denied that racial segregation carried implications of racial inferiority. Any such notion, he said, "is not by reason of anything found in the act, but solely because the colored race chooses to put that construction upon it." Henry Billings Brown, however, had never known the fear of white rebuff or of standing out as one not fit to associate with certain other persons: the shame of untouchability, as if black would rub off on white if elbows accidentally bumped on a crowded streetcar. He hadn't known the fear of overstepping racial demarcations, of inadvertently stepping ahead of a white customer in a drugstore, and arousing latent hostility. Brown had known nothing of the immediate effects and less of the cumulative effects of racial segregation, how, as Paul Trévigne had put it back in 1877, it "tends to degrade" individuals.

One of the biggest advertisers in the *Louisiana Weekly* was the seventy-five-year-old Galenol Company of Atlanta whose best-seller was a skin whitener.

Shortly before the end of World War II, a young black girl was asked what she thought ought to be done with Hitler after his defeat. Without a moment's hesitation, she replied:

Paint him black and bring him over here.

One year older than the century, A. P. Tureaud was unavoidably reliving his own youth through his children in the late 1940s and early 1950s, forced for the second time to peer personally into the dark corners of the human spirit, to confront the euphemism of "separate but equal" with which southerners attempted to mask bigotry, to experience again the stigma, the lost opportunities, the frustrations and wounds, to endure again the humiliations of racial prejudice. However deep these wounds, whatever visceral reactions he suppressed, he persisted nonetheless in his purpose. In the tradition of Desdunes and Martinet, he would build the bridges between the races without resorting to the rhetoric of violence, adhering rigidly, almost religiously, in his long fight for racial equality and ultimately harmony, to the legal language of the courtroom.

By 1951, there were six black lawyers practicing in Louisiana, five more than in 1947, the beginning of a trend toward blacks hiring black lawyers at last. The pressure on Tureaud to be everywhere at once had not, however, abated, and he was spending less and less time in his sparsely equipped little walk-up office in a predominantly black section of town. He was the senior among them, the one with years of courtroom experience. He knew the white judges in Ouachita and New Iberia and St. Helena parishes. The years of waiting and watching in their court-rooms and conferring with them in their chambers had familiarized him with their individual professional styles. He knew the white lawyers against whom he contended. He knew exactly what he was up against: the men, their strengths, their weaknesses, and their repertoires of legal arguments. Perhaps most important, he knew how the white legal frater-nity dealt with uppity Negro lawyers. "Nigras" when they wanted to be polite; "Nigguhs" when they didn't care. Still, he soldiered on in his soft-spoken but nonetheless determined way. No case was too big, no com-plaint too small, no insult too humiliating.

By 1951, Tureaud was catching the attention of the federal courts with his arguments and was beginning to scratch at the outer coat of paint on the local caste system. New Orleanians were finding him an increasingly skilled opponent, his confidence bolstered, perhaps, by his winnings: the teachers' salary-equalization case that had made his repu-tation, a voting rights case he'd won that had added luster to it, the recent suit in behalf of blacks' admission to the graduate and profes-sional schools at LSU after twelve years of rejection; and tangling with the university's biggest legal guns had given him invaluable experience. It was apparent to all, black and white both, that behind Tureaud's quiet, dignified mien there lurked the strength and will of a tiger that made his legal acumen and strong sense of purpose that much more effective. But what they were seeing was only the beginning.

Blacks' access to the highest levels of public education, the law and graduate schools, was a significant triumph, the first advance blacks had made on public education since Reconstruction. As such it was psycho-logically exciting as well as socially and politically significant.

Trained in inferior schools, blacks, however, were not prepared to take advantage of this progress. The Heman Sweatts and George McLau-rins were still the exceptions at mid-century, and if the scarcity of well-prepared students persisted, the court victories in Texas and Oklahoma and Louisiana would be meaningless.

In the early 1950s, Tureaud's attention, like that of a good many other American lawyers and educators, was focusing on the lower levels of education where graduate and professional students were born intellectually and psychologically. NAACP planning had begun to concentrate on improving blacks' access to all the educational advantages whites took for granted, on reversing what had seemed for so long an ineluctable trend of providing for black children vastly inferior educational opportunities no white parent, teacher, or administrator would have tolerated. The "equal" in "separate but equal" had never really existed, except on paper.

It was hardly a secret in Louisiana or anywhere else in the Jim Crow South that the lion's share of taxes was pumped into the best of the public facilities which were reserved for whites. The budgets devised to finance the schools allotted to the two races were particularly lopsided. In 1944–45, near the end of World War II, in which 900,000 blacks risked their lives for principles that didn't always apply to them, taxpayers in nine states—Alabama, Arkansas, Florida, Georgia, Louisiana, Mississippi, North Carolina, South Carolina, Maryland—and the District of Columbia were spending an average of $88.70 on each white primary-school child and $46.95 on each black primary-school child. In Louisiana, the differential was even higher: $113.30 for each white child compared to $34.06 for each black one.

Across the South as a whole, school terms averaged 173.5 days a year for whites, 164 days for blacks. In Louisiana, whites went to school 180 days, blacks, 156.7. Southwide, the states spent 427.6 percent more money per white child in school property. Louisiana, with a 561 percent greater investment per white child in school property, exceeded even the regional average.

Undergraduate education for blacks was suffering similarly. Southern taxpayers were supporting colleges and universities for white students eleven times more generously than they were supporting these institutions for black students. Louisiana taxpayers were supporting colleges and universities for white students fifteen times better than they were supporting them for blacks.

An unidentified black educator at the Colored Industrial High School in West Palm Beach, Florida, described in 1948 to the syndicated columnist Fred Hechinger at a regional conference the Catch-22 of black education:

They don't teach us what they blame us for not knowing.

These tangible, objective shortcomings without question devalued blacks' education, but dollars and cents didn't tell the whole story. They

ignored, for example, the damage whites, who both fed on and reinforced the inferiority of blacks' schooling, inflicted on the alumni of
whom nothing much was expected.

The author Richard Wright, who grew up in Jackson, Mississippi,
relived a disturbing moment of his youth in his autobiographical *Black
Boy*:

> "What grade are you in in school?" a white woman asked him.
> "Seventh, ma'am," Wright replied.
> "Then why are you going to school?" she persisted.
> "Well, I want to be a writer," he mumbled . . .
> "You'll never be a writer," his antagonist declared. "Who on earth put
>   such ideas into your nigger head?"
> "Nobody," Wright answered.
> "I didn't think anybody ever would," she said.

In her autobiographical *I Know Why the Caged Bird Sings,* Maya
Angelou described what passed for a high-school education in her native
Stamps, Arkansas. Her experience was not atypical.

There was no real high school for blacks in Stamps. Angelou went to
the Lafayette County Training School, an inelegant building on an
unlandscaped dirt hill that was in fact nothing more than a training
school. If they went to college at all, and most didn't, its graduates were
expected to go not to the state university for an academic degree and
preparation for a profession, but to the agricultural and mechanical
school where young black men were trained as carpenters, farmers,
handymen, or masons, and young black women were trained as maids,
cooks, or baby nurses.

In Angelou's year, the black community in Stamps went all-out on
the day of the graduation ceremony. Angelou's grandmother closed her
store. The graduating seniors wore new outfits, oiled their legs and
brushed their hair back. The band played, the choir sang, and the local
Baptist minister led the audience in prayer.

Then the white speaker from Texarkana, clearly a state official,
described the changes about to come to Stamps. A new art teacher had
been hired to teach at the all-white Central High School. New micro-
scopes and chemistry equipment had been purchased for Central's laboratory. And when the speaker, who was running for office, was elected,
the black community of Stamps could be sure the Lafayette County
Training School, nursery for some of Arkansas Agriculture and
Mechanic's best football players, would have the "only colored paved
playing field in that part of Arkansas." At which point the "hush-hush

magic time of frills and gifts and congratulations and diplomas" ended for Maya Angelou.

Wright and Angelou, of course, went on to forge brilliant careers as writers, but most blacks in those days fulfilled their schools' lower expectations of them. In 1960, advertisers in the classified section of the *Times-Picayune* were looking for a "Head coach ... white," a "Young man white" to train as district manager of a national concern, a "white service station manager," a "Service station attendant, colored"; "Colored maintenance man," "Neat colored woman to do housework." By this time separate but *un*equal had worked so well that some blacks didn't want to succeed anymore, were afraid to try. Truck driver was high enough, a father advised his son; lawyer was a "white man's job."

Nor did the objective criteria take into consideration the effects, as Thurgood Marshall had demonstrated so clearly in Heman Sweatt's suit against the University of Texas, of blacks' isolation from the dominant white culture with which they must cope, whether they were in the first year of elementary school or the final year of law school, if they hoped to be successful in the marketplace, at the counsel's table in the courtroom, or in the operating theater of the hospital.

The edifice had, however, begun to crumble as black lawyers like Marshall and A. P. Tureaud, Marshall's man in New Orleans, hacked away at its main supports. The NAACP's victories in voting rights cases and graduate and professional education suits had made it the organization most hated and feared by the white South, a conspiracy of "outside influences" that "come down here," as a white secretary in a rural Virginia school put it, and "stir the Negroes up. Tell them: 'See what the white folks have in their schools? You ought to have that in your schools, too.'"

Initially, the lawyers would have settled for the equalization of facilities in separate schools for blacks and whites—the requisite number of coats of paint, up-to-date textbooks, adequate teaching staffs, the crumbling ceilings and leaking pipes repaired, basic necessities taken for granted in white schools. Then in the mid-1930s, black leaders had begun to have doubts that the massive infusions of money that equalization of facilities would require would do the job they wanted done, and they wondered whether they might have to abolish segregation itself. There was little agreement among them.

In 1935, the *Journal of Negro Education* had devoted its entire July issue to the question of "The Courts and the Negro Separate School." Contributors complained bitterly about the notorious inequality of facilities provided for blacks but were divided on the issue of whether to solve the problem by demanding equalization via the courts or whether to attack segregation head-on.

W. E. B. Du Bois, one of the founders of the NAACP, editor for a quarter century of its monthly magazine *Crisis,* in whose pages he thundered against racism as it was practiced in the United States of America, and in 1935 a faculty member at Atlanta University, was convinced that so long as "racial animosities and class lines" defined American society, blacks needed separate schools. In those majority-white public schools in the North to which black children were admitted, he wrote, voicing the concerns of many black parents then and later, the youngsters were not "educated," they were "crucified." To force them into schools where "the white children, white teachers and white parents despised and resented the dark child, made mock of it, neglected or bullied it, and literally rendered its life a living hell," amounted to "refinement of cruelty."

Howard University professor Alain Locke, on the other hand, felt that racially mixed schools would better reflect the real world with all its hostilities and fears. In an unsegregated atmosphere, "the student is better conditioned to the eventual stress he must undergo in the black community." However, he warned, as if he had had a vision of the 1950s and 1960s, desegregation would undoubtedly encounter "temporary setbacks," and any such movement ought to prepare for "retributive community sentiment and behavior in some instances."

Elaborating poignantly on Paul Trévigne's half-century–old argument against segregated schooling in New Orleans, *Journal* editor Charles H. Thompson articulated the case for mixed schools that in the end prevailed:

> [T]o *segregate* is to *stigmatize.* . . . We segregate the criminal, the insane, pupils with low I.Q.'s, Negroes and other undesirables. . . . [W]e all know that segregation is practically always initiated by the whites . . . on the basis that Negroes are inferior and undesirable. Thus, when Negroes allow themselves to be cajoled into accepting the status defined by the separate school, they do something to their personalities which is infinitely worse than any of the discomforts *some* of them *may* experience in a mixed school.

The argument was by no means settled, however. The discussion reverberated outside and inside the NAACP offices for a decade and a half. Outside, black teachers and principals feared for their jobs if desegregation became the goal. Economic reprisal was always a threat. Black parents, like W. E. B. Du Bois had said, feared to expose their children to the resentment they knew would surface the minute a black child entered a formerly all-white school.

Inside the organization's offices, some staff members thought an attack on segregation was premature. Others thought it was going too far. Thurgood Marshall knew that eventually they had to attack *Plessy* head-on, but thought that for the time being judges would be more cooperative in ordering equalization of facilities than in approving blacks' applications to white schools. The parent organization was "convinced of the futility" of the separate-but-equal formula but recognized similar futility in jumping the gun, and settled down to "work for the day when the same and not equal opportunities are open to all." In the meantime, they would use equalization suits as "steps toward our goal."

In New Orleans in 1946, A. P. Tureaud was assembling one of those "steps."

For his civil-rights legal work, Tureaud had acquired a part-time colleague, Daniel Ellis Byrd, a light-skinned Negro with a full head of wavy gray-streaked black hair and a handsome oval face accented by a pencil-line mustache and an ever present well-chewed but unlit cigar clamped between his teeth. He was a native of Marvell, Arkansas, who, like the youthful Tureaud, had moved north to find greater opportunity, only to find racial discrimination instead.

He became a civil rights activist in his high school in Gary, Indiana, graduated from Northwestern University, and played several seasons with the Chicago Globetrotters—later the Harlem Globetrotters—before moving to New Orleans in 1937. He found race relations "terrible" there and soon joined the NAACP. Courses offered by the Lasalle Law School, a Chicago-based correspondence school, provided him with enough of a rudimentary background to assist Tureaud, whom he knew socially and as a fellow member of the NAACP.

In 1941–42, he was president of the NAACP's New Orleans branch and in 1946 was executive secretary of the statewide conference. He'd celebrated his thirty-sixth birthday that year and begun his thirty-seventh year by putting together a formal petition from black parents of Orleans Parish to the local school board in which they vigorously protested conditions in their children's schools.

Local school authorities were not unaware of these conditions. In their annual reports they had consistently deplored the overcrowding of the schools assigned to blacks, whose enrollments, equally consistently, increased over the years, often necessitating the assignment of two students to one desk. What school authorities failed to publish, the local black newspaper, the *Louisiana Weekly,* made sure the public knew: how the schools for black youngsters were "poorly lighted, poorly ventilated, poorly arranged and not large enough to accommodate the number of students who are to be in attendance."

A committee of local educational activists in 1938 had hired Alonzo

Grace, Connecticut's education commissioner, to take a hard look at New Orleans's schools. He and his staff of prominent northern educators found conditions deplorable throughout the city's two systems, white as well as black, which had virtually ignored modernizing trends in education since the early years of the twentieth century. But the investigators saved their harshest words for the neglected schools provided for black children, who had to endure the "wide gulf in educational opportunity dating far back into the history of the state and region."

The Grace report, which came out in 1939, changed very little in the city's public schools. Dan Byrd was acutely aware that before he was born, the NAACP had been formally protesting conditions in the city's black schools and the answer had invariably been "The matter will be taken under advisement." Allowing himself the luxury of hyberbole under the circumstances, he estimated the number of petitions at more than five hundred.

The members of the school board traditionally had maintained a veneer of courtesy, which made possible a continuing conversation between petitioner and petitioned. It had not, however, indicated the board's acceptance of blacks' demands, and now in 1946 Byrd was not particularly sanguine about the fate of his latest query.

He filed his petition on May 3, 1946. He focused on the "glaring" inequalities that had become standard at the local schools allotted to black children. He stuck closely to fundamental academic discriminations: 82 percent of the blacks' schools operated on double sessions—known as "platoons"—while schools for white children, functioning at only 69 percent of capacity, had empty classrooms; black children read from out-of-date textbooks; crippled, deaf, speech-impaired, and blind black children lacked the special classes readily available to white children. Nor were the business education and certain vocational classes that white children enjoyed accessible to black youngsters. Cutting to the heart of the complaints, Byrd accused the city of New Orleans of spending only 37 percent—a little more than a third—of the available school funds on its black students' schools, although the total enrollment in the two systems was nearly the same.

And Byrd didn't include the understaffing at Johnson Lockett—two teachers for four first-grade classes and two for three third-grade classes—the cold and milkless lunches at Robert R. Moton, the failure to repair Lawless Junior High after a helicopter fell on it, or the rusted furniture at Harding where the teaching staff had been called on to kill two snakes that had wandered into the building.

Byrd's first hint that this petition, too, would be taken under advisement, probably forever, came within a week after he sent it off. School board secretary Jennie Roch formally acknowledged its receipt, but explained that it had arrived too late to be included in the agenda scheduled for discussion at the May 6 meeting. She had been instructed to notify Byrd that the board would arrange a conference with him and his associates "at sometime in the near future."

May passed. June came and went. July arrived. The summer was half over. Not much time remained if repairs were to be made on schools before they opened in September.

His ears laid back now, Byrd curtly reminded the school board of its promise of a meeting. He and his colleagues had accepted the board's promise "in good faith," and had "assumed the attitude that the Board, while being an intelligent group of persons, was unmindful of the flagrant violation of the Equal Protection Clause of the Fourteenth Amendment to the United States Constitution." Byrd "respectfully" requested the board to set a date to discuss the matter.

At last the board responded. A meeting would be held July 25 at the board's headquarters on Carondelet Street in the heart of New Orleans's commercial section.

A. P. Tureaud appeared for Byrd and his colleagues who had in the meantime organized themselves into a Citizens' Committee on Equal Education. Tureaud was at ease addressing the school board, having appeared for plaintiffs with similar petitions for more than a decade, and he did his dignified, eloquent best to urge correction of "discriminations" in the city's public school system. The board heard him out but seemed far more interested in discussing white student absenteeism, which was reported in considerably more detail by the *Times-Picayune.*

Once again, the board promised to take the blacks' pleas "under advisement," although Byrd and his committee got the impression the board intended to respond immediately: either to deny the blacks' allegations or to set out in writing a "program for eliminating" the inequities they complained about.

Byrd twiddled his thumbs for another three weeks, then wrote to the board about what he had regarded as a commitment to the city's blacks. Byrd's reminder, Jennie Roch replied a few days later, had been submitted to the board at a recent meeting, and she had been "directed" to notify him that at the meeting on July 25, the board had given the committee "as much information as it was possible to give on these matters." Once again the circular file had swallowed blacks' hopes.

A new school superintendent, Lionel J. Bourgeois, had been appointed that year. Although he'd come up through the white system as was traditional—teacher, principal, district superintendent of high schools, assistant parish superintendent, and now finally full superintendent—and no one really knew how much he understood or even was familiar with conditions in schools for blacks, he seemed to be genuinely sympathetic to blacks' concerns. He told Tureaud he "agreed 100 percent" that black children at several local schools were being "deprived of an equal opportunity for education with children in more favored situations, particularly because of the necessity of installing double sessions to take care of the great numbers." Bourgeois stood, he said, "squarely upon a platform of equal opportunity for all children who attend the public schools."

Publicly—and presciently—he went even further, too far, in the end, for the school board, which was still in 1946 elected largely by the white majority in New Orleans. He told a reporter for the *Louisiana Weekly* that "the Negro in the community can be an asset morally, sociologically, and economically. Any narrow policy that neglects this very important segment of our population is certain to bring about problems and conditions this community may ultimately find difficult to solve."

Unfortunately, however, he told Tureaud, he had "inherited a backlog of problems" which were making the burdens of his office "heavy to the backbreaking point." He hoped eventually to wheedle $20 million from the state legislature—which the state constitution assigned to finance the schools from the revenues of various tax funds—for school construction and repair, including two high schools and several elementary schools for blacks. He planned also to convert some white schools to blacks' use.

If all went well, he hoped for an additional $500,000 a year of operating-expense revenues with which he planned to equalize pupil-teacher ratios in all schools, to install kindergartens in every black elementary school that had none, and to add psychological, dental, and medical services for Negro youngsters on the same basis they were available now for whites.

He asked the black community's patience—he couldn't change the habits of a century in a semester. Ultimately, however, the school board exhausted even Bourgeois's patience.

The months dragged on. The board sat on its hands. Bourgeois warned its members that blacks were threatening to go to court. He suggested that if the board couldn't find equitable solutions to blacks' concerns, the courts would, and he even added the possibility of racial integration of the schools to his list of dire prophecies. But no one took him seriously.

In April, 1948, not quite two weeks short of two full years since Dan Byrd had submitted his petition, Bourgeois told Tureaud that in good conscience he could no longer ask the black community for its forbearance. He could not in his position advocate "court action," but he would not oppose it, either. Byrd, who had been eager for it for some time, interpreted Bourgeois's comment as "asking for such action indirectly and," he added, putting the spurs to Tureaud, "if we fail to produce the desired action then I feel we should close the doors."

At this point, Tureaud needed little urging from either Bourgeois or Dan Byrd. Events in New Orleans had been moving along and had begun to focus on the all-black Macarty Elementary School in the city's Ninth Ward.

Every city had then—and most still have—an impoverished and run-down Ninth Ward where except near election time the garbage is picked up irregularly, street lights don't always work, weeds overrun vacant lots, drainage facilities block up, sewage collects in the streets, and police protection, along with sidewalks, stops at the boundaries. New Orleans's Ninth Ward, which was an industrial area crisscrossed by railroad tracks, bisected by the polluted Industrial Canal, and scarred by factories, sprawled over the eastern edge of the city from the river to Lake Pontchartrain.

Small shotgun frame houses and mom-and-pop groceries scattered through the area were home and livelihood to a racially mixed working-class population. Before the city constructed two mammoth public housing projects there in the 1940s, the area had a small-town feel about it despite its industrial overcast. After erection of the projects, the Ninth Ward gained a reputation as a place of crime and violence. The black schools in the area were some of the worst in the city.

The ramshackle Macarty School, looking every minute of its age—it had opened in 1861—blended in with the landscape. Its warped floors, mildewed ceilings, and overcrowding made it a likely place for trouble to start.

There wasn't enough political clout in the entire Ninth Ward to get the bulb in a streetlamp changed or the trash picked up on anything resembling a regular basis. City officials found it easy to ignore residents' complaints about their streets and neglected vacant lots, and school board members had no trouble ignoring the umpteen irate letters from Wilfred S. Aubert, Jr., a dock worker and local civic leader who'd spelled out for them the details of the overcrowding at Macarty, which two of his children attended. Aubert had come to Tureaud independently seeking direct legal action.

Aubert's eagerness to take his protests into court belied the difficulties inherent in persuading black men and women to seek redress through the courts during the 1940s and 1950s. Courthouses, with their white judges, all-white juries, white staffs—except maybe for the janitors—had too often seemed hostile to black interests in the past, too anxious to put black men in jail and keep white men out. Fear held people back. So did ignorance, poverty, and sometimes just plain inertia.

Of them all, fear of white reprisal was the worst. A black's hold on his or her job in a white-controlled economy in which most blacks worked for whites was tenuous at best. Often it was enough for a white supervisor just to suggest to his black employee that of course they agreed on segregation as the wisest policy for all concerned, black as well as white. Parties to legal suits against the white establishment risked heavy losses.

Aubert, however, was angry, and his anger sent him straight to A. P. Tureaud's law office. Tureaud immediately set the legal machinery in motion for a suit against the Orleans Parish school board.

The procedure was similar to that of suing the board for teachers' salary equalization. First, the customary petition to the board, which Tureaud carefully registered, requesting a return receipt, when he mailed it. He reminded the board that Dan Byrd's petition of two years before had never been given the promised "due consideration." The conditions complained of in 1946 had not been corrected, and it looked from where the black lawyer sat as if "the Negro children of this City face another year of gloom, despair, and frustration." If Tureaud's prognosis was accurate, he could delay no longer. He would now "be compelled to take such legal action as may be warranted." He planned to attend the regular meeting of the school board the following night. He would discuss the matter with the membership then.

The conversation that night, May 21, 1948, was as inconclusive as ever. Tureaud reiterated what Dan Byrd had said in the petition submitted two years before, adding that although the board had since made "a few improvements," black children in New Orleans still attended school "under difficult circumstances." There still existed in the city's schools, he charged,

> many discriminations against Negroes, although the board is familiar, I'm sure, with recent decisions of the United States Supreme Court regarding equalization of educational facilities.

Board members assured Tureaud that they were in complete sympathy with blacks' needs. It was just that funds weren't available, although of what little money there was for school improvements, a large chunk, they promised, would go to blacks' schools. To which Tureaud simply repeated his threat of legal action unless "these inequities are removed immediately."

For Tureaud and Byrd, the cavalier handling by the Orleans Parish school board of the Macarty parents' petition served only to underline the fact that legal action was the only way to get social action in New Orleans.

The black community could wait no longer. Byrd's Citizens' Committee had "refrain[ed]" from court action until school superintendent Bourgeois had "exhausted every means of converting the public" to his program for bringing all of the schools of New Orleans "up to par." But they had waited in vain.

Following his set-to with the school board—the veneer of courtesy that marked the dialogue couldn't hide the passions that simmered beneath—Tureaud shot off a copy of the latest petition to the Inc. Fund's New York office along with a request for the "skeleton form recommended for use" in assembling a law suit against a local school board. He'd missed by only a few days Thurgood Marshall, who was out of town, explained one of Marshall's assistants, adding that before leaving, Marshall had talked about the possibility of the New Orleans group pressing a law suit similar to one filed previously and now awaiting trial in Virginia. And he briefly outlined the procedure followed there: petition to the local school board, then on into federal court when the reply was either not forthcoming or was unsatisfactory. He promised Tureaud copies of the Virginia lawyer's papers as soon as he had them in hand.

On May 30, 1948, Tureaud filed the suit in behalf of the Auberts.

Walter and Macedonia Nichols's experience in protesting conditions at the Hoffman School, which their two youngsters attended, had been much like the Auberts': the school board had "done nothing to provide a safe, well-lighted and comfortable building for the use of the Negro Children in this community," and the Nichols family was only too anxious to join the Auberts' suit. The case (unpublished) was titled *Rosana Aubert* [Wilfred's daughter] v. *Orleans Parish School Board*. It landed in Judge Herbert Christenberry's court.

It was Christenberry's first civil rights case. He'd been appointed only six months before. Neither the black plaintiffs nor the defendant school board could have known then that the former tough federal prosecutor, a relentless cross-examiner, would tend, when he became a judge, as one of his law clerks later put it, "to favor the little guy. When he saw the little guy getting a raw deal, he'd come to his aid."

In his formal complaint, Tureaud argued for application of the "separate but equal" formula to academic conditions in the Orleans Parish schools, which in 1948 was still official NAACP policy in matters involving elementary and secondary education. He declared that the facilities provided for "Negro children's education are vastly inferior" to facilities provided for white children, and, therefore, "in violation of the Fourteenth Amendment to the United States Constitution, the laws of the United States and the Constitution of Louisiana." Though undoubtedly weary of the necessity for such frequent reiteration, he once again listed the disparities in the facilities provided for whites and blacks about which he and Byrd had been petitioning the school board for years unsuccessfully, and he asked the federal court for an injunction

> forever restraining and enjoining the defendants from making any distinction based upon race or color in the facilities or opportunities provided by the defendants for the education of white and Negro children . . . in Orleans Parish.

The board stalled another full year before answering Tureaud's complaint. When the answer came, it was a denial, paragraph by paragraph, of the lawyer's charges, along with a firm declaration that there was

> no substantial inequality between the rights and privileges afforded to the white and the negro race and therefore there is no actual controversy between the parties.

What small "inequities" existed the board promised to remedy. It also issued a warning intended perhaps to scare off black plaintiffs in the future but at the same time highly revealing of its own nervousness:

> [I]nvoking the process of this court . . . cannot serve to accelerate the program; it may even retard it.

At the public hearing held on December 19, 1949, Tureaud stood alone against the school board's lawyers. Once again he hammered away at the educational inequalities suffered by his clients and the other black children of New Orleans.

The school board's main line of defense was the improvements that already had been made since the suit was filed a year and a half before. The blacks' suit, the board's lawyer said, was now out of date and "totally at variance with the facts." It should be dismissed.

The judge, however, made short work of that argument. "I get around a little myself," Christenberry said, and "know what the situation is." One of the schools he'd seen he described as "disgraceful." He did, however, agree to consider the board's request.

Finally, on July 12, 1950, more than four years after Dan Byrd had taken the original petition enumerating the deficiencies in the city's schools for blacks to the board, and, coincidentally, one day before the board announced final approval of an architect's design for the fourth new school approved in the past year—three of them for white students—Christenberry announced the first of his decisions in the first legal suit brought by blacks against the Orleans Parish school board since Arnold Bertonneau's in 1878. Not his final decision on whether he would accede to the blacks' request for an injunction barring racial discrimination in the public schools, only his preliminary finding that his court did in fact have jurisdiction in Wilfred Aubert's case against the school board. He refused to dismiss it on that ground, as the school board had asked, and he refused to dismiss it on the basis of the board's claim at the December hearing that subsequent improvements in schools for black children had made Tureaud's complaint obsolete. "If this motion were granted," Christenberry explained,

> and assuming that the defendants continue to make changes and improvements, there would be no end of amendments and as a consequence, trial of this case might be postponed indefinitely.

The overall tenor of his announcement was an implied invitation to Tureaud and his clients to persist in their quest, however exhausting it might be. But by summer, 1950, the color of the NAACP's mood had changed.

At first, Inc. Fund chief counsel Thurgood Marshall had been skeptical of attacking racial segregation in elementary and secondary schools. He wasn't sure the U.S. Supreme Court was prepared yet to follow up its rulings opening public graduate and professional schools to black students, and he still thought southern judges were more likely to cooperate in equalizing facilities than in ordering whites' lower schools to let down the barriers to the admission of blacks. Although national sentiment against race discrimination and the black vote was increasing everywhere, albeit snaillike in the South, white southern sentiment, ripened over two centuries of living the gospel of black inferiority, was not ready for integration, particularly not in the schools, where the association of the races was unavoidable. One could ride or not ride a bus, eat in a restaurant or not, sit on a park bench or not. In schools there was no choice. Nor were there effective ways to avoid the inevitable fostering of social relationships that could not but follow race mixing.

Hodding Carter, editor of the *Delta Democrat-Times* in Greenwood,

Mississippi, and a self-confessed "southern liberal," predicted it would be "tragic" for blacks, whites, the South, and the nation if school integration were forced on a reluctant population, black and white, by federal law or a Supreme Court decision in the manner of *Sweatt* and *McLaurin*. In 1949 he had written:

> The southern Negro, by and large, does not want an end to segregation in itself any more than does the southern white man. The Negro in the South knows that discriminations, and worse, can and would multiply in such event. He knows that those things which he does want—the vote, educational opportunities and the rest—are more readily attainable in a South that is not aroused against federal intervention. . . .
>
> The white South is as united as 30 million people can be in its insistence upon segregation. Federal action cannot change them. . . . If the Federal Government is concerned with the plight of a racial minority, it should be concerned also with the general problems and predicaments of the area in which that minority principally dwells.

Marshall nonetheless was besieged. Social scientists like Alain Locke at Howard had been preaching the evils of racial segregation for some time. The young warriors on Marshall's staff and others in the organization were becoming increasingly vocal on this issue.

Experience had plainly indicated that "separate but equal" was not a workable formula, that whites' schools, even though southern state governments were making frantic attempts to stave off school integration by allocating increasing amounts of money to improve blacks' schools in the late 1940s and early 1950s, would remain state budget beneficiaries over the long run. Observers have speculated since that time whether school desegregation would have become the crusade it did if the "equal" requirement of the separate but equal program had been carried out in good faith.

The question is purely an academic one, however, because Marshall succumbed to the combined arguments of the social scientists and the eager young lawyers on his staff. At an NAACP Lawyers Conference in the spring of 1950, "certain policies" were established, the most significant of which was that the NAACP would "make an all out fight against segregation and that there would be no attempt made for 'separate but equal' facilities for Negroes from the kindergarten up to the graduate and professional schools."

The lawyers would no longer be satisfied with the infusion of up-to-date textbooks that would soon be dog-eared again, a few coats of paint that wear and tear would once again darken, and repair of the leaky toilets that would break down again in short order, so that the process would have to be started again. They wanted no less than access to what Marshall's old professor at Howard, Charlie Houston, had taught him to go after: the eradication of race as caste and of life as second-class citizens that *Plessy* had imposed fifty-odd years before.

Charlie Houston, the man whom Federal Judge William H. Hastie later called the Moses who guided the black legal fraternity "through the legal wilderness of second-class citizenship," was dead now, but Thurgood Marshall had absorbed enough of his idealism and his tactics to carry on. Working out of the national office in midtown Manhattan and commuting to antebellum courthouses in little town squares guarded by the ubiquitous Confederate soldier frozen in granite, and to modern stone buildings in congested southern city streets, monuments to post–World War II urban development, Marshall and his team began to collect a representative group of cases illustrating a variety of discriminatory practices in public schools.

With the change in strategy came a heightened militancy. The respectful petitioning and accommodation, the humble demeanor and patience of the lawyers were replaced by a new fighting spirit. Marshall himself, on a visit to New Orleans during a critical period, pumped a crowd gathered at St. John the Baptist Church full of the newfound vitality that already had begun to drive the professionals:

> We have gotten [he thundered] out of the idea of going around and pleading. Nobody ever got anything that way. Uncle Tom himself did not do so well at it. We are going to take our bandanas and have a big bonfire. We are going to stop pleading and begging. We are going to build up a fighting organization of Negroes not only willing to fight, but anxious to fight for their rights.

The new fighting spirit of Thurgood Marshall and his legal infantry spread and caught fire among blacks throughout the South. It was accompanied by an innovative approach to the presentation of legal evidence that put a whole new spin on the inequities in the education of black youth.

Even as Judge Christenberry was encouraging Tureaud to pursue the Auberts' suit against the Orleans Parish school board, the Inc. Fund lawyers were collecting a representative group of similar suits illustrating a variety of discriminatory practices in public schools. Many white southerners viewed the NAACP in those days as a band of crafty conspirators from New York who paid poor and unschooled blacks handsomely to participate in the school segregation cases. In fact, the Inc. Fund lawyers did not choose the plaintiffs; the plaintiffs chose the Inc. Fund, and some of them paid a high price for the privilege.

The lawyers, however, were lucky enough, as they plunged at last into the crusade for public school desegregation, to be approached by five plaintiffs who'd been the victims of "glaring" discrimination, as NAACP policy specified, the correction of which would "benefit a large number of Negroes." Without asking for it, the lawyers also got geographical diversity—a case each from the deep South state of South Carolina, the northern state of Delaware, the upper South state of Virginia, the border state of Missouri, and the District of Columbia, the segregated federal enclave that served as the nation's capital. Each one was a chapter describing a single area of the South; together they amounted to a revealing book of racial segregation in all its ramifications as it was being practiced in America in the early 1950s. As the cases accumulated at the U.S. Supreme Court, Justice Robert H. Jackson wrote a friend that he had read the brief Albion Tourgée had submitted in Homer Plessy's case fifty-four years before and was surprised to learn that "there is no argument made today that he would not make to the Court. . . . The question is again being argued whether his position will be adopted and what was a defeat for him in '96 be a post-mortem victory."

The first suit originated in Clarendon County, in the Dixiecrat state of South Carolina, a state with a long tradition of quarreling with the federal government over whether Columbia or Washington had the upper hand. In the last century, die-hard states' righter and Vice President of the United States John C. Calhoun worked out a set of political principles that allowed a state to nullify an act of Congress—in the 1950s, as southern states looked for precedent on which to base their protests of school desegregation, Calhoun's writings came to stand for a whole canon of states' rights. In this century, too, the state had produced Strom Thurmond, governor and Dixiecrat candidate for president. In 1950, he was running for the U.S. Senate on a platform of racial segregation.

Clarendon County was an outback of rich cotton land where the ticking of the clock had hardly been heard since slavery ended. Black people, who accounted for 71 percent of the county's population, had long been caught in the unending cycle of debt and destitution, the two chief attendants on ignorance, that had befallen so many of the region's sharecroppers not only in South Carolina but in Mississippi, Alabama, Louisiana, and wherever else white farmers rented land to black tenants.

Blacks' schools reflected the general poverty: outdoor toilets, no running water, up to seventy pupils in a class. Whites' schools weren't palaces, but there were at least up-to-date textbooks, a school lunch program, and free bus service. The state spent $148.48 on each white child, $69.95 on each black student. When the black children went to school at all—they could go only after the farm chores were done—they had no buses to take them there, and some had to row a boat to school when the Santee Dam backed up and flooded the roads they usually walked. A lot of youngsters either didn't go or dropped out after the first few years; 35 percent of all blacks over the age of ten in Clarendon County were illiterate.

Grounded in ignorance, blacks' docility had led white Clarendon County to boast about what one businessman called its "good bunch of nigras," happy and contented with the various denials that defined their lives. White complacency was about to end.

Black Clarendon County's first request was for a bus to take its children to school. But when School Superintendent R. W. Elliott was approached, he immediately said no, falling back on the old excuse that the white community, which bore the brunt of the tax burden, could hardly be expected to pay an even larger share.

Black Clarendon County, however, stood firm, despite threats of reprisals and violence. Under the tutelage of Thurgood Marshall's staff and the Inc. Fund's representative, Harold Boulware of Columbia, like Tureaud an alumnus of Howard University's law school and a veteran of the teachers' salary equalization wars in his native state, black Clarendon County translated the denial of a school bus into a full-blown violation of the federal Constitution's Fourteenth Amendment requiring "equal protection of the laws."

Marshall directed black Clarendon County to recruit twenty plaintiffs for a legal suit. Inc. Fund lawyers tried to enlist as many participants as possible to protect the suit from too many future losses as some people inevitably dropped out, often because of fear. After an eight-month search, the twenty were at last found. Harry Briggs, who signed up for his son, nine-year-old Harry, Jr., was first in alphabetical order; the dictates of legal custom put the suit in his and the school superintendent's names. It was *Briggs* v. *Elliott*. It was filed in federal court in November, 1950, and the plaintiffs were demanding not equalization of facilities, but desegregation of all public schools.

Former secretary of state and Supreme Court Justice James F. Byrnes, having succeeded Strom Thurmond, was governor of South Carolina when the Briggs case came to trial in 1951. As a congressman in 1919, he had called for the deportation of all blacks demanding racial equality. Unreconstructed three decades later and aware of the potential in the Briggs case for stirring up trouble, he attempted to defuse it by pouring money into blacks' public schools before the courts required even worse. Some $84 million of a projected $176 million, 69 percent of it for blacks' schools, was quickly appropriated and put to work. In 1951–52, thirteen southern states lavished about eight times as much for school construction and maintenance as they had in 1939–49. If money could buy segregation, they were willing to spend it.

The trial in a packed federal courtroom in Charleston began on May 28, 1951. A special three-judge court had been convened because the *Briggs* case, like Roy Wilson's against LSU the previous year, challenged state authority—in this case the statutory and state-constitutional requirement of racial segregation in the public schools.

Senior Judge John J. Parker of Charlotte, North Carolina, and the Fourth Circuit court of appeals who'd handed Marshall his first appellate victory—Melvin Alston's salary equalization suit back in 1940—was the ranking judge. Marshall sized him up as substantially more enlightened than George Bell Timmerman of Columbia, the outspoken white supremacist district judge who sat beside Parker, but unlikely to chart any new legal course that entailed undermining the settled principles of the fifty-five-year-old *Plessy.* District court Judge J. Waties Waring of Charleston, as confirmed an antisegregationist as Timmerman was a segregationist, was the third member of the panel. Marshall was certain he could count on Waring, but he feared it would be in dissent.

Marshall had developed his argument as the logical lower-school extension of *Sweatt* and *McLaurin* at the university level. But he had brought with him to Charleston more than the legal arguments. Robert L. Carter, his chief assistant at the Inc. Fund as well as a fellow alumnus of Charlie Houston's activist law school at Howard and a veteran of the segregated World War II Air Force with a reputation as an uppity black officer with an attitude bordering on defiance when defending his race, had never heard of Paul Trévigne. But he had been reading the current writings of social scientists who had come to view racial segregation in subjective psychological and sociological terms, and he had persuaded Marshall of the usefulness of testimony that segregation per se held the potential for inflicting permanent psychological damage on children. Some of these experts had come to the crowded, sweltering Charleston courtroom with him.

Following the strictly legal part of his argument, Marshall set the scene for his experts, telling the court that South Carolina's segregated school system pointed up blacks' exclusion

> from the group that runs everything. The children see it, and they
> see they are compelled to go to inferior schools. The Negro child is

branded in his own mind as inferior; he thus acquires a road block in his mind which prevents his ever feeling that he is equal.

You can teach him the Constitution, anthropology, citizenship, but he knows it isn't true.

Several well-known authorities in the fields of education and psychology supported and elaborated on what Marshall had said. But Dr. Kenneth B. Clark, a thirty-seven-year-old social psychologist and assistant professor at City College of New York, and his dolls stole the show. Clark and his wife, Dr. Mamie P. Clark, also a psychologist, had been studying the pathology of racism for more than a decade and publishing their results in obscure academic and scientific journals. In 1950, Kenneth Clark had prepared a report for the Mid-Century White House Conference on Children and Youth summarizing the effects of racial prejudice, discrimination, and segregation on personality development in children, black and white. It was this that had caught Bob Carter's attention.

In his own testimony, Clark described the testing of children he and his wife had been doing. As he told the court in Charleston about the tests, they seemed simple, and in retrospect perhaps obvious, although at the time they were considered pathbreaking. He merely asked the children to respond to a group of racially specific dolls. Which doll would the child like to be, the brown doll or the white one? Which most closely resembled himself or herself? Which was the nice doll, which the bad one? Sometimes he used crayons and asked the children to draw their answers in color. He tested children in segregated schools, including a group down in Clarendon County, and he tested children in mixed schools. Interview piled on interview and test on test until the Clarks had examined some four hundred children, and they began to see patterns in the results: "The majority of these Negro children at each age indicated an unmistakable preference for the white doll and a rejection of the brown doll."

By the time Clark came to the court in Charleston, he was confident enough of his findings to declare unequivocally that Clarendon County's black children, "like other human beings who are subjected to an obviously inferior status in the society in which they live, have been definitely harmed in the development of their personalities." He had concluded from his investigations, he said, that the damage to black children's self-esteem was permanent and prevented them from developing into healthy personalities. Other witnesses corroborated Clark's testimony, and several described the effects of segregation as detrimental to white children as well, producing confusion and guilt feelings in them.

Politicians, legal philosophers, and other social scientists lambasted the blacks' lawyers reliance on Clark's kind of testimony. Lawyers, they argued, oughtn't to replace the time-tested rules of legal evidence with the gossamer tenets of psychology. Even the Inc. Fund staff wasn't entirely convinced, and one of its young lawyers referred to Clark's occupational gear as "those damned dolls."

Nor was the court convinced. Marshall's pretrial assessment of the three individuals' jurisprudence had been accurate. As Waring described their posttrial conference, Parker had "just set his feet on Plessy against Ferguson and said, 'We can't overrule'" that. Timmerman spoke up for the state's right to operate its schools under its constitution and laws and concurred in Parker's opinion. Waring himself dissented.

Summing up the case for South Carolina, Parker ordered school officials to bring facilities for black children up to speed. He left the method of correction to local authorities "so long as it is done in good faith," and gave them six months to file a report "showing the action that has been taken."

Beyond that, however, the court would not go. Management of the public schools, Parker declared, following the pattern set by Justice Henry Brown and himself setting the pattern, not for the last time, for contemporary judges confronted by similar suits over the next several years, was a local responsibility and did not tolerate interference by the federal government. The Constitution, he added, gave the states the "police power," i.e., the power "to legislate with respect to the safety, morals, health and general welfare," which included public education. Neither *Plessy* nor its progeny, Parker said, ever had been overruled. They were still the law of the land.

Parker carefully distinguished between education at the graduate level, citing *Sweatt* and *McLaurin,* and education at the "common school level" where, he wrote, "as good education can be afforded in Negro schools as in white schools." He disputed Kenneth Clark's testimony with a generally held belief, also testified to by experts, he said, that "mixed schools will result in racial friction and tension and that the only practical way of conducting public education in South Carolina is with segregated schools."

The constitution and laws of South Carolina remained intact. Harry Briggs, Jr., and the children of the other plaintiffs would have to make do with the new pencils and books, gymnasiums and laboratories the court had ordered.

Along with a carton of cigarettes, Harry Briggs, Sr., who'd pumped gas at Carrigan's service station on Main Street in Summerton, South Carolina, for fourteen years, ever since he came back from the South Pacific where he'd been with the navy, got fired the day before Christmas after he put his name to the suit against the local school system. His credit not only at the Summerton bank but for a radius of twenty-five miles was cut off. Suppliers threatened the motel where his wife, Lisa, had worked as a chambermaid for six years, and she got a week's notice. A lot of blacks in Clarendon County couldn't get their cotton ginned that season.

J. Waties Waring, the lone dissenter on the three-judge court, was the son of a slaveholder who, with his brothers, had fought for the Confederacy. Waring himself had been reared in the palmetto society of clannish Charleston on what Hamilton Basso in *The View From Pompey's Head*—and later Waring himself—called southern Shintoism, the worship of ancestors. He belonged to the city's elitist organizations, including the Charleston Light Dragoons, a group that traced its roots to pre-Revolutionary days. After a brief tenure as corporation counsel—city attorney—and a season as campaign manager for the racist South Carolina senator "Cotton Ed" Smith, he'd gone, on Smith's recommendation to FDR in 1941, to his reward on the federal district bench.

As a child and young man, Waring had had some misgivings about race relationships in his native city, but the subject was taboo in the fashionable section of Charleston where he grew up, and, like Skelly Wright in New Orleans, he'd accepted the way things were. After he became a judge, he began to read: Myrdal's *An American Dilemma* and other works on race relations. He began to travel, leaving Charleston and sitting on federal courts in other parts of the country. He foresaw the trouble that was on its way.

He met it head-on. He desegregated his courtroom, saw that federal juries were biracial, and named a black man to his staff as bailiff at a time when a black court officer was a rarity in any American courtroom.

He began to uphold the claims of black plaintiffs in civil rights suits: a peonage case at which many southern judges would have winked, a teachers' salary equalization suit. While *Sweatt* v. *Painter* was malingering in the Texas trial courts prior to its appearance in the U.S. Supreme Court, Waring boldly ruled in a similar South Carolina case that the state had three choices: to establish a serious law program at the state college for blacks, to admit a black applicant to the white law school, or to shut down the white law school altogether. Following Thurgood Marshall's successful suit to strike down the white primary, *Smith* v. *Allwright,* Waring outlawed South Carolina's attempt at evasion with a few choice words carrying, perhaps, a special significance because of their origin in Charleston, launching pad of the Confederacy and one-time home of John Calhoun. It was time, he wrote, for South Carolina to rejoin the Union, to fall in step with the other states and to adopt the American way of conducting elections.

"Racial distinctions," he ruled, "cannot exist in the machinery that selects the officers and lawmakers of the United States."

White Charleston and white South Carolina were outraged by what they regarded as betrayal. Waring watched a flaming cross burn on his lawn. Hate mail overflowed his mailbox, and the lower house of the legislature voted to buy the judge and his wife one-way tickets out of South Carolina.

Nevertheless his decision stood. The U.S. Court of Appeals for the Fourth Circuit upheld him, as did the U.S. Supreme Court.

Harry Briggs's case was the most flammable of all, but Waring didn't flinch. He'd often passed the Clarendon County schools on his way from Charleston to the central part of the state, and he'd been shocked by the "awful little wooden shacks" that passed for blacks' schools. His dissent rang out.

Waring couldn't alter the outcome of *Briggs.* He could, however, record his protest for posterity. He paid tribute to the plaintiffs' courage in bringing the suit, then put everything he had into a verbal slap in the face for his colleagues:

> If a case of this magnitude can be turned aside and a court refuse to hear these basic issues by the mere device of admission that some buildings, blackboards, lighting fixtures and toilet facilities are unequal but that they may be remedied by the spending of a few dollars, then, indeed people in the plight in which these plaintiffs are, have no adequate remedy or forum in which to air their wrongs. If this method of judicial evasion be adopted, these very infant plaintiffs . . . will probably be bringing suits for their children and grandchildren decades or rather generations hence in an effort to get for their descendants what are today denied them.

His contempt apparent, he added, "I want no part of it."

The ostracism, the hate mail, the obscene telephone calls crescendoed. When lightning struck a neighbor's home, the neighbor put a sign on it: Dear God: He Doesn't Live Here. Ultimately, they drove him out of his courtroom in Charleston, away from the place his family had lived for nine generations, and sent him to live and die among strangers in New York.

The majority's opinion, however wrongheaded the plaintiffs and their lawyers believed it was, had in fact served its purpose and opened the way for the Inc. Fund team to take the case to the highest court of all where, with any luck, the issue would be settled differently—and finally—so that Harry Briggs, Jr., and the other children whose parents had joined the suit might be spared the trauma of doing it all over again "decades or rather generations hence in an effort to get for their descendants what are today denied them."

Marshall and his colleagues, however, hadn't been so foolish as to bet the future on one case. Having no illusions about the outcome of *Briggs,* the lawyers were on their way to Topeka, Kansas, even before Judge Parker announced his court's decision. There they were scheduled to prepare, once again in collaboration with local lawyers, for the next trial of a public school segregation case, which was to begin shortly.

The details of the Topeka case differed from those of the Clarendon County case as did the two locales, the former one a border state that retained only enough of its southernness to *permit* elementary school in first-class cities—those with populations of more than 15,000 when the law was passed in 1879—and the latter a deep South enclave subject to both constitutional and statutory *requirements* of statewide school segregation. The overall thrust of the two suits was, however, exactly the same: a demand for the end of racial segregation in all public schools.

In Topeka, Oliver Brown's nine-year-old daughter, Linda, had to walk a mile every morning just to meet the school bus that took her to the all-black Monroe School, a dark, gloomy-looking redbrick structure twenty-one blocks from her home. Her itinerary included walking on the grassy strips between the tracks of the still-active Rock Island Railroad's switching yard.

She often wondered, as she passed the pretty all-white Sumner School just five blocks from her home, why she couldn't attend it. The explanation was that although Kansas as a border state was not quite in or of the South, it was also a Jim Crow state in which custom had accomplished what the law had neglected, and public facilities, including hotel accommodations for visiting New York lawyers, were segregated. The public schools in Topeka were actually segregated by local law.

Despite the obvious dimness of his prospects, Oliver Brown, a railroad welder and part-time minister, had tried to enroll his daughter in the Sumner school the year before, but she'd been rejected. He took his complaint to the local office of the NAACP, which had been considering litigation for some time and saw in Linda's situation a viable case.

The pressure of work back in New York kept Thurgood Marshall from flying off to Kansas with his staff. There were too many cases now, as the Inc. Fund encouraged its lawyers in other southern states to develop suits opposing school segregation. The chief couldn't handle them all. In his place he sent his trusted lieutenant, Bob Carter, the mainspring behind introduction of psychological and sociological testimony in these suits.

Carter's spending his youth in East Orange, New Jersey, had not protected him from racism. He had trained for battle at East Orange High School where black students had not been allowed the use of the swimming pool except late on Friday afternoons. His first public protest was joining the white boys at the pool one day after basketball practice. In his NAACP work, he had a sense he was "doing something for my people and also doing something for myself." As a federal judge sixty years later, he looked back on those years as "the most exciting period in my life."

Carter brought along to Topeka a whole new crew of expert witnesses—sociologists, psychologists, and combinations of the two—to give scholarly credence to the testimony of the plaintiffs who totaled eight by the time the trial opened on June 25, 1951. Oliver Brown testified to the hazards of his daughter's daily commute to the Monroe School. The other parents followed with their own children's horror stories. The academics backed up Kenneth Clark's testimony in Charleston regarding the negative effects of racial segregation on the personality development of children.

The now-usual three-judge panel assigned to decide such cases was unanimous in its decision, which was announced on August 3, 1951. Walter A. Huxman, a flinty former governor of Kansas and a veteran of twelve years on the U.S. Court of Appeals for the Tenth Circuit, spoke for the trio.

In an appendix, the judges conceded the validity of the social scientists' claims, that the

> [s]egregation of white and colored children in public schools has a detrimental effect upon the colored children. The impact is greater when it has the sanction of the law; for the policy of separating the races is usually interpreted as denoting the inferiority of the Negro group. A sense of inferiority affects the motivation of a child to learn. Segregation with the sanction of law, therefore, has a tendency to retard the education and mental development of Negro children and to deprive them of some of the benefits they would receive in a racially integrated school system.

The appendix, however, carried no force in law.

Huxman's opinion itself, which did have the force of law behind it, made no such allusions to the experts' testimony. The judges had decided, he said, that the city's white and black schools were substantially equal, that there was no "willful, intentional or substantial discrimination ... between the colored and white schools." Linda Brown, they had concluded, could not in fact attend Sumner school, although they did note that the U.S. Supreme Court itself had in recent years "show[n] a trend" away from the old established formulas written into *Plessy*. Considering what had happened in Heman Sweatt's and George McLaurin's suits against the state universities the previous year, it was not impossible, Huxman noted further, that that very court would soon find racial segregation in the lower schools unconstitutional. His court, however, was bound by precedent until the higher court spoke.

The two panels of judges, the first in South Carolina, the second in Kansas, had made virtually the same decision: segregation that conformed to the separate-but-equal formula was not unconstitutional. But the tenor of the two opinions put them at opposite ends of the judicial spectrum. Huxman's practically invited the U.S. Supreme Court to rewrite the rules, and Huxman conceded some years later that he and his colleagues would have preferred to find Topeka's school segregation law unconstitutional, but the continuing presence of *Plessy* had restrained them. Parker's opinion was defensive, daring the Supreme Court to intervene in matters affecting schools in the Great Nullifier's home state, a foreshadowing in fact of the judge's future role when the issue of school segregation returned to his court a few years later.

In October of that same year in Delaware, two more cases came to trial, and still another suit, which had originated in Prince Edward County, Virginia, was awaiting trial, now scheduled for February, 1952. The little cluster of segregation cases that the august justices of the U.S. Supreme Court were destined to confront in the very near future was nearly complete.

At the same time black parents in the two Carolinas, Texas, Georgia, and Arkansas had begun to take their complaints against their local school systems into court. And in New Orleans, A. P. Tureaud was reworking Wilfred Aubert's suit for equal facilities into one demanding the dismantling of school segregation itself.

In July of 1935, a group of educators and other black leaders had used an issue of the *Journal of Negro Education* to debate whether courts were the best forums in which to urge their cause and whether they should fight for separate but equal or go for the brass ring, desegregation itself. Seventeen years later, in July, 1952, a new generation of black leaders came together in the same journal to discuss not whether—that had been decided—but how.

CHAPTER 9

Small Cracks in the Wall

J udge Christenberry's decision in July, 1950, to allow Wilfred Aubert's suit against the Orleans Parish school board to continue in federal court came fifteen years after a municipal judge in Baltimore had ordered Donald Murray admitted to the law school at the University of Maryland, the NAACP's first successful attempt to crack the color bar in education. Fifteen years marked by early moments of indecision as the organization struggled with its collective conscience to decide between the relatively mild separate but equal program and the more radical desegregation of the public schools, and later moments of spiritual elation and earthly resolution once the decision to charge the San Juan Hill of racism was made. Author Ralph Ellison described the mood upswing to his fellow author Robert Penn Warren as the "affirmation and assertion of identification," the emergence of the "real identity of a people who have been here for a hell of a long time."

As the 1950s opened and the biggest push was launched for blacks' civil rights to date, the descendants of African slaves were beginning to make the white majority dance. No unconditional surrenders yet, but scattered little victories, encouraging, for all their small size, to a man like Tureaud, who was engaged in a long, lonely, and frustrating quest for a time when racism would survive only as part of a historical record, but not part of daily life.

Take just his own experience. He had argued before and won over to his point of view federal judges Skelly Wright, Herbert Christenberry, and, six months later, Ben C. Dawkins, Jr., of the Federal District Court for the Western District of Louisiana. Dawkins had issued an order similar to Christenberry's in a case Tureaud, who was still the Inc. Fund's chief strategist and litigator in all of Louisiana, had filed against the Ouachita Parish school board charging racial discrimination much like that in the New Orleans schools. Earlier he had been working on a facilities-equalization suit similar to *Aubert,* this one against the Iberville Parish school board. Even before Judge Wright had a chance to hold the usual hearings, however, the board, spooked perhaps by the hovering specter of full desegregation later, folded, admitted that facilities for black children did not in fact come up to those for white children, and invited the judge to order them equalized.

Tureaud worked alone. His partners, Ernest Morial and A. M. Trudeau, Jr., had adjoining offices, but all three were independent, only occasionally joining together on particular suits when one or the other needed help. Tureaud did not even have a law clerk, only a secretary to take his telephone calls and type his correspondence. His successes nonetheless have been attributed to his meticulous preparation of his cases: his careful research, his willingness to write and rewrite the briefs until they met his high standards, his only mentors the Inc. Fund lawyers headquartered in New York, fifteen hundred miles away.

Despite Christenberry's encouragement, Tureaud did not return to his courtroom with the *Aubert* suit. Rather, he fashioned a new one out of its parts, one that more closely coincided with the national organization's recently announced policy of hitting racial segregation broadside.

During the months Aubert had been pending in federal court, Superintendent of Schools Bourgeois had continued to urge equalization of educational facilities for the black children of New Orleans, the only official in the South, observers commented a little later, to favor racial equality. He'd twisted the arms of school board members privately and spoken out at board meetings. Although black leaders opposed them on the ground that they were hand-me-downs, another reinforcement of blacks' second-class citizenship, and white parents opposed them because they brought blacks into white neighborhoods, Bourgeois had tried to have several schools converted from white to black use to relieve overcrowding temporarily. But he'd succeeded only in provoking the state legislature into passing a bill prohibiting conversions without the approval of 70 percent of the property owners in the school area.

His personal feelings aside, Bourgeois had seen what was coming, but his prophecies of court action were thought to be alarmist and were ignored by his still confident employers. New Orleanians were more concerned about whether bomb shelters would be racially segregated in the early days of the 1950s, a high point of the cold war with the Soviet Union. At the time, fallout, social as well as radioactive, from the A-bomb seemed more of an immediate threat to southern tradition than the fanciful notion that a custom so ingrained as school segregation would come undone in some vague future. The fear that white New Orleanians might have to travel to kingdom come in racially mixed company commanded more urgent attention.

White New Orleanians nonetheless got even with Superintendent Bourgeois. They fired him. The charges were "inefficiency, incompetency and unworthiness" and were based on some political miscalculations and missteps the superintendent had actually taken, although there was some disagreement over whether the punishment fit the crimes. It was generally acknowledged that Bourgeois's real offense was his too "favorable" position on "Negro education." Bourgeois was the first casualty of the New Orleans school segregation crisis. He would not be the last.

In 1950, Dan Byrd had been made a regional field secretary for the NAACP's Inc. Fund, which meant he was the group's troubleshooter from Florida to Texas. One of his first jobs was organizing the plaintiffs in the school segregation suit Tureaud was assembling to replace Aubert's.

New Orleans remained Byrd's home base. As the 1950s opened, he was still wearily writing and gathering parents' signatures on petitions complaining about conditions in the city's public schools for blacks. He would present the documents to the school board, then, while he waited for the board to respond, go off on his field trips through Alabama and Mississippi to confer with the principals or parents' organizations and community groups about local race problems. When he returned to New Orleans weeks later, he very likely still would have received no reply from the school board.

In late 1950, among Byrd's stops on his thirteen-hundred-mile odyssey through his deep South beat, was a meeting of the Ninth Ward Civic Improvement League at that same Macarty Elementary School where the Aubert suit had originated. The league had been organized largely to promote black voter registration and thereby to pressure city hall for better city services in the long-neglected neighborhood. In 1950, however, the school issue was paramount. It was November. School had been in session for two months now, and the parents of Macarty pupils were in a mood to march.

If anything, conditions had worsened at Macarty since Byrd put together the futile petition to the school board in 1946. It was still one of the most rundown facilities in the city system—not only in the contemporary system, but in the system's entire history. The building had been meant to accommodate 1,200 children, but in the 1950s, 2,536 were packed in. The lunchroom had been built to hold 150 children but was feeding 800 and doubled as a third-grade classroom. The library was being used as a classroom for one of the two fifth grades. There were no dressing rooms for physical education classes, hardly any storage space for files or equipment, and limited office space for the staff—the principal and two secretaries, all with desks, were crammed into a twelve-foot-by-twenty-foot room.

Some youngsters received only two and a half hours of instruction a day even though several teachers worked double shifts. There were too many children, too few teachers, and too little time, a situation that not infrequently caused teachers in such schools to skimp even on the basic requirements and led to a willingness to promote any child who could wash a blackboard.

Dan Byrd found that night in the dilapidated firetrap of a school an overflow crowd no longer willing or able to contain its fury. The meeting's chairman, Leontine Goins Luke, a neighborhood community activist whose minister-father had founded the Ninth Ward Civic Improvement League, was so disturbed that she rushed from her critically injured nephew's hospital room to take charge of this meeting.

Byrd promised an immediate investigation and was able that same night to channel the parents' anger into a movement for legal action.

Macarty parents had little reason for optimism. Some had been through it all before with Wilfred Aubert, and it was far from certain that what Dan Byrd was proposing that November night, although his upbeat presentation was persuasive, would be any more effective the second time. If simple equalization hadn't succeeded, there seemed little reason to believe the more drastic full-scale desegregation would. Their kids would probably be out of Macarty anyway, maybe even out of junior high and high school before any improvements were actually made. For Macarty youngsters, race was destiny from cradle to grave. The fact that loomed largest in their lives was the one for which they were least responsible.

Byrd's—and the NAACP's—hope was that the U.S. Supreme Court, via Harry Briggs and Linda Brown and the other black youngsters whose suits were moving along through the lower federal courts, would in the near future declare racial segregation in all of America's schools unconstitutional. Failing that, the fallback plan was for the long-frustrated blacks in Clarendon County, Topeka, New Orleans, and wherever else racial segregation in public education was a way of life, to make equalizing the facilities and opportunities in the dual systems so expen-

sive that segregation would collpase under the strain. One observer estimated that new capital outlay alone would amount to between $50 and
$100 million in each state, or more than a billion dollars over the whole
South. Add to that the operation and maintenance of the new black
schools at the higher level—probably half a billion dollars a year—and
the small price tag on desegregation might begin to look tempting.

Byrd had no trouble collecting signatures to the new suit Tureaud
planned to put together as his RSVP to Judge Christenberry's invitation
to persist. Upwards of ninety parents put their own names and those of
their children on the paper Dan handed around, so intense were the feelings that night. Although her only child was twenty-four and long gone
from the New Orleans schools, Mrs. Luke signed on. So did Wilfred
Aubert for his four children. The usual concerns about joining in legal
action seemed to evaporate in the city's cool November air.

Oliver Bush, president of the Macarty Parent-Teachers Association,
was one of the first. Without a moment's hesitation, he added the names
of his eight school-age children, five of whom attended Macarty. His oldest, Earl, 16, gave his name to the suit. When it was filed in federal district court two years later, it would bear the name *Earl Benjamin Bush* v.
Orleans Parish School Board.

Oliver Bush had less cause than most black men to fear reprisal. His
job as salesman for the all-black Louisiana Industrial Life Insurance Company would not be jeopardized, although he did take the precaution of
discussing the matter with the president. There was some concern about
possible attacks on the company's state licensing, but the president
assured Bush that his job was indeed safe.

The steam power generated that night at the Macarty parents' meeting seemed forceful enough to send a locomotive across America. In
fact, results of the protests would be a long time coming.

Dan Byrd would need time for his investigation. Documenting the
complaints was a tedious process.

Tureaud in the months following the meeting had barely time to tie
his shoes and tuck in his shirttails. In addition to his private practice and
the work connected with being Louisiana's only black notary, he was still
cleaning up odds and ends of the suits against LSU's law and graduate
schools, working on public school segregation suits in Baton Rouge and
St. Helena parishes, taking legal action to desegregate City Park—opening Municipal Auditorium to blacks was still in the discussion stage—
and handling legal matters for the Louisiana Education Association, a
statewide organization of black teachers. He had just stepped down as
president of the NAACP Louisiana State Conference of Branches, but
remained active in NAACP affairs both statewide and locally. He did

legal work for the Knights of Peter Claver and kept his hand in the affairs of the local Progressive Voters' League, which he'd founded in 1949 to promote black voter registration.

Byrd's research confirmed the validity of the Macarty parents' grievances. Tureaud set about turning his investigator's facts and figures into still one more petition to the Orleans Parish school board charging racial discrimination in public schools. He concluded with a paraphrase of the NAACP's latest policy: "Segregation is discrimination: Negroes get the separate but not the equal."

In mid-February of 1951, the gods loosed the first in a series of thunderbolts on the city. Pressured by returning black war veterans as well as organizations such as the Knights of Peter Claver, Archbishop Joseph Rummel, spiritual leader of the largest Catholic diocese in the South and becoming known as a liberal in racial matters, announced that he would no longer tolerate racial segregation in local Catholic churches, not in the pews, at the confessional, or at the Communion rail where blacks were traditionally served last. He went further and declared that "Black children and youth should have equal opportunities with White children, that will enable them to aspire to vocations in life that are honorable as well as useful . . . " He stopped short of desegregating parochial schools, but he came much too close for white New Orleans's comfort. White Catholics, who made up about 40 percent of the city's 600,000 population, suffered in silence this time, as they had two years before, in 1949, when Rummel canceled a Holy Hour service because the procession would be racially segregated. But their silence did not mean that they acquiesced.

Later the same month, the black-owned *Louisiana Weekly* reported that two of the local daily newspapers had used the title "Mrs." before a black woman's name and had run photographs of the new middleweight champion of the world, the black prizefighter Sugar Ray Robinson.

That spring representatives of the state NAACP organization met in Hayes, Louisiana, to map a strategy for an all-out assault on racial discrimination in Louisiana's schools. A. P. Tureaud explained that the NAACP intended never again to stop at the demand for equal facilities. From now on it was all or nothing.

And that summer the national NAACP went south, to Atlanta, to hold its annual meeting. It was the first time in forty-two years. President Truman sent the delegates greetings in which he reiterated past demands for enactment of civil rights legislation so that "these rights—on equal terms—are enjoyed by every citizen." The delegates themselves resolved "to achieve the fullest integration of Negro teachers and other

Negro school officials as well as Negro students in all of our public school systems."

On November 12, 1951, while they pondered how best to dump the man they saw as the nation's most prominent civil rights sympathizer, President Truman, from the Democratic ticket in 1952, southern governors meeting in Hot Springs, Arkansas reaffirmed their dedication to traditional southern standards of education. Governor Fielding Wright, the Dixiecrats' vice presidential candidate of 1948, opened the issue when he declared:

> Regardless of what others may say, we in Mississippi are determined that the segregated education system shall be maintained.

Should events conspire to produce another split in the Democratic party, which seemed a distinct possibility in late 1951, the governors had begun to talk about Governor Byrnes of South Carolina as their spiritual leader. Too old at seventy-two to run for national office, at least by the standards of the 1950s, Byrnes's strong position on school segregation in his own state during the blacks' recent assaults on the tradition lifted him a little above the run-of-the-mill governors, gave him added cachet. Indeed, he was already making plans to turn over his state's public schools to private institutions such as churches, should the U.S. Supreme Court find racial segregation unconstitutional.

On November 12, too, the very night Governor Wright was trumpeting his segregationists' call to arms, A. P. Tureaud in New Orleans, petition in hand, was marching on the local school board, which was, perhaps, no less determined than the blunt and outspoken Mississippian. Ninth Ward residents filled the room to overflowing.

This was not, however, just another futile hat-in-hand gesture on Tureaud's part. This was a lawyer building his case, taking the first step in the procedure, what judges called exhausting the administrative remedies before coming into their courtrooms. The procedure was meant not only to keep matters that could be solved elsewhere out of the courts but to minimize friction between states and the federal government by reserving the courts as a last resort. Had, for example, any one of these state bodies responded to black New Orleanians' complaints, had some spirit of compromise emerged at any one of the confrontations, the saving in court time and money alone is inestimable in a case that involved forty-one separate judicial decisions during the prime of its life. Not to mention the human toll: the expenditure in emotions, the spiritual hurts, the psychological maiming.

Tureaud undoubtedly knew the school board's response before he left home that night. But it had to be done. The petition was part of the procedure. Judges threw out cases when lawyers cut corners.

It was evident at this meeting that Tureaud had caught some of Thurgood Marshall's fire. He wasn't asking this time, he was telling the board. He wasted no words on what he previously called the school board's responsibility to bring blacks' schools up to par. He immediately launched into his clients' demands that the board "at once" end its seventy-five-year-old policy of segregating black and white children in New Orleans's public schools. If the board refused, he warned, and they knew now from Aubert's suit that Tureaud was a man of his word, "legal action will be taken."

There was less new in the board's response. His flaming red hair and brusque manner dramatizing his position, Dr. Clarence Scheps, an administrator at Tulane University as well as an Orleans Parish school board member, answered: "This is a grave question and we're in no position to discuss it now." The board would take it under advisement. Again.

Previous petitions submitted by blacks frequently had not been given the courtesy of an answer. Now in late 1951, with recent U.S. Supreme Court decisions desegregating graduate departments in Texas, Oklahoma, and Louisiana universities ringing in their ears, the members of the Orleans Parish school board at last took Tureaud's demands seriously. They hastily passed the petition to the city attorney for a legal opinion. His office replied immediately, reminding the board that article XII, section 1, of the state constitution of 1921 required that

> Separate free public schools shall be maintained for the education of white and colored children between the ages of six and eighteen years.

It was the city attorney's position that

> [a]ny action on [the board's] part, irrespective of . . . individual feelings or opinions about this matter, that would tend to do away with or abolish complete segregation of the two races in your schools, would be plainly in contravention of the law that you have been sworn to uphold.

Two days later, the board responded to Tureaud publicly and formally. The members had given his petition "serious and thoughtful consideration." That is, the city attorney's office had gotten the school board off the hook. "After careful study," the members had concluded that

[s]uch a radical change of policy could not, at this time, serve the best interests of the system. The board believes, rather, that such a departure from tradition and custom, quite apart from the fact that such action by the Board would be illegal, could result only in chaos and confusion and further, quite probably would cause a very serious worsening of race relationships in the community as a whole.

Tureaud's seriousness and newfound contentiousness combined with the threat of a court suit notwithstanding, the five members of the Orleans Parish school board unanimously denied his petition.

While Tureaud readied the Bush case for the federal court, he continued to exert pressure on the school board to improve the facilities and opportunities for those children then making their way through the grades: children who probably would never taste the fruits of desegregation; it would be too late for them.

Even while the board members closed ranks and stood resolute against any "radical change of policy," their five pairs of eyes had finally fastened on the clock that was ticking away the final hours of racially segregated public education in New Orleans. Only the amount of time left was in doubt, and the board reacted to Tureaud's pressure with a belated program of pacification by equalization not unlike Governor Byrnes's prescription for South Carolina when Harry Briggs's case against the Clarendon County school officials took wing: $60,000 here, $162,000 there, $182,000 somewhere else, and the announcement in late January, 1952, by Charles R. Colbert, head of the city's planning and construction office for city schools that

We plan to eliminate pot-bellied stoves as heating plants, to provide adequate lighting in all classrooms, eliminate fire hazards and put the toilet and sanitary facilities in good condition.

Cafeterias would be renovated or installed in schools where children now had to eat lunch in their classrooms. Paint would be liberally applied to corridors, classrooms, and wherever else age and dirt had gotten the best of the buildings.

Colbert had been hired the year before to plan and supervise construction of city schools, at which time he had observed that local public schools for Negroes were a "total disgrace to the educational system of our city." Over that year he had developed plans for the renovation of seven all-Negro schools at a cost of $1 billion, and rudimentary plans for five others, all of which were to be "freshen[ed] up generally to provide teachers and pupils with more attractive atmospheres in which to teach and learn." Schools too dilapidated to be properly or profitably recon-structed would be replaced.

Tureaud and Byrd, firmly committed to full desegregation, were not diverted from their purpose for a minute by the school board's unaccus-tomed generosity, but went about their business of developing their legal case. Another administrative hurdle fell when Tureaud dispatched the Macarty parents' petition to the state board of education in Baton Rouge along with the Orleans Parish school board's denial "of the relief prayed for." He asked the state authorities to reverse and set aside the local school board's action and "that your honorable body order the said Orleans Parish School Board to comply with the demands contained in the petition."

The early months of 1952 brought Tureaud news of the develop-ments in Virginia and Delaware. On March 7, Federal District Judge Albert V. Bryan, speaking for the three-judge court convened in Rich-mond, Virginia, to decide whether or not the 117 students at the tumble-down all-Negro Robert R. Moton High School in rural Prince Edward County, would be admitted to the vastly superior local all-white high school, wrote that they would not. Nothing Tureaud hadn't heard before. The court would grant that the Fourteenth Amendment to the federal Constitution required equal facilities for all races, and Bryan listed with some particularity the deficiencies at Moton High that "frankness" had required the defendant school board to admit: poor science facilities and equipment, no industrial arts shop, no gymnasium or showers or dress-ing rooms, no teachers' rest rooms, no infirmary—all of which were taken for granted at the white high school.

And he ordered the school board to "pursue with diligence and dis-patch" a program to replace the Moton buildings, which had been put up originally as temporaries, and facilities with a new building and new equipment and "otherwise remove the inequality in them." Like the judges in South Carolina and Kansas, however, that was as far as the Vir-ginia court would go. Virginia history as well as Virginia law and custom militated against black and white sitting together in the same class-rooms.

During the trial, which lasted a full week, the court had heard "emi-nent educators, anthropologists, psychologists and psychiatrists" testify that racial segregation stigmatized Negroes as "unwanted" and implanted "unjustly" in them a "sense of inferiority" in relation to others. The judges had found the testimony highly debatable, and they had also listened to "equally distinguished and qualified educationists and lead-ers" vouch for the other side that "given equivalent physical facilities, offerings and instruction," the Negro would receive in a separate school the same educational opportunity as he would in the class room and on the campus of a mixed school. Each witness offered cogent and appealing grounds for this conclusion.

Reviewing the evidence presented by both parties, the court had discovered in the traditional patterns of racial segregation

no hurt or harm to either race.

Oliver Hill, Melvin Alston's lawyer in his salary equalization case against the city of Norfolk and the local NAACP lawyer who'd represented the Moton High School students, although he had wondered in the beginning whether Prince Edward County, about as culturally southern as you could get in Virginia, was the wisest choice for a test case, had never for a minute wondered what the judges would say. What Bryan said and how he said it, as it turned out, however, set the NAACP lawyers up for the next step.

We were [Hill explained] trying to build a record for the Supreme Court.

The good news from Delaware that followed the bad from Virginia more than compensated for the latter. Though it lay several hundred miles to the north, Wilmington, Delaware, was culturally closer kin to Virginia than Pennsylvania. Delaware's young men had fought for the Union in the Civil War, but most of the state actually stretched below the Mason-Dixon line, and slaveholders had flourished in its southern environs. It was a true border state, a place where North and South met in an often uneasy alliance. As the 1950s opened, southern Delaware's conservative farmers, who controlled the state legislature, were willing to barter their votes for favorable tax rates—"sweetheart" laws—on the big corporations drawn to the area around Wilmington in return for northern assistance in keeping the states' blacks subjugated. As a result, not a single high school for blacks existed in Delaware south of Wilmington, and all public schools in the state were racially segregated. Jim Crow regulated employment, public accommodations, and etiquette statewide.

It was in connection with public school facilities in and near Wilmington, the urban outpost at the north of the state, that the Inc. Fund's Delaware cases against racial segregation in the schools originated. They essentially followed the pattern set in South Carolina, Kansas, and Virginia: dissatisfied black parents protested the inequities in their children's segregated education and contacted the local NAACP lawyer. This one was named Louis A. Redding. He was an Ivy League–educated, experienced activist who worked almost alone in his state, the A. P. Tureaud of Delaware. He turned the parents' protests into formal legal complaints and filed them in the local federal court.

Sarah Bulah had called on Redding when her daughter was denied a ride to the black school on a state-operated school bus; Ethel Belton had appeared in Redding's Wilmington office with seven other black parents whose children had been refused, like Linda Brown in Topeka, admittance to a white school nearer and superior to their black school. Francis B. Gebhart's name came first in alphabetical order among the members of the State Board of Education, and the cases, which were filed, argued, and decided in tandem, were called *Belton* v. *Gebhart* and *Bulah* v. *Gebhart.*

Redding originally took the two cases to the federal court in Wilmington and asked for the usual three-judge panel to hear them. The state attorney general, however, contended that because they challenged state law, they should be heard in a state court, which in Delaware meant Chancery Court. Chancery Court had what is called "equity jurisdiction"—lawyerese for justice decided on the basis of fairness rather than on the strict rules of law. In Delaware the Chancery Court arbitrated various matters affecting the large and growing resident population of multi-million-dollar corporations plus, what was more important to Ethel Belton, Sarah Bulah, and Louis Redding, the civil rights of blacks and other matters of human relations.

The plaintiffs were in luck. The new young (thirty-eight-year-old) state chancellor, Collins J. Seitz of Wilmington, was a devout Roman Catholic—like blacks, a minority in Wilmington—with a reputation for upholding ideals of Christian brotherhood as well as a record for judicial integrity, legal acumen, and a sense of fairness. As the result of a previous suit initiated by Redding, Seitz had already desegregated the University of Delaware of which he was an alumnus, and Inc. Fund lawyers had high hopes when their case against racial segregation in Delaware's lower public school fell to him.

Seitz did not disappoint them, although the breadth of his decision, which he announced on April 1, 1952, may have surprised some. He began in the usual way by recapping the blacks' complaints, but then forged ahead into virgin territory. "Experts," he explained, referring to the testimony of psychiatrist Frederick Wertham of New York, who'd examined both white and black children attending Delaware's segregated schools—a first—had testified to the "harmful over-all effect of legally enforced segregation in education upon Negro children generally." It was, Seitz went on, "no answer to point to numerous Negroes who apparently have not been so harmed." It must be admitted that segregation

> leads to lack of interest, extensive absenteeism, mental disturbances, etc. Indeed, the harm may often show up in ways not connected with their "formal" educational progress. The fact is, [Seitz declared, his forcefulness establishing his opinion as a landmark in the annals of public school desegregation] that such practice creates a mental health problem in many Negro children with a resulting impediment to their educational progress.

Which was exactly what Louis Redding, Robert Carter, Thurgood Marshall, and A. P. Tureaud had hoped to hear but hadn't expected: judicial vindication of what they'd been saying all along. The Kansans had acknowledged that legally enforced segregation had "a tendency to retard the education and mental development of Negro children," but it was a pale acknowledgment compared with Seitz's, and it was tucked away in an appendix. Seitz included his much harsher indictment in the body of the opinion itself.

Seitz, however, had still another surprise in store for both parties to the suits. First, like his fellow judges in the other states, he dredged up the origins of the "separate but equal" formula in *Plessy* and its offspring, conceded that the United States Supreme Court had not overturned that decision, declared that he would like to see it overturned, but believed that though its reversal was "in the wind," it must come from that Court, not this. Like his fellow judges, too, Seitz enumerated in some detail the deficiencies in the Negroes' schools involved in these two cases—his plain, unelaborate listing requiring more than two and a half pages in the court reports. He concluded that school facilities for whites and blacks in and around Wilmington were not equal, and dutifully noted that under similar conditions, "some courts have merely directed the appropriate State officials to equalize facilities." So far he was running with the herd.

Seitz, however, had his own ideas about what was equal and what was not. He set aside the issue of segregation's constitutionality and focused on how to ensure equal education to Delaware's black student body. It was obvious, he implied: send them to the place where it was. It seemed to Seitz, he said, summing up his final bombshell, that when a plaintiff

> shows to the satisfaction of a court that there is an existing and continuing violation of the "separate but equal" doctrine, he is entitled to have made available to him the State facilities which have been shown

to be superior. To do otherwise is to say to such a plaintiff: "Yes, your Constitutional rights are being invaded, but be patient, we will see whether in time they are still being violated."

It wouldn't wash in Seitz's court, and he, like Waties Waring in South Carolina, wanted no part of it. His next sentence made American civil rights history:

> [S]uch a plaintiff is entitled to relief immediately, in the only way it is available, namely, by admission to the school with the superior facilities.

It was the first time an American court had ordered the racial desegregation of a white school at that level. It was the Inc. Fund's first real victory below the university level, and Thurgood Marshall pronounced it "most encouraging" and a "valuable precedent" for the justices of the United States Supreme Court to note when they confronted the package of segregation cases coming to them at that very moment.

Seitz hadn't quite finished yet, however. He still had a light slap on the wrist for the defendants. The school board had protested that the state may not be "ready" for nonsegregated education and that a "social problem" could not be "solved with legal force." Retorted Seitz:

> The application of Constitutional principles is often distasteful to some citizens, but that is one reason for Constitutional guarantees. The principles override transitory passions.

The school boards against which the two suits had been brought would, of course, appeal.

Back in New Orleans, another term had passed. The only change at the Macarty Elementary School was the accumulation of another year's grime, another year's wear and tear on the desks and blackboards, and another series of classes passed on with less than adequate preparation.

"Appropriately," as the *Times-Picayune* put it, on Friday, the thirteenth of June, after a series of strident public hearings on the matter, the Orleans Parish school board announced its decision to convert three all-white schools to Negro use. Though it had been made clear that conversions satisfied no one, the board argued that its program would provide forty-five more classrooms for black children, and along with the later conversion of the Edward T. Merrick School, take two thousand youngsters of the platoon system at a modest price. Conversions were considerably cheaper, and white taxpayers, who insisted they paid the lion's share of the taxes, were not, the board believed, anxious to finance more schools for black children.

Dr. Scheps, speaking for the board, explained its decision:

> With the school board confronted by a suit for equal facilities and with my own deep conviction that all children are entitled to equal educational opportunities, it is unrealistic as well as unjust, to retain a white school which is not needed when it can be converted for Negro use where it is desperately needed.

Lest anyone think the Macarty parents' threat to take the board into court had softened his opposition to desegregation in the schools, however, Scheps added:

> I think the principle of segregation is a part of our way of life. . . . The school board must respect the customs of the community.

In Chicago that summer, Republicans met to nominate Dwight D. Eisenhower for president of the United States. The prominent New Orleans lawyer John Minor Wisdom, local organizer of Americans for Eisenhower "even," as he said later, "before Eisenhower was for Eisenhower," announced at the convention that Louisiana cast "thirteen hard-earned votes" for the general, who represented the internationalist/liberal wing of the party; two of the state's fifteen votes went to Senator Robert A. Taft, who represented the isolationist/conservative wing.

Wisdom's announcement marked the finale in a rough-and-tumble internecine war between old- and new guard Louisiana Republicans whose political behavior that year had sunk to new lows even by Louisiana standards. Unpublicized ward and precinct meetings had been held in isolated fishing camps. One group met in Pilottown, a hundred miles downriver and accessible only by boat, although eight of the nine delegates lived in New Orleans. Hidden meetings, which the Wisdom faction referred to as "up in Brittmar's bathroom" in honor of Brittmar Landry, a Taft faction lieutenant and chief of concealment, were common. The Taft people scheduled one meeting at the home of a Negro midwife on the assumption the swing vote in that ward, one of the grande dames of New Orleans, wouldn't attend; when she appeared at the meeting, passers-by were brought in off the street to offset her influence. Disruptions marked several meetings, and one delegate had been seen slipping his brass knuckles to the bartender in a nearby room just before the police arrived. Democrats had voted openly at Republican caucuses, registrations had been entered in defiance of election law, votes had been counted in partisan interests, and unfavorable ballots had been torn up.

The result inevitably was a bifurcated delegation to the national convention in July. The national committee at a closed hearing voted to seat the Taft delegates. Wisdom, however, lawyer that he was, prepared the Eisenhower faction's case as if he were taking it not to the credentials committee but into a federal trial court.

The meeting of the credentials committee was held under the bright lights of the new medium, television. Wisdom's easy charm, sense of humor, and good looks—alert blue eyes highlighting a craggy profile undamaged by a large aquiline nose—didn't hurt his case, which he argued before an estimated television audience of seventy-five million. Wisdom got up there with a pointer and easy-to-read six-foot-by-six-foot charts illustrating the legitimacy of his delegates. He followed this up with a parade of witnesses: a pretty white girl, a "frowzy" housewife, an old black, a young black, an old Republican, and a new Republican. Somebody for everybody. All that was missing, remarked one commentator, was a "Chinese Jew." A 104-page legallike brief, a plethora of affidavits and photographs, and a booklet, "The Louisiana Story," completed his documentation of what he—and others now—were calling the "Louisiana Steal."

In contrast, the Taft people offered virtually no documentary evidence and shortly conceded defeat in the interests of party "harmony," and to minimize damage to the party in the November election. Some observers believed, however, that a deal had been made with the credentials committee, whose members hoped its seating of Louisiana's Eisenhower delegation would put them in a better tactical position to recommend seating the Taft factions from the contested delegations of Georgia and Texas.

A registered Republican since 1929 when he was a student at Tulane Law School, a time when there were only nine hundred of his political persuasion in all Louisiana and "half of them were dead or moved to Texas," Wisdom had hoped over the years to establish a true two-party system in the state as an antidote to the accumulation of uncurbed power in one party that led to the ascendancy of the politicians like Huey Long. In 1948, he formed the first Dewey-Warren club in the South, a place for Louisiana's now fifteen-hundred registered Republicans to call home. He'd also wanted to wrest control of the local Republicans from the leadership of John E. Jackson, whose little clique had been entrenched at the head of the local party for thirty years.

Now in 1952, as the number of registered Republicans in Louisiana testified, Wisdom's day had come. He'd accomplished both his goals and at the same time secured the Louisiana Republican delegation to the national convention for Eisenhower. Wisdom replaced John Jackson as the leader of Louisiana's Republicans and campaigned vigorously for the general in the months ahead. Eisenhower didn't forget it, either.

Others remembered it, too, although for different reasons. For years afterward, New Orleans tour guides stopped their buses in front of the Wisdoms' big antebellum house in the Garden District and with understandable if not entirely justifiable pride pointed it out as the home of the fellow who'd made Eisenhower president.

The platform that emerged from the Republican convention was hardly calculated to win black votes; in fact it represents the birth of the party's much-discussed future "southern strategy": its later blatant courtship of the white South. The delegates that summer expressed the usual platitudes about race, "condemn[ing] bigots who inject class, racial and religious prejudice into public and political matters." But they also made it clear that it was "the primary responsibility of each state to order and control its own domestic institutions," presumably, although not specifically, its public school systems. Federal intervention wasn't needed or wanted. Editors of the NAACP's monthly publication *The Crisis* saw the calls for states' rights as a euphemism for permission to "cheat, discriminate against, segregate, beat, maim and otherwise mistreat their dark citizens without interference from the Federal Government."

The Democrats didn't have to dump Harry Truman in 1952. He didn't run.

The Louisiana delegates to the Democratic National Convention held later in July, also in Chicago, were led by the prima donnas of the state party: Governor Robert F. Kennon, chairman; ex-governor Sam Jones, the two United States Senators Allen Ellender and Russell Long, the mayor of New Orleans Chep Morrison. With them came a dozen or so men who aspired to the formers' offices plus the ubiquitous Leander Perez, who, though he customarily avoided public office, was second to none in his determination to insinuate his influence.

The states' righters dominated the group, the mind-set of the southern bolt in 1948. In 1952, the Louisianans had gone so far as to pass a preconvention resolution declaring their independence from the regular Democratic Party, should an unpalatable candidate win the nomination. Perez and Kennon made veiled threats to support the Republican candidate if that happened, and moderates, who opposed Truman's programs but saw the extreme sectionalism of the Dixiecrats as self-destructive, had little influence within the delegation.

Early convention demands for loyalty to the national party in the form of an oath to support its chosen candidates provoked a family feud among the Louisianans, and Leander Perez, savoring memories of 1948, announced he would "consider it an honor to be thrown out of this convention." The haggling continued almost up to the minute of the voting on the nomination. Only then did the Louisianans, threatened with the loss of their right to vote on the candidates, yield, and even then their capitulation was half-hearted at best.

The civil rights plank was less bland than the Republican's but not exactly startling: a rehash of Democratic successes achieved through federal action and a provision urging congressional reform of rules governing the filibuster, a major obstacle to passage of civil rights legislation in the past, so that, as the platform committee put it, "majority rule prevails and decisions can be made . . . without being blocked by a minority in either House."

The Louisianans labored strenuously for the candidacy of Senator Richard Russell of Georgia, the perennial southern favorite, but they remained in their places when the convention nominated Truman-type liberal Adlai E. Stevenson, governor of Illinois, for president, and the sop to the South, Senator John J. Sparkman of Alabama for vice president. But the Democratic Party remained intact that year. Nobody, not even Leander Perez, walked out. Governor Byrnes's services would not be required.

When the reports from the two conventions were all in, the NAACP was hard-pressed to recommend any of the candidates. The board of directors liked Stevenson for the "clarity and courage of his pronouncements" on reform of the filibuster rules and his support for a fair-employment practices committee. The board was "impressed" by Eisenhower's statements on ending segregation in the nation's capital and the military as well as his apparent concern for equal employment opportunities, although in this latter connection, his statement fell short of endorsing a fair-employment practices committee, and he had never supported congressional reform. The civil rights records of both vice presidential candidates were, declared the board, "unsatisfactory," and the two men were urged to "re-examine their positions." What the board could recommend wholeheartedly was that blacks register to vote. It directed all NAACP branches to conduct an "all-out campaign" for a nationwide registration of five million black voters in time for the November election.

As the summer of 1952 waned, A. P. Tureaud was still trying to provoke a response from the state board of education to which he had sent a copy of his petition to the Orleans Parish school board nine months before. Neither his original communiqué nor his attempt to jog the board to a reply the following February had been answered. In August he sent a registered letter, reminding the board of his previous dispatches and "respectfully" asking its reaction.

The state board of education, via its secretary, the devout segregationist Shelby M. Jackson, who liked to boast he'd been shaped in the same mold as the great Stonewall, delayed another two weeks before answering. Finally, on August 27, 1952, days from the opening of school for the 1952–53 term—the delay making improvements at Macarty this term virtually impossible and subjecting the black youngsters and their parents to still another year of despair—Jackson dictated a reply, the standard rebuff to which Tureaud had long before become calloused. The board, said Jackson, had received the petition about which Tureaud had recently inquired. Jackson himself doubted the state agency had jurisdiction over the New Orleans school board. The petition nevertheless, he assured Tureaud, was "being studied and considered in connection with the general problem of providing adequate education and educational facilities for all the schoolchildren of Louisiana."

The following day, August 28, the supreme court of Delaware upheld Chancellor Collin Seitz's order to admit black students to all-white schools in that state. The attorney general would, of course, appeal to the U.S. Supreme Court. But for blacks, the high state court's decision represented an encouraging signal.

Shortly after, on September 5, 1952, A. P. Tureaud made his move. Along with a similar suit got up in St. Helena Parish where Dan Byrd's investigations had a white school enrollment of 1,060 enjoying facilities worth $200,000 and a black enrollment of 1,675 making do with facilities valued at $51,000, all presided over by a white school superintendent who claimed that neither whites nor blacks were interested in desegregating, Tureaud marched into federal court in New Orleans and filed the second suit brought by Macarty parents against the Orleans Parish school board. Wilfred Aubert's had been mild in comparison, asking only for equalization of facilities. The Bush suit was challenging segregation itself. If the court upheld the Macarty parents, it would invalidate all Louisiana's requirements, including constitutional requirements, of racial segregation in its public schools. It was to be a true test of federal supremacy, as Louisiana battled for its rights and traditions with vigor, imagination, and spirit unmatched in any other southern state.

Herbert Christenberry would have every reason to feel relieved that the court clerk's odd-even numbering system, which was still in operation in 1952 but which later succumbed to lawyers' manipulation of it and had to be changed, had allotted number 3630 to his judicial partner at the Federal District Court for the Eastern District of Louisiana, J. Skelly Wright.

In the fall of 1952, after two years on the bench, Wright had a reputation as an efficient, diligent judge whose impatience with lawyers' dilatory tactics sometimes brought out an imperial tone in his remarks from the bench. Off the bench, he looked in his conservative clothes as much like the high school teacher he'd been as the judge he'd become. His speech was incisive, his manner dignified and quiet, though he dominated any group of which he was a part. Most important, he had crossed his personal Rubicon two years before when he ordered the law school at LSU desegregated posthaste.

Wright's first move was to get in touch with Judge Hutcheson, still chief judge of the U.S. Court of Appeals for the Fifth Circuit, and his superior officer in the judicial service. Because the Bush suit challenged Louisiana's constitutional requirement of "separate free public schools" for whites and blacks, it was Wright's "opinion" that a three-judge panel was "necessary." Would the chief judge appoint one?

Before Hutcheson had a chance to answer, A. P. Tureaud had received instructions from the national office in New York: he was to hold this one in abeyance until the U.S. Supreme Court ruled on the cases from South Carolina, Kansas, Delaware, and Virginia then awaiting argument. Wright and the defendant school board acquiesced.

It was a quiet beginning for a case that within the decade was to tear the social fabric of the city while it consumed thousands of hours of legal and judicial time, involved not only the two local district court judges— Christenberry was consistently named to the three-judge panels as the suit progressed—but also the seven judges of the Fifth Circuit court and the nine judges of the U.S. Supreme Court. New Orleans would never be the same again, for which one segment of its people damned the case and the courts and another praised God.

CHAPTER 10

"[W]e Together Have Created a Miracle"

T he rally for the Republican presidential candidate on October 13, 1952, was held in one of New Orleans's public squares to avoid local laws that would have required the crowd to be segregated—in the Municipal Auditorium, for example. There was a carnival air about it. Al Hirt, vice chairman of the local musicians' union, led his twenty-piece band through the 60,000 spectators lining Canal Street, ten- to twenty-feet deep in some places—20,000 more than the number that had turned out for the Democratic candidate the previous Friday. There were floats, balloons, and all those people pushing and shoving to get nearer the center of the action in Beauregard Square.

The former chairman of the Louisiana delegation to the Democratic National Convention in July, Governor Bob Kennon, had been as good as his word. An unrepentant supporter of states' rights, he couldn't overcome his dissatisfaction with the spirit of compromise inherent in the choice of the Democratic candidates or the party's platform, and shortly after his return from Chicago, he'd met clandestinely in a Baton Rouge graveyard with the new local Republican national committeeman John Minor Wisdom and let Wisdom talk him into committing his political support in the 1952 presidential campaign to Wisdom's own candidate, General Dwight Eisenhower. Kennon was the first of the southern governors to declare his intention. He was followed shortly by Byrnes of South Carolina and Allan Shivers of Texas as well as Senator Harry F. Byrd of Virginia. The influential Democrat Richard Russell of Georgia didn't actually support the Republican candidate, but only stayed home throughout the campaign, silent as the tomb.

When Governor Stevenson arrived at Moissant Airport outside New Orleans the previous Friday, Kennon had been caught stuffing his "I Like Ike" button into his pocket before greeting the Democratic candidate. He hadn't joined the sixty-car cavalcade into the city, or attended the reception for Stevenson and Democratic officials from ten southern states at the Roosevelt Hotel, or joined the torchlight parade up Canal Street. Kennon hadn't in fact stayed around long at all, only long enough to observe the minimum in good political manners by shaking hands with his fellow governor; then he'd flown off to Shreveport, leaving Frank Ellis, the new Democratic national committeeman, to introduce Stevenson at the rally that night.

Now as Beauregard Square in central New Orleans filled with darkness, Kennon found himself introducing General Eisenhower to the crowd. Kennon knew his crowds, and he pushed all the right buttons: the Civil War, recollections of his own life as a Democrat, Louisiana's support for the Dixiecrats in 1948, and the "un-American" character of the Democratic platform four years later. The crowd roared its approval at every comma, and when he described Eisenhower as a Democrat at heart, adding "We are for him," Louisianans, convinced the regular Democrats were bent on selling out the South to blacks and northern liberals, went wild.

Eisenhower himself wasn't more eloquent, though he told them what they'd come to hear. Beginning with "Ladies and Gentlemen," then switching to *"Mesdames et Messieurs,"* the general won their hearts immediately. Then he went to work on their minds. He made his position perfectly clear: he "deplore[d]" and he promised to resist "federal encroachment upon rights and affairs of the states." Militant segregationist campaign rhetoric was soft-pedaled that year, replaced by the politely uttered but veiled allusions whose implications no one misunderstood. He didn't have to mention schools or southern tradition. The crowd knew what he meant.

He was more specific about the offshore oil issue. The Republicans, he said, deplored, too, as well as "federal encroachment upon rights and affairs of the states," the federal "attack on the tidelands," which he described as "part of the effort of the [Democratic] Administration to amass more power and money." Eisenhower strongly favored "recognition of clear legal title to these lands in each of the forty-eight states." Twice, he noted, both houses of Congress had voted to recognize traditional ownership of the offshore, mineral-rich territory, and both times President Truman had vetoed the legislation. Boos and catcalls. He himself would not.

State ownership of these lands, he said, was a "long recognized concept" that had not "weakened" America or "impaired the orderly development of such resources." Where would the government draw the line? After the annexation of Louisiana's, Texas's, and California's tidelands, he couldn't help but wonder about the fate of Pennsylvania's coal-bearing waters, Minnesota's iron ore, Florida's fisheries, Maine's kelp, even the real estate New York and Massachusetts had so laboriously reclaimed from submerged areas along their coasts. So many states were vulnerable.

The pushy federal foot, he charged, had gotten in the door. He repeated his support of state ownership, which provoked the biggest cheers of all. Governor Kennon led them, leaping to his feet and waving his hands over his head.

In contrast, the crowd had received Governor Stevenson's remarks of the previous week quietly. He'd said little that white Louisianans had wanted to hear. He'd opened with a strong, though brief statement, of his belief in "minority rights." He had, he said, but one comment to make. It saddened him that

[a]fter 2,000 years of Christianity, we need discuss it at all.

Having alienated a healthy section of the assembled crowd, he'd then launched into the Democratic case for national ownership of tidelands oil. He sympathized with Louisianans in their disappointment in the U.S. Supreme Court's vesting their ownership in the federal government two years before, but believed congressional gifts of national assets to individual states an unwise policy, whether it was submerged coastal lands, national parkland, or any other public territory. He believed it the duty of the President to "conserve the national assets," and he hoped the states and the nation, between them, could work out some mutually agreeable solution to the problem. He concluded with a timely warning against going "behind the Supreme Court decisions, saying that this one is wrong and acting accordingly . . . whether they involve submerged lands or the seizure of the steel industry." Or even, he might have added, as the segregation cases made their way to the U.S. Supreme Court, racial mixing in the schools.

It was definitely *not* what his audience had come to hear, and Stevenson couldn't even make amends by delivering his three concluding—and noncontroversial—paragraphs in French. He earned polite but not energetic applause.

It was the 108,000 registered black Louisianans who kept the state's ten electoral votes away from Eisenhower in the November election.

Despite the Republican candidate's impassioned reception in New Orleans and the Democratic candidate's lukewarm-bordering-on-cool, Stevenson took not only New Orleans, but also the state and the South except for Florida, Tennessee, Texas, and Virginia. Wherever blacks were registered, they voted in solid blocs for the regular Democratic candidate, who spoke fluently, as well as French, their common language of civil rights.

Eisenhower's dominant language of the campaign in the South had been Dixiecrat, albeit minus any blatant racism, and he won in those pockets of New Orleans, Louisiana, and the South that had voted heavily for the Dixiecrats in 1948. Leander Perez himself had proudly presented the Republican with a whopping 93 percent of the popular vote in his own Plaquemines Parish. Eisenhower nonetheless lost statewide, 306,925 to 345,027 (47 to 53 percent), and he won the presidency without most of the South. The tears he made, however, in the political fabric there, solidly Democratic since the mass disenfranchisement of blacks following the U.S. Supreme Court's decision in *Plessy* v. *Ferguson* a half century before, demonstrated the potential for a rebirth of the Republican party in the South. There was already enthusiastic talk about the future.

Midway between the election on November 4, 1952, and the new President's inauguration on January 20, 1953, on December 9, 1952, the four school segregation cases that had accumulated at the U.S. Supreme Court, along with a fifth case picked up in the nation's capital, which was still as racially segregated as it had been when A. P. Tureaud lived there thirty years earlier, were scheduled for presentation. The array of legal talent assembled for the occasion was dazzling.

Thurgood Marshall had already participated in one capacity or another in fifteen cases before the nation's highest tribunal. His arguments had won thirteen of them.

His opposite number, who was arguing Harry Briggs's case for South Carolina, was the eminent John W. Davis, Democratic candidate for president in 1924 and veteran of no fewer than 141 Supreme Court cases and even at seventy-nine a formidable figure in the courtroom. Marshall knew the lawyer's tactics well; as a student at Howard he'd often gone down to the Court to listen when Davis appeared for one of his corporate clients. Comparing him with other lawyers who'd appeared before him, Justice Oliver Wendell Holmes had pronounced Davis "more elegant, more clear, more precise" and "more logical" than all the rest.

Davis had known Governor Byrnes of South Carolina when both men were members of the House of Representatives, and Byrnes, who considered Davis "the ablest constitutional lawyer of the time," went to his old friend when he needed a high-powered talent to argue South Carolina's side of Harry Briggs's case. After reading the records in the case, Davis, who believed ardently in both states' rights and stare decisis—lawyers' shorthand for abiding by precedent, in this case *Plessy*—agreed to take it on. He believed, he told Byrnes, that the lower court had been right on the money when it denied black children access to the state's white schools.

Briggs and its progeny were Davis's last arguments. Before the Supreme Court announced its final decision in the segregation cases in May, 1955, he would be dead.

Virginia sent its chief law enforcement officer, Attorney General J. Lindsay Almond, to present its case against the Negroes of Prince Edward County. He'd been a lower state-court judge in Roanoke for more than a decade and a Congressman for two terms. His passionate argument for maintaining separate schools for Negro—or "nigra" as he called them—and white children would do no harm to his gubernatorial candidacy.

Ten days before the scheduled oral argument, Thurgood Marshall set up housekeeping in a suite at Washington's Statler Hotel, one of several racially desegregated local establishments—although it was said at the time that most of these places that allowed blacks to book rooms reserved their lower floors for them in order to diminish their visibility on the elevators. Robert Carter, assigned to argue the Kansas case, came and went. Spottswood Robinson III, legal historian and technician par excellence who some years later was appointed a federal appellate judge, brought his problems with the Virginia case there. James Madison Nabrit, Jr., whose illustrious past included arguing—successfully—against the white primary at the Supreme Court in 1927 and establishing the first serious course in civil-rights law at Howard University, of which he would later become president, came there to discuss the District of Columbia suit. The lawyers got little sleep during those tense days before their court appearances. According to Marshall, they'd "fuss 'n fight" the nights away, testing their ideas, honing their points, and in the process building the confidence they'd need on December 9. At one point they went up to Howard and held a moot court, during which they presented their cases to mock judges who shot them down with probing questions. When the great day arrived, the Inc. Fund lawyers were ready.

The courtroom was packed long before the arguments began—promptly at 1:35 P.M. Four hundred people waited outside in the Great Hall. Many of the spectators were black, emphasizing that it was their two and a half million children attending segregated schools in whose behalf these cases had been brought here.

The atmosphere of the courtroom was as cold as the December day beyond the oak-paneled walls and the red velour curtains, and it did nothing to undo the knots in an attorney's stomach to watch the audience rise as the crier smashed down his gavel and the nine black-robed, somber-faced justices filed in and took their seats. For all its chilliness, however, the U.S. Supreme Court was perhaps the last place in Washington where the elaborate equipment of bureaucracy had not attached itself, and the advocate of a cause presented his arguments to the highest level of decision maker.

Marshall had faced these same justices when he argued Heman Sweatt's suit against the University of Texas two years before. The question now was whether he could persuade them to take the next step, to cross that dangerous intersection, and declare public school segregation itself unconstitutional. As lawyers, these men, even in their self-imposed isolation that was supposed to foster objectivity, could understand the requirements of legal training. Could they also understand what overcrowding, leaky toilets, out-of-date maps, tattered textbooks, and all the other humiliations that went with second-rate elementary and high school education did to a child's psychological development? Could the Inc. Fund team convince the Court, three of whose members were southerners and had grown up in racially segregated schools—Hugo Black of Alabama, Tom Clark of Texas, and Stanley Reed of Kentucky—that even if the fiscal gaps could be closed, separate could never ever be equal.

The NAACP characterized the two days of argument as a "dramatic contest between youth and age, with the young men of the NAACP battling for a new order in which racial distinctions are banned and the older men of the opposition defending the southern 'way of life' with its racial taboos." In Louisiana, state officials were monitoring the Court proceedings closely and were already talking about working on plans to continue school segregation, should the Court ban the present system.

As the leading attorney for Linda Brown's suit, Bob Carter led off the arguments before the Supreme Court. When he returned to the counsel's table, he looked a little shell-shocked by some of the justices'—especially Felix Frankfurter's—probing questions, most of which, that day and the next, involved the justices' deep concern for the effect of any move on their part to interfere in the operation of state segregated school systems. Thurgood Marshall and his opponent John W. Davis were at their best that day when their turns came: precise, clear, articulate.

The range of references over the two days of argument was broad: in addition to the ghosts of *Plessy, Sweatt,* and *McLaurin,* the dominant figures in the precedents cited, the ghosts of Gunnar Myrdal, W. E. B. Du Bois, the expert witnesses who'd testified in the lower courts on the effects of racial segregation on children, and even California's Japanese-Americans forcibly dislocated during World War II, were disinterred. Neither side's basic assumptions altered one whit, however. The debate still focused on the Fourteenth Amendment's "equal protection of the laws" versus the state's right to administer its own domestic affairs.

When the last advocate sat down at 3:50 on December 11, 1952, following nine and a half hours of argument, the justices had not only the kernels of the parties' collective wisdom to digest, but they also held amicus curiae briefs from the American Civil Liberties Union, American Federation of Teachers, American Jewish Congress, American Veterans Committee, and the Congress of Industrial Organizations, plus what may have been the most important outsider's comments of all: a thirty-two-page brief submitted by the solicitor general's office. It had been written by the solicitor general's ace civil rights attorney, Philip Elman. Citing John Marshall Harlan's color-blind Constitution, Elman largely urged the NAACP's arguments for desegregating schools on the Court. But Elman, a former law clerk to Felix Frankfurter and still close enough to the justice to be on the receiving end of Frankfurter's concerns should the Court order immediate wholesale racial desegregation of the public schools, also urged the justices to go slowly—as slowly as was humanly possible without falling over backward. Citing the logistical and psychological problems such a decision would engender—invalidation of old laws, formulation of new ones, dislocations of teachers and students—Elman suggested that the Court

> take into account the need, not only for prompt vindication of the constitutional rights violated, but also for orderly and reasonable solution of the vexing problems which may arise in eliminating such segregation. The public interest plainly would be served by avoidance of needless dislocation and confusion in the administration of the school systems affected.

He wanted no one to mistake the government's advice against undue haste as affecting the merits of these cases. He did, however, want to remind the Court that

> racial segregation in public schools has been in effect in many states for a long time. Its roots go deep in the history and traditions of these states.

Its demise would not be accomplished easily or simply.

Following the arguments, the justices retreated to the inner sanctums of their minds to digest what they'd read and heard and to debate among themselves what they would do. John Davis wasn't worried. He was overheard as he left the Court that final day predicting to one of his colleagues that he was sure the states had won. Five-to-four at worst, he thought, but optimistically, six-to-three.

Spring marched implacably onward. The silence of the Supreme Court was earsplitting. Americans waited. And waited. Then waited some more. Other cases involving segregation—in transportation, various public facilities, and schools—that had been initiated in the lower courts, including Oliver Bush's case against the Orleans Parish school board, languished on hold while the judges and litigants waited to see what the highest court in the land would do about the cases before them.

As ordered by Chancellor Seitz the previous April, two white public schools in Delaware—an elementary school and a high school—began to admit Negroes. Psychiatrist Frederick Wertham, who'd tested white and Negro children attending segregated schools prior to testifying at the trial of the NAACP's suit in that state, wondered how the children involved were affected, and he returned in February, 1953, to re-test children transferred from segregated to integrated schools six months before. Some of the children had been part of the original study. Although, Wertham admitted, "the period is short and the number of cases small," it was clear to him that

> all the Negro children of this study who changed from segregated to integrated schools made distinctly better academic progress than they had shown before.

Their teachers knew it; their parents knew it. And the children themselves knew it, although they had been surprised.

The better facilities alone—access to up-to-date dictionaries and reference books, smaller classes, courses they'd never heard of before—contributed to the children's progress. But the "most potent" factor, Dr. Wertham thought, was the improved emotional motivation. "The conflicts caused by state-ordained segregation" had been removed. It was true there'd been some minor incidents: "transitory" name-calling and occasional "embarrassing" giggling and laughing in the early days. But the transition had largely proceeded smoothly.

Dr. Wertham could only conclude that the overview of February, 1953, reinforced his previous findings:

> The abolition of segregation removes a handicap that interferes with the self-realization and social adjustment of the child.

Finally on June 8, 1953, as the Supreme Court's 1952 term was winding down, the justices emerged from their isolation just long enough to order the five cases brought back for still another session of argument, posing specific questions they wanted answered. The first three involved whether the authors of the Fourteenth Amendment had or had not intended the measure to deal with segregation in the public schools and, if they had, how. Had they expected future Congresses to take care of it, or were they relying on the nation's judges to interpret their wishes. The last two questions asked exactly how school desegregation could be accomplished. Some Court watchers believed the content and phraseology of the questions indicated the justices had already made up their minds to abolish segregation in the public schools, although Felix Frankfurter, in a scribbled note to the chief justice, said the questions as posed, "by looking in opposite directions . . . would not tip the mitt."

An invitation was extended to the United States attorney general to participate. Justice Robert Jackson, himself a former attorney general, had suggested, and the other eight had agreed, "that the new administration [Eisenhower had become President in January, 1953], unlike the old, might have the responsibility of carrying out a decision full of perplexities; it should therefore be asked to face that responsibility as part of our process of adjudication." At which point the justices retreated again into silence while they awaited the rearguments, scheduled for October 12.

The NAACP was disappointed but urged continued patience and faith in resolution of the conflict by law, not by the kind of "hysterical mob appeal" resorted to by Governor Byrnes and his next-door neighbor Governor Herman Talmadge of Georgia, who were talking about turning the public schools in their states over to private institutions, should the Court order wholesale desegregation.

In New Orleans, lawyer Tureaud was able to spend his now well-honed skills on the racial desegregation of the state university's undergraduate departments. Nearly three years after desegregation of its law school, these were still off-limits to black students.

By this time, Tureaud was known to have the best law library of any local black attorney, and, using its availability as the pretext, young black lawyers on Saturday afternoons brought their sandwiches and soft drinks to his office where they talked away the hours, sharing experiences and problems, posing the legal conundrums that engage eager young law school graduates, and imbibing, along with their colas, the older, more experienced man's sense of their common profession. Tureaud's sense of himself as social engineer was contagious, and he transmitted to many a young black colleague in those days that it was the law, their own calling, that would in the end be responsible for the slaying of the dragon Jim Crow. He gave them hope, encouragement, and above all, by his own example, sketched for them a model of what they themselves could do, of how they could contribute to the social revolution that was then in the making.

The social revolution of which the racial desegregation of the rest of Louisiana State University was a small but essential part. This desegregation institution by institution was a cumbersome process. Even after the public law schools in Texas and Louisiana were pried open, the segregation policies at the public universities in Georgia, Mississippi, Alabama, Florida, the Carolinas, Virginia, Arkansas, and Tennessee had to be attacked individually.

The attorney general of Tennessee, although thoroughly convinced that "strife and turmoil" would follow the "letting down of the bars," had approved the admission of three blacks to the professional schools at the state university. At the time he had issued a most unsouthern statement:

> We must [he said] bow to the inevitable. . . . The opinions of the Supreme Court become the law of the land, notwithstanding any opinions that may be entertained by any individuals, however sound such opinions may be.

At the other extreme and a more typical example was the University of Virginia whose law school had had to be desegregated by federal court order.

The NAACP was desperate for the funds to keep the program alive. The additional suits required to finish the job at this one-at-a-time pace, said Walter White, executive secretary of the organization, would run into who-knew-how-many thousands of dollars. Even Thurgood Marshall was worried. As he had told NAACP members earlier in 1953, as the organization came closer and closer to victory, his own job became more difficult. Not only was the opposition solidifying, but "our lukewarm friends run to cover." Time consuming, enervating, and expensive as the process was, however, the organization couldn't stop now. Failing action by Congress, a political impossibility, or the President, also a political impossibility at the time, litigation was all that was left.

If the job was to be done right, all the circles closed and all the corners squared, the undergraduate had to follow the graduate schools. The process had to be undertaken again and again and again, every excruciating step of it.

Local NAACP leaders had been discussing such a suit against LSU for some time but had been unable to find a suitable plaintiff. They required one not only academically qualified and willing to face the social and emotional consequences of being the first black to invade a formerly whites-only territory, but one whose character was unassailable. Another fiasco like Roy Wilson's at LSU Law School could ruin them.

Tureaud was in this one up to his eyebrows, his involvement visceral as well as cerebral. The plaintiff who finally came forward was his only son, A. P., Jr., about to graduate in the spring of 1953 from New Orleans's all-black Joseph S. Clark High School. All his life, his teachers had told him he had to do better than the white kids because he'd be judged by harsher standards. He'd done well among the black students, despite the overcrowding at Clark and the old hand-me-down textbooks. Now he wanted to see what he could do in competition with whites. The personal consequences of desegregating a major section of a university would be considerably more painful than what Rodolphe Desdunes's son Daniel had faced when he tried to desegregate the passenger cars on the Louisville and Nashville railroad back in 1892, though in June, 1953, when he shot off his application to the registrar at LSU, young A. P. didn't imagine his own as the usual sort of test case or as requiring unusual fortitude.

Young A. P.'s story is no prettier than any other black plaintiff's in those days. In addition to the constant legal wrangling in and out of courts and the perpetual exposure to public scrutiny, which carried its own vulnerabilities—the young women in the family joked about the bombs hitting their front bedroom first, but the fear was real—the nightmarish experience exacted an emotional toll of the entire family, but especially young and old A. P. It had been "easy enough," Tureaud commented in the midst of it, to be

> on the other side as counsel, advising a client, but when you are both client and counsel it is a different story.

The elder Tureaud knew he had only himself to blame. Whenever young A. P. had accompanied him to Baton Rouge on some legal errand during the siege of the university's law school, the older man would exclaim:

> Look at that library! Look at this campus!

And the next thing he knew, his son had set his heart on LSU. With A. P.'s record in high school—a general average of 89 and a school medal for excellence—he could have gone to the all-black Xavier or Dillard or

Southern and ranked at the head of his class. But it was LSU or bust.

He wanted desperately to be a regular student at the state university, to join in the fraternity high jinks and cheer the Tigers on sunny fall Saturday afternoons. LSU at the time offered a unique course of arts, science, and the law that could be completed in six years, and young A. P. was sure it had been meant for him. Southern University offered a similar course, but it failed even to approach LSU's "level of scholarship and intensity."

That there might be serious consequences of his action didn't really occur to young A. P. He didn't ask his father's advice and the elder Tureaud didn't offer it. It wasn't an emotionally demonstrative family. Its members shared objective information but not feelings. The young man figured that with the graduate and professional schools already integrated, thanks to his father, the way had been paved. A. P., however, also had led something of a sheltered life in the still black Seventh Ward of New Orleans. He knew discrimination but not compared to what a black Mississippi sharecropper's offspring experienced. He'd also known a wider world. He'd gone to the racially mixed summer camp near Philadelphia, Pennsylvania. His parents had made it a practice to expose their children to cities, people, and ways of life outside the South. At seventeen, young A. P. was "idealistic." He truly believed "there'd be some fuss in the press for a while, then it would die down," and he'd go on to LSU and "have a great time."

He never imagined what really happened to him at LSU would, never in his wildest dreams thought he would endure three long months of inconclusive court battles, or that when he finally entered his beloved university, would think he had descended to hell. The attitudes there terrified him, the epithets shocked him, the cold and determined resistance depressed him.

The summer of 1953 dragged on as he waited for LSU's answer to his application. Finally, on August 1, the university officially rejected him, and a week later, the inevitable but not unexpected letter arrived at the Tureaud home on Pauger Street. He had been turned down "in line," the registrar told him, with the university's "policy of not admitting Negro students" to the section to which the youth had applied. Although a hundred or more blacks were enrolled that summer in LSU's graduate departments, LSU President Middleton explained to a newspaper reporter, the university admitted blacks only to those graduate schools whose courses were not offered elsewhere to Negroes.

The Tureauds' next stop had to be federal court, and the elder Tureaud immediately put together their formal complaint, the main point of which was that nowhere else in Louisiana could young A. P. pursue the course of study he had chosen. Southern University had tried to create such a program, but had not so far been successful. Lawyer Tureaud sent the first draft of the document to Bob Carter at NAACP headquarters in New York. He wanted an expert's opinion. He had heard that LSU

> intend[ed] to make a last ditch fight and [he] would not like to have any loop holes in [the] procedure.

When he finally filed the case, it was assigned to Judge Wright. Skelly was just back from his annual busman's holiday in New York City where he liked to stretch his legal legs a little in another court, gargle a little spaghetti with clam sauce at Chez Vito's, and take in a few games at Yankee Stadium. Lawyers who argued in his court during those summers remembered his clock-watching on game days and his increased impatience with any hint of delaying tactics. Skelly loved that month on the Federal District Court for the Southern District of New York. He called it the "Big Leagues" and he thought of the judges there as all-stars.

Tureaud requested a three-judge court. His case seemed to have all the elements specified in the U.S. Code: LSU's president was certainly an "officer" of the state, and the order denying young A. P. admission to the university had been issued by LSU's board of supervisors, by definition "an administrative board or commission acting under State Statutes." Tureaud hoped the case would be assigned to the same trio—Wright, Christenberry, and Borah—that had ordered Roy Wilson admitted to LSU's law school three years before.

But Wright refused this time to convene one, explaining that it was "unnecessary . . . the issues have already been passed upon in this court." This latest suit was, after all, not the first but the fourth time such a suit had been filed against LSU. All three previous suits had resulted in the court's requiring the university to open graduate departments to blacks, and this past June, a black recipient of an advanced degree had marched in the LSU commencement parade for the first time in the university's history. As far as the judge was concerned, the questions Tureaud was raising about LSU had already been answered, and he had as well the U.S. Supreme Court precedents of *Sweatt* and *McLaurin* to back him up. Instead of contacting the chief judge this time, Wright scheduled a hearing for September 8. He alone would decide A. P.'s case.

The courtroom was packed that morning. The eighteen attorneys representing LSU went a long way toward filling it. All of them were alumni, all were donating their services.

Finding the difficulties of acting as lawyer, plaintiff—and not incidentally, concerned father—too much to cope with at one time, the elder Tureaud had asked one of his law partners, A. M. Trudeau, to take care of the usual paper work that required the services of a local lawyer, and had persuaded Bob Carter to drop everything in his New York office and hurry South to handle the trial itself. It was never easy for black lawyers from the North to work southern courts. Hotels refused them rooms, restaurants refused them food, taxies refused to stop for them, and they were almost entirely dependent on friends—like the Tureauds, for example, whose house was always open to visiting lawyers—for housing, meals, and rides. Carter nevertheless came.

A veteran of the U.S. Supreme Court as well as lower federal courts all over the South, Carter knew the ropes. The applicant, he said, was seeking admission to LSU's undergraduate school of arts and sciences because he couldn't get the course of study he wanted to pursue at Southern University. The facilities at Southern simply weren't equal. In addition to the difference in facilities, he continued, there was a substantial disparity between the two universities' spending for students. LSU's annual budget of $12 million and enrollment of some 6,400 students broke down to an expenditure of about $1,875 per student. In contrast, Southern's annual budget of $2 million for some 1,900 students broke down to an expenditure of only $689 per student.

Laurence Brooks, who'd lost LSU's case against Roy Wilson to Tureaud three years before, was again captaining the argument for the university. If he was aware of impending threats to the southern way of life—and who in America wasn't in the summer of 1953?—he didn't show it but soldiered on clinging desperately to the Lost Cause of his century.

As he had Wilson's case, Brooks asked the judge to dismiss this one. Racial segregation, he declared, was

> necessary in this state to preserve and to promote more friendly relations and mutual understanding between white and colored persons.

The progress of blacks over the last few years and the absence of race riots in the state proved, he explained, the wisdom of the policy, and the state was acting within its constitutionally delegated police powers in excluding them from schools reserved for whites.

Leander Perez, however, unreconstructed Dixiecrat and now one of the South's most strident voices for segregation, turned legal argument to racial diatribe. Before he was finished, Mrs. Tureaud regretted she had come to the hearing. She would not, she vowed, come again.

Perez shocked young A. P. as well as a lot of other people in the courtroom that day when he called the youth "the only ungrateful 'nigra' in the state of Louisiana," and added contemptuously:

LSU's refusal to admit young Tureaud does not constitute irreparable injury to the youth . . . the harm is done to LSU by having the institution hauled before the court.

The session ended at 12:45 P.M. on Judge Wright's promise to make his decision promptly, possibly before the end of the week, in any case before the opening of the academic term at LSU.

Wright made good his promise. Just three days later, on September 11, he issued the injunction Tureaud had requested. He began his opinion by reminding the university of his previous injunction prohibiting the institution from barring blacks to certain other departments. He had found, he said, that the combined arts and sciences/law course offered by Southern University was "not substantially equal" to the comparable course offered by LSU, and for anyone who doubted his judgment, he attached a lengthy appendix detailing the inequalities between the two schools, from the number and qualifications of the two faculties to the most minute differences in their curriculums. Based on these inequities, he had decided to enjoin the university from refusing admission not only to A. P. Tureaud, Jr., but "all others similarly qualified and situated . . . at the same time, upon the same terms" as "other residents and citizens of the state." Young Tureaud's suit thus became what the university had most hoped to avoid: a class action. LSU must admit A. P., but the university also could no longer discriminate against any black applicant to the combined arts and sciences/law program. It was a limited course of study which the university was obliged to open to blacks. It was that combined arts and sciences/law curriculum that Wright had found wanting at Southern University, and it was this program and only this program to which he was requiring A. P.'s admission.

Wright had been governed, he explained in his conclusion, by the best known of the U.S. Supreme Court's precedents, beginning in 1938 with Lloyd Gaines's suit against the University of Missouri and ending with his own decision in *Wilson* v. *Board of Supervisors* in 1950, which that court had refused to reconsider, and including the law and graduate school suits, *Sweatt* and *McLaurin,* all of which, like Tureaud's suit, had involved only inequities in state-operated educational facilities for blacks.

He didn't say so, but the implication was strong that none had involved the issue of racial segregation *per se,* and he needn't consider that in A. P.'s case.

Within days, young A. P. gathered together his gear and headed for Baton Rouge. His mother later told a friend that one of the hardest things she ever had to do was send him off to the university, but she'd been unable to share her fears.

Her fears were not baseless. The young man's emotional troubles were just beginning and his legal troubles weren't over yet. He and his father were met in the registrar's office by Lawrence Brooks with the news that the university had asked for a new trial and an order to postpone the imposition of Wright's injunction. He was sorry, but A. P. wouldn't be able to register that day.

The elder Tureaud immediately telephoned Skelly Wright, who just as quickly set a date for a new hearing: September 16, still in time for young A. P. to enter the university this semester. The elder Tureaud was optimistic.

On the appointed day, several members of the university's legal team, including Leander Perez, who'd rearmed his missiles for the occasion and enlivened the proceedings with some of his increasingly familiar racial tirades, returned to the district court and asked the judge to set aside his injunction. Wright had been wrong, they insisted, when he refused to convene a three-judge court at the outset.

Wright refused their request. His judicial oath, he explained, required him to "follow the teachings of the Supreme Court," and he affirmed his previous ruling. The university immediately filed a notice of appeal to the United States Court of Appeals for the Fifth Circuit.

Momentarily unperturbed by the threat of further legal battles, young A. P. returned to Baton Rouge. The historic moment of his registration in LSU's freshman class, the first known American black in the institution's history to enter the undergraduate section, took place on September 18, 1953. LSU considered his registration conditional and subject to further court action.

Nevertheless, this second attempt of A. P.'s to enter the university went smoothly enough. Officials were polite if not open-armed, and he was given a single room in a stadium dormitory, a course of study that included English, math, advanced Spanish, military science, and physical education, along with the traditional freshman haircut and instructions to attend the next football game in traditional freshman attire, pajamas. All in all, said his father, who had accompanied him back to the LSU campus: "He has become 'regular.'"

Behind the older man's pride, though, old fears still lurked, and he contacted a friend in Baton Rouge, asking him to keep "a watchful eye" over his son "so that no harm will come to him."

As he suspected, it was indeed too soon to crow. Disturbed by the events of the past week, J. Stewart Slack of Shreveport, chairman of the university's board of supervisors, within days warned that the institution intended to reverse the tide:

The authorities of the University feel that the decision admitting a Negro to the academic department is destructive to the entire educational system built under the constitution of the state, and every step possible will be taken in an effort to get this ruling reversed.

While LSU's attorneys concentrated on the legal remedies to their difficulties, young A. P., whose early euphoria soon turned to something more akin to agony, concentrated on relief of his own increasingly intolerable situation. He wasn't "spat upon or pushed in the corridors," as some black undergraduates were later. He was never explicitly threatened. The strategy seemed to be to wear him out.

Some three thousand foreign students were enrolled in LSU courses that year, many of them dark-skinned Asians from whom the bronze-colored A. P. was virtually indistinguishable, and he would overhear white students discussing him in his presence, how they'd "lucked out, not having a class with him." One went so far as to ask A. P. himself if he had seen "that nigger Tureaud."

Most people at LSU, however, knew who the "nigger" was. Radios, their volume turned high, were concealed outside his window; a dead cat was hung on his doorknob. An administration promise that the university would "treat him the same as anyone else" was broken right off when a faculty member announced that she'd been teaching for thirty years, "had never taught a Negro before and wasn't going to start now." Other faculty members "down-graded" A. P.'s academic work.

Robert Collins of New Orleans, who'd entered the law school on Roy Wilson's heels and would later become the first black judge to sit on a federal court within the Fifth Circuit, was in his final year when young A. P. Tureaud arrived on campus. Collins remembered well the "sense of isolation" he himself had felt on his arrival, but at least he had a roommate, fellow New Orleanian Ernest Morial. A. P. was alone. More alone than he'd ever been before.

He had no social life at all. These few blacks in the graduate programs were just enough older to ignore him. Activists back in New Orleans, worried that the young man might abandon ship prematurely, informed friends in Baton Rouge that Tureaud was "being treated in anything but a brotherly and Christian manner." Could anything be done "to make him feel more at home and at ease"?

The young man felt "locked in," committed, and didn't want to quit. But he wasn't sure how long he could hold out in the face of the hostility and isolation. It wasn't getting any easier.

The elder Tureaud was pulled in opposite directions. The NAACP, which had invested heavily politically, financially, and psychologically in the case against LSU, was insisting A. P. remain at the university. Roy Wilson's forced withdrawal from the law school three years before was still fresh in the attorneys' minds, still smarted. The organization could ill afford another episode like that.

Young A. P.'s agony was pulling his father the other way. So were the boy's mother and the rest of the family. The seventeen-year-old was, after all, his son, and the boy's pain was his as well. Long years ago, he had seen "the hurt" in his people, had recognized their "need," and his entire adult life had been directed toward alleviating their misery. But his own family, his only son, had not been involved until now. Had he Abraham's strength and faith? Had young A. P. Isaac's?

The U.S. Court of Appeals for the Fifth Circuit made the decision for all of them when on October 28, 1953, its verdict reversing Skelly Wright's of the previous month was announced. It was Wright's failure to convene a three-judge court that had tripped him up. Chief Judge Hutcheson, writing for himself and Robert T. Russell, after reviewing the literature of three-judge courts, declared that he and his colleague were "in no doubt that the suit from which this appeal comes was one for three judges and that the district judge was without jurisdiction to hear and determine the application for injunction."

Wright was plainly disappointed and baffled as well, wondering whether these two judges "decided I was going too far or maybe too fast." He saw Hutcheson's opinion as one that could only compound his own difficulties, which had begun to include, not hate mail yet, but some fairly trenchent criticism. "How can a white judge in the South and aware of the facts concerning the two races," went a letter from a Baton Rouge elementary school principal, "rule to place Negro students in white educational institutions . . . I know of no surer way of tearing our nation apart than by forced intermingling of the two races." As Wright described his predicament when the court of appeals reversed him, he

was swimming upstream as far as the local community was concerned, and then to have a critical opinion reversing what I had done didn't improve my position any.

He could, however, be somewhat consoled by the dissent, which had been written by the third member of the panel, the soft-spoken Alabaman Richard T. Rives.

Rives's precourt record on race was mixed. Personal experiences with racial injustices in his native Montgomery and a brief repugnant flirtation with the Ku Klux Klan had pushed him in one direction; political pressures had pulled him in another, and he once went so far as to coach the Montgomery Board of Registrars in frustrating a black voter-registration drive. On the Fifth Circuit, to which Truman had appointed him in 1951, he was still feeling his way. Eventually he would become one of that court's most passionate advocates of black equality before the law, and as Oliver Bush's case was later buffeted about in judicial forums, Rives and Skelly Wright would become firm allies as co-members of the various three-judge district courts on which they served together. But all that came later. In A. P. Tureaud's case, he applied quite a different set of citations from those chosen by the chief judge—a not uncommon occurrence in judicial opinion-writing that sets a reader to wondering sometimes whether the authors are discussing the same case—and came to the conclusion that in Wright's decision not to convene a three-judge court, Wright had

> commendably . . . shouldered the responsibility imposed upon him by law.

Having no force in law, it was, however, small comfort, and on November 9, Wright, as instructed by the higher court, vacated his order requiring LSU to enroll A. P. Tureaud, Jr.

The elder Tureaud immediately telephoned his son and told him to "start packing." He'd explain when he got to LSU.

On arrival, his father explained the court decisions to young A. P., relieving the boy not only of the agonies that had dominated his days at the university but of any guilt he might have felt about leaving, letting down his father, the NAACP, his people.

"I could know now it's not on me," A. P. the younger recalled some years later. "I didn't quit. I was forced to leave."

Robert Carter had asked the university to allow A. P. to remain in school pending final consideration of his case by the U.S. Supreme Court. Carter was worried. It was entirely possible, he thought, that A. P.'s departure might convince some of the justices on that Court, then in the midst of deliberations on the five all-important school segregation cases, that "the time is not ripe for desegregation of minors of an impressionable age."

But the university, on advice of counsel, had lost no time in making the departure official, telling its first black undergraduate that his "registration in the LSU undergraduate division has been cancelled" as the result of recent court actions.

A. P. was on his way home by that time. He had six weeks' work to catch up if he was going to be able to compete with the other freshmen at Xavier University where his older sister was enrolled.

The elder Tureaud vetted his emotions in two ways. He first filed a petition for certiorari—the formal request to be heard—with the U.S. Supreme Court asking reversal of the Fifth Circuit's decision. He next addressed an NAACP rally in New Orleans. Intemperate would be an exaggeration, but it was not the quiet, dignified A. P. Tureaud New Orleanians knew who thundered:

> We know our rights, we have been exercising them for a number of
> years. There is no force on God's green earth to stop integration.

On November 16, the U.S. Supreme Court, at Tureaud's request, suspended the judgment of the U.S. Court of Appeals for the Fifth Circuit, pending the full Court's consideration of Tureaud's petition for certiorari. But it was too late for young A. P. Safely enrolled at Xavier, he had vowed at his departure from LSU: "I'm never coming back here. I don't care how you work it out."

As the new year opened, Tureaud's case floated in personal and legal limbo. The elder Tureaud wasn't at all sure he could persuade his son to return to LSU under any circumstances. He was "not only fighting the boy but his whole family." In the meantime another plaintiff had come forward. The university, on advice of counsel, was disinclined, however, to accept any new applicants until the U.S. Supreme Court settled the matter. Given the turmoil within those hallowed marble halls as 1954 opened, it might not be soon.

The re-argument of the five segregation cases in that Court originally scheduled for October, 1953, had been postponed. On September 8, Chief Justice Vinson died of a heart attack, leaving the Court headless in the midst of its deliberations regarding perhaps *the* most significant cases of the century.

Observers who believed the Court had made up its mind before the re-argument was ordered necessarily believed Vinson, in presiding over the early deliberations, must share the praise or blame for the final decision. Moreover, it had been a unanimous Vinson Court which had decided the two leading cases, *Sweatt* and *McLaurin,* that had established the atmosphere for initiating the five suits now pending in that

Court. Chief Justice Vinson had written both of them. J. Waties Waring, the dissenter on the federal court which had upheld public school segregation in South Carolina, believed Vinson would have decided these cases the way the Supreme Court finally did. But Waring didn't think the chief justice would have been enthusiastic about it. Other observers thought Vinson might have been inclined to hold public school segregation unconstitutional but that he was shaky at best and in his shakiness might have dissipated the momentum for unanimity. Felix Frankfurter regarded his chief's death as an omen, the first indication he'd ever had that "there is a god."

On September 30, 1953, President Eisenhower repaid one of his political debts and named as Vinson's successor Earl Warren, sixty-two-year-old Republican governor of California who'd run for vice president in 1948 on the ticket with Governor Thomas E. Dewey of New York and had swung the California delegation to Eisenhower at the 1952 Republican convention, even though his behavior all but destroyed any presidential ambitions Warren himself might still have nurtured. Warren's experience was political, not judicial. He had an infectious smile, but his personality, by Washington standards, was bland. No one expected much of him. "He had been hired," remarked one of his biographers later, "as the colorless manager of a team of all-stars."

On December 7, 8, and 9, 1953, the segregation cases were finally reargued in the Supreme Court. Once again the parties and the justices played to a standing-room-only house, with people lined up in the corridor waiting to get in.

The new chief justice was taken by surprise by the tenor of the arguments during this, his first, view of the participants in the segregation cases. He'd prepared for emotional appeals from the plaintiffs and cool constitutional discussions from the lawyers for the states. He found, however, the opposite to be true. Thurgood Marshall, "cold as steel," as Warren described him later, avoided all emotion and hammered home the legal arguments while John Davis not only pushed all the emotional buttons with his oratory but himself broke down once or twice and forced the Court to pause briefly while he composed himself.

During the three days of re-argument, counsel for the opposing sides of the segregation suits addressed themselves to the five specific questions asked by the Court the previous June. After exhaustive historical research, each side came to different conclusions on the meaning of the Fourteenth Amendment. The Inc. Fund lawyers agreed that Congress had intended it to abolish racial segregation as a "last vestige of slavery." The amendment, they reasoned, had envisaged the establishment of complete equality for all persons regardless of race. Equality was denied to blacks so long as their children were barred from white schools. They believed the states understood all that when they ratified the measure, and they urged immediate admission of black children to the schools of their choice.

Opposing counsel tried to convince the justices it had *not* been the intent of Congress or the states to outlaw public school segregation. As for the question of how desegregation could be accomplished, John Davis, maintaining that it couldn't, caught the mood of his colleagues when he warned the Court:

> Neither this Court nor any other court . . . can sit in the chairs of the legislature of South Carolina and mold its educational system. . . . [I]f it is found to be in its present form unacceptable, the State of South Carolina must devise the alternative. What they would do, I don't know.

He did know for certain, however, that "if the testimony is to be believed, the result would not be pleasing."

On July 20, 1953, Governor Byrnes of South Carolina, whom President Eisenhower had known since the war when Byrnes headed the Office of War Mobilization, had lunched at the White House. His presence there undoubtedly reminding the President of the 158,000 votes South Carolina Democrats had cast for the Republican in November, 1952, thanks to Byrnes's support, the governor had come to Washington to plead in the political arena his state's case for maintaining public school segregation. Byrnes was "well aware," Eisenhower wrote in his diary later, "of my belief that improvement in race relations is one of those things that will be healthy and sound only if it starts locally" and that "prejudices, even palpably unjustified prejudices" would not "succumb to compulsion." Byrnes played skillfully on the President's feelings. He brought up the potential for riots and other manifestations of racial hostility, should the Supreme Court abolish school segregation, and elaborated at some length on his opinion that southern states would immediately close their public schools. Neither consequence could have been very appealing to a first-term President.

The governor hoped, he said, the new administration would not feel "bound by the position previously taken by the Democratic administration" when the attorney general appeared in the high Court in December. He hoped further that the Department of Justice would recommend that the Court follow the half century of precedents that permitted separate but equal facilities for Negro and white children. Failing that, could the attorney general advise the Court to defer to the states' Tenth Amendment powers to regulate their own domestic affairs?

The President listened attentively, but was noncommittal. Governor Byrnes would have to go down the street to the attorney general's office when legal questions were involved.

Eisenhower had had mixed feelings about the government's participation in these arguments since Attorney General Herbert Brownell first mentioned the Court's invitation. On constitutional grounds, he didn't think the executive department ought to be involved in what he considered a judicial matter. As he saw it, the Constitution had given the President the authority to enforce what the judges said, but not a license to take a stand on every constitutional question that arose. Brownell ultimately convinced Eisenhower there was nothing constitutionally improper in either the Court's invitation or the Department of Justice's acceptance. Although Eisenhower made some contributions to the final brief, he disassociated himself from all but the legislative and legal history it contained. He wanted no part of Brownell's strongly held conviction that public school segregation was unconstitutional.

During Governor Byrnes's July, 1953, trip to Washington, he did visit Attorney General Brownell at his office. Brownell heard the governor out politely and promised to consider his request. Byrnes had one last one. Could the attorney general see his way clear to assign lawyers to the government's brief-writing who hadn't previously participated in this task, lawyers who might inject some new ideas into the discussion. Brownell replied that it seemed a reasonable enough request, but remained noncommittal.

In late November, the indefatigable Byrnes sent Eisenhower a draft of John Davis's brief for the South Carolina defendants in the school suits. The document contained a discussion of the "right of a state in the exercise of its police powers to make distinctions between people, provided such distinctions are not arbitrary and unreasonable." He still hoped the government would take the same position.

In his reply, Eisenhower remained noncommittal, deferring again to the attorney general, who, the President said, was acting "according to his own conviction and understanding."

When the government's brief was published, it bore both the signature and unmistakable style of the same Philip Elman who'd written the government's brief for the arguments the year before and once again left no doubt in anyone's mind where the nation stood:

> The Fourteenth Amendment [declared J. Lee Rankin, the assistant attorney general who actually presented it in Court] does not permit any discrimination based on race or color.
>
> The Court can find only one answer.

When these plaintiffs stood before the Supreme Court and charged that "the only reason for segregation is color, the Court must say that the Fourteenth Amendment does not permit this to happen."

On the question of what to do about it, should the Court decide to declare school segregation unconstitutional, this brief took up where Elman's previous go-slowly brief had left off and recommended sending the cases back to the lower federal courts for decisions on how, in the light of local conditions, a Supreme Court order should be enforced.

Re-argument ended at 2:42 P.M. on December 9. Once again the justices retreated into public silence as they attempted to unravel the constitutional puzzles these cases presented. For five months more they held their peace. On March 30, 1954, Justice Jackson suffered a heart attack that hospitalized him.

That spring Eisenhower invited South Carolina's chief counsel to one of his White House stag parties, seating him within speaking distance of Chief Justice Warren and regaling Warren during dinner with stories of what a great man Davis was. As the President and his guests adjourned to another room for after-dinner coffee and brandy, Eisenhower took Warren's arm and spoke of the growing fears among his southern friends of what Warren's Court was going to do. "These people are not bad people," the President told the Chief Justice. "All they are concerned about is to see that their sweet little girls are not required to sit in school alongside some big overgrown Negroes."

When John McDonogh, the millionaire who'd left a good part of his fortune to the city of New Orleans for a public school system, died in 1850, he'd asked in his will that local schoolchildren honor his memory each year with gifts of flowers. In 1898 a bust of McDonogh on a pedestal, with the figure of a boy and girl reaching toward it in gratitude, was unveiled in Lafayette Square. Year after year, the children were bused in on the first Friday in May to lay wreaths at McDonogh's feet while bands played and the mayor gave keys to the city to each school's delegation. White children went first, black children went last, usually following a long wait under the hot May sun.

Until May, 1954.

That year black parent-teacher organizations and other community groups protested on the grounds that the wait was humiliating for black children and reinforced the notion of white superiority. Black parents were persuaded to keep their children home.

The success of the boycott, however—the exhilaration from the rare display of black solidarity, the pain caused in other quarters when only 34 of the 32,000 black children enrolled in the public schools showed up at the monument that day and a perplexed Mayor Morrison stood on the steps of

City Hall, a bunch of unclaimed keys in his hand—was almost immediately submerged in the news that came from Washington three days later.

On May 17, 1954—the date, one day short of the fifty-eighth anniversary of *Plessy* v. *Ferguson,* could hardly have been an accident—Chief Justice Earl Warren announced the U.S. Supreme Court's decision in the five segregation cases. There had been no prior warning. Only the presence of Justice Jackson, who'd left his hospital bed to sit with his brethren for the occasion, had hinted that something important was about to happen.

In exile in New York for his betrayal of white South Carolina, former federal judge J. Waties Waring had had a "little hunch" this might be the day, and he'd spent the morning making notes in case the press wanted a comment from him. Shortly after noon the phone rang. An excited Henry Moon, NAACP public relations chief, was on the line. He wanted the judge to know: it was indeed the day. Moon himself was listening to Washington over the telephone. Waring and Moon called back and forth for a few minutes, then a radio newsbreak told Waring all he needed to know: racial segregation in America's public schools was unconstitutional.

The time was 12 noon on May 17, 1954, ninety-one years after Lincoln issued the Emancipation Proclamation, eighty-six years after the states ratified the Fourteenth Amendment, and fifty-eight years after Henry Billings Brown announced the U.S. Supreme Court's decision in *Plessy* v. *Ferguson.* It had taken all those years to turn the freedman into a legally free man, to rededicate America to the ideals of its Constitution, to write at last the death warrant for Jim Crow. This day broke the twentieth century into two parts, leaving behind the tired and worn shibboleths of race and making way for a second Reconstruction based on an equality of opportunity not often seen previously on these shores. If only America was equal to the task.

The chief justice himself had written the Court's opinion, which was called *Brown* v. *Board of Education of Topeka*—little Linda Brown's suit had been the first of the five to reach the Court. In a thirty-minute recital remarkable for its dispassion, his nontechnical but nonetheless austere language belying the turmoil he knew would ultimately surface, he had built premise upon premise, down-playing the formidable body of constitutional precedents, the 157 cases that had been decided on the basis of separate but equal since *Plessy,* and relying on the data and conclusions of the Kenneth Clarks, until he arrived safely at his destination:

Does segregation [he asked rhetorically] of children in public schools solely on the basis of race, even though the physical facilities may be

> equal, deprive the children of the minority group of equal educational
> opportunities?

He answered for all of the eight justices who flanked him on the bench:

> We believe that it does.

But it wasn't the disparities in educational costs or teaching loads or
quality of the textbooks that had counted in the justices' decision, it was
what the black Creole newspaper editor and teacher Paul Trévigne had
complained of nearly eighty years before:

> To separate [minority children] from others of similar age and qualifi-
> cations solely because of their race generates a feeling of inferiority
> as to their status in the community that may affect their hearts and
> minds in a way unlikely ever to be undone.

He concluded with the Court's final declaration, eloquent in its simplic-
ity:

> [I]n the field of public education the doctrine of separate but equal
> has no place. Separate educational facilities are inherently unequal.

Some years later, former judge Waring and Chief Justice Warren met
in New York City. They chatted awhile, then Waring, laughing, said: "I
felt greatly relieved when you decided the Clarendon School case. I'd
been very lonely up to that time."

"Well," the Chief Justice replied, "you had to do it the hard way."

In his opinion for the Court, Warren had, in effect, given the justices'
answer to the first three questions they had asked counsel the previous
June. He had not, however, answered the last two, the ones involving
how the Court could/should/would enforce its strong words. Here the
justices were still unsure of themselves, and they invited counsel in all
the cases to return later to further elaborate on this complex and potentially terrifying question.

Never mind. As of May 17, 1954, Jim Crow, *Plessy,* and separate-but-
equal were dead. Only the funeral rites remained. Louis Martinet,
Rodolphe Desdunes, Paul Trévigne, John Marshall Harlan, triumphant at
last, their cause vindicated.

John Davis immediately wrote the Clarendon County, South Carolina, school board's lawyer: "We have met the enemy and we are
theirs."

There was jubilation that night in the New York apartment of the J. Waties Warings. There was whiskey set out in the little dinette and plenty of ice and water to wash it down. People began to drop in about eight. Henry Moon came. Alan Paton, the South African writer and protester against apartheid in his own country, was the first to arrive and the last to leave. He even made a little speech, but for Paton as well as for others there, what made the occasion "unforgettable" was a short talk by Walter White, executive secretary of the NAACP. It was, as Paton described it later, "full of pride, joy, humility, and controlled emotion . . . pride and joy in being," as Paton could not be, "the citizen of a country that had justified his long, deep, and at times one must admit undeserved devotion."

White began by saying he hadn't expected the Court's decision that day, but, like Waring, he suddenly "had a feeling. . . . And there was a sort of funny quiver inside." As he talked informally to the roomful of friends that night, he recollected the cases and courts, the legal stalwarts and the plaintiffs, some of whom had risked so much but still stood firm. He paid tribute to John Marshall Harlan's *Plessy* dissent, to J. Waties Waring's steadfastness a century and a half later, and even to those unidentified justices who'd been reluctant to join the Court's opinion that day but had ultimately found the inner resources to do it. And he concluded that

[W]e together have created a miracle.

Walter White was proud and full of joy, just as Alan Paton had said, but he was nobody's fool. He knew as well as anyone in that room that May 17, 1954, was not an end, only another beginning.

CHAPTER 11

Rebel Yell

O n the night of May 17, 1954, as the white and black populations of seventeen states and the District of Columbia stretching in an arc from Delaware to Texas, all their schools segregated by law, wondered what tomorrow would bring, Bonnie Wisdom gave a forty-ninth birthday party for her husband John, President Eisenhower's Louisiana campaign manager in 1952, one of the founding partners at a small but prestigious New Orleans law firm, Wisdom and Stone. The Wisdoms still lived in the elegant Greek Revival house on First Street in the Garden District with its lacy cast-iron railing around the balconies, and the tour buses still stopped in front, the guides still pointing out that there lived the fellow who'd made Eisenhower president.

Both Wisdoms were old Louisiana and New Orleans, members of that caste that rarely, except for birth, marriage, and death announcements, has its photographs in the newspaper. Bonnie's credentials were perhaps even more impressive than her husband's. She'd grown up on thirty thousand acres of sugarcane in La Fourche Parish. Her great grandfather, George Matthews, had been chief justice of the Louisiana supreme court. In 1836, he'd astonished a good many Louisianans when he'd refused to order the re-enslavement of a local bondwoman who'd been taken to France by her owner, then returned to Louisiana. "Being free for one moment in France," he'd said in his court opinion, "it was not in the power of her former owner to reduce her to slavery again." His conclusion was well enough remembered that Justice Benjamin R. Curtis quoted it two decades later in his dissent to the U.S. Supreme Court's declaration that the slave Dred Scott, despite his brief sojourn in free territory, was still a slave.

John Wisdom's ancestors had come to New Orleans in the 1840s via Virginia and Kentucky. His father, Mortimer Norton Wisdom, had been a prominent local insurance executive and cotton broker who'd made and lost several fortunes and dabbled in politics. John had grown up in the New Orleans elite's world of racially segregated private schools: Isadore Newman High School, from which he went on to his father's alma mater Washington and Lee at Lexington, Virginia, where southern gentlemen were in the habit of educating their sons, and Tulane Law School, where his grandfather had been a member of the first graduating class. He belonged to the exclusive Boston and Louisiana clubs, and several old-line Carnival organizations despite his few drops of Jewish blood on his mother's side. He attended high church, Christ Church Cathedral (Episcopal), and he moved comfortably and effortlessly in the highest levels of New Orleans society. In the noblesse oblige tradition, he also gave generously of his energies to various local charitable organizations. He described himself as "probably liberal generally," but not "conspicuously so." If Louis Auchincloss had written about upper-class New Orleanians instead of upper-class New Yorkers, it was the Wisdoms and their friends whose lives he would have chronicled.

John Minor Wisdom was a fully credentialed, card-carrying white southerner. There was, however, one important issue on which he departed radically from the majority of his fellows. He believed that racial segregation was "plain wrong ... dead wrong. Slavery was dead wrong—and we're paying the price of slavery. And segregation is just a refined version, in some places, of slavery."

The guests at Wisdom's birthday party that warm and rainless evening in May, 1954, shared his southern heritage and traveled in the same high echelons of local society. Nearly all had had forebears who'd fought in 1874 with the White League at the Battle of Liberty Place to unseat the biracial Reconstruction government. Wisdom's own father, a private in the Crescent City White League, had been among the street fighters.

All of the guests had been raised in a strictly segregated society, and Wisdom knew for certain that not all shared his sentiments on racial matters. Nonetheless the mood that night was confident if sober. No one, least of all the Wisdoms, who'd discussed the recent court cases and recognized the inevitability of the Supreme Court's announcement that day, had been surprised by it. When the conversation turned in that direction, no one even raised an eyebrow. The "general consensus" of these establishment New Orleanians, old friends whose talk flowed uninhibited as they sat around the Wisdoms' drawing room that evening, was that in their city at least, there would be a "peaceful transition." No one predicted delaying tactics, obstruction, or violence. Wisdom himself at the time, though he came to think otherwise later, believed it had been a "good idea" for the Court to "postpone" fashioning the remedy for segregation for a while. The deferment, he'd decided, would provide "extra time in which to make adjustments."

Their confidence couldn't have been more misplaced or their assessments of their city and region more wrong. Since the end of World War II in 1945 and the return of black soldiers from a war in which only the top sergeant was entitled to a superiority complex to the still segregated society where a black officer was still a "nigger," the black's "place" had been changing, a millimeter at a time, as black voters, university students, jury members, athletes, and railroad car passengers nudged whites to move over and share the space. The U.S. Supreme Court's decision in *Brown* v. *Board of Education,* white southerners feared, held the potential for pushing them completely off balance.

Those six little words—"Separate educational facilities are inherently unequal"—had now flashed the news around the earth that long-held and deeply cherished living patterns were in mortal danger in the American South, a world its white residents had imagined was as firmly implanted as America's rocks, rills, and templed hills. The high Court's ruling was received by white southerners, with nearly the same fury that had greeted Union General William Tecumseh Sherman's slash-and-burn march across Georgia the century before.

There were, of course, many Souths. The drawing rooms of aristocratic New Orleans and the magnolia-scented mansions of Charleston, the posh hotels of Miami and the steel mills of Birmingham belonged to the same family of states as the small-town grocery stores of the coppertone Louisiana timber country, the hillbilly cabins of the Ozarks, the sharecroppers' shanties in the cotton-rich delta lands and the railroad flats of Atlanta.

There was also one South. It had been created by slavery, cemented by secession, and recreated by post–Civil War adversity. The lords of the mansions, the shopkeepers behind their counters, and the sunburned farmers astride their tractors had been bound together by timeless certainties of race, pride of place, and a combative spirit that often masked the fears, the shame, the guilt, and embarrassment connected with human oppression.

They didn't agree on much, these aristocrats and merchants and dirt farmers. But they voted the Democratic ticket, and they stood together in their low opinion of the blacks who lived among them.

When they worried out loud about what the Supreme Court had just done to them, they didn't express concern that better educated blacks were potential competitors in the labor market or that black voters threatened the political status quo. The ordinary southerner didn't usually come right out and say he or she believed blacks were intellectually inferior, although references to blacks often implied childlike natures, buffoons at best, and white employers weren't above discussing black household servants as they passed the carrots around the dinner table, as if they didn't really exist. What concerned them most about the Supreme Court's ruling on the schools were sex, syphilis, and the disruption of a social system that they thought satisfied everybody, black as well as white.

The biggest, meanest bogeyman of them all was sex. The fear of polluting whiteness with blackness, symbol, as Tom Wicker put it in *A Time to Die,* "of the evil in man and nature, the blackness of life . . . that dark side a human senses in himself, admit it or not. White fear was the fear of blackness, the fear of the worst in man and oneself." Wicker explained slavery as a way of holding "the evil in mankind" in check.

Segregation, slavery's successor, kept it not in check but, second best, out of reach and often out of sight. Race mixing in the public schools, which white southerners were convinced would lead, when all the controls had snapped, to interracial marriage, a mulatto South, would transfer the darkness to white skins and white souls.

Look magazine's national affairs editor William Atwood heard parent after parent voice the fear that sooner or later, "some Negro boy will be walking his daughter home from school, staying for supper, taking her to the movies . . . and then your southern friend asks you the inevitable, clinching question, 'Would *you* want your daughter to marry a Nigra?'" Atwood called the driving white concern "sexual neurosis."

There were other fears, too. When white southerners reflected on racial desegregation in the public schools, they didn't focus on clean, scrubbed, beribboned children like Ruby Bridges poised on the brink of her great educational adventure in her best dress. Not all of them could recite the statistics, but many of them could describe in plain English what Archibald G. Robertson, one of the legal team who'd argued the Virginia segregation case before the Supreme Court had told the justices: "Negroes constitute 22 percent of the population of Virginia, but 78 percent of all cases of syphilis and 83 percent of all cases of gonorrhea. . . . Of course the incidence of disease and illegitimacy is just a drop in the bucket compared to the promiscuity; the white parents at this time will not appropriate the money to put their children among other children with that sort of background."

Southerners never tired of telling anyone who'd listen that, as they'd told the Swedish social scientist Gunnar Myrdal, their "Negroes are happiest among themselves." A friend of Georgian Louis Lomax once told him, "I talked to my cook; she is a sweet old Nigra woman who has been with us for years and she told me she didn't want her grandchildren going to school with white children." Lomax claimed he never met a white man, North or South, whose cook wanted to integrate anything.

Dan Seward, a white peanut grower in rural Virginia, once described an old employee to the author William Styron: "We have a wonderful relationship, that Negro and myself. By God, I'd die for the Negro and he knows it, and he'd do the same for me. But Ernest doesn't want to sit down at my table, here in this house, and have supper with me—and he wouldn't want me in *his* house. And Ernest's got kids like I do, and he doesn't want them to go to school with my Bobby, any more than Bobby wants to go to school with *his* kids." Bobby, in fact, had spread a banner across an entire wall of his room.

TWO . . . FOUR . . . SIX . . . EIGHT!
WE DON'T WANT TO INTEGRATE!

was what it said.

Lillian Smith, southern author and early white spokeswoman for racial equality, summed up the regional mystique in *Killers of the Dream:*

We southerners learned our . . . lessons too well.

I do not think our mothers were often aware that they were teaching us lessons. . . .

We were taught to love God, to love our white skin, and to believe in the sanctity of both.

By the time we were five years old we had learned, without hearing the words, that . . . segregation is right. . . . [W]e believed God . . . had made the rules concerning . . . Him and our parents . . . and Negroes.

These were our first lessons. . . . They were taught us by our mother's voice, memorized with her love, patted into our lives as she rocked us to sleep or fed us.

Over the years, Smith had been constantly reminded that her white skin was her "glory" and the "source of [her] strength and pride." Whiteness, she was told, was "a symbol of purity and excellence," and she was admonished to remember that her "white skin proves that you are better than all other people on this earth."

This was the South that bonded once again in a common cause after May 17, 1954, reacting to the federal insult in the way in which southerners were most practiced: red hot defiance. "Never!" the extremists yelled, their voices strident. They clenched their fists as they pounded on the lecterns in the legislature. They waved their arms as they damned the Supreme Court at county fairs that election summer. And the voices of moderation fell silent, leaving the way open for the hard-core opposition to take charge.

"The Court expected some resistance from the South," said Earl Warren. "But I doubt if any of us expected as much as we got."

Newspaper editors in the border states, whose schools would be the first to open their doors to black children in obedience to the Supreme Court's orders, in general supported the first of the Court's desegregation rulings. If they weren't enthusiastic, they weren't rabble-rousing, either. But they were soon drowned out by papers lower down in the South, papers like the Jackson, Mississippi, *Daily News,* which added appreciably to the atmospheric pressures with its banner headline "Blood on the Marble Steps," its oath that Mississippi could not and would not even "try to abide by such a decision," and its accusation that the inescapable violence waiting down the road was on the head of the U.S. Supreme Court.

In Washington, the President called together the three District of Columbia commissioners, the administrators of the federal enclave's Congress-controlled government at the time, and told them that the District, which as a party to one of the five school segregation cases before the Supreme Court had opposed desegregation, should now take the lead in desegregating its public schools. As the seat of the American government, Eisenhower said, Washington should be the "showpiece" of the nation.

He had already had asked his secretary of labor, Martin P. Durkin, to announce that contracts issued by the District of Columbia would contain clauses barring racial discrimination in employment and had put one of his top aides in charge of overseeing desegregation in the military. He had in mind to also desegregate veterans' hospitals and other installations where federal money was spent.

But beyond that he could not or would not go. Buffeted by his own contradictory beliefs, he was ambivalent on the matter of the nation's public schools. On the one hand, he had a commitment to states' rights as firm as a Dixiecrat's, which he'd amply demonstrated during the 1952 campaign, plus an abiding feeling that the "hearts of men" could not be changed by law or judicial fiat.

On the other hand, he was convinced that racial discrimination was "morally wrong"; he was confident the South was on its way to solving its racial problems, and he pointed to the recent desegregation of public universities in no fewer than twelve border and southern states. Such a process, he realized, was "painfully slow," probably "too slow to fit the aspiration of many Negroes," but he thought it would "insure orderly integration."

He stated categorically in his memoirs that he did in fact approve the Supreme Court's decision in *Brown* v. *Board of Education,* but if he did, he was mighty quiet about it. In his public pronouncements, he remained aloof from the struggle over the public schools for the entire eight years of his presidency.

In addition to meeting with the District of Columbia commissioners following announcement of *Brown,* as it soon was abbreviated, Eisenhower also met with his chief advisers, Sherman Adams and Jim Hagerty, to discuss the implications of what the Supreme Court had done and to prepare for the inevitable press conference questions. He'd joked with Attorney General Brownell about it, venturing the hope that the Court would hold the case over until another president's administration, then had added more seriously, "I don't know where I stand, but I think I stand that the best interests of the United States demand an answer in keeping with past decisions."

He seemed to think that the justices had jumped the gun. He was concerned, he told Adams and Hagerty that day, that some of the most embittered of the southern states might well carry out their officials' threats to shut down their public school systems, and he feared for the children of both races who would be trapped in dungeons of unlearning.

He didn't really want to discuss *Brown* publicly at all. He didn't like venturing into the risky business of approving or disapproving Supreme Court decisions, a practice, he felt, that had the potential to "lower the dignity of government, and . . . in the long run be hurtful."

His generation didn't discuss matters of race in public, and the President wasn't comfortable doing it. He liked to talk about "inalienable rights" and maintaining "justice and freedom," but he was reluctant to apply them to specific situations. He told Adams and Hagerty that day that if he was asked about *Brown* at his next press conference he would talk about his own constitutional powers as simply as possible, and, he hoped, with finality.

Just two days after *Brown,* when Harry Dent of South Carolina, a reporter for the Columbia *State and Record,* and later one of President Richard Nixon's chief advisers for Republican southern strategy, asked Eisenhower whether he had "any advice to give the South as to just how to react to this recent Supreme Court decision banning segregation," the President replied:

> Not in the slightest. I thought that Governor Byrnes made a very fine statement when he said, "Let's be calm and let's be reasonable and let's look this thing in the face."
>
> The Supreme Court has spoken and I am sworn to uphold the constitutional processes in this country; and I will obey.

Chief Justice Warren, who needed every bit of support he could salvage for his Court, went to his grave twenty years later still believing that had Eisenhower, one of the most popular presidents in living memory, spoken out in favor of the Supreme Court's ruling in *Brown,* had urged "every good citizen to help rectify more than eighty years of wrongdoing by honoring that decision," resistance to it would have been substantially less, and "we would have been relieved . . . of many of the racial problems which have continued to plague us."

But the President was silent, and Americans heard instead the voices of resentment and resistance, the unapologetically shrill tirades of men like Mississippi's James O. Eastland, about to open his campaign for a third term in the United States Senate, warning,

> I know that southern people, by and large, will neither recognize, abide by nor comply with this decision. We are expected to remain docile while the pure blood of the South is mongrelized.

They heard Georgia's governor Herman Talmadge express his outrage by quoting President Andrew Jackson's alleged wrathful comment on the U.S. Supreme Court's 1832 decision holding his—Talmadge's—state's Indian land laws unconstitutional: "'Well, John Marshall has made his decision, now let him enforce it.'"

Within hours after the Court announced *Brown,* Talmadge had his attorney general, Eugene Cook, in touch with his counterparts in the other sixteen states whose schools were racially segregated by law. Not one of them, Cook found, intended to submit docilely to the ruling, but were already devising legal tactics to maintain segregation in their states' schools. These were the men who over the following decade would draft the laws of resistance for their legislatures and defend their schools' policies of evasion in the courts. This century's Defenders of the Faith.

Compared to the incendiary reactions to *Brown* in other areas of the South, Louisiana and New Orleans responded quietly and calmly. Governor Kennon, his states' rights mantra abandoned for the moment, saw no cause for alarm, but took a wait-and-see position:

> The Louisiana legislature and the local school boards have already done much to provide new school facilities. No school board in Louisiana is faced with a new emergency today. We have ample time to work out the problem.

Louisiana State University President Troy Middleton, whose institution was still in the courts trying to keep young A. P. Tureaud out, refused to comment. State Superintendent of Education Shelby Jackson, whose department oversaw the schooling of Louisiana's 325,000 white and 200,000 black children, also declined to comment.

The New Orleans newspapers, more sad than angry at this point, a subdued resentment substituting for the open defiance all around them, actually urged compliance. The *Times-Picayune,* its history of racial conservatism notwithstanding, predicted "considerable turmoil" but reluctantly advised southerners, despite their "disappointment and frustration," to

> shoulder the burden the court has placed upon them and work soberly to redirect their educational effort along lines that will be adaptable to all and at the same time will preserve the vitality.

The *Item* spoke similarly, warning its readers that the court's decision, "however unpopular,"

> is the law of the land and must be complied with. . . . Deep emotions, it is true, are stirred. . . . But wisdom calls for calmness and moderation, for reflection, and discussion of ways best to live with the decision.

Clarence Scheps, president now of the Orleans Parish school board, the target of Oliver Bush's two-year-old suit that had been hanging in limbo pending the Supreme Court's decision in the other segregation cases, wanted time to study the high court's opinion before he discussed the board's position. His first impression, however, indicated that *Brown* would "have no immediate effect on the New Orleans public school system." He thought "several years" might elapse before there was any "change in our local situation."

The Kansas-born superintendent of the city's schools, James F. Redmond, who'd come from the Chicago school system only the year before, bringing a reputation as a crackerjack administrator, also wanted time to study *Brown* before he commented. He hoped for directional signals from the state legislature.

Sam Rosenberg, a wiry little civic-minded local lawyer with an elfin way of working backstage, had been hired two years before by the school board as general counsel. The very day the Supreme Court announced its decision in *Brown,* he telegraphed the clerk of the Court to request a copy of the full decision. After reading it carefully with his trained lawyer's eyes, he got in touch with the senior Tureaud and persuaded him to hold back the Bush suit until the high Court announced its prescription for remedying segregation in the schools.

The spiritual leader of Catholic New Orleans, Archbishop Rummel, had been pulling away from racial segregation for some time, and when in mid-February of 1951, he'd seemed to sail dangerously close to desegregating local parochial schools, he'd scared the living daylights out of those New Orleanians who'd looked to them as refuges should the worst happen in the public institutions. In 1954, the fearful got a respite. Rummel didn't take that next step as might have been expected following *Brown.* He did, however, hint that it was only a matter of time. His school superintendent, Monsignor Henry Bezou, reacted to *Brown* with a long and warm approval and an earnest expression of anticipation that "integration may prove to be a pattern for better and more enlightened relationships on all sides in the days that lie ahead."

Louisiana's was the only southern state legislature in session when *Brown* was announced, although Governor Byrnes planned to call South Carolina's into extraordinary session within days, and Georgia's, in a previous session, had inserted a provision in the most recent appropriations bill that all state funds would be cut from any school that desegregated. Lawmakers all over the South soon seized the issue and rode it like oil sheiks on flying carpets.

Brown gave the members of the Louisiana legislature, which was dominated at the time by die-hard segregationists from the northern part of the state, every cause for alarm, and in their anxiety, their trumpets of defiance effectively silenced those elements that might have, as the *New Orleans Item* had advised, suppressed their emotions and reflected calmly on the future they faced to discover "ways best to live with the decision." The lawmakers had to accomplish their aims without Governor Kennon's help; he was hoping for a federal court appointment, Eisenhower's expression of gratitude for the Democrat's assistance in 1952, and it would hardly do to publicly oppose the highest federal Court of them all. He did, however, without hesitation sign the bills that came out of the legislature.

First, the lawmakers censured the U.S. Supreme Court for its "unwarranted and unprecedented usurpation of power." Two of the three dissenters in the legislature lost their seats two years later.

The legislators followed up the resolution with the first of 131 measures they were to pass opposing desegregation over the next decade—more than any other southern legislature—a statute requiring all public schools to remain segregated and withholding funds and accreditation from any school that defied the ban. It effectively rendered the local school boards powerless, caught between state and federal orders.

Then they passed the first of several so-called pupil placement laws, which established elaborate criteria for the transfer of students from one school to another, carefully excluding race as one of them, and leaving the decisions to local school authorities. Surviving constitutional tests longer than other measures, it proved to be the most popular with school boards throughout the South and remained on the books to plague black plaintiffs by delaying, if it couldn't entirely stop, school desegregation.

They tied up the package with a constitutional amendment specifying that all "public elementary and secondary schools . . . shall be operated separately for white and colored children." The constitution of 1921, on which the state was still operating, already required racially segregated schools; to save it from the inevitable legal challenge, the new amendment's main premise was shifted from racial considerations to promotion and protection of "public health, morals, better education, and the peace and good order of the state." That is, they slipped it out from under the Fourteenth Amendment's prohibition of racial discrimination by the state and based it on the state's police power, the term adopted for that vague and still controversial plethora of unenumerated powers reserved to the states by the Tenth Amendment to the Constitution. The requirement, the legislators were careful to emphasize, the commands of the troublesome Fourteenth Amendment pounding in their heads, was decided "not because of race." Submitted later to the voters, the lawmakers could congratulate themselves on their accurate assessment of the public's opinion of *Brown*. It passed 217,992 to 46,929, a ratio of nearly five to one. Leander Perez's Plaquemine Parish signed in with an astonishing margin of forty-eight to one.

By then the lawmakers were running out of steam. The Supreme Court not yet having issued final directives, the legislature had no more specific targets to shoot at just now. They'd gone about as far as they could go, at least for the moment.

It wasn't far enough for Leander Perez, who, like many racial conservatives, as the cold war against the Soviet Union droned on through the 1950s, had discovered that the civil rights movement, which had in fact the support of the American Communist Party, could be equated with what he and they believed was an international Communist conspiracy to weaken the United States by mixing what they considered inferior black genes with superior white genes. As a political issue it had sex appeal. Its advocates believed it held the potential to attract support from outside the South, to nationalize the opposition to civil rights, which was giving the South a bad name. Which was the way Perez looked at Brown: "nothing more or less than a fellow-traveler blank check to the pro-Communist decrees for forced racial integration, regimentation and the ultimate amalgamation of the American people to our certain destruction and, in the end, the surrender to the worldwide communist conspiracy." Perez devised a comprehensive plan to phase out and ultimately abolish the state's entire public school system by handing it over to private concerns controlled by local school boards. Aside from the bill's having been hastily drafted and full of legal holes, Perez's proposal was a little too bold for the lawmakers at this juncture—although it was no more daring than what the governors of Georgia and South Carolina had been talking about for years—and they took no action on it.

What Perez did bring out of that noisy session of the legislature was formation of the influential Joint Legislative Committee to Maintain Segregation, which led the legislature's opposition to *Brown* for nearly a decade. Its sole mission was to obstruct desegregation of the state's public schools, and its power extended to authority to inspect state government and local school board records.

The committee was composed of four state senators and five members of the state house of representatives, but its chairman was the man to watch. His name was William M. Rainach. He told nearly everyone he met to "call me Willie," and many did. He came from Summerfield in Claiborne Parish, a northern citadel of staunch segregationists, and he wore wide ties with Confederate flags emblazoned on them.

He was forty-two years old in 1954. He'd been in politics for seventeen years, the legislature for six, but hadn't yet found an issue he could ride to higher office. Race, however, turned out to be the one. He saw his power surge, as the hundreds of fan letters cheering on his dogged resistance to *Brown* came in from Louisianans in all parishes, all walks of life, some scribbled in pencil, others neatly written in ink. They soon set him thinking about being governor.

On the Joint Legislative Committee to Maintain Segregation, Rainach and Perez teamed up: two burn-the-house-down mind-sets united in a common purpose. They were "Willie" and "Judge Perez" to each other.

Perez, as he preferred it, worked behind the scenes, devising strategy and drafting legislation. Rainach, who wasn't a lawyer, hit the campaign trail, first drumming up support for the constitutional amendment the legislature had just passed and calling the NAACP names—"arrogant, alien" . . . "hellbent to impose a foreign system of life that creates strife and confusion"—then trying to cleanse Louisiana of the organization's influence completely: protesting the presence of books by black writers such as Richard Wright and Langston Hughes on public library shelves, lecturing state education Superintendent Shelby Jackson on the content of public school textbooks, monitoring the content of national magazines circulating in the South, and hectoring the editors of those he found wanting in sympathy for the white South. Earl Long, when he was governor of Louisiana, used to say that Rainach would deliver one of his racial tirades, then go home, "get up on his front porch, take off his shoes, wash his feet, look at the moon and get close to God."

Long's sarcasm notwithstanding, Louisiana, along with most of her southern sister states, was ripe for resistance in the summer and fall of 1954, a near-perfect culture in which to grow racial dissension. Taking advantage of the climate, and meeting no opposition, not from the President himself, not from local community leaders, not from rank-and-file white Louisianans, Perez and Rainach welcomed the development of the Citizens' Council movement born that summer in neighboring Mississippi, and they prepared to import it, promote it, and assume its leadership.

Citizens' Councils were the white South's grassroots solution to the race problems *Brown* promised, direct descendants of the White Leagues that had created racial havoc during the last decades of the nineteenth century and watered down versions of the Ku Klux Klan, though the contemporary vigilantes professed to abhor violence and to adhere to strictly legal tactics, boycotts instead of bullwhips.

They were the brainchild of a Lawrenceville- and Yale-educated, aristocratic-looking local circuit judge in Senator Eastland's Sunflower County, Mississippi, Tom Pickens Brady (rhymes with laddie and may originally have been spelled B-r-a-d-d-i-e). Days after *Brown* was handed down, Brady had been prevailed upon by members of his audiences, whom he'd lectured on the dire future consequences of the ruling, to put his speech into writing. Working furiously for ten days, Brady readied for immediate publication what amounted to a segregationist's manifesto, a little paperback book entitled *Black Monday* and subtitled *Segregation or Amalgamation . . . America Has Its Choice.* It put into words what a lot of southern whites were feeling.

In the plainest possible language—Brady said later that in 1954 "an appeal was needed in words of one syllable"—and lacking even a pretense of civility, he urged every "patriotic American" to "condemn" *Brown* and "to do all that he can to see that it is reversed." He outlined in some detail his understanding of racial origins, which he based on what he called scientific evidence, and concluded that blacks had missed out on so many steps in their evolution that they were, in mid-twentieth century, decidedly inferior beings unfit to exercise the rights, privileges, and responsibilities of citizenship in a democracy. Blacks had, Brady declared, been "handcuffed by heredity" and, egged on by the Communists who recognized that a "mongrelized race is an ignorant, weak, and easily conquered" one, were seeking amalgamation with the white race as a way to mix the genes and improve their mental capacities. They had found, he said, a convenient and easily persuaded ally in the United States Supreme Court, or what Brady called the "new Sociological Supreme Court."

In that Court's application of the controversial Fourteenth Amendment to the federal Constitution, which Brady described as "filled with dynamite," it had "usurp[ed] the seats" of the state legislatures and taken over "the duties of the Congress." In so doing, it had handed down an "erroneous decision which breaks all long-established rules of law, violates the principles of stare decisis, and adopts sociological assertions instead of laws." The country must not submit "blindly."

When Brady looked into the future he saw young blacks, "the veterans, who under the Truman and Eisenhower Administration and in the armed services drank deep from the flagon of non-segregation . . . who were attended by white nurses in hospitals, who were in barracks with white men," yearning to "again sample its flavor in other phases of our national life." Playing on whites' deepest ingrained fears, he foresaw some "young Negro schoolboy, or veteran . . . who considers the counsel of his elders archaic perform[ing] an obscene act, or mak[ing] an obscene remark, or a violent overture or assault upon some white girl" and rationalizing his behavior in the Supreme Court's abolition of racial segregation in the public schools. Rather than concluding *Brown* with the traditional "it is so ordered," Brady said, that "myopic tribunal" ought to have ended with "*Après nous le deluge.*"

In conclusion he offered a number of suggestions by which Americans, particularly southerners, might ameliorate the ruling's effects: such practical measures as creation of a separate state into which blacks could be herded, popular election of Supreme Court justices and the attorney general, amendment of all state constitutions to insure separation of the races in the public schools, or, if all else failed, replacement of the public systems with private education. Above all, the situation called for the total destruction of socialist and Communist ideas and programs in America and reestablishment of the patriotic values on which America was founded. It was, Brady said, alien Communist principles that had brought on the racial revolution that culminated in *Brown,* and it was these that had to be exorcized if national calamity was to be averted.

Of all Brady's suggestions, his proposal for the organization in every southern state of resistance organizations made the biggest splash. Within a month, a group of 75 to 100 Mississippians had organized the Indianola Citizens' Council (Indianola was the seat of Sunflower County). Within a year this little nucleus of passionate segregationists had grown into an area-wide apparatus claiming 300,000 members and inspiring a disparate cluster of American states to unified action. Governors and gubernatorial hopefuls joined. So did state legislators and the mayors of countless little southern towns. Businessmen, professional men, sat alongside rank-and-file southerners.

In April of 1955, Willie Rainach established Louisiana's first Citizens' Council in Homer, seat of his native Claiborne Parish. By January, 1956, he had formed the Association of Citizens' Councils from thirteen parish units and installed himself as president. By the first anniversary of the birth of Citizens' Councils in Louisiana, twenty-eight of the state's sixty-four parishes had units, and claimed 75,000 to 100,000 members.

Dignified by the memberships of leading local politicians and professional men, the Citizens' Council movement appealed to the no-longer-latent fears of whites throughout the South and became a formidable force in the southern crusade to preserve segregation and states' rights. At first the councils were content to isolate the few liberals and moderates left and to instill the fear of God in blacks who might have had some notion of claiming rights under *Brown*. Once they got up a full head of steam, however, they were satisfied with no less than entirely silencing their opposition, including the NAACP, which they set out to burn to the ground.

These were the people who set the tone and mood of the southern white community over the next decade. When, toward the close of the decade, their numbers began to drop, their voices only grew louder and shriller.

It was not the climate anticipated that sunny day back in May when A. P. Tureaud had crowed that the date would "mark the turning point in world events," and Thurgood Marshall was "so happy [he] was numb." Despite the early restraint shown by its press and school officials, New Orleans, as 1954 inched toward 1955, gave off some clear signals about how its white population really felt.

To woo blacks away from trying to integrate the municipal golf course in City Park, the Morrison administration was hastily developing separate recreational facilities, including an eighteen-hole golf course for blacks in another part of the city. The mayor predicted it would be "one of the finest recreational areas for Negroes in the nation."

That summer, the rank and file of the City Police Mutual Benevolent

Association voted overwhelmingly (529 to 42) against admitting black officers to its membership. Blacks had served on the local police force for four years.

Emperor Haile Selassie of Ethiopia visited the city that year, raising difficult questions of protocol within the Morrison administration, which were answered much the way they might have been fifty years ago. The state department had instructed the city to treat him "normally along the lines of what he is—the head of a foreign state," and he was given a formal reception, a grand tour of the harbor, and an official dinner. Local black participation in the festivities, however, was played down as much as possible, and several white community leaders boycotted them entirely. With some difficulty, the mayor found lodging for the emperor and his staff at the posh Roosevelt Hotel. Hotel officials, however, warned that neither he nor members of his party would be allowed in the bar or restaurants.

Outside New Orleans, the inevitable violence erupted. On July 5, a brick was thrown through the window of attorney Richard Millspaugh of Lake Charles, an active member of the local NAACP branch. "Keep Negroes where they belong," the attached note said. The next day, a brickbat was heaved through the window of Arthur V. Giron, an Opelousas teacher with no known black activist affiliations.

In Baton Rouge, representatives of a newly organized rival of the Citizens' Councils, the Southern Gentlemen, called on Governor Kennon in late August and invited him to join. The governor expressed his "sympathy" with the group's views, but declined its invitation and suggested the men offer their services to Willie Rainach's legislative committee on segregation.

Washington, D.C., and some of the border states didn't wait for judges to tell them what to do. As schoolhouse doors opened in September, 1954, less than four months after *Brown* was handed down, black and white children were going to school together in Arkansas, Delaware, Maryland, Missouri, Tennessee, and West Virginia. Not in every school in every district of these states. West Virginia, for example, had completely integrated twelve and partially integrated thirteen of its fifty-four districts, all with small black populations; eighteen districts with larger black populations were waiting, and eleven had no black pupils. The numbers in all states prophesied slow progress. But they'd made a start.

The deep South was something else. Black youngsters attempted to enroll in all-white Baton Rouge and Gretna, Louisiana, schools, but were abruptly turned away. Three states—Georgia, Mississippi, and South Carolina—had sworn to resist opening their schools to blacks even if it meant closing every one of them. And a mixed group of seven states—

Arkansas, Florida, Maryland, North Carolina, Oklahoma, Texas, and Tennessee—had asked the justices for permission to appear at the next oral argument, now scheduled to begin December 6.

Picketing by members of the National Association for Advancement of White People (NAAWP), another newborn racist group to protest *Brown,* was reported at three schools in south Baltimore. Milford, Delaware, a small generally quiet city in a rural section of the state, hovered for several days perilously close to violence, which also had been fomented by members of NAAWP. School openings in the deep South proceeded serenely and normally. No one there had even considered desegregating them that term.

As the aftermath of *Brown* transformed itself into the foreground for the upcoming arguments before the Supreme Court, the President's 1952 supporters in the South, particularly Governors Byrnes of South Carolina, Kennon of Louisiana, and Shivers of Texas, again tried to cash in some IOUs. Again they begged Eisenhower, "bombarded" him, as Attorney General Brownell put it, as they sought to keep the federal government out of these arguments. If school segregation was entirely outlawed by the Court, they warned, it would mean the shutdown of public education in the South.

Back in May, John Wisdom had hoped the time lapse between the Supreme Court's two pronouncements would mean time and opportunity for the besieged South to make "adjustments." His calculations hadn't included what was becoming more and more apparent as the segregation crisis developed. The time lapse was being used to best advantage by troublemakers and rabblerousers bent on keeping southern leadership from making those adjustments.

CHAPTER 12

"With All Deliberate Speed"

ertrude Stein once said it was whites she was worried about, not blacks: "The Negro can take care of himself. . . . It's a case of pity the poor persecutor. Whites . . . have stood still in an effort to keep the Negro down."

Full of the hope generated by *Brown I,* a clear signal, it was believed, that the nine white justices of the highest court in the land at last understood that racial segregation and the inequality prohibited by the Fourteenth Amendment were linked by indissoluble chains, blacks wasted not a day or an hour during the fifty weeks between the Court's first and second *Brown* decisions. As white resistance grew, black resolve stiffened.

While Thurgood Marshall and his staff went about the business of preparing their next round of arguments for the Supreme Court, the NAACP went about its business of preparing for the desegregation of public schools, instructing its branches in "every affected area to petition their local school boards to abolish segregation without delay." The NAACP Louisiana State Conference of Branches immediately went on a campaign to secure twenty thousand new members, a voter registration campaign to increase black voters in the state by 100,000, and legal attacks at all levels of public education. Inspired by Monsignor Bezou's post-*Brown* enthusiasm, A. P. Tureaud planned to work on New Orleans's parochial schools to desegregate by the following fall.

Confident that the Supreme Court would see the actual school desegregation his way, Thurgood Marshall stirred up the delegates to the NAACP's annual meeting in Dallas in July with his promise/threat to "negotiate as long as there is substantial evidence of good faith on the part of the school authorities. By September, 1955, if a school board has not been able to integrate but its good faith is unquestioned . . . we would continue negotiations." But—and it was a big "but" that he added—

> if we are then convinced that a school board will not follow the law and that there is no longer good faith involved, we will petition in behalf of aggrieved parents and take the case into the courts to get the full measure of compliance.

The U.S. Supreme Court had been slightly reconstituted since its decision of the previous May. Robert Jackson, who'd left his hospital bed to sit with his brethren for the Chief Justice's announcement of *Brown,* had died of a heart attack on October 9, 1954. A month later, President Eisenhower had replaced him with John Marshall Harlan, a New York corporate lawyer and grandson of the first John Marshall Harlan, whose observation in his dissent to *Plessy* v. *Ferguson* in 1896 that "Our Constitution is color-blind" had assured his place in American constitutional history. People wondered at the time whether as a Supreme Court justice, the second Harlan's corporate connections or his blood would tell, and in the end, both did. On most matters he became known for conservatism. On matters of civil rights, he more often followed his grandfather's lead.

Southern senators delayed Harlan's confirmation for four months, until March, 1955, and the Court postponed the final *Brown* arguments originally scheduled for December, 1954, until April 11, 12, 13, and 14, 1955. Marshall and his cadre of lawyers all came back, battle weary but buoyed by their victory of the previous May: Bob Carter again representing the Browns of Topeka, Kansas, where the walls of segregation had begun to crumble; Louis Redding representing the Delaware plaintiffs, several of whom were now attending formerly all-white schools; James Nabrit and George Hayes representing black pupils in the District of Columbia, where schools were about to complete their first term on a desegregated basis, where, Nabrit volunteered, the transition had been nothing short of "amazing" over the past year; and Spottswood Robinson representing Harry Briggs of Clarendon County, South Carolina, the state that, along with Virginia, whose plaintiffs Marshall himself was representing, had become the nerve center for southern resistance to last year's high Court ruling.

As did his Inc. Fund colleagues, Marshall urged the Court to order public school desegregation "forthwith," by which he meant the opening of the 1955 term, September, 1956, at the very latest. In reply to those who predicted the direst consequences as a result of undue haste—disturbances and upheavals not excluding bloodshed and violence—he cited not only Kansas, the District of Columbia, and Delaware as examples of school desegregation proceeding more or less serenely, clouded only by a minor confrontation in Delaware, but he reminded the justices of earlier voting rights and university desegregation cases out of which the awful prophecies never materialized. He dismissed the commonly employed objection that where tradition was so deeply entrenched a court order might not be obeyed. He was sure, he said, that

> the people in the South are no different from anybody else as to being law-abiding.

Adverse developments, he explained, would need only

> a firm hand of government to say, "We are going to desegregate." And that is it.

On the other side, from which the legal patriarch John Davis was conspicuously absent—he'd died in Charleston only a few weeks before, on March 24—the lawyers begged for time, for unspecified deadlines somewhere west of infinity. South Carolina, Virginia, they weren't Kansas or the District of Columbia or even Delaware. Archibald G. Robertson for the state of Virginia was particularly defiant, opening his argument with the flat challenge that fifty-five of his state's ninety counties had already passed resolutions indicating their opposition to "compulsory integration." He berated the justices for their preoccupation with the "emotional and psychological effects upon Negro children" while they ignored "what the emotional and psychological effects will be upon the white children." He criticized the Court's taking nearly sixty years to change its mind about *Plessy* v. *Ferguson,* then expecting a rural Virginia place like Prince Edward County where black children far outnumbered whites "to adjust itself to this revolutionary decision." If the justices had any doubt about Virginia's resolve, they had only to refer to the appendix to the state's official brief in which the work of a recently (since May 17, 1954) appointed special legislative commission was described:

> the Commission, working with its counsel, will explore avenues towards formulation of a program within the framework of law designed to prevent enforced integration of the races in the public schools of Virginia.

In its original school desegregation ruling of the previous year, the Court, "in view of the nationwide importance of the decision," had invited the attorney general of the United States to participate in this final argument. Despite the pleas to the President by southern governors, Department of Justice lawyers put together, and Attorney General Brownell submitted, the federal government's recommendations in a brief to the Court. Solicitor General Simon Sobeloff, who'd once been an adviser on civil rights to the governor of Maryland, presented the oral argument to the justices.

Urging them to avoid setting deadlines and emphasizing the necessity for consideration of local conditions in any formula they devised, the government's discussion was notable largely for its spirit of compromise between the "get-out-of-my-face" posture of the southern school boards and the aggressive "forthwith" demand of the black plaintiffs. The President himself was reported to have contributed a passage pleading for "understanding and good will" for his southern friends who were about to be ordered to alter the customs and mores by which they had lived for more than two centuries.

The justices also had invited the attorneys general of those states "requiring or permitting segregation in public education" to submit briefs and appear as amici curiae at this final argument before the Court decided the destinies of the 50 million people—11 million of them children—in seventeen states: the eleven states of the old Confederacy plus Delaware, Kansas, Kentucky, Maryland, Oklahoma, and West Virginia. Attorneys general from only Florida, Arkansas, Oklahoma, Maryland, North Carolina, and Texas had accepted the Court's invitation. The message that emerged from their combined presentations emphasized the potential for the federal courts gagging on the flood of litigation that was bound to follow the outlawing of segregation, the widespread hostility among southerners in both high and low places to this federally imposed revolution, the complexity and magnitude of the problems desegregation fore shadowed, and the urgent need for enough time to solve them.

Officials from the deep South states of Mississippi, Alabama, Georgia, and Louisiana were conspicuously absent. Louisiana's attorney general, Fred LeBlanc, taking into account his state's strong opposition to desegregation and the frantic race in the parishes to equalize educational facilities, had discussed with some of his fellow attorneys general what his response to the Court's invitation ought to be. The reason behind his declining it was jesuitical and spoke volumes about the future of race relations in his state and the southland in general:

We are not parties to any of the segregation suits before the Supreme Court. The thought among attorneys general is that if we did file briefs, we would be bound by the decree rendered in the case; whereas if we did not file we would not be bound directly by the decree. It may be that if any integration decree is to be enforced in Louisiana, additional suits will have to be filed against the State Department of Education and the school boards around the state.

Once again it was Chief Justice Warren who wrote the Court's opinion, read it to the public on May 31, 1955, and absorbed the severest of the aftershocks. Impeach Earl Warren billboards soon cluttered the American landscape from the Atlantic to the Pacific, the Canadian border to the Gulf of Mexico.

Like its predecessor, *Brown II,* as it was abbreviated, was short—seven paragraphs—dispassionate, and straightforward. Leaning on *Brown I*'s "fundamental principle that racial discrimination in public education is unconstitutional," Warren directed that "all provisions of federal, state or local law requiring or permitting such discrimination must yield to this principle."

To A. P. Tureaud, the Court clearly meant to cancel Louisiana's constitutional provision requiring segregation in its public schools as well as the legislature's recently enacted statute that withheld funds from public schools that desegregated and the one that assigned authority over student transfers to local school officials. To Leander Perez, who'd tried unsuccessfully to legislate public education in Louisiana out of existence following the Supreme Court's decision of the previous May, and state senator Willie Rainach, whose strident voice in opposition to *Brown I* retained all of its earlier venom, Chief Justice Warren's words meant that his Court had assumed powers to which it had no constitutional right whatsoever.

Following that first outburst of stern judicial authority, the Court's tone mellowed some. In the matter of remedy, there was something for everyone, but satisfaction for no one. On the assumption that a plan of implementation handed down from Washington would be substantially harder to sell to southerners than a locally devised program, the justices returned—or in legal language "remanded"—to the federal district courts from which they'd come the four cases in which the school boards had prevailed against the black plaintiffs. (The fifth case, from Delaware, had been decided in favor of the black plaintiffs, and the state already was proceeding with public school desegregation.)

Back in the lower courts, the judges were instructed to reappraise the cases under the constitutional principles enunciated in *Brown I* and *Brown II* and in the light of local conditions. In fashioning decrees, they were directed to take into consideration each individual locality's unique administrative and logistical problems inherent in "adjusting and reconciling public and private needs." At the same time, they were ordered to make sure the "vitality" of the principles of *Brown I* and *II* was not "allowed to yield simply because of disagreement with them." This last warning was reported to have been the contribution of the newest justice, John Harlan. If it hadn't the power or failed to prophesy the long life of his grandfather's "Our Constitution is color-blind," it had a certain ring to it and explained gracefully as well as earnestly the thrust of the Court's declaration that it would brook no nonsense.

The justices set no timetable for America's schools to desegregate, only ordered that the defendant school boards make a "prompt and reasonable start" toward compliance with its directives. They left the lower courts in charge of desegregation's pace, requiring only that the process be accomplished "with all deliberate speed," a cryptic oxymoron whose ambiguity under the circumstances created a loophole large enough for all nine justices, the attorneys general of the seventeen affected states, and the fifty-eight federal judges distributed throughout the southern circuits to march through.

The burden of enforcing the Court's decree fell hardest on these lower federal courts, which the justices instructed to retain jurisdiction, or supervision, during the entire period of transition from the standard dual to a desegregated unitary school system. The task proved more difficult and required a longer period of time than anyone imagined in May of 1955. In Oliver Bush's case against the Orleans Parish School Board, supervision by the federal district court would last twenty-one years, counting from the day of the district court judge's decision.

These fifty-eight federal judges to whom the Supreme Court was assigning this special responsibility, scattered throughout twenty-eight southern districts, were all white, all male, and all southerners. Only five had been born outside the South, and 51.3 percent of them had been born in the districts in which they served. Only five had attended law schools outside the South, and 56.1 percent had attended law schools in their home states. Prior to being appointed to the federal bench, 89 percent had held public offices in their home states. Their ties with their districts ran deep.

While their life tenure on the federal bench made them invulnerable to the political pressures that dogged state judges periodically, especially at election time, they were still members of their communities, which were going to feel the brunt of the Supreme Court's orders to desegregate the public schools. Their judicial independence did not lessen their concern for their own or their families' standing there. They all knew what happened to Waties Waring of the federal district court in Charleston, South Carolina, when he wrote that the public schools of Clarendon County ought to be desegregated. As Lieutenant Governor S. Ernest Vandiver of Georgia put it on receiving word of the Supreme Court's decision in *Brown II,* southern federal judges were

> steeped in the same traditions that I am. I know that they will assume a reasonable attitude in the enforcement of the decision. Thank God we've got federal judges.

From the judges' point of view, *Brown II* had guaranteed that their courtrooms would be the center of frequent and intense racial conflict, and the judges themselves would be caught in the crossfire between the local white establishment to which they belonged and which expected them to defend their traditional southern way of life, and the black plaintiffs who expected them to uphold the Constitution as interpreted most recently by the United States Supreme Court.

The reactions of black civil rights activists ranged from lukewarm to warm. None were hot. The official statement of the NAACP's board of directors and officers spoke more to hope than anticipation, expressing confidence that the "whole American people will support this historic decision to open up new avenues of democracy for all the children of our nation." The organization and its local branches stood "ready to cooperate with all officials" on such programs. At the same time it again directed every last one of its chapters in the seventeen affected states to petition their school boards that very summer, gently prod them to action. Wherever school officials refused to act, black parents and their children were urged to bring law suits in the federal courts. As Louisiana's attorney general Fred LeBlanc had foreseen, those states that had not been segregated before the Supreme Court decision could conceivably continue to operate their schools on a segregated basis.

Thurgood Marshall and Bob Carter collaborated on a more detailed analysis of the Court's decree and the NAACP's relationship to it, which was published that summer in the *Journal of Negro Education.* Overall, the two lawyers who'd nursed the five original segregation cases through the perilous shoals of federal court litigation for the better part of the past three years agreed that, with reservations, the decision was "a good one," the formula "about as effective" as they could have expected. Their major concern was that "in the deep South, with rare exceptions, desegregation will become a reality only if Negroes exhibit a real militancy and press unrelentlessly for their rights."

If they failed to follow through, Marshall and Carter warned, "nothing would be done." If on the other hand, they maintained the momentum that had brought them this far, kept the adrenaline flowing, *Brown II* was

> a ticket to desegregation which is now available to every parent and child who needs it and wants to use it.

Reflecting readers' viewpoints, editorial comment across the white South was somewhat less shrill than that following *Brown I,* though it was wary. In some quarters, *Brown II* was welcomed and interpreted as capitulation by the Court, even approval of delay. Elsewhere, the old stridency surfaced once again. For every paper like the *St. Petersburg* (Florida) *Times,* which predicted that despite the Herman Talmadges and their fellow extremists, "within ten years progress in human relations will be made even in the worst states," there was at least one like the *Shreveport* (Louisiana) *Journal* that complained that "no man or group of men ignorant of, or indifferent to, the South's problems can arbitrarily tell the South how to solve these problems." The ruling, said the editor, made a "mockery of states' rights."

The two largest newspapers in New Orleans came down almost as far apart. The *Item*'s tone assumed that compliance with the Supreme Court's decision meant desegregation of the public schools and cautioned against extremism. The city was "fortunate," the editors declared,

> in having judges of the high caliber of J. Skelly Wright and Herbert W. Christenberry, both of whom are thoroughly familiar with local conditions and will bring to this problem the wisdom and patience it demands.

The *Times-Picayune* assumed exactly the opposite—the continuation of the old separate-but-equal arrangement:

> There is no question of "integration" it seems to us. The court uses "racial discrimination." There is a lot of difference between compulsory integration and racial nondiscrimination in planning and developing a school system.

The editors urged local school authorities to continue their recent efforts to buy off blacks by upgrading their schools. Louisiana's parishes, they admitted, could hardly "hope to continue with unequal facilities and still not suffer disorderly consequences."

The newspaper's sentiments coincided with those of state senator and Citizens' Council movement leader Willie Rainach, who commented to a fellow state senator that it "look[ed] like the *Times-Picayune* is coming along with us rather well editorially," and that month had goaded the legislature into passing an extra $33 million appropriation for equalizing educational facilities. He continued to radiate optimism publicly:

> Integration [he'd explained in support of his appropriations bill] will destroy our public school system in Louisiana. We are going to keep segregation, come what may. This means that we must preserve segregation in our public schools, regardless of cost. Equal facilities are a necessary part of the solution.

To Rainach's chagrin, however, Governor Kennon, whom the NAACP's Dan Byrd had so recently "respectfully" reminded of the school desegregation suits already filed in federal court, of the twelve additional suits ready for filing across the state, and of black parents "pressing for action in other places to bring about equal education for their children," after keeping the senator waiting until the last minute of the legislative session, vetoed the bill. With so many demands on its money, Kennon explained, the state simply couldn't afford to get into the school construction business, which traditionally had been left to the individual parishes. Rainach was angry but publicly put the best face on it he could: "The governor made a very serious error in placing other things above the welfare of the school children of our state." Privately, he called the bill's defeat.

> merely a skirmish in the opening phases of this fight.... [W]e at least had the minimum gain of demonstrating our strength in the legislature.

The governor was not, however, entirely deaf to the politics of race. Included in the regular school appropriation was more than $4 million for capital improvements, all calculated to ward off desegregation suits at white institutions, to various black schools maintained by the state: Grambling and Southern universities, the State School for Deaf Negroes, and a new Negro trade school for New Orleans.

In response to the Supreme Court's second decision in *Brown,* Kennon made no allusions to his relatively mild comment on *Brown I,* a year ago, his seeming willingness to "work out the problem," but climbed right in with the protesters now:

> I am convinced the majority of the people of this state want their schools segregated. So long as I am governor, I will try to follow the wishes of the people.

Senator Rainach had found the Court's decree "milder" than he and his fellow segregationists had expected. "It gives us room," he said, "to continue our fight," and within the week, Rainach, Attorney General LeBlanc, Leander Perez, who'd immediately branded the Court's ruling as "unlawful," "Communistic," and a "disgrace to the country," and others of their persuasion were meeting in Baton Rouge to make plans for bypassing the Court. For "strategic reasons," they explained, they couldn't disclose what they had discussed.

One of their schemes became immediately evident. His school equalization appropriations bill vetoed by the governor, the ever resourceful Rainach prepared to fight the segregation battle in the courts and set off for the State Board of Liquidation, an appropriations body that acted for the legislature in fiscal matters when the lawmakers were not in session. There he asked the board to release $100,000 in state funds to be used by Louisiana's school boards in employing "the best brains in the state" to defend them against the court suits they anticipated being filed by blacks. The state board approved his request unanimously, and the legislators okayed the appropriation by mail ballot overwhelmingly.

In 1955 terms, $100,000 looked like a lot of money. Thurgood Marshall, however, quickly put the opposition's new weapon into perspective. The funds had been appropriated, he said, "to scare you . . . make you think you can't win in court." And Clarence A. Laws, state NAACP official, vowed to "match dollar for every dollar misappropriated and misused by opponents of freedom and opportunity to win implementation of integration in public schools." His organization, he vowed, would test "to the limit" the legality of this "nefarious" grant.

In New Orleans, school board President Clarence Scheps was looking at a public school population of 71,248; nearly half was black (34,600). During the previous year or so, the race for equalization had resulted in the opening of four new schools for black children and a reduction of 2,291 in the number of black pupils forced to attend school on the platoon system. Whether the spaciousness of the buildings or their ultramodern features would have an effect on the NAACP's determination to pursue desegregation remained to be seen. The announcement of *Brown II* and the Supreme Court's resolve to enforce public school desegregation nationwide certainly had had no effect on the rigid segregationist posture of the school board. Scheps issued a statement on behalf of the members immediately following Chief Justice Warren's reading of *Brown II*.

Essentially it was an elaboration of what he'd said following *Brown I:* the NAACP shouldn't hold its breath while it waited for the local schools to desegregate. He didn't mention the three-year-old Bush case against the school board, but that it was on his mind was clear. He did, however, lay out in the plainest English how he and his colleagues felt about race mixing in the schools. His statement set the scene for a fight:

> The Supreme Court's final ruling on segregation can have no immediate effect on the New Orleans public school system. It must be remembered that our local schools are part of the state system and as such are governed by the regulations of the state board of education and by the statutes and constitution as interpreted . . . by the attorney general of Louisiana.
>
> Beyond this, however, we are aware that the legislature, the people of the state and the people of our community have declared themselves overwhelmingly in favor of the maintenance of a separate but equal school system for Negroes.
>
> The five members of the Orleans Parish School Board are in unanimous agreement that the education of both races can proceed more effectively under a segregated system.

Scheps quickly denied all implications of "prejudice" or "defiance" of the Supreme Court. Board members, he explained, wanted only to "make available to all children the fullest advantages of our great public schools." They hoped a "lawful and honorable way" could be found by the state to "preserve our segregated schools." School Superintendent Jim Redmond refused to comment except to promise that "as the school board's chief administrative officer I shall follow whatever the board dictates."

Between the Supreme Court's announcement of *Brown I* and *II*, A. P. Tureaud, his son's suit against Louisiana State University still pending in the United States Court of Appeals for the Fifth Circuit, had succeeded in convincing lower federal courts to order the racial desegregation of three of the state's other institutions of higher education: Southwestern Louisiana Institute in Lafayette, McNeese State College in Lake Charles, and Southeastern Louisiana College in Hammond. That very spring he had been honored by the local Insurance Executives Council with a testimonial at which he was dubbed "Mr. Civil Rights of Louisiana." His response to *Brown II* spoke more of his fears than his hopes.

Black lawyers were in short supply in the South of 1955. He himself was stretched to the limit. In addition to his private practice and young A. P.'s suit, he had two school desegregation cases—the local Bush case and a similar one in St. Helena Parish—already filed in the lower federal courts, and another in East Baton Rouge almost ready for filing. White lawyers, even if they were sympathetic, could ill afford the loss of clients taking civil rights cases would inevitably entail. There weren't enough attorneys anywhere to turn the ideals of *Brown II* into reality, and Tureaud could only hope

> that it will not be necessary in those states which do not have cases before the Supreme Court to force legal action compelling desegregation.

Following publication of his statement in the *Times-Picayune,* the mild-mannered Tureaud received a sample of the hate mail that would soon become standard as the struggle for the soul of the New Orleans schools was on. It was addressed to "A. P. Tureaud, negro," and it was notable largely for its vehemence:

> You seem to be typical of the "Educated" negro who is stooging for the communist front organization known as the N.A.A.C.P.
>
> Your fears are well founded when you express your concern over what the white race will do when any attempt is made to mongrelize the races. When the time arrives, we will make our fight openly and with determination as befits a SOUTHERNER.

> J. W. Mabry, President
> Anti-Communist League of America
> Birmingham Alabama Chapter

After a quarter of a century as a civil rights lawyer, Tureaud wasn't a man to be cowed by a few ill-tempered words. Following *Brown II,* he was, as always, crouched on his mark, waiting only for the pop of the starting gun to propel him forward.

Chief Justice Warren had begun his recital of the Court's decision at noon on May 31. Before the day was out, Tureaud had sped an urgent letter to Sam Rosenberg, the Orleans Parish school board's lawyer. Would Rosenberg get his *Bush* papers in order immediately so that the case "may be heard at the earliest possible moment"?

Rosenberg's reply was, in contrast, laconic. The school board's lawyer discerned no need for haste. In fact he wanted time "to study and analyze the effect" of the Supreme Court's decision in light of the Louisiana legislation and constitutional amendment adopted in 1954 following *Brown I* reaffirming the state's commitment to segregation in its

This aerial view, looking upriver toward Baton Rouge, explains why New Orleans is called the Crescent City. Founded in 1718, it combines old-world charm with new-world bustle. The hundred-year struggle to integrate its schools that climaxed in 1960 revealed a darker side of the city. *(National Archives)*

The first Battle of New Orleans, 1815. Upwards of four hundred free blacks fought with distinction alongside General Andrew Jackson's three thousand white troops; their nurses had tended the wounded. Despite the general's public expressions of gratitude, the war veterans returned home to their former lowly status, "object[s] of scorn," as Hippolyte Castra, a black Creole poet, put it. *(New Orleans Public Library)*

When John McDonogh died in 1850, he left half his considerable fortune to the public schools of Baltimore, where he was born, the other half to the schools of New Orleans, where he'd made it. He included "every poor child and youth of every color" in his bequest, but educating blacks violated Louisiana law at the time, and city officials ignored that provision in his will. *(Earl K. Long Library, University of New Orleans)*

The rotunda of the St. Louis Hotel in New Orleans was the city's main auction mart before the Civil War, dealing in slaves as well as objects. New Orleans was a major distribution point for slave traffic flowing from the East to plantations beyond the Mississippi. *(Courtesy of The Historic New Orleans Collection, accession number 1974.25.23.4)*

Popular nineteenth-century novelist and twice-wounded Confederate veteran George Washington Cable was thoroughly committed to the southern way of life before the Civil War. By the 1870s, he was convinced slavery had been a terrible mistake. In his book *The Silent South* and in his lectures he begged southerners to speak out against its lingering effects and the injustices being visited upon Negroes in the post-war South. But his pleas were in vain. His audiences maintained their silence. *(Courtesy of The Historic New Orleans Collection, accession number 1993.127)*

Supreme Court Justice Henry Billings Brown of the abolitionist state of Massachusetts wrote the majority opinion in *Plessy* v. *Ferguson*, 1896. The issue involved separate accommodations for black passengers in railroad cars, but it effectively imprisoned black Americans in Jim Crow schools, hotels, restaurants, hospitals, even some graveyards for more than fifty years. *(Collection of the Supreme Court of the United States)*

Plessy's latter-day champions. United by the politics of race and the specter of federal intrusion on states' rights, southerners bolted the regular Democratic Party convention in 1948 and reconvened in Birmingham, Alabama, where they organized the States' Rights Democratic Party—Dixiecrats—and nominated then-Governor Strom Thurmond of South Carolina for president. *(AP/Wide World Photos)*

Justice John Marshall Harlan of Kentucky, former slave owner, was the sole dissenter in *Plessy* v. *Ferguson*, maintaining that "Our Constitution is color-blind." It was Harlan, however, who had the last word when in 1954 the Supreme Court declared segregation in public schools unconstitutional in *Brown* v. *Board of Education*. *(Collection of the Supreme Court of the United States)*

Give 'em hell, Harry! President by succession, Harry Truman wanted to be elected in his own right in 1948. Despite his alienating the white South with his talk about blacks' civil rights and the Dixiecrats' challenge to his Democratic Party, he got his wish. Blacks helped provide the margin of his surprise victory.
(National Archives)

We like Ike! Dwight D. Eisenhower, 1952 Republican nominee for president, flanked by his Louisiana chairman, New Orleans lawyer John Minor Wisdom, and his wife, Bonnie. At the national convention, Wisdom led the movement to unseat Robert A. Taft's Louisiana delegates and replace them with Eisenhower's. In 1957 Eisenhower appointed Wisdom to the U.S. Court of Appeals for the Fifth Circuit, which in effect wrote America's civil rights law over the next decade. In recognition of Wisdom's judicial championship of civil rights, President Bill Clinton awarded him the Medal of Freedom.
(AP/Wide World Photos)

Friendly enemies. John Davis, left, and Thurgood Marshall, opposing counsel in the legal struggle over segregation in public schools, chat before oral argument in the U.S. Supreme Court, 1952. Davis, a former Democratic presidential candidate whose courtroom skills Marshall had long admired, represented the state of South Carolina, which supported the traditional segregation. Marshall represented blacks trying to outlaw it. *(AP/Wide World Photos)*

The *Brown* Court. Top row: Tom C. Clark, Robert H. Jackson, Harold H. Burton, Sherman Minton; bottom row: Felix Frankfurter, Hugo L. Black, Chief Justice Earl Warren, Stanley F. Reed, William O. Douglas. In 1954, these nine men launched a social revolution when they unequivocally and unanimously declared that racial segregation in public schools "deprive[d] the children of the minority group of equal educational opportunities." One of *Brown*'s offspring was *Bush* v. *Orleans Parish School Board*, which was responsible for desegregating New Orleans's public schools, although not without a fight. *(Fabian Bachrach, Collection of the Supreme Court of the United States)*

Chief Justice Earl Warren swears in President Eisenhower, 1956, two years after the Warren Court ruled in *Brown* v. *Board of Education* that racial segregation in public schools was unconstitutional. Warren always believed that had Eisenhower publicly supported *Brown*, many of the problems it caused would not have arisen. But Eisenhower, like many Americans in positions of influence, maintained a rigid silence during the critical period. For his part, Eisenhower considered his appointment of Warren as chief justice the "biggest damn fool thing I ever did." *(Library of Congress)*

The black Creole lawyer A. P. Tureaud, light-skinned enough to "pass," nonetheless lived as black. He spent forty-plus years in Louisiana's courts arguing for the civil rights of his fellow blacks, including their right to attend schools traditionally reserved for whites. As his daughter, Jane, put it years later, he'd seen "the hurt," he knew "the need," he wanted to "right the wrongs." *(Amistad Research Center, Tulane University, New Orleans)*

Joseph McKelpin, left, and A. P. Tureaud. McKelpin, a black teacher in the New Orleans public school system, was the plaintiff in the suit against the Orleans Parish School Board to equalize the salaries of black and white teachers. It was the lawyer Tureaud's first big civil rights case. When it was successful, McKelpin was promptly fired. *(Peter W. Clark)*

LEFT: Daniel Byrd, NAACP functionary in Louisiana and A. P. Tureaud's right-hand man, minus the ever-present unlit cigar. Byrd's saturation bombing of the Orleans Parish School Board with complaints about the poor quality of education provided for black youngsters in New Orleans laid the groundwork for the court suit that desegregated the city's schools.

BELOW: Oliver Bush. He volunteered his son Earl as plaintiff to the suit that ultimately desegregated the New Orleans public schools. Bush worked for a black-owned insurance company and was invulnerable to white reprisal—a consideration that kept many blacks from joining desegregation suits.

(Louisiana Weekly *Collection, Amistad Research Center, Tulane University, New Orleans)*

Thurgood Marshall, far left, then Supreme Court Justice Marshall, delivers a eulogy at A. P. Tureaud's funeral in 1972.
Marshall and Tureaud worked together on Louisiana civil rights cases beginning in the 1930s with the teachers' salary equalization suits. Marshall and his assistants often stayed with the Tureauds during those years when local hotels were closed to blacks.
(New Orleans Clarion Herald)

State senator and White Citizens' Council potentate William "Call Me Willie" Rainach wearing his trademark tie. Segregationist to his core, he turned the 1959-60 Louisiana gubernatorial election into a referendum on race. *(Courtesy of the Noel Memorial Library, Louisiana State University-Shreveport Archives)*

Soulmates. Just inaugurated governor of Louisiana, Jimmie ("You Are My Sunshine") Davis greets fellow segregationist governor Ross Barnett of Mississippi, left, and an unidentified well-wisher at right. Much of Davis's first year in office was spent trying to keep blacks out of New Orleans's white schools. In 1963, Barnett won national notoriety when he tried to block the admission of James Meredith, a black Air Force veteran, to the University of Mississippi. *(Gasquet Collection, Louisiana State Archives)*

Leander Perez, autocrat of his native Plaquemine Parish, made his money from oil and his reputation from demagoguery. In 1948, he'd been one of the architects of the Dixiecrats' secession from the Democratic Party. In 1960, he was the pit bull of racial segregation in Louisiana, the brains behind the state legislature's strategy, and the power behind the White Citizens' Council. *(Louisiana Collection, State Library of Louisiana, Baton Rouge)*

The Mayor. DeLesseps S. "Chep" Morrison, left, *Time* magazine's "Most Progressive Mayor of the Decade, 1940-1950," takes the oath of office for the fourth time. During his four terms (1946-62), Morrison made the port of New Orleans a competitor with Miami as the "Gateway to Latin America," expanded tourism, and brought in new industry, but remained silent on the most critical social problem his city faced: the racial desegregation of its schools in 1960. *(New Orleans Public Library)*

Orleans Parish school officialdom in 1954, when the U.S. Supreme Court ruled that racial segregation in America's public schools was unconstitutional. Seated, left to right: School Board members Celestine Besse, Clarence Scheps, president, Emile Wagner; standing, left to right: member Theodore Shepard, school superintendent James Redmond, and member Matthew Sutherland. Scheps predicted *Brown* would "have no immediate effect on the New Orleans public school system." All but Scheps and Besse retained their positions through the crisis that climaxed in November of 1960, long enough to experience *Brown*'s effect. *(Earl K. Long Library, University of New Orleans)*

Elected to the School Board in 1956, Louis Riecke
served as vice president during the crisis of 1960.
When at last the board reluctantly capitulated to
the federal court and began to plan for public
school desegregation, Riecke's lumber business
suffered serious financial losses. He told everyone that his dog was the only friend he had left.
(Earl K. Long Library, University of New Orleans)

Lloyd Rittiner, elected, like Riecke, to the
School Board in 1956, served as president—
and lightning rod—of the board during the
crisis of 1960. Poison-pen letters filled his mail
box; hate calls monopolized his telephone line.
His engineering business lost money, and
bricks were hurled at his trucks.
(Earl K. Long Library, University of New Orleans)

Appointed School Board attorney in 1952, Samuel
Rosenberg warned the board two years later that
the Supreme Court meant business when it
declared racial segregation in public schools
unconstitutional. During the local school crisis,
Rosenberg worked largely behind the scenes.
(Earl K. Long Library, University of New Orleans)

Rosa Keller tells young readers the facts of library life. As a board member of the New Orleans Public Library, Keller was largely responsible for its desegregation. She was also one of the few prominent white New Orleanians to speak out for public school desegregation. *(New Orleans Public Library)*

Archbishop Joseph F. Rummel of New Orleans. An early champion of racial integration, the German-born prelate tolerated no discrimination in his churches, but he dragged his feet when he was faced with the problem of his schools, which made up the largest single system in the state and for a time provided a convenient refuge for white parents unwilling to send their children to integrated public schools. *(New Orleans* Clarion Herald*)*

Maurice "Moon" Landrieu. As a freshman member of the Louisiana legislature, he and a handful of colleagues bucked the tidal wave of segregation statutes pushed through the state house and senate to stop school desegregation. He was warned he was digging his political grave. But when he ran for mayor of New Orleans in 1969 he was rewarded with 99 percent of the black vote. His major achievement as mayor was opening the upper echelons of city government to black men and women. In 1978, President Jimmy Carter appointed him Secretary of the Department of Housing and Urban Development. *(Louisiana Weekly Collection, Amistad Research Center, Tulane University, New Orleans)*

J. Skelly Wright, federal district judge for the Eastern District of Louisiana from 1950 to 1962. Growing up in the Irish Channel section of New Orleans, he was "just another southern 'boy.'" Later, exposure to the bitter fruit of racial discrimination forced him to rethink his heritage. As a judge, he set about enforcing *Brown* v. *Board of Education* in his native city with all the certitude and toughness of a convert, despite the white majority's vilification and ostracism of him and his family. *(Library of Congress)*

Self-described as "no swinging liberal," Herbert W. Christenberry, Skelly Wright's judicial partner on the federal district court for the Eastern District of Louisiana during the New Orleans school crisis, nonetheless believed that "you should do every-thing under the law to guarantee the constitutional rights of Negroes." He supported Wright in every civil rights case on which they sat together. *(AP/Wide World Photos)*

The U.S. Court of Appeals for the Fifth Circuit, whose jurisdiction stretched from Texas to Florida, the heart of segregation country. This court "backed me every step of the way," said federal district judge Skelly Wright. Top row: Warren L. Jones, Benjamin F. Cameron, John R. Brown, John Minor Wisdom. Bottom row: Richard Rives, Chief Judge Joseph C. Hutcheson, Elbert Parr Tuttle. *(Courtesy of the Fifth Circuit)*

The cheerleaders hurl insults and obscenities, which alternated with tomatoes, rotten eggs, and spittle, as the William Frantz Elementary School, their neighborhood white school, integrates. They maintained their vigil for the entire 1960-61 school year. *(AP/Wide World Photos)*

A veteran of the race wars at six: Ruby Bridges at home, November 1960. The first black child to enter the William Frantz Elementary School since Reconstruction, she had to walk through lines of white hecklers to get there. She spent her first year alone with her teacher; her very presence had virtually emptied the school of white pupils except for a few stalwarts. (*UPI/Bettmann*)

Ruby Bridges Hall, 1992: wife, mother of four lively sons. Her experience desegregating the William Frantz Elementary School (illustrated here by the Norman Rockwell painting "The Problem We All Live With") led her to an interest in child psychology and to the conclusion that her role in New Orleans's school crisis was a necessary part of a larger plan for her life. She saw the "pieces of the puzzle falling together" when she created a program she called "parenting" in which she acts as liaison between a school and the parents of its students, urging them to get involved in their children's education. (*Steve Lasky*)

The night after "D-Day", the White Citizens' Council massed in the Municipal Auditorium, a forum consistently denied Thurgood Marshall because, city authorities declared, he was too "political." The fiery speeches made at this pep rally were consistently interrupted by cries from the audience to "Send 'em back to Africa!" *(UPI/Bettmann)*

King Zulu and his zany entourage. The Zulus, who clowned their way through downtown sections of the city, tossing coconuts to the shouting crowds, were one of the most popular attractions of Mardi Gras. Resentful of the vicious white opposition to school desegregation in late 1960, they threatened to boycott the event in February 1961. *(National Archives)*

Mardi Gras. Rex, King of Carnival and Lord of Misrule, leads his entourage through the cheering crowds on the day of days. Until the 1990s, krewes were strictly segregated. When a city ordinance forced their desegregation, some of the oldest, most prestigious krewes stopped parading. *(National Archives)*

public schools. Rosenberg was accordingly asking the federal court for an extension of ninety days in which to file his papers. Tureaud immediately dispatched Rosenberg's letter to Bob Carter at NAACP headquarters in New York. Carter thought ninety days was "too much time." The court, however, politely granted it.

Meanwhile Tureaud prepared to march on the school board during its regular semimonthly meeting at its headquarters in the Nicholas Bauer Building on Carondelet Street. Privately, board President Scheps had reassured Senator Rainach, who had indicated concern about petitions to the school board, that the members were "determined to use every legal and honorable means at its command to preserve our present segregated school system." Two board members were even then preparing to leave for Baton Rouge to call on the attorney general in connection with Oliver Bush's suit to end racial segregation in the city's public schools. Scheps would have a copy of the suit forwarded to the senator. He was not to worry.

The meeting of the Orleans Parish school board on June 27 offered standing room only when Tureaud appeared to present black New Orleans's case for ending racial segregation in the city's schools. He made his first point by distributing to the four board members—all but Scheps who was absent—copies of *Now Is the Time* by Lillian Smith. This book, like her other work, was a plea for moral and intellectual leadership against racial discrimination and segregation.

Tureaud went on to review the tedious history of blacks' petitions for educational parity with white New Orleanians, and reminded the men that "separate but equal" was no longer of concern. A hush settled over the room and his voice rang out when he read from the Supreme Court's most recent ruling. He defined for the board its responsibility to begin immediately desegregation of the schools under its jurisdiction and offered the assistance and cooperation of his organization, which he said was "ready and willing to supply technicians trained in carrying out a program of desegregation." His conclusion belied the gentleness for which he was known, although his creamy voice remained calm:

I know that you are not unmindful of the fact that you must yield to the constitutional laws of the United States whether you like it or not.

The members of the school board had appeared to listen intently, but, as if they had heard it all before, no one commented when Tureaud sat down. The men immediately moved on to other pending business.

Opposition to *Brown II* was hardening fast, its purveyors increasingly impassioned not only privately but publicly. Among the personals that ran periodically in the *Times-Picayune* that summer, one stood out:

> Knights of the White Christians
> Need the help of all loyal Southern White Christians to protect and preserve segregation, states' rights and traditions of the South. Write P.O. box 2370, New Orleans, Louisiana.

Six weeks after the Supreme Court's ruling in *Brown II,* less than three weeks after the Orleans Parish school board meeting at which Tureaud had presented the case for public school desegregation, on July 15, 1955, the United States Court of Appeals for the Fourth Circuit showed the South a way out of its dilemma. The opinion for the special three-judge court was written by the seventy-year-old veteran of thirty years on the bench, John J. Parker, who had been able to find support in the federal Constitution to uphold the equalization of black and white teachers' salaries in 1940 but whose constitutional tolerance for civil rights had run out in Harry Briggs's case against the Clarendon County school board a decade later.

Now Harry Briggs's case was back, remanded, as the Supreme Court had directed, to the special three-judge district court from which it had come. The dissenter in the first Briggs case, J. Waties Waring, had been replaced on the panel by seventy-four-year-old Armistead Dobie, Roosevelt appointee, Democrat, and former dean of the University of Virginia Law School; he had once been overheard to call the social scientist Gunnar Myrdal, cited by the Supreme Court in *Brown I,* "a foreign Communistic anthropologist." Otherwise the panel remained the same as it had been during the first Briggs adjudications: the ardent segregationist George Bell Timmerman and the moderate Parker. Briggs's second time around, the panel was unanimous.

The judges acknowledged that

> Whatever may have been the view of this court as to the law when the case was originally before us, it is our duty now to accept the law as declared by the Supreme Court.

They could not this time simply instruct the school board to get on with equalization of educational facilities. But what they came up with was not a big improvement over the old formula. It sounded better than it was.

The jurists "restrained and enjoined [school officials] from refusing on account of race to admit to any school under their supervision any child qualified to enter such school, from and after such time as they may have made the necessary arrangements for admission of children to such school on a non-discriminatory basis with all deliberate speed as required by the decision of the Supreme Court in this case."

That is, rather than set a deadline for making "the necessary arrangements," reshuffling school districts, or in any way ordering desegregation, the judges had shifted the onus back to the plaintiff. If Harry Briggs, Jr., now fourteen and in the eighth grade, really wanted to go to an all-white school, he could not be refused admission, but it was up to him to persuade school officials to "make the necessary arrangements" for his entry. The court set no deadline; presumably the school board could take its own sweet time since no one yet knew what "all deliberate speed" meant. The decree was barely a decree at all. But the worst was yet to come.

Being one of the first lower federal courts to confront the problem of implementing the Supreme Court's orders in *Brown II,* the three judges set out to define with some particularity "exactly what the Supreme Court has decided and what it has not decided in this case." The following passage became known as the "Parker doctrine." It set back school desegregation years.

It has not decided that the federal courts are to take over or regulate the public schools of the states. It has not decided that the states must mix persons of different races in the schools or must require them to attend schools or must deprive them of the right of choosing the schools they attend. What it has decided, and all that it has decided, is that a state may not deny to any person on account of race the right to attend any school that it maintains . . . if the schools which it maintains are open to children of all races, no violation of the Constitution is involved even though the children of different races voluntarily attend different schools, as they attend different churches. Nothing in the Constitution or in the decision of the Supreme Court takes away from the people freedom to choose the schools they attend. The Constitution, in other words, does not require integration. It merely forbids discrimination. It does not forbid such segregation as occurs as the result of voluntary action. It merely forbids the use of governmental power to enforce segregation.

In December, 1952, during the first oral argument of the original segregation cases, Justice Felix Frankfurter had warned:

Nothing could be worse from my point of view than for this Court to make an abstract declaration that segregation is bad and then to have it evaded by tricks.

Over the decade following the Fourth Circuit's decision in Harry Briggs's case, Frankfurter's fears were soon realized. Parker had in effect given resistance a good name as well as made it legitimate.

He had set the precedent for allowing students what became known as "freedom of choice," also called "local option" and "open enrollment." Taking advantage of white reluctance to send white children to all black schools and of black reluctance to intrude where blacks were obviously not wanted, school boards rather than redistrict children of both races into desegregated reality, lived off the Fourth Circuit judges' decision for years.

Young A. P. Tureaud's case against Louisiana State University, begun two years earlier when the institution's registrar had rejected his application for admission to the freshman class entering in September, 1953, was also a casualty of institutional delaying tactics. At midsummer, 1955, A. P. was happily settled as a rising junior at the all-Negro Xavier University in New Orleans. He could look on dispassionately now as his case bounced from court to court. He thought he would probably graduate before it was settled.

But it faded into the background that summer while his father concentrated on the three-year-old Bush suit against the Orleans Parish School Board. Circumstances had changed since the case was filed in the fall of 1952. As Judge Parker had said, what had been the law no longer was. The two Brown rulings had killed any vestiges of separate-but-equal that remained, which gave him precedents on which to build. But the state legislature had tried to pull them out from under him. Which put Tureaud in the unenviable position of defying local law and lawmakers who'd plainly shown just how angry they were.

Tureaud nonetheless wasn't one to hang back and wait for the school board to move. He knew his petition had undoubtedly already followed all the rest of the petitions to the board he'd filed over the past decade: into the wastebasket labeled "under advisement." Having alerted school board legal counsel Sam Rosenberg immediately following the announcement of *Brown II* on May 31 to his intention to revive the Bushes' suit, Tureaud sat down to rewrite his arguments in the light of the new developments.

When he filed his amended suit with the federal court on August 20, 1955, he demanded both a declaration that Louisiana's post-*Brown* constitutional amendment preserving segregation was unconstitutional and a court order immediately desegregating the city's public schools.

Once he'd studied the Supreme Court's decisions in the two *Brown* cases, Sam Rosenberg had concluded that they were indeed the law of the land, and he'd warned the school board it "must comply with all reasonable speed." Long drawn-out litigation would not only prove expensive, but it was doomed from the start. Rosenberg was the only man in local school officialdom to stand against the prevailing winds of sentiment, not because he was eager to desegregate, but because he was eager to comply with the law.

It was not what the board wanted to hear. Dependent for reelection on the majority voters of New Orleans (white) with whom the members were in fact largely in basic agreement, the board was not nearly ready to capitulate, and Rosenberg's advice was ignored. The board in fact vowed publicly to defend Bush's suit against it "vigorously, aggressively, and capably."

Taking advantage of the state's special war chest of $100,000 recently appropriated to help individual localities fight desegregation in their schools, the Orleans Parish school board allowed Rosenberg to recuse—disqualify—himself from the approaching court battle, although he remained general counsel in charge of all other legal matters involving the board. The members, after first consulting with Willie Rainach's committee on segregation, hired a well-known local lawyer, Gerald Rault, who shared the committee's and the board's enthusiasm for perpetuating school segregation, as special counsel to defend it in the courts against the crescendoing onslaughts of the black plaintiffs. Leander Perez, whose war stories of his bouts with the federal government were known all over the state and whose reputation for courtroom agility was unmatched, was engaged to advise Rault.

For this job, from which Rault could expect to reap political as well as personal satisfaction and professional rewards, he was to be paid $25,000 a year. The state was to dig into its special appropriation for the first $10,000, and the local school board would have to dig into its own pocket for the rest. For court appearances he was to get $150 a day extra, and for legal work outside New Orleans another $150. Dan Byrd grumbled that the lawyer stood to clear "at least $30,000" for defending the school board against the local blacks, big money in 1955.

Not if A. P. Tureaud had anything to say about it. Following the state legislature's approval of the funds, members of NAACP branches in Louisiana demonstrated that they were no longer the submissive men and women their white neighbors thought they knew and understood, that the courts had given them the confidence to throw their bandanas on the bonfire and to assert their rights, fight for them if necessary. No fewer than 225 NAACP members from twenty-seven Louisiana branches volunteered as plaintiffs, should the organization decide to test the constitutionality of the legislature's appropriation to fight it. By the end of

August Tureaud had selected eight names from four of Louisiana's largest parishes and had started a suit against the state attorney general in state court at East Baton Rouge contesting the legality of the use of the $100,000 grant for the purpose of "maintaining and enforcing the official maintenance of segregation" in Louisiana. Tureaud's chances of winning in a state court were dim and he must have known it, but he couldn't very well take a strictly state matter into a federal court, and he couldn't let the state get away with this without a fight.

It wasn't, however, much of a fight. Judge J. Coleman Lindsey of the Nineteenth judicial court at East Baton Rouge, told the black plaintiffs he had "searched in vain for any taint of unconstitutionality or illegality" in the procedures followed by the board of liquidation which had approved it, the state legislature which had voted for it, or the attorney general who was handing the money out. The attorney general in fact, against whom the suit had been specifically brought, had, in Lindsey's opinion, "the sworn duty to do precisely what he has done." Accordingly, as the attorney general had asked, Lindsey was dismissing Tureaud's suit. Plaintiffs would be assessed court costs.

Outside New Orleans, anger at the school desegregation decisions was spilling over into action. In August, a federal district court issued an order prohibiting University of Alabama officials from denying admission to Autherine J. Lucy, who'd been rejected previously because of her race. She enrolled at the school that fall, but her stay was brief, cut short by the riots and violence that broke out as soon as she appeared on the campus.

The little town of Greenwood, Mississippi, showed Americans in every section of the country just how angry southerners could get. On August 31, the sodden, mutilated body of Emmett Louis Till, fourteen years old, from Chicago, Illinois, was recovered from the Tallahatchie River near Greenwood, three days after the boy had been kidnapped at gunpoint from his uncle's home in Mondy, where he'd been visiting his country cousins. It was said that he'd "wolf-whistled" at a white woman.

The two men charged with the crime confessed to the kidnapping to the arresting officers, but denied the killing, although a year or so later they told a writer for *Look* magazine they hadn't

> intended to kill the nigger . . . just whip him and chase him back up yonder.

But the boy had made the mistake of showing them a picture of a white girl he said he knew back in Chicago and bragged o' what he'd done to her! I counted pictures of three white girls in his pocketbook before I burned it. What else could I do? No use lettin' him get bigger!

Local Greenwood white men and women contributed money for the men's defense. The prosecution produced no witnesses, and the defendants didn't testify. The jury—all white, male "qualified electors"—took one hour and five minutes to acquit them.

You and Segregation by Governor Herman E. Talmadge of Georgia came out that year, its clarion cry for continued segregation rallying white southerners to the flag from Virginia to Texas. There was nothing new in it; it was only an echo of Tom Brady's *Black Monday* published the previous year; it was no more temperate, only possessed the enhanced political cachet the author's high position offered. Talmadge revived all the clichés: how *Brown I* and *II* had insulted states' rights, the prophecy that racial mixing in the schools meant interracial marriage, the politicization of the U.S. Supreme Court, its citation in *Brown I* of more authorities on sociology and psychology than references to the laws and Constitution, and the relationship of civil rights advocacy to the international Communist conspiracy. All together, Talmadge concluded, the Supreme Court's decisions in the segregation cases had placed in the hands of the NAACP "the power and authority to destroy the public school systems of many sovereign states."

Dan Byrd reported to Thurgood Marshall in late August that black plaintiffs who'd joined the school segregation suit in St. Helena Parish, the companion case to New Orleans's Bush case, were being intimidated. A branch of the Southern Gentlemen had been organized there at midsummer, and by the end of August its members were overseeing the hiring and firing of public school personnel. A black teacher was fired because her father had signed the court papers. A janitor was let go because his brother was a plaintiff; not so veiled threats were making the rounds of the school system.

All of which did nothing to ease tensions in New Orleans, where struggles over segregated public schools were bringing out the worst in some people and the best in others. On September 12, 1955, a delegation of white New Orleanians led by Rabbi Julian Feibelman and Rosa (Mrs. Charles, Jr.) Keller stalked into a meeting of the Orleans Parish school board waving a petition signed by 179 white New Orleanians and demanding that the board members "honor the laws of the United States" and "make plans for the immediate integration" of schools in their jurisdiction.

Following brief introductory remarks by Feibelman in which he sharply criticized the board's hiring of special attorney Gerard Rault "to circumvent and defy the law"—a "misusage of public monies," he called it—Rosa Keller read the petition in its entirety to the board. Feibelman had written it but had asked Keller to present it to the board.

I'm Jewish [he'd explained] and that makes a difference.

When people in New Orleans talked about the city's elite, the name Rosa Freeman Keller was often the first they offered. She was the second of three children born in New Orleans to a prominent businessman, Alfred Bird Freeman and his wife Ella—both Georgians who'd migrated to New Orleans in the early part of the century bringing along the Coca-Cola franchise for Louisiana. The drink had caught on there about the way it had in the rest of the country, and Freeman had quickly risen to local fame and fortune.

Education-wise, his daughter Rosa was a product of the city's segregated public schools, the Newcomb Music School in New Orleans, and Hollins College in Hollins, Virginia. Socially, she'd been educated at debutante parties and Mardi Gras balls. Her father and brother both had been reigning kings of carnival.

Her access to the highest social circles was limited some now by her marriage to Charles Keller, Jr., a Jew, but her entrée into business and political New Orleans was still open. She had, in fact, campaigned for DeLesseps Morrison's election as mayor in 1946, and he'd never forgotten the debt. If he didn't always approve of her civil rights activism, ladylike though it was—marching in the streets wasn't her "cup of tea"—the door to his office was usually open to her. Among businessmen, she was not above trading on her family's name, and she delighted in taking local black leaders into the inner sanctums of bankers and industrialists when she had some problem of race relations with which she needed help.

The results were mixed. In gratitude for her help in his political campaign, Morrison appointed Keller to the library board. She behaved quietly for a year, "trying to look nice, doing my homework," but then began to agitate among her fellow board members, segregationists all, for desegregation of the city libraries. Following *Brown,* it had become an issue in New Orleans as black organizations pleaded with city officials for access.

After returning home from meeting after meeting physically nauseated from the board's resistance, Keller told Morrison she'd have to resign. To her surprise, he told her he thought she was right about desegregation, and after meeting with city officials, he made library integration official policy. It was the only public facility in New Orleans that desegregated without a court suit or the threat of one.

Her attempt to integrate the Orleans Parish Medical Society during the previous year had no such happy ending. In her capacity as chairman of the board of Flint-Goodridge Hospital, a black institution, she went to the current president of the medical society, Alton Ochsner, world-famous surgeon, founder of Ochsner Hospital, and one of the elitest of the city's social elite. All she could think of was Captain Queeg in *The Caine Mutiny* when she suggested admitting black physicians to the professional society: "His face began to twitch, his hands nervously moved things around on his desk, his eyes darted around quite strangely, and he mumbled incoherently," then flew into a passion using language that made her blush.

Keller's civil rights activism had evolved slowly, beginning during World War II when she volunteered to fill her recently deceased mother's seat on the Young Women's Christian Association's board of directors. She learned more than the logistics of testing air raid sirens and checking black-out precautions in the Ninth Ward. The "Y" was one of the rare interracial organizations in the city, and she met for the first time black women who weren't servants but were "self-respecting and well-educated, women who could and should have been welcome anywhere." Women, moreover, whose existence she'd never known before.

And she was appalled that the people she worked with so "convivially" at the "Y" were unacceptable in white hotels, stores, restaurants, public parks, even, to her horror, churches. All of which, combined with her disgust and anger at Nazi treatment of the Jews at about the same time, turned Keller into a confirmed and energetic participant in the struggle for blacks' civil rights.

She went from the "Y" to boards at the Urban League (interracial), Dillard University (black), Flint-Goodridge Hospital (black), and the Amistad Research Center, a depository for black history on the Tulane University campus. She became an important connection between the black and white communities in New Orleans and an outspoken critic of racial segregation in public facilities.

Her husband, a West Pointer and veteran of World War II fighting, tried to talk her out of her activism: when she replied with no hesitation: "You fought your war. This is my war and someone's got to do it. I've gone too far to stop." They had some "sticky" times of it, although he came around eventually. Her father's friends at the exclusive Boston Club suggested he tell her to "shut up." Friends argued with her:

"These niggers don't want what you say they want."

"Who have you talked to?" she would ask.

"The cook," was the invariable reply.

She attributed their attitude to a fear of change. Nevertheless, the heaviness of the opposition sometimes made her question her principles. She "couldn't go to a party or a wedding or anything without getting attacked," and she would get to thinking that maybe she was "wrong after all."

But not for long. "You can't," she declared, "just sit back and let things happen."

Members of the Orleans Parish school board and School Superintendent Jim Redmond, who was also there the night of September 12, 1955, received Keller's pleas somewhat less politely than they had received those of A. P. Tureaud and Dan Byrd in the past. They heard her out, but they made no secret of their hostility. They listened impatiently to her hope that the city not "close its eyes, harden its heart and ostrich-like pretend that no such issue as school desegregation exists." Segregation, she warned,

> now is legally wrong. In addition to this, and not less important, segregation is morally wrong. It offends, if not actually defiles basic ethical and religious teachings of the major religious bodies of the Catholic, Protestant, and Jewish faiths.

And she concluded with an appeal for action: that school officials immediately settle down, look the facts of constitutional law in the face, and study the city's social, economic, and geographic environment

> with the purpose in mind of drafting a plan by which integration or desegregation of schools of Orleans Parish may go forward as soon as possible.

The men were stunned into fury, "practically threw us out," Keller recalled some years later. "[S]uch howling and screaming you never heard." They expected opposition from Tureaud and the others from the black community who'd appeared at their meetings. They did not expect such language from a prominent white woman. They could only imagine the kind of trouble Rosa Keller could stir up for them. The newly organized White Citizens' Council within two weeks had collected fifteen thousand signatures on a petition urging the school board to "take every possible action to prevent integration of white and colored children in the same schools of New Orleans and continue the principle of separate but equal facilities."

By 1955, Keller was accustomed to the slights and snubs at cocktail parties by people she'd danced with as a debutante, people crossing the street to avoid her, anonymous phone calls informing her husband she was "sleeping with a nigger." But she was entirely unprepared for what happened shortly after her debut at the school board's meeting. She had vastly underestimated the opposition's desperation.

Her children were upstairs studying and her husband was out one evening when a member of the board, whom she declined to identify publicly, came to her door. Recognizing her caller, she opened it without hesitation.

To her astonishment, instead of offering the usual greeting, he pulled a little gun out of his pocket—"scared the hell out of me"—and launched into a tirade, called her a Communist, and demanded an apology for what she'd said to the school board. When she was able finally to collect herself, she simply looked him in the eye and said:

If you shoot me it's going to make BIG newspaper headlines.

He had planned, he said, to confront Rabbi Feibelman that night, too. Feibelman had been getting hate mail and obscene phone calls since the school board meeting, but so far no unruly callers with murder on their minds. In the face of Keller's bravado, however, her visitor turned and walked away. Keller, her hubris dissipated, collapsed on the floor. The incident so unsettled her, she couldn't tell anyone about it for years.

On December 1, 1955, a special three-judge court made up of Judges Skelly Wright and Herbert Christenberry of the New Orleans division of the federal district court for the Eastern District of Louisiana, plus Wayne Borah of the Fifth Circuit court of appeals—the same trio that had decided in 1950 that Roy Wilson could not be rejected by LSU's law school—presided over the first open court hearing of the Bush case against the Orleans Parish school board. Waiting for the U.S. Supreme Court rulings on school segregation had cost them more than three years and the meter was still running.

On hand for Bush and the ninety-odd other black plaintiffs were Tureaud plus a veteran of the Supreme Court school segregation battles, Robert Carter, who with Thurgood Marshall had supervised Tureaud's paperwork: the complaints, the briefs, the motions, and other legal whatnot required for court proceedings.

The power of the state was amassed at the defense table: no less than the state attorney general Fred LeBlanc, flanked by the new school board attorney Gerald Rault, and W. Scott Wilkinson, a Shreveport lawyer increasingly involved in defending segregation suits.

Tureaud and Carter presented the plaintiffs' side in their usual straightforward way. They said nothing about the psychological damage of segregation that had won the Supreme Court case for them but concentrated on the legal and constitutional issues. Federal law and the Supreme Court's decisions, Carter declared, were equally "clear." Racial segregation was "unconstitutional in the field of education."

The lawyers for the school board demanded the judges dismiss the suit. Failing that, however, they made some sociological arguments of their own. Denying that the question of race per se was the reason they were contesting Earl Bush's admission to an all-white school, lawyers for the school board had gone to local psychologists, psychiatrists, law school deans, and Orleans Parish school officials to collect their data, and had come to the hearing with thirty-five affidavits and other exhibits in which their experts testified in essence that racial mixing in the public schools would undermine if not destroy the state's ability as well as its constitutional authority to "protect public health, morals and welfare," the authority implicit in the Constitution's Tenth Amendment.

Using the comparative scores of white and black students on the Metropolitan Readiness Tests, which had been used for years in the local school system to measure a child's readiness to handle the social, psychological, and academic demands of school, Superintendent Jim Redmond had characterized black children as intellectual liabilities. Those scores revealed, Redmond had said, that black children in every grade, one through twelve, scored lower than white children, that in fact the evidence amply supported "the generalization that Negro pupils are from 1.5 to 3.4 grades below the level of achievement attained by white pupils."

Clarence Scheps in his affidavit made out black children as social and cultural misfits. The "average Negro child," he said, "in the main, comes from a deprived home with the educational attainments of his parents extremely low . . . homes which do not contain facilities of a sanitary nature almost taken for granted in the homes of the average white family," homes lacking in the "social and cultural opportunities considered normal for the white child."

> How [he asked] can the Negro child, coming from such an environment, with a lack of social and cultural advantages, be expected to compete on even terms in a community of white children?

He answered his own question. He believed it would be "tremendously disadvantageous and unfair to the white children of New Orleans to force integration" in the schools. White parents didn't want it, "very few" black parents wanted it, and the effects of it would be "disastrous." He urged the court not to order it.

As was customary, the three sphinxes gave no indication of the direction their thoughts were taking. Past performance pointed to reliance on precedent, *Brown I* and *Brown II*.

But resolution of the Bush suit was more complicated. "With all deliberate speed" had not been tested yet; what it would mean to this trio was anybody's guess. Judge Parker had shown them an easy way out. Would they take it?

CHAPTER 13

Revisiting the Civil War in Legal Dress

S ix inches of rain fell on New Orleans on February 15, 1956, flooding at least part of every section of the city and retarding the efforts of street cleaners to remove the mountain of debris left by Rex and his convivial court, King Zulu and *his* followers, and the near million Mardi Gras revelers who'd danced in the streets the day before. Nursing the usual morning-after headaches, New Orleanians trudged solemnly off to Ash Wednesday church services. About the time the aspirin took effect, the afternoon paper was on the street, its eight-column front-page banner headline screaming:

N.O. PUBLIC SCHOOLS ORDERED TO BEGIN DESEGREGATION PLANS

If Federal District Judge Skelly Wright had arrived in New Orleans on a gunboat, torn down Confederate emblems, and replaced them with American flags, then marched to the customhouse, a military band playing "Yankee Doodle" the way Union General Ben Butler and his troops had done nearly a century before, he could not have shocked and disturbed the townspeople more than he did the day he announced his court's decision in the Bush suit against the Orleans Parish school board. He was the first district court judge within the Fifth Circuit's jurisdiction—the deep South from Texas to Florida—to issue an injunction ordering a school board to abolish racial segregation in its schools. As state senator Willie Rainach said, "the battle" was now "joined": the white majority against the black minority, the state government against the federal, and the local school board trapped in the middle, its freedom of movement blocked now by the one, now by the other.

The legal and constitutional issues had given Wright no trouble. The Bush suit was obviously the next generation of *Brown,* the offspring necessary for perpetuation of the parental features, and he had already settled in his own mind the meaning and implications of *Brown.* Looking at it first through the lens of the American history he once taught, he'd found a place for *Brown* as "the Civil War over again in legal dress." What the Supreme Court had done, he explained later, was to "indicate clearly that the time had come to pay full respect to the outcome of the Civil War, to the constitutional changes that it wrought."

Then he'd put *Brown* into the context of the Court's own precedents. After it decided the Texas Law School case, *Sweatt* v. *Painter,* in 1950, which he himself had quickly followed up with his order to desegregate the law school at Louisiana's state university the same year, Wright figured the justices had to "either retrogress in their movement toward equality or . . . to finally reject *Plessy* and the idea of separateness." The justices seem to have crossed their Rubicon at about the same time Wright crossed his, and *Brown I* was less a "giant step" than a lot of people had thought. By mid-1954, the constitutional "steps were all taken." The Court's decision in *Brown I* had "exhilarated" Wright, but it hadn't surprised him.

He wished the Court had supplied him with guidelines, indicated "what kinds of plans would be successful," and imposed a "time frame" for school desegregation to begin. But even lacking these, he'd found the mandate of *Brown I* and *II* compelling; "nothing, just nothing, could stand in the way of desegregating." *Brown,* he added, "did not in my judgment admit of any exceptions, however creative and resourceful" its opponents might be.

The *Bush* decision, like the *Brown* decision, came in two parts. The three-judge panel—District Court Judges Wright and Christenberry plus circuit Judge Borah—disposed of the major constitutional issue, which was the state legislature's post–*Brown I* defiance of federal authority, in a terse no-nonsense per curiam opinion announced first. The 1954 amendment to Louisiana's constitution and the statute requiring or permitting racial segregation in the public schools of the state were, the three judges chorused, "invalid under the ruling of the Supreme Court in Brown."

Christenberry and Borah then withdrew from the case and turned it back to Wright, in whose court it had originated, to issue the decree. It was here that his fears, hopes, and political sensitivities showed.

He had kept his own counsel during the weeks since the December hearings, answering the questions asked by his younger brother Jim, to whom he was close, but elaborating on them very little. He wasn't accustomed to sharing his philosophical journeys into legal and constitutional matters with either family or friends. He still had no law clerk with whom to discuss the fine points of decision writing, and once again he set off alone to cross a treacherous sea.

Aware of the potential for trouble in a federal court order to reshape the traditions of a city that hadn't changed "significantly for a hundred years," Wright tried to time it well. His opinion had been ready on the Monday before Mardi Gras, but he deliberately postponed making it public until after the holiday frenzy ended, when he hoped the calm of Ash Wednesday, beginning of the Christian season of repentance, would work to his advantage.

But he didn't allow his concern for white reaction to dissipate his resolution. Too many times he had driven through rural Louisiana, passing all those tumble-down one-room schoolhouses for black youngsters set apart from the "new little brick buildings" reserved for whites. He knew that "a Negro school would always get secondary treatment in the matter of buildings . . . up-keep, and . . . teachers. You name it and they would come out second." The picture that stuck in his mind long after the event was of a typical shanty for black pupils he'd seen set just off the road to Baton Rouge. Water stood high in the schoolyard following a soaking by one of the daily monsoonlike downpours, and a man was carrying the children, one by one, on his back to the privy perhaps fifty yards away. Wright knew these youngsters and all the others like them were "tied to the segregated slum where the social, intellectual, and educational damage . . . [began] the day they [were] born."

In the six years since he had crossed his personal Rubicon, his "earlier indifference," as he called the escapades of his youth, had vanished, and his own courtroom had become one of the "havens of refuge" for the "helpless, weak, outnumbered" and the "victims of prejudice and public excitement" that his judicial hero Hugo Black had written about. His opinion supporting the Bushes' claims fell neatly into the pattern. The defendants, that is, the members of the Orleans Parish School Board, Wright declared sternly, were prohibited from "requiring and permitting segregation of the races in any school under their supervision."

He elaborated on what his fellow judges had said about the unconstitutionality of the legislature's attempts to preserve segregation in the local schools, pointing out where the amendment to the state constitution and the specific statutes, including the pupil placement act, fell short. Then his tone moderated some.

Compared with the severity of some of his later opinions, those he wrote after he lost patience with the local school board's intransigence, Wright's *Bush* opinion was conciliatory. He spoke softly this first time, hoping to win some hearts, but he left no doubt that he held the big stick of federal authority in reserve.

He set no deadlines for desegregating, but allowed the board "such time as may be necessary to make arrangements for admission of children to such schools on a racially nondiscriminatory basis with all deliberate speed as required by the decision of the Supreme Court in *Brown* v. *Board of Education of Topeka.*" He assured the city's white majority that his granting of the injunction the black lawyers had asked for did not mean he would order the public schools of Orleans Parish "completely desegregated overnight, or even in a year or more." Rather, as the Supreme Court had also instructed the lower courts, "local school problems" would be carefully considered.

And then in an uncharacteristic nonlegal passage in which black Coast Guard stewards and cooks marched between the lines alongside blind Christmas Eve partygoers separated by race and black school children who had to be carried to the privy when it rained, Wright reached out in humility and hope to the collective conscience of this heavily Catholic city. At the same time, he let white New Orleanians know that he, not so long ago just "another southern 'boy'" himself, understood.

He had scribbled the two paragraphs just the Sunday before on the back of a Mardi Gras ball program while Helen sipped her morning coffee in bed. Like a CIA operative, Wright kept his personal and professional lives in separate compartments. He didn't tell her what he was writing, and he didn't read it to her afterwards. She was unaware he was drafting perhaps the most eloquent passage of his career:

> The problems attendant desegregation in the deep South are considerably more serious than generally appreciated in some sections of our country. The problem of changing a people's mores, particularly those with an emotional overlay, is not to be taken lightly. It is a problem which will require the utmost patience, understanding, generosity and forbearance from all of us, whatever the race.

But he could not yield, and he could not allow New Orleanians to yield. He had set his course:

> But the magnitude of the problem may not nullify the principle. And that principle is that we are, all of us, freeborn Americans, with a right to make our way, unfettered by sanctions imposed by man because of the work of God.

Wright's decision scored a direct hit on New Orleans at a time when the entire white South, writhing in the grip of insecurity and fear, was sending out all the classic signals of panic. The prevailing moods ranged from honest soul-searching up to and including violence.

Over the decade following the Supreme Court's decision in *Brown,* all of the various frames of mind were reflected in the federal courtrooms of the South, as local lawyers dug out doctrine and precedent to sustain segregation and at the same time survive judicial scrutiny. Wright's decree, simultaneously conciliatory and firm, his deliberate appeal to the religious among his fellow New Orleanians standing out starkly against his sternly delivered directive to the school board, was an anomaly among district court decrees in the South during those years. Wright's opinion took its place some distance along the judicial spectrum from John Parker's of the previous July, which had illumined a way out of the woods for southern whites, even though Wright's "such time as may be necessary to make arrangements for the admission of children to such schools on a nondiscriminatory basis with all deliberate speed" was word-for-word Parker and a paraphrase of the Supreme Court.

The time element, however—the lack of a firm deadline—was all the two rulings shared. The dynamic was entirely different. Having explained away the Fourteenth Amendment as a passive instrument that only forbade "the use of governmental power to enforce segregation," Parker required nothing from school officials and expected nothing. Wright's decree explicitly ordered the end of school segregation the minute it was practicable to stop it, and it was clear he expected the initiative to come from school officials. Whereas Parker put the responsibility on the Negro who'd been disabled and weakened by the system he had to abolish, Wright put the responsibility on the strong and powerful to undo as soon as they could the damage they'd done.

There was little uniformity among the South's federal judges as they struggled over the next decade to reconcile their communities' traditions with their oaths of office. Their courtrooms became theaters of confrontation, with all America watching the show. In the absence of specific instructions from the Supreme Court, it was every man for himself. Many found that between compliance and circumvention, there was a good deal of room for individual discretion.

A judge could dismiss a case or demand a plan, allow delay, or devise his own plan. What a district judge did, in the end, came down to personal predilection. And when state officials or local school boards applied the pressure, dozens of federal judges found ways to avoid carrying out the orders of the United States Supreme Court in *Brown* v. *Board of Education of Topeka.*

Some judges had no stomach for racial desegregation at all. The outspoken octagenarian and avowed segregationist William H. Atwell of Dallas, Texas, sitting temporarily in Brooklyn, New York, some thirty years before, had been censured by the local bar association for insulting a black attorney appearing before him. In the mid-fifties, he was semiretired, just helping to clear the local federal court docket, but his advanced age had not extinguished his fire. Following *Brown,* he steadfastly maintained that "the real law of the land is the same today as it was on May 16, 1954." The first chance he got to adjudicate a suit on that basis, he did. As if it really was May 16, 1954, and *Plessy* v. *Ferguson* was still the law of the land, he dismissed the suit of black parents seeking admission of their children to white public schools in Dallas with the declaration that "when similar and free schools are furnished to both white and colored . . . there then exists no reasonable ground for requiring desegregation."

Judge Wilson Warlick of North Carolina let it be known that he was a "states' rights individual"; if he "had anything to do with schools in North Carolina," he wouldn't "let the federal government have any part of it." Although the Supreme Court had stated clearly that the "vitality" of *Brown*'s constitutional principles could not "be allowed to yield simply because of disagreement with them," Judge Sterling Hutcheson of the federal district court for the Eastern District of Virginia, pushing the Supreme Court's order to "adjust and reconcile public and private needs" to its limit, and blurring the line between understanding of community problems and defiance of Supreme Court directives, ruled on remand of the Prince Edward County school case, one of the original five that comprised *Brown,* that to demand the "mixing of the schools, resulting in closing them, would be highly and permanently injurious to children of both races."

In Louisiana's Western District, Judge Ben C. Dawkins, Jr., of Shreveport, heart of the state's strongest segregationist sentiment, had to be prodded and scolded by the appellate court into obedience of the Supreme Court's orders, and he admitted at one hearing that if he had his way, he'd "still be on *Plessy* v. *Ferguson,* separate but equal." Judge Gordon West of Baton Rouge had been overheard to confess that he "considered the Fourteenth Amendment unconstitutional and a great tragedy."

All these recalcitrant judges risked reversal by higher courts, and each of them had decisions overturned. Judge Dawkins only shrugged: "It's all part of the game."

One of the most difficult problems the district judges faced was the vagueness of what constituted the "racially nondiscriminatory school system" the Supreme Court justices had imagined when they assembled *Brown II.* Parker's essentially passive position that the Court had not intended to require the "mixing of white and Negro children in the schools," but only the abolition of discrimination, clashed with the Kansas court's holding that maintenance of separate schools for blacks and whites was unlawful, even by mutual agreement between the two races.

It was Parker's, however, that most appealed to judges who were taking the heat. After Parker spoke, almost any plan for public school desegregation that fell short of blatant defiance of the Supreme Court's orders encountered little difficulty in federal courtrooms. One after the other of the district judges freely granted the school boards the delays they asked for, readily settled for token plans, and approved weak programs that kept most blacks in segregated schools even beyond the time when those in the first grade when *Brown II* was handed down would have graduated from high school.

Of the plaintiffs whose names appeared on the original segregation cases, only Linda Brown of Topeka, Kansas, ever attended a desegregated school; her family moved to Springfield, Missouri, where she entered the desegregated Central High School. Harry Briggs, Jr., was a thirteen-year-old seventh grader when *Brown I* was handed down, but even he was out of school before Clarendon County school officials made "the necessary arrangements" for admission to its schools "on a nondiscriminatory basis with all deliberate speed." Spottswood T. Bolling, Jr., of Washington, D.C., where school desegregation had begun immediately following *Brown I,* transferred to Spingarn High School where one white student attended classes with sixteen hundred black ones. When Dorothy Davis graduated from Moton High School in Prince Edward County, Virginia, in 1956, it was still all black, and the entire state was mired in a massive resistance program to keep it that way. Already a high school senior when *Brown I* was handed down, Ethel Louise Belton of Wilmington, Delaware, also graduated before her school could be desegregated; some of the younger Delaware plaintiffs whose names did not appear so prominently on the suit did, however, attend desegregated schools.

No one, *U.S. News and World Report* discovered in an April, 1956, survey of federal district judges hearing segregation suits, was "anxious to issue ultimatums with time limits." Of the 2,147,798 school-aged black youngsters in the deep South (Alabama, Florida, Georgia, Louisiana,

Mississippi, Texas) in 1955–56, 2,782 were going to school with whites, all of them in Texas.

"With all deliberate speed," assumed to be the U.S. Supreme Court's way of allowing time for school officials to plot courses of compliance, to prepare parents and pupils psychologically for the changes they would have to make, to work out the complicated logistics of administrator- , teacher- , and student-reassignment, back-fired. When put to the test, "with all deliberate speed" helped *Brown*'s opposition a good deal more than it helped its supporters, allowing whatever moderates there were time for procrastination and the bitter-enders time for organizing and arming.

In retrospect, it has been suggested that the local school boards were under too much pressure in the deep South states to act on their own, that at the time they might have welcomed firm, clear-cut guidelines and time limits from the courts, which would have absolved them of the blame for compliance. Without such directions, they either foundered or resisted.

In New Orleans, School Superintendent Jim Redmond's response to Skelly Wright's order to desegregate was cautious. He was not about to embark on any such radical program, or even comment on the federal Court's decision until he had word of "what steps to take" from the school board and "our special attorney, Mr. Rault." Mr. Rault was also cautious, unwilling to comment until he'd had time to study the ruling.

Standing in for the new school board president, Celestine P. Besse, who was out of town when Wright released his opinion, the old board president Clarence Scheps stood firmly on the principles he'd enunciated on this issue over the years. He reaffirmed the board's strong commitment to racial segregation in the city's schools and promised to appeal the federal court's decision. Asked if plans had been made to desegregate, just in case the board's appeals to the higher courts failed, he replied:

Absolutely not. We will not integrate.

On his return to New Orleans, Besse reiterated the board's determination to "use every legal and honorable means to preserve segregation," renewed Scheps's pledge to appeal, and instructed Rault to prepare the papers immediately. Neither Scheps nor Besse explained how he would simultaneously uphold the state and federal constitutions, both of which he had taken an oath to support and each of which now demanded diametrically opposed action.

The *Times-Picayune* predicted no good would come of Wright's Ash Wednesday ruling, that resentment would only grow as pressure on the South increased, and a federal Court order could not "change public feeling." If the judge intended racial mixing in the schools, then in the editors' view, the court was "crediting the school board with superhuman power."

Louisiana's legislators were undeterred by the district court's invalidation of their post-*Brown* statutes and constitutional amendment that had contemplated retention of racially segregated schools throughout the state. Defeat in the courts only spurred them to new pinnacles of defiance, and they took their cause again into the mean streets of politics.

The United States Congress itself set the example. Harry Flood Byrd of Virginia, one of the Senate's most influential members, whose reputation for integrity had won him political leverage beyond the borders of his own state, and who might have used his popularity to sponsor a movement for compliance with *Brown I* and *II,* instead was busy during the nine months following the announcement of *Brown II* stirring up resistance to public school desegregation all across the South. The movement was a legacy of the Dixiecrat protest against the regular Democratic party's failure to support states' rights in 1948. But by 1956, attitudes had hardened, as the *Times-Picayune* said, in response to the increase in pressure on the South. The rhetoric and ramifications of this contemporary maneuver were second only to those of secession the century before.

Byrd and the Dixiecrats' candidate for president in 1948, Strom Thurmond of South Carolina, now Senator Thurmond, were working backstage in the Congress to rally support for a public challenge to the Supreme Court's decision. Thurmond wrote the first three drafts of the document they put together. It required six altogether, most of them demanded by delegations from the border states who wanted Thurmond's warlike wording toned down. Finally on March 12, 1956, Senator Walter George of Georgia read the "Declaration of Constitutional Principles" as it was officially known, or the "Southern Manifesto" as it soon came to be called, into the *Congressional Record.* Its origins in the United States Congress made it the most prestigious opposition to the Supreme Court to date.

Nineteen southern senators and eighty-two members of the House signed it. Both Louisiana's senators, Allen Ellender and Russell Long, added their names, as did the entire eight-man Louisiana delegation to the House. Waverers were strong-armed, and only the pluckiest refused: Senators Albert Gore and Estes Kefauver of Tennessee, the latter a potential vice presidential candidate in 1956, Lyndon B. Johnson of Texas, Senate majority leader at the time and not asked to sign, and twenty-four intrepid members of the House.

This document of defiance was grounded in the Tenth Amendment's guarantee of states' rights. The lawmakers scolded the justices of the Supreme Court for their "clear abuse of judicial power" in their "unwarranted" decision of May 17, 1954, the climax, the legislators added, visions of past tidelands oil put-downs as well as lost voting rights suits marching in their heads, of a "trend in the federal judiciary undertaking to legislate, in derogation of the authority of Congress, and to encroach upon the reserved rights of the states and the people."

Neither the federal Constitution nor the Fourteenth Amendment to it, the southerners contended, mentioned education, and the Supreme Court justices had no business using it to club the South into compliance. It was an "unwarranted exercise of power" and served only to create "chaos and confusion" in the states "principally affected."

The lawmakers "commend[ed]" those states that had "declared the intention to resist integration by any lawful means," and "pledge[d]" themselves to "use all lawful means to bring about a reversal of this decision . . . and to prevent the use of force in its implementation."

When the Georgia senator finished reading, the manifesto's author, Strom Thurmond, took the floor to explain the need for the document, with which he hoped to win the support of "all people who love the Constitution." Using his own state of South Carolina as the model, he described how "outside agitators" employing "racist lawyers" had disrupted the "harmony which has existed for generations between the white and Negro races." It was these "troublemakers" who'd made Harry Briggs and the other Clarendon County blacks dissatisfied with sending their children to tumbledown schools in a rowboat because the local school board refused to assign them a bus. He claimed that Clarendon County schools for Negro children were now superior to those for white youngsters, though the Negroes continued to seek admission to white schools, leading Thurmond to conclude that they were really interested not in improved education but in "the mixing of the races." For moral and social as well as political reasons, he said, the United States Supreme Court had set a "dangerous precedent."

The Southern Manifesto not only breathed new life into resistance to the Supreme Court's decisions in the segregation cases, but it enhanced the respectability of the opposition, if any of the state legislatures needed it. Louisiana's didn't. The adrenaline was flowing freely.

Immediately following Skelly Wright's announcement of *Bush,* state senator Willie Rainach had chided the federal Court for presenting the "sorry spectacle" of southerners, which all three of the judges of the Bush suit were, "plunging their own state into sorrow and strife" and the white children of Louisiana into "moral and intellectual chaos." He solemnly swore that "the people of Louisiana will not integrate," and threatened that

> Moves will be met with countermoves, decrees with laws, and political court decisions with political strategy. There will be no compromise. We will fight and fight until we have finally won.

Privately, he whistled another tune: "I fully agree with you," he told a friend, "that we face ultimate defeat in the federal courts and all legal action is merely a delaying tactic. . . . We will be forced to the private system for schools, parks, and recreational facilities before the matter progresses much further."

Over the next four or five years, his cynicism notwithstanding, Rainach was tireless in his efforts to fulfill his pledge. With the creative and resourceful Leander Perez as technical director, Rainach schooled the Louisiana legislature in obstruction tactics as effective as any in the South. Once underway, this resistance movement became increasingly difficult to stop. Its political appeal made it increasingly impossible for voices of moderation to emerge and be heard above the din.

The first order of business in Baton Rouge that summer of 1956 was a formal statement of policy vis-à-vis the southern view of America's unique structure of federalism, the fragile relationship between the states and the nation. In this their hour of crisis, the lawmakers revived an obsolete and long-dormant eighteenth-century political theory known as the doctrine of interposition. Popularized in the regional press following the Supreme Court's decisions in *Brown I* and *II,* it quickly became the battle cry of opposition to the Court's orders throughout the South.

Ignoring Article VI of the federal Constitution, which made it the "supreme Law of the Land" binding on all the states, and pretending the Civil War, which was supposed to have settled the issue of state versus federal supremacy once and for all, had ever happened, the doctrine of interposition was based on a proposition last articulated in 1831 by the hardcore states' rights advocate and vice president of the United States John C. Calhoun of South Carolina. He'd gotten it from the Virginia and Kentucky Resolutions of 1798 and 1799 passed by the two state legislatures to publicly protest Congress's passage of the Alien and Sedition Acts.

As Calhoun put it, the "General Government emanated from the people of the several States, forming distinct political communities and acting in their separate and sovereign capacity, and not from all of the people forming one aggregate political community." The Constitution, as Calhoun defined it, was thus a compact to which each state was a "party" and the "several States, or parties, have a right to judge of its infractions." In his view, Article VI notwithstanding, none of the states had relinquished their sovereignty to the nation at the Constitutional convention of 1789, but had retained the authority to "enlarge, contract, abolish the General Government's power at its pleasure." What the states had given, the states could take away.

Calhoun, who wanted to be president as much as Willie Rainach a century later wanted to be governor of Louisiana, was urging the states to protest the tariff of 1828 which he saw as destructive of the South's cotton-based economy and the prelude to a later frontal attack on the institution of slavery itself. Regional feeling against the tariff was running nearly as high following its enactment by Congress as that against the Supreme Court's decision in *Brown* v. *Board of Education of Topeka* in the mid-1950s and its Louisiana offspring *Bush* v. *Orleans Parish School Board* in 1956.

Closely following Calhoun's reasoning, the example of Virginia, and setting an example for the legislatures of North Carolina, Arkansas, and Texas, the Louisiana senate and house, on May 29, 1956, enacted a concurrent resolution telling the federal courts "hands off" the state's public schools. Inspired by the recently released Southern Manifesto, the lawmakers "solemnly" declared the Supreme Court's decision of May 17, 1954, the federal district court's derivative decision in the local Bush case, and "any similar decisions that might be rendered in connection with the public school system and public parks and recreational facilities" affecting Louisiana to be "in violation of the Constitution of the United States and of the State of Louisiana." They intended to take "all appropriate measures honorably and constitutionally available to [them], to void this illegal encroachment upon the rights of the States."

Not a nay was heard when the resolution came up for a vote. Under the skillful shepherdry of Willie Rainach, who looked to interposition as a way of focusing "the searchlight of public opinion on the integration issue," it passed the house 82 to 0 and the senate 37 to 0.

For all its propaganda value, interposition was only a resolution, a formal expression of the way the lawmakers felt on the particular issue. At most it was a declaration of intent articulating the state's commitment to noncompliance with federal court orders to desegregate schools. It made agreeable reading for local segregationists and political hay for its supporters. But it had no force in either statutory or constitutional law.

Tactically, it provided the legislators with a foundation on which to build a structure of legal defiance, a rationale for proceeding with the orgy of vengeance on the federal government's "illegal encroachment upon the rights of the several States." Realizing perhaps the futility of the strategy, they didn't bother this time around to invoke the state's police power, which had proven following their rampage after *Brown I* in 1954 to be an empty euphemism, but had come right out and legislated separation of the races everywhere they could think of. Laboring through the long, hot months of June, July, August, and on into the fall of 1956, the Louisiana legislature implicitly nullified the federal court's orders in *Bush* v. *Orleans Parish School Board* by enacting statutes requiring racial segregation in the schools of all cities having a population of more than 300,000 (New Orleans, the subject of the only suit decided to date, was the only one to qualify) and the assignment of teachers on a racially segregated basis. Giddily the lawmakers had gone on to continue operation of all public parks, playgrounds, community centers, swimming pools, golf links, "or other recreational facilities," on a racially segregated basis. Railroad station waiting rooms, toilets, and participation in athletic events followed.

This last effectively killed plans in the works for LSU to play football and basketball against Big Ten schools, all of which had some black players. Even Little Leagues felt the pinch as white parents scurried to withdraw their children from mixed leagues and form white ones.

Fearful of a flood of black applicants to LSU's undergraduate departments following the Fifth Circuit's final ruling in January that in effect the university must admit A. P. Tureaud, Jr., and the U.S. Supreme Court's refusal in early May to reconsider the case, the state legislature responded with still another strategy to avoid the racial desegregation of classes there. What Leander Perez couldn't accomplish in the courtroom—he was still on the university's legal team and had participated in its appeal to the Fifth Circuit—he intended to achieve in other quarters. This time he resorted to a little legislative sleight of hand.

Under Perez's expert tutelage, the lawmakers enacted two statutes that proved lethal to black college and university students throughout the state. Their sweep embraced the recently desegregated McNeese State College, Southwestern Louisiana Institute, and Southeastern Louisiana College, as well as LSU.

The first measure, Act 15, required an applicant to any state institution of higher education to present a certificate of scholastic eligibility and good moral character signed by his or her high school principal and parish school superintendent. Its failure to enunciate any standards, leaving everything to the discretion of the local school officials, was troublesome enough. When the law was applied in conjunction with Act 249, which remolded the Teacher Tenure Act to make advocacy of racial integration in any state educational institution grounds for dismissal, it was dynamite. Leander Perez was salivating:

With these laws it won't be long before we purify our colleges.

His pleasure was, however, premature. The catch the segregationists hadn't anticipated soon became apparent. To whom did the laws apply? First-time applicants or students already enrolled, or both? By the time the issue was resolved, the acts were authoritatively interpreted to mean both categories of student, and Willie Rainach could smile his big crocodile smile as black student numbers dropped precipitously. But A. P. Tureaud had brought three suits challenging the constitutionality of Acts 15 and 249, and both the federal district and Fifth Circuit courts had agreed with him.

Skelly Wright had made short work of the suits. He found the state legislature's attempts to "purify" Louisiana's colleges and universities "more subtle" than the Orleans Parish school board's to retain racial segregation in the city's public schools, but hardly subtle enough to get by a federal court. The Fourteenth Amendment, he reminded the lawmakers, quoting a seventeen-year-old U.S. Supreme Court decision in an Oklahoma voting rights case, "nullifies sophisticated as well as simple-minded modes of discrimination."

Round one to the NAACP. Round two to Rainach and Company.

On March 1, 1956, just under two weeks after A. P. Tureaud won the Bush suit in federal court, Attorney General Fred LeBlanc, in close collaboration with Rainach, accused the NAACP of subversion and violation of Louisiana law, rendering the organization virtually impotent for the next five years. There had been no advance warning, and NAACP officers had had to scramble to secure their files in Tureaud's law office and send their money to New York headquarters before the state seized it.

LeBlanc and Rainach had resuscitated a state statute originally passed in 1924 to castrate the Ku Klux Klan by requiring its membership be made public, a statute that had lain comatose but that had not been repealed in the three-decade interim. They checked into state judge J. Coleman Lindsey's court in Baton Rouge and asked for an injunction prohibiting the NAACP from conducting business in the state and in effect to dissolve it for not turning over the required names and addresses.

Bob Carter came down from New York to stand in for Tureaud who didn't argue the case because he was a co-defendant in it. Carter invoked the U.S. Constitution's protection of free speech and assembly and accused the state officials of harassing the NAACP for its active resistance to racial segregation, but what mattered as much if not more than these objective criteria was what he told the court about the feelings of every NAACP member in Louisiana, even across the South, where similar attacks on the organization were being made:

> If we made our membership public, we are afraid in small communities it would serve to single them out for intimidation and economic pressures.

Disregarding the differences between the NAACP and the Klan, particularly the latter's preaching of racial and religious hatreds and its reliance on violence to achieve its ends, the *Times-Picayune* was quick to remind its readers that Carter's argument was one of those "used by or on behalf of the Ku Klux Klan" against the statute when it was before the legislature in 1924. Judge Lindsey himself had been in the state legislature when the statute at issue now passed, and he reminded those gathered to hear the suit argued that the NAACP was "one of the principal groups to prevail upon the legislature to pass that law."

Lindsey's comments and his recent judicial support for the state's allocation of public money to fight integration still fresh in their minds, the NAACP's lawyers saw little hope for survival in his court and filed a petition to have the case removed to federal court. After that, the jurisdictional disputes, which even Skelly Wright found "highly unusual" when he finally got the case, tangled until they appeared virtually insoluable. The attorney general confessed he was "confused, just like everybody else."

Lindsey ignored the transfer request and issued the injunction LeBlanc had asked for, prohibiting the Negro organization from doing business in Louisiana, even from holding meetings or participating in law suits until it turned its membership lists over to the state. Wright scolded him for retaining jurisdiction after the case had gone to federal court, but he felt powerless to take any action on it until it had made its way through the state system.

Caught between the two systems and under the state's injunction to cease and desist, the NAACP suspended all activities in Louisiana pending definitive judicial resolution of its status.

Almost completely paralyzed, Louisiana branch officials tried to maintain a minimum level of operation, informally raising funds for or donating their dues to the national organization, still a legally permissible activity, and setting up shadow groups to carry on the work. But a scrappy new state attorney general, Jack P. F. Gremillion, kept tightening the screws until at last several of the state branches said "ouch" and essentially capitulated. In December, 1956, three branches, including New Orleans, surrendered their membership lists to the secretary of state, and the resulting publicity accomplished exactly what the Louisiana officials had intended: the reduction in NAACP numbers. By 1957, NAACP membership in New Orleans had dropped from 4,750 to 1,300. Statewide it dropped from 13,190 members and sixty-five branches to 1,698 and seven branches. In rural areas the organization was effectively silenced for the rest of the decade. Even in New Orleans, its voice was subdued.

Bob Carter's fears of reprisal that he'd voiced at the hearing in Lindsey's courtroom proved well grounded. Willie Rainach got hold of the membership lists and distributed them to local newspapers and Citizens' Councils. The daughter of Dorothea A. Combre, president of the Louisiana state conference of NAACP branches, was suspended from her state job, threatening letters were numerous, and an "atmosphere of fear" prevailed at Lake Charles, Mrs. Combre's home. Café owner Frank Davis of Coushatta refused to drop out of the Red River branch of the NAACP; the mayor imposed a nightly curfew on his operations, his landlord raised his rent, starving Davis out of business. A black deputy sheriff in Shreveport was fired for speaking up for desegregation.

Not surprisingly, since Willie Rainach had his fingers in both pies, the attacks on the NAACP coincided with the rise of the Citizens' Councils in Louisiana. By April of 1956, first anniversary of their birth in the state, they claimed a New Orleans membership of twenty-five thousand, a statewide membership of fifty thousand to one hundred thousand, chapters in twenty-two of the sixty-four parishes, and a cozy relationship with Louisiana's leading lawmakers.

Rainach functioned as chairman of the Joint Legislative Committee to Maintain Segregation as well as president of the statewide Citizens' Council association. State representative John S. Garrett, vice chairman of the segregation committee and its spokesman in the Louisiana house, was a high official of the state councils and later succeeded to Rainach's positions in both. William M. Shaw, the segregation committee's general counsel, was also executive secretary of the state organization of Citizens' Councils. All three came from Claiborne Parish, in the heavily segregationist north of the state. Their proximity made cooperation that much easier; their professional connections made them that much more powerful.

The New Orleans branch was ostensibly under the leadership of the respected ex-president of the Louisiana Medical Association, Dr. Emmett L. Irwin, but it was usually Leander Perez who was pulling the strings in the back room: bankrolling it, recruiting members, making the table-pounding speeches, and devising the strategies.

On March 20, one month after Skelly Wright had raised their hackles with his ruling in *Bush,* the New Orleans chapter held a Confederate-flag waving rally in the local Municipal Auditorium calculated to plant fear in the hearts of any local blacks who might contemplate exercising their rights under the recent court orders. Georgia attorney general Eugene Cook and Georgia's former house speaker Roy Harris, the irrepressible roving ambassadors of segregation, came over from their home state to lead the anti–Supreme Court oratory, and a house-to-house canvass was launched to recruit fifty thousand members. Before the end of the month, the membership chairman reported record numbers of enrollments, exceeding all expectations. Within two years the New Orleans chapter was being ballyhooed as the largest Citizens' Council in America.

Turning up the volume of the sentiment for segregation, the Louisiana School Boards Association passed a resolution urging the state legislature to keep up the good fight against federal encroachment. The group warned black teachers and administrators that "their professional welfare would be greatly jeopardized" if racial segregation in the state's public schools were abolished.

Skelly Wright confided to a friend shortly after he released his *Bush* opinion that the position taken by Archbishop Joseph Francis Rummel, spiritual leader of the Catholic Archdiocese of New Orleans, was "the only thing that saves the situation from absolute madness."

The eighty-year-old, German-born Rummel, former pastor of St. Joseph of the Holy Family Church in Harlem where as a much younger man he'd taken his first lessons in American race relations, was in the habit of speaking his mind on controversial social issues. He had been the first Catholic bishop to circulate a resolution in May, 1954, supporting the United States Supreme Court's decision in *Brown* v. *Board of Education of Topeka,* and just months before *Bush* was announced, in the fall of 1955, matching his words with swift, forceful action, he had disciplined Catholic congregations in Jesuit Bend, a hamlet about fifteen miles south of New Orleans, and in Belle Chasse, a New Orleans suburb, for refusing to allow black priests to say Mass. The Vatican itself had commended the archbishop and urged all American Catholics to join the fight against "inhuman" racial prejudice.

Almost immediately after Wright handed down the Bush ruling, Rummel followed his long-standing custom and issued one of his periodic pastoral letters to the clergy and laity within his jurisdiction:

Racial segregation as such is morally wrong and sinful because it is a denial of the unity and solidarity of the human race as conceived by God in the creation of man in Adam and Eve.

Rummel freely acknowledged his church had segregated blacks ever since the Civil War, but denied the "arrangement" had been intended to be "permanent." He found it "amazing" that considering the "neglect and barriers to which they have been exposed in education, housing facilities, contact with stable institutions, and the more dignified ways of life," that blacks had survived as intactly as they had.

Again, he stopped short of setting a date for desegregating the local parochial schools, which, as private institutions, were out of reach of Louisiana's newly enacted segregation statutes and made up the largest single school system in the state, but a large majority of the families using the schools, like those using the public schools, wanted them to remain segregated. His letter was widely interpreted to mean the process would begin for the archdiocese's 60,000 white and 12,000 black students the following September.

His words, when priests read them out at mass on Sunday, February 19, rocked the half million Catholics in the archdiocese, which included, in addition to Orleans Parish, ten other Louisiana parishes and six smaller ecclesiastical units between Little Rock, Arkansas, and Jackson, Mississippi. A few priests refused to read the letter, and a cross was burned on the archbishop's lawn. Leander Perez, a devout Catholic, accused the Catholic hierarchy of "turning against their own people." Catholic lawmakers indicated they would ignore Rummel's moral prodding.

For the archbishop, the most disturbing reaction came from Emile Wagner, a prominent Catholic layman as well as a member of the Orleans Parish school board. Wagner and several dozen of his fellow rebels organized the Association of Catholic Laymen for the stated purpose of "investigat[ing] and study[ing], in all its aspects the problem of compulsory integration of the black and white races."

Piqued at Wagner's hubris and the challenge to his leadership, Rummel accused Wagner of trying to "embarrass and handicap the proper authority designated according to the sacred Scriptures, canon law, and tradition for the decision of questions of moment within diocesan administrations." Following several unproductive exchanges of letters, Rummel threatened the members of the association with excommunication if they continued in the direction they were headed. The laymen capitulated, though sullenly, and disbanded, though reluctantly.

On July 31, Rummel, who'd already removed the "colored" and "white" signs from Catholic church pews, announced parochial schools would begin desegregating on a grade-a-year schedule in September, 1957. The rectory was picketed and church contributions fell off drastically. Citing "certain difficulties"—it was common change knowledge in New Orleans that state legislators had threatened to take away church tax exemptions if parochial schools desegregated—the archbishop, his eyesight failing and his diminished physical strength draining his stamina, announced that his pastoral letter of the previous February 19 "still holds true as a guide of Catholic conduct," but the schools of the New Orleans archdiocese would remain segregated at least another year.

With the Orleans Parish school board's appeal of *Bush* still pending before the judges of the Fifth Circuit, all the schools in New Orleans, parochial and public, opened in September on the traditional segregated basis. Schools for black students were still overcrowded, schools for white youngsters had empty classrooms, and black parents were still showing up at school board meetings to protest makeshift arrangements that allowed lunch rooms, health classrooms, and gymnasiums to be set up simultaneously in the same thirty-eight-feet-by-eighty-three-feet space. School Superintendent Jim Redmond saw no substantial relief down the road. For all the progress made in the black schools of New Orleans, it could have been 1936 or 1946.

Nineteen fifty-six was an election year. The national card featured a return bout between the Democrat Adlai Stevenson and the incumbent Republican President Dwight Eisenhower. Civil rights planks in the platforms of both parties were flabby. Platitudes barely distinguishable one from the other, both were attempts to attract the black vote in the northern cities without alienating the white South and thereby precipitating another bolt like that of the Dixiecrats in 1948.

The Dixiecrats had lost the battle then, but had perhaps won the war, having substantially enhanced their bargaining power within the regular party. In 1956, they agreed to accept a "moderate" platform and a "moderate" candidate, and they got both. Except for an occasional outburst of support for the U.S. Supreme Court's decisions in the segregation cases, Stevenson was the very model of moderation.

Eisenhower's outlook on civil rights remained noncommittal. The Southern Manifesto, its high potential for further roiling the waters of opposition practically guaranteed by the vehemence of the document combined with the political stature of its authors, did not alarm the President. Asked about it at his press conference on March 14, two days after the congressmen issued it, he said:

Now, the first thing about the manifesto is this: that they say they are going to use every legal means. No one in any responsible position anywhere has talked nullification; there would be a place where we get to a very bad spot for the simple reason I am sworn to defend and uphold the Constitution of the United States and, of course, I can never abandon or refuse to carry out my own duty.

He went on to explain southern feelings: "the people who have this deep emotional reaction . . . were not acting over these past three generations in defiance of law. They were acting in compliance with the law as interpreted by the Supreme Court of the United States under the decision of 1896." Now that the law had been reinterpreted by that same body, it was going "to take time for them to adjust their thinking and their progress to that." He believed that ultimately they would approach their problems "intelligently and with patience and understanding." He concluded:

I do deplore any great extreme action on either side.

Only weeks before the Republicans were to meet in San Francisco in late August of 1956, the President had told an aide he was convinced the Supreme Court's decisions in *Brown* had seriously retarded racial progress, and shortly afterward he telephoned Deputy Attorney General William P. Rogers, asking him to soften a civil rights passage Rogers was planning to write into the party's platform. The next day he telephoned Attorney General Brownell, already in San Francisco, and had him delete that "the Eisenhower Administration . . . and the Republican Party" supported *Brown*. The President pointed out that Supreme Court decisions were not "actions" of his administration. Brownell interpreted the President's own "action" as evidence he was still not prepared to say whether or not he believed *Brown* had been "correctly" decided. After some discussion—the attorney general was thoroughly committed to civil rights—the two men compromised with "The Republican Party accepts the decision of the U.S. Supreme Court that racial discrimination in publicly supported schools must be progressively eliminated," which carried as much force as the Democrats' platform pronouncement that the Supreme Court's rulings in *Brown* had "consequences of vast importance."

Eisenhower didn't campaign in Louisiana in 1956. His advisers had told him it would be "a waste of time" for him to "visit the South this year," and he limited his political appearances largely to the mid- and far-western states, punctuated by brief calls in Richmond, Virginia, and in Jacksonville and Miami, Florida, and several nationally broadcast television addresses.

As it turned out, the President didn't need to campaign in Louisiana. He won the state anyway, the first time since 1876 a Republican had taken its electoral votes, prompting John Minor Wisdom, still the Republicans' man in Louisiana, to remark that two-party politics was once again a reality in his native state. In the South, Eisenhower again took Florida, Tennessee, Texas, and Virginia, giving him 67—more than half—the South's 128 electoral votes.

Black voters across the country, disappointed by Stevenson's equivocation on civil rights, were reported to have abandoned their traditional Democratic ties and contributed heavily to the overwhelming Republican victory. In Louisiana, it was said blacks voted Republican to show their disgust with Democratic state legislators' flagrantly racist post-*Brown* maneuvers and reelection campaigns in 1956.

On the state level, Governor Robert Kennon, barred at the time by the Louisiana constitution from succeeding himself, retired to Baton Rouge to practice law, and Earl Long was elected over a slate of six candidates that included Mayor Chep Morrison of New Orleans in his first of three runs for governor. Like his late brother Huey, Earl was not a blatant racist. Neither was he an integrationist. He paid his dues to southern tradition, standing, he said, "one thousand percent behind segregation," and after he was elected in 1956, he responded to the state's white opposition to *Brown* and *Bush* by yielding without a fight to the legislative leadership and unhesitatingly signing every last one of the obstructionist measures enacted that year.

He knew all the code words, the racist jokes, could even contribute a few earthy ones of his own. But Earl's main political agenda, also like his brother's, was geared to improving the health, education, and welfare of poor Louisianans, in which category he included blacks, and in these matters he did not discriminate. During Earl's first administration, 1948–52, recognizing the potentially big rewards of black enfranchisement, he'd gotten some 100,000 blacks registered to vote, raising Louisiana's total to more than 160,000. As he'd figured, they repaid him by voting overwhelmingly for him in 1956.

Which frightened Willie Rainach, ambitious young future gubernatorial candidate, nearly out of his white skin. And he stepped up his campaign to purge black voters from the state's rolls; the "illegally registered" he called them. His Citizens' Council members fanned out across the state, investigating registration records and disqualifying blacks for errors in "spilling," as one of them wrote on an affidavit, for miscalculations of age or mistakes in grammar. By the end of the year, they'd culled 11,000 black voters from the rolls.

In New Orleans in 1956, Israel M. Augustine ran for one of two vacancies on the Orleans Parish school board due to the resignations of Clarence Scheps and Celestine Besse. Had he won, Augustine would have been the first black to join the board since Louis Martinet and three others were appointed in 1877. Augustine, however, lost. Elected to fill the two vacancies were Louis G. Riecke and Lloyd J. Rittiner.

The school board that was to successfully stave off public school desegregation in New Orleans for the next four years was in place now. It was the creation of a group of women reformers who'd worked for Chep Morrison's election as mayor in 1946 and in their eagerness to clean out political corruption in their city had gone on to reconstitute the school board, gradually filling it with youngish civic-minded business-men with firm commitments to public schools and reputations for integrity and independence.

Theodore H. Shepard, Jr., elected in 1952, was a local shrimp importer. Emile Wagner, elected on the same ticket, was the scion of an old New Orleans family that had come to the city in the early eighteenth century. He'd gone to the segregated local parochial schools, graduated from Loyola University, and was now an officer, soon-to-be-president, of the Hibernia Homestead and Savings Association, for which the new school board lawyer Gerald Rault was counsel.

Matthew Sutherland, elected in 1954, was a fourth-generation New Orleanian, a product of the segregated local public schools, and in 1956 general counsel for the Pan American Life Insurance Company. One of the new members, Louis Riecke, ran a small family-owned lumber com-pany, was active in Charity Hospital and several local welfare organiza-tions and had been president of both the local and state Young Men's Business Club. The other new man, big, affable Lloyd Rittiner, was also a product of the segregated local public schools, had a degree in mechani-cal engineering from Tulane and in 1956 owned the Rittiner Engineering Company, which he'd founded. He was an enthusiastic member of the Dads' Club at Edward Hynes Elementary School, where his two children were enrolled.

Of the five, the stocky, dark-haired Wagner was the only hater, the only one who belonged to the Citizens' Council. Ironically, he'd been Skelly Wright's closest friend at Loyola Law School, and was remem-bered by the Wright family later for the many days he'd driven Skelly home after classes, then sat talking with the future judge for hours in front of the Wright house on Camp Street. It was in fact Wright who'd recommended Wagner's candidacy for the school board when the reformers were looking for someone to run in 1952. Wright and Wagner weren't friends anymore.

Neither Riecke nor Rittiner had supported Wright's ruling on the

Bush suit. Both had run on a platform of preserving racial segregation in the public schools and pledged to fight to the legal limit all attempts to desegregate them. But neither these two nor Sutherland and Shepard were filled with the kind of hate men like Wagner and his confederates Rainach and Perez displayed. Like Skelly Wright and so many others, they'd grown up in a segregated society as intrinsic to their lives as breathing in and breathing out. Over the next four years they would be personally torn between clinging to their cherished traditions and defying public sentiment, professionally torn between obeying the commands of the state and carrying out the orders of the federal court.

Not one political figure of stature in all of Louisiana that year advocated compliance with either the law of the land or the local federal court's ruling in *Bush*. As Skelly Wright contemplated the wreckage, he thought he could "stand a little encouragement" and was grateful when he received it from friends who'd read his widely reprinted Bush opinion—the *New York Times* described it as calculated to "stir the heart."

But the outlook for changing either the minds or the mores of his fellow southerners seemed bleak in 1956. The number of white moderates on racial questions in New Orleans was never high, and those few seemed paralyzed by the growing and stiffening opposition. Wright was deeply concerned that "unless we get some help from our leaders and our papers in this area, it will be a long time before the light shines through."

CHAPTER 14

Smashing More of the Old Family China

O ne morning early in 1957, the year that marked the one hundredth anniversary of the U.S. Supreme Court's decision to deny the Missouri slave Dred Scott and all other American blacks the "rights and privileges" of American citizenship, the Reverend Abraham Lincoln Davis, pastor of the New Zion Baptist Church and the most influential black clergyman in New Orleans, met Mayor Chep Morrison in a municipal building hallway.

Genially greeting the local black leader who had for some years been his closest contact with the black community, Morrison remarked, "Reverend, I hear you're suing us."

The mayor was referring to the suit Davis and several fellow black ministers who'd organized themselves into the Interdenominational Ministerial Alliance, had persuaded A. P. Tureaud to file against the city in federal court. Titled *Davis* v. *Morrison,* the suit asked the court to kill one of New Orleans's—and the South's—most sacred cows: the state laws relegating black passengers to the back of the bus, or, in New Orleans's case, the trolley cars as well, in principle, what Homer Plessy had futilely sued for in 1892. Like the Comité des Citoyens, the clergymen, who together represented a sizable chunk of New Orleans's black population and knew the power of the pulpit, which was beyond the reach of white economic reprisal, wanted the offensive laws requiring segregation on public transportation declared unconstitutional and the practice stopped.

Davis was forty-three years old in 1957. He'd come to New Orleans from Bayou Goula, Louisiana, where he was born, just over two decades before. He'd built his New Zion Church up from ninety to eight hundred members. Until black riders in Montgomery, Alabama, boycotted that city's bus line into submission the previous year, opening all sections of public vehicles operating in the Confederacy's first capital to blacks and whites on equal terms, Davis had kept his feelings about racial segregation quiet publicly. After Rosa Parks, the modern Homer Plessy, refused to give her seat to a white passenger and to move to her traditional place at the rear of a Montgomery City Line bus one dreary afternoon in December, 1955, had been tried, convicted, and fined, and Davis, along with the rest of America, had watched Montgomery's black population retaliate by refusing to patronize the local transit company, he took his protests against segregation straight into the pulpit.

Using the slogan "New Orleans Negroes Will Not Dance While Montgomery Negroes Walk," black New Orleanians had already, for the first time in history, boycotted Mardi Gras balls and parades when Davis officially broke his public silence and told a mass meeting of 2,500 blacks gathered at the Union Bethel African Methodist Episcopal Church that he and they were "tired ... of sitting behind screens"—the movable signs that designated white and black seating on public transportation. While Citizens' Council recruiters were out knocking on doors to raise their membership by 50,000, Davis called for "100,000 Negroes in this vicinity to rise up and let Perez and his followers realize that the time is out for segregation and for all that this evil monster stands for." The meeting collected $3,000 for Montgomery's militants, who were enduring bomb threats, assaults, and arrests, court suits, harassment, and humiliation in retaliation for flexing the new muscles they believed *Brown* had given them.

The success of Montgomery's blacks demonstrated vividly to both races throughout America, including the Reverend Davis and his colleagues in New Orleans, the potential of blacks' economic power and the depths of their determination. The New Orleans clergymen, however, preferred to solve the problem of bus and streetcar segregation in the courts rather than the streets, although they never ruled out the latter should the former fail.

Tureaud devised the legal arguments while the ministers got out the petitions and publicity, mobilized financial support, and orchestrated rallies and meetings. The charismatic young Martin Luther King, Jr., the Thomas Payne of the Montgomery boycott and one of a new breed of educated, politically savvy, and perhaps most important of all, self-confident black leaders who were replacing the fragmented, more docile older generation in the South, came over from the Alabama capital, his incantations rousing the crowds that gathered in New Orleans's black churches to cheers.

Black New Orleans in the end had no need to strike against the local bus and trolley line. The legal strategy worked. *Davis* v. *Morrison* wound up in Skelly Wright's court. After hearing arguments from both parties plus the state of Louisiana which had filed the usual motion to dismiss the suit, Wright ruled that Louisiana's laws requiring racial segregation on public transportation were unconstitutional and void

> in that they deny and deprive plaintiffs and other Negro citizens simi-
> larly situated of the equal protection of the laws and due process of
> law secured by the Fourteenth Amendment to the Constitution of the
> United States.

That same day, Wright issued essentially the same ruling in connection with a similar suit Tureaud had filed protesting racial segregation in city-operated parks and recreational facilities. As expected, attorneys representing the city and the park concession announced they would take their cases to the U.S. Court of Appeals for the Fifth Circuit. They warned that the judge's rulings must not be put into effect until all avenues of appeal were exhausted. Following a talk with the city attorney, Alvin Liska, and other local authorities, Wright agreed to withhold the injunction Tureaud had asked for pending final court action. In the South during these litigious days, that usually meant not only the next highest appellate court but ultimately, the United States Supreme Court.

A. P. Tureaud was spread thin that year. In addition to the two cases against the city, he had a dozen petitions, some of which were out of date, pending before parish school boards throughout the state, and black parents in the city were still complaining about overcrowding in their children's schools.

According to the latest figures published by the *Louisiana Weekly,* a grand total of 10,817 black students went to school in platoons: half from 8 A.M. until noon, and the other half from noon until 4 P.M. Besides feeling educationally short-changed, black parents considered their children's idle half day a direct invitation to delinquency, and the large classes and long days added unnecessary strain on their teachers. The most overcrowded schools were those for black children in the politically powerless and economically disadvantaged Ninth Ward where at Robert Moton school, dedicated less than a year before, 2,200 youngsters were on the platoon system. Once again frustrated parents were petitioning the school board, their voices rising in direct proportion to the casualness of the school board's dismissals of their requests. Any one of the meetings of outraged parents held the potential for an explosion, the fragments falling into Tureaud's office.

He already had eight court suits, including appeals of the Bush case against the Orleans Parish school board, pending in one local court or another. Much later, Skelly Wright would speculate that it was the excessively heavy case load the black lawyer and his Inc. Fund associates bore as they tried to keep abreast of legal battles across the South that prevented them from pressing the Bush case, five years old in 1957, as aggressively as they might have.

When 1957 opened, the Bush case was awaiting decision in the United States Court of Appeals for the Fifth Circuit, to which Orleans Parish school board attorney Gerald Rault had taken it. On March 1, a three-judge appellate panel unceremoniously dismissed it and upheld Skelly Wright's order of the previous year that the city's schools must desegregate.

The Fifth Circuit court's future role in the civil rights revolution of the 1960s was not yet blindingly obvious largely because the number of civil rights cases coming to the court in the mid-1950s was still too small for patterns to be discerned. There were, however, signs, and the court's decision in the Bush suit was one of them.

The three judges who decided it were Alabaman Richard Rives, who'd supported Skelly Wright's orders to desegregate Louisiana State University's undergraduate departments a few years back and whose opinion ultimately had prevailed; John Robert Brown, Nebraska-born lawyer more recently from Houston, Texas, who'd gotten out the Texas vote so efficiently for Eisenhower in 1952 that the Republican had taken Brown's adopted state; and Elbert Parr Tuttle, Eisenhower's first appointment to the Fifth Circuit in July, 1954, less than two months after the Supreme Court's announcement of its decision in *Brown*. The California-born, Hawaii-reared, and Cornell Law School–educated Atlanta Republican had lined up Georgians to vote for Eisenhower in 1952, and, although the state had voted two to one for the Democrat Stevenson, Tuttle's efforts, like John Brown's in Texas, had been rewarded with an appointment to the appellate court. After the civil rights movement was over, Claude Sitton, who'd reported the agonies of the period for the *New York Times,* told an interviewer:

> Those who think Martin Luther King desegregated the South don't know Elbert Tuttle and the record of the Fifth Circuit Court of Appeals.

It was Tuttle who wrote the court's opinion in Bush's case. Its strength, its close reasoning, the way Tuttle laboriously dismantled school board attorney Rault's case, point by point, leaving no doubt of his meaning, ought to have alerted plaintiffs and defendants all across the deep South to where this relatively new judge was heading. Particularly his concluding analysis of the Fourteenth Amendment:

> However undesirable it may be for courts to invoke federal power to stay action under state authority, it was precisely to require such interposition that the Fourteenth Amendment was adopted by the people of the United States. Its adoption implies that there are matters of fundamental justice that the citizens of the United States consider so essentially an ingredient of human rights as to require a restraint on action on behalf of any state that appears to ignore them.

A disgruntled Louisiana attorney general, Jack Gremillion, called the Fifth Circuit's ruling a "dangerous precedent which will have repercussions throughout the state." An equally disgruntled Gerald Rault applied to the Fifth Circuit for a rehearing. The judges refused. He then petitioned the U.S. Supreme Court to consider the case. That Court also turned him down.

Normally, no respectable lawyer recommends that his client continue to press litigation involving an issue already definitively decided by the Supreme Court, but in the late 1950s and 1960s, the strategy was part of the South's policy of massive resistance. Any tactic that bought a year or two of delay in racial desegregation was worth whatever it cost. Desperation was the prevailing mood, and lost-cause litigation threatened to choke the federal courts to death, the legal and constitutional issues at stake less important than the politics.

Rault's bosses, elected officials all, were determined to fight until the last legal recourse had been taken, and Rault sat down immediately to search for some unexplored point, some loophole that had escaped his sharp lawyer's eye, some way he could keep the city's gates shut against the federal wolf. Once again he applied to the Fifth Circuit, charging that the black lawyers in the *Bush* suit had failed to file a $1,000 bond required by the court. Again the Fifth Circuit turned Rault down, telling him he'd waited too long to complain. Rault's request for a rehearing at that level as well as a request that the Supreme Court consider the case was also denied. Which was less important to the school board lawyer than the fact that he'd bought nearly a year of precious time.

Looking for more, Rault returned to Wright's court, contending that the state legislature had stripped the local board of control of its schools in 1956. Rault's bosses, he argued, were powerless to comply with the judge's orders.

Wright required only three short paragraphs to dispose of Rault's arguments. He concluded wearily:

> It would serve no useful purpose to labor this matter. The Supreme Court has ruled that compulsory segregation by law is discriminatory and violative of the Fourteenth Amendment. . . . Any legal artifice, however cleverly contrived, which would circumvent this ruling . . . is unconstitutional on its face. Such an artifice is the statute in suit.

Over the three years following Wright's initial ruling on racial segregation in the New Orleans schools in 1956, Rault filed no fewer than seven appeals of the *Bush* case.

Rault, however, could not at the time have perceived the dynamic that was to drive the Fifth Circuit judges through the next decade of civil rights contention. A new coalition was building there, an alliance of men committed to no longer reading the Fourteenth Amendment the way southern law schools had traditionally taught it since *Plessy,* but in the revolutionary way the U.S. Supreme Court had read it in May of 1954. Richard Rives, John Brown, Elbert Tuttle, their jurisprudence now partially unwrapped, were waiting. They needed but one more to make a majority on what was then a seven-judge court. They had, of course, no way of knowing that day they announced their decision in the latest appeal of *Bush* that the fourth horseman was on his way.

Late in 1956, Wayne Borah, whose courtroom style Skelly Wright had long admired, announced he was retiring from active duty on the Court of Appeals for the Fifth Circuit after more than three decades of public service, all but five of those years spent on the federal bench. He retired officially on January 1, 1957, but was still available to sit on occasional panels although freed from the arduous full-time routine.

He'd been a regular on the special three-judge district courts with Wright and Christenberry ever since the desegregation of LSU's law school in 1950, and they would miss his support and guidance. They would not, however, be disappointed in his successor.

A seat on the U.S. Court of Appeals for the Fifth Circuit was a juicy plum coveted by every United States attorney, district judge, and political IOU holder within the six-state circuit. The salary of $25,500 in 1957 was considerably less than a crackerjack lawyer could earn in private practice, but it was comfortable and certain, guaranteed for life.

Along with the independence and security that went with a lifetime appointment, the job offered prestige and intellectual challenge. Prior to the influx of civil rights cases, which didn't reach flood stage in the Fifth

Circuit until the early sixties, there was time for writing jurisprudentially interesting and provocative opinions and for developing a viable philosophy of law at a leisurely pace.

Perhaps most important, the appellate bench was well removed from the battleground that district court judges like Wright and Christenberry faced regularly, the intervals between conflicts diminishing significantly since the U.S. Supreme Court had handed down *Brown* v. *Board of Education*. Appellate judges were less exposed to local pressures and alliances. The actual parties to the litigation remained faceless, and an appellate judge was rarely called upon to enjoin a golf or bridge partner. The passions of the trial were absent, their existence only implicit between the lines of the printed record of the cases. It was as good a life as a judge could find this side of the U.S. Supreme Court.

Borah's resignation started the rumor mills grinding immediately. Tradition decreed that Borah being a Louisianan, the seat go to a fellow Louisianan.

Panicky, state senator Willie Rainach, although preoccupied while the legislature was adjourned with his organizational work for the Citizens' Councils, of which there were now thirty-six scattered across the state, got in touch right away with both his United States senators. He'd read in the newspapers that the Republican administration was considering federal district judges Wright and Christenberry for the vacancy created by Borah's resignation, although both men were Democrats.

"Recent decisions by these judges," Rainach complained to Senator Russell Long,

> make them completely unacceptable to a vast majority of the people in Louisiana.

Rainach hoped Long would

> take every possible step to see that neither of these men is confirmed to this high office. This also applies to all others similarly *hostile* to our laws and institutions.

Long's reply was polite but noncommittal. He preferred to postpone discussion of the matter until the President's final choice for Borah's court seat was before the Senate.

Senator Allen Ellender, who'd received a similar letter from Rainach, was equally noncommittal, though somewhat more eloquent. Like Rainach, he deplored the Supreme Court's decision in *Brown*, which, he said, threatened to "wreck our educational system and retard racial relations in the South." He assured Rainach he was as "deeply against integration as anyone in the South." On the other hand, he was willing to concede that

> Judge Wright and Judge Christenberry have simply followed the mandate handed down by the Supreme Court just as have all other Federal judges who are complying with what the Supreme Court has decreed to be the paramount law of the land. They are in a position where they either have to carry out the Court's mandate, or cast off their judicial robes and resign.

In his retort, Rainach cited with obvious approval the example of Federal District Judge William Atwell of Dallas, Texas, who had consistently ignored *Brown*'s mandate and continued to operate under *Plessy*'s old "separate but equal" authority. Rainach wanted to see the federal bench populated by more judges like Atwell, who took "oaths of office to uphold the Constitution of the United States, and not the opinion of the Supreme Court, which may or may not be in keeping with the Constitution."

Ellender was unmoved. During his entire twenty years in the Senate, he'd supported the President's nominations except for only two he believed obviously incompetent. It was, he explained, the "President's prerogative to nominate men of his own choosing for Federal judgeships, and it is rather difficult for the individual Senators to raise objections, unless it can be shown that the person so nominated is clearly not qualified."

Former Louisiana governor Bob Kennon, who'd risked his political neck to lead the parade of Democratic governors into Eisenhower's camp in 1952, felt he deserved the judgeship and calculated that his friendship with the President's closest adviser, former New Hampshire governor Sherman Adams, gave him a shot at it. Forty years later, Eisenhower's first attorney general Herbert Brownell, who was an influential part of the judge-selection process, wrote in his memoirs that Kennon was ultimately passed over because he had remained a "staunch segregationist."

In the end it was not Wright or Christenberry or Kennon who got the much-coveted call. It was John Minor Wisdom, the man who'd persuaded Kennon to support the Republicans, who'd built a viable political party out of the little band of fewer than one thousand Republicans registered in the Louisiana of 1929, who'd persuaded the 1952 Republican convention to seat Eisenhower's rather than Taft's Louisiana delegates, and who'd stayed on in Republican politics long enough to persuade his state to vote Republican in 1956. Deeply appreciative of the loyalty and yeoman's service Wisdom had given the party and the President, Eisenhower also had come to like Wisdom personally during their periodic though brief White House meetings and discussions of southern politics. Wisdom always believed the decision to appoint him to the Fifth Circuit had been made not by Sherman Adams or Herbert Brownell or any of the usual presidential advisers, but by his new friend, the President himself.

Again Willie Rainach protested to his senators. Not only was he worried about Wisdom's lack of judicial experience, he wrote to Allen Ellender in Washington, but he was suspicious of Wisdom because of his service on the board of the racially mixed Urban League's local branch. The organization's liberal racial policies had recently come under the magnifying glass of the local Citizens' Council, which had been instrumental in getting the Urban League evicted from the Community Chest after a twenty-five-year membership. The charge, undocumented and unspecified, involved participation in Communist activities, but everybody knew the League's racial policies were its real problem. Rainach felt the appointment to the appellate court of a man affiliated with such a suspect organization was "almost equivalent to the appointment of a member of the NAACP," and he warned the senator, whose 1960 reelection campaign loomed not so very far ahead, that Wisdom's appointment to the Fifth Circuit "might well be construed in that light by the people of this state."

Ellender reiterated that it was his policy to "go along with presidential nominations, unless it can be shown that the person is incompetent or clearly unqualified." He would be guided, he said, by what he read in the record of the hearings to be held by the Senate Judiciary Committee.

In fact, at the time, the influence of southern senators on the selection of federal judges had diminished since the Supreme Court had handed down its decision in *Brown* v. *Board of Education,* and Ellender lamented the fact that a senator could "no longer, under the rules of the Senate, object to the nomination of anyone because he may be 'obnoxious' to that Senator."

Prior to *Brown,* recommendations of the senators from the districts involved in judicial appointments were important to a president. After *Brown,* the southern senators tended to recommend candidates with public records indicating opposition to *Brown.* As a result, the Eisenhower administration frequently nominated men to southern judgeships without asking for recommendations. It had to be done carefully, however, lest nominations antagonize southern lawmakers and jeopardize confirmation.

Brownell recalled in his memoirs that it was done by choosing "persons of outstanding quality." He might have added that one "outstanding quality" Eisenhower's nominees had in common was a record of partisan loyalty, and their views on *Brown* and other matters outside party politics were not always visible to the naked eye.

John Minor Wisdom's constitutional theology wasn't crystal clear to his sponsors on the eve of his nomination. His law practice was largely corporate, and he hadn't talked publicly about *Brown* or desegregation or race matters in general. He'd worked hard to restore the Republican Party in Louisiana and that was about all that was known. What he would do on the court of appeals was anybody's guess.

The fact that Camille F. Gravel, Jr., Louisiana's Democratic national committeeman whose public approval of racial desegregation nearly lost him his influential position, strongly supported the Republican Wisdom might have tipped somebody off. The fact that Emmett Irwin, president of the New Orleans Citizens' Council, and Robert Chandler of Shreveport, chairman of the States' Rights Democratic Party in Louisiana, showed up at Wisdom's confirmation hearings before a subcommittee of the Senate Judiciary Committee in Washington to testify against him indicated something about public perceptions of the nominee.

Questions regarding his participation in the Urban League did arise, but Wisdom slithered over them smoothly, explaining that he'd joined in order to promote harmonious race relations in economic matters: the Urban League, he assured his inquisitors, was not concerned with integration in the schools or in social relationships. His previous service on the President's Committee on Government Contracts, a group of presidential appointees charged with overseeing federal contractors' compliance with the nondiscrimination clause in their agreements, he rated similarly: he was the only southern member and had sought only to promote wider understanding; he emphasized that sanctions against noncomplying employers never had been invoked.

At one point in the proceedings, Chairman Eastland, who claimed he had "special pockets" in his pants where he carried civil rights bills and had developed blocking judicial appointments he didn't like to a high art, leaned over to Wisdom and whispered, "Don't worry about this hearing, there is nothing to it."

A few miscellaneous questions followed, including one regarding the nominee's deportment during a Mardi Gras celebration. Wisdom denied he ever had been disorderly but observed tartly that it was not unusual for Carnival revelers in New Orleans to consume a considerable quantity of alcohol.

When at last all the questions had been answered and all the charges defended, Chairman Eastland declared simply: "I am satisfied."

Local gossip attributed Eastland's easy satisfaction to traditional Washington wheeling and dealing. The deal was rumored to have been made when Wisdom interceded with the attorney general in behalf of Ben Cameron's appointment to the Fifth Circuit two years before—Wisdom was one of those who admired Cameron's legal skills—and cemented when Cameron subsequently supported Wisdom under similar circumstances. Together, the two transactions found sufficient favor with Chairman Eastland to prevent him from opposing the Louisianan, despite what the Mississippi senator might ordinarily have considered blots on Wisdom's record. Wisdom always suspected Eastland was counting on his being "another Cameron."

Although their polling of Louisiana lawyers had indicated widespread support for Wisdom's appointment, Senators Ellender and Long still refused to commit themselves for or against until they had thoroughly digested the transcript of the hearing. In the end, Wisdom was confirmed by voice vote "without objection" on June 26, 1957, and no one except the two senators themselves knew whether they answered "aye" or remained silent.

Not three months after he'd taken his seat in July of 1957, the new judge offered the first clue to his habits of thought on an appropriately dramatic occasion. That September, just three hours before they were scheduled to be strapped into the electric chair, he stayed the execution of two black men convicted of raping a white woman on the streets of New Orleans. The accused, Wisdom had concluded, had been denied a fair trial due to systematic exclusion of blacks from the trial jury. Not quite what the deep South expected from its judges, though in Wisdom's case, it was only the beginning.

Wisdom was part political functionary, part social and political historian particularly conversant with the southern experience, part constitutional scholar, and part avid student of Shakespeare and Marlowe, and he knew how to employ all the parts as superstructure for his judicial opinions. Scholarship as well as civil rights soon became his specialty.

The players were all in place now. "The Four"—Rives, Tuttle, Brown, and Wisdom—as the sturdy little unit was labeled, had come together to reassemble the Fourteenth Amendment in the deep South after Redemption and early twentieth-century judges had undone it. Three of the four were Republicans beholden to no one in the heavily Democratic South, unburdened by fears of disappointing their "friend the senator" or any impulses to look over their shoulders, as Tuttle put it later, when they followed the directions they were certain the federal Constitution had given them. The fourth, Richard Rives, the lone Democrat, had come a long way since he coached the Montgomery (Alabama) Board of Registrars on how to legally keep blacks from registering to vote. After upholding Skelly Wright's decision not to convene a three-judge court in young A. P. Tureaud's suit against LSU, he'd gone on to throw his judicial support to the black boycott of Montgomery's buses and to write a two-fisted opinion holding that requiring racial segregation on public transportation was as clear a violation of the Fourteenth Amendment as was requiring racial segregation in public education. He thought of himself as "not really pure on this question of bigotry . . . but I think my own experience is some indication that people change their views as they go along." A friend of Rives's son, an outspoken advocate of racial justice before he was killed in an automobile accident, believed that Rives had "wanted to live the new South his son talked to him about."

Together these four presided over the civil rights revolution in the deep South during the late 1950s and the 1960s, upholding national policy and protecting nationally guaranteed rights in the place they were the least popular, and taking, as Wisdom once put it, "the monkey" off the backs of the district judges.

The district judges, the Skelly Wrights and Herbert Christenberrys, the men for whom the parties to litigation were not abstractions but real faces, many of them contorted with hate and hostility, the men to whom the passions of the trial were not contained in the small print of the transcripts but erupted right there in their courtrooms, at last had solid, reliable support. Skelly Wright said later, in gratitude for the Fifth Circuit judges:

They backed me every step of the way.

Despite southern opposition and threats of a filibuster—Senator Allen Ellender of Louisiana, for one, had stockpiled forty hours worth of material with which to talk the "vicious and obnoxious" bill to death—the Congress passed, and the President, because he was concerned in 1957 about the "stature of our leadership in the free world," signed the first civil rights bill since Reconstruction. It wasn't much of a bill. It created a civil rights commission in the executive branch and a civil rights division in the Department of Justice, but its fangs had been filed down, the price southern Congressmen had extorted for their acquiescence. The section authorizing the attorney general to initiate legal action against civil rights violations had virtually disappeared, and the attorney general's authority was limited to proceeding only against threats to voting rights. Deputy Attorney General Rogers described it as handing "the policeman a gun with no bullets." The bill's main virtue was its role as a herald of civil rights bills to come. Attorney General Brownell himself, author of the original, stronger bill, regretted the weakness of the final version, but believed it "paved the way" to the future, contributing to the demise of the filibuster, so long an effective obstructionist's tool, to the later passage of more comprehensive and powerful civil rights legislation, and, most important, to an expanded role for the federal government in protecting civil rights.

The bill's reach did not extend to public school desegregation, which was proceeding as slowly as ever. The numbers of racially mixed school districts in the border states were increasing. South of Kentucky little was happening. Not one elementary or secondary school had desegregated in Alabama, Georgia, Florida, Mississippi, South Carolina, or Louisiana.

In New Orleans, Theodore Shepard, who'd succeeded to the presidency of the Orleans Parish school board—which had recently been "commended" by the local Citizens' Council "on its position regarding segregation and integration matters in view of the position which has prevailed in the community for generations"—told reporters that nothing had been done toward desegregating the local public schools and that he couldn't even contemplate it now. He rather thought the legal battles the school board had mapped out would drag out racial mixing in the schools for at least eight or ten more years.

To the suggestion that some of the underused schools reserved for white students be converted for use by black students who were crammed into overcrowded buildings, many of them substandard, Shepard countered that neighborhood property owners would immediately protest the inevitable downward slide in the value of their homes. "They would kill us," he argued.

All September, New Orleans, along with much of the western world, watched as the full force of white southern rage at the Supreme Court's decision in *Brown I* and *II* erupted in Little Rock, Arkansas. Young John Chancellor, Chet Huntley, and David Brinkley, just then discovering the power of the television image, were showing Americans, with an intimacy rarely achieved by newspapers, helmeted troops in battle fatigues patrolling an American city's streets, their fixed bayonets the only barrier between a human wall of howling segregationists and nine black teenagers assigned to desegregate Little Rock's formerly all-white, architecturally stately Central High School.

The disturbance seemed all the worse for its being unexpected. The upper-middle-class Little Rock civic leadership had chosen to desegre-gate a school attended largely by the children of working-class families. At the same time they left the suburban high school recently built for youngsters like their own untouched. The establishment seemed entirely unaware of the social dynamics involved, entirely insensitive to the possibility that poor whites, politically impotent, psychologically inse-cure, and materially disadvantaged, might well resent being told to do what they considered the dirty work of desegregation while the powerful and influential walked off scot-free.

To the city fathers' surprise, the whites took their revenge. They turned the well-groomed grounds around Central High School into a combat zone fiercely contested by the state in the person of the two-term governor, Orval E. Faubus, who was hoping to buy a third term using racial confrontation for currency, and the federal government, whose Court had ordered Little Rock to begin desegregating its public schools, and whose chief executive, President Eisenhower, though he'd vacillated and in the end acted only reluctantly, had dispatched the troops to make sure the Court order was obeyed. It was the first time since Reconstruc-tion that federal troops had been sent to keep order in the South.

The governor wasn't really a committed racist. He came from Greasy Creek in the Ozarks where race was secondary to economic sur-vival, and he hadn't made race an issue in his first two campaigns for governor. By 1957, however, *Brown*-born segregationist sentiment had intensified, and to friends who tried to dissuade him from interfering with Little Rock's public school desegregation, Faubus replied with final-ity: "I'm going to run for a third term, and if I don't do this, Jim Johnson and Bruce Bennett [Arkansas's leading segregationists] will tear me to shreds."

In the long run, the southern federal judiciary, the Skelly Wrights and others of his ilk, as well as the rule of law triumphed at Little Rock. The nine black students did finally enter Central High School, although many of the twenty thousand white students, who behaved as if they'd been apprenticed to the Ku Klux Klan, made the blacks' welcome as mis-erable as they could. Tacks strategically placed on a black youngster's desk seat, unprintable names shouted in the corridors, hot soup spilled on a black student's clothes in the cafeteria, lockers broken into at the gymnasium, surreptitious bumping, pushing, and tripping out on the gym floor, pelting with wet towels afterward, comprise only a partial list of the torments the newcomers were forced to endure—the perpetrators added nothing new to the annals of teenage torture, but it was no less hurtful for its banality.

Nevertheless, only one of the black youngsters failed to finish the first year at Central High. Three graduated from Central High, the most notable being Ernest Green, who eventually became an assistant secretary of labor in Washington; he returned to Little Rock two decades later as the featured speaker at the twentieth reunion of his high school class. When Faubus finally succeeded in closing all Little Rock public high schools in 1958–59, the rest had to forage elsewhere to finish their secondary educations. All nine did, and most earned college degrees.

Shortly after the incident at Little Rock, United States Attorney General Brownell resigned to return to his New York City law practice. His deputy, William P. Rogers, succeeded him.

Speculation soon surrounded Rogers's refusal to permit federal prosecution of agitators in the Little Rock crowds despite strong recommendations by Department of Justice officials to do so. St. John Barrett, a young lawyer in the new Civil Rights Section, for one, feared such failure "might encourage persons ... to interfere with" future court-ordered school desegregation. Some said the Eisenhower administration had already absorbed more than its share of criticism for its resort to the use of troops. Others suggested it was the price paid for easy Senate confirmation of the new attorney general. The Little Rock newspaper editor Harry Ashmore wondered publicly if the Eastland-dominated Senate Judiciary Committee's approval of Rogers had not been "one of the most singular political deals in recent years."

The lessons of Little Rock were lost on a lot of people who might have profited from them. The ugly confrontation, the presence of paratroopers patrolling the streets of an American city, the economic fallout as businessmen shunned dealing with Arkansans or settling in Little Rock, did not prod the civic leadership of New Orleans to prepare the city for the school desegregation ordered the year before. The silence only became more noticeable, particularly to militant segregationists, who wasted no opportunity.

After Little Rock, sentiment for permanent separation of the races in the schools metastasized. Southern white spines were stiffened by still another defeat at the hands of the federal government; segregationists escalated their attacks on the area's few—and shrinking number of—moderates and liberals. As Louisiana's governor Earl Long commented to Willie Rainach about this time, "a lot of people aren't with you, but they're scared not to be."

The politics of the period pointed up the widening chasm southwide. Just as he'd hoped, Arkansans reelected Faubus by a landslide in 1958—and 1960, 1962, and 1964. Segregation, combined with his victimization by the federal government, made powerful appeals in these uncertain times, and their impact extended beyond Faubus himself. Congressman

Brooks Hayes of Arkansas was soundly whipped by the militant segregationist Dale Alford, for whose candidacy Faubus had worked. Over the three years following Faubus's attempt to face down the federal government, 77 percent of the southern gubernatorial contests were won by diehard segregationists.

In New Orleans in 1958, political patterns paralleled those drawn in Arkansas and other sympathetic states of the South. A. P. Tureaud lost his first—and only—race for the U.S. Congress to the segregationist incumbent F. Edward Hébert. It was the school board race, though, that drew New Orleanians' attention away from Mayor Morrison's lackluster campaign for reelection to a fourth term. John P. Nelson, a former district attorney and a declared racial liberal who'd found moral support for integration in his Catholicism, was challenging incumbent and fellow Catholic Emile Wagner, who'd found support for segregation in *his* religious principles. Although the real issues were often lost in the smoke screen of charges that Nelson was involved in the so-called international Communist conspiracy—the knee-jerk answer in the 1950s to any equation in which racial liberalism was a factor—Nelson based his campaign on the school board's obligation to obey Skelly Wright's order to desegregate the local schools. He warned that "sooner or later" New Orleanians would have to comply with the federal Court's directive, like it or not. Wagner vowed to use every means he could "morally justify" to prevent integration, which he described as one of the "most ominous problems that have ever beset the board." Wagner won, three to one.

As if Little Rock had never happened, the Louisiana legislature returned from its recess refreshed and revved up to go to work on what little public resistance to public school segregation remained. Leander Perez was in his usual place behind the scenes, studying measures passed by other states and preparing drafts of bills to fit Louisiana's particular circumstances.

Willie Rainach's speeches and statements had helped to keep the issue of race before the public between legislative sessions. Under his direction, Citizens' Councils scattered across the state claimed to have purged some thirty thousand black voters from the rolls using gimmicks such as refusing to accept affidavits from blacks countering challenges to their registration, requiring identification of black registrants' witnesses by a Citizen Council member and a law enforcement officer, and the old standby, the "constitutional interpretation test" of new registrants. "By this time next year," Rainach crowed, "Louisiana will be a shining example to the nation on how to thwart the NAACP."

On the legislature's return, Rainach resumed his throne at the head of the Joint Legislative Committee to Maintain Segregation—now known as the Rainach Committee—to which the other lawmakers and even Governor Long, dependent on a large black constituency but too politically cautious to risk an open clash with the segregationists, deferred as quietly and unceremoniously as birds to a squirrel at the feeding dish. It was all in the natural order of things. Rainach soon discovered he could win support for any measure designed to preserve white supremacy. He had nearly all political Louisiana from the Governor down to the assembly's newest members in a hammerlock.

The dynamic duo, Rainach and Perez, was once again in control. Under Rainach's leadership and the expert legal guidance of Perez, whose interest in a statewide private school system to replace the public institutions hadn't changed since he first gave voice to it immediately following the U.S. Supreme Court's decision in *Brown* v. *Board of Education,* three major bills aimed at the establishment of such a private system emerged from the state legislature in 1958.

Act 256 authorized the governor to close any school that integrated and to distribute public school property to private school groups established by Act 257. Act 258 provided for state tuition grants to students attending the new private institutions. He intended, Rainach warned, the threat of Louisiana's preparation for privatization to serve notice that "we mean business, that the federal government is playing with fire in this matter." Governor Long, reluctant but unwilling to oppose Rainach, signed all three bills.

Two additional statutes and a constitutional amendment, all three measures affecting public school operations, should the systems unaccountably survive the previous assaults on them, also whizzed through the state assembly and the senate and governor's office in 1958. Act 259 was a revamped pupil assignment law to replace the one Skelly Wright had declared unconstitutional in his 1956 Bush opinion. Act 187 guaranteed teachers' salaries during time lost as a result of school closing due to desegregation, and the constitutional amendment provided for state control of both private and public schools. Their thoughts perhaps returning to the two state representatives who'd opposed the anti-*Brown* constitutional amendment in 1954 and lost their seats in 1956, the lawmakers gave these new measures their solid support.

Not everything went Rainach's way that year. To his chagrin, a New Orleans branch of the Louisiana State University opened in 1958 on a totally desegregated basis.

Redeeming a campaign pledge he'd made in 1956, Earl Long, looking to the next gubernatorial election looming just ahead in 1959, strong-armed the city out of a piece of land near Lake Pontchartrain where the university could at last be built.

Who could attend classes there, however, immediately became an issue. To solve the dilemma—state law prohibited integration and federal court orders prohibited segregation—Long persuaded the legislature to establish a branch of the all-black Southern University not far from the new LSU, which first became known as LSU-NO, then later, UNO—the University of New Orleans. The intent was to divert black students quietly from what was considered the main attraction.

The scheme backfired. On the books, both universities had to be open to all races. The federal courts would have stood for nothing less. But no whites applied to Southern while some two hundred blacks applied to the new institution its first semester.

Long didn't resist. "The feds are behind the niggers," he'd commented to a friend following the confrontation at Little Rock. "I'll be damned if I'll make a fool of myself like Faubus." Shelby Jackson's state education department resisted, however, claiming that the federal courts' decisions requiring LSU in Baton Rouge to admit blacks to its undergraduate classes didn't apply to the new university.

Tureaud once again took his problems into federal court and in record time—within a half hour after hearing the arguments—Judge Christenberry issued an injunction requiring LSU-NO to admit blacks. The Fifth Circuit later upheld the judge's action.

Two hundred blacks entered the new institution when it opened in September. It was the first university system in the deep South to be fully integrated. It had required a decade of litigation.

Legal efforts to muzzle the NAACP in Louisiana were renewed in 1958. The last attempt—1956—to get rid of the exasperating organization having ended inconclusively in a jurisdictional squabble between the state and federal courts, and the United States Supreme Court having just that summer decided in a similar Alabama case that forced disclosure of membership lists violated the due process clause of the Fourteenth Amendment, the legislators had to come up with a new device to harass the association. Act 260 required local NAACP branch officials to file an affidavit annually, attesting that no officer of the parent body belonged to any group "cited by the House of Congress [sic] Un-American Activities Committee or the United States Attorney General, as Communist, Communist front or subversive."

Although his resources were overextended, A. P. Tureaud nevertheless took on the added challenge. Citing nine recent legislative measures opposing desegregation as well as the recently enacted Act 260, which he found to be "part and parcel of a plan to preserve racial segregation in public schools and in other places of accommodation," he disputed the constitutionality of the 1958 act in federal district court.

The courts, too, were feeling the pressure of numbers, and it would be some time before Tureaud would have judgment on his suit. The docket for the Eastern District of Louisiana was becoming increasingly unwieldy, "approaching four times the national average per judge," Skelly Wright told a friend. He declined to spend his usual month sitting on the district bench in New York City that year, but he did finally persuade Chief Judge Hutcheson of the Fifth Circuit, with whom he'd begun pleading back in 1954, to allot him a law clerk. His first one, Peter Powers, fresh from Harvard Law School, arrived that fall.

Approaching the end of his first decade on the federal court, Wright, if he looked back, would have seen the contrails of his decisions in racial desegregation cases that had begun with *Dean* v. *Thomas,* the 1949 suit involving blacks' voting rights in Washington Parish. Following that he'd plunged headlong into Roy Wilson's suit for admission to Louisiana State University's law school—he still pointed to that case as his "Rubicon," after which he could never again be just "another southern 'boy.'" In the milestones department, young A. P. Tureaud's admission to the university's undergraduate departments came next. *Bush,* the capstone of his career thus far, followed. In early 1958 his recent orders to desegregate New Orleans's parks, recreation facilities, and transportation were pending in the appellate court. His popularity among his fellow New Orleanians approached that of someone who'd deliberately smashed a dozen pieces of the old family china.

The only time his fellow citizens uniformly applauded Wright was the day in 1958 that he, Christenberry, and the recently robed Wisdom, sitting together on one of the special district courts, ordered local sporting events desegregated. Segregated athletic contests, required by Act 579, which had been among the various bills passed by the state legislature in 1956, were costing the city money, as it was the black boxer Joe Dorsey, Jr., who estimated he was losing nearly $10,000 a year by not being able to fight whites. Dorsey filed a suit to get the law annulled.

The city fathers could not, of course, publicly support him, although they had already seen profits from football weekends melt away when Army refused to play Tulane in New Orleans the year before because of Act 579. They could, however, lend a hand surreptitiously.

Capitalizing perhaps on what they may have regarded—mistakenly—as Wisdom's naïveté, several prominent New Orleanians phoned him asking him to "set aside" the troublesome law. Thirty-plus years later, the judge could chuckle over the incongruity in men he suspected of membership in the local Citizens' Council wanting a segregation statute nullified, but at the time, he didn't "take kindly" to people "improperly calling a judge in a case to influence his decision."

Dorsey's wasn't the sort of case the judges had problems with. Wisdom wrote the opinion for himself, Wright, and Christenberry. Together they cut the arguments of the State Athletic Commission, against whom Dorsey had filed his suit, into shreds, then took *Brown* down from the shelf of precedents once more, augmented it with principles from Wright's opinion in *Bush*, ruled that the section of Act 579 that prohibited the races from competing against each other in athletic contests was unconstitutional, and issued a temporary injunction restraining the athletic commission from enforcing the act.

The fact that the despised *Brown* principles underpinned the court's decision in Dorsey's case seemed not to matter when money was at stake. New Orleanians were so pleased with the result that voluntary desegregation of several hotels, restaurants, and bars soon followed. Wisdom always thought a lot of people in the South of the late 1950s were ready to desegregate at least these sorts of public functions, but were, as Earl Long had said, "scared." With a court order to blame, they were willing. One of Wisdom's callers had in fact told him exactly that:

> Of course, we can't desegregate voluntarily but we would not object to an order ordering us to desegregate.

It was, however, the last time Skelly Wright did anything as a federal district judge that his fellow New Orleanians approved of. That same year they had to confront his court-directed reality of desegregation in their city parks, recreation facilities, and transportation after the Fifth Circuit upheld his decision and the U.S. Supreme Court refused to hear arguments. Some of them didn't much like it.

As the example of Montgomery had vividly demonstrated, racial segregation on buses was a deeply revered custom not always graciously abandoned in the South, and Wright shrewdly eased the city into the new order as gently as possible. He received word of the Supreme Court's refusal to hear the case on a Monday. The official papers arrived in his chambers on Wednesday. He wasted no time. Memorial Day weekend, when use of public transportation should be light, loomed immediately ahead.

Wright wanted desperately for his orders to desegregate to go "through successfully" and "with the least possible turmoil." He sat down with city attorney Liska and discussed how it could be worked. He secured the cooperation of the mayor, the police department, and the

New Orleans Public Service Company, which operated the city's buses and trolleys. The Montgomery experience had taught bus companies throughout the South the financial realities of race, and the New Orleans corporation was only too glad to cooperate with the judge.

Then he waited until midnight Friday, when the local newspapers had been put to bed, to issue his order to desegregate. One minute later, at 12:01 A.M., Saturday, May 31, just as he'd planned it, bus drivers and motormen all over New Orleans glanced at their watches, stopped their vehicles, and walked down the middle aisles while passengers—plainclothesmen from the New Orleans Police Department sprinkled discreetly among them just in case—solemnly and silently watched. Matter-of-factly, the drivers picked up the signs that for so many years had designated separate seating for whites and blacks, carried them to the front of their vehicles, and deposited them on the floor like pieces of junk.

Then it was all over. The barriers had fallen. A "very dramatic non-event," as one reporter referred to it.

William R. Adams, a local black physician who'd been part of the ministers' suit against the city, urged his fellow blacks to be "quiet, orderly, and of good behavior" in celebration of their victory, explaining that he wasn't asking for any less manhood but only suggesting that "we'll make more friends by courteous good behavior than by ruthlessness and belligerence." White New Orleanians, he added, should not "lend an ear to radical advice emanating from certain quarters." Revius Ortique, a local black lawyer, recalled a confrontation between the city's black and white leadership: "We said to the leaders of the white community, 'Look, you guys, *this* judge will put people in jail if they don't obey.'"

As events spun out, "*this* judge" didn't have to put anyone in jail. Police had prepared for trouble, but incidents were few: some minor shoving, a little name-calling, a slight decline in bus and trolley ridership. For a few days one old white man not ready to let go drove to bus and trolley stops to offer white New Orleanians rides. No one, however, accepted his largesse.

There was some grumbling about the arrogance of judges, an occasional verbal desire to "tar and feather" Skelly Wright, and finally, the burning of an eight-foot-high kerosene-soaked wooden cross on the Wrights' lawn. The judge thought it was probably "a Ku Klux Klan thing. It wasn't the work of an amateur," but dismissed it calmly as "just someone looking for publicity." Eleven-year-old Jimmie thought it was "neat" and "great fun," and went off bragging to his friends that "we got a burned cross." In most quarters it was thought to be the rare "act of a fanatic," few recognizing the depth of feeling behind the gesture or that it might be a portent of things to come.

CHAPTER 15

"The Only Thing Necessary for the Triumph of Evil Is That Good Men Do Nothing"

(EDMUND BURKE)

George Washington Cable, son and grandson of slave owners, who turned to blacks' civil rights for the text of his essays during the late nineteenth century, had not been born to social reform. On the contrary. He'd been born in New Orleans in 1844 to a prosperous local businessman and his wife and had grown up in a rambling wooden house on spacious grounds. Typical of its time, place, and caste, it was surrounded by large galleries constructed to catch any breezes blowing through the magnolias, live oaks, and fig trees on the property, and there were fireplaces inside to take the edge off the raw dampness of winter. Eight slaves lit the fires, tended to the lawns, cooked the meals, kept the house clean, and nursed the children.

The Cables were thoroughly committed to the southern cause. When the city fell to Union forces in 1862, Cable's mother and two sisters—his father had died in 1859—balked at taking the required oath of allegiance to the United States, were forced to register as enemies of it, were threatened with imprisonment, and were ultimately banished to Confederate territory. Sold, as Cable said, on "Union"—he feared secession—"Slavery, and a White Man's Government," young George accompanied his little family to Mississippi where he enlisted in the Confederate cavalry and was wounded twice before being discharged after Appomattox. During the war he'd carried books in his saddlebags, and by the end of it, his reading had led him to question not only the effectiveness of secession but also its political morality.

After the war, he'd worked as a columnist and reporter for the politically conservative *Daily Picayune,* but within a few years he resigned to write novels and short stories in which he crafted the scenes and traditions of his native city as lovingly as he did those of his heroes and heroines. Fame, fortune, and international critical acclaim followed, his work being compared favorably with that of William Dean Howells, Mark Twain, and Henry James. In outlook, his writings seemed no different from those of his white contemporaries, and he couldn't turn out his fiction fast enough to satisfy his publishers.

Also after the war, however, as he grimly followed the social, economic, and political upheavals his beloved South was enduring, he began to question his intellectual and emotional moorings, searching again for answers in books: historical tomes and the documents on which America had been built. By the early 1870s, his studies had convinced him not only that slavery was a terrible wrong in the past, but that the effects of it still haunted the present and were dragging down the postwar South.

In 1875, he wrote two letters to the editor of the *New Orleans Bulletin,* which had loudly opposed the racial desegregation of the New Orleans schools earlier in the decade. Signing himself simply "A Southern White Man," Cable suggested the argument over racial segregation in the New Orleans public schools was much ado about nothing; he himself couldn't imagine what harm brief social contacts with black children in desegregated schools could possibly cause white children who'd been nursed by Negro women and whose parents had spent their youth playing with slave children. The *Bulletin* published Cable's letter alongside a rebuttal by one of its own editors. Cable in turn shot off a spirited reply to the editor. But the *Bulletin* refused to publish this second missive, and the editor advised its author to put it away for ten years; on rereading it a decade later, he said, Cable would be ashamed of his foolishness. Cable did save it, noting on it not the editor's advice but that he had published his views ten years prematurely. He busied himself over the following decade with church-sponsored humanitarian projects, then, during the early 1880s, with a particularly successful effort to bring some semblance of reform to prisons and asylums, locally and nationally.

But the Negro's plight continued to trouble him, and in 1884 he decided the time had come, for good or ill, to discuss the subject of race publicly again. He could remain silent no longer. His novels in progress, he moved to a back corner of his desk while he concentrated on what he considered "the greatest social problem before the American people today . . . the presence among us of the Negro."

Persuaded by his success in changing some practices of the penal system during the past few years that he had only to awaken his people's social and moral consciousness to injustice and the indicated reforms would follow, he began to lecture throughout the South. Careful to disavow any intention to bring about social equality, and concentrating on the wrongs of slavery and its lingering effects, he managed at first to avoid the wrath of local politicians and newspaper editors.

Encouraged, his boldness grew. Standing before a national audience for the first time—the annual meeting of the National Social Science Association in Saratoga, New York, on September 11, 1884—he attacked contemporary subjugation of blacks and challenged southerners to confront their racial problems squarely as well as to remove the long list of discriminations and inequities, all of which he described in exquisite detail.

When the white supremacists got through with him, he was limp. He had been so sure of his arguments, so certain that his South was home to equally outraged white men and women who were entirely aware of the "wrong and folly of these things" and "silently blush[ed] for them" but withheld "their open protests only because [their] belief is unfortunately stronger in the futility of their counsel than in the power of a just cause." Cable thought that because the people he described had unhesitatingly come forward, encouraged after his lectures in small southern towns, to shake his hand and tell him how closely their own feelings coincided with his, that these "good southern people"—the men and women "in whom the community placed most confidence and pride"— would come forward similarly in their communities, speak out, and assume responsibility for leading the South into a new era of race relations.

He was wrong. He'd known he would face opposition, but he was unprepared for the vehemence of the personal abuse, particularly by newspaper editors, churchmen, and politicians, all of whom had built-in forums and constituencies, and he looked around in vain for the thousands of "good Southern people" in whom he'd placed his confidence. Support was nowhere to be found.

As he wrote in the first pages of his 1885 essay "The Silent South," he had discovered that the moral conscience of the region was symbolized by the "brave, calm, thoughtful, dispassionate, sincere" character of the revered Robert E. Lee, whose likeness stood in the center of New Orleans's Tivoli Circle. But, Cable continued, that conscience might as well have been carved, like the monument, out of white marble. In this time of crisis, it remained "all too mute."

Booker Washington himself admired Cable and provided him with factual information for his essays. But, lest he lose the support of southern whites for his own programs and his increasingly respected Tuskegee Institute, the black leader required the writer to keep their relationship secret. He rather thought, he told an acquaintance, that there were "many in the South who *think* as Mr. Cable does but have not the moral courage to express their sentiments." Some professed to believe race relations were progressing as rapidly as possible; others, that Cable was pushing a natural social evolution unnaturally. Time, not noisy protests, they agreed, would solve the problem.

Not even Cable's closest friend in New Orleans would, or could, admit he agreed with the writer's views, although he did. And when Cable brought together a group of like-minded college presidents and faculty members, clergymen, judges, lawyers, physicians, and business-men in an informal organization of correspondents for the purpose of publishing papers on the subject of race relations, the men abandoned the project within a couple of years, their appetite for addressing such inflammatory subjects more than satisfied. Ultimately exiled to Northampton, Massachusetts, where he lived the rest of his life, Cable cried out in agony to one of his old colleagues:

> Men of the South must speak out. How on earth is deliverance from error and misrule ever to come if the men who hold places of trust and influence cannot or do not give their counsel to the people?

Three-quarters of a century later, on July 15, 1959, nearly seven years since the *Bush* suit against the Orleans Parish school board was filed in 1952, and three and a half years after Federal District Judge J. Skelly Wright had ordered the same board to begin "to make arrange-ments for admission of children . . . on a racially non-discriminatory basis with all deliberate speed," the parties to the suit—except, of course, those who'd graduated from high school or college in the interim—were back in Wright's courtroom. The necessary "arrange-ments" had not been made, or even thought about, and the black plain-tiffs to the suit were there to press their cause.

Black education in New Orleans, overcrowded and understaffed, had continued to deteriorate, with black elementary school buildings expected to bulge in the fall of 1959 to hold an average 114 percent of their capacity while white elementary school buildings operated at an average 73 percent.

A. P. Tureaud was in his usual place in the courtroom, this time to raise the temperature of his attack on local public school segregation via a request for another injunction against the school board, whose mem-bers had so far successfully resisted any compliance with Wright's orders in *Bush*.

There was some agitation for the NAACP to start a separate suit demanding desegregation of Benjamin Franklin High School, a special facility for gifted students. Both Tureaud and Thurgood Marshall, however, had rejected the proposal on the grounds that another suit in New Orleans would bring only "confusion and harm" but "no advantage." Tureaud also had school suits still pending in East Baton Rouge and St. Helena parishes. PTAs in New Orleans's Ninth Ward were still petitioning the school board to alleviate the overcrowding there, but no one seemed to be listening. Southwide, Louisiana was still one of the five holdouts against *Brown,* along with Alabama, Georgia, Mississippi, and South Carolina. School desegregation was still limited to the border and south central states.

Gerald Rault was sitting at the defense counsel's table ready to defend the school board's honor against this latest assault by the black lawyer. The Fifth Circuit court of appeals just this past month had rejected a petition in which Rault had argued that the state legislature had taken away the school board's authority to desegregate New Orleans's schools no matter what the federal judge said. Wright, Rault argued, should never have declared the state statute unconstitutional without a definitive interpretation of it by the Louisiana supreme court.

Reminding Rault that this was the third time in as many years that this case had come before the appellate court, their tone suggesting that they were tired of Rault's delaying tactics, the panel of judges had made short work of Rault's claims and upheld the district judge. This very day the Fifth Circuit had denied the indefatigable Rault his request that they hear his case still another time.

During the past summer, 1958, the U.S. Supreme Court had come down hard on Orval Faubus's obstructionist tactics in Little Rock and declared that the "constitutional rights of children . . . can neither be nullified openly and directly by state legislators or state executive judicial officers, nor nullified indirectly by them through evasive schemes whether attempted 'ingeniously or ingenuously.'" While they "sympathize[d] with the position of the [school] board in the face of the frustrating conditions which have confronted it," the justices fully expected its members to assume their responsibilities under *Brown I* and *II,* and they hammered home as hard as they could that the states must operate their schools "consistently with federal constitutional requirements as they apply to state action." Which meant getting on with school desegregation with dispatch. There was to be no further evasion of the law. The decision was explicitly tailored for the circumstances in Little Rock, but it fit Louisiana perfectly, and the Inc. Fund was anxious to test its mettle there. Thurgood Marshall had sent lawyer Constance Baker Motley down from national headquarters to give Tureaud a hand.

Mrs. Motley presented the black plaintiffs' main argument to the court. Having "refrained," she reminded the judge and Rault, "from seeking further relief from the Federal Court in the past in order to give the defendant school board a reasonable length of time in which to make whatever arrangements ... necessary" to desegregate the city's schools, she noted that three and a half years seemed an inordinate amount of time. It was "apparent," she said, that the school board had not "proceeded to make the necessary arrangements," and she asked the court to order the board to devise a plan within a month, by August 15, that would begin school desegregation in New Orleans this coming fall.

It was Wright's first day back after a month on the federal district court bench in New York where the legal traffic was nearing gridlock. It was a pleasure he had denied himself the previous year because of heavy docket pressures on his home court, but he had resumed his summer trips again in 1959, his own court having been singled out by the Senate Appropriations Committee for its record of disposing of cases with dispatch and by the Administrative Office of the United States courts as "a marvelous demonstration of efficient judicial administration."

Wright had talked by telephone with Thurgood Marshall in New York and conveyed the impression to the chief Inc. Fund lawyer that he would "act swiftly and favorably" on the black lawyers' motion, which was one of eighteen motions scheduled to be heard on July 15. It was Wright's welcome home.

In his opening remarks, Wright reminded the school board of its failure to take his school desegregation order seriously, much less obey it. "Other than appeal" his decision, he noted caustically, "the board has done nothing to comply with that order." As he talked, his dissatisfaction with the school board's performance became increasingly apparent.

In the austerest possible prose but in the strongest possible tone, he ordered the board to "prepare, present and file in the record of this case ... an overall plan covering the complete desegregation of the public schools in this city." There was no allusion to the U.S. Supreme Court's requirement of "all deliberate speed" this time. There already had been too much deliberation and not enough speed. Without referring to Mrs. Motley's deadline, he set a specific time limit within which he expected the board to comply: March 1, 1960—just seven-and-a-half months ahead. To start the deliberations and debate, he suggested the board consider desegregating a grade a year beginning with the first grade until all the classes were mixed.

He concluded with a plea to the good sense of establishment New

Orleans, to those George Cable seventy-five years before had called the men and women "in whom the community placed most confidence and pride":

> The choice [said Wright] as to whether New Orleans will become another Little Rock is not the school board's alone. Our news media, our public and private leaders, our churchmen and the public generally will share the responsibility of that decision. It is only with their hope, their intelligent and active support, that the board will be able, without civic excitement, to comply with its duty under the law.
>
> This court has every confidence that these responsible influences on our community life will take their places, as they have in the past, on the side of law and order.

The white parents in Wright's "public generally" immediately grumbled that black children (7,000) far outnumbered white ones (4,000) in the city's elementary schools, the implication being that no white parent in his or her right mind would send a child into such a racially lopsided environment.

For all the influence it had in New Orleans, the Supreme Court might never have spoken about Little Rock. School board vice president Lloyd Rittiner had no intention of complying: "We have several legal steps which can be made by March. We don't think this is the proper time to integrate the schools and hoped Judge Wright would delay his decision until these appeals could be ruled on by the Supreme Court." Matt Sutherland pleaded state law that forbade the racial desegregation of Louisiana's public schools, and Emile Wagner said he'd see the schools closed before he would approve desegregation. He wanted no part of the "educational jungles and moral swamps of Washington and New York." He publicly pledged his support for state-subsidized private schools. In fact, before the year was out, the school board got its way temporarily. On October 9, Wright met in his chambers with both Tureaud and Rault and agreed to postpone the deadline for the school board to produce a plan from March 1, 1960, to May 16. No reason was given.

A. P. Tureaud was less than optimistic to begin with. Wright's order, he said, was "too slow. It gives the city too much opportunity for delay and evasion," and he prophesied that several more of the plaintiffs, whose number had dwindled by 1959 from the original ninety-plus to thirty-nine, "will have finished college" before the judge's plan could benefit them. Tureaud anticipated considerable opposition by segregationists, and he was right. The militants stepped right up, all ready to intimidate Wright's "responsible influences on our community life" before they could organize.

State representative John Garrett of Claiborne Parish, vice chairman of Willie Rainach's segregation committee and the state senator's protégé, vowed at his press conference a few days later that Louisiana's laws being perfectly "clear" on the subject, the New Orleans school system would "continue to operate on its present basis"—if it operated at all. Judge Wright could go fly a kite. Rainach himself, who already had announced his candidacy for the governorship that year, told an applauding luncheon meeting of the local Young Men's Business Club that Wright was "inviting the people down here to participate in their own destruction." Within a year, that same YMBC, fifty-one to forty-one, recommended closing the local schools over desegregating them.

Of all the "responsible influences on our community life" that the judge had counted off in his latest desegregation order—"our news media, our public and private leaders, our churchmen and the public generally"—the civic leadership to which he had desperately appealed for support, the only one to stand by him publicly was the local Catholic archbishop, although in his weakened condition his efforts only underlined his impotence and invited further attack by the segregationists in his flock. Eighty-two years old in 1959, Rummel had maintained his silence ever since he faced open rebellion among his parishioners three years before when he supported Skelly Wright's order for public school desegregation, but now he was ready to speak out again. Going beyond a general statement issued by the Catholic Bishops of the United States at their annual convention the previous November condemning racial segregation, Rummel promised to integrate the 71,069 white and 12,137 black students in the parochial schools of his archdiocese "at the earliest possible moment and definitely not later than when the public schools integrate."

It was not Rummel's most vigorous statement, but at his age he had more weariness in him than vigor, his energy sapped not only by his years but also by his parishioners' determined opposition to his earlier statement that racial segregation was "a mortal sin" and his previous declaration to desegregate parochial schools. Emile Wagner's organization of a laymen's crusade against racial mixing had been perhaps the most personally devastating. In addition to pickets outside the rectory and the cross burned on its lawn, petty but nonetheless humiliating harassments had plagued black parishioners—white men, for example, blocking the path of a black youth inside the sanctuary because the boy had chosen a pew near the front of it. Together such incidents had effectively undermined the archbishop's will to carry out his earlier plan, and in the summer of 1959 he had not yet fully recovered. This latest announcement of his resolve to desegregate lacked the old wallop.

Except for Archbishop Rummel's publicly stated intention to desegregate the schools under his control, establishment New Orleans—the business community, the press, teachers, civic organizations, trade unions—retreated into silence. Confronted with the shrill determination of militant segregationists to prevent the local public schools from desegregating, New Orleans's haut monde hid from the most important issue in its recent history, torn between the roles of skeptic and ostrich.

While Montgomery's business elite was using its influence with the city fathers to make sure appropriate schools were chosen for desegregation, while Dallas's businessmen were buying advertising space on city streetcars to support school desegregation, and Atlanta's leadership, learning from Little Rock's mistakes, was drawing up a workable school desegregation plan, New Orleans's leadership, regularly reassured by school board members and other political figures that Little Rock couldn't happen here, were "out" to anyone who tried to draw their attention to the gathering storm. The city was left essentially leaderless.

Skelly Wright was particularly critical of the bar associations, whose members, he felt, succumbed to the social and economic pressures of the moment and failed in their responsibility to make the public aware of what the law was and to support the efforts of the federal courts to enforce the Constitution. He believed their reticence "caused a great part of the delay in getting *Brown* off the ground."

The local newspapers reflected their subscribers' views on race. There had been moments in its 122-year history when the *Times-Picayune* had demonstrated its ability to lead public opinion—during the post–Huey Long scandals, for example—but this critical period in race relations as Wright's deadline approached was not one of them. Ignoring entirely the fact that the local school board was operating in violation of a five-year-old Supreme Court order that the local federal district court judge had made specifically applicable to New Orleans, the paper seized every opportunity to cheer on Gerald Rault's obstructionist tactics, heartily approving his efforts to "exhaust every legal avenue" to avoid school desegregation. The editors still "deplored the change of position on the part of the supreme court [sic] of the United States which created our dilemma."

Chep Morrison, *Time* magazine's "Most Progressive Mayor of the Decade, 1940–1950," was as conspicuously silent as the rest of the city's leadership. In January, 1958, eighteen months before Skelly Wright set a concrete deadline for school desegregation, Morrison had confessed his "firm belief that those who shout the most get the greatest amount of integrated facilities" and announced his intention to "maintain a calm, cool attitude and to attempt every possible way to remove the causes that would create agitation among the races." Less than a month before Wright made his deadline public, Morrison told a friend privately that "on performance I believe we are doing better than any other southern state in two ways—in keeping down mixing and in not having any trouble. Maybe we have been a little smarter than other people who blow their horns so often." Because, he said a little later, New Orleans had sponsored what Morrison called "truly equal facilities," the local "Negro population hasn't wished to mix with white people." He'd gone to some pains, for example, to keep greens fees low at the new Negro golf course in order to discourage blacks from trying to use the one at City Park, which the federal courts had ordered desegregated.

In sum, no one of any stature or capacity for leadership in New Orleans, following Skelly Wright's setting of a deadline for a public school desegregation plan, was ready to speak out in support of the judge, the law, or the Constitution. No one even considered planning what the city ought to do. The issue of race had once again silenced the South. No individual or group around whom George Cable's quietly convinced southerners or the "responsible influences on our community life" to whom Skelly Wright had appealed emerged from the obscurity of the silence, and the road was thus cleared for the demagogues—members of the Citizens' Councils, Willie Rainach, Perez, and others of their ilk for whom the upcoming gubernatorial election would provide the most important forum to date.

By the Fourth of July, 1959, the traditional kickoff date for Louisiana's gubernatorial election campaigns, no fewer than eleven candidates, including a little-known Lake Charles insurance man and a New Orleans taxi driver, had joined it, lending it the aura of a horserace more than an important political contest to determine the next state government. The number of candidates was not unusual. Open to anyone who could come up with the $210 filing fee, the state's first primary typically drew a large field. And since hardly any in such a large number of contestants ever won the majority required for nomination, a runoff was almost certain.

Which was when the fun began. The minute the results of the first primary were announced, the swapping started in earnest, the losers offering their support to the highest bidding winner in exchange for promises of legislative favors, patronage, or even—not unheard of in Louisiana—money. The dynamics of deciding which candidate had the best chance to cross the finish line first and finding exactly the right price to buy and sell for made politics the popular sport it was in the state.

Six of the eleven candidates entered in 1959 were political nonentities. All of them together would probably collect no more than 2 or 3 percent of the vote. They were in the race hoping to pick up just enough votes to join the postprimary bargaining and win promises of obscure government sinecures. The five serious candidates that year were sixty-nine-year-old Monroe oil and media mogul James A. Noe; William J. Dodd, Governor Earl Long's lieutenant governor from 1948 until 1952 and the state comptroller in Long's present administration; Mayor DeLesseps Morrison of New Orleans, to whom his long-time political enemy Earl Long liked to refer as "Delessoups" and his "tuppy"; ex-Governor Jimmie H. Davis; and state senator Willie Rainach. The winner would be a significant force in the political manuvering for control of New Orlean's schools.

Lusty, gusty Governor Earl Long, barred by the Louisiana constitution from succeeding himself but not ready at sixty-four to renounce his throne and live out his days quietly on his farm in Winnfield, had induced Jimmie Noe, who served briefly as governor following the death in office of Oscar K. Allen in 1936 and had been a strong supporter of Huey Long's brand of populism, to come out of retirement and head a Noe-for-governor, Long-for-lieutenant governor ticket. It was widely rumored Long meant for Noe to resign after inauguration to allow his lieutenant governor to succeed him. This scheme for securing another term as governor was said to have won over an earlier one in which Long would resign as governor in time to run in the first primary legitimately. It was discarded because Long feared being out of power and leaving the state government, particularly the payroll, in the present lieutenant governor's control for too many months.

In the campaign of 1959, the old trouper was not, however, himself. A combination of fatigue and all-round poor physical condition contributed to the deterioration of his personality, and following a period of incoherence, verbal abuse, and use of rougher-than-usual language on the floor of an uncooperative state legislature, he was spirited away in a National Guard plane to an asylum in Texas; he was later transferred to Southeast Louisiana State Hospital at Mandeville. By the Fourth of July he had escaped from his keepers, fired the state director of hospitals plus the head of the hospital at which he'd been incarcerated, and was back on the campaign trail, white coat, red suspenders, Panama hat, and all.

He opened his campaign on July Fourth in Ville Platte, where a large crowd, curious about the governor's health following his recent ordeal, had gathered. "I just wanted to let you see for yourself that I'm not as dead or as crazy as they say I am," he thundered.

All the announced candidates including the Lake Charles insurance salesman and the New Orleans taxi driver appeared at Ville Platte that day, and Long denounced them all with equal venom, plurally as "rascals," "cowards and liars," collectively as comparably low-life creatures. He labeled ex-Governor Davis, who hadn't yet formally announced his candidacy and wasn't there to defend himself, "the biggest jelly bean that ever lived" and came close to slandering Mayor Morrison and comptroller Dodd, accusing them of being puppets of the local vice king Carlos Marcello.

Despite the return of his old rambunctiousness, however, people said he looked tired. He'd lost some weight and he had trouble keeping his teeth in, jamming them back in midsentence. His abbreviated speeches were skeletons of his former harangues. He fell asleep at a meeting of his campaign staff the following morning, and on his return to Baton Rouge later in the week, he was too tired to cope with official business. On July 11, he went off on an extended tour of the West, returning at the end of the month looking refreshed and reinvigorated. He and the aging, politically impotent Noe campaigned across the state that fall on a typical Long platform: more roads and bridges, higher old-age pensions, pay raises for state employees, support for organized labor, cheap automobile license plate fees, more money for higher education, and, last but not least, "peaceful race relations."

But the jokes had lost their edge, and the governor hardly ever worked the crowds the way he used to. Now he was driven as close as possible to the speakers' platforms in an air-conditioned Cadillac or a police squad car. His obvious physical decline combined with the adverse publicity in connection with his earlier detention in mental hospitals had withered his political support.

"How could I vote for him in that condition?" asked a man in one of Long's crowds. "He probably wouldn't live until inauguration if he got elected."

Bill Dodd, a political crony of Earl Long's, though the two men were locked in a constant off-again, on-again personal feud during both of Dodd's terms in Long's administrations, lined up with the other candidates that Fourth of July in Ville Platte. He didn't have much to say then, but promised to formalize his platform shortly.

New Orleans Mayor Chep Morrison kicked off his second campaign for governor the same day, making most of the same stops his opponents made—Eunice, Erath, Lake Arthur, Cameron, Lake Providence—but also making every effort not to cross Earl Long's path any more than necessary. He made it clear even in the short talks he gave that he was going to base his campaign on the comparison between what he called the "broken promises" of the Long administration, which "weren't worth the paper they were written on," and his own record as mayor of New Orleans. What he had done for the city, he planned to do for the state.

He was in his fourth term as mayor now, and a new city charter prohibited him from running again. He was only forty-six, still handsome, politically astute enough to forge a ticket of solid civic-minded candidates for the other state offices open in 1959, and as far as anyone knew, he was clean as a whistle.

Over the past twelve years, he'd brought New Orleans up from the sixteenth busiest port in the United States to the second and made the city a competitor with Miami as the "Gateway to Latin America." He'd expanded tourism, brought in new industry, cleared slums, and chased the gambling dens across the river to Jefferson Parish, although the strip-tease joints still operated openly in the city. His city hall office, decorated with autographed photos of nationally known churchmen, prominent baseball players, television celebrities, and United States Senators plus several Miss New Orleanses, Miss Louisianas, and Miss Confederate Daughters of America in company with the mayor, testified to an ever broadening circle of acquaintances—and ambitions—beyond New Orleans.

At the beginning, before his financial backers began to pull away, Morrison's drawbacks seemed to be few, the major one being the reluctance of the heavily Protestant rural north to vote a southern Catholic, particularly one from the "big city," into the governor's mansion. But he was confident of the *Times-Picayune*'s support; the paper had loyally stood by him since his first campaign for the state legislature back in 1939. Labor liked him, and he'd made a decent showing against Earl Long in 1956, Morrison's first try for the governorship. At the Fourth of July kick-off, he appeared to have a good chance to win.

Even though ex-Governor Davis hadn't announced his candidacy before Independence Day and he wasn't standing with the others at Ville Platte and the other stops, his shadow loomed over them, his name arising in conversations, speeches, and the news stories of the following day. Harnett T. Kane, a longtime observer of and commentator on Louisiana's history and culture, described Davis as a rather "more complex character than some realized," even an "enigma to those around him." Moon Landrieu, who was running for the state legislature that year on Chep Morrison's ticket and who was to find Davis a formidable opponent during the approaching school crisis in New Orleans, described him as a "sweet, gentle guy on the surface and a tough politician below" it. Landrieu confessed to retaining a strong personal affection for Davis many years afterward.

Davis began life as one of eleven children born to a Jackson Parish sharecropper. No one in his family was certain of his birthdate, whether it had been 1901, 1902, or 1903. Nineteen hundred two was the date finally settled on, which would make him fifty-seven years old during the first primary of 1959.

He was picking cotton on the family farm at seven, had become a competent farmer by the time he was ten. He graduated from Beech Springs High School, then worked in the sawmills summers and washed dishes during the terms to pay his way through a nearby Baptist college. To find money for graduate school, he returned to Beech Springs High School to teach and later transferred to a local elementary school. In 1927 he received his MA from Louisiana State University, where he had sung in various musical groups and organized the popular quartet, the Tiger Four. He was not an intellectual—singing was his first love—and he once confessed he'd never read a book after he left school.

When Davis left LSU, he divided his time between a couple of minor political offices and singing appearances. People fell for his engaging diffidence in the one and his simple way of presenting his songs in the other.

In 1944, he ran for governor and won by conducting a programless, platformless campaign in which he promised a respite from the turbulence of the post-Huey years, a period of amiability and peaceable relations. As he stood on the platforms tapping his feet and strumming his "gitar," his sincere look frozen on his not unhandsome face, the voters took to him and sent him strumming right into the governor's chair.

His four years there were lackluster. He didn't seem to have much in the way of convictions, and he didn't like making decisions. Faced with a serious problem, he was apt to leave the state, often for Hollywood, where he'd acted previously in a couple of grade-B westerns and hoped now for a bigger role. He churned out songs the way other governors between 1944 and 1948 were churning out legislative plans: the famous "Your Are My Sunshine" plus lesser-known "Bedbug Blues," "Bear-Cat Papa," "High-Power Mama, Get Yourself in Gear." His regime was generally characterized as "plain, do-nothing government," and he slid into political anonymity when it was over.

In 1959, Davis began his second campaign for the governorship with what observers called his "usual vanilla diet." His theme was "harmony and unity," though he also made the usual kind of political promises—expansion of the state's public health services, college scholarships for deserving students, aid to farmers and planters, help for the aged, and improvement in corrections institutions. But, aware of the large role religion played in the lives of many Louisianans, he preferred to talk about the Biggest Election of Them All rather than any plans he might have for returning prosperity to his declining state. Nearly everyone in Louisiana heard his peroration at least once and many heard it more than once:

> I look beyond this election. I look beyond all elections. I look to the time when they're going to take me ... to some silent city on the hill. . . . They'll take us to a place where there are no small men; no bigshots and no little-shots; no rich men and no poor men; where six feet of earth makes us all the same size. And when they take me there, I want people to say that I was decent and honorable and respectable and I did the best I could to serve all the people. And that's the only reward I want for serving as governor.

On July 2, Willie Rainach Day in his hometown of Homer, the sentinel of the southern way of life announced his candidacy for governor and changed the whole complexion of the race. Rainach had already resigned as head of the state's Association of Citizens' Councils to devote full time to the campaign, explaining that "every bit of information indicates the showdown will come shortly after the new governor takes office." He presented himself to the crowds on the Fourth of July as the only candidate "you know whose stand on this vital issue is staunch enough to provide the leadership that's going to be necessary over the next four years." He hoped eventually

> to bring the entire nation to the viewpoint of the South, but it will require executive power that will stand up to the federal government.

Early in the day, Long had told the crowd he planned to "reduce" the noisy segregationist to "a good, kind, ordinary, indulgent citizen." To which Rainach had replied, "We'll see who reduces who to what."

Had it not been for Rainach's entry into the gubernatorial campaign during the summer of 1959, the other candidates would have plodded on in the well-worn political ruts, Morrison and Noe/Long outpromising each other, Davis preaching love, the nonentities quickly disappearing into oblivion. Without Rainach's goading, the other candidates would undoubtedly have established themselves matter-of-factly as bona fide segregationists and let it go at that. Willie Rainach, however, having seen with his own eyes the harvest of votes his neighbor to the northeast, Orval Faubus, had gleaned from his use of race as an issue, entirely changed the tenor of the campaign. From the moment he announced his candidacy, the race issue drove the candidates, with Rainach cracking the whip.

Until that year, Louisiana's gubernatorial elections had been less bedeviled than other sections of the deep South by the politics of race.

The Long brothers, who'd dominated Louisiana politics for the previous three decades, had sublimated racial to economic issues. There had even been times when one or the other of them had actively solicited the black vote. Now in 1959, ranting against the "mixing of the bloods," Willie Rainach stepped into the vacuum.

Like Chep Morrison's, Rainach's political life had begun with his election to Louisiana's legislature in 1940, where his first fourteen years as a lawmaker had been singularly unremarkable. When in 1954, early in his second term as state senator, the U.S. Supreme Court handed down its decision in *Brown* v. *Board of Education,* he'd grabbed the issue and raced for the political goal posts. By 1959, he hadn't many yards to go for a touchdown.

His massive grassroots movement to establish the Citizens' Councils across his state had given him a solid political base. His leadership as chairman of the Joint Legislative Committee to Maintain Segregation and his well-publicized attempts to persuade his colleagues to enact statutes maintaining racial segregation during the five years since *Brown* had made Rainach a household name. His current efforts to purge Louisiana's 159,000 registered black voters from the rolls were making him a hero among segregationists.

Rainach characterized this election as "the most eventful and decisive" since Louisianans elected Francis Nicholls governor in 1876, after which white government returned to the state, federal troops were withdrawn, and Louisiana, said the state senator, enjoyed seventy-five years of peace—until whites "went to sleep and let the NAACP and the Communist Party bring pressure on the [United States] Supreme Court." He boasted that he, Willie Rainach, and only he, was "in a position to help unite the South" and promised he would work toward restoring southern influence in both national political parties.

Operating out of a storefront headquarters in Shreveport, its walls papered with blow-ups of pictures of Jimmie Davis leading an orchestra at a California nightclub where blacks and whites were allowed on the same dance floor, he lashed out at all the candidates. Earl Long, he charged, had

> deserted the white people after the big Negro vote put him in office last time.

Morrison

> won't stand up for Louisiana rights. Jimmie Davis won't stand up for anything, and Jimmie Noe is already on record as opposing the segre-

gation states' rights people. I got into this race to preserve peace between the races. It's a country club radical like Morrison with the NAACP backing who will get us into racial trouble.

He accused Morrison of pressing New Orleans hoteliers to rent rooms to blacks, of wanting to desegregate Pelican Baseball Stadium, and of allowing the desegregation of trolleys and buses on his watch. He reprinted and distributed as a flyer a letter to Jimmie Davis in which a long-faithful Davisite switched his political loyalty to Rainach:

> The next Governor of Louisiana is going to be under tremendous pressure to integrate our public schools. . . . We don't want our children to be the guinea pigs in sociological experiments. The rapes, murders and violence that have followed integration of the schools in New York, Chicago, Philadelphia, Washington, and other Northern cities must not happen to our children . . . we must have a Governor *who will not yield.*

This voter was no longer convinced of Davis's political fortitude and intended to vote for Rainach, "who has led the fight for segregation in this state, who has shown that he has the courage and ability to lead us to victory."

Although roundly denounced for mixing what was supposed to be nonpartisan public service with partisan politics, Orleans Parish school board member and resident segregationist Emile Wagner joined his friend Willie Rainach's team as campaign manager for the First and Second Congressional Districts. Wagner vehemently denied he was violating any law or code of ethics.

> As an individual [he declared] I am firmly convinced that Willie Rainach stands for the best interest of the board . . . I have a right and obligation to support him and foster the good of education in this state.

Earl Long's response to Rainach's campaign was almost a dismissal, a perfunctory accusation that the segregationist wanted to "fight the Civil War all over again," after which the governor stumped the state scattering his promises of roads and hospitals and bridges like rice at a wedding. Davis took Willie more seriously and advanced from a "100%" to a "1,000%" segregationist. Without entirely dropping his "harmony and unity" goals he began to reach out for the Citizens' Councils' support, promising the continued racial segregation of the public schools, no "compromise on the issue of states' rights," and a stop to federal agencies like the Civil Rights Commission's interference with "the rights that the Constitution specifically reserves to Louisiana."

DeLesseps Morrison was a segregationist but not a hard-core racist. During the years he served as mayor, he'd steered a moderate course that appeared to benefit both races and offend neither, and both races contributed to his mayoral campaigns. The members of his own political organization, the Crescent City Democratic Association, were white, but he had successfully enlisted blacks' support for his administrations by working through the black community's political leaders—the black clergy, most notably the prominent black clergyman A. L. Davis, and various autonomous black political and labor organizations. Besides which, he viewed the crescendoing surge of federal court decisions as unstoppable.

But this election was different. If Morrison couldn't win the governorship this time, he would be out as mayor and have no political base when next the office became vacant, in 1964. It seemed it was now or never for Chep Morrison, and the political necessities required him to court the substantial segregationist element among the state's voters.

Back in the spring of 1959, before either Jimmie Davis or Willie Rainach formally entered the race and Earl Long looked like the candidate to beat, Morrison had in fact attempted to win Leander Perez's backing. But his record on race—his regular denunciations of civil rights legislation, his boast that he'd been "sued by the NAACP more times than any public official in Louisiana"—hadn't satisfied the kingmaker, and the mayor's ambition and independence had alienated him. Morrison was left to face the pit bulls alone.

Morrison's star began to fall and Jimmie Davis's to rise as the first primary vote on December 5 approached. The *Times-Picayune,* which had been faithful to Morrison through his legislative and mayoral races as well as his one previous run for governor, suddenly shifted its support to Davis, explaining that the editors did "not believe that Mr. Morrison would be in a position to rally various political factions and consolidate diverse legislative elements in support of a forward looking and effective program for the whole state."

New Orleans financial leaders, fearful that the firebrand segregationist Rainach might otherwise win, began quietly to move their money into Davis's campaign from Morrison's. The night before the primary, Morrison made one last appeal to the voters; in retrospect it falls into the category of famous last words:

I'm proud to step forward and say that if every city in the South and in the nation could have handled its race problem as well as New Orleans there would not be any problem.

When the 840,000 votes were tallied the next night, Morrison had won more than any of the other ten candidates—278,900, or 33.1%—but not the majority he needed. He'd done well in urban Catholic Louisiana, especially in New Orleans, but had lost the rural Protestant north to Davis (213,500 votes, or 25.3 percent) and Rainach (143,059 votes, or 17 percent); Rainach pulled 11 percent of the vote in New Orleans, Morrison's home base as well as the immediate target of school desegregation. Dodd trailed all the major candidates.

Long before Louisianans went to the polls, their current governor knew his struggle was hopeless. He and Noe carried Winn Parish, his home base, as well as several other parishes in the western and north-central part of the state, but ended up in fourth place, even lost his seat as a member of the Democratic State Central Committee, an upset he hadn't bargained for. The runoff, set for January, 1960, would be the first time since 1928, when Huey Long won the Louisiana governorship, that a Louisiana gubernatorial second primary was run without a Long candidate.

The 1959 gubernatorial primary, whose trends the approaching runoff confirmed, altered politics in Louisiana for some years to come. Longism itself fell into the dustbin of history. The fundamentalist rural Protestant north, overwhelmingly segregationist, had seized control from the French-flavored, mellower Catholic south, urban and more racially tolerant, and race had replaced economics as the major political issue. This last trend persisted in Louisiana politics through the 1960s, 1970s, and 1980s.

The immediate result of the 1959 gubernatorial primary was to drive the state inexorably into the violence of 1960. As well as being a blatant appeal for Willie Rainach's support in the upcoming runoff, Jimmie Davis's postelection statement marked the beginning of the new trends:

The vote that has been cast in the first primary has proven ... that the majority of the voters of Louisiana want to preserve state sovereignty and the right of self-determination in internal matters. The second point ... is that there are forces at work that will undermine by tactics fair or foul the rights of an overwhelming majority of our citizens.

The first gubernatorial primary that year also marked the political demise of Willie Rainach. He'd had to give up his seat in the state senate to run for governor, and his failure to qualify for the runoff the following month deprived him of an official forum. He enjoyed a brief period in the limelight as the bargaining for his support following the first primary made him a much-sought-after ally. Urged by the top state political broker Leander Perez, Rainach rather favored Davis, who knew he needed Rainach's backing to win the second primary, and on December 29, the ex-senator and the governor-to-be made their deal. After considerable dickering over price, Rainach agreed to endorse Davis's candidacy in the runoff in return for Davis's support for Representative John Garrett's succession to the chairmanship of Rainach's old segregation committee plus a Davis-created, Rainach-chaired state sovereignty commission authorized to work with other southern state officials in forming a southern coalition to promote the region's interests in the rest of America.

"I don't think," said Rainach in explaining his support of Davis, "there is anyone . . . who would take as strong a stand as I would take, but I do believe Jimmie Davis would take the next strongest stand in the state of Louisiana."

As for those stories Rainach had spread regarding Davis's making music at an integrated California nightclub, they were exaggerated, Rainach said now. "We never found that matters were as they had been reported." The bargain insured Davis's alignment with the most militant of the segregationists, a runoff campaign calculated to intimidate whatever racially liberal or even moderate voices remained as the 1950s closed on Louisiana, and the inevitability of the racial confrontations in New Orleans in 1960.

The voting on December 5, 1959, had brought a one-day respite from the torrents of racially charged rhetoric washing over the state. Within twenty-four hours afterward, however, publicly bidding for the backing of Rainach's army of segregationists in the runoff, Davis set the tone for the rest of the campaign with a tirade against the NAACP:

> I hope not one of them votes for me because I don't want their vote. I'm not a hater but there comes a time when you must stand on your principles. We know what is good for the country and we don't want someone from New York running our state.

Davis himself, he declared, intended to "lay it on the line—support the principles we stand for down here in the South."

It was not the kind of race the genial Davis would have run had he been in control. His natural instincts led him to avoid fights, and in his ideal world, he would have sung and strummed his way into the governor's mansion in 1960 the way he had in 1944, all smiles, friendly hand-shakes, and ballads about lovesick cowboys.

But Davis wasn't in control this time, and the bland old theme and the mellow style, having failed him in the first primary, would in January, 1960, be as useful as an extra wheel on his father's hay wagon. Leander Perez and his Citizens' Council were in control now, and it was Perez who took charge of Davis's campaign now that Willie Rainach's was dead.

Convinced that Mayor Morrison couldn't win and confident that Jimmie Davis, once installed as governor, would do what he was told, Davis's financial supporters in the primary stayed with him. The New Orleans *Times-Picayune* followed along, regularly reminding New Orleanians how many blacks had voted for Morrison in the first primary. Organized labor, usually a strong Morrison partisan, surprised a lot of people and supported Davis. The Orleans Parish school board member and voluble segregationist Emile Wagner publicly switched his loyalties from Rainach to Davis. When the board asked for his resignation for once again mixing in partisan politics, Wagner refused, arguing that Davis's opposition to federal interference with the city's schools coincided with the board's concerns. Although he vacillated, even Governor Long finally announced he was going to vote for Davis.

Chep Morrison never had a chance. Voters raged at Moon Landrieu, running for the state legislature from New Orleans's Twelfth Ward on Morrison's ticket:

> I wouldn't vote for you if you're associated with Chep Morrison if you were the last man on earth!

Davis characterized his opponent as a pawn of the NAACP, forcing him immediately on the defensive. But nothing Morrison could say in rebuttal had the same effect on voters as had Davis's charges that the mayor was soft on race, that racial desegregation of New Orleans's public libraries, transportation, and city parks had happened on his, Morrison's, watch, and that those of New Orleans's voting precincts that were predominantly black had, like the *Times-Picayune* said, voted for him in the first primary. Segregationists distributed photographs of Morrison jumping into a swimming pool with blacks.

Old Jimmie Noe, campaigning now for Morrison after his own defeat in the first primary, rapped the segregationists' knuckles for deliberately whipping voters into a frenzy of fear on the issue of race, but his effort was futile. Racial segregation had already been inflated to monstrous proportions. There was no other issue in January, 1960. Public service, education scholarships, attracting new industry to boost the state's economy—none of them amounted to a bag of rags compared with the risk of a white child's being required to go to school with black children, possibly to sit alongside a Negro in the classroom, perhaps to share a locker in the gym.

The combination of the Citizens' Councils' grassroots movement under the leadership of the indefatigable Leander Perez and Willie Rainach, united to defeat Chep Morrison through the inflammatory issue of race, couldn't be stopped. If there were Louisianans out there who were less committed to racial segregation, their voices had been drowned out or entirely silenced.

When the voters went to the polls on January 9—the segregation issue had brought out 88 percent (more than 900,000) of the 1,140,000 Louisianans registered, 57,744 more than had turned out for the first primary—they sent Davis into the governor's office by a 71,847-vote margin (7.8 percent). He took all sixteen parishes that had gone heavily for Rainach the month before and averaged 75.5 percent of the total vote in the segregationist northern section of the state, carrying some parishes by up to 90 percent. Morrison carried only twenty-two of the state's sixty-four parishes, all of them in the south, none by such large margins as Davis gathered in the north.

Davis won the general election that followed on April 13 without even campaigning, trouncing both the States' Rights Party candidate Kent Courtney and the Republican candidate Francis C. Grevemberg. He took office on May 10, marking the occasion by leading his horse Sunshine up the Capitol steps and by reaffirming the principles of his campaign. In his inaugural address, he promised to "preserve segregation" and to "maintain our way of life without compromise, without prejudice, and without violence." The great state of Louisiana, he vowed, would solve its "problems without interference from those outside our borders," and he himself swore to "jealously guard the right to our self-determination in internal matters." He planned, he said between interruptions for applause,

> to cooperate with the federal government [but] I will not permit interference with those rights that the constitution reserves to Louisiana.

And from the moment he stepped down from the dais until his term ended four years later he did his political best to encourage the state legislature to live up to his promises.

Jimmie Davis was no Huey or Earl Long. He was an amiable ex-farmer and a country and western singer trapped for the second time in the body of a troubled state's chief executive officer, and his taste for wielding power hadn't developed significantly since he'd last held the office. He smiled a lot and reassured his financial supporters he wasn't about to turn their world upside down. When divisive issues arose, he was still apt to go dove hunting or grab his guitar and tour the state's charitable institutions. As one member of the state legislature put it, he and his colleagues felt like "a bunch of helpless men searching for a seeing-eye dog."

He was heavily in debt to the state's segregationist leaders, and Willie Rainach, for one, never let him forget that it had been he, Rainach, and his supporters who had returned the former governor to office. Although Davis wasn't the most militant segregationist in the state, he was not unwilling to continue to let himself be manipulated and maneuvered by those who were. In effect, he abdicated his authority to king-maker Perez and the ruling clique of legislative demagogues from his own north. As the new decade opened, the segregationists had the state of Louisiana by the throat.

CHAPTER 16

"Get Ready for War!"

W hite tension and black restlessness following *Brown* were heightened throughout the South in 1960 by the organization on a national scale of the movement that became known as "sit-ins." On February 1, several well-dressed black freshmen from North Carolina Agricultural and Technical University, fed up with the humiliations of racial segregation, sat down at a whites-only lunch counter in the F. W. Woolworth store in Greensboro and demanded to be served. Their tactics, spreading quickly to neighboring Virginia and South Carolina, then to Tennessee and Florida, and eventually to Louisiana, alerted segregationists that a new militance had been born in the younger generation of blacks, an impatient group dissatisfied with the slow progress their elders—A. P. Tureaud's generation—were making toward winning their fair share of American democracy's benefits. The new activists, who belonged to organizations with names like Congress of Racial Equality (CORE) and Southern Christian Leadership Conference (SCLC), which were springing up to challenge the NAACP's effectiveness, touched off three years of energetic protests through the South, punctuated by painful episodes of violence that ended the lives of eighteen people, most—but not all—of them black.

The sit-ins reached Louisiana in March when a group of Southern University students were arrested for integrating whites-only lunch counters in Baton Rouge. The New Orleans chapter of CORE sent a representative group of its members to the organization's Action Institute in Miami to learn the philosophy and tactics of Gandhian, non-violent, passive resistance. They returned to find the rest of the members already planning to integrate the lunch counters on Canal Street, New Orleans's largest and busiest shopping center. By the time the sit-in movement reached Canal Street, the city was embroiled in its own protest against racial discrimination in the marketplace.

Henry Mitchell, a black physician with an office on Dryades Street, the city's second largest shopping center, had noticed that "just thousands" of black shoppers regularly bustled in and out of the Ben Franklin, Roy's Shoe Store, and the dozens of other white-owned stores in the Dryades area, but that he never saw any blacks working as cashiers, clerks, or managers. Figures backed up Mitchell's observations: blacks accounted for 70 to 80 percent of the merchandise sales there, but black employees made up only 34 percent of the workforce, and of that, only 12 percent held any job better than a janitor's.

Mitchell mentioned his concern to a group of black leaders that included the Reverend A. L. Davis, who hadn't led a blockbusting cause since his successful assault on racially segregated public transportation. Davis, Mitchell, and the others formed an organization they called the Consumers' League. Young black lawyers Lolis Elie and Tureaud's law partner Ernest ("Dutch") Morial offered free legal counsel, and the movement to alter the balance of trade on Dryades Street began.

At first the white merchants seemed more bemused than worried, and they answered the Consumers' League demands for hiring and promoting blacks with a flippant

> Go ahead. Demonstrate, and march all you please. You're not gonna keep the black folks off Dryades.

Mayor Morrison was furious when upwards of two thousand blacks staged the first civil rights march in New Orleans in living memory. What sort of picture of the city did militant black demonstrators show travel agents and their clients the tourists, a staple of New Orleans's economy, or corporate executives looking for a place to settle their companies, or new university faculty moving to the area? And he asked "all of the respectable, honest and solid Negro citizens of New Orleans to take steps to stop those of their race who are acting against the overall good of the community."

His implication that local blacks were "Uncle Toms" and had an obligation to stop their aggressive leaders from trying to right what they believed to be a wrong of long standing only rekindled blacks' resentment, and the Consumers' League threatened to sponsor a formal boycott of the Dryades district stores just before the big spending period at

Easter. The "dead" look on Dryades Street two days before the holiday changed the mood of the white management, and discussions that ultimately led at least to some modest successes for the league now began in earnest. The black group, which struck one neighborhood after another over the following year, eventually negotiated, boycotted, and picketed a total of 152 blacks into white-collar jobs in traditionally resistant supermarkets, drug stores, and department stores. Where white merchants remained adamantly opposed to the change, blacks took their money elsewhere, boycotting some of the white establishments into bankruptcy.

Mitchell recalled the Dryades Street crusade as a "very, very emotional type thing." Black leaders were gratified not only by their tangible successes but also by the demonstration of a willingness on the part of their community to mobilize against racial discrimination. It was clear now that an untapped reservoir of solidarity existed, that a new interest in self-determination had been awakened outside the consciousness of individuals like A. P. Tureaud and A. L. Davis and that it existed very near the surface of the collective psyche.

Lloyd Rittiner, forty-four, had rotated to the presidency of the Orleans Parish school board in December of 1959. He was no integrationist. He believed in the segregated system he'd grown up in, considered it to be in the "best interest of the people of New Orleans of both races to have separate schools." Following his election to the board in 1956, he'd echoed the words and certainty of tone of his predecessor, Clarence Scheps, and pledged to all those who'd voted for him he would fight to the legal limit any and all attempts to desegregate the city's public schools.

In early 1960, Rittiner had begun to feel the pressure from the federal court on the one side and the state government on the other and had gone on record as "favoring integration to the extent that it is necessary to comply with the law" if—and only if—he was faced with the choice between integrating and closing the schools.

"If you have an integrated school system the people would have a choice" of sending their children to either integrated or private schools. If the schools closed, the only alternative was private schools, and, he added balefully, "I don't think most of the people could afford private schools."

As soon as he settled into the school board presidency, he'd worked out a plan to poll the parents of school-age children. He wanted to know how *they* felt. Would they choose to desegregate or slam the schoolhouse doors?

When Skelly Wright succumbed to the board's pleas for extra time to draw up a blueprint for school desegregation, and extended his deadline two and a half months, from March 1 to May 16, the board used the time not to formulate a plan, but to solicit public opinion. Rittiner hoped, no doubt, to reinforce his own position as well as to "wake up the people to the problem they face."

Over the objections of Emile Wagner, who protested that the results would not reflect the views of those property owners who paid for the schools but sent their children to private schools, Rittiner mailed postcards to the parent or guardian of every child enrolled in the city system. He or she was to indicate a preference between

1. I would like to see the schools kept open even though a small amount of integration is necessary; or
2. I would like to see the schools closed rather than be integrated even in small amounts.

In a study published in March, the local NAACP branch had reminded local blacks how out of balance the two divisions of the public school system were, how the numbers of facilities for black children were spiraling downward and the strains on the overcrowded schools were spiraling upward, how teachers in some black schools were teaching two grades simultaneously, and, most important, perhaps, how continued segregation meant the continued "exclusion of Negro children from the mainstream of American society" and the resultant psychological injury.

When the school board sent out the postcards in April, several black organizations protested that "partial integration does not answer the situation of a totally integrated public school system." A. L. Davis, however, fearing the alternative, urged "all parents to vote 'yes' for integration and to keep the schools open." Mrs. Ethel Young, president of the New Orleans Parent-Teachers Council, the local citywide synod of black PTAs, echoed Davis, adding only her own sense of urgency to it:

We *must* save our schools.

The results of the poll jolted Lloyd Rittiner. He'd fully expected white parents to prefer a "small amount" of integration to closing the schools. However, four out of five whites (81.86 percent of the 63 percent who responded) checked number 2. An overwhelming number (94.56 percent of the half who replied) of blacks checked number 1. Totaled together, black and white parents would have made a substantial majority for open schools. Despite that and the fact that black children were a majority in the city's schools, their parents' ballots had as much influence with the board as their numerous petitions had had over the past decade.

Dredging up the ever-useful excuse regarding who financed the schools, Rittiner exacerbated simmering indignation in the black community by announcing he would ignore blacks' votes and "abide by the wishes of the white people because they are the people who support the school system and elect us to the school board." Although he'd been "surprised" by the results of the poll, it was, Rittiner explained,

> evident now how the white people feel about the school integration. I, for one, will not go contrary to the wishes of the white people.

Alone among public influences, WDSU, the leading local television station, owned by Edgar Stern, Jr., whose wealth put him beyond the reach of Citizens' Council retaliation, was taking its first tentative steps toward what was to become over the next year one of the few voices for law and order in New Orleans. In April, while parents were still making up their minds how they would mark their postcard ballots, WDSU editors had urged them to vote for open schools, calling school closure "a form of suicide." Now, following Lloyd Rittiner's announcement of the poll's results, they focused on what they saw as a leadership vacuum in the city. Not one New Orleanian of stature had taken a position on the postcard poll, either before, during, or since. It was as if, complained WDSU,

> most community leaders are trying to look the other way. Few people want to talk about it. The newspapers play it down. . . . It seems to us that New Orleans is drifting in an atmosphere of unreality toward a catastrophe which, if it occurs, could seriously hurt this city.

At the school board's regular meeting on May 9, six days after the poll's results were announced, vice president Louis Riecke wondered whether it was safe to advertise for bids on $160,000 worth of school buses for the coming year, given the precarious position of the city's schools at that juncture.

Shortly before the results of the poll were announced, a delegation of black parents appeared at a school board meeting in behalf of thirty-five black high-school students with the required IQs of 120 or more who wanted to enter the all-white Benjamin Franklin High School for gifted students. The group's leader complained that the city's schools designated for the use of blacks did not offer adequate college preparation, and thereby denied the youngsters opportunity for full development of their potential. Rittiner explained that under state law, black children may not attend any school designated for white children, but told the group the board was investigating the possibility of providing a Benjamin Franklin–type program for black students.

May, 1960, as the sixth anniversary of *Brown* approached, 749 of the 7,016 school districts in the seventeen southern and border states that had been strictly segregated in 1954 had desegegrated. Not one of them was in Louisiana, and the president of the school board operating the state's largest public school system was still leaning on the constitutionally discredited "separate-but-equal" formula that had grown out of the sixty-four-year-old now defunct *Plessy* v. *Ferguson.*

As the state, state courts, and federal court battled it out that spring and summer of 1960, the legal maneuvering was complicated enough to make an ordinary lawyer cry. With A. P. Tureaud in hot pursuit, Attorney General Gremillion was in and out of the state courts where he generally got both a sympathetic hearing and a verdict in his favor, while school board attorney Gerald Rault pressed his cause in Skelly Wright's court and the Fifth Circuit court of appeals where he never faced a sympathetic panel and more often had to settle for a judicial scolding. For the general public, it wasn't easy that summer to follow what was constitutional and what was not.

The main events took place in Skelly Wright's courtroom, beginning with the school board's unapologetic failure to show up with a plan for local school desegregation. A postcard poll had upstaged a federal court order. The judge was running out of patience, and the week before the May 16 deadline, he'd warned Rault:

> I will tell you now publicly what I have already told you in chambers. I am not going to hold any member of the school board in contempt, no one is going to jail if they do not present a plan by May 15, but

and it was a "but" that resonated beyond the courtroom's oak-paneled walls and through the city for a long time afterward:

> if they do not present a plan, I will come up with one myself.

Rittiner and his colleagues couldn't say so publicly, of course, but they undoubtedly welcomed Wright's ultimatum. John Wisdom always believed the local school boards in the deep South states were under too much public pressure to act on their own, that they hungered for clear-cut guidelines and time limits from the courts, which would absolve them of the blame for compliance with *Brown*.

As ordered, the Orleans Parish school board reported to the judge on May 16, one day short of *Brown*'s sixth anniversary, their briefcases empty. They did not bring along a plan for desegregating the city's schools either immediately or in the future.

As he'd said, Wright didn't "want to put anybody in jail," that would "just make martyrs of them." But he did want to "force them." Years later he explained his feelings:

> I guess you get yourself in a position where you get yourself convinced you are right and there's no retreat from that. At least there is no retreat for someone who wants to live with himself. . . . I became convinced that not only was I right in following the Supreme Court but that what I was doing was morally and socially right, so I was going to do it. I could have cut corners, I could have delayed, I didn't have to be aggressive about this, and still be within the structure and commands of the Court, but I became convinced I was right, so I moved.

He admitted that he, like other federal judges in the South caught in his position, had "no expertise" in devising such plans or administering a school system. Nonetheless he plunged ahead and coolly ordered the school board to accept what he called his own "desperation" plan.

In his order, Wright reviewed the tedious history of his rulings, reminding the board that since his original decision in *Bush* back on February 15, 1956, the board had had ample time to get on with school desegregation. He'd already given them one healthy postponement, from March 1 to May 16, 1960. It was, he intimated, enough.

He set the opening of school in September, only three-and-a-half months away, as the new deadline, not for a plan now, but for the actual start of desegregation in "all public schools in the City of New Orleans." The procedure would be "remarkably simple":

> A. All children entering the first grade [ironically, those born in 1954, the year of *Brown*] may attend either the formerly all-white public school nearest their homes, or the formerly all-Negro public school nearest their homes, at their option. [Wright chose the first grade, he explained, because children of that age were "not color conscious; they haven't been taught to hate."]
>
> B. Children may be transferred from one school to another, provided such transfers are not based on considerations of race.

Desegregation was to progress stepladder-wise upward a grade a year until all the grades were racially mixed. Wright was the first federal judge in the Fifth Circuit to actually set a specific date for the start of public school desegregation.

Considering the options open to him, Wright's plan was moderate. He did not abolish the traditional dual system of education with the stroke of a pen, and he'd included the free transfer provision as a sop to white New Orleanians. Nonetheless the city was "stunned."

That afternoon, school board members huddled for more than an hour behind closed doors on the third floor of the board's offices. Even the transoms were tight shut. Rising voices occasionally pierced the silence outside, then, cautioned, fell back to near whispers.

When the five members emerged close to 6 P.M., they had come to no decisions. Vice president Riecke, for one, was pessimistic about the board's ability to keep the schools open and segregated. He feared Wright's order might well be "the end of the line." Speaking for his colleagues, Lloyd Rittiner, who was convinced that the "NAACP will try to register just as many Negroes as possible in every school in town," said board members felt Wright's order wasn't "clear"; they meant to consult Attorney Rault before taking any action.

Attorney General Gremillion said an appeal of the judge's order was certain, and, as predicted, Rault immediately asked the Fifth Circuit court of appeals to stay Wright's order.

In the meantime, the school board wanted to talk with the governor as soon as possible. They needed to know *how* he intended to keep his campaign promises to maintain racial segregation in the schools. Louis Riecke thought it was "time for Davis and Rainach to make good."

Davis readily agreed to a meeting. He'd told the state legislature only a few hours after Wright issued his order that he, Davis, was determined to preserve segregation "without prejudice and without violence." Two days later he issued a longer statement to the press, but this, too, lacked any specific plans. Other than expressing his deep "regret that Judge J. Skelly Wright has failed to recognize the serious situation which exists in our Southland" and reassuring "all of our people that we will continue our legal efforts to protect their rights," thereby maintaining "peace and harmony with dignity and the good will of all our races within this great state," Davis could only promise—again—

> We're going to do everything we can; we'll use every means we can . . . no one is interested in segregation more than I am.

The Citizens' Council of Greater New Orleans celebrated Skelly Wright's order to the school board along with the sixth anniversary of *Brown* on May 17 with a rally at the Municipal Auditorium. School board member Emile Wagner sat on the speakers' platform alongside the big guns of segregation: national Citizens' Council President Roy Harris, local council President Emmett Irwin, and the ubiquitous Leander Perez. Local Citizens' Council membership had dropped since Willie Rainach had resigned his office to run for governor, but the stalwarts could still draw an enthusiastic crowd in the name of a good cause.

Wagner proposed a plethora of segregation-preserving statutes for the state legislature to consider and pledged he would vote to close the New Orleans public schools before he would submit to integration, "a fate" he described as "worse than death."

Leander Perez led Roy Harris to the microphone and introduced him with the eloquence befitting the distinguished visitor. Never reluctant to further inflame already smoldering racist passions, Harris urged his cheering audience to

Get ready for war!

Wright's order brought out the killer instincts in the state legislators who'd returned to Baton Rouge in mid-May for their regular session. Now that Wright had turned what had been treated almost like an abstract issue for debate into a concrete threat, the lawmakers settled in for a full season of 100-degree heat, limp collars, and serious sabotage.

Wellborn Jack of upstate Caddo Parish had fantasized a scheme for seizing the New Orleans schools, one he thought would have "amazed" the federal court were it known at the time. Articulating his colleagues' as well as his own frustrations and feelings of defiance, Jack wanted to appoint a whole new school board and a new school superintendent, then

> with fifty state troopers come down here [to New Orleans] at four in the morning and knock down the door to the school board offices.... When the employees came to work, the new superintendent would have met them and said "I am the boss. Sign this loyalty oath or you're fired."

When the former superintendent arrived at his office,

> we would have taken him in custody and put him in jail.

Jack went so far as to suggest at a legislative strategy session that his plan be tried out. The lawmakers said no, at least to its terrorist particulars. But Jack's scheme to evict the school board and take over the New Orleans schools appealed to them and stuck in their heads, its future usefulness a definite possibility.

Working inside the newly air-conditioned Capitol that summer, the legislators steamrolled their ideas for preserving school segregation into state law. The New Orleans delegates, although it was their schools that were primarily affected, had not in the summer of 1960 yet assembled a united front. Opposition to the bills ranged from weak to nonexistent, a few scattered individuals but no cohesive block.

Leander Perez was masterminding the segregation statutes through the various committees and onto the floor of the two chambers. One of the first was to create a Davis-backed state sovereignty commission. Willie Rainach, no longer a state senator, was in town and preening himself to accept the chairmanship of the new commission for which he had exchanged his support in the recent gubernatorial campaign.

Wobbling at the brink of political extinction following his defeat in the first gubernatorial primary, Rainach envisioned the new position not only as a just reward but also as resuscitation—a high profile and politically powerful independent chairmanship of a liberally funded cabinet-level department. Davis, then jockeying with Rainach for leadership of the segregation issue, imagined a considerably less exalted and less powerful body that would operate under his, the governor's, firm control.

Despite a disgusted Rainach's charge that Davis was breaking promises made when as a candidate he "came to me after the primary and wanted to enlist my support," and despite the South Louisiana Citizens' Council's urgent telegram to Davis reminding him it had been Rainach's endorsement "that made you governor . . . for the second time," the commission that emerged early in the session was Davis's and his alone. It was not independent; it was not powerful; it was not liberally funded. And as Davis undoubtedly knew the once so ambitious ex–state senator would, Rainach declined the chairmanship, clearing the way for the governor to appoint one of his own political intimates, then faded into obscurity.

From then on, the governor, following his charge to a joint session of the legislature on opening day to "implement that portion of [his] inaugural address dealing with the maintenance of segregation, law and order," concentrated his official actions during the rest of the session on sponsoring and signing the bills the lawmakers proposed, wrote, and passed. He said little of any note in public and left strategy to Perez and his floor managers. His standard answers to questions regarding the all-important question of school segregation, the question that had every parent of a school-age child in the state, but especially in New Orleans, nearly frantic, was that public schools would open on schedule in September still racially segregated. He did not invoke interposition, and he confessed that means were still being "studied," which was not particularly reassuring to the parents and children involved.

Members of the Orleans Parish school board trekked to Baton Rouge periodically to consult with him and other state officials, after which Davis issued his usual bromide:

> The people of Orleans parish and the state of Louisiana can be assured that every necessary legal step will be taken to preserve and maintain segregation in this state.

The attorney general telephoned from Las Vegas on his way home from the 1960 Democratic convention in Los Angeles and promised to file a suit in state court within days after arriving in Louisiana, but he refused to reveal its nature. No one—not the attorney general, not the state superintendent of education, Shelby Jackson, and certainly not the governor—was willing to answer questions or divulge details of their plans.

In rapid succession the lawmakers passed bill after bill intended to preserve racial segregation in public schools at any cost. Some were reruns of earlier bills already ruled unconstitutional by Skelly Wright. Others originated in the 1960 legislative session.

The legislators reinstated the pupil assignment law and again authorized the governor to close all public schools in the state when a court ordered any one of them racially integrated. They protected the salaries of employees whose schools the governor closed, and, looking toward the establishment of private systems, the lawmakers included in it authority for Louisiana's school boards to "sell, lease, or otherwise dispose of" the property of any school forced out of business. They reinstated the power of the state legislature to classify schools by race in a statute not substantially different from one they had passed in 1956 and which Skelly Wright, upheld by the Fifth Circuit court of appeals, had declared unconstitutional. They even made it a misdemeanor punishable by fines and/or imprisonment to furnish a desegregated school with supplies or textbooks. Smarting from Wright's recent order to desegregate six state-operated schools scattered across Louisiana, they reinstalled the tradition of segregation there and authorized the governor to close them if integration was threatened.

Not all of the measures attacked school desegregation directly, but there was no question in any Louisianan's mind, black or white, who were the targets of an act making it a crime to give birth to two or more illegitimate children. They passed a similar act denying welfare assistance to such families, and to combat sit-ins in Louisiana's cities, they substantially strengthened the state's trespass laws.

In their frenzy to stop racial mixing in the schools, they made public their previously whispered threat to revoke the Catholic archdiocese's tax exempt status if Archbishop Rummel went through with his announced intention to desegregate parochial schools when the public schools desegregated. When a group of black parents tried to enter several black boys of "above average ability" in an all-white Catholic high school, the archbishop could only respond dolefully that this wasn't "the time to integrate due to material losses that may be incurred by the Catholic school and church."

Following Skelly Wright's definitive order of May 16, letters to the editors of the local newspapers, reflecting public reaction, reached flood stage. Lloyd Rittiner even took his crusade for open schools there, reminding white parents that private schools were currently charging more than $600 a year tuition. There was also fuller news coverage of the developing school crisis. In February, there'd been virtually no column inches in the *Times-Picayune* devoted to the subject of school desegregation. In the last two weeks of May, the number of column inches had risen to 320, and it continued to rise thereafter.

Among all the thousands of words, however, none addressed the issue of obedience to the law and Constitution. Toward the end of June, the *Times-Picayune,* which had never hesitated to take firm stands on Communism, political candidates, or any other controversial matter the editors considered of interest to their subscribers, finally published its first editorial on the school crisis that year. The editors deplored but "recognize[d] the naked power of the supreme court [sic] under our Constitution to change its mind" about *Plessy* as precedent, as well as the "binding effect of such decision on trial judges who bear the onus of carrying out the supreme court's [sic] mandate." As if, however, the Constitution existed apart from the practical dilemma facing the city, a document for debating but not to be taken seriously, these same editors ignored its demands and couched the city's critical condition in terms of personal preference:

> The choice as to whether closed schools are to be preferred to integration is one which the people themselves must make. We would not presume to make it for them.

White PTAs and other school organizations across the city began to make their choices in end-of-term meetings. Three basic views emerged from the Babel. The Jean Gordon School PTA was one of the few to ask for a "concerted effort" to keep schools open, though the membership wished they could also be kept racially segregated. More usual was the resolution passed by the Dads' Club of Gentilly Terrace Elementary School, which out-and-out opposed the desegregation of the public schools as "contrary to the best interests of the children." The dads of Gentilly Terrace were convinced desegregation "would destroy the school system as we know it today and lower its standards, and will ulti-mately be a threat to the survival of the white race in this community." The C. J. Colton Dads' and Boosters' Club asked the school board to immediately reveal plans for operating a private school system in the event the public schools had to close, and pledged to support the board in "whatever efforts it undertakes to see that the schools of this city remain segregated." If black PTAs were discussing the matter, their con-versations and votes and resolutions were not reported.

School board officers Rittiner and Riecke stumped the city in behalf of open schools.

> The school board has not given up [Rittiner told the President's Co-operative School Club] but in my opinion we have come to the end of the road. I am hopeful we can work out a plan more palatable than the judge has presented. I think the judge would be susceptible to a sug-gestion from us.

Rittiner consistently pointed out the unworkability of any private school system and threw himself into an urgent plea for action:

> Don't sit back [he would say] and think this is going away. You've got to face it.

But the heartiest applause he got always came at the start of his talks, when he established his credentials as a committed segregationist.

The opposition to school desegregation in the spring and early sum-mer of 1960, which included the governor and all the members of his administration plus a large majority of the state legislature—the entire state government—alternately supported and prodded by the White Citi-zens' Councils throughout the state, was well-organized, voluble, and picking up momentum every day. Daily life in New Orleans was regu-larly punctuated during those tension-filled months by Citizens' Council–sponsored rallies, broadsides, even occasionally threatening telephone calls to known or suspected racial moderates.

For any wavering group, the Citizens' Council stood ready with a pamphlet calculated to dispel all the doubts and to bolster segregationist resolve, or, as its prototype, "The Citizens' Council's Answers to the Questions of the Francis W. Gregory Parent-Teacher Association," which was widely circulated, put it,

> to set at ease the minds of our citizens upon whom a campaign is being waged by certain elements to confuse and stampede them into a belief that they must accept integration of our public schools. If our white people will remain firm and steadfast there will be no integration.

When the New Orleans PTA Council, the citywide association of white PTAs, passed a resolution calling for a "concerted effort" to keep the public schools open despite the federal court order to desegregate them, local units roundly criticized the parent organization. A week later, the measure was declared null and void, and council officers threatened to expel any local PTA unit that approved it. The all-white Louisiana Teachers' Association met and voted to support the governor and the state legislature through the school crisis.

New Orleans in the spring and summer of 1960 desperately needed leadership. For six years, the only voices heard above a whisper had been segregationists'; the more militant they felt, the louder they talked. They were winning control by default.

The mayor said nothing publicly about the approaching crisis. His standard answer to pleas to keep the schools open was a promise to "do everything in my power to assist," but that it was "a matter which must be resolved by the State Legislature." He and Police Superintendent Joseph I. Giarrusso worked out a joint press release, a "statement of aims, policies and advice" in connection with maintaining "law and order" in New Orleans "during the coming days and weeks," their euphemism for the September opening of the public schools on a desegregated basis for the first time. But in the end, Morrison did not release the statement to the public.

He refused even to appoint a race relations committee for the city that had been promised and been two years in the planning. Given the turmoil swelling in the city, his public relations man, David McGuire, doubted "whether representatives of the extremist groups of either end of the problem would be willing to sit down around one table for an amicable discussion and consideration of race relations problems." More to the point, as Morrison began to think about a third gubernatorial race in 1964 despite his being a lame-duck mayor, the appointment of such a committee would be interpreted, McGuire feared, as a "pro-integration move." Morrison later told A. L. Davis he would ultimately appoint the promised committee, but, still smarting from his recent beating at the polls, added, "in the meantime, the Governor is 'carrying the ball,' and, of course, the people selected him, not me, to handle this matter."

The city's establishment also maintained its silence. Four years had passed since Skelly Wright's first ruling in *Bush* and nearly three since the disturbances at Little Rock had dramatized the price of the politics of confrontation. But the men of substance still averted their gaze.

When Betty Wisdom, whose credentials included membership in an old and respected New Orleans family as well as kinship with several similar families—she described her father as having practically been "born on the board of Mardi Gras"—looked back on the turbulence of 1960, she said she thought these men had convinced themselves that "the Chamber of Commerce wouldn't let [school segregation] happen. The mayor wouldn't let that happen. The governor promised that won't happen."

Harry Kelleher, a successful corporate lawyer who'd been born at the top of the local power structure, looked back later and admitted that his friends and associates were "probably inclined to let events take their course, and . . . probably inclined to the status quo." He was not, however, altogether certain that "there was anything that could have been done":

> You had a segregationist legislature . . . a segregationist governor, and the segregationists were in complete control of the legislature, and they were grinding out this legislation . . . and it's presumed to be constitutional until the court says it's not.

"They kept a steady stream coming," he added, his voice rising. "It's expensive and burdensome to undertake litigation of that sort and most people didn't have any taste for it. . . .

It's lame, but I think a true explanation.

The first public move by any citizens' group in New Orleans toward keeping the public schools open in the face of Skelly Wright's order was made by an organization called Save Our Schools, or SOS as it soon became known. Actually organized by Rosa Keller, Gladys Kahn, and a group of their racially moderate/liberal uptown friends in the fall of 1959, it had operated underground until after a crucial school bond issue passed, then surfaced in the spring of 1960 with a public announcement of its intention to use "all legitimate means [to further] a statewide system of free education and to offer support to all elected or appointed public officials in their efforts to continue free education."

The local Citizens' Council immediately asked state and federal authorities, including the House Un-American Activities Committee in Washington, to investigate the organization's financial backing. SOS was never investigated, but the officers had understood the threat of it from the outset and had made a deliberate decision to avoid any taint of Communist affiliation. As Ann Dlugos, one of the first members Keller recruited and a "bonafide WASP" who became the group's first secretary, put it,

> Communists—that was what we didn't want to be called. We didn't care if they called us nigger-lovers. And we didn't care if they called us integrationists. But we really weren't out of the McCarthy era.

Betty Wisdom became public relations director. Sympathetic representatives of the local white Protestant, Catholic, and Jewish clergy were enlisted to lend the group respectability. After consulting with A. L. Davis and other local black leaders, SOS officers made a conscious decision to keep the organization white, the better to establish a rapport with the white community at this crucial time, particularly those parents who'd indicated on their postcards they preferred closed to integrated public schools. It was these men and women who were SOS's main targets.

The membership's motives were mixed. Southern liberals like Rosa Keller believed racial segregation was morally wrong. Ann Dlugos had internalized the social gospel she heard at church every Sunday as a child and young woman; history courses at Sophie Newcomb College, the women's division of Tulane University, and work with the League of Women Voters had taken up where the preachers left off. Peg Murison, vice chairman, had brought her Chicago-learned racial attitudes with her when she moved south with her husband in the 1940s.

Economic reprisal, a constant threat to many New Orleanians, was not a concern for SOS members. Not all were as rich as Keller, but most were middle class and either professionals or the spouses of professionals, out of reach of the Citizens' Council. Dlugos's husband was in a brokerage office; Murison was the wife of a physician. Mary Sand, president, was married to a federal forest service official.

Keller had been born in Georgia and grown up in New Orleans. Dlugos had grown up in Alabama, Jack Nelson in Gulfport, Mississippi. Betty Wisdom was New-Orleans born and bred. Others were transplanted "foreigners." Sand had come from Wisconsin, and when she testified later before the state legislature, the *Shreveport Times* ran a full-page ad about it. "Mrs. Norbert H. Sand was born in Madison, Wisconsin" was all it said. All it had to say.

SOS membership eventually approached fifteen hundred, the ranks augmented by Tulane faculty and their spouses. It was a healthy number for a group of its kind, but a mere drop in the ocean of local segregationists.

The group made it clear from the beginning it was not advocating integration or desegregation or racial mixing of any kind. The words never passed their lips publicly. Besides the fact, however, that the organizers and a substantial portion of the membership had desegregation in mind from the beginning, it had become apparent that "open schools" had to be the partner of desegregation, and "open schools" was in fact a euphemism for desegregation.

SOS opened an intensive campaign to alert New Orleanians to the dangers of closed schools, stressing the high cost of private education and the potential for an increase in juvenile delinquency, loss of federal funds, the sacrifice of such student health benefits as physicial examinations and immunizations, and, last but by no means least, the economic stagnation as new industries removed New Orleans from their lists of desirable locations.

The group disseminated information about the school crisis, including legal issues not covered in the local newspapers. The members flooded white sections of the city with news letters and press releases in the effort to reverse the results of the postcard poll.

The return mail ran about ten to one against SOS. Nonetheless the organization persisted. Members could expect calls from Gladys Kahn any time after 7 A.M. with her "battle plan for the day."

A board member from Help Our Public Education (HOPE), an Atlanta group similar to SOS, spoke to an SOS-sponsored public meeting, advising New Orleanians that "once people have the facts—once they fully comprehend the drastic implications of public school closings—they will prevent such a tragedy." SOS brought the publisher of the *Arkansas Gazette* over from Little Rock and an industrialist from Norfolk, Virginia, where schools had also been closed, who warned New Orleanians of some of the "drastic implications" with which they had become acquainted through firsthand experience.

Clergymen belonging to the organization wired Governor Davis:

> We have already seen in other Southern states the disastrous results and the futility of school closure. We earnestly hope and pray that your leadership will prevent similar tragedy in Louisiana.

Rosa Keller went to the besieged school board president and offered her group's help, but it was rejected. The only way she could help him now, Rittiner said, would be to persuade Isadore Newman, a fashionable private school, to integrate first. Hoping to create a climate more favorable to keeping the public schools open, SOS members used their social and professional contacts and buttonholed the city's important businessmen. Wouldn't they use their influence to speak out for keeping the schools open? A few church groups declared themselves in favor of open schools, but the local civic leadership maintained its long silence.

SOS proved to be no match for the segregationists. Gladys Kahn's early morning zeal and her coworkers' diligence and industry notwithstanding, it was another case of too little and too late. The segregationists had stolen a six-year march on the group and spent their time profitably. They had whipped the state legislature into a frenzy of opposition to school desegregation, forced the issue into the gubernatorial elections, taken control of the winner, clamped their hands over the mouths of dissenters, and stampeded the school board into a tight corner. Attitudes had ossified, and the press releases and news letters SOS sent out began to elicit more obscenities than rational discussion.

Increasingly panicky in its precarious position between the state government and the federal court, uncertain of its authority, the Orleans Parish school board worried about September. None of the members—not Rittiner, Riecke, Shepard, or Sutherland, and certainly not Wagner—really wanted the schools racially integrated. Integration they saw as an invitation to citywide rebellion and violence. But nobody wanted them closed, either. Locked schools invited chaos in both the long and short run. About all that was certain that summer was that New Orleans was headed for more trouble.

At its regular meeting on May 24, the first since Wright issued his stunning order, board members put together a long and detailed statement outlining their plans to deal with the increasingly perilous situation. Number one was still another pledge, the umpteeth of its kind, to "continue to fight this order in the courts of the land" and "to use every legal means"—New Orleanians could recite it in their sleep—"to preserve a segregated school system." Rault was authorized to keep up the legal fight.

Board members acknowledged they were trapped between the order to integrate and "present state laws" that kept them from going ahead and could only be altered by the people through the state legislature. They concluded they had not a clue at this time "whether the schools will be opened or closed this September," but were basing board policy and future "purchases, personnel, placements and other matters" on the premise they would be open. The statement was approved four to one— Wagner objected to its implied "invitation to the people to change the statutes."

A month later, Wright's May 16 order to desegregate in September was still pending in the appellate courts, and the school board had taken no steps to implement it when on June 20, an anxious overflow crowd forced the transfer of the regular meeting from the board offices to the auditorium of nearby Rabouin High School. Boos and cheers shattered the usual orderliness of the gathering as board president Rittiner, over Emile Wagner's objections, read from letters that had come to him, including one from Archbishop Rummel virtually begging New Orleanians to accept "the moderate form of gradual integration proposed by Judge Wright as a sound temperate interpretation of the American way of life and, incidentally of the Christian way of life." Four or five smaller church groups added their pleas to keep the schools open.

But the voices for desegregation were few and considerably softer than those of the segregationists, who'd come out in force. Mrs. Bernard J. Gaillot, Jr., a Catholic housewife who was soon to become one of New Orleans's most vocal militants, in one of her early public assaults on race mixing, branded integration a "mortal sin." Jackson Ricau, a journalist and prominent member of the local Citizens' Council, urged the school board to switch to a private school system, and council president Emmett Irwin charged that SOS's real agenda was not open schools but racial integration. Calling New Orleans a "testing ground," he advised the board to exhume the twentieth-century's version of old John Calhoun's nullification doctrine, what modern southerners called "interposition" and which the state legislature had passed as a resolution in 1956.

Irwin's suggestion was the one that most appealed to the board that night. It carried a sense of seriousness as well as an urgency about it. It also transferred the burden to act from the school board to the governor, whose responsibility interposition ultimately would be.

Davis, however, wasn't ready to take that big a step. At a news conference two days later, he backed the school board down some, declaring that "interposition would be the last thing before secession." He said he and Attorney General Gremillion were exploring several avenues open to the city's school board, but avoided giving a direct answer on whether he would close the schools rather than see them desegregated.

On June 26, the board took another direct hit on its insistent efforts to stop school desegregation in September. The Fifth Circuit court of appeals, speaking through its stalwarts Elbert Tuttle and John Wisdom,

344 • The Second Battle of New Orleans

in a one-sentence per curiam ruling denied Gerald Rault's request for a stay of Wright's May 16 order.

The third judge on the panel, the Mississippian Benjamin F. Cameron, perennial dissenter in the burgeoning number of civil rights cases coming into the court, did not sully his record in this one. He questioned Wright's authority to singlehandedly overturn a state statute, declared the lower court judge's May 16 order "not . . . sustainable," then warned that

> if any considerable number of the six thousand nine hundred eighty-two Negro children who were eligible to enter the first grade of the New Orleans public schools in September should demand entrance into "the formerly all white public school nearest their homes," nothing but chaos could result and the enforcement of the order would be accompanied by nothing but harm to the children, the parents and teachers of both races and to the entire community.

As instructed, Rault took the case to the U.S. Supreme Court, but that Court having adjourned for the summer and time being of the essence, Justice Hugo Black on July 10 alone refused to stay Wright's order.* The federal court order stood, as the September opening of the New Orleans schools loomed closer and closer.

Lloyd Rittiner, whose position was undergoing some not-so-subtle changes, touched off a controversy with a statement on television that "integration in Orleans parish public schools cannot be avoided and there is no answer to the problem except to comply with the judge's decision if the schools are to remain open." Emile Wagner, demanding equal time from the media, assured New Orleanians the schools most likely would open in September, but they would be operated not by the local school board but by the legislature and the governor, who would take them over. He also said he'd been approached by three groups urging him to become a candidate for mayor on a segregation platform in 1962, but he was not, he said, giving it serious thought "at this time." That summer he stumped the city advising his cohorts in the Citizens' Council to organize educational cooperatives "as an emergency measure should interposition fail."

It was not only Rittiner among the board members, however, who'd recognized "the end of the road" when they saw it and were ready to give up the fight before the public school system was destroyed. Riecke, Shepard, and Sutherland were also beginning to crack under the unac-

*When it returned in October, the full Court concurred.

customed strain on the board's joints. They began to assume the inevitability of some racial mixing in the city's schools. Shepard promised to "cast my vote for open schools." He hoped they would remain segregated, but he was ready to accept them "either way, so long as they stayed open." Sutherland, although up for reelection by a white majority that had so far shown no such signs, agreed with Shepard:

> [I]f we can't open segregated schools ... then we we should open with token integration. I would integrate two or three grades just to buy time and attempt to prevent violence.

And he began to talk about the possibility of resurrecting the so-called pupil placement plan as a way of limiting the number of black children entering white schools. The plan appeared to be available again. Although the local federal district court, later affirmed by the Fifth Circuit judges, had thrown Louisiana's pupil placement law out in 1956, the U.S. Supreme Court had allowed a similar measure in Alabama to stand, taking a "wait and see" position on whether school districts in that state would attempt to use it to discriminate against black youngsters trying to enter white schools. Now Louisiana's legislature was fashioning a similar measure designed to finally pass judicial muster.

As if encouraged perhaps by the school board's changing position, a few small voices were heard supporting open schools, desegregation and all. A PTA here and there, a group of thirty Methodist ministers, a coalition of ninety-four clergymen of all denominations, who believed New Orleanians had been hoodwinked by politicians into believing that "through some fictitious legal device," public education could be privatized at no extra cost to the taxpayer, stuck their hands in the fire with no apparent burns, but no apparent effect, either.

The opposition to school desegregation was still outshouting everyone else. In addition, a serious movement for private education had begun. The White Educational Association, an umbrella group organized to help white parents set up cooperative schools, incorporated that summer and soon claimed a membership of two hundred. The first of the cooperatives also applied for a charter shortly afterwards.

The state legislature having provided him with the statutory bedrock, Attorney General Gremillion marched on the civil district court for Orleans Parish on July 25 and asked Judge Oliver P. Carriere to prohibit legally the school board from taking any steps whatever toward the desegregation of the New Orleans schools. He claimed the legislature had taken the responsibility and authority for designating the racial makeup of Louisiana's schools out of the school board's hands and put it in the legislature's. Since the federal judge, Skelly Wright, had ignored the state's interest in the matter, he had no authority to proceed with his own desegregation plan in such a high-handed manner.

Lloyd Rittiner was disappointed. He had thought the state was as close to the end of its legal road as he was, that there was

> absolutely nothing the governor or the attorney general can do to maintain a segregated school system in Louisiana

and he greatly feared continued opposition could only result in the destruction of the local schools. Gremillion was sorry, he said,

> that Mr. Rittiner is getting the jitters. Such activity on his part will only lead to uncertainty.

It took Judge Carriere just four days to announce his decision. He did exactly what the attorney general had asked, noting that if the school board objected, it was free to close the schools. Taking a page from John Parker's model for reluctant desegregators written back in 1955 following *Brown II,* Carriere added that

> *the United States Constitution does not require integration; it merely forbids discrimination.*

The school board responded gloomily by announcing it was now prohibited from planning or even thinking about the desegregation of the schools that September 8.

The lines of convergence were implacably narrowing as the state of Louisiana and the federal government, like sumo wrestlers, locked themselves into a final embrace. Black PTAs continued to prepare parents for the opening of school, now less than six weeks off, but, Tureaud reported to Thurgood Marshall in late July, "there is much uncertainty as to what will be the procedure for registering children in the first grade."

> It looks like New Orleans may be the next battle ground for massive resistance or closing of the schools in the state or interposition.

CHAPTER 17

War—In the Legal Sense

As the summer of 1960 marched inexorably toward fall, the approaching day of school desegregation starkly real and at the same time too fantastic to be real, the struggle for power in Louisiana intensified beyond anyone's expectations. Had these events occurred in some central European monarchy, tanks would have rumbled in the streets and infantrymen marched.

In Louisiana, however, no military juntas conspired to unseat the elected state government, no cabals plotted to oust the constitutionally appointed judges from their chambers. *Coup d'état* was not only a foreign word but a foreign concept and a foreign fact of life.

In Louisiana, the politicians played out their aggressions in the courtroom, on the floor of the legislature, and in the voting booth. In the immortal words of Robert Jackson, U.S. solicitor general, attorney general, and Supreme Court justice,

> Struggles over power that in Europe call out regiments of troops, in this country call out battalions of lawyers.

The NAACP was still fighting for its life in Louisiana in the summer of 1960. The resolution of the state's efforts to muzzle the organization still had not been finally settled by the courts. This past February, a three-judge federal district court—Wright and Christenberry, who seemed to be joined at the hip on civil rights matters, plus John Wisdom, who'd been plunged into the middle of the civil rights wars immediately after his appointment to the appellate court in 1957—had repulsed Attorney General Gremillion's pincer attack on the black group. First, they had ruled unconstitutional the old anti–Ku Klux Klan Act of 1924 that required the organization to disclose its membership, wryly commenting on the fact that the measure had been a dead letter for nearly three decades, uninvoked until after the agitation for school desegregation and other civil rights made it politically useful.

Further, they said, those few NAACP branches that complied with the state law had found, as the organization's lawyers had predicted, that some members were "subjected to certain economic reprisals." Teachers, particularly vulnerable to Louisiana laws denying employment to anyone who believed in school desegregation, had resigned from the NAACP in panic, and the membership had been reduced "significantly," bearing out the United States Supreme Court's conclusion in a similar Alabama case that such state statutes have a distinct "deterrent effect on the free enjoyment of the right to associate."

The other arm of the state's attack on the NAACP, Act 260, which required such organizations operating in the state to file annual affidavits declaring that none of their officers was a member of any group cited by the Communist-hunting House Un-American Activities Committee or had any Communist affiliation, the trio of judges reduced to absurdity. They had nearly laughed it out of court during a hearing when Attorney General Gremillion stood up and told them with a straight face that some nine hundred organizations in Louisiana had complied with the law. One of the judges had retorted that there were more than nine hundred organizations operating in the Ninth Ward of New Orleans alone. Writing formally for the law reports, the judges soberly declared that

> The statute would require the impossible. It is clearly unconstitutional.

Good news for the NAACP.

But Gremillion wasn't through. There was still the Supreme Court, and although he must have known he hadn't a prayer of persuading the justices to reverse the lower court, the temptation to keep the meter running was irresistible, and he asked that Court to review the district court's ruling on the grounds that it had failed "to recognize that sovereign right of the state to exercise its police power" and denied to Louisiana "the right to protect itself against associations dominated and controlled by Communist or subversive leadership."

All A. P. Tureaud could do he did, which was to ask the high Court to reject Gremillion's appeal on the ground that the justices had already settled the matter in the Alabama case. But the final fate of the NAACP in Louisiana still hung in the balance. It would hang there through the rest of 1960 and into 1961 while the justices deliberated, the organization's membership all the while unsure of itself and carefully watching its step.

The intricate legal maneuvering over school desegregation continued. Local Judge Carriere's order prohibiting the school board from desegregating on the opening day of school flew directly in the face of Skelly Wright's federal court order to do it. A. P. Tureaud had no alternative. The "stubborn" Creole did what he had to. He returned to Wright's courtroom, the only game in town Tureaud had a prayer of winning, and asked the judge to put a stop to obstruction of school desegregation. The lawyer could only hope his winning streak would continue.

In the meantime, the local branch of the NAACP was assuming schools would open as scheduled on September 8 and was informally—and cautiously—instructing the parents of children ready to enter the first grade "how to carry out our program against vulnerable spots," i.e., the twenty-eight all-white elementary schools near which black families lived and the obvious targets for desegregation. Arthur Chapital, a local postal worker and president of the New Orleans NAACP chapter in 1960, explained:

> We must be ready to move, now that there is hope of accomplishing the intent of at least eight years of painstaking court action.

Shelby Jackson, state superintendent of education, had something to say about that. Handily reelected in 1960 to the position he'd held for the past twelve years, he warned during an interview in Baton Rouge that black teachers would lose their jobs and black children their chance for an education if desegregation was "forced." Jackson didn't see why, he said, "we have to abide by the wishes of a small minority when it is evident that a large majority of both races want the schools to remain as they are now."

There was standing-room only at school board meetings late that summer. Frightened by the crosscurrents churning up their city and the rumblings of the governor's tough talk and indecision filtering down from Baton Rouge, New Orleans parents were crowding into board sessions trying to find answers to what they considered the life-and-death questions about the status of their schools. But the board's agendas focused on housekeeping matters—what to do about insurance premiums then due, about contracts already let for school renovation and repair, about the five thousand employees who, in compliance with one of the few new state segregation laws not yet declared unconstitutional by Skelly Wright, had to be paid through any desegregation crisis. The school board offered no solace or reassurance, only more promises to study the issue.

Deeply concerned now, they began to badger Mayor Morrison himself, and he at last showed some concern of his own. He wrote the governor asking "exactly what is the status of this matter" and offering "all the aid that is within our power to accomplish in the aim of seeing the schools open on a segregated basis." At the same time he commissioned city attorney Alvin Liska to evaluate the city's legal status.

Davis assured the mayor he would take every step possible to keep his city's schools the way he wanted them but revealed no definite plans, only promised to keep Morrison "advised of future developments." Liska reported he could see no legal way to accomplish what Davis and Morrison intended. All of which was discouraging enough for Morrison to suggest "a small percentage of integration" might ward off "lots of trouble and lots of mixing." Then he lapsed back into his accustomed silence.

On August 17, Governor Davis at last came up for air after months of secret plotting and strategy sessions and made his move. Acting in his "sovereign capacity," he superseded the Orleans Parish school board and put the city's schools under his own personal "control, management and administration," then ordered the schools to open on September 7, a day ahead of schedule. Following his dramatic announcement, he remained secluded in the governor's mansion, refusing to comment.

A grinning Attorney General Gremillion was happily handing out copies of the governor's order in Davis's office at the state Capitol. He hotly denied the move involved interposition or even a step toward interposition. It was, Gremillion explained, only a move to "let Louisiana run its schools as it sees fit." It was designed, he added euphemistically, to "let the legislature and the legislature alone come up with a plan for integration and to leave to them what is deliberate speed in desegregating the schools."

Board President Rittiner's first reaction was confusion. Who was going to pay the school system's bills?

His more considered reaction was pessimism. He simply didn't think, as he'd been saying for some time now, especially since May 16, when Wright's desegregation plan lifted the responsibility from the school board's shoulders, that defiance of the Supreme Court was any longer a viable option. Now he was even pointing out the inconsistency in "teaching of the Constitution of the United States to school children, and on the other hand, defying the ruling of the Supreme Court." This wasn't the Lloyd Rittiner who'd sworn to preserve school segregation when he was elected to the school board in 1956.

Board Vice President Riecke and Matt Sutherland shared Rittiner's pessimism regarding the workability of Davis's order. Emile Wagner, who'd spent his summer whipping up support for maintaining school segregation, could hardly contain his elation, however. The governor's action he found "in accordance with the promise he made to the people of New Orleans and to me." Wagner believed it gave Davis a "golden opportunity" to make history, to "rally the conservatives of the nation to the end that we can turn to the right the thinking of the people in this country," a change in political direction Wagner believed had been "sorely needed" ever since Franklin Roosevelt was elected president.

Leander Perez was of the opinion that the governor's takeover of the local schools *had* to work if the children were to be saved, if New Orleans was not to become another Washington, D.C., where, he charged, school desegregation had sent "thousands of white families" fleeing to the suburbs "pursued by the Communist front of the NAACP, backed by the United States government." He could only despair that "This country is in a hell of a fix."

Recognizing the possibility that the governor's defiance of a federal court could result in closing the public schools and thus jeopardize their own futures, particularly those of the seniors among them, a group of white New Orleans high school students took a bus to Baton Rouge carrying a petition to the governor. They begged him to keep their schools open. Davis refused to see them. His executive secretary, Chris Fraser, accepted the petition for the governor. He asked who was sponsoring them.

SENIOR RICHARD BASS: We sponsor ourselves.
FRASER: What organization out of New York asked you to come here today?
BASS: No organization.
FRASER: How much are they paying you all?
BASS: No one is paying us anything.
ANONYMOUS STUDENT: Is that a joke—or what?
FRASER (who'd learned some segregation-speak himself during his service with the governor): No one believes in education more than Governor Davis. . . . The Governor has taken control of the situation. . . . He has spent a lot of sleepless nights. . . . You're going to have schools. Don't you worry about that.

But New Orleanians *were* worried. Their letters to the newspapers and to city officials, their coming out in record numbers for school board meetings, and now in late August, a substantial drop in back-to-school retail sales reflected their deep concern.

As the prospects for the closing of public schools in September grew, along with an increasing awareness, particularly inside the threatened city, that the state government's belligerence wasn't solving the school system's problem, a second organization had joined the small, largely SOS-led chorus bold enough to speak out for life. This new organization called itself the Committee for Public Education (CPE), and its members did not view the closing of the city's schools as a desirable or even a viable alternative to racial desegregation.

Not that the CPE people wanted the schools desegregated. Most of them didn't. Although SOS and CPE took identical public positions—both advocated open schools despite desegregation—CPE members were not the racial liberals SOS members were, and in fact it was the fundamentally conservative makeup of CPE that made all the difference.

CPE stationery listed as directors Clarence Scheps, who'd vigorously fought Skelly Wright's court orders during his term as school board president, and Sam Rosenberg, the regular school board attorney removed from the desegregation battles when Gerald Rault was hired. Most CPE members looked at school desegregation through lenses more or less like Scheps's and Rosenberg's. One of the group's founders characterized herself as a "segregationist but a law-abiding citizen first."

Many of them parents of students living and attending public schools in the largely white uptown and similar districts out along Lake Pontchartrain, they themselves had little to fear from desegregation but much to fear from the closing of city schools. Which was where they focused their energy and left discussion and resolution of the racial problems to the local partisans.

CPE couldn't arrest the movement for private cooperative schools started by parents frightened equally by the prospects of racial desegregation and by public school closings. No fewer than twenty-four cooperatives either had been chartered or were at some other early stage of organization by the end of August.

What CPE did was to bring respectability to a long-suppressed desire on the part of the public to support open schools. CPE hadn't perhaps the clout the city's civic and business leaders might have brought to the cause had they been willing, but CPE on the other hand was broad based: not exactly grass roots but not without influence, for all its middle-class aura. Morton Inger in his *Politics and Reality in an American City: The New Orleans School Crisis of 1960* compared CPE's status to that "of an advance motorcycle escort that guarantees the safety of the marchers in a parade through hostile territory."

Although the white professional educational associations—the New Orleans Classroom Teachers Association and the Louisiana School Boards Association—continued to back the governor's efforts to retain racial segregation in the schools at all cost, a small surge of support for CPE's position brought several other groups into the open: Episcopal, Methodist, and United Church of Christ clergy led off, the United Packinghouse Workers of America, and the Central Labor Council of New Orleans joined up, and the Junior Chamber of Commerce allowed that the city's best interests would be "served if schools are kept open," although its membership also still condemned the federal government "for its infringement on the constitutional rights of the state of Louisiana."

CPE members were the people Lloyd Rittiner considered his constituency, the people who'd undoubtedly checked "I would like to see the schools kept open even though a small amount of integration is necessary" on the postcards he'd sent out this past spring, and the organization's public support for open schools emboldened Rittiner and the three other moderate members of the board to use whatever strength they had left on preparing to comply with the federal court order. Joined by School Superintendent Redmond and the ubiquitous Rosenberg, who seemed to be everywhere at once as the pace of the conflict quickened, the four organized themselves informally into a committee designed to function without the obstruction of the fifth board member Emile Wagner, whom Rittiner accused of informing his friends in the Citizens' Council of every move the others made.

Unhesitatingly, CPE officers went after the Davis administration and in an open letter "implore[d]" Davis, the attorney general, and the others

> to put aside the false opiates you have been administering to the public; and in assuming your roles of leadership, begin to prepare the citizenry for the problems they must face in September.

The alternative, CPE president Robert C. Lancaster warned,

> must inevitably lead to the violent eruption of emotions when the euphoria bubble ultimately breaks.

But, fearful of harassment, CPE members preferred behind-the-scenes operations. There were rumors that it was the school board itself, along with Sam Rosenberg and maybe even Skelly Wright—although given Wright's ethical scruples his participation seems unlikely—who organized CPE in the first place. Rosenberg did handle the legal details of incorporation, and board president Lloyd Rittiner was the featured guest speaker at the group's organizational meeting, after which the board's connection with CPE was close if not formal or official.

There was talk in New Orleans's legal community, following the filing of A. P. Tureaud's suit in federal court to stop the Davis administration from blocking Skelly Wright's latest desegregation order, that Tureaud's case wasn't strong enough to accomplish his purpose. Sam Rosenberg got it in his head—rightly or wrongly—that the NAACP wanted to lose this round, force the schools to close, and thereby "dramatize the issue" to galvanize public opinion. As a member of CPE, and committed to open schools, Rosenberg couldn't risk it. Quickly and quietly, he flushed out no fewer than thirty-one parents of white public-school children willing to put their names on a legal suit, then found a local attorney, Charles E. Richards, who would be willing to intervene in the *Bush* case to keep the schools open—segregated or desegregated, CPE didn't care, so long as they stayed open. Rosenberg settled down in Richards's office for the night of August 16 to prepare the suit that CPE took into federal court next morning, the very day the governor announced he was taking over the New Orleans schools.

Called *Williams* v. *Davis* (for Harry K. Williams, one of the white parents, and Jimmie H. Davis), the CPE suit deliberately disassociated from Tureaud's suit and avoided the issue of racial segregation altogether. In fact, CPE asked Skelly Wright to dissolve his desegregation order and thus create the conditions under which Davis and the legislature could allow the schools to remain open. Wright's refusal a foregone conclusion, however, the Williams suit asked alternatively that the judge declare the entire package of antidesegregation statutes then on the books unconstitutional and prohibit state officials from interfering with the operation of the public schools. On its face, the suit appeared neutral on the race issue. Realistically, it was an endorsement of Wright's desegregation order. It was the first time in the eight-year history of *Bush* v. *Orleans Parish School Board* that white parents went on public record as opposing the behavior of the state government in connection with the New Orleans schools.

Recognizing the identical purposes in Tureaud's *Bush* and CPE's *Williams* suits, though there was not a moment's cooperation between the two, Wright consolidated them and scheduled a joint hearing for August 25. Then he set about the business of bringing in the major [named] defendant, Governor Davis, who one day was seen laughing and joking with newsmen while he talked about the time being ripe for a showdown with the federal government; the next day no one could find him at all when federal marshals tried to serve him with a summons. Secretaries at the Capitol hadn't laid eyes on him for hours; state troopers denied all knowledge of his whereabouts, although lights blazed and voices could be heard in his office and his limousine was parked outside. One summons was taped to the spot on the floor where it fell when a secretary refused to accept it; a Plexiglas shell protected another that had been dropped under similar circumstances. Davis ignored them all. The question on everyone's mind was Where's Jimmie?

The man who had vowed to "fight to eternity" for his state's right to disobey a federal court order could hardly appear with his gubernatorial dignity intact as a defendant in that very court, and Davis didn't. The marshals had, however, found Attorney General Gremillion, a co-defendant, at home, and handed him his summons. He and several members of his staff had come. Thurgood Marshall had come down from New York. And Gerald Rault, who felt he'd exhausted every available legal device in the school board's struggle against desegregation and was on the verge of resigning as its special attorney, made his final public appearance for the board. Local attorneys, members of the press, and a parade of spectators elbowed each other as they crowded into the courtroom. They saw and heard considerably more than they'd expected.

Attorney General Gremillion outperformed all the rest. The scion of an old Donaldsonville, Louisiana, family and proud of his ancestry, he'd been developing his professional skills and hardening his character in the business of law enforcement, first in a district attorney's, then in the attorney general's office, ever since his graduation from LSU Law School in 1937. In the summer of 1960, he was in his first year of his second term as the state's attorney general. He'd joined the stampede to Davis early in the campaign and, with the *Times-Picayune*'s hearty endorsement largely on the basis of his vigorous defense of states' rights, he'd easily won reelection on Davis's ticket.

At forty-six, he was moderately good-looking. His oblong face showed only the first signs of fleshiness, his full head of hair curled gently, and the appearance of youth had not yet entirely disappeared. His overall appearance, however—his ruddy complexion, beefy body structure, and aggressive stance—accurately mirrored his persona: feisty.

A self-styled "doer, not a reader," the chief law enforcement officer in Louisiana found himself "too busy in action" for the kind of contemplation serious reading required. Back at Catholic High School in Donaldsonville, he'd already earned a reputation as a scrapper, and "What's Jack fighting about today?" led off many a student conversation. It seemed to Gremillion then, and nothing had happened to change him over the intervening years, that "everything [he] put [his] hand to turned to controversy."

He claimed to hold Skelly Wright in the highest regard and attributed the judge's determination to carry out school desegregation to the fact that he was "duty bound to the federal statutes." But when Wright and the other two judges at the hearing on the consolidated *Bush* and *Williams* suits committed what Gremillion maintained was a breach of federal procedure—in the interests of speed they'd introduced several affidavits in lieu of testimony which the attorney general hadn't read, then refused to postpone further proceedings until he read them—he slammed a law book down on the defense table, then jumped up and shouted

You are running over us roughshod!

Judge Rives, over from the Fifth Circuit court of appeals for the occasion, told Gremillion in his soft, mellifluous Alabama accents to sit down, he'd have adequate time to examine and reply to the documents. Gremillion sat, but his mutterings about justice and the Constitution could be heard throughout the courtroom. When CPE attorney Charles Richards began to read from one of the contested affidavits, Gremillion could stand it no longer. He charged toward the courtroom door shouting

I'm not going to stay in this den of iniquity!

Spotting representatives of local black PTAs among the spectators, the attorney general interrupted his flight just long enough to spit on them. Followed out by Emile Wagner, Gremillion could be heard pacing the corridor and bellowing about the "kangaroo court" he'd just left.

A hush settled over the stunned courtroom as the hearings continued, though not before Rives whispered to his neighbor on the bench Herbert Christenberry that "we've got to do something about that young man," then ordered the United States attorney's office to prepare appropriate contempt charges against Louisiana's attorney general.

The affidavits at issue were read as scheduled in the open courtroom, but when Rives asked for the state's testimony, there was only silence. Gremillion's staff had collected his papers and followed him out.

Thurgood Marshall made a brief argument urging the court to block the state's interference with the local school desegregation and concluded that

This is no longer a case of Negro children seeking their constitutional right. This is now a challenge of the officials of the State of Louisiana to the sovereignty of the United States. The duty of this court is clear.

The court saw it Marshall's way. In a per curiam opinion—it was becoming obvious that Skelly Wright wrote the per curs coming out of the three-judge courts, but his colleagues were trying to deflect some of the heat from him by taking equal responsibility for authorship—issued on August 27, just two days after the hearing, the judges supported the plaintiffs, Bush and Williams. They ruled firmly unconstitutional all Louisiana statutes putting responsibility for school desegregation in the legislature's hands as well as Governor Davis's takeover of the Orleans Parish school board, and they ordered the again-legitimate elected parish school board to get on with the ordered desegregation*

At the same time, the court ordered Attorney General Gremillion to return to the courtroom at 10 A.M. on September 12 to defend himself against charges of criminal contempt for his "misbehavior" there two days before. The unrepentant, almost cocky Gremillion proudly told reporters that the Louisiana District Attorneys Association, "along with a number of other capable attorneys," had "volunteered to defend" him.

Gremillion's conceit notwithstanding, the attorney general's mouth had been put out of commission, at least temporarily. Louisiana's laws obstructing school desegregation, having been declared unconstitutional, were also out of commission, their only use now to the legislators who'd gone home to campaign for reelection on the basis of them. Theoretically, nothing stood in the way of school desegregation in New Orleans now. But only theoretically.

Implicit in CPE's *Williams* suit was the need for further delay of desegregation to allow the school board members time for ironing out administrative details with which they had previously refused to cope. Chaotic visions of overcrowded school buildings, confusion over teaching assignments, classroom disorganization, were doing a dance of death in Superintendent Redmond's head as he contemplated the opening of the city's schools in just over a week. Board member Ted Shepard was hoping for at least a year's postponement, and Rittiner, Riecke, and Sutherland, painfully aware of the lack of planning and preparation on their part, were talking about approaching Skelly Wright for one last commutation of the city's sentence. Predictably, Emile Wagner had "no interest in," nor would he "discuss the matter" with his old friend Judge Wright. He planned to ask the governor to close the schools when desegregation came too close for comfort.

At a special meeting at noon on August 29, the school board—again,

---

*Seven months later, on March 20, 1961, the U.S. Supreme Court affirmed the special district court's judgment.

all except Wagner—met briefly, discussed Wright's latest order, and agreed to ask him for the postponement needed to make arrangements. Together they walked solemnly across Lafayette Square to the federal building on lower Camp Street and were in Wright's chambers by 12:55 P.M. They sat informally around a big table. No records were kept of their conference, they just "laid it right out." Having gone along with the state legislature and the governor these past four years, the school officials told the judge they were now ready to comply with his order. There was only one catch. They once again required time to tend to the logistics, muddled now beyond any quick repair. Two months or so would probably do it, they said.

It was the first affirmative action Wright had had from the school board, and if they kept their promise, that, too, would be a first. Rittiner read sympathy in Wright's tone and demeanor.

They didn't, however, exactly level with Wright. All they said was certainly true, but they didn't say all that was true. They didn't discuss with Wright Matt Sutherland's upcoming race for reelection to his seat on the board.

Sutherland was a champion of open schools, but, discouraged by the intensity of the opposition, he'd been on the verge of resigning from the board. Then CPE came along. Some of the opposition seemed to be softening, at least a little, and he was confident enough now in late summer to run again. "If you run and get elected," his colleagues told him, "then we'll know we're on the right track. If you run and are not elected, then we're gonna think seriously whether we should continue." They wanted reassurance that their confidence in the white majority's preference for open schools, despite the result of the postcard polling, had not been misplaced.

Board members also failed to discuss with Wright their plan to make moving from one school to another as complicated and time-consuming as possible by reviving the old pupil placement plan, which was enjoying renewed vigor in the South following the U.S. Supreme Court's support of it. From the board's point of view, the further delay and discouragement of desegregation imposed by the plan's required qualifying tests offered New Orleans its best hope of limiting the number of black students who could be admitted to white schools. The smaller the numbers, they reasoned, the calmer the early days of the traumatic transition.

The board, Wright said later, "shielded" him from their intention, and he "just took it on faith that they were going to comply with [his] order" to desegregate the first grade citywide. State senator Adrian G. Duplantier observed much later, after he himself had become a federal judge, "Skelly could have told the school board to go stand on their heads. He could have integrated any or every school in the city" with the stroke of a pen. But the meat ax was not Wright's way. As politically astute as any candidate for public office, he knew he needed more support than he had at that moment, and he knew where it had to come from. He gave the board no answer that day. He said he wanted to think about it, discuss it with the parties to the legal suits.

He conferred with A. P. Tureaud for two hours that afternoon. The black lawyer found it hard to believe that after eight years the school board needed two more months; to him it was simply another obstruction and he vigorously protested any further delay of school desegregation. Following the meeting he shot off a petition to the U.S. Supreme Court asking the justices not to allow Wright to yield to the school board's pressure. After eight years of litigation, he told the Court, "the only relief obtained in this case is a change of attitude of the school board from open defiance of the *Brown* decision to interminable delays."

Charles Richards, who was still speaking for the thirty-one white parents who participated in the *Williams* suit, told Wright he thought the school board ought to be given any reasonable time to formulate plans. His only interest was in keeping the schools open.

Gerald Rault seconded the board's pleas during the meeting with Wright. But next morning, he told his employers that over the years since his appointment as special attorney, he'd done all he could for them. He'd now come to the end of his legal rope, and he resigned on the spot, leaving the board without a guide through the heavy weather that lay ahead. Rittiner was surprised and "sorry" to see him go, but recovered quickly and asked the redoubtable Sam Rosenberg, who'd continued to handle regular school board business during Rault's tenure and was already involved up to his ears in desegregation matters, to slip quickly into Rault's shoes.

Skelly Wright took twenty-four hours to weigh the various personal, professional, and political considerations that the school board's request involved. Every idea he had only emphasized his own vulnerability and the precariousness of his position as he faced the desegregation of the city's schools with only the Constitution for cover. It was a traumatic time for him as well as for New Orleans.

Publicly, he presented a stoic mien. Privately, as he contemplated the complications of delay, he wrestled not only with the public issue but also with his own emotions. He liked to think "personal hate" did not motivate the attacks on him and his family, that people looked at him now not as their friend and neighbor Skelly Wright but only as the imper-

sonal "instrument by which [the white majority's] way of life was threatened." Few other federal court judges had encountered what Wright was
facing in New Orleans, however, and it was one time in his life that he
could not find a suitable precedent to follow. The human aspects of judging could not be reduced to a set of case numbers.

He was glad now that he had developed a habit of keeping his own
counsel over his ten years of judging. His appearance had changed some
during that time—his face was a little fleshier, he was balding, and there
was no clump of hair in which to anchor his glasses on his head as he'd
been accustomed to doing—but the part of him that went through life
solo remained in place, and knowing that 88 to 90 percent of the people
in New Orleans "hated" him, he stuck close to the courthouse during the
day, lunched alone at a nearby private club, and retreated to his home in
the uptown section of the city after work, thereby avoiding as many personal confrontations as possible. Once he thought a passerby may have
tried to push him into traffic, and he took to walking as far from the curb
as he could get. Acquaintances sensed he was "shocked" that he'd been
"turned on by his own people. It hurt a lot," they said.

His wife, Helen, was beginning to feel the hostility. Shopping in local
department stores was no longer a pleasure as she watched the smiles
on clerks' faces freeze when she handed them her credit card. Women
she'd worked with for years in local civic associations began to snub her.
Crank phone calls and nasty letters multiplied.

New Orleanians were heaping criticism on the judge for sending his
thirteen-year-old son Jimmy to the private Metairie Park Country Day
School, and just that past spring the judge had considered moving the
boy to a local public school. Then after some soul-searching, he thought
better of it. He didn't believe Jimmy, well adjusted where he was and had
been since nursery school, should "suffer" for the predicament in which
his father found himself. The gesture, Wright said, had a "little aspect of
the heroic about it that offended" him.

It was against this background that Wright wrestled with the
Orleans Parish school board's appeal for still one more delay, an appeal
that could not itself be considered in a vacuum but was fraught with
political implications, national as well as local.

Wright wasn't at all certain the men really needed two months to get
the system's affairs in order, and it was then that it occurred to him that
just over two months would bring the day of desegregation down to election day—November 8—and what they actually had in mind was to delay
desegregation until Matt Sutherland was safely reelected. As a judge,
Wright was accustomed to searching out precedents—an ingrained habit
of mind now—and as he unwound the reels of memory, he returned to

his days in the United States attorney's office twenty-five years before, recalling that a staff rule-of-thumb barred seeking indictments of political figures during an election campaign and thereby making martyrs of them. It wasn't, he said, a strong precedent, but it was there, and he began to look at desegregation delay as a useful device for lowering the emotional decibels of the event if it could be separated from election politics. He also felt he needed the school board's support as much as the school board needed his—they needed each other now—and he saw his acquiescence to its appeal as one way to improve their relationship.

At the same time Wright was considering the school board's proposal, he was also weighing the prospects of his getting help from Washington when the time for enforcement came. He later claimed that national political ramifications relayed to him as he turned the question of postponement over in his mind prevented immediate school desegregation even if the school board had been willing, and this factor also influenced his decision on whether or not to order the two-month deferral the school board wanted.

There are two contradictory versions of Wright's dealings with the Department of Justice during that eventful summer of 1960: his and the department's.

The way Wright remembered it, he feared another Little Rock if he failed to prepare for the worst, and he asked the justice department for troops, marshals, "all the help [he] could get," since he found himself virtually alone and "helpless" with no way to enforce his order and aware that he could count on neither the local nor state police for assistance. Near the time of the school board's capitulation and its subsequent discussion of postponement, Wright recalled that Harold R. Tyler, Eisenhower's new assistant attorney general for civil rights, flew into New Orleans one August night, consulted not with Wright but with U.S. attorney A. Hepburn. Many, then within hours flew back out. In Wright's version of events, Many reported the next day to the judge that President Eisenhower, who saw the election of his vice president, Richard M. Nixon, in 1960 as a "vote of confidence of his policies over the past seven and a half years," had strongly suggested that Wright defer the desegregation of the New Orleans schools until after that election. As Wright told it twenty years later:

> Many said that we do know you have this problem; we want to help you with this problem, but if you proceed to force the integration now before election there will be much greater problems than if you wait until after the election. He made it clear to me that if I waited until after the election, that they would give me all of the support I needed.

I don't think anyone was crude enough to suggest to me that they wouldn't give me any support if I didn't wait. . . . But it was clear to me that if I did wait they would. There's no doubt about that.

Except in Tyler's recollections. Tyler recalled an August, 1960, Saturday afternoon when the customary weekend silence in the Department of Justice was broken by an urgent telephone call from Augusta, Georgia, where Eisenhower was vacationing. Jim Hagerty, the President's press secretary, came on the line.

"The President wants to talk to you," he began.

Tyler, who had a voice like an AK–47, snapped to attention. "Yes, *sir.*"

Eisenhower had been reading about events in New Orleans, he said, and he inquired into Tyler's plans. Tyler replied he was sending extra marshals to the city.

Eisenhower: "I'm telling you now, young fellow, if you need military assistance, don't hesitate. I'm not going to stomach violence. If there is any, I'll crack down hard." He added that he'd send troops if necessary, "election or no election," and concluded with his own description of the Louisiana legislature as "crazy."

Tyler's reconstruction of his visit to New Orleans also clashed with Wright's. Tyler remembered seeing Wright at his home where he'd gone to reassure the judge of the department's intention to support the federal court with whatever manpower it took. He denied that any suggestions for postponement of school desegregation until after November 8 had come either from Attorney General Rogers or from his own, Tyler's, civil rights division, and the President had certainly made it clear where *he* stood.

Whichever version is true, Wright proceeded on the premise that delay in this instance represented the better part of valor, and on August 30, he offered the school board ten more weeks, until Monday, November 14, to plan for school desegregation and prepare the city to open its traditionally white educational facilities to its black citizens, facilities shut up tight against the latter for more than three-quarters of a century.

School board President Rittiner was much relieved. He foresaw the city's schools opening in September "without confusion" now, and he looked forward to implementing the pupil placement plan, predicting that under its provisions for retarding desegregation, the city could look forward to "probably not more than a dozen" black children entering all-white schools. The board ordered Superintendent Redmond to prepare a long-range plan for facilitating the grade-per-year integration Wright had ordered.

Mayor Morrison broke his silence once again to say he was "pleased" at the outcome of events. He reiterated that he favored "maintaining the southern way of life and all steps should be taken to preserve it." He hoped people would use their "good judgment" when the day of desegregation finally arrived, "to minimize any trouble that might come up." Like Lloyd Rittiner, he was confident the pupil placement procedures would keep "mixing to the barest minimum."

Governor Davis was "glad" the judge had granted the delay but warned that postponement was after all only postponement and did not "represent any enduring solution to the problem that faces the citizens of our state." Emile Wagner, running for unpledged elector on the States' Rights Party ticket, pronounced the deferment no more than a ploy "to lull the people to sleep" until after election. His political blood brothers Leander Perez and other segregationists, however, viewed it as an opportunity for the governor and the legislature to revive the recent summer's frenzy of opposition.

September opened with news from the U.S. Supreme Court, which, although officially adjourned until October, had met in chambers to consider both A. P. Tureaud's request to nullify Wright's postponement of school desegregation and Attorney General Gremillion's appeal to return the New Orleans schools to the control of the governor. The Court's refusal to listen to either case and its dismissal of both represented to Thurgood Marshall the justices' impatience with excessive litigation and their clear signal that the time had come to get on with the matter at hand, the racial desegregation of America's public schools, which they themselves had ordered six years before. Legal opinion in Washington, looking at the specific cases involved, viewed the Court's action as opening the doors of all 118 New Orleans elementary schools to any qualified pupil without regard to race, an increase of sixty-five schools to which black children were now eligible to transfer.

That same day, Governor Davis, who had a tendency to respond physically to emotional stress—he'd succumbed to exhaustion and dehydration on his way to the Democratic National Convention in July and again following his attorney general's recent shouting spree in the federal court—came down with what at first seemed to be a gall bladder attack. He canceled a hunting trip to Wyoming which he'd been planning for several months, underwent a battery of tests, conferred with his physicians about his physical condition and his political advisers about school desegregation and confronted the dilemma of whether to enter a hospital for surgery immediately when the illness was acute or to wait until later when he should be in less pain but when the school situation might have become acute. He spent the next several days engaged in similar activities, then on September 12, his doctors released him with a clean bill of health. Surgery would not be necessary. No gallstones had been found, and the function of Davis's gall bladder was "satisfactory." They wanted to make it clear that the governor was "organically sound and fully capable of carrying out all the duties of his office."

> What he had [they concluded] was dyspepsis, which is chiefly due to
> the stress of his campaign and his office.

Within two more weeks he felt well enough to perform as the featured speaker at a Baptist church music conference in Alexandria, where he blended his natural folk humor with serious discussion of religious music and at the same time got in a plug for a song he had recently recorded, "Known Only to Him."

Although his stamina at least in public belied the statistics, and age had not tempered the sharpness of his tongue, Leander Perez became sixty-nine in 1960. He decided then that thirty-six years as district attorney of Plaquemines Parish, which he'd called home for all his sixty-nine years and which he'd ruled, as sole monarch, for almost all his professional life, was enough, and on September 2, he suddenly resigned, abdicating in favor of his son, Leander H. Perez, Jr., who as assistant district attorney had been practicing for this moment for some time.

Not that Perez the First had run out of energy or strong words at sixty-nine. He'd been as busy as ever that year: the brains behind not only an unpledged elector slate currently being added to the ballots in time for the presidential election in November, but also the state legislature's passage of its packet of laws to preserve school segregation, and a Citizens' Council's attempt in February to resegregate New Orleans's public transportation system on the grounds that white New Orleanians were afraid to ride the desegregated buses and trolleys. His fiery speeches were eagerly awaited wherever segregationists gathered in Louisiana. Just a few days before his resignation from official public service, he'd provoked the usual applause and hog-calling from an overflow crowd in nearby Chalmette when he blamed the "Zionist Jews" for the civil rights movement and accused them of raising the funds to keep SOS, CPE, B'nai B'rith's Anti-Defamation League, and the NAACP afloat in the choppy seas of racial controversy. After closing the public libraries in Plaquemines Parish to blacks, he'd ordered the removal of all books that even mentioned the United Nations—he believed it was a club for Zionists—works published by UNESCO, any writing that smacked of a "liberal viewpoint" or spoke, however remotely, with favor about the Negro race.

Wipe that filth off the shelves [he'd commanded].

Perez had no intention of abandoning his work in the service of racial segregation just because he was sixty-nine. In fact, he explained that he was resigning in order to have more, not less, time "to devote to the serious public issues and problems which threaten the welfare of our people." He hoped, he said, that his fellow citizens would in the future

> adjourn factional politics and close ranks against the common enemy and fellow travelers who would force unmoral racial desegregation upon our children to destroy their personal safety and well being, and who would destroy our white civilization, so that in the end our nation may be easy prey to the Communist vultures.

The next day, September 3, ex-Governor Earl Long spent some of his last breaths urging the retention of open public schools. Following his political humiliation in the 1959 gubernatorial election, he had lowered his expectations and campaigned for the Eighth Congressional District's seat in the United States House of Representatives. He defeated his opponent and looked forward to a new political life. But while the ballots were still being counted, he had a heart attack and was rushed to the hospital.

Haggard-looking now, woozy from sedation and dependent on pumped-in oxygen to support his weakening body, he held his last press conference lying in bed at Baptist Hospital in Alexandria. He said he was "glad" it was Davis and not he who had to lead the battle of the public schools, then added: "I hope he can keep the schools open." Two days later, on September 5, he died. The legend, however, lived on. Although it fell somewhat short of his brother Huey's, like Huey's, too, it seemed to grow in the telling over the years.

September saw America's schoolchildren return to classes. In the slowly desegregating South, plans like Skelly Wright's—one grade-per-year beginning in the first grade—were popular. In Knoxville, Tennessee, twenty-eight black first graders enrolled in racially mixed classes at eight formerly all-white schools. In Houston, Texas, six-year-old Tyrone Day, son of a local bank custodian and a seventh-grade English teacher at an all-Negro school, joined thirty white classmates at the Kashmere Gardens Elementary School. Twenty-one other black children had applied for transfers, but the pupil placement plan in operation there had ruled eleven of them ineligible. Ten applications were still pending when school opened. Following the U.S. Supreme Court's refusal to grant a delay, there were no incidents in either Knoxville or

Houston, although Houston officials were opening white schools to Negroes only under "protest and duress." In Little Rock, Arkansas, only sixteen of the seventy-four black students who applied to attend white high schools survived the stringent provisions of the state's pupil placement law and were approved for admission.

CHAPTER 18

"If the Fight Can Be Kept in the Courts, Everything Will Work Out"

O n September 7, New Orleans's public schools opened racially segregated as they had every year since the Democrats, returned to power at last following the 1876 election, "redeemed" the city's and the state's educational institutions. Black enrollment had risen during the past year from 49,121 to 52,581.

White enrollment showed an ominous trend. Before a single plan for desegregation had been made public, before one application for student transfers had been received in the school board offices, before one black first grader had appeared at a formerly white school, white pupils had began to abandon the local public schools. Overall numbers of white students had dropped from 40,498 in 1959 to 38,112 in 1960. Privately, school officials admitted that the new cooperatives springing up across the city—twenty-four had either been chartered or were at some other early stage of organization by the end of August—as well as other private schools and the parochial institutions were drawing off substantial numbers.

Undoubtedly uncomfortably aware that his counterparts in San Antonio, Texas, Raleigh, North Carolina, and St. Louis, Missouri, had desegregated their schools—Archbishop Joseph E. Ritter of St. Louis had actually threatened to excommunicate anyone who opposed his action—Archbishop Rummel had sent around one of his pastoral letters to be read at all the parishes in the diocese on Sunday, August 21. In it he had warned "of the danger of chaos and moral irresponsibility which is latent in the prevailing efforts to nullify or circumvent or even defy a ruling proclaimed by the supreme legal authority of our country." He was appalled at the possibility that the city's schools might close, and he regretted the burgeoning of private schools, which, far from providing a solution to New Orleans's problems, promised only to exacerbate financial and administrative difficulties as well as make education the exclusive province of the well-to-do.

With a buildup like that, Rummel could logically have been expected to follow up his previously announced intention to desegregate parochial schools by setting a firm date. The public school deadline did not seem out of the question. Such an announcement would coincide with the high moral tone he'd adopted from the beginning and have the added practical advantage of preventing white refugees from the public system from flooding and probably overcrowding his parochial institutions.

Instead, he braked suddenly and asked Catholics only to pray for "an early solution of the race problem in our midst and to bring about a propitious response to the challenge for compliance with the ruling on the integration of our public school system of education." He reiterated that "in principle we are committed to the racial integration of our Catholic schools," but again he set no date for putting the principle to work.

U.S. Attorney Hep Many was the cliché of the courtly southern gentleman, a bridge-playing crony of Judge Wisdom's, with whom he'd worked on Dwight Eisenhower's campaign for the presidency in 1952—for which he'd been rewarded with appointment to his present position. A native New Orleanian, he was also a sworn enemy of legally enforced racial discrimination and had yearned to tear down the Whites Only signs in public places long before Skelly Wright had made them illegal.

He had, however, personal reservations about school desegregation. Not the principle of it; he believed in that. But he deeply feared total integration. He estimated a white school could absorb "5, 10, 15, 20 percent of Negroes" without any problems. He felt, however, that when a school became "35, 40 percent black . . . you have a black school. The blacks dominate because the blacks use language and . . . means of coercion that whites have been forbidden to use. It's a different ball game. And when it goes all black, all you have is a holding action."

But these sentiments were purely personal. As U.S. attorney, he was entirely committed to the rule of law, and he'd recently told a local civic group,

> The Constitution is no pious declaration of principles. It and its amendments are the law of the land. . . . The ruling of the court may

be agonizing but we must live with it. . . . What the court orders is law.

A justice department lawyer who worked with Many during these trying times, both a Yankee and a veteran of the Little Rock and other wars, found the New Orleanian's support of federal policies "unusual for southern United States attorneys."

Many was concerned about Archbishop Rummel's most recent pastoral letter. It seemed to him "less than the way things should be that the Catholic Church would be a refugium for white parents who didn't feel there should be any black faces in their schools." He asked for an audience with diocesan school officials and found himself confronted by a roomful of berobed prelates. As he told it later, he quickly made his "pitch" for parochial school desegregation in tandem with that of the public schools, but made little impression on the assembled churchmen. When he recognized the futility of further argument, he began to take his leave. One of the conferees remarked,

"Mr. Many, what you have asked of us, it would not be prudent."

Many was not in the habit of biting his tongue, and his dulcet tones, once provoked, turned immediately to acid. A devout Anglican Catholic, he was not unacquainted with Christian principles. Drawing himself up to his full six feet, he answered as tartly as he ever had: "Excellency, it comes with some embarrassment on my part to remind you that the founder of our religion is not known for his prudence. Good day, sir."

Parochial schools opened in September as scheduled. They were fully segregated.

While the majority of the Orleans Parish school board planned for the November 14 school desegregation, Emile Wagner continued to insist that the city's schools would remain segregated. In a steady stream of speeches, he contended that the legislature would take over the local school system, which then would be abolished and replaced by private schools financed by the state. The majority rebuked him publicly at an open meeting of the board, but Wagner stood firm. He was, he said, "giving the people the thing they are asking for."

At last, on September 26, School Superintendent Redmond announced the drill for students wanting to transfer from one public school to another. For youngsters in kindergarten and grades two through twelve, the procedures hadn't changed, and permits would be liberally distributed so long as physical facilities and teaching staffs could accommodate them.

On paper, the procedure for transfers in grade one looked simple enough—a request in writing to Superintendent Redmond submitted between September 27 and October 7. No mention was made of any limitations, interviews, intelligence or psychological testing, health or moral standards, the youngster's conduct record, or any other of the intangibles the state's revived pupil placement plan allowed.

No one in New Orleans had even the vaguest idea how many applications to the first grade would involve desegregating a school. It was perhaps one of the most crucial questions in all the years of litigation. Would applications flood the school board offices, or would they amount to a trickle? Predictions varied.

The big map hanging in the school board's Department of Research and Planning showed the location of white and Negro schools as well as the residences of every public school student. When schools opened on September 7, sixty-five white and fifty-three Negro elementary schools accommodated an estimated 4,000 white and 7,000 black first graders. Twenty-eight of the city's white elementary schools stood close enough to Negroes' residences to encourage blacks' application for admission. Most were in older residential areas where blacks and whites had lived in close proximity for years. Those along or near the more recently developed Lake Pontchartrain/Gentilly/City Park areas to the north, almost suburban in their social climate, had no Negroes living near them.

School board vice president Louis Riecke expected fewer than a hundred transfer applications from blacks citywide. He estimated twelve to twenty-five youngsters would actually be admitted.

Superintendent Redmond put the number at one hundred. He recalled testimony he'd given to the federal court early in the *Bush* litigation indicating that "Negro pupils are from 1.5 to 3.4 years below the level of achievement attained by white pupils." The figures, he said, "still hold good." One of his young assistants volunteered that black children assigned to classes with whites would hold the latter back. Redmond was counting on the pupil placement plan to avoid that.

A. P. Tureaud wasn't optimistic. The racial climate was hardly conducive to the mixing of blacks and whites. He himself was getting hate mail. Tureaud didn't think every black parent in New Orleans was anxious to send his or her six-year-old off to a white school where hostility between the races seemed not only possible but probable. He felt six-year-olds were "too small to start alone in a white school" and many would choose to remain in the Negro school with their older sisters and brothers. He estimated the board would get sixty-five to seventy-five applications, of which about half would make the grade.

Skelly Wright's order had imposed no limitations on the number of transfers from school to school. He had assumed the good faith of the school board's promise to comply. He was still assuming desegregation would be citywide.

An uneasy quiet engulfed the city through September. The legislature had gone home, Jimmie Davis was nursing his dyspepsis, and the public schools had opened without incident. New Orleanians were tensely watching and waiting and wondering, as school board members struggled to work out a desegregation plan they hoped would not disturb the city's equilibrium.

The only way the Orleans Parish school board had of keeping school desegregation to a minimum and at the same time complying with the judge's order was to apply the widely used pupil placement act to student transfer applications. Designated Act 492 by the state legislature, the measure established certain criteria these applicants had to meet. The first two held a certain logic: "availability of [class] room and teaching capacity in the various schools" and the "availability of transportation facilities." Tangible, objective requirements, hard to manipulate when the underutilization of several white elementary schools had been widely published and bus and streetcar schedules were readily available.

After that, school officials were on their own, authorized to use their judgment on a variety of subjective criteria devised by political partisans and intended for political use; using standardized psychological and intelligence tests, they were to evaluate the home environment, including the morals, general behavior, and personal standards, of every six-year-old applicant for a school transfer and to measure each one's readiness to assume the responsibilities of the first grade.

The editors of the *Louisiana Weekly* were deeply distressed when they saw the length and complexity of the requirements. It seemed obvious to them that the purpose of the plan was "to preserve the present segregated school system" by keeping school desegregation "to a bare minimum."

Sam Rosenberg, who had become a kind of maître d' of desegregation now that the machinery had been installed, noted, however, that Alabama's pupil placement statute, of which Louisiana's was a verbatim copy, was the only post-*Brown* state enactment involving the relationship between the races that had survived U.S. Supreme Court scrutiny, and after he assured Skelly Wright that the board would apply it absolutely without discrimination on the basis of race, he advised Superintendent Redmond and the board they could put it to work immediately as they sorted through the transfer applications that had begun to arrive.

By the October 7 deadline, only 135 of the total 6,482 black six-year-olds and only one of the total 3,335 white six-year-olds had applied for the transfers. After a cursory study of the pile, board president Rittiner estimated that "there would be no more than two Negroes in any one white school" even if all 135 survived the stringent requirements of the pupil placement plan, which Rittiner described as insurance that "no child, white or colored, will be admitted to a school for which he is not suited." He emphasized that the plan would be administered "fairly."

The facet of the pupil placement plan that appealed particularly to the four-man school board majority, operating now almost exclusively without Emile Wagner, was what they believed to be its objectivity. In their minds, batteries of scientific tests for every criterion the statute described could be administered to the applicants, the scores carefully measured, and the children to desegregate chosen on the basis of the numbers. It was as if a computer had been put in charge of a process that demanded very human decisions. Board members in fact affectionately referred to their method as "the machine."

Rigidly following such mechanical procedures, the men believed, freed the volatile issue from politics and, perhaps even more to the point, themselves from responsibility for the final decisions, a welcome respite now that their isolation from their own white community was rapidly increasing and their allies proportionately falling off. In the minds of many New Orleanians, they had capitulated to the enemy the minute they undertook to comply with Skelly Wright's desegregation order.

During the time Lloyd Rittiner was shuffling through the applications for school transfers, he also conferred with several of the city's top business and professional leaders. He tried to impress upon them the potential for disturbance and disorder that would inevitably accompany a school crisis in November, and he asked them to buy an ad in the newspapers opposing school closing and urging orderly desegregation when the day finally arrived. The sound of their voices, he felt, could make all the difference.

They were polite. They didn't refuse outright but instead deflected the conversation to peripheral considerations such as racially segregated toilets and classes segregated by sex. They did not offer the support the board president considered essential if the city was to survive the looming social upheaval intact, but returned to their aeries from which they silently watched while increasingly larger clouds isolated the members of the school board. Not only did these aristocrats promise Rittiner nothing; they also insisted that even the meeting itself be kept secret—they didn't want their association with him known at all.

School board members began to get threatening telephone calls at night. Friends began to avoid them, and the press was referring to them as the "four surrender members." Rittiner's engineering business began to suffer financially. It was rumored that Leander Perez had warned major oil companies to take their trade to another firm or face a tax increase. Several times Rittiner's young daughter was told in vivid detail when she answered the phone exactly how her father was going to be killed.

The board nonetheless trudged on through the complicated process of selecting the children to carry out the desegregation and the schools they would enter. The youngsters took the required aptitude tests and submitted to interviews by psychologists and other "scientific" observers who reported on their dress as well as their test scores. The job consumed the better part of a month.

As New Orleanians, black and white, awaited the final decisions of school officials regarding the who, the where, and the how many, other developments temporarily kept them turning the pages. Interest in Attorney General Gremillion's hearing for contempt of court vastly overshadowed that in the New Orleans Classroom Teachers Association's resolution "to work to keep New Orleans public schools open," even though this was not only the first statement of its kind from any teachers' group but also a reversal of its previous position.

Gremillion could hardly contain his pride in the fact that every district attorney in the state had signed his pleadings, and his counsel included state representative Wellborn Jack, who'd suggested not long before that the Louisiana legislature roughly dismantle the New Orleans school system. Finding a judge to decide Gremillion's case proved more difficult. Rives, Wright, and Christenberry, having been the victims of the attorney general's spleen, disqualified themselves immediately. Several other judges also turned down the assignment. Judge Edwin F. Hunter, Jr., of Lake Charles and the federal district court for the Western District of Louisiana, protested strongly on the grounds that he'd boarded at Gremillion's "mama's house when [he] was goin' to law school," and the attorney general, his LSU Law School classmate, had remained "one of [his] dearest friends." Hunter finally agreed to sit on Gremillion's case when he was told that just then "Gremillion needs a friend."

U.S. Attorney Hep Many prosecuted the case, bringing in witnesses who'd watched and heard Gremillion's previous court performance and showing the packed courtroom pictures of Gremillion on national television calling Rives, Wright, and Christenberry a "kangaroo court." Unaccustomed to being a defendant, the attorney general rose to speak, only to hear Hunter cut him off:

"Sit down, Jack, this isn't your day to talk. You had your day in court and you talked too much."

Wellborn Jack's defense of his client denied none of the accusations but rationalized Gremillion's outburst with a comparison to the manager of a team that had played 150 games and not won a single contest in six seasons. Under such circumstances, he reasoned, the attorney general deserved to explode:

> You would do anything. There's not a man who could have stood it. He was in the heat of the battlefield. In the heat of the courtroom we all say things . . . but he's sorry. He will not do it again. . . . This man just had had all he could stand.

No one, not even the defendant, was surprised when the judge found him guilty. "No one not in my position," Hunter began, "can appreciate the sadness I feel on this occasion," but, he continued, Louisiana's chief law enforcement officer had shown "a lack of respect for the judicial process that cannot be condoned," and he issued a five-minute admonition to Gremillion, concluding:

> Neither zeal, good intentions or devotion can alter the due processes of law and the respect all should have for the law. . . . Are you ready for sentencing?

Gremillion replied that he was and began to grope for the $5,000 in his pocket in the event the sentence was a fine, at the same time catching the eye of a friend in the courtroom who'd brought another $10,000 just in case. But Hunter imposed no fine. He let his old friend off with a light rap across the knuckles: a sixty-day jail term, which he suspended on the condition Gremillion agree to serve eighteen months of probation. The judge concluded with a characterization of the attorney general as a "fighter" and

> the world loves a fighter, but he fought out of bounds.

Gremillion, said Hunter, was free now to fight again, to continue on his crusade against school desegregation, but he was to do it in an orderly fashion.

Gremillion, usually the picture of pugnacity itself, broke down then and sobbed for joy. His eyes were still wet as he left the courtroom and lost himself in the hugs and handshakes of family and friends.

Not long afterward, the attorney general found himself in Skelly Wright's courtroom once more, this time in his official capacity as counsel for the state mineral board. As he seated himself on the witness stand, Wright leaned toward him, so close Gremillion "could feel him breathing."

"Jack," Wright began.

"Yeah, Judge," Gremillion replied, expressionless and wondering what to expect.

Wright: "It sure is nice to have a case not involving segregation, isn't it?"

Thurgood Marshall had been in town for a convention that past May. Mayor Morrison had once again denied him use of the Municipal Auditorium to give a speech on the grounds it "would promote controversy and was not in the interest of the people of New Orleans," although the mayor had raised no such objections when Governor Faubus had asked to use it. As if he would like to have been one of them, Marshall in his speech, which he finally gave in the auditorium of a parochial high school, put his imprimatur on the student sit-ins then taking place at lunch counters across the South. This broad movement, he said, precisely described the depth of feeling among southern Negroes "sick and tired of being pushed around in a democracy that fails to practice what it preaches."

The movement had already ended in sixty-nine southern communities when it finally hit New Orleans on September 9, two days after the city's schools opened for the 1960–61 term. The young protesters were, however, in plenty of time to further roil public sentiment as New Orleanians wondered what lay ahead for them on November 14.

The siege began when five black members of CORE's local chapter and two white Tulane University graduate students sat in at the F. W. Woolworth lunch counter on Canal Street. Backed by new statutes enacted by the state legislature that past session to deal with such situations, police arrested them and charged them with disturbing the peace and criminal mischief. Undeterred, the young people staged more sit-ins, augmented by picketing outside. At the mayor's direction, police put them all in jail. Finally, Morrison banned all sit-ins and picketing. It was his "determination," he explained,

> that the community interest, the public safety, and the economic welfare of this city require that such demonstrations cease and that henceforth they be prohibited by the police department.

A. P. Tureaud's daughter Elise, midway through college at the time of the sit-ins, begged her father to let her join them.

"But, Daddy," she pleaded, "you do your thing. I have to do mine."

Tureaud didn't like it. He held no brief for confrontational politics, and the law and the courts remained for him the preferred route to racial justice. He was also a father as well as a lawyer, and he was reluctant to risk his daughter's involvement in what he considered a dangerous adventure. Her connection to him, the city's foremost fighter for blacks' civil rights, he believed added to the danger—"no tellin' what they'd do to you," he argued—but he finally relented and gave her a long list of "thou shalt nots," the gist of which boiled down to "keep on walking. Don't stop. They can't pick you up if you keep going." Her promises notwithstanding, the father in him had been "very distracted" until she returned home safely.

The sit-ins continued into early October, then tapered off as increasing numbers of arrests and diminishing funds weakened both the demonstrators' will and wherewithal. Downtown New Orleans quieted and shoppers returned to the stores.

There was considerable speculation that the commotion and disruption of business, first on Dryades in the spring, then on Canal Street in the fall, would compound the problems of school desegregation in November. Mayor Morrison himself warned that the demonstrators would "antagonize the rank and file of the people who are not a party to either extreme," and the *Times-Picayune* predicted the protesters would earn only the "contempt of the majority." A. P. Tureaud, however, shrugged off their concerns. He'd heard the talk, too, he said, but he figured "the people saying that were not with us in the first place. The people against the Negro being admitted to public schools would be against it whether or not there were sit-ins or demonstrations."

The Orleans Parish school board was losing precious ground in its fight to comply with Wright's desegregation order. Feeling the first of several financial pinches, the members had felt compelled to reject bids on a $10 million bond sale because interest rates, forced up by the desegregation uncertainties according to one bank, were too high.

The board's determined reliance on the "machine" they had constructed out of the pupil placement law to solve its desegregation problems proved none too popular in New Orleans among either segregationists or desegregationists. Emile Wagner, for one, didn't like it and said so publicly. He thought it was "wrong" and "if properly applied would result not in token integration but in total integration." If improperly applied, it amounted to a "deceit" and would inevitably be ruled unconstitutional by the courts. He made no attempt to mask his disappointment over the school board's refusal to put its trust and confidence in the governor.

Black parents were furious when on October 27, School Superintendent Redmond announced that through the winnowing process required by the pupil placement law, only five first-grade black girls and no boys—Redmond said later no boys had passed the tests—had survived the rigorous testing and interviewing. Five out of 135 applicants. Fifty-two failed the scholastic aptitude tests, thirty-nine had not complied with the "established procedure," twenty-two had not made the "readiness score in comparison with group to which transfer is sought"; "possible effect upon family relationships" had disqualified eight, "psychological effect upon the pupil" had kept out six more, and "not of proper age," "distance from home to school," and "lack of available room and teaching capacity of school" had disabled one each. If anyone suspected the truth—that board members had manipulated their "machine" by instructing it to find no more than ten qualified applicants—it was not discussed publicly. Dean John B. Furey, a white administrator at all-black Dillard University, did publicly protest the transfer of so few children into a "hostile school environment" where they would "continue to be treated as ... inferior[s]." He thought the five little girls

> must be literally shaking in their boots. . . . There is widespread belief among the Negro people that the series of tests that have been administered to the transfer applicants are devices to discourage further applications for transfers. The parents are looking forward to a systematic program of embarrassment, humiliation, and harassment designed to compel Negro children to withdraw from the white schools and to discourage further applications for transfer.

The board instructed Redmond to keep the names of the children who'd been selected secret, even from the members. Emile Wagner in particular was not to know. They feared the information falling into segregationists' hands would result in threats and pressures on the black families to withdraw their children.

Even more fatal to the school board's position, however, although it didn't become apparent immediately, was its choice of schools to desegregate. All that summer Rosa Keller and her friends and neighbors had sat around the Kellers' swimming pool planning for school desegregation. They picked out a couple of elementary school buildings in their neighborhood: Lusher, which was operating at 60.3 percent of capacity, and Wilson, which was operating at 72 percent.

There were significant advantages to using schools here in addition to their obvious capacity to absorb more children. Uptown was one of the local neighborhoods where blacks had lived for generations interspersed among the white well-to-do. Slave quarters on the master's property had given way to the homes of paid domestics and groundskeepers, which had in turn been replaced by the modest residences of independent blue-collar black families. Black children were already scattered through the neighborhood, and many children of both races already knew each other. In addition, many of the white children attending these two elementary schools were the offspring of Tulane and Loyola university faculty members, and it was thought, correctly or incorrectly, that racial tolerance was part of their upbringing. Taking all these factors into consideration, Keller and her colleagues concluded that black children would find acceptance easier at Wilson and Lusher than in some other sections of the city, and the PTAs of both schools formally requested the school board to send black children to their institutions.

But school authorities had become obsessed by the "machine" they'd created. Superintendent Redmond replied to the PTA representatives that the pupil placement plan required applicants, and no one from the university section had applied. Redmond and *his* colleagues felt they had to find schools where the achievement level of the white first-graders equaled, or, preferably, fell below that of the black newcomers. As Sam Rosenberg told it, "putting black children in the first grade to compete with children who had a higher achievement level" could only mean "additional stress on the children that were beginning the desegregation process."

A visiting school official from Norfolk, Virginia, had warned the Orleans Parish school board: "Don't make the terrible mistake of picking poor schools," but nobody heard him. The lesson of Little Rock civic leadership's insensitivity to the social dynamics of desegregation in a disadvantaged neighborhood had been lost over the scant three years since New Orleanians, along with most of America, had followed the disturbing events at Central High School.

Limiting its search for appropriate schools to those where the white and black achievement levels more or less matched, the Orleans Parish board careened straight for disaster. When they saw that William Frantz and McDonogh 19, both elementary schools within a five- or six-block radius of where the five little "tokens" lived, met the requirements, they confidently predicted both academic and social success for the girls, all of whom ranked above the average achievement of pupils at the two schools.

They looked at the demographics and saw that though the neighborhood was predominantly white, it was racially mixed. They looked at the schools themselves and saw that Frantz was operating at only 82.1 percent of its capacity and McDonogh 19 at 79.9 percent. From the perspective of the board, all white, no one particularly attuned to the dynamics of race, Frantz and McDonogh 19 appeared ideal choices, and they mortgaged their uptown CPE and SOS support to downtown opposition.

Rising at the epicenter of New Orleans's Ninth Ward, William Frantz and McDonogh 19 were the worst possible choice of schools from which to launch racial desegregation. Just from a tactical standpoint, their proximity to each other made it easier for segregationists to concentrate their forces, and their proximity to neighboring St. Bernard Parish to which Leander Perez's influence extended made wider protest easy. From the standpoint of the social and economic realities, it was one of the city's neighborhoods most vulnerable to confrontation, perhaps even violence.

Racially mixed the Ninth Ward was, but not in the agreeable way uptown was, which was more what the school board had in mind for desegregation, had they been able to recognize it when it was offered. In 1960, nearly 25 percent of the city's black population lived in the Ninth Ward. Many were crowded into one of the city's two largest housing projects, trapped there in one of the last low-rent areas left in the city. The run-down condition of their Macarty School that had prompted the petitions to the school board, then the *Aubert* and *Bush* suits, tells their story eloquently.

Ninth Ward whites were not much better off. Originally settled by German, Italian, and French immigrants, the area began life as a truck-gardening section in the nineteenth century and remained a predominantly white working-class section in the twentieth. Over the fifteen years since the end of World War II, white New Orleanians had been moving to the northeastern outskirts of the city, out toward Lake Pontchartrain, as fast as swampland could be reclaimed, leaving the Ninth Ward to those who couldn't afford to move. Many of them had been defeated in the competition for material success and were least equipped psychologically to handle the added humiliation they believed racial desegregation of their children's schools would impose. That they lived in a housing project already had demoted them to the level of the black families who lived in the nearby all-black project. "At least I'm not a nigger" counted for less now than it once had. The prospect of black children transferring from the neighborhood black schools to the neighborhood white schools promised the final injustice. The outlook for the peaceful desegregation the school board members hoped for was bleak. Further inflammation of class and race hostility seemed more likely.

No one in the Ninth Ward knew in October of 1960 that their own

Frantz and McDonogh 19 had been chosen for the city's first school desegregation in November. The names of the schools were as closely guarded as the names of the children. But back in August, Frantz parents had already been worried enough to join the White Educational Association during its early days of establishing alternatives to public education.

While school officials were still ironing out the logistics of the fast-approaching deadline for school desegregation, rumors swept the city that the governor was going to call a special session of the state legislature to enact the measures necessary to put a stop to it. Disturbed as they had not been previously and convinced that such a session would mean "chaos," the group of top local businessmen who had secretly met with Lloyd Rittiner in September to discuss the city school system's plight, all heavy contributors to the governor's 1959–60 re-election campaign, went to Baton Rouge in late October—again secretly—to discuss with Davis what they'd heard. Still unwell following his attack of dyspepsis, he was in bed and being fed intravenously. Nonetheless he patiently heard out their pleas not to recall the legislature to stop the scheduled school desegregation. Aware of his visitors' financial clout, Davis promised to think about it, although the New Orleanians came away believing he was leaning toward granting their request. Given the governor's skill in avoiding direct commitments, however, they weren't sure.

The realization that the Orleans Parish school board meant to actually comply with Skelly Wright's order to desegregate the city's schools on November 14, however, spurred the governor to action, and the day following the board's announcement that the children who were to do the job had been chosen, on October 28, Davis, pressured by Citizens' Councils, his State Sovereignty Commission, and the legislature's noisy Joint Legislative Committee to Maintain Segregation, retaliated with a summons to the lawmakers to return to the capital on November 4—ten days before the desegregation was scheduled to begin—for a special twelve-day session. The terms he issued were general—instructions to legislate "relative to the school children of the state," for the "protection and preservation of the powers reserved to the state of Louisiana" including the "police power of the state." But the tone suggested a showdown between the state and federal governments was in the making.

Following a secret session with district attorneys and lawyers from all parts of the state, the joint committee on segregation prepared a dozen bills designed to tie up school desegregation for years. The seventeen members of the New Orleans delegation, angry at being left out of the planning for a legislative session dealing with the schools in their own city, telegraphed the governor for copies of the bills, but the administration and its leaders ignored them. And Davis went off to a football game while what came to be called the Second Battle of New Orleans shaped up. Representative Wellborn Jack's earlier fantasy of revenge on the Orleans Parish school board nearly became a reality.

Governor Ross Barnett came over from Jackson to speak at a $10-a-plate dinner given by Louisiana's States' Rights Party, still hoping to make electoral mischief in November. Barnett was confident, he said, that the local lawmakers would "act swiftly and boldly to prevent the modern-day carpet-baggers from again taking over operation" of the New Orleans public schools and volunteered that his own Mississippi and its neighbor Louisiana had "never been closer than they are today, as we join hands in meeting the common threat of the federal government's cynical play for Negro votes in the presidential election next week."

What state senator Adrian Duplantier of New Orleans later described as "bedlam" broke out on November 4 when the 140 members of the state legislature—39 senators, 101 representatives—officially convened in their respective chambers at the state Capitol, all but the top leadership still in the dark about the specifics of the proposed measures. Duplantier characterized the session's purpose as essentially "delay," the lawmakers being already aware that "there was really nothing that was going to be effective," and compared the legislative mind-set to that of a defendant in a criminal trial who knows he'll ultimately be convicted but nonetheless stalls as long as possible in the hope that "something good may happen," witnesses may die, "all kinds of things happen." The result, he added, was to "give an audience to people to raise hell."

Leander Perez installed himself as chief strategist, after which the governor abdicated in favor of his floor leaders and left them to steamroller the program for preserving public school segregation into state law. They were unimpressed and undaunted by testimony against their proposals, most of which addressed the futility of reenacting measures already pronounced unconstitutional, from SOS and CPE members, the Louisiana Civil Liberties Union, the American Association of University Professors, and other groups, including irate parents from New Orleans and Baton Rouge. Perez simply retaliated by organizing demonstrations of picketers carrying Keep Our Children White placards onto the floor of the house. The bills sped through both houses with only token opposition from a few members of the New Orleans delegation and even fewer from non–New Orleanians.

Maurice "Moon" Landrieu, who represented New Orleans's Twelfth Ward in the house in 1960, emerged a hero of the opposition during that turbulent legislative session. Although warned against behaving as he did, he himself believed his votes against the segregation measures, despite his inability to effect the outcome, profited him a decade later when he was elected mayor of New Orleans largely through the support of black residents whose voting registration had increased significantly during the intervening ten years.

Landrieu's resistance to Louisiana's determination to maintain racially segregated schools had developed slowly, the product of three decades of shaping experiences. He'd grown up in the heart of racially segregated New Orleans, played ball in the streets with the black boys in his blue-collar neighborhood, but otherwise, like Skelly Wright and most young white men of his generation, had conformed unquestioningly to the local etiquette of race relations. Nobody told him to be unfair or deliberately unkind, but nobody suggested he invite the neighborhood's black youngsters to play in his yard. He read mostly the sports pages of the newspapers, and he was a lot more aware of Lou Gehrig's and Babe Ruth's batting averages than he was of Adolf Hitler's racial pogroms of the 1930s and 1940s.

A prominent athlete at all-white, all-male Jesuit High School, Landrieu went on to all-white Loyola University on a baseball scholarship. As an undergraduate, he branched out into debating and other politically oriented campus activities and was eventually elected student body president. "All of a sudden" politics became what he wanted to do with his life.

Landrieu went on to Loyola's law school where the Jesuits on the faculty "instilled . . . a sense of conscience" that went beyond his parents' lessons in good manners and human kindness, and he came to the conclusion that he couldn't square racial segregation with Christianity.

He made friends with the first two black students admitted to the institution. It was the first time he'd met blacks on an equal social and economic level, and the fact that he and his black friends couldn't eat together in a restaurant "angered" him. When he heard the news of the U.S. Supreme Court's decision in *Brown* v. *Board of Education,* he found himself "terribly relieved" and exclaimed to one of his black friends, "Thank God, it's over!" It wasn't, of course. His euphoria soon changed to disillusionment when no downtown restaurant would cater the campus law club's end-of-the-year banquet because it had two black members. Landrieu resolved the impasse by throwing a seafood party in his own backyard.

Two years of military service further broadened his horizons, after which he returned to New Orleans and opened a small law practice in a poor neighborhood. Half his clients were black, and he found himself once again reevaluating his native city's customs and mores.

The presidency of the United States his ultimate goal, in 1959 Landrieu ran for the state legislature. He was twenty-eight years old. The primary was his first political contest, and he was the first in his family to run for office. That campaign and the subsequent runoff, focused as they were on the issue of segregation, "forced" him to "think more about race, in a broad sense."

Asking for Chep Morrison's endorsement provoked questions from the mayor's handlers about Landrieu's politics and comments such as "we assume you believe in the southern way of life." But Landrieu had come too far by then, and he answered tartly, "not if you mean what I think you mean." When a politically savvy friend advised him to present himself as a segregationist, he answered succinctly:

Bullshit.

But he won a place on Morrison's ticket and handed out Morrison's literature as he campaigned door to door. People slammed their doors in his face, called him "nigger lover," and swore not to vote for him. But when they went to the polls, more did than didn't. In the first primary, he got more than twice as many votes—3,538—as his closest opponent—1,681—in a field of five candidates. In the runoff he got just under twice as many—5,857—as his only opponent—2,980.

The veterans had advised him, following his swearing-in during the regular session of the legislature the previous May, to "let this session go by and learn and listen." But that wasn't Landrieu's way. So when he raised his hand and strode to the microphone to object to a resolution one of the segregationists had introduced—urging not a vote against it, but only a chance to discuss it—his boldness stunned the entire house into silence. Returning to his room at the Capitol House Hotel that night, Leander Perez and Willie Rainach were waiting for him at the side door. Rainach waggled his finger in the freshman lawmaker's face and warned:

We know your kind and we're gonna get you.

From that day forward he was a marked man, a "wild-eyed liberal," in the eyes of segregationists, though he was less an obstructionist during the regular session that summer than he became during the special session in November.

This special session convened at 1 P.M. on November 4. The house chamber was packed with advocates on both sides of the segregation issue, some wielding American flags, others Confederate emblems. Davis's floor leaders had planned an accelerated schedule for passing the twenty-nine-bill package, which, according to one representative, was "dumped" on the members' desks and under a suspension of the usual rules, referred immediately to the administration-controlled judiciary committee without even being read. Under normal procedures, the bills would have gone to the House Committee on the Affairs of the City of New Orleans, but these were not normal times and speed was of the essence.

Several lawmakers objected to the juggernaut tactics, but fear of being branded an integrationist kept them quiet. Only the representative from New Orleans's Twelfth Ward, Moon Landrieu, who was already on the leadership's hit list, spoke up. He wanted to read the bills before he voted; he didn't know what they provided. But the drivers of the juggernaut couldn't afford mature consideration or prolonged public debate, and he was voted down, 93 to 1.

The morning after this first special-session meeting, Landrieu dropped in at a Catholic church on his way to work. He needed to think about the "terrible decision" he had to make during the coming weeks. As he and his fellow representative from New Orleans and his roommate in Baton Rouge, Salvador Anzelmo, whose Italian background had earned him his own share of ethnic discrimination during his student days at LSU, left the church and started toward the Capitol, Landrieu told his friend:

Sam, they can't eat me. You know, the hell with 'em. I ain't gonna do it.

And he didn't. If, as he'd been warned, he was digging his political grave and never got to be president, as he was convinced at twenty-nine he would, he asked himself "so what?" He could always go back to practicing law.

Confronted with the hardest choices of his career, Landrieu felt the "fire in [his] belly" at last. He recognized the futility of his position, had been reminded of it often enough by colleagues, friends concerned for his future, and, most dramatically, by the daily vote counts. He persisted nonetheless, and voted against every bill that directly affected New Orleans during that stormy session—seventeen of the twenty-nine bills that came up for passage. He told the full house he would not be "coerced, intimidated or threatened" into voting for any measure that threatened to jeopardize "law and order." Shortly afterward, Sam Anzelmo announced he stood "shoulder to shoulder" with Landrieu and he himself voted against sixteen of the seventeen bills that affected his city.

Chep Morrison's biographer, Edward F. Haas, has speculated that had the mayor and his powerful Crescent City Democratic Association (CCDA) united with the seventeen-member legislative delegation from New Orleans to oppose the administration's segregation package, a "full-scale struggle for legislative power could possibly have drained administration forces and raised the cost of victory." But the mayor kept his peace too long, his two CCDA floor leaders regularly voted with the administration's forces, and the New Orleans delegation had been unable to come up with a unified plan of action. It was every man for himself. The men's private comments ranged from "the worst legislation I've ever seen" to "it won't make any difference," but with only infrequent exceptions their public positions paralleled the administration's leaving Landrieu and his friend Sam Anzelmo alone in the cold.

In the senate, the two renegade representatives were supported with some regularity by the thirty-one-year-old freshman Adrian Duplantier and president pro tem Robert Ainsworth. "It made no sense," Duplantier explained, "to close the public schools. Places that had tried it had just had absolutely terrible experiences with it and a year later had to reopen them." For that kind of statement and the mildly desegregationist positions he occasionally took in the senate, Duplantier, who came from one of New Orleans's oldest families and whose grandfather's great-grandfather had been Lafayette's aide-de-camp, heard his children called "nigger lovers" at school and saw segregationists throw trash at his house.

Robert A. Ainsworth, Jr.,'s great-grandfather had been a sergeant in the Confederate army and members of his family remembered Louisiana's carpetbag governments. A native New Orleanian, the senator himself had grown up in the same blue-collar neighborhood as had Skelly Wright and had graduated two years ahead of Wright from Loyola Law School. He had once argued a case before the U.S. Supreme Court and what stuck in his head was his feeling of

> how little these men knew of conditions in the South.

It was rumored that Ainsworth, who'd been elected to the senate in 1950, had gubernatorial ambitions, and he had been Jimmie Davis's personal choice for president pro tempore of the upper house in 1960. He was trapped now between conflicting loyalties:

> [I]t would have been easy for me to say these are segregation bills, [he told the senate] and I might as well vote for them because they're going to pass anyway.

But, he explained,

> I do not want to see the time when the physical forces of the state of Louisiana would have to meet the physical forces of the federal government.

We are, after all, American citizens. There are grave dangers attendant upon implementation of these bills that could cause disorder or even bloodshed in my city. I do not want another Little Rock.

It was Ainsworth, after quietly refusing to continue as the governor's point man in the senate during this special session, who led Duplantier, his most frequent ally, and a handful of senators in hopeless opposition to the most destructive of the segregationists' measures. Occasionally they could coax nine or ten of their colleagues to join them, even twelve if the proposed bill was truly "outlandish," but their little group could exert no pressure on the remaining twenty-seven to twenty-nine hardliners.

All told, the four New Orleanians' protests proved feeble and futile, and the segregationists made mincemeat of them, although not without the usual indispensable accompaniment of the rhetoric that politicians believe keeps them in office. Nobody wanted to return home branded as an "integrationist" or a "summer soldier"—a legislator willing to accept token integration. Every speaker opened his address with an account of his grandfather's service for the Confederacy. A few of the lawmakers suggested putting a federal marshal or two, even a judge, in jail to assert their state's sovereignty.

By November 8, four days after the session opened, the entire twenty-nine-bill package had sailed through both houses of the legislature: an interposition statute—not a resolution this time, but a statute—invoking state authority to nullify "unlawful encroachments" by the federal government on Louisiana's public schools. Everybody was in his seat for the interposition statute and it passed unanimously, the several regular dissidents' scruples notwithstanding. It set the tone for and gave substance to all the subsequent legislation.

Having established the state's legal position vis-à-vis the federal government, the lawmakers went on to reinstate school closing measures previously pronounced unconstitutional by federal district and appellate court judges, then generally reauthorized state control over public schools and took away the elected school board's authority.

Despite the warnings of dire consequences by his hand-picked senate president pro tem, Bob Ainsworth, Governor Davis signed the bills as fast as they arrived on his desk, finishing the last of the batch at 7:16 P.M., on November 8. Ordinarily they would not have become law until January 4, 1961, twenty days after the session ended. To expedite matters, however, and thereby use them to influence the crucial events of November 14, the governor certified the lot as "emergency" legislation, making them effective the minute he signed them. WDSU in New Orleans accused the lawmakers of carrying on with an "air of reckless-ness and desperation" and called on the legislative leaders to "ask them-selves how far they're willing to push this city down the road to disaster in pursuit of a lost cause."

The transfer of authority and responsibility from the Orleans Parish school board to the state and Davis's subsequent appointment of a com-mittee from the legislature to run the city's schools brought even Mayor Morrison into the fray. One of his floor leaders, Edward LeBreton, intro-duced an amendment requiring the takeover committee to be made up of New Orleans legislators. The measure was defeated although LeBre-ton himself was named to the group. The others came from widely scat-tered areas of the state.

Mayor Morrison at last was "shocked" at the behavior of the law-makers. Angry and disturbed by their antics, he lashed out at them for the secrecy with which they'd surrounded their plans, the "steamroller tactics" employed in their sessions, and their failure to consult with or appoint members of the New Orleans delegation to positions of influence on matters involving city affairs. Morrison found it "just as wrong" for an outsider to "try to run our Orleans school affairs as it is wrong for the United States supreme court [sic] to dictate to the people of Louisiana." To which Wellborn Jack, still nursing his fantasy of taking the Orleans Parish school board hostage, replied cockily:

Home rule goes out the window when you fight this battle of segrega-tion.

Watching the show in Baton Rouge from his chambers in New Orleans, Skelly Wright was acutely conscious of the "emotionalism that had been stirred up in many of the people." While he was also equally aware that the legislative attacks were politically motivated by men who depended on issues like racial segregation to remain in office, he was nevertheless beginning to "get a little concerned that it might become actually physically difficult to integrate the schools on the day appointed."

The first indication that the winds of public opinion might be shifting came on November 8. The breeze was mild, hardly strong enough to reverse the course, but nonetheless welcomed by those in the trenches. As the governor ended his eight-hour bill-signing marathon, the election returns began to come in.

On November 8, 1960, Massachusetts Senator John F. Kennedy won a cliffhanger of an election over Eisenhower's vice president Richard M.

Nixon, a Democratic victory Eisenhower mourned as a "repudiation" of his own eight years in the White House. But neither the national race nor Leander Perez's unsuccessful struggle to elect a slate of States' Rights Party candidates to the electoral college held as much excitement for New Orleanians that year as the local school board election, which was fought largely on the issue of school desegregation. This was the race that held the most serious implications for the future of race relations in New Orleans, that provided the headlines and captured New Orleanians' attention.

Matt Sutherland had overcome his early reluctance to run for reelection when a group of prominent local business and professional men had quietly come to him, adding their pleas to those of his colleagues and offering to pay his expenses. His announcement of his candidacy made his and the school board majority's position absolutely clear. There was no tiptoeing around desegregation with euphemisms now. It was too late for that. Sutherland's stand was unmistakable:

> I am a Southerner by background and a segregationist by conviction.
> I have fought hard to maintain our traditional segregated schools . . .
> for six turbulent years. The schools have lost every law suit on this
> issue. The choice is inescapable now between compliance with fed-
> eral law and total loss of our public school system. Preservation of our
> uniquely American system of free publicly supported schools for
> everybody seems to me paramount.

The alternative—the "creation of a caste system in education, providing for the favored few, and leaving out those who are unable to afford it"— promised only "chaos and disaster."

Sutherland had three opponents: John Singreen, the Citizens' Council's candidate; Caryl H. Vesy, a young attorney to whom Skelly Wright himself had taught federal procedure at Loyola University Law School— he called himself a "moderate," but always managed to leave his audiences with the impression that he preferred closing to desegregating the schools; and Marie V. McCoy, a "100%" segregationist who wanted to be in a position to share her woman's "understanding and wisdom" with the governor when he took over the schools. None intended to comply with Skelly Wright's desegregation orders, which made for a heated and sometimes nasty atmosphere.

Sutherland's safe position as assistant general counsel for the Pan-American Life Insurance Company gave him immunity from economic retaliation, but not from the constant telephone harassment and threats to himself and his family. As the campaign crescendoed, the Sutherlands had to ask friends in each block to monitor their children's progress as they walked the six blocks between home and school each day.

The specter that one of these three potential troublemakers might actually replace the calm and politically balanced Sutherland, join forces with Emile Wagner, and precipitate a more dangerous situation than the one already looming—close the schools, perhaps, inhibit the local economy, ruin the city's reputation, turn New Orleans into a Little Rock—had at last apparently penetrated establishment New Orleans's collective consciousness.

On November 1, as the campaigners began the last lap before election a week later, the *Times-Picayune* made its choice. In a front-page editorial, the paper endorsed the incumbent Matt Sutherland, congratulating him and his colleagues on their single-minded devotion to the "needs of educable children" and their resistance to the "intrusion of politics" into the board's operations. The editors allowed that in the present crisis, the members had had no other option, having lost some thirty-five appeals in the courts, but to recognize the federal court orders. But it was a grudging acceptance, and a lingering air of regret pervaded the written words. The editorial substantially boosted Sutherland's standing with the voters, but its failure once again to endorse the constitutional and legal imperatives did nothing to soften the general public's opposition to Skelly Wright's order.

On November 4, the day the special session of the state legislature opened, life at last stirred within the local community of business and professional men. A hastily assembled "Committee of 100" prominent New Orleanians, headed by an eighteen-member executive committee that read like a combination who's who in business and industry, social register, and scrapbook of Mardi Gras programs, came out of their closets and publicly endorsed Sutherland's reelection. It was a tepid statement and failed to address either the desegregation issue or the constitutional questions but only supported Sutherland as an individual of "integrity," "proven experience," and one who could be counted on to "insure the continuance of a favorable business and economic climate in New Orleans." Almost any New Orleanian, with the exceptions of Emile Wagner or other Citizens' Council members, could have joined it.

Three days later, on November 7, the day before election, the committee took out a newspaper ad, but its message came nowhere near what Lloyd Rittiner had urged them to say about law and order when he met with the members that past summer. It was large, three-quarters of a page in size, but as lukewarm as the committee's first statement: "We believe that we and our children will all have a better future if Matt Sutherland is re-elected to the School Board."

It did, however, bear the individual signatures of members of the city's ruling class: business leaders such as Darwin S. Fenner, vice president of the Merrill Lynch brokerage firm and permanent resident on the pinnacle of prominence in New Orleans; Richard W. Freeman, owner of the local Coca-Cola plant—his sister Rosa Keller's work for racial integration seemed only to have previously hardened his own heart against it; leading lawyers such as Harry Kelleher; civic leaders such as Joseph M. Jones, chairman of the Tulane Board of Administrators; Mardi Gras royalty, including 1961's king-designate, Laurence Moore Williams.

Next day, Sutherland won. His 55,494 votes—55.6 percent—were almost double those of his nearest rival John Singreen, who received 31,367—31.4 percent. McCoy came in third, and Vesy trailed them all.

Sutherland's decisive victory was interpreted as a sign that white New Orleanians preferred token integration to closing the schools. It was also interpreted, just as the board had hoped, as a vote of confidence in its program to comply with Skelly Wright's directive. The men felt encouraged now to abandon their former passivity and actively work toward the federal-court ordered desegregation.*

Once the election was over, establishment New Orleans retreated again into its habit of silence. Nothing was done to prepare for the fast-approaching desegregation deadline, except by the U.S. Department of Justice, which dispatched a large contingent of marshals to the city. Just in case.

Mayor Morrison said and did nothing. The "Committee of 100" was not heard from again. And Archbishop Rummel, hospitalized in Baton Rouge as the result of broken bones suffered in a fall and with a subsequent bout of pneumonia, failed to exert the usual moral pressure. The plan to desegregate parochial schools simultaneously with the public schools had been changed; parochial schools were now scheduled to desegregate after public school desegregation was "successful." The encouraging little flurry of public support did not last beyond election day, and Skelly Wright stood virtually alone again, he and the school board locked together, their only source of political nourishment each other.

The names of the children chosen to desegregate the two New Orleans schools remained a closely guarded secret, known only to

---

*Under instructions from the state legislature, secretary of state Wade O. Martin, Jr., himself a committed segregationist, refused to certify Sutherland's election, and Sutherland served the entire six years without his commission.

School Superintendent Redmond and Ninth Ward black-community leader Leontine Luke, who was helping to prepare the children and their apprehensive parents for the job they'd been chosen to do. Luke was visiting the children's homes

> to encourage the people, and to assure them that they would not be harmed in going to school. However, that was only my great belief—because I did not know whether or not they would be.

On the morning of November 10, three armed state troopers drove the legislature's committee appointed to operate New Orleans's schools to the city, then stood guard outside the school board's offices while the lawmakers went through the formalities of hiring teachers, administrative personnel including Jim Redmond as superintendent, and other board employees, and while they rechanneled school board funds into a special bank account set up by and under the control of the legislature, exclusively. Lloyd Rittiner could only stand aside while his recent negotiations for the $2 million bank loan he needed to meet the schools' November 23 payroll went up in smoke.

He hadn't, however, reckoned with Skelly Wright's determination to maintain the authority of the federal court. Within hours, CPE lawyer Charles Richards, on behalf of the plaintiffs in the *Williams* suit, was back in Wright's courtroom asking for an order prohibiting the lawmakers from closing the city's schools. The judge immediately issued a temporary injunction forbidding all state interference with the New Orleans schools as well as enforcement of all the new state laws enacted at the legislature's special session. City police mounted a twenty-four-hour guard on Wright's home.

President Eisenhower had given no public indication that he would send troops to New Orleans, but it was noted in the press that a detachment of U.S. Marines was stationed at the naval base across the river. Speaking from Washington, Assistant Attorney General for Civil Rights Harold Tyler remarked that

> If the fight can be kept in the courts, everything will work out.

The school board, all except Wagner, who was in Baton Rouge meeting with the new state sovereignty commission, conferred formally about 5:30 P.M., but spent the first half hour arguing over whether their meeting was legal. At six, Sam Rosenberg, fresh from Skelly Wright's chambers, burst in to assure them it was. Wright's restraining order, he said, had put them back where they'd been before the legislature tried to take over. Rittiner, Riecke, Sutherland, and Shepard were in control again. After which the board formally approved the transfer of the five little Negro girls to white public schools on Monday next, November 14.

United States marshals fanned out to deliver copies of Wright's restraining order to the officials named in it, including Governor Davis, Attorney General Gremillion, legislative leaders, the district attorneys of East Baton Rouge (the section of the capital that included the Capitol) and Orleans parishes, and other local law enforcement officers who posed a potential threat to the planned program. They caught the governor, natty in his peaked cap and khaki hunting outfit holding a rifle in his left hand, relaxing on the porch of the mansion. He accepted the writ, but declined to comment on whether or not he would obey it, and after telling the marshal "you should have been on that dove hunt with me," disappeared inside the house.

Davis was not, however, without resources himself, and after conferring with segregation leaders—members of the State Sovereignty Commission, the legislative committee on segregation, and a recently created "interposition" committee—behind closed doors guarded by armed state troopers, the governor announced his decision to call another special session of the legislature to begin Sunday, November 13, before the present special session had officially ended and just hours before the five first-graders, whose names and schools had—miraculously—remained secret, were scheduled to desegregate the Orleans Parish schools. House Speaker J. Thomas Jewell explained that "technical changes" were needed in the legislation enacted in the still ongoing special session.

On Saturday, November 12, the *Times-Picayune* announced that its editors had come around to the school board's way of thinking about the city's crisis and admitted that "damage to be done the school system through forced integration will not be as great as total destruction of the system through closing of the schools."

That same day Thurgood Marshall, in town to lend a legal hand where he could and planning to stay at least through D-Day on Monday, went with A. P. Tureaud to federal court once again to ask for a federal injunction to prevent state officials from interfering with the school desegregation scheduled for two days hence. It was a Saturday, and Wright was not in his chambers. Asked by reporters about NAACP strategy in the event of the legislature's moving to close the schools, Marshall replied:

Whatever moves the Legislature makes, we'll countermove. I assume the schools will be open. Selective closing of schools is illegal and if two are closed then all should be closed. Once you start closing schools it's no longer a Negro problem.

That night, state superintendent of education Shelby Jackson declared Monday, November 14, "a statewide public school holiday." Lloyd Rittiner went into a full tailspin. "We don't know whether he has the legal authority to do this," the board president groaned. "The school board has been ordered by a federal judge not to interfere. To keep from being held in contempt, we may be required not to observe such a holiday." Sam Rosenberg's best legal opinion was that there being no precedent for Jackson's extraordinary proclamation, the board probably wasn't obligated to comply with it. Rittiner immediately announced that schools in New Orleans would open as planned "no matter what" and instructed principals, teachers, and students to report at the usual time, 8:45 A.M. Simultaneously, house Speaker Jewell and Lieutenant Governor Clarence C. Aycock telegraphed the city's school principals warning that "penalties are provided for any violations" of state law. New Orleans police were put on twelve-hour tours of duty.

The proximity of the inevitable clash between the federal and state governments notwithstanding, Thurgood Marshall announced that the four black first-graders would "go to school as planned." A few days before, Superintendent Redmond had called Ruby Bridges's parents into his office to explain the school board's plans for the day of desegregation and to reassure them of the federal marshals' ability to protect the children. Redmond himself was concerned. Nothing he had experienced as teacher or administrator in the Kansas City or Chicago schools, where he'd matured professionally, approached the frenzied atmosphere in which he now found himself. He spoke calmly and clearly to his callers but concluded the interview with "Do you believe in praying, Mrs. Bridges?"

"Yes," she replied.

"I'm going to be here now," Redmond continued, "but you may not see me any more, because they're going to pretty near hate me as much as they're going to hate you. All I can ask is to pray, and pray for me also."

The D Word

Monday, November 14, the day white New Orleanians had dreaded for the entire eight years, two months, and ten days since A. P. Tureaud had first filed the *Bush* suit in federal court, dawned a typical late fall day: slate gray and sullen, the air heavy and still. Lloyd Rittiner had circled the date on his desk calendar and scribbled under it "D-Day." He undoubtedly had meant the D to stand for desegregation, but as the day shaped up, it could have stood equally well for defiance, demonstrations, disorder, distress, disturbances, or even disaster.

The previous night Skelly Wright had canceled Shelby Jackson's school holiday for today and forbidden the legislature to send state troopers to interfere with school desegregation in New Orleans. Nonetheless the troopers, wearing plainclothes and hastily commissioned as sergeants-at-arms to the legislature, had set out early for New Orleans, their orders to keep black children out of the city's white elementary schools. Even as the policemen were approaching the principals' offices, black children were preparing to enter two of the white schools, but Jackson hadn't been told which ones, and he was taking no chances. He dispatched his deputies to all of them.

When Jackson telephoned Rittiner personally to discuss Rittiner's counterorders to school employees to report to work despite Jackson's holiday proclamation and the board president's assurances to parents that their children would be protected, Rittiner, whose patience had run out after four years of court proceedings and the emotional strain of recent months, told his caller he didn't "give a goddamn" who Jackson was; he, Rittiner, was not going to close the city's schools. And he didn't.

Every last one of New Orleans's 123 public schools opened that morning. Some opened late. Teachers at the William C. Claiborne school met together first to determine their legal status; assured they were protected by the federal court order, they started classes. Citywide, one hundred teachers were absent, up from the normal fifty-five to sixty.

Some schools were not well attended. A newspaper spot check of elementary buildings throughout the city revealed about half the total enrollment present. But all of the schools opened. They were the only ones in Louisiana that did.

Local police, who'd barely had time to recover from the downtown lunch counter sit-ins in September and October, had been stationed at all the elementary schools in the city. There was some concern that New Orleans's police might look the other way if blacks were attacked, as they had in some other southern cities, but Chief Giarrusso had gone on television the night before to inform the city that while he didn't expect to enjoy enforcing integration of the schools, he did expect to have peace in the streets. His officers were under orders to disregard all personal feelings about race.

At approximately 9:25 A.M., the arrival of two automobiles at the all-white William Frantz Elementary School, a nondescript brick building in a normally quiet neighborhood of the Ninth Ward, started the day off. At the same time an important new chapter in deep South history opened as the struggle to make the high principles of *Brown I* and *II* reality began.

The first vehicle to arrive was a brown-and-white sedan belonging to the federal marshal who drove it. A native New Orleanian, he had been chosen especially for his familiarity with the alleys and byways of the city in case a quick getaway should be necessary.

Out of the car popped a little black girl, Ruby Bridges. Her mother, Lucille Bridges, had told her only that she was going to a new school— she'd gone to an all-black kindergarten the year before—and that there were people who weren't going to like her being there, might even "hate" her. When Lucille assured her daughter they couldn't hurt her, not with all the marshals there to protect her, Ruby's final comment was an offer to pray for her antagonists.

Even at six, Ruby was a rather self-contained private person not given to temper tantrums or other displays of emotion. Her mother's warning notwithstanding, she found it hard to understand the shrieking that was coming from the crowd of women gathered near the school. Alerted by the large concentration of police amassed at Frantz, they had dropped the breakfast dishes and hurried to the school to boo, scream, and call any blacks who showed up to enter the neighborhood white school ugly names.

Too young, too, to understand the momentousness of the occasion, Ruby had, however, dressed appropriately in her best—white pinafore, bright blue stockings, shiny black shoes—both for her first day in a new school and for her role in helping to move the 250-year-old city, still mired in legacies slavery had left, into a new age of race relations.

Lucille, smart in blue sweater and plaid skirt, her blue-black hair shining, got out of the car with Ruby. One of the marshals had told her on the way down: "Mrs. Bridges, you're going to be called everything but a child of God." He urged her, however, not to respond whatever the provocation. She knew the marshals were armed. She felt safe with them, and she did whatever they asked.

Lucille had waited a long time for this day. Born in the mid-1930s, she was one of eight children of Mississippi sharecroppers. She had ached and the "tears used to run down my eyes" when the big yellow school bus rumbled down the dirt road on its way to pick up the white farmer's youngsters farther on.

Lord, God, I wish I could go to school,

she'd whisper, though she knew full well she had to spend her day in the fields picking corn and cotton until the crop was all in—late October or November. After that there was wood to be sawed, fertilizer to be hauled, and a thousand other chores for the young woman, who was as strong as a field hand, even a mule, maybe, when she had to be.

Three or four months out of the year—those between the fall harvest and spring planting—were all that black children could be spared to attend the shanties that passed for blacks' schools in rural Mississippi where Lucille grew up. She hungered for more than the little reading and writing she learned there, and she supplemented her formal education during stolen moments with the local black schoolteacher to whom her mother occasionally rented out a room during the term. She never forgot for a moment why she was sending Ruby to the all-white William Frantz Elementary School. The childhood deprivation still seared.

Lucille had been only nineteen when Ruby was born in September of 1954 on that same farm in Mississippi. She and her husband, Avon, had grown up together as neighbors and his education had been as spotty as hers, his youth also having been largely spent working the land. Farming was all he knew when the army shipped him off to the Korean War.

When Ruby was born, he had only just come home after receiving a Purple Heart for wounds suffered rescuing a white soldier. The army had taught him to repair automobile engines, and, faced on his return with steadily diminishing income if he stayed on the farm, he scooped up his little family when Ruby was about six months old, and set out for New Orleans.

Like many refugees from the rural South, they settled in the Ninth Ward with its poorly lit and half-paved streets. Avon got a job in a gas station through a cousin and was able to rent a small white shotgun house with a front porch and a yard, elegant compared with the pineboard sharecroppers' cabin they had left. For the next six years, until Ruby was chosen to help desegregate the city's schools, the family lived, as Avon put it, "real quiet like." Two more daughters and a son were born, and as D-Day dawned, Lucille was expecting her fifth child.

Easygoing Avon was not particularly interested in the movement for racial desegregation. He felt black people had their "place," that even in the war, "fighting side by side," he told Ruby later, "we were still black and they were white and we just didn't mix." To a man whose formal education had ended at the sixth grade, all-black Johnson Lockett where Ruby'd gone to kindergarten seemed adequate, and she was doing so well he didn't see any point to her leaving.

But the strong-willed Lucille insisted. "I'm a hard person," she explained. Her conviction that Ruby and her younger children coming along would get a better education in a desegregated school gave her the strength to withstand the hostility she and Ruby were meeting on their first trip to the Frantz School.

Jesse Grider, wearing the yellow armband that identified him as a federal marshal, was already out of the car and waiting for Ruby and her mother on the sidewalk. He was not a New Orleanian but had been imported to participate in the events of D-Day. On his way home to Louisville, Kentucky, from his honeymoon, he'd gotten word he was needed temporarily in New Orleans, and he'd flown right out. His dry sense of humor and soft voice with the blue grass of Kentucky in it belied the toughness of which he was capable and which had in fact already been tested as a Louisville police officer and as a federal marshal at Little Rock.

Two more marshals from the second car followed. There were about 150 marshals in town at the time. The extras, brought in, like Grider, for D-Day, had been scattered unobtrusively in hotels and motels around the city. Their access to FBI intelligence, added to what their own undercover people had gathered, allowed them to monitor the mood of the city, and they had prepared for trouble.

Until 8 A.M. that morning when word of the large police presence at Frantz had spread through the neighborhood, the identity of the schools and the names of the children to desegregate them had remained a secret. When a member of the state legislature cornered Superintendent of Schools Jim Redmond and demanded the names of the children "so we can send people out to their homes to make sure they won't come to the schools," Redmond, although in his heart of hearts he believed "this thing was pushed too rapidly" and his precarious position among the few New Orleanians who had chosen to obey the federal court gave him a "hollow, empty feeling," had nonetheless steadfastly refused to hand the names over.

"Don't look back," Lucille Bridges instructed Ruby, as the little group started toward the school, and Ruby didn't. Not for the entire eternity the short walk required. If her face betrayed her fright, her purposeful stride forward revealed an inner strength, and, exerting all the determination her six-year-old spirit could muster, she mounted the steps to the three-story building. Each step seemed as high as heaven.

"Two, four, six, eight. We don't want to integrate" along with "Glory, glory segregation" chanted to the tune of "Battle Hymn of the Republic" were just distinguishable in the cacophony of insults shouted from the sidewalks. The threats were extravagant—"If my mother was for integration, I'd string her up" was one—the outward and visible signs of an inner anger suppressed longer than anyone perhaps realized.

The school board's choice of the politically powerless, materially disadvantaged, and psychologically impoverished Ninth Ward as the site for the city's first school desegregation since Reconstruction was not working out the way the men had planned. The placards the women were waving that morning told their story succinctly, revealing the source of the hurt beneath the bravado:

IF YOUR [sic] POOR, MIX. IF YOUR [sic] RICH, FORGET IT. SOME LAW!

Now that the reality of school desegregation was upon them, the parents of white children in the Ninth Ward had translated their fears into the language of hate. Frightened and frustrated, they saw themselves as victims, mugged by history.

[I]t felt like you were beating your head against the brick wall,

said Muriel Schneider, who had prayed over desegregation "long and hard" the previous summer and concluded that it was not "God's will." The mood in the Ninth Ward was feral.

Jesse Grider's eyes, alert for signs of trouble, darted from one screaming woman to another as he escorted Ruby and her mother into the Frantz School. Skelly Wright had met with the marshals in his chambers at seven that morning. He'd prepared copies of the court order for each of the men, signed it "to make it look more legal than usual," affixed a gold stamp, blue ribbon, and the seal of the court, then rolled it up into impressively official-looking cylinders. He instructed the marshals to flash the documents at any state troopers who tried to bar the way. If the troopers pulled guns, however, the marshals were to back off immediately. Above all, they were to protect the children.

Grider had inspected the Frantz School carefully the day before, Sunday, and had memorized the entrances and especially the exits. Then he had visited Ruby at home and assured her parents that he and his crew were well trained, that they could handle about any situation likely to arise the next morning.

Now, as he walked beside the little girl and her mother, shielding them from the spittle and rotten eggs that the crowd had begun to lob their way, he hoped he hadn't misspoken. Now, he had just one thing on his mind:

> to make damn sure that whatever happened, I got [Ruby] out of the school and I protected her, which I think I would have been prepared to do regardless of cost.

The flow of adrenaline slacked off some when the marshals and the two Negroes stepped inside the school, although Ruby required some little time to stanch the stream of tears that had suddenly begun to spill over onto her face. The taunts of the mob across the street faded, and the formalities of Ruby's enrollment proceeded smoothly. Even the state trooper lingering in the hall, who had made no move to keep Ruby out and who described himself to Grider as an observer, left meekly at the federal marshal's bidding.

Grider settled down for the day in Ruby's first-grade classroom. No other child joined her that first day.

As originally planned, Ruby was to have had company. Five girls had survived the rigorous testing required by the pupil placement plan. Three had been assigned to nearby McDonogh 19, Ruby and another to Frantz. But it was discovered at the last minute that the parents of one girl had not been married when she was born—although they subsequently married. Both the school board and Skelly Wright, fearing repercussions from the Citizens' Council as well as the effect of publicity on the child, had agreed to drop her name.

Only 105 of Frantz's 575 pupils showed up at all that day. Some, like little Bobby Suitor, whose mother came from Ohio and had herself gone to elementary school with black children, had tried to get there, but had been turned back a block from the school by a police officer who told him there'd be no school that day.

Born in Costa Rica, Daisy Gabrielle had come to New Orleans at the age of seven, attended the city's segregated schools through the seventh grade, then left to work in her father's restaurant. Intellectually insatiable, however, she had since then read independently, particularly in comparative religion, and concluded that essentially it was brotherhood that made the world go around.

When school desegregation seemed inevitable in the late summer of 1960, and the petitions protesting it arrived at the Gabrielles' housing-project apartment, Daisy refused to sign them. On D-Day, she did the only thing her conscience would allow. She left her two-year-old with a neighbor as she usually did on school days and walked the three blocks to Frantz School to deposit her six-year-old daughter Yolanda in the first grade. She was totally unprepared for the torrents of abuse: "nigger lover," "kill her," "Communist," "who's paying you?"

That afternoon as she sat playing with the baby on one of the small grassy areas outside her apartment, two neighbors ganged up on her. "Daisy," they began, "you've got a child in Frantz, haven't you? You must be crazy! Don't you know there's a nigger there? You'd better go get that kid home fast, or she'll catch their diseases."

Daisy replied: "There's only one little colored girl."

The visitors exchanged knowing glances. "Daisy," said one, "we didn't know you were a nigger lover," and they walked away.

Daisy Gabrielle was one of a small minority among Frantz School parents; her visitors represented the white majority of mothers who appeared at intervals all day long to pluck their sons and daughters from Frantz classrooms, every departure marked by a round of applause from the howling pack, which numbered between 500 and 600 before the day was out. By 1:20 P.M., only fifty white children remained at their desks.

Outside, the sun burned away the haze from the Mississippi, exposing the carnival of color created by the oleanders and crepe myrtle framing the little wooden houses nearby. Black squad cars cruised slowly through the narrow streets. Patrolmen wearing gold-striped blue trousers, black boots, and white helmets diverted the uncommonly heavy traffic away from the school area. At midmorning, a contingent of police reinforcements arrived in a corrections department bus, but they made no move to disperse the women, and the women made no move to leave.

Newsmen covering the events of D-Day named them the "cheerleaders."

Having prepared the black children for their ordeal that morning, black-community impresario Leontine Luke visited the sites to see how things were going, to lend a hand where needed. As the hostile mobs swelled, Luke recognized very few of her neighbors among them, and she began to think, as did SOS President Mary Sand, Lloyd Rittiner, School Superintendent Redmond, and others, that Leander Perez had had them bused in to stir up trouble.

A few blocks away from Frantz, at McDonogh 19 Elementary School, a three-story stucco building typical of late nineteenth-century school construction—it opened in 1884—similar scenes were being enacted that November morning. Only the numbers were different. There, three six-year-old hair-ribboned black girls—Tessie Prevost, Gail Etienne, and Leona Tate, who soon became known as the "three little niggers"—also accompanied by a force of marshals, marched into the formerly all-white school.

Tessie thought the noise and the crowd made it seem like Mardi Gras, and "it was a long time before we realized what went on." Gail was "terribly afraid" that "if these people could get at me, they would kill me." Twenty years later, Leona still had an aversion to crowds.

The yelling, the taunts, the boos, jeers, and insults—"Kill them niggers" one man shouted over and over—cut through the morning mugginess just as it had over at Frantz. "Stay away," strangers warned parents on the streets. "Stay away," friends whispered to them, "or your children may get hurt."

The file of white women converging on McDonogh 19's classrooms to extricate their children continued throughout the day. When it was over, the number of white pupils at McDonogh 19 had dwindled until only forty were left.

The grandmother of one of the little black girls entering McDonogh 19 accepted the disorder and demonstrations with stoicism. Her granddaughter, she said, her voice filled with regret as well as resignation,

can get through these mobs; she was born to, and one way or another, she'll have to do it for the rest of her life.

Black New Orleanians in the crowd that had assembled at McDonogh 19, outnumbered and outshouted, had nevertheless watched with considerable pride as the three six-year-olds walked resolutely together into what was for them a hostile place, and had applauded and cheered. They sensed that something had ended and something else was starting.

As one of them put it that day, "we're beginning to win our fight."
"Amen, amen," came the response.

Down at the federal courthouse, Skelly Wright was trying to juggle
the urgent business generated by the school desegregation crisis with
the regular business scheduled for that Monday. He had set several pretrial conferences for November 14, but when the lawyers began arriving,
he told his secretary: "Let 'em wait, let 'em wait." And after they waited,
interruptions delayed them time and time again while Wright, as calmly
as he could under the circumstances, prepared still another order rein-
ing in the rambunctious state legislature bent on stopping school desegregation.

As was his wont, he was managing his emotions efficiently. To Louis
Claiborne, his law clerk that year, he seemed "preoccupied" and "especially purposeful," nothing more. There was "no visible anger, no noticeable flush of excitement; nor any desperation, much less panic."

Which does not mean he had no doubts. The black robes, the austere dark suits, the calm manner, in fact concealed a not untroubled man.
On this issue of school desegregation, 99.95 percent of him was firmly
convinced that his position was the right one, legally and morally. But
the opposition he'd been getting—not that from the state legislature,
which he recognized as politically necessary, or the unruly crowds now
surrounding the schools, which he discounted as impersonal, but from
local businessmen and civic figures, many of whom were his friends—
gave that last little part of him twinges.

And he worried that 1930's "just another southern 'boy'" had not
evolved enough. He was concerned about his feelings on shaking hands
with blacks, confessing it was "different," even "difficult," "you don't
erase a whole life in a few years. . . . I still suffer from my background."

His doubts notwithstanding, there was no retreat now, not if he
wanted to continue to live with himself, and he hunkered down to do the
job, willing to go head to head however formidable his opponent.

He had been surprised at the small number of children assigned to
desegregate the schools, as had the Negro families involved. Lucille and
Avon Bridges had thought it "was for all the colored to do." They would
never have consented to Ruby's participation had they known she would
be alone. Like Ruby's parents and the others, Wright had assumed a citywide movement when he ordered the school board to begin desegregation with the first grade that fall. Too late, he realized the truth.

To elude state police who were "on the prowl" for the list of children,
School Superintendent Redmond had been driving around the city a
good part of Saturday, D-Day minus two. At about 2 P.M., Wright con-

tacted him. They met a few minutes later. Redmond handed him the names. It was the first time the judge had seen them. He asked, "Is that all?" Redmond carefully explained the complexities of the pupil placement plan that the board had adopted for selecting the children.

Wright was as disappointed as the black parents. He'd wanted to avoid such lopsided numbers, especially the situation Ruby Bridges was facing, the lone black child so noticeable in an ocean of white faces, so vulnerable to ridicule and scorn, possibly even violence, and, cruelest of all, so isolated. On Sunday, he paid an informal call on Ruby and her family. They appeared calm, unruffled by the emotional buildup around them.

Months before the deadline for D-Day in New Orleans, Leander Perez had set up one command post in his Baton Rouge hotel suite and another in the office of the secretary of state. From these two hideaways, he was continuing to channel a steady flow of segregation measures to his allies in the senate and house.

The last-ditch struggle by the legislature had begun Sunday afternoon, D-Day minus one. The galleries in the thirty-four-story state Capitol had filled by 2 P.M., although the session wasn't scheduled to begin until three. State police circulated among the army of placards, the majority of which advocated continuance of segregation:

NIX ON MIXING!
WHITE PEOPLE MUST HAVE WHITE SCHOOLS!
WE'RE NOT IN CUBA! WE DON'T WANT DICTATORSHIP HERE!
WRIGHT IS WRONG!

Lulls in the proceedings after they began provoked the crowd to loud demonstrations. The racket was only barely drowned out from time to time by the noise of the electronic vote recorder, and it emphasized rather than masked the presence of the outwardly dispassionate white-jacketed black waiters handing out the traditional cups of coffee to the debaters. At one point Speaker Jewell had to interrupt the proceedings to clear the floor of segregationists distributing literature to the delegates.

Support poured in from the outback. A telegram from members of the Ouachita Parish school board was typical:

The white citizens of Monroe and Ouachita parish are supporting you and the governor one thousand percent. Let's battle the U.S. courts to the bitter end and learn once and for all whether the state of Louisiana, its legislature and its governor are going to run the affairs of our state or whether or not traitors like Skelly Wright and a Communist Supreme court is going to take over, and run our state. We . . . ask that no stone be left unturned in this all important fight to preserve our traditional way of life. If we lose this fight then we have lost it all.

High on the show of public support, the lawmakers moved with dispatch, again suspending the rules in order to eliminate debate and leaving the New Orleans delegation, whose schools were the only ones involved at the time, behind and gasping for breath. This little group of legislators finally had to ask for time out to read the bills and resolutions their colleagues were urging on them with such unaccustomed speed and rarely achieved unity.

The lawmakers had begun by firing Jim Redmond for refusing to reveal the names of the children scheduled to desegregate the city's schools and Sam Rosenberg for going to the federal court with CPE's lawyer. Rosenberg admitted he never thought "the legislators and governor would go as far as they did." They returned control of the Orleans Parish schools to the legislature, dismissing the school board—all except Emile Wagner. They forbade banks to lend the board money, reaffirmed Shelby Jackson's call for a school holiday next day, and appointed special "sergeants-at-arms" to guard every New Orleans elementary school against desegregation the following morning.

Skelly Wright had been watching the proceedings on television. He felt he had allowed state officials ample time and opportunity to comply with his orders voluntarily. He understood as well as anybody that individual politicians "were doing what they felt they had to do . . . to stay elected." But as a federal judge he could not tolerate their open rebellion; he could not allow the state of Louisiana to triumph in this contest of wills.

At 9:45 P.M. Sunday, less than twelve hours before classes were scheduled to begin in New Orleans's schools, he struck back. The lopsided voting had hardly been recorded when, at the request of the school board, he ordered the holiday canceled and cited its author Shelby Jackson for contempt of court. He restored the Orleans Parish school board to control of the city's schools as well as Jim Redmond and Sam Rosenberg to their respective offices.

Then he took the boldest, most extraordinary step of his judicial career to date and perhaps even afterward. He issued a comprehensive, formal, and official restraining order not only against the governor, members of Davis's administration, and legislative leaders, but against every single member of the state legislature; the order prohibited any and all interference with the next morning's scheduled school desegregation. No judge had ever enjoined an entire state legislature.

At the same time Wright, in an effort to keep the state/federal contest of wills confined to the courtroom and out of the streets, asked the federal government for its help in enforcing his orders: not for the use of the 102nd Airborne, which had kept the peace in Little Rock, but for the Department of Justice's participation as friend of the court in an upcoming November 18 hearing to consider the constitutionality of all this hastily passed legislation to stop school desegregation. The department had been a regular in the Supreme Court for some years, but had appeared only a few times in the lower federal courts. Its acceptance of Wright's invitation represented a giant step into civil rights litigation. Through its taking a firm stand, Wright hoped, he said, to "find a peaceful solution to the problem created by the state's interference with the orders of the court. To do otherwise was to risk anarchy."

Wright's boldness astonished the lawmakers. Their ammunition supplies temporarily exhausted, they adjourned until morning.

In a telecast that night Governor Davis belted out his pitch for continued school segregation. He predicted that the drama being played out at that moment in Louisiana would "take its place in history as one of the most critical and trying times in the history of our state." The legislation being enacted in this special session of the legislature, Davis believed, represented

> the determination of the majority of citizens of our state to preserve intact those principles upon which our nation was built and has prospered and to resist weakening the fabric of which our nation was made.

Davis was reluctant, he said, to provoke a physical clash "between our state and the forces of the federal government." Such a confrontation "would settle nothing except to prove which side had the greater might." It was, however, his position, and he was "convinced" his was the "position of the overwhelming majority" of Louisianans, that

> we must jealously guard our rights and we cannot abdicate our responsibility.

On the Monday morning that followed, the state legislature was hard at work even before the four little black girls had arrived at their schools. As the first order of business, the lawmakers, ignoring Skelly Wright's sweeping injunction prohibiting them from interfering with the New

Orleans schools, once again dismissed the school board. A member of the New Orleans delegation called the bill "the child of a warped brain." But the ardent segregationists from north Louisiana still held the reins, and measures opposing school desegregation continued to command overwhelming majorities.

With A. P. Tureaud and Dan Byrd monitoring the proceedings on the radio, preparing petitions for restraining orders, and rushing them to Wright down at the federal courthouse as fast they could get them on paper, it was difficult to follow who was in and who was out of office that day.

The legislators, though, they knew, and their fury increased as Wright's boldness foiled scheme after scheme, and their rhetoric became proportionately vindictive. State Senator Speedy O. Long, a distant relative of the late governors, suggested that every Louisianan

> Fire your colored maid and let her go back to her quarters and pass the word. Do not patronize any establishment that employs colored people. They'll pass the word around. They won't want to come into white schools if they know they are going to have their income cut off.

And State Senator John Garrett of Claiborne Parish, one of the leading segregationists, urged that Skelly Wright

> be arrested before the sun goes down.

Meeting with a group of eight hundred Louisiana school administrators that day, state education Superintendent Shelby Jackson, although under the cloud of a contempt citation from the federal court, got a five-minute ovation for his rousing address, his plea for a "united front" in the fight against integration and his declaration that

> There is no law, either federal or state, that requires integration of schools. There is nothing in the United States Constitution which says you shall have integrated schools. . . . However, the Louisiana constitution requires segregated schools.

Attorney General Gremillion was promising, as D-Day proceeded, to seek dismissal of the federal injunctions against the legislature, the governor, the other state officials, and himself. The federal courts, he charged, had taken over the New Orleans school system and were "trying to run the state of Louisiana."

New Orleans School Superintendent Jim Redmond, his wife's warnings to be careful ringing in his ears and tailed by United States marshals all the way to the office, got to work early that day, after which he huddled for most of it with other school officials. He'd "never dreamed" there'd be so much trouble, and he accused Leander Perez of sending in busloads of outside agitators to foment disturbances at the two desegregating schools. Although he'd nearly lost his own job, he put the best light he could on the day's events, commending teachers and other school employees for staying on theirs. When he met the press late that afternoon, he ventured that the "worst" was over.

Board President Rittiner shared his confidence. He pronounced D-Day a "helluva day" but believed, like Redmond, "the worst" was over and predicted "the people of New Orleans are going to accept the inevitable." He expressed his pride in "the way the people of Orleans Parish reacted to what must be an unpleasant situation." He urged them to obey "the supreme law of the land" and explained that as things stood now, if compliance failed, the schools would have to be closed. There was no alternative. The choice was not his. It was theirs.

Matt Sutherland spent D-Day riding around the city with other members of the board, trying to avoid being served with a subpoena by the state. He hoped the legislators realized, he later told the press, that he and his colleagues had been caught between the devil and the deep blue sea, that they had done everything in their power to comply with the lawmakers' orders. "Only when the federal injunction was issued, when the issue was forced," he wanted everyone to know, did the board capitulate.

Lloyd Rittiner, Jim Redmond, Sam Rosenberg, Matt Sutherland: neither haters nor integrationists. This day symbolized to them all serious personal conflict, the difficult choice between defying deeply cherished local traditions for which they had some feeling, and doing their civic duty as public officials. Had they chosen to bow to public sentiment at the end, they, too, like Shelby Jackson, would have gotten a standing ovation. When they chose to obey the federal court order at last, to keep the city's schools functioning, and at the same time to sponsor what was token integration, they stood alone. They got no support from anyone in authority, no nod of approval from anyone in a position of leadership—social, civic, political, or commercial—no word of encouragement from a single establishment institution.

Skelly Wright, on one of the rare occasions his law clerk had yet heard him curse, blamed the disturbances of D-Day on the failure of Mayor Morrison to exert his leadership. Morrison blamed everything on Leander Perez and Willie Rainach.

That morning, Wright, who felt Morrison's refusal to rally the city's establishment behind compliance with the law and the Constitution had contributed mightily to the day's disorders, telephoned the mayor, whom he knew well, and put the immediate problems to him straight:

> You know as well as I do that every time we've had a problem of this kind, we've kept the crowd back at least 200 yards. Your police chief is letting them on neutral ground.

Only weeks before, Morrison had had young black men and women jailed for sitting in at lunch counters and peaceful picketing on Canal Street. Now he was noncommittal about the failure of local police to take action. The police chief, he told Wright, was in charge. He had the mayor's full confidence.

As D-Day edged toward D-Day plus one, Morrison, concerned for the "reputation of our community" and "our ability to compete for trade and commerce," praised "the good judgment of our people" which he believed had spared New Orleans "the troubles that have befallen many of our sister southern cities." The booing and jeering, after all, were "all part of the American way of life."

Louis Claiborne, a young member in good standing of New Orleans's haute monde as well as Skelly Wright's law clerk in 1960, went to a party after he finished work at the courthouse that night. The events of the day came up in casual conversation—after the steamiest gossip had been thoroughly digested. Someone mentioned the judge in a tone not meant to flatter. Claiborne leaped to his defense. No one, however, took the young man seriously. No one wanted to believe that his old friend Louis had defected to the enemy. Everyone there took it for granted Louis was only perfunctorily showing his loyalty to his employer. It was at that moment that Claiborne began to understand "the enormity of the task Judge Wright faced and the personal obloquy he would endure."

Remote from the disturbances in the Ninth Ward geographically, culturally, and psychologically, New Orleans's aristocracy maintained its customary silence, leaving Wright and the law and order he represented to the rabble-rousing vultures. Declared one who had watched events unfold in New Orleans over a period of time:

> You get violence where it's asked for—and it has been here.

The grandmother of little Tessie Prevost, the first black child to step inside McDonogh 19 that morning, saw fit to include the city of New

Orleans in her prayers that night. "Lord," she added to her customary modest requests,

> you have started giving New Orleans your attention at last. The whites are screaming at Tessie and me, but that's because they know they're bad, and they'll soon be punished, soon now that You've decided to take a hand in our lives here.

CHAPTER 20

Courage

T he Lord was not alone in lavishing attention on strife-torn New Orleans during that fall of 1960. Reporters and camera-men from the national wire services AP and UPI, the televi-sion networks NBC, CBS, and ABC, the newsmagazines *Time, Life, Newsweek, The Reporter, The Nation, Commonweal, New Republic,* and leading national newspapers including the *New York Times,* and *New York Herald Tribune* plus members of the foreign press—English, Swedish, and Australian—converged on "The City That Care Forgot" and recorded for all the world's eyes and ears what one observer described as a scenario for a "South American revolution."

Following the disturbances at Little Rock in September of 1957, southerners had made the Arkansas capital the symbol of racial con-tention, most of them desperately hoping their own cities could avoid the same mistakes. After D-Day in New Orleans three years later, Little Rock's days as the most frequently cited example of what not to do about school desegregation had ended. The people of Memphis and Dallas and Atlanta had replaced Little Rock with New Orleans. As two of Little Rock's formerly all-white high schools, including Central High where the trouble occurred, quietly absorbed eleven blacks into its student body in 1960, all eyes had shifted to New Orleans, which, as Louisiana's attorney general Jack Gremillion had predicted, was making the Little Rock of 1957 "look like a picnic."

Unwilling perhaps to expose the raw feelings that lurked beneath New Orleans's famous cultured and cosmopolitan veneer, the conservative local press covered and published skeleton accounts of events, the barest minimum required to give readers some notion of what was going on in their city. It was the national media, the outsiders, come to record the daily dramas of desegregation, that captured the revealing incidents describing a city stretched to the very limits of civilized behavior. It was the television cameras that caught the murderous glares of the mobs, the woman exhorting her child to "hate the niggers." A reporter for *Ebony* overheard state representative T. J. Strothers "jestingly," so he said, call for a rope to hang white parents still sending their children to integrated schools. Harnett T. Kane, long an observer of Louisiana culture, watched a "saddened woman" turn away as she remembered the song from *South Pacific* that warned "You've got to be taught to hate." New Orleanians, she said, were "giving them postgraduate lessons in hating one another."

The cameras also burrowed, better than the human eye could, beneath the studied stolidity of the children, especially the black children on whom the media tended to focus its attention, as they took their daily walks through the lines of hostile spectators. It was the camera that was quick enough to catch the way the youngsters' eyes widened, or their little arms suddenly tightened against their sides.

Despite the disturbing elements of her entry into her new school, Ruby Bridges, without tears or complaints, set off for Frantz alone with the marshals on Tuesday morning, D-Day plus one. Her mother had told her to pray if she was frightened. Only forty-five white children were left at Frantz, only twenty, at McDonogh 19. Citywide, ten thousand pupils were absent from local schools that day.

The crowd that surrounded Frantz, however, had increased to a thousand on Tuesday. One woman shrieked at Ruby:

> You wanna be white, we'll make you white! We're gonna throw acid in your face!

Another woman screamed that she intended to poison Ruby, a threat she repeated with such regularity that Ruby grew afraid to eat certain foods. She began to hide her peanut butter sandwiches in a supply cabinet and pour her milk into the paste pot.

Psychiatrist Robert Coles, gathering material for his book *Children of Crisis,* talked with several of the demonstrators at Frantz and McDonogh 19. He found that their protests against admitting the black children to the white schools often had as much, if not more, to do with private emotional pain in their own lives as with the presence of the little Negro girls suddenly in their midst, and "Mrs. Patterson," as Coles called the woman who threatened to poison Ruby, was actually protesting her own loneliness, the poverty out of which there seemed to be no way, and the emotional injury caused by her hard-drinking husband.

At Ruby's insistence, Lucille stayed home with her younger children on Tuesday. She wanted to maintain as normal a routine as possible, although she was acutely aware of and tried to compensate some for the strain under which her oldest daughter was functioning. At the same time, she felt it was important to maintain, too, her customary disciplinary standards. "[T]wo bads," she explained, "won't make Ruby a good girl."

Avon Bridges was nervous. The impact of his experiences in Korea had not worn off, and the dangers attached to Ruby's transfer to the white school, about which he'd been apprehensive from the beginning, added to his alarm. Avon went off that day to Smith's service station where he'd worked for four or five years, but Smith already had gotten calls from neighborhood whites warning him to fire Avon or face a boycott of his business. Summarily discharged, Bridges grew morose, lost his appetite, and had difficulty sleeping. He was out of work for several months. He could, Lucille explained, have worked on the river front, but NAACP officials feared it would be too easy to push him off the dock, and they urged him to wait for something less dangerous. Hecklers got the Bridgeses's telephone number and threatened the family at all hours. A. P. Tureaud's office, which itself was receiving regular bomb threats, screened the family's mail. Both Lucille's and Avon's parents back in Mississippi were threatened. Their credit at the local grocery store was cut off, and they lived in fear for their lives.

Tall—six foot three inches—muscular Charles Prevost, father of Tessie, first black child to enter McDonogh 19 on D-Day, was a sorter at the local post office, a job that gave him the financial security to see his family through the school crisis. He often sorted his own mail and had read the obscenities and threats before he got home from work. He'd graduated from college and had wanted to be a lawyer, but the money ran out, and he'd settled, like many educated black men in those days, for the post office where federal regulations prohibited job discrimination on the basis of race.

It was Dora Prevost, Charles's mother and Tessie's grandmother, a tall, erect, hazlenut-colored woman with white hair, who held the family together emotionally during the school crisis. She lived next door, and Tessie spent almost as much time there as she spent at home.

When Dora was young, she had wanted to be a nurse, but, like Lucille Bridges, she hadn't been able to go to school, and she had

worked as a domestic most of her life. Also like Lucille, she was determined that her children and grandchildren would get an education.
She felt in her bones that "things were going to be better for the black
man," and when they were, she wanted the black man to be ready to
assume his place in American society. Education, she knew, was
important, and when her own children were young, she and her husband had walked to work to save the nickel carfare so their youngsters could go to school. Now, a generation later, it was Dora who held
firm when her son and daughter-in-law might have wavered in the face
of the hostility at McDonogh 19. As her daughter-in-law, Tessie's
mother, put it:

> The truth is, I might have taken Tessie out, returned her to a Negro
> school. I held firm because my husband held firm, and we both held
> firm because of Tessie's grandmother. My husband and I were angry
> and scared, but she never gets scared, and if she gets angry only she
> knows it . . .

Dora worried as hard as Tessie's parents, but she didn't weaken; she
kept her fears to herself, making a point of smiling and joining Tessie in
a dish of ice cream at the end of each stressful day.

About midmorning on Tuesday, police stopped a carload of teenagers, one of a dozen that was racing through red lights on busy Canal
Street shouting segregationist slogans and waving Confederate flags.
Later that morning, they arrested seven men, two youths, and two
women who were among the band of some 350 rowdy white students
from nearby all-white Francis T. Nicholls High School who marched on
Frantz and McDonogh 19. Only the presence of mounted police, who
fleshed out the ranks of the nightstick-armed patrolmen, kept the
demonstrators from breaking into the schools.

Skelly Wright accused the police department of being "politically
motivated" and maintaining only a bare minimum of law and order.
Police Chief Giarrusso, who'd grown up in the white schools of New
Orleans, had joined the force in 1946 before any blacks were admitted,
regarded racial segregation as a "way of life," a "habit"; he explained
some years later that he and his department, whose members were
"set in their ways," had been "ill-prepared" for the federal court's
order to desegregate the city's schools and they had done their best to
avoid "chaos." He sat on the steps of McDonogh 19 Tuesday afternoon
and summed up his department's duties, which he saw as somewhat
limited:

We shall not be bullied or pushed around by anyone, and we shall stand ready to do our job. . . . Enforcement of federal orders is the responsibility of United States marshals and not . . . the New Orleans police department. . . . Our position is solely to preserve peace and maintain law and order.

Sara Tomlin, a teacher at nearby all-white Kohn Junior High School, found she had to suspend classes late every afternoon, when the cheerleaders reassembled to jeer Ruby home. Neither she nor her students could concentrate while the shouting and cursing continued outside.

Governor Davis called for calm, but not for obedience to a federal court order:

I know feeling is running high in New Orleans because of the fact that the big majority, and in fact practically all, of the people do not want integrated schools. I think it is timely and in order for me to suggest that people restrain their emotions and above all things keep a cool head.

On Tuesday night, more than five thousand people massed in the Municipal Auditorium, the forum consistently denied Thurgood Marshall because he was too "political," and stomped and shouted their feelings at a Citizens' Council rally. Willie Rainach warmed up the crowd, urging white Louisianans to

bring the courts to their knees. . . . Let's empty the classrooms where they are integrated. A day lost can be made up; a week, a year lost is not fatal. . . . But once bloods are mixed, that is forever fatal.

Repeatedly interrupted by cries of "Send 'em back to Africa," speakers attacked the federal courts, the local school board, and supported the police department's low arrest record, explaining that patrolmen were "ashamed" to guard integrated schools. The legislature's committee on segregation chairman John Garrett demanded that Skelly Wright and the federal marshals be thrown in jail.

Seven grade-school age white children, four in blackface and three with no makeup, hugged and kissed onstage, after which emcee and council president Emmett Irwin asked the crowd, "Is that what you want?" and the hall broke into a riot of boos. Concessionaires hawked Confederate flags and rebel army caps in the aisles.

It was Leander Perez, though, who brought the crowd to orgasm when he shouted

Don't wait for your daughter to be raped by these Congolese. Don't wait until the burr-heads are forced into your schools. Do something about it now!*

Egged on by the previous day's and night's orgies of hate, an estimated two thousand white teenagers on Wednesday, D-Day plus two, diverted attention away from the besieged desegregated schools and onto the streets of downtown as they marched on city hall and the school board's offices, rocking automobiles driven by blacks and throwing bottles and insults. Spotting a black house painter on a scaffold, they tried to shake him off, then hurled rocks at him when they were unsuccessful. Another gang tossed bags of ice at Negro bus passengers. One black man was stabbed. Blacks retaliated with bricks, stones, and Molotov cocktails. One white man was shot.

When motorcycle and mounted police proved ineffective in clearing the streets, they summoned fire trucks and turned the rioters back with hoses—just minutes before the crowd reached the school board's offices. At first district police headquarters that night a line of some two hundred whites and Negroes waited to be booked.

Mayor Morrison went on television that night to deplore the violence, the "disruption of traffic and the necessity of diverting the police from their normal duties." He appealed to New Orleanians to keep their children off the streets and described how disturbances like the one just winding down would destroy what was closest to his heart, the city's reputation. At an urgent closed-door meeting next day, he persuaded 160 leading citizens to issue a statement commending the mayor, the police, and the city council for doing their part in preserving law and order. Neither the mayor nor the civic leaders even mentioned the school board or the legal and operational difficulties it was facing. Neither took a position on school desegregation or responsibility to the law and the Constitution.

On Thursday, November 17, D-Day plus three, parents of the four little black girls who'd desegregated the two schools gathered in A. P. Tureaud's office for an NAACP-sponsored press conference. Their common ordeal had drawn the families together. Three of them met twice daily at McDonogh 19 as they shepherded their children to and from school; Ruby's family, though isolated at Frantz, was drawn into the circle through the ministrations of Leontine Luke, the neighborhood leader who'd continued her interest in them after helping to prepare the families for the desegregation and now that Ruby's father—and Leona Tate's,

---

*The *Times-Picayune* published most details of the Citizens' Council rally. The paper omitted, however, any reference to the children in blackface as well as Perez's call to arms.

too—had lost their jobs, was distributing food and clothing along with her moral support. Neither the parents' names nor their addresses were divulged to reporters at the press conference. The photographer for the *Times-Picayune* was permitted to shoot his pictures only after the participants had turned their backs. When the group portrait appeared in the newspaper, all that could be seen was a solid wall of ramrod-backed men and women cemented together by their common purpose and a determination already tested in combat. Nothing said at the Citizens' Council rally, nothing that had happened at the two desegregated schools or in the streets had stopped them. The words they spoke reinforced—made official, in a sense—the impression the picture of them conveyed:

> We are not afraid, we are determined to keep our children in school
> and we believe our government will protect us.

By the end of the first week of desegregation, the white boycott of McDonogh 19 reached 100 percent. It remained so for the rest of the school year.

During the Thanksgiving holiday, Leander Perez pried open the public schools of neighboring St. Bernard Parish for the "dispossessed" white children of New Orleans. By January, 1961, School Superintendent Jim Redmond estimated that 601 of the 1,019 pupils formerly attending Frantz and McDonough 19 had either voluntarily accepted St. Bernard's largesse or had been bullied into accepting it by the Citizens' Council. Another 132 were attending various other private and public schools, including the new cooperatives that had sprung up over the summer to take care of such refugees. Two hundred eighty-six New Orleans children were not going to school at all.

At Frantz School, although the majority of white children left within days of Ruby Bridges's appearance on the front steps, many within hours, a few trickled back over the following weeks, and it was for these children and their parents that the hecklers reserved their most venemous abuse. One woman asked her black neighbor to mind her children while she joined the hecklers. Federal marshals protected the black children and their families at least from physical harm, but the white parents were left to their own devices in the beginning.

The Reverend Lloyd A. Foreman, pastor of nearby St. Mark's and Redeemer Methodist churches, was one of these. The cheerleaders could hardly wait for him to appear with his five-year-old daughter Pamela Lynn, whom he was escorting to the Frantz kindergarten. The women had their eggs ready to hurl and the epithets poised on the edge of their tongues long before the grim-faced pair came in sight each morning. Sometimes the women blocked the way, at other times they shoved the clergyman. His response was calm but firm:

Take your hands off me. Talk to me, but don't touch me.

They heaved rocks through the parsonage windows and spattered red paint over the exterior walls. Foreman had to move five times in a month to stay ahead of them. They defaced his churches with creosote and tar and heckled him during his Sunday sermons in which he incorporated contemporary themes with Christian principles, Gandhian precepts, and other topics of tolerance and brotherhood. Demonstrators outside the church distributed literature linking him with the "Communist-inspired NAACP." No arrests were made.

The harassment of Daisy Gabrielle did not end with her one-woman defiance of the hate-mongers' army on D-Day. She had concluded after the afternoon visit from her neighbors that "neighbors change. Principles don't," and she continued to defy the neighbors by escorting her daughter Yolanda through the lines of booing and taunting women, the child's wide eyes and pert bangs proclaiming young innocence, her white-knuckled grip on her mother's arm, her terror. The torment soon escalated beyond the immediate participants and the immediate neighborhood, and it became the whole family's battle.

The mob at Frantz began to follow Daisy and Yolanda home, then to heave rocks and garbage through their kitchen window. Economic retaliation, however, especially against vulnerable semiskilled and unskilled workers—not only the Gabrielles but others, too—proved the most effective deterrent to back-to-school movements on the part of white parents and children.

Daisy's husband, James, supported her decisions utterly, and his job as a $230-a-month water-meter reader for the city ought to have been beyond the reach of vengeance, but the taunts and threats of fellow workers combined with a salary cut put his working life in jeopardy. James wasn't fired; he was hounded out of his job. His reputation as a "nigger-lover" followed him, and he was unable to find another. The Gabrielles' small savings dwindled.

SOS President Mary Sand's six-year-old daughter was repeatedly threatened on her way to public school out near Lake Pontchartrain where the family lived—miles from the war front—but when Sand complained to city police, the answer came back: "Serves you right, lady."

Only when a wire-service reporter phoned police headquarters and promised to write a story about police indifference to the little girl's safety did police respond and mount a guard on her.

Sand herself received a funeral wreath she never ordered, and a can of red paint was thrown at her front door. A newspaper ad stating she would pay high wages for ten laborers sent an army of black men to her home early one Sunday morning.

Construction work stopped on local schools in mid-November as a result of "unsettled" conditions, and the members of the school board were themselves all but immobilized, as the state legislature and Skelly Wright batted them back and forth. They felt more a cat's prey, pushed first by one paw, then the other, than the dignified and dedicated public servants they were.

Vice President Louis Riecke, whose lumber business was steadily losing money as a result of his position on school desegregation, walked his dog every afternoon, telling anyone who would still listen to him that his pet was the only friend he had left.

Former friends crossed the street to avoid speaking to Matt Sutherland, although they'd recently reelected him to the board. He was summarily ousted as president of the Louisiana School Boards Association at its first meeting after D-Day. The threats and cursing of the telephone callers at night persuaded him to prohibit his young children from answering its ring.

Among the poison-pen letters and the other hate calls, Lloyd Rittiner was telephoned promptly at 4 A.M. every morning and given the same warning: "We're gonna . . . blow your brains out." His engineering business was still losing money, inching ever closer to bankruptcy, and when his trucks rolled down a city street, bricks were thrown at them. At one point, two of the city's leading businessmen made a lunch date with him at a French Quarter restaurant, but they insisted in dining in private, still not wanting to be seen with him. They offered to help the board so long as their anonymity could be preserved.

Rosa Keller, watching the events of November, 1960, spin out in ways she had not anticipated when she and her friends had sat around the swimming pool planning the desegregation of nearby uptown elementary schools, was prompted to ask: "Is this a civilized society—or isn't it?"

For their parting shot from the first twelve-day extraordinary session of the state legislature, which expired at midnight on November 15, D-Day plus one, its members once again evicted the Orleans Parish school board, provoking Skelly Wright to issue still another restraining order against them, his second within twenty-four hours. The lawmakers did not, however, return to their homes. Governor Davis had already called another session, this one to begin at one minute past midnight on Wednesday, November 16, and to last for thirty days.

United States Senator Russell Long gave them a pep talk at a joint session that first day. He told them about his twelve years in the federal body and how he had consistently been a member of the "southern team . . . fighting to preserve the customs and traditions of our section of the nation." He described for them some of the difficulties endured by his "southern team," a definite minority on Capitol Hill, and congratulated the Louisianans, envy tinging his tone, for having "all the votes you need to pass anything you desire."

In addition to sufficient numbers of votes, the Louisiana legislators had a reservoir of anger on which to draw, a consequence of the ugly confrontations at the two New Orleans schools and in the city's streets, and the governor's lieutenants had even less trouble steering his second package of segregation bills through both chambers than they had had during the previous session. Of the approximately forty-five measures— bills, resolutions, concurrent resolutions—passed during the thirty days, only about a dozen drew even token opposition. House members, like Moon Landrieu and other members of the New Orleans delegation or other southern parishes, cast a grand total of thirty-seven votes against the entire package. Senators, also largely from the New Orleans delegation—Bob Ainsworth and Adrian Duplantier their leaders—or other southern parishes cast a total of eighty-three nays.

Much of the legislation enacted during this second session, recycled from the first special session, was remarkable mostly for its propaganda and nuisance value. Although one of the lawmakers' most ardent champions, and still hoping to defeat desegregation in New Orleans, the Times-Picayune begged the legislature to pass only "good" and "sound" bills "calculated to be effective and constructive over the long term" and to discard the "futile and disruptive proposals" that distinguished the previous session.

The legislators got the propaganda out of the way first, commending the white parents who'd withdrawn their children from Frantz and McDonogh 19 for their "courageous stand" and "brave fight," and urging others to keep their children away from the desegregated schools. They condemned Skelly Wright, "Communist forces," and "others outside the state" who had brought the school crisis on New Orleans, and reaffirmed racial segregation in the public schools to be the "public policy of the State of Louisiana." At one point, they reasserted the viability of the "separate but equal constitutional doctrine," then took pains to assure "Negro citizens that the Louisiana Legislature's determination to destroy forced integration in the State is not based upon any animosity or ill-will toward the Negro race, but is based solely upon its determination to defeat subversive attempts by the disloyal persons and organizations to drive a wedge between our races and bring trouble, anxiety, and heart-break to our Negro children."

On November 23, a mourners' march commemorating D-Day nine days earlier wound through the pink marble chambers of the legislature bearing a miniature coffin holding a blackened doll labeled "Smelly Wright." The lawmakers gave the performance a standing ovation.

The legislators, however, were not so captivated by their own inflammatory rhetoric that their creative juices stopped flowing, and they did manage during this second session to bring the New Orleans school system closer than ever to the brink of catastrophe. Frustrated in his attempts to annex the city's schools, Governor Davis tried to buy them.

Skelly Wright's several restraining orders notwithstanding, Davis persuaded the legislature to again declare the regular elected Orleans Parish school board defunct and any action its members took illegal. In his mind and that of strategist Perez, this meant that Lloyd Rittiner, Louis Riecke, Matt Sutherland, and Ted Shepard could not handle public funds.

First, the lawmakers put "all banks, lending institutions, firms, corporations, and individuals" on notice that these men, with the addition of School Superintendent Redmond, had no authority to conduct school business. When the Whitney National Bank continued to cash school board checks, the legislature removed it as fiscal agent for the state.

Then to tighten the stranglehold, they ordered all banks holding school system funds to transfer them to a special account controlled by the legislature. It was the legislature's most menacing attack to date. It trapped the local banks, like the school board, between the state and federal governments, and it immediately brought the school crisis home in the most effective way, through the pocketbook.

The school board needed $2,100,000 to meet the payroll due on November 23. On November 22, Jim Redmond announced the board had no money. When payday actually dawned, the lawmakers relented and released some of the funds, but only enough to pay those school system employees who had "complied with the constitution." Those who "willfully, knowingly and voluntarily implemented school integration in New Orleans" were out of luck. The list included Jim Redmond and Sam Rosenberg, both of whom the legislature had again fired, plus the teachers at Frantz and McDonogh 19.

For himself, Redmond wasn't concerned. He borrowed on his life insurance, a tactic that allowed him to maintain his independence throughout the crisis. It was the teachers facing the approaching holidays about whom he was worried. Whatever their personal feelings about race, however hard the pressures on them to leave their posts, however emotionally draining the disturbances outside the two schools, the teachers at Frantz and McDonogh, carried on. Many were forced to confront habits of thought and behavior formed over decades. All were forced to deal every day with tension, fear, and uncertainty. No small matter was the trauma of defying the governor—an unusual experience for an elementary school teacher—along with their professional organization, the Louisiana Teachers Association, which officially endorsed, during its convention in late November, continuation of racial segregation in the public schools and vowed to resist Skelly Wright's "usurpation of power" and the "resulting encroachment of state sovereignty." The teachers at Frantz and McDonogh 19, though they far outnumbered the pupils, had remained on duty. As one of their number explained:

I didn't like it, but I also couldn't walk out on my job. That would be unthinkable.

As they went about administrative tasks assigned by the school board to keep them busy in schools with only a handful of students or, in the case of McDonogh 19, just the three little black girls, a "kind of school spirit" emerged, and someone wrote a song about it: "Frantz School Will Survive." Now the state legislature had decreed that their payday would be payless.

Sam Rosenberg swung into action. He went to an old friend, George Dreyfous, a wealthy local lawyer and staunch civil libertarian, co-founder of the Louisiana League for the Preservation of Constitutional Rights and the Louisiana Civil Liberties Union. Known among his friends as fearless and independent, he had testified several times in Baton Rouge against the legislature's attempts to countermand the federal court's recent orders and been subjected to the customary abuse segregationists heaped on people whom they considered traitors. Rosenberg had only to ask, and Dreyfous immediately loaned him $100,000 to pay the Frantz and McDonogh 19 teachers.

The school board itself offered to back interest-free loans for financially strapped teachers, and local department stores extended generous credit terms. But these were short-term solutions, and every school system employee in New Orleans suffered for months under the arbitrary rule of a vindictive state legislature, every paycheck in as much doubt as the last.

The uncertainty [said one] is almost as bad as the poverty.

Now that he had the money, Davis appeared to be in control. But instead of using his power to blackmail school officials into submission, he persuaded the legislature to take the first steps toward establishing a separate private school system. Senator Long had suggested such a strategy when he addressed the lawmakers at the opening of the session, though he also warned it would be an expensive and difficult enterprise due to the fact that "your right and ability to do it ... is being undermined by the usurpation of power by the federal government, particularly the judiciary and executive branches." Nonetheless they forged ahead with a program for tuition grants for children attending private nonsectarian schools in the hope that "all peoples within our state shall respect deeply-felt convictions," and authorized the substitute school board, recently recreated for the umpteenth time, to "sell, lease or otherwise dispose of" public school property, a measure calculated to bankrupt the local school system, and put its assets to use in a legislature-controlled private system.

United States Senator Jacob K. Javits, New York Republican, had been monitoring events in New Orleans, and he suggested in a telegram to President Eisenhower that he seize the "moral opportunity in which the President can speak most appropriately for the conscience of the country." He would like, Javits said, to drop by the White House and discuss the possibilities with the President. The President, however, turned the senator down. In a "Dear Jack" reply, Eisenhower indicated that he, too, had been "staying in close touch" with the "developing situation" in New Orleans, but it was his judgment that the kind of meeting Javits suggested would be "inadvisable at this time," the matter requiring "great delicacy."

Down at the Yankee courthouse, Skelly Wright had missed little, if any, of the action on any front that fall. He had the FBI reporting to him daily on the safety of the little black girls, and marshals on the floor of the legislature phoning him the latest developments there.

Sam Rosenberg was following the proceedings on the local radio station broadcasting live from the floor of the house and senate. He had recruited a small squad of volunteer lawyers unashamed to allow their names on school board pleadings, and together they were turning out requests for injunctions restraining the legislators as fast as the bills were enacted, often appearing at Wright's home in the middle of the night. "Never hesitate," the judge had told Sam, and Sam didn't. Aware of all the angles, Rosenberg had even prepared writs of habeas corpus—the legal term for demanding release from unlawful imprisonment—in case state troopers actually arrested Jim Redmond who was still refusing to reveal the identities of the children attending Frantz School. Emile Wagner claimed he wanted to "make arrangements to get [the white children] in school," but Redmond discerned the mind of a bully at work, and said he'd be "hanged and quartered" before he'd release the names.

Skelly Wright was doing his best to carry on as if nothing unusual was happening, playing golf every Saturday, meeting his teaching commitments at Loyola Law School, running his courtroom in the same calm, efficient way he'd run it for the past decade, and trying to ignore the petitions for his impeachment circulating in Baton Rouge and the newspaper photograph of his effigy beside the front steps of the Louisiana Capitol, a swastika painted on its back, a hammer and sickle on its front, and a placard labeling him "J. Wrong."

At the same time he was emerging to the national audience that saw him on the nightly newscasts as a man of mettle, one of the most courageous federal district judges in the South. *Time* named him to an "honor roll without precedent in the U.S. legal annals," the list of federal judges who were blazing the trail for justice in southern civil rights cases during the six years since *Brown* was decided. He was grateful when friends, particularly fellow judges, sent him a few precious words of support, and found it "most comforting" when the retired federal district judge, J. Waties Waring, run out of Charleston for his heretical views on blacks' voting rights and school desegregation in his native South Carolina a decade ago, implored Wright to "go on," accompanied by the "admiration and thanks of one who can appreciate what you are doing." Elizabeth Black (Mrs. Justice Hugo L.) wrote Helen Wright how much she and her husband appreciated Skelly's "courageous fight to uphold the same constitution that Hugo is fighting for." The Supreme Court justice hadn't been back to his beloved Alabama since his Court decided *Brown*—there just never seemed to be a "good time," Elizabeth explained sadly. There was hardly a favorable letter that didn't feature the word "courage" prominently.

There was also hate mail, which was not limited to correspondents in the South or New Orleans but originated at all points of the compass. The main themes involved the tyranny of federal courts, their jeopardization of states' rights, biblical origins of racial segregation, the potential in school desegregation for racial mongrelization, and the perfidy of Communists and "Zionist Jews." Most of these letters came from private citizens, although chambers of commerce and American Legion posts were also represented. Some of it bordered on the illiterate, much of it was obscene, and all of it was intemperate.

Closer to home, New Orleanians unleashed a campaign of ostracism against all three Wrights: Helen and thirteen-year-old Jimmy, as well as Skelly. The victims tried not to let the hurt show, but they couldn't always hold their feelings back.

When malicious rumors of a romance between the judge and a woman who lived down the street were started, he and Helen visited their neighbor and her husband, and the two couples laughed it off together. Considerably more difficult for Helen was the behavior of one of her close friends, a local establishment woman. As the school crisis headed toward its climax, Helen's friend announced suddenly one day she was "ashamed to be seen" with the judge's wife. "Well," replied Helen in the sternest voice she could muster under the circumstances, "you need never be ashamed again," on which sour note another friendship ended. All of a sudden, Helen recalled thirty years later, couples who'd invited them to dinner in the early days of Skelly's judgeship and to whom the Wrights had become "quite close" were "among the missing."

Even in what the judge called the "protected community" of the Metairie Park Country Day School, young Jimmy took a good deal of verbal abuse—and at least one physical attack—from the children of people his father called "all the nice families." Jimmy, however, heavily involved in athletics that kept him at school almost until the dinner hour, was in fact somewhat insulated much of the time from the main impact of the school crisis, a school bus ride away in New Orleans.

At home, however, there was no escape. Plainclothes New Orleans police officers, working in eight-hour shifts, were camped in the basement recreation room twenty-four hours a day. Federal marshals called for the judge in the morning and returned him to Newcomb Boulevard after five—it was his unvarying custom to work a nine-to-five day, and not even a school crisis or his battle with the state legislature could change that. Always available for emergencies, as he'd assured Sam Rosenberg, he rarely, however, brought work home.

The telephone rang incessantly. Home alone one night, Jimmy listened to a caller ask, "Is the nigger-loving Communist at home?" Unruffled, Jimmy replied, "No, I'm sorry, the nigger-loving Communist isn't home. Would you like to leave a message?"

There was relief at the office, where the usual daily federal court fare, which didn't diminish during these tense days, distracted, and someone else screened the telephone calls. Wright's secretary Martha Scallon recalled her return from lunch one day during which the rest of the staff had also been out and the judge was answering his own phone for an hour or so. "'My God,' he exclaimed, 'is that the kind of calls you've been getting?' He just couldn't believe the obscenities."

The staff was tense during these troubled times, and Scallon also remembered the day a local newspaper photographer accidentally dropped a flashbulb during a picture-taking session. It exploded, and

Martha, her usual serenity abandoned, "shot right up in the air."

Wright's Irish Channel origins gave him perhaps some of the feistiness he needed to stand firm against the entire state government and the large number of white New Orleanians who opposed his uncompromising position. It was said by people who knew him well that it was frequently his Irish Channel background talking through his school desegregation rulings.

His past had not, however, endeared him to establishment New Orleans. He was not and never could be one of their own, however diligently he strove.

Establishment New Orleanians were much more accepting of their fellow elite John Minor Wisdom, who, though somewhat insulated on the appellate court and safely removed from the front lines at the district court, was fully as adamant as Skelly Wright in upholding the civil rights he also believed were mandated by law and the Constitution—approving Wright's rulings in the school desegregation case whenever they were assigned to him, voting rights and trial procedures at other times. Wisdom got a good deal of mileage out of his membership in an old New Orleans family, the right carnival Krewes, the right clubs, and the right social circles.

His telephone rang a lot, too, during the school crisis, but New Orleans's overall reaction to Wisdom's judging was substantially less visceral. He claimed to have lost no close friends, that in fact most of them defended him although they disagreed with him. One story that made the rounds during the school disturbances in 1960 involved the judge's visit to the bar at the Boston Club one late afternoon. Another member accosted him.

"Well, John," he asked with a smile, "what have you done to us white folks today?"

Wisdom extended his blue blood hand in friendship to Skelly Wright during this troubled time, and they became friends as well as colleagues. Wright was appreciative, even encouraged, but their association could not shore up his position among white New Orleanians. It was too late for that.

Wright speculated that there were New Orleanians who attributed Wisdom's strong judicial support for blacks' civil rights to his strain of Jewish blood. Wright himself didn't, but he did believe that whatever little backing he had for his own position on local school desegregation came from the Jews of New Orleans. SOS had attracted a number of Jewish members. Rosa Keller wasn't Jewish herself, but her husband was, and she attributed her own position on civil rights to her late-blooming awareness of discrimination against Jews. There was also Rabbi Julian

Feibelman at Temple Sinai, Sam Rosenberg at the school board, Edgar Stern, Jr., owner of television station WDSU, and then, as life for the Wrights became more difficult in the fall of 1960, Stern's mother Edith. A local civic leader and philanthropist as well as the daughter of Julius Rosenwald, philanthropist and financier of black education during the late nineteenth and early twentieth centuries, Edith picked them up, just telephoned one day out of the blue, introduced herself, and invited them to dinner, beginning a long and fast friendship. Wright believed these people supported him "because they had felt discrimination over the years" and were "still discriminated against in New Orleans in certain ways—socially and what not."

During this time, Wright's concern was for his family and the effect the vilification was having on Helen and Jimmy, on his parents and those brothers and sisters that still lived in New Orleans. He was reluctant to contact friends; he didn't want to "tarnish" them, to "let whatever is on you rub off on them, so that they might suffer." A habitual loner himself, especially since he became a federal judge, he isolated himself increasingly.

He tried not to dwell on the crank calls, the hate mail, the personal attacks, the political diatribes and threats. He knew he was "hated by 80 to 90 percent of the people in New Orleans" and "assumed" there was good reason "to put marshals and police in the house." He knew his judicial stands had removed him from consideration for promotion to the Fifth Circuit court of appeals, the natural next step for a district judge in Louisiana, that United States Senate Judiciary Committee Chairman Jim Eastland would never let the name of J. Skelly Wright reach a confirmation vote. Young Jimmy rather thought his father "enjoyed" the battle, even "thrived" on it, "drew strength and personal satisfaction from what he was doing because, dammit, it was right. He believed it was right and that was his reward."

The judge did, however, find himself constantly "assur[ing]" himself he was right. Worse, he also began to worry about "what could happen to you, whether they would try to frame you. . . . I even thought about anything that I had ever done that I can't stand public exposure on. . . . I kept racking my brain for something that might be embarrassing." Nonetheless he neither slowed his pace nor diluted his determination. The harassment seemed to strengthen rather than weaken his resolve.

As the four little black girls at Frantz and McDonogh 19 were finishing up their first week of work in their new schools, the legal match between the state and the federal governments was resuming in Skelly Wright's courtroom. Lloyd Rittiner said it was the thirty-seventh time, the Bush case had been argued in court, but most people had lost count.

The second-floor courtroom in the old Post Office Building was so crowded that November 18, four days after D-Day, with attorneys who had spread themselves and their papers across four large tables and with litigants and members of the press that only a few members of the public got seats. Deputy federal marshals confined hundreds of would-be spectators to the first-floor lobby.

Once again representing the school board, Rosenberg, who wanted still another delay of school desegregation, captained his battery of volunteer lawyers. Board members Louis Riecke, Shepard, and Sutherland as well as School Superintendent Redmond sat with them. Lloyd Rittiner wasn't there, and Emile Wagner was sitting with Scott Wilkinson, the Shreveport lawyer who was representing the substitute school board the legislature had appointed to replace the elected officials.

Not yet returned to his New York office, Thurgood Marshall, accompanied by A. P. Tureaud and his partners A. M. Trudeau and Ernest Morial, argued in behalf of *Bush*'s black plaintiffs that so far only four black children out of fifty thousand had entered white schools although the case had been in litigation for eight years and it was clear that no amount of time would bring cooperation from the state legislature. Marshall asked the court to deny Rosenberg's request for another delay.

State Attorney General Gremillion, still on probation for his intemperate outburst during the August hearing, had brought four assistant attorneys general with him. Together they were representing state officials named in various actions.

U.S. Attorney Hep Many, Assistant U.S. Attorney Prim B. Smith, Jr., plus Gerald Choppin from the Civil Rights division of the Justice Department were there in their supporting role as friends of the court. And Charles Richards, still representing the thirty-one white plaintiffs who protested state interference with New Orleans schools the previous summer, was back arguing against enforcement of the legislature's latest bills to obstruct desegregation in the city. As he looked over the group assembled that day in the courtroom, Richards said he felt like he was "playing a dime store piccolo in a symphony orchestra."

There were no surprises that day. The issues had been litigated time and again in the recent past. No one had anything new to say, Jack Gremillion kept his temper under control, and the members of the public unable to get seats missed very little. Reduced to its essentials, the anticlimactic hearing elaborated still another time the flash points of state versus federal conflicts, Gremillion and Wilkinson waving the state flag, Thurgood Marshall, Hep Many, and Charles Richards supporting federal law and the Constitution, Sam Rosenberg once more caught between them. As Marshall put it,

This is not a case of getting some children into school. It is a question of whether or not a federal court can protect its jurisdiction.

The judges, too, had heard it all before. Consolidating the various cases, they needed less than two weeks to come to a decision. They announced it on November 30, a per curiam opinion, but, like the others of that ilk, undoubtedly written by Skelly Wright.

The court refused Sam Rosenberg's request for another delay of school desegregation. Sympathetic to the school board's desperate plight and "persuaded of the School Board's good faith," the judges nonetheless felt, practically paraphrasing Thurgood Marshall at the recent hearing, that the "history of this litigation leaves some doubt about the advisability of further postponing an inevitable deadline." It made no legal sense, they said, to delay "still longer the enjoyment of a constitutional right which was solemnly pronounced by the Supreme Court of the United States more than six years ago."

The court's main quarry, however, was the interposition statute that had been the first measure enacted following the appropriation providing for the lawmakers' salaries during the special session, the measure that set "the tone" and gave "substance to all the subsequent legislation." Historical step by historical step, the court dissected it and reduced it to a "mere statement of principles, a political polemic" and "not a *constitutional* doctrine." It "amounted," The judges concluded, quoting another federal district judge's analysis of a similar Alabama statute, " 'to no more than a protest, an escape valve through which the legislators blew off steam to relieve their tensions.' "

Once interposition had been shot down, the rest of the legislative package enacted during that first special session, its separate parts interlocking so that together they formed a "single scheme" calculated to "preserve a system of segregated public schools in defiance of the mandates of the Supreme Court and the orders of this court in *Bush*," "falls of its own weight." Those measures that had been recycled from previous legislative sessions for passage in this most recent one, plus all the new general statutes whose "sole purpose" was to "defeat the constitutional right of colored children to attend desegregated schools" were, the judges had concluded, "all unconstitutional."

Their impatience apparent, the judges minced no words but bitterly chided the legislators for their use of stylistic stratagems as "euphemism" to reinstate an enactment already voided by the court, "patent subterfuge" to disguise their ulterior motives by invoking "constitutional processes," "evasive schemes" to indirectly nullify constitutional rights, and "specious" argument to divert their opponents from the real issues. The state lost by a landslide.

The *Times-Picayune,* after commending the governor, "other executive officials," the state legislature, and the local school board for their valiant and long hard fight to preserve segregation in the public schools, acknowledged the day after the court had spoken that

> As much as we dislike it, it appears that opponents of desegregation of New Orleans public schools are at or near the end of the road on which they can continue to wage legal war against integration.

But in Baton Rouge, an unrepentant house of representatives passed a resolution charging that the court's decision was "palpably dangerous and constitute[d] a threat to the survival not only of state governments everywhere but to the survival of the Constitution of the United States." The joint legislative committee on segregation chairman John Garrett threatened to reenact the interposition statute.

Governor Davis had no comment. Attorney General Gremillion was "disappointed" and claimed acidly that he'd never "heard of a state legislature being enjoined by a federal judiciary without rhyme or reason."

School board members in New Orleans individually hoped the state legislature would leave them alone now to operate the schools and that white parents would return their children to Frantz and McDonogh 19. Collectively, however, they were less sanguine and immediately authorized Sam Rosenberg to appeal their request for further delay of desegregation to the Supreme Court.

The justices responded quickly, as all the parties to the suit had requested, and firmly supported the lower federal court. They were both unanimous and brief, striking down interposition in the clearest and firmest English: "The main basis for challenging this ruling is that the State of Louisiana 'has interposed itself in the field of public education over which it has exclusive control.' This objection is without substance. . . . The others are likewise without merit."

As the *Times-Picayune* had indicated, the federal district court's decision of November 30—plus the subsequent rejection of the state's position as untenable by the U.S. Supreme Court—marked the beginning of the end of the legal struggle for the New Orleans public schools. Although these were by no means the final decisions, the battle had reached its legal climax. The contenders had only to walk off their sweat.

Their creative imaginations apparently wearied, the state's lawmakers, although Governor Davis recalled them in special sessions three more times, keeping them at their desks continuously from November 4, 1960, through February 26, 1961, spent their considerable oratorical energies abusing Skelly Wright, the federal government, the U.S. Supreme Court, the elected New Orleans school board, and racial segregation's enemies wherever they might be. But they came up with little that was new or even useful, and the federal judges had only to reissue their restraining orders, changing little more than the dates.

Only the governor seemed undaunted in his determination to wrest control of the New Orleans school system—and its funds—from the elected school board, and he handed the legislators bill after bill designed to accomplish his purpose, after which he would appoint a substitute school board comprised of Citizens' Council members and campaign supporters. Before the year was out, the legislature had fired the elected school board no fewer than seven times, the bills flying always into one of Skelly Wright's legal blockades.

Simultaneously, the controversy over the school board's money continued unabated, and the board's bills mounted. On December 21, two days before payday, the federal district court, in another per curiam opinion written by Skelly Wright, took the lawmakers to task for their efforts to bring "financial chaos" to the board, and summarily unfroze the board's funds. The judges—the usual trio of Wright, Christenberry, and Rives—ordered local banks to honor school board checks, prohibited the legislature from transferring school funds into its special legislative account, and cited Lieutenant Governor Aycock, house Speaker Jewell, and state education Superintendent Jackson for contempt for refusing to pay the salaries of Redmond, Rosenberg, and the teachers at Frantz and McDonogh 19.

Piqued, the legislators, who were now meeting in an unprecedented third special session, were not so easily brought to their knees. Next day, the day before payday in the Orleans Parish schools, they adjourned for the Christmas holidays, refusing to release the funds to meet the payroll and condemning and censuring local school officials. In their resolutions they insisted on calling Redmond the "former" school superintendent, and his associates the "former" Orleans Parish school board.

Local banks, however, did begin to honor school board checks, though only in the amount of about $728,000, less than half of the $1.9 million that meeting the whole school system payroll would have required. Most school employees were not paid for December until January.

Although he had been thwarted almost daily by the federal court, Davis nonetheless wasn't through. Soon after the judges struck down the interposition doctrine and the pile of statutes derived from it, New

Orleanians began to hear rumors of the governor's interest in levying a sales tax to finance the private school system he had convinced the lawmakers to authorize. Sure enough, within hours after the third special session of the legislature opened on December 17, his floor managers introduced a measure raising the state sales tax by a penny—from two to three cents—to bankroll tuition grants to school children. On December 22, he addressed a joint session of the legislature:

> I have never been more determined to continue to fight for the principle of state sovereignty than I am at this moment. I never have been more convinced that the people of our state expect me—as a state official—to continue to use every resource available to me to protect and preserve those principles upon which our nation grew and prospered. I have never been more hopeful that the citizens of our state, along with their elected officials, will present a united front to the forces that would seek to destroy a system that is the fabric of democracy.

His determination, his conviction, and his hope notwithstanding, Davis was beaten now. Early in the debates over the tax increase, he had asked the house Ways and Means Committee to show the world that Louisianans would "never put a price tag upon principle," but in the end, Louisianans did. No one, not even the *Times-Picayune,* which editorialized against it, was willing to pay the extra penny for racially segregated education, and when the votes were counted, Davis had not been able to attract the two-thirds majority the state constitution required for a tax increase. The legislature adjourned for the holidays on December 22, deeply divided on the tax issue, defeated by the federal court, but still defiant.

Inspired perhaps by the persistence and bravery of Daisy Gabrielle and the Reverend Lloyd Foreman, a few terrified white children led by scarcely less terrified parents began to trickle back to the Frantz School in December, though none returned to McDonogh 19 where Tessie, Gail, and Leona were learning to read and write alone with their teachers in the eerie quiet of an empty building. The movement was helped substantially by members of SOS who organized a carlift to transport white children to and from school.

Two volunteers to a car, the drivers slipped quietly up to a less accessible side door to load and unload their passengers, successfully eluding the hecklers for some time. But Citizens' Council members soon traced the drivers' names and addresses through their license tags, and opened a campaign of harassment on still another front, burning crosses on SOS members' lawns, strafing automobiles with rocks, and telephoning obscenities along with threats of arson, kidnapping, beatings, even murder. After SOS member Peg Murison's car window was broken by bricks and the perpetrators tried to claw their way into the vehicle, her husband began to accompany her on her daily trips to and from the Ninth Ward. No arrests were made.

SOS president Mary Sand, whose husband's job with the federal forest service was as secure as a job could be, along with Prim Smith, assistant U.S. attorney, visited the white housing project in December, knocking on apartment doors and attempting to persuade residents to send their children back to school. A few agreed, tempted perhaps by the intervention of federal marshals whom Sand had persuaded to assume responsibility for the protection of white as well as black children on their way to and from school. At one point white attendance rose to a high of twenty-three. But tire slashings, broken apartment windows, and threats of job losses militated against their ability to hold out more than a few days. Attendance soon dropped back and remained at ten for the rest of the academic year.

After police sent Bobby Suitor home on D-Day with the story that there would be no school that day, his Ohio-born mother kept him home for more than a month, afraid he would be hurt. She and her husband, James, were friendly with the Gabrielles, and she often told them she wished she could be "that brave."

She got her wish shortly. On the family's return from a holiday trip to Ohio, they decided to send Bobby back to the Frantz School, presumed to be a safe option since federal marshals had taken over protection of the children. At first harassment was limited to neighborhood ostracism because of the Suitors' friendship with the Gabrielles. Then it escalated to rock throwing and broken windows.

Then the dirty work began. The Suitors had no phone, which shielded them from obscene and threatening calls. But the mail kept coming, "filthy, dirty words that people don't even need to know how to spell." The loan company seized pieces of furniture and the automobile—not because payments had fallen behind; they could have made a deal on that issue, but, as the collector made clear, because Bobby had returned to Frantz. Jim lost his job at the Henderson sugar factory, was unable to find another—his reputation followed him—and the family finally had to leave town before he found work.

The harassment finally got too much even for the Foremans and the Gabrielles. Foreman persisted as long as he could, each day another harrowing test of his will and his faith. Ultimately, however, he, too, yielded and moved to another part of the city.

Fourteen-year-old Marie Gabrielle had once been a popular student, but now her friends all shunned her and she left school. Three of the younger Gabrielle children required police protection when they traveled back and forth to their parochial schools. Yolanda had nightmares and began to cry a lot. Even the baby, responding to the family's emotional upheaval, had become cross and fussy.

On December 14, exactly a month after D-Day and the beginning of their ordeal, the emotional and economic burdens, the frustrations and sense of futility having proved too much, the Gabrielles could stand it no longer and left New Orleans for Rhode Island, where they settled in a small town outside of Providence, near James's parents. Americans who had watched their agony on the nightly news hours were appalled that it had come to that. Their defeat was felt as high as the White House itself from which Daisy Gabrielle received a post-Christmas message:

> Our nation must continue her steady advance toward equality before the law for all men and each one of us must do his share to make certain that we have a government of laws, not of men. If all of us will, like yourself and your family, stand up to be counted in the cause of human dignity, even though personal sacrifice be involved, these goals will be one day attained.

The four little black girls continued to tramp resolutely into the two beleaguered schools. Their welcome was, however, no warmer, and to protest their treatment at the hands of the cheerleaders, whose ranks had not thinned and whose venom had not weakened, black New Orleanians were threatening to boycott Mardi Gras. The loss could be bad for business. The all-Negro Zulu parade was not only one of the major attractions of the biggest annual tourist event in one of America's most tourist-oriented cities, but it contributed heavily to the support of a whole panoply of subsidiary industries involving musicians, cab drivers, cooks, waiters, caterers, beauticians, cleaners, pressers, and dance hall owners. Despite the potential for economic hardship imposed on individuals as well as the city, local blacks were incensed enough at white New Orleanians to go through with the boycott in order to "awaken more of our people to the seriousness of the current situation and the responsibility that is theirs."

The city had in fact already slumped. November's downturn was worse than August's back-to-school sales slide. Beginning the first week of school desegregation, it became apparent that the school crisis was having an impact on the local economy. The legislature's seizure of school board funds added to the problem. In addition, there were reports, privately discussed but publicly unconfirmed, that the hotel and restaurant trade was off more than 30 percent. Empty tables were spotted in the French Quarter's fanciest restaurants, and visitors could still reserve hotel and motel rooms a week before the annual Sugar Bowl game. The manager of Maison Blanche, a leading local department store, reported November sales had dropped 35 to 40 percent below those of November, 1959. Cab drivers reported that fares fell off after sunset, and the manager of a clothing store remarked that blacks were "afraid to come downtown and whites aren't out much either." Even the barkers outside the night spots on Bourbon Street failed to draw the normal number of customers.

The decline in revenues, however, also had its upside in that it accomplished what court pressures, legislative oratory and near riots had failed to accomplish. Local businessmen, reluctant for so long to support their school board or condemn violence for fear of Citizens' Council retaliation, were at last persuaded that something had to give, and on December 14, one month after D-Day, a three-quarter-page ad signed by 105 "Business and Professional People of Greater New Orleans" appeared in the *Times-Picayune*. It urged a drastic change in local white attitudes.

For the first time since the U.S. Supreme Court announced *Brown* as the law of the land in 1954, since Skelly Wright made *Bush* the law of Louisiana in 1956, a prestigious group of white New Orleanians publicly advocated abiding by the decisions of "our legally constituted courts," pledged its support to the "duly elected school board of the Parish of New Orleans," and demanded an "immediate end to threats, defamation and resistance to those who administer our law." The signers called for "an end to street demonstrations" and implored their fellow citizens not to allow the "education of our youth" to be "interrupted." They wanted to see "dignity . . . restored to our community." A long time coming, and signed by only one of the city's top establishment members, Darwin Fenner—Richard Freeman, Joseph Jones, Harry Kelleher and Laurence Williams had not signed it; it was heavy on business and professional men, light on social register and Mardi Gras figures—the ad nonetheless signified the beginning of the end of the fear that had stalked white New Orleans for so long. Within days, 120 parents of children in local public schools announced that they supported the statement "wholeheartedly." Asked if it accurately represented the views of parents generally, they answered, "We must emphatically say it represents the feelings of thinking parents."

At Tulane University, 319 faculty members signed a similar statement supporting the business and professional men, 120 Protestant, Catholic, and Jewish clergymen signed an appeal for "brotherly understanding," and the executive committee of the New Orleans bar association for the first time deplored "irresponsible attacks upon the integrity of the judges performing judicial functions" as well as "any utterance impugning the integrity of the judicial system."

Mayor Morrison still had not got the point. Silent during the crucial months leading up to school desegregation, inclined to agree with the political and social views of the "Rainach-Garrett forces," if not their desire to "create trouble and stimulate agitation," Morrison blamed the outside press for many of the city's troubles and was embarrassed by the widespread publicity his city was getting.

Partly, he felt, the cheerleaders were performing primarily for the television cameramen and argued that the newsmen themselves were responsible for the jeering, egg-throwing, and cursing demonstrators who congregated at the desegregated schools, then rushed home to see themselves on the regular newscasts. He claimed to have watched a camera crew "actually setting up a scene."

His main concern, however, as always, was for the city's image before the television-watching, newspaper-reading world. He had, he said, "spent most of his official life trying to build the economy and good name of New Orleans." He deeply regretted the "general impression nationwide" that the city was now a "sea of turmoil and violence." Such a picture, he argued, was exaggerated and "very bad" for business and the tourist trade; he was even now trying to dissuade blacks from boycotting Mardi Gras at the same time he was telling the rest of the world that Mardi Gras would proceed as scheduled on February 14.

In all the years since *Brown* and *Bush,* Morrison had never publicly uttered a word of support for the law, the Constitution, or the local school board, only complained that the "serious consequence" of the federal court order had been the "damage . . . done to the reputation of our city." He did not change his pitch now.

His solution to the turbulence roiling the atmosphere of the city now was to try to strike a deal with the newsmen he so disliked, suggesting a three-day moratorium on news coverage of school desegregation. When newsmen counterproposed that police cordon off an area around the schools from which demonstrators would be barred, Morrison replied that the time had not arrived for such stringent measures.

SOS member Betty Wisdom saw the press through a different lens.

She also regretted the "black eye" New Orleans was getting as a result of the disturbances the media was documenting daily. But she believed the newsmen had accomplished something no one else had during the crisis. Defending the performance of the press in a letter to the *Nation,* she credited the reporters' dissemination of the horrors with "stir[ring] local power structures to action." She heard that the pictures and stories of the debacle in New Orleans had been "instrumental in convincing the people of Dallas and Atlanta that such things must not happen to them." Perhaps most important, she concluded, was the picture that went out over the airwaves of the principal actors themselves:

The racists' great mistake [she said] has always been that they have allowed the press to see the inner nastiness of their souls.

CHAPTER 21

Let the Healing Begin

Simultaneously frightened by the specter of continuing financial loss and buoyed by the favorable reaction generated by the mid-December ad in the *Times-Picayune* calling for support of "our legally constituted courts" and the "duly elected school board," business, professional, and civic leaders of New Orleans seemed to think it was shrewd as well as safe now to be seen in public with the likes of Lloyd Rittiner, Louis Riecke, Ted Shepard, and Matt Sutherland. After nearly five years of public silence (*Bush*'s fifth birthday was coming up on February 16, 1961), punctuated occasionally by secret meetings with select board members and equally secret contributions to Sutherland's recent reelection campaign, the city's elite was at last ready to stand behind the school board publicly. The days of skulking into private dining rooms to discuss the city's crisis furtively over lunch had at last ended.

In a complete about-face, a group of prominent New Orleanians decided that one way to unite their fellow citizens behind the board was to throw a party: to give a public testimonial dinner honoring the local heroes on the school board who had worked hard and conscientiously to maintain the public schools even while they were being ambushed on every flank. So far their reward had been only public scorn, which may have reached its climax in mid-January when they were summarily ousted from the Louisiana School Boards Association. Political scientist Morton Inger believed that that testimonial dinner, on January 30, 1961, marked the beginning of the end of the school crisis: "the fever was broken," he said, but cautioned that "the patient was still ill."

Louis Riecke, who'd recently rotated to the board presidency, had ridiculed the idea of a dinner when Sam Rosenberg sounded him out on the subject. But when he saw the overflow crowd of 1,650 New Orleanians gathered in two of the Roosevelt Hotel's largest dining rooms to break bread with school superintendent Redmond and the four board members—Emile Wagner, the fifth, was not invited—Riecke confessed he had been profoundly moved.

New Orleans entrepreneur Lester Kabacoff thought the reconciliation had come at the right time, that the prior "upset" had given the community a necessary opportunity to "blow their top and get it over with," had provided a catharsis beneficial to both white racial moderates revolted by the violence and white extremists whose anger was purged by it. Without the "upset," he seemed to think, the truce might not have been possible.

Harry Kelleher's position at the top of New Orleans's power elite made him the perfect choice for keynote speaker at the dinner that January night. The grandson of both a Confederate cavalryman and a Union soldier, he came from old New Orleans money, had grown up amid the quiet grandeur of impeccably groomed grounds and large decorous homes on Nashville Avenue in the uptown section of the city. He'd gone to the local public schools, of which he claimed to be a strong supporter, although he sent his own children to the private Metairie Park Country Day School. He'd earned his law degree at Tulane in 1931.

He modestly claimed his hands were not on the local "levers of power," but his membership on Tulane's Board of Administrators and the Rex Mardi Gras Krewe, his prominence in the legal community, and his close association with local establishment figures ensured that what he said that night would be listened to carefully.

Kelleher saw himself as a "transitional" figure in twentieth-century Louisiana, a throwback to what he called the "archaic paternalism" of the old ways and at the same time a modern progressive southerner:

> [W]e had servants, and they became the responsibility of your family. They were ill, you saw to it they got medical care. Their children, grandchildren, or anyone else got in jail, got in trouble, anything else, you got 'em *out*. They needed surgery, you saw it was *provided*.

His fellow elite had grown up in the same milieu: "black people were never their enemies. They were their fellow citizens, their friends—sometimes their very devoted friends." Like his associates, Kelleher had grown up in the "separate but equal" society and had listened at his grandmother's knee to her romantic tales of the old South and the Lost

Cause. Unlike some of his associates, however, he was not unwilling to face the changes taking place in the South:

> I felt that *Brown* marked a turning point, a milestone in history. The realities of the situation were that changing social and moral values ... dictated a change in public education and that reality needed to be faced up to and recognized and dealt with intelligently and responsibly. It was just that simple.

Believing, by January of 1961, that there was a "real possibility of violence," that only "riot, civil disorder and commotion" could result from the confrontation between state and federal governments, the black community, and white extremists, Kelleher opted to "comply with the rule of law." Now that the legal remedies were exhausted, he thought he could say

> to men of good will, "now look. All this litigation is at an end. We must decide we will or we won't comply with the rule of law,"

and when a group of civic-minded New Orleanians called on him at his law office and asked him to be the main speaker at the testimonial dinner they were planning, he muttered something about his not being much of a speaker, but he accepted the challenge.

Ralph N. Jackson, one of the dinner's sponsors and master of ceremonies for the evening, explained the program as a "public display of public support for the principle of law and order and preservation of public education in New Orleans." He reminded the all-white audience that the *New York Times* had recently run an editorial asking "where are the Southern moderates?" To which Jackson replied:

> This gathering tonight is an excellent and adequate answer to that query. We are here.

Introducing Harry Kelleher, Jackson glowed: "If the face of the mob on Carondelet Street [address of the school board offices and goal of the rioters on D-Day plus two] is our worst face, our speaker tonight represents our best face—the aspect with which we would like to face the nation and world at this time." Harry Kelleher stepped up to the microphone.

He opened with his own regret—and what must have been the regret of every white man and woman in that room—that the U.S. Supreme Court had seen "fit to reject the constitutional valididty of the doctrine of separate but equal facilities." He himself had thought the doctrine had been "approaching reality in New Orleans" and was only sorry "such progress could not have continued."

He applauded the school board for fighting the good fight to "maintain the schools in our traditional manner," then explained that the choice the board confronted today between "compliance with federal court orders or the closure and eventual destruction of our school system" was the very same choice the community faced.

He was there to tell that community that the past was past now, that

> whether we like it or not, now we must recognize that things will never be quite the same again.

People would have to stop and think, undergo "an agonizing reappraisal," and decide whether "we believe in due process of law, or government by men, and second, whether we believe in public education." And he challenged his audience to "go forward." Neither New Orleans nor the South could "afford to go backward."

Eleven weeks had passed between D-Day in mid-November, 1960, and the love feast at the Roosevelt Hotel at the end of January, 1961. Christmas had come and gone. The four little black girls had been inundated with dolls and books and cards from all over the world. There had even been a card from former first lady Eleanor Roosevelt. Tessie Prevost acidly recalled some years later that they also had received packages containing roaches, rats, and horse manure. Only a dozen or so of the usual demonstrators had shown up to keep a virtually silent vigil on the morning in early January when schools reopened after the ten-day Christmas holiday. Thirteen white children returned to Frantz; no white children returned to McDonogh 19.

The boycott of McDonogh 19 was never really broken that term. For the rest of the school year, Tessie, Gail, and Leona studied alone with their white teacher. The girls eased their loneliness by playing little games in which their new friends, the federal marshals who accompanied them to school each day, starred as imaginary "boy friends."

But their early fears had not yet dissipated. Gail was still having nightmares and awoke each morning with a dread of going to school. Leona was disturbed by the lights shining in her window at night and the knowledge that her house had to be guarded by marshals. Tessie still found going to school "scary." Nonetheless the six-year-olds got out of bed and went every day, steadfastly walked the gamut of hostile eyes trained on them and hostile voices boxing their ears.

Their isolation was relieved only once and then but briefly when Gregory Thompson, ten, and his eight-year-old brother, Michael, recently moved to New Orleans from Alabama in the hope of easing Michael's asthma attacks, defied the protesters and entered the school under the protection of the federal marshals. They were the first white children to set foot in McDonogh 19 since the boycott began in mid-November.

Their father, John Thompson, a $73-per-week clerk at Walgreen's drugstore, had initially put them on the school bus each day for the long ride to a white public school in neighboring St. Bernard Parish, but soon noticed his older son was reading from the same textbooks he'd already studied back in Alabama, and was mad enough to transfer the boys to McDonogh 19. An outspoken man with a ninth-grade education, a boyish face, and a preference for cigars, Thompson explained his rationale:

> I was raised a segregationist but I've a mind of my own. I lived with Negroes in the service and I know no black rubbed off on me. I know integration has got to come and there's no use trying to live like a hundred years ago.

The temperature dipped into the low thirties those mornings the Thompson boys went to McDonogh 19, chilly for New Orleans even in January and February, but the hecklers were undaunted and warned the "traitor" to "go home." At first the "traitor" had no intention of submitting to their pressure—"if they come here, they'll have to mess with me," he vowed—but in the end, the women left him no choice.

On the grounds that her other tenants were disturbed and talking about leaving, Thompson's landlady evicted the family from its four-room apartment, and the protesters set up a picket line in front of Walgreen's. It cost Thompson his job. Three days after his boys entered McDonogh 19, the Thompsons hastily grabbed their still-wet laundry from the line, packed their belongings, and disappeared, their destination undisclosed.

Ruby Bridges doggedly continued on at Frantz where she enjoyed the undivided attention of her teacher, the only person the little black girl could "play with, talk to," or play the pranks of a normally mischievous six-year-old on. The lone black child and the lone white adult, together for almost the entire school day during that school year, developed, Ruby recalled, a "nice relationship."

Psychiatrist Robert Coles took an interest in the four black six-year-olds that term and began visiting them at home, probing them for clues to the ways they were handling their emotional anxieties, how the turmoil in their daily routine was affecting them. Coles's work is reminiscent of psychologist Kenneth Clark's earlier attempts to plumb the depths of children's racial awareness and attitudes that were publicized when he testified for the plaintiffs in the legal cases against school segregation that resulted in *Brown* v. *Board of Education* in 1954. In his *Children of Crisis,* Coles in fact cited Clark's early writings on children and race.

Instead of using brown dolls and white dolls to trigger children's responses to skin color and its implications as Clark did, however, Coles, finding that drawing came easily to young children, carried paper and crayons or paint with him on his regular visits to the children's homes. Sometimes encouraging them to draw whomever and whatever they wanted to, at other times gently guiding them toward a particular subject, the psychiatrist was able through the youngsters' choices of form, color, and subject matter, to discern otherwise private feelings. Keeping in mind that his findings could not be separated from each individual's age, family relationships, mental and physical well-being, neighborhood influences, and the other factors that contributed to a child's total environment, he came to believe nonetheless that the factor of race figured prominently in the development of the children's personalities.

Ruby Bridges was Coles's first subject. Her drawings, upwards of two hundred executed in the relaxed atmosphere of friendly banter and shared Cokes over several years, provided Coles with a map to her emotional life.

For the first four months, Ruby used her brown and black crayons exclusively for depicting soil, or the ground, which she consistently covered with green grass. In her portraits, including a self-portrait, she differentiated between whites and blacks at first by omitting a prominent feature from her black subject—an eye, an ear, a mouth, a finger—and drawing her white subject considerably larger than her black one as well as properly constructed.

When she finally did attempt to distinguish her subjects by race, her use of the brown crayon was unusually restrained—just enough to indicate skin color. Coles eventually summoned the courage to ask her why. She replied evenly:

> When I draw a white girl, I know she'll be okay, but with the colored,
> it's not so okay. So I try to give the colored as even a chance as I can,
> even if that's not the way it will end up being.

In his visits with Ruby and other children in New Orleans and in his travels across the South over a four-year period—at one point Coles had a list of twelve black and twelve white children whom he visited regularly—the psychiatrist discovered in his talks with them and their parents and in their drawings, however childishly executed, that significant common threads ran through the youngsters' lives. He found, for example, that most children, black or white, became aware of differences in skin color by the time they were two and a half or three. By the time they were six, they were clearly connecting skin color to social status, sensing that whites were the "in" party, the achievers, and blacks were the "out" party, the unsuccessful.

Tessie Prevost once apologized to Coles for the state of the streets around her home, essentially dirt roads with ditches on each side. "The colored," she explained, "don't get good streets with cement on them as easy as the white." At six, Ruby knew, if she didn't fully understand, the protocols of race. Her mother had already taught her to respond to whites' requests with a brisk "Yes, ma'am" and to wait until white customers had been served before she bought her own Coke.

Coles also found that by the age of three, black children had already learned the stratagems they believed they needed for survival in a predominantly white world: cunning, speed, and a certain alertness in the presence of the bigger, stronger, and more politically powerful white children. Before they were three years old, the idea that they were the weaker race had been deliberately planted deep in their psyches. A black mother whom Coles did not identify by name summed it up for him:

I guess we all don't like white people too much deep inside. You could hardly expect us to, after what's happened all these years. It's in our bones to be afraid. . . . But . . . we have to live with one another, black with white, I mean. I keep telling that to the children. . . . It's like with cars and knives, you have to teach your children to know what's dangerous and how to stay away from it, or else they won't live long. White people are a real danger to us until we learn how to live with them. . . . I don't let my kids get fresh about the white man even in their own house. . . . They'll forget, and they'll say something outside, and that'll be it for them, and us too. So I make them store it in the bones, way inside, and then no one sees it. . . . [M]ostly it's buried. The colored man, I think he has to hide what he really feels even from himself. Otherwise there would be too much pain—too much.

Coles found, too, in his studies of white children and their parents that although viewed as dominant with the power and freedom to manipulate blacks, they were no less troubled than blacks by race and the issues it raised. Fear, though different from Ruby's, never failed to enter their calculations of any given interracial situation. One example he used to illustrate his point was a blond, freckled, and lively boy whom he identified only as Jimmie: a schoolmate of Ruby's for several years and as such called upon to play a role in the social drama of school desegregation in New Orleans.

Jimmie took to drawing for Coles enthusiastically. His parents had been no happier than other white parents at the presence of Ruby Bridges in their son's school, but they didn't want him to waste a term, and they sent him back as soon as they thought he would be safe.

His early drawings left no doubt how he felt toward blacks. He gave them animal features, made their brown skins look dirty. He was reluctant to draw Ruby at all. When Coles finally persuaded him, he shrank her in size, omitted her feet altogether, and colored her a brown-black much darker than she really was.

Then over time, Jimmie began to humanize his drawings of Ruby, but he continued to confine her to the yard outside the building, explaining to Coles that

> The teacher said it won't be long before we go back to normal. She said that if most kids still stay home and the people still make all the noise in front of the school, then they'll send Ruby away and the trouble will be over; she said Ruby still isn't a regular member of the school, but that we have to be polite anyway.

It didn't quite work out that way. Ruby stayed on, resolutely making her way each day through the crowd's continued harassment.

But the healing that had begun at the dinner honoring the school board seemed to have penetrated at least some Ninth Ward homes. Coles noticed that Jimmie's parents stopped calling Ruby a "nigger" and began to call her a "nigra"—a southernism carrying implications of affection, even limited respect, but not yielding on the concept of black inferiority. They moved from ignoring Ruby's presence at Frantz to asking their son about her schoolwork and behavior.

Coles watched fascinated as Jimmie's drawings changed perceptibly. In the early days, the boy had characterized his school as a besieged tumbledown building with unsubstantial walls. As its occupants developed school spirit and as confidence returned, Jimmie's drawings transformed it into a normally sound and pleasant place, the dominating structure in the neighborhood. He diminished the demonstrators in size, and even began to put Ruby inside the building, although he usually consigned her to one section of it. He abandoned the Negro dialect he had attempted to adopt when speaking of her, and began to draw her house, which he had previously drawn as one of a jumble of ramshackle buildings under a sunless sky, as an erect and sturdily constructed place with grass, flowers, blue sky, and sun, this last, Jimmie's ultimate seal of approval. For Jimmie, at least, the season of hate seemed to have petered out.

As the sun obligingly pushed away the morning fog to expose brilliant blue skies for Mardi Gras on February 14, King Zulu stepped onto the Poydras Street Wharf from his "royal yacht"—a local salvage company tugboat in real life—and boarded the tinseled float awaiting his royal presence. Crowds had been lined up for hours along Poydras, a major thoroughfare, to watch, cheer, and, with a little luck, to catch the painted coconuts tossed out by the king and his attendants.

Two weeks had passed since the festivities at the Roosevelt Hotel honoring the local school board. On the surface, the city appeared to have quieted some. The numbers if not the fervor of the women who still gathered to jeer the black children at Frantz and McDonogh 19 seemed to have diminished, and their rancor was no longer the main center of attention in New Orleans. As political scientist Morton Inger remarked, however, the city had a long climb ahead of it before its health was completely restored, particularly that of the black community, where anger over the whites' reception of the six-year-olds at their new schools, the racial arrogance of the state legislators, and the lack of black support from the mayor, for whom many blacks had voted, called for retaliation. Blacks responded with the best weapon they had: Mardi Gras.

All through December, January, and early February, black groups threatened to boycott the city's biggest party—and one of its major sources of revenue. Explained community activist Leonard L. Burns, New Orleans's black carnival organizations, which were called social aid and pleasure clubs rather than krewes and functioned during the rest of the year as community service groups, intended "to prove to the boys in Baton Rouge that we all stand together and can put as much pressure on them as they can on us." If the boycott succeeded, the Zulus would not parade, and no black money would be spent on ball gowns, liquor, catering service, decorations, or all the other things it took to make a Carnival. "This hate business," Burns warned, "works two ways, and is sharper than a two-edged sword."

The movement, however, only partially succeeded, although opponents of the Zulus' parading had kept the pressure on until the last minute. But they hadn't reckoned with Chep Morrison's determination to reconstruct the image of his city that had been communicated to the outside world during the disturbances of the past several months. They had underestimated his resolve to present a calm and unified city, not only to reassure tourists that New Orleans remained the merry and mellow Mardi Gras city they remembered, but also to convince business-men and industrialists seeking a site in which to settle that the city had recovered from its recent indisposition. And he and Police Chief Giar-russo had dropped in unannounced on a meeting of the Zulu Aid & Plea-sure Club to twist a few arms.

Except for the mayor's guarantee of the Zulus' safety during their march, the details of the deal made were not disclosed, but ten minutes after the two city officials left, club officers announced that the fifteen members present had voted unanimously to go through with the parade. At which point, Lucy Washington, the official Queen Zulu for 1961, threatened with a boycott of a tavern she owned in a heavily black sec-tion of the city, abruptly abdicated her throne.

Time was when it was considered wise to catch the Zulu parade early in the day because the plans for its route sometimes disintegrated as the day wore on and the bar stops became more frequent. This year, however, it didn't matter much. This year it was a subdued, joyless affair. Not the make-believe quality of the holiday or King Zulu's gaudy fin-ery—gold-colored shoes, straw skirt over black tights, sequined jacket, and silver crown—could dispel the gloom.

Four lonely floats less than exuberently tinseled, King Zulu's in the lead, his face hidden by makeup and his identity a secret, snaked, quietly rather than rambunctiously as in other years, between Poydras and North Claiborne, hugging the area nearest downtown. When asked where the queen was, a tight-lipped attendent on number two float where she normally sat replied: "We didn't have a queen." The witch doctor fol-lowed along puffing on a foot-long cigar, and the Eureka brass band did its best to revive spirits, but a pall hung over the crowd, and the king reigned "hurriedly and worriedly" rather than merrily. A few coconuts were handed out—not thrown exuberantly this year—but solemn-faced police guards with dogs kept what few spectators had remained beyond arm's length. North Claiborne, ordinarily mobbed, was nearly deserted now, and several of the most popular taverns had closed. The forty-third annual march of the Zulus was a bust.

Leonard Burns was, however, gratified by the "gains realized by the Negroes of New Orleans ... by the citywide unity of purpose. The Negroes did not dance as usual; they did not attend Carnival parades; they did not leave their homes on Mardi Gras day (other than the degrading Zulus) and they have shown the white merchants the effect of their buying power by not spending for Carnival."

The gloom accompanying King Zulu's Mardi Gras performance and the sharply diminished support for the celebration by the black commu-nity turned out to be a minor blip on the total Mardi Gras screen. Away from the mixed emotions and despondency that afflicted the king and what was left of his court, it was a city on the mend that the maskers saw, no less festive than last year's celebration when Rex, Lord of Misrule, had rolled along these same uptown streets with his royal retinue, listening to the same cheers and inhaling the same familiar aromas of whiskey and hot popcorn and wieners cooking.

Revelers jammed Canal Street and St. Charles Avenue where stately old homes had been draped with the royal flags of past Carnival kings. Mechanics, as they had long been accustomed, abandoned the garages at which they labored during the rest of the year, clerks their desks, students their books, and got themselves up in funny hats and false mustaches, clown suits and diamond tiaras. A few masked mannequins in shop windows wore costumes; others wore half masks above the latest fashion in spring suits and dresses. The shop windows themselves wore festive banners of green, gold, and purple, traditional Mardi Gras colors.

Street vendors hawked camellias and candied apples, a banjo player in a skeleton suit found a pillar to lean against while she strummed, the little coins developing a rhythm of their own as they plinked into the tin cup beside her feet. Children rode on their fathers' shoulders or perched on stepladders. Babies cried and whistles shrieked; balloons burst and men and women laughed together. The sounds crescendoed to a roar.

Laurence Moore Williams, civic leader and businessman, made a regal Rex. His selection had the air of a coronation about it. He was the fourth in his family to play a leading role: his grandfather had been king in 1909, his sister queen in 1926, his daughter queen in 1954.

He sat erect astride his throne, which had been secured to a truck costumed as a circus wagon. Behind him a twenty-two-float retinue lined up: a twelve-piece Dixieland band plus a vehicle fitted out with animated moving heads, rolling eyes, and waving arms all with amplifying systems blaring out tunes from *Music Man, Kiss Me, Kate, Brigadoon,* and other well-known hit musicals that illustrated that year's theme, the Magic of Music.

As was traditional, Rex began his six-mile trek from his headquarters uptown into the heart of the festivities downtown about 10 A.M. Trinkets flew through the air along the way, the crowd yelling, jumping, sometimes catching them, sometimes missing, then scrabbling along the ground to retrieve a fistful of doubloons or a string of beads. The cortege paused at the usual stops along the way: at City Hall, to exchange toasts with a beaming Mayor Morrison; at the Boston Club, where 1961's queen, Virginia Borah, daughter of retired Federal Judge Wayne Borah, awaited her king; and at the exclusive Pickwick and Louisiana clubs for additional injections of champagne.

The disturbances of the past several months in the lower Ninth Ward seemed far removed in time and space as the marchers and bands passed the cheering crowds that had gathered virtually all day until the setting of the sun over the western suburbs alerted revelers that the party was about to move indoors—to their homes, hotels, bars, restaurants, and dance halls.

Then about seven thirty, the parade of Comus, elitest of the elite, followed by cakewalking hooded flambeaux carriers lighting up the balmy New Orleans night, set out on the final march of the day and of the 1961 season, whose twenty-five parades since Epiphany had distracted New Orleanians at least briefly from the difficult decisions still to be made about their city. Later that night, the most exclusive balls were staged in the Municipal Auditorium, Rex, Comus, their queens and courts, meeting there for the first time, the gala atmosphere that night belying the auditorium's recent past as a regular rallying place for the local White Citizens' Council.

Louisiana's lawmakers were among the last to get the message that New Orleans's school crisis had peaked and was beginning to wind down. They had adjourned their fourth special session on February 14 and on February 15 were back at their desks to begin the second special session of the year, the fifth since early November. They had spent more than half a million tax dollars—$168,000 for each of the first three special sessions—and were about to appropriate another $178,000 for the fifth. (Little business was conducted at the fourth special session. Members passed a couple of inflammatory resolutions including one condemning NBC newscaster Chet Huntley to perdition for misrepresenting the South in his "White Paper on Sit-ins" broadcast December 20, then adjourned until noon on February 14.) Like wounded animals, they still had a snarl or two left in them.

The lawmakers' early efforts to prevent public school desegregation, then to undo the token desegregation the courts had imposed having failed, they hoped in this fifth session to contain it. Governor Davis kept his legislative schemes secret until the last minute. An early meeting with his strategists was so secret that Leander Perez, arriving late, had trouble getting in and had to knock several times before the door to the governor's office was opened.

Then on the afternoon of February 15, thirteen bills were dropped into the house hopper. In this final session, the legislators did not initiate any new battles with the federal government, but concentrated instead on bills designed to afford white parents, like those who'd withdrawn their children from Frantz and McDonogh 19, an escape from the racial mixing they so despised.

The most important of the bills of this session comprised a single, carefully constructed package, the keystone of which was an act giving each local school board authority to suspend public elementary and secondary schools within its jurisdiction if in a parishwide election a majority of voters gave their consent. The bill masqueraded under the title of a "local option" law, but in fact, as Matt Sutherland put it, it was a "one-way street. If the majority votes to close the schools we would have to oblige them. But if the people vote to keep them open, the state ... will still refuse to recognize a school system under token integration and won't give it funds to operate."

The same day, the next block was put in place. Both houses authorized the money to pay for the private school system contemplated by the "local option" law. Grants-in-aid had been authorized earlier, but when the governor's tax increase to finance them was defeated, nothing more was done. Now they robbed the Public Welfare Fund of $2,500,000 in tax proceeds for tuitions, then threw in another $250,000 a month from the same source for current private school operating expenses. Flanked by executives from U.S. Rubber and the Borden Company, corporate parents of a new firm scheduled to break ground in the New Orleans area shortly, the governor predicted a private school system supported by his grant-in-aid tuition plan would "attract more people to Louisiana than we could handle." Senators and house members, including both New Orleans delegations, voted for the measures unanimously.

Tightening the noose, the lawmakers next found a way to keep recalcitrant school boards in line. Firing the renegades hadn't worked in New Orleans. Now they tried packing the boards with partisans, beginning in East Baton Rouge, which was under a federal court order to desegregate. The plan was for the governor to add four members to the seven then serving on the board; added to the two Davis loyalists already on the board, the new members would give him a total of six and a majority of one. Despite the fact that the East Baton Rouge board had voted 5 to 2 in an emergency meeting against the packing plan, this not-so-subtle insurance against parish schools remaining open though desegregated passed the senate 26 to 9 and the house 78 to 15. Bob Ainsworth, Adrian Duplantier, and other New Orleanians in the senate voted against this one, as did Moon Landrieu, Sam Anzelmo, and other New Orleanians and south Louisianans in the house who could easily imagine the rope around the necks of their own school boards.

The most controversial of the measures that went into the segregation package that session, the measure to hold the package together by enforcing its provisions, imposed fines on anyone caught inducing others to attend integrated schools, and authorized financial rewards to be paid to informers. It was debated at some length, and Franziska Heberle, a Baton Rouge social worker who'd grown up in Nazi Germany, warned the senate committee holding hearings on the bill that conditions in her adopted state were coming perilously close to those

> prevailing in Germany immediately before the Nazis took over in 1933 . . . a period when people felt they couldn't speak up for what they knew was right. They thought it would harm them or their relatives, their employer would not like it, or it would endanger their business. . . . Others thought politics was not their concern. They wanted to be neutral. . . . Neutrality in these times actually gives support to an aggressive minority.

The bill passed both houses overwhelmingly. Not even Ainsworth, Duplantier, Anzelmo, or Landrieu voted against it.

On February 20, six days before the session officially ended, the governor signed the package. As was customary for these special sessions, the bills were designated emergency legislation and went into effect immediately.

Louisiana's legislative record of the previous several months, its main theme one of defeat after defeat at the hands of the federal court, made depressing reading for the lawmakers themselves, for Governor Davis's administration, and for segregationists throughout the state. Now in the spring of 1961, the only hope of establishing the long-wished-for private segregated school systems lay with the recently enacted local option law, flagship of the fifth special session, and the governor and the lawmakers were eager to test it. If it fell, the whole package would ultimately fall.

St. Helena Parish, already under a court order to desegregate its schools, was chosen as the guinea pig. A small parish of red dirt hills, piney woods, and strawberry patches lying about a hundred miles north-northwest of New Orleans on the Arkansas border, it was a poor parish. Per capita income of $894 fell below the state average of $1,147 and the national average of $1,974. School ended in May each year to free youngsters to help with the strawberry harvest. An unidentified local official characterized it as "strictly a country parish . . . where the only industries are welfare and politics." Even with tuition grants, there would be few St. Helenans able to afford private schools if voters opted to close the public system.

Nonetheless, the referendum was held, voters consented to the school closing, 1,147 to 56, and A. P. Tureaud challenged the law that had made it possible in federal court. The judges of the special federal district court considering Tureaud's suit—Circuit Court Judge Wisdom replacing Circuit Judge Rives who'd begged off the grinding special district court duty because of his wife's poor health, and district judges Wright and Christenberry—were caught a little short of precedent, and they took the unusual step of asking the attorneys general of the other forty-nine states to brief them on the two main issues to which they believed the case boiled down:

1. Would abandonment by a state of its public school system deprive children of rights guaranteed by the Fourteenth Amendment?
2. Would the answer be the same if the abandonment were on a local option basis after a vote of the electorate authorizing county school authorities to close the public schools?

Twenty-eight attorneys general replied. Seventeen said the Constitution required states to provide public education; eleven said it didn't. They divided largely along regional lines.

Yankees like Attorney General Walter F. Mondale of Minnesota assumed federal supremacy and agreed that abandonment by a state of its public school system, with or without a referendum, would deprive children of the Constitution's guarantees. Attorney General Richard Ervin of Florida and his fellow southerners agreed that the Constitution neither guaranteed nor granted all children free public education, that such a right could be determined only by the "will of the majority of the state itself."

The court announced its decision on August 30, just over a week before Louisiana's schools were scheduled to open. It was a per curiam, but bore all the features of John Wisdom: his erudition, the detailed analysis for which circuit judges had the time and a stylistic eloquence only rarely glimpsed in the work of trial judges whose opinion-writing time was severely limited by the daily demands on their courtroom presence. That Wright and Christenberry had contributed significantly to the constitutional logic of it, however, was obvious.

The local option law, the trio had decided, was clearly unconstitutional, a "transparent artifice" designed, they said, to deny black children's "constitutional right to attend desegregated schools." Despite the measure's studied avoidance of racial references, the judges exposed the lawmakers' scheme to use it as the foundation for a white private school system, fitted their findings into the context of the social and economic dynamics of St. Helena Parish where private schools—the so-called option—were neither affordable nor available to the large majority of children, and concluded that privatizing the public schools spelled the "end of school education for all children in the parish, white and Negro, except a handful of well-to-do white children." The referendum that purported to measure the majority's will was, the judges said, irrelevant when constitutional promises were at issue—"no plebescite can legalize an unjust discrimination" was the way they put it. The local option law on which the desperate segregationists' hopes had been concentrated could not stand.*

---

*The following February, the U.S. Supreme Court affirmed the lower court's decision.

CHAPTER 22

Lessons Learned

hortly before the judges announced their ruling on the constitutionality of the local option law, on August 21, 1961, Skelly
Wright was speculating on the outlook for the New Orleans
schools as preparations for their September 7 opening went forward. His
disturbing memories of the previous year inevitably mingling with his
hopes for the current term, he told an acquaintance he had "reason to
believe that the atmosphere has improved materially."

Wright could not but have been aware that the local picture was not
all blue skies and sunrises. Although four more city schools, including
Lusher and Wilson, whose PTAs had offered them up for desegregation
the previous year, were scheduled to receive black children in September, the number of black children had once again been drastically limited
by the requirements of the pupil placement law. Of sixty-six transfer
applications received from black children, only eight had been chosen.
SOS members were energetically holding coffee parties at which they
tried to persuade white parents to keep their children in the desegregating schools. Their success rate was not high.

Private segregated education was thriving, siphoning off increasing
numbers of white children from the public schools. Applications to the
private schools springing up across the city and supported by contributions, the kitty set aside by the state legislature for the purpose, and the
newly created tuition grants—$2 a day for a 180-day school year, $360
per pupil—poured in faster than they could be processed. Emile Wagner
recruited a group of local segregationists to establish the New Orleans

Educational Foundation, a school-board–like organization to supervise the private system and administer the grants-in-aid, which had so far survived federal court scrutiny.

Originally limited to supporting nonsectarian, nonprofit institutions, largely children attending the hastily thrown-up little cooperatives, the grants-in-aid plan was later modified by the legislature to include those attending profit-making institutions. As a result students at the best private schools in Louisiana received state money to help pay their tuition: Metairie Park Country Day School, Isadore Newman, École Classique, and Miss McGehee's where the local debutante crop prepared simultaneously for college and "coming out."

At the same time, plans were afoot to build at least five more alternative schools for white children in Orleans Parish alone. The $2.5 million reserved for the grant-in-aid program, although supplemented by the legislature-mandated $250,000 a month, was dwindling fast, and the state treasurer complained publicly that "if we are going to set up private schools all over New Orleans, it's going to take a lot more money than we have."

The state legislature still had New Orleans's school money tied up, and Shelby Jackson had devised a scheme for starving the city into submission by stopping all state education department/Orleans Parish school board communications as well as funds for textbooks, supplies, school milk and lunch programs. Skelly Wright finally had to threaten Jackson, house speaker Tom Jewell, and lieutenant governor and senate president Clarence C. Aycock with contempt of court citations in order to loosen the state's grip on New Orleans's money.

But it was too late for some items in the budget. Financial famine had taken a large toll. Scheduled school construction, much of it earmarked for black schools to alleviate some of the overcrowding those like Macarty, had stopped abruptly during the crisis, and the cityscape was pockmarked with foundations waiting for superstructures, shells of classrooms waiting for renovations, and vacant lots where buildings had been planned now overgrown with weeds and strewn with trash.

With all the cause for pessimism, however, the atmosphere of New Orleans during the final weeks before schools opened for the 1961–62 term had, as Skelly Wright had said, "improved materially" over the previous summer's helplessness and hopelessness.

For one thing, the new Kennedy administration had gotten involved in the local crisis early on. Attorney General Robert F. Kennedy had unhesitatingly acceded to Skelly Wright's request to retain the Republican United States attorney in New Orleans, Hep Many, who normally would have resigned when the administration changed on January 20 and made way for a Democrat. Neither party politics nor his personal distaste for massive school desegregation, however, had influenced Many's conduct of the federal office, and he had demonstrated many times his unswerving support of the federal courts. When Wright telephoned Burke Marshall, the new assistant attorney general for civil rights, to request Many's retention, Wright was looking mainly for continuity in the U.S. Attorney's office while the crisis continued, but he was also worried about the political views and loyalties of a Democrat who would, in effect, be chosen by the two Louisiana senators. Senator Ellender, in fact, who'd supported Many's original appointment in 1955, having had no idea "he was going to turn coattail," already had "three or four" candidates in mind for Many's job.*

In February, 1961, the President himself, in sharp contrast to Eisenhower, went public on the New Orleans school crisis and called on the moral authority of his office to congratulate educators, parents, and other New Orleanians who were working to keep public schools open for their "quiet intelligence and true courage." In a telegram to a conference on schools sponsored by the U.S. Civil Rights Commission at Williamsburg, Virginia, Kennedy declared that

The whole country is in their debt,

then went on to "pay tribute to the school children and their parents, of both races, who have been on the frontlines of this problem. In accepting the command of the Constitution with dignity, they, too, are contributing to the education of all Americans."

That summer saw Burke Marshall and John Siegenthaler, special assistant to the attorney general, dispatched to southern cities, including New Orleans, which were either in the process or on the brink of desegregating their schools. They were to scout out the racial terrain before schools opened in September. The President hoped, Marshall explained, "to get the country ahead of its problems" rather than to let them "build up" the way Little Rock had.

On their visit to New Orleans, Marshall and Siegenthaler talked "quietly and privately" with key figures involved in the desegregation: Skelly Wright, Hep Many, A. P. Tureaud, Harry Kelleher, state senator Bob Ainsworth, who agreed to serve as the justice department's eyes and ears in the legislature, Jack Gremillion, and Police Chief Giarrusso. They wanted, Marshall said, "not to be surprised." They wanted advance

---

*Many remained in the U.S. Attorney's office through 1961. The attorney general invited him to stay longer, but Many refused. He did not choose, he said, to preside over the "second reconstruction" of his native city. He went into the private practice of law.

notice of any need for a federal "physical presence"; at the same time, they hoped to defuse the crisis aspect of the situation sufficiently to obviate any need for that presence.

In their talks with Giarrusso, Marshall and Siegenthaler assured the police chief that sixty U.S. marshals would be standing by at Camp Leroy Johnson on the lakefront, prepared to cooperate with local law enforcement if they were needed. But Giarrusso had been "living with and studying the problem" for several weeks, and he was confident his department could handle anything that might arise. This year, Giarrusso promised,

> We know now more about how to handle the problem and I'm sure
> we learned something last year.

It seems that a lot of New Orleanians "learned something last year." As preparations for the opening of the 1961–62 school term went forward, the scenario for desegregation had been completely rewritten.

Perhaps the most important factor in the change of mood was the new mayor. From the very beginning of his tenure, there was every indication that Victor Hugo Schiro's (pronounced Skée-ro) decisive, no-nonsense manner would contribute substantially to a change in the city's behavior.

On D-Day in the fall of 1960, nearly a year after his disastrous loss to Jimmie Davis in the gubernatorial race, Chep Morrison still aspired to Davis's office. But political doors had begun to close. His persistent public neutrality on the issue of school desegregation had alienated people on all sides of the question: blacks who resented his failure to support the court orders to desegragate, white segregationists who doubted the firmness of his commitment to "separate but equal," and moderates more tolerant of token desegregation than of disturbances like those of 1960, which Morrison had done virtually nothing to curb.

There was also the problem of the city charter, which allowed the mayor only two successive terms after the 1954 date of its adoption. Morrison was already in the middle of his second. If he was to shed his lame-duck feathers and run again in 1962 in order to retain his political base until the next—1964—gubernatorial election, he had to persuade New Orleanians to amend that charter.

The referendum was set for April 15, 1961, and he began hastily to mend his political fences, beginning with his courtship of Ninth Ward voters with new lights for the Richard Lee playground and extensive street repairs throughout the area, explaining that "since there has been so much anti-City sentiment in the area of Frantz and McDonogh schools," he wanted to see "stepped up activity on street work in this area. . . . [T]hese people have been bitter against the City government, and I think this will help to offset their bitterness."

It was all for naught. On April 15, enough New Orleanians suspected Morrison's motives—his political ambition—or simply opposed tinkering with the city charter as a matter of principle to defeat the amendment Morrison needed to salvage his sinking career.

The governorship all but a dead letter now, Morrison began to fish for an appointment in the Kennedy administration, and on June 13, he accepted its nomination of him as U.S. ambassador to the Organization of American States. The local NAACP branch, whose members were not only angry over the mayor's position on school desegregation but had never forgotten his refusals to allow Thurgood Marshall use of the Municipal Auditorium, wrote the Senate Foreign Relations Committee opposing Morrison's appointment. The Senate nonetheless confirmed the nominee, and he took office July 17.

On July 20, city council president Vic Schiro, a councilman for seventeen years, was elected by fellow councilmen to fill the remaining nine months of Morrison's term, which expired in May, 1962. His acceptance speech was brief. He focused on the future of New Orleans as a business and industrial magnet city—even as he spoke, the National Aeronautics and Space Administration (NASA) and the Boeing Aircraft Company were considering a former army ordnance plant in the New Orleans area as the site for producing the booster stage of the Saturn missile, a plum that would mean employment of an estimated ten thousand. He said nothing about school desegregation.

But it didn't take him long to come around to that subject. On August 8, following the school board's publication of the names of the schools to be desegregated in a month, the new mayor put the city "on notice" that "law and order" would be enforced. He considered the board's early announcement of its plans advantageous. "Surprises," he explained, "always have an element of emotion and create trouble."

After that, though no integrationist himself, he grasped the reins firmly and drove the city safely past any hazards that remained. He was so confident by mid-August that he invited the national press to cover the further desegregation of New Orleans's schools. He promised there would be no attempt by the city to restrict coverage in any way. He did remind reporters that they were "guests of our city" and must "conduct themselves accordingly." He was sure that "our city will give the national press very little to report here next month."

He had every reason to believe what he did. The school board itself, no longer racked by competing state and federal demands, was no longer writhing in torment but was confronting the desegregation of the city's schools head-on. They'd had transfer procedures worked our by early April. In May they'd advertised for bids on new laboratory equipment and school refurbishing, and with little fuss had chosen a new school superintendent, O. Perry Walker, a native New Orleanian with thirty-nine years experience in the local school system, to succeed Jim Redmond, who'd resigned in a dispute over salary.* And all summer they kept in close touch with Chief Giarrusso.

Even the local power structure, having discovered the effect of civil disturbances on profits, caught the change of mood and rallied around peaceful school desegregation. On August 11, a select group of the city's aristocracy met at International House "to consider a plan aimed at avoiding trouble at the September opening of public schools." Socially and economically homogeneous but politically diverse, the group included Richard Freeman; Darwin Fenner; Charles Keller, Jr.; Lester Kabacoff; and Charles G. Smither, a prominent insurance mogul who had signed the newspaper ad endorsing Matt Sutherland's reelection to the school board; plus the segregationist publisher of the *Times-Picayune* John Tims; Clifford F. Favrot, a real estate magnate and financial backer of Governor Davis's; A. L. Schlesinger, a real estate broker and devout southerner but opposed to the legislature's vicious attacks on the federal courts; and Raburn Monroe of Monroe and Lemann, one of the city's most prestigious law firms.

Fenner chaired the meeting. He explained briefly that a statement he'd brought for his colleagues to consider had been worked out by a committee of twenty prominent men from every congressional district of Louisiana, and, assuming enough signatures could be gotten, it would be published shortly. He showed them a six-paragraph "Declaration of Principles" that reflected the various viewpoints of its authors and the men Fenner was trying to persuade to sign it. It urged the eventual amendment of the federal Constitution to ensure the states of their right to "determine the basis on which their schools should be operated," but in the meantime firmly supported compliance with the "final decisions" of the U.S. Supreme Court, and concluded that

---

*Redmond was earning $23,000 a year and wanted a $7,000 raise, but the board claimed it could afford only $3,000. Board President Riecke thought the harassment Redmond had endured over the previous year was a larger part of Redmond's story than was generally acknowledged, that his feelings had been hurt after he'd taken the abuse, then was denied what he believed was his just reward.

He joined the educational administration division of the national consulting firm of Booz, Allen and Hamilton in New York City, stayed two years, then returned to Chicago as superintendent of schools. He later retired to Benton Harbor, Michigan.

The time has come for the reasonable men and women of Louisiana to express their views and to assume positions of leadership in this critical social problem.

On August 31, the men at the meeting, calling themselves the Committee for Louisiana, published their "Declaration" in a full-page newspaper ad signed by three hundred other leading citizens of New Orleans. As declarations of principles go, it was weak, less forceful than the statement of the past December, which only Smither, Fenner, and Schlesinger of this group had signed. But it was a substantial advance over the empty silence of the year before.

The Greater New Orleans Federation of Churches gave the "Declaration" its support and asked local churchgoers to observe Sunday, September 10, and Sunday, September 17, as days of special fasting and prayer for "peaceable and lawful solution to the problems which confront our community as a result of racial tensions." Tims's *Times-Picayune,* after seven years of editorially encouraging defiance of the U.S. Supreme Court's decision in *Brown* and Skelly Wright's ruling in *Bush,* conceded defeat, and in a front-page editorial on September 3, two days before public school children were scheduled to register for the 1961–62 term and four days before the term was scheduled to open, the editors urged that there be "no repetition" of 1960's disorders. Like the authors of the "Declaration," their hope for the South's future lay in a constitutional amendment recently introduced in Congress by Senator Herman Talmadge of Georgia and Representative Hale Boggs of Louisiana to preserve state control over public schools. While the amendment was pending in Congress, they said, again echoing the authors of the "Declaration,"

> Like it or not, the nation's law, as interpreted by the highest court in the land, calls for desegregation of public schools.
>
> If we are to continue to have a government of law and not of men, we must respect that law.

Segregationists in the legislature met in Baton Rouge in August and September to discuss strategies for firming up the muscle in the grant-in-aid measure, tenure for teachers in private schools, and the controversial pupil placement law, almost all that had survived Skelly Wright's cleaver. Convinced that "Rome is burning," Leander Perez tried to persuade the lawmakers to open one more special session, but he stood alone. They seemed not to have much stomach for it then, and they contented themselves with protesting a Justice Department attempt to persuade the courts to remove New Orleans pupils from St. Bernard Parish's segregated schools to which they'd fled from Frantz and McDonogh 19 the previous year. Governor Davis wowed the Southern Governors' Conference later that month when he gave a stirring rendition of what he called his "old meal ticket, 'You Are My Sunshine.'"

On August 31, the same day the "Declaration of Principles" ran in the *Times-Picayune,* Mayor Schiro met in his office with school board members, Superintendent Walker, Sam Rosenberg, Chief Giarrusso and one of his assistant chiefs, plus Glenn P. Clasen, the city's chief administrative officer. They discussed in detail "the future integration situation" and police department plans for the coming week.

The mood was positive, and parents were assured that children attending all schools would be safe. Board President Riecke believed that over the past year "the feeling of the community has changed." New Orleanians realized now, he thought, that nothing more could be done to preserve separate schools, and desegregation was "the law of the land."

Chief Giarrusso took the upcoming opening of city schools as a personal challenge and announced in advance the ground rules he and his department had laid: streets would be barricaded one block in each direction from the desegregating schools; up to sixty uniformed plainclothes police would be stationed at each of the six schools; parents would be permitted to escort their youngsters to the buildings but would be required to leave immediately; "agitators would be arrested."

On the evening of September 5, following the first day of registration, Harry Kelleher moderated a discussion broadcast simultaneously by three local television and eight local radio stations. The participants— all white—included the mayor, School Superintendent Walker, Darwin Fenner, and Charles Smither, Chief Giarrusso, banker Joseph Simon, Jr., labor union president A. P. Stoddard, and Young Men's Business Club president Malcolm Munday. Their pitch was a fervent plea to all New Orleanians to maintain law and order during the critical next few weeks while, as Schiro reminded them, "the whole world is looking at New Orleans"—including, though the mayor didn't say so out loud, the people who would decide where to locate a new production line for Saturn missiles.

The following evening, Charles Smither moderated a discussion among the four school board members. It was broadcast over WYES-TV, and the participants, like those of the evening before, stressed the necessity to obey the law, the futility of boycotting schools, the public's obligation to respect the rights of parents whether they sent their children to public or private schools, and the mayor's promise that "law and order will be maintained around our desegregated public schools."

The buildup succeeded. Thursday, September 7, dawned cloudy and warm with a high of 86 degrees and scattered afternoon thunder showers, a typical September day in New Orleans. The only disturbances that day originated in the heavens.

No demonstrations, incidents, or episodes broke the quiet as schools opened. The pleas of the city's leadership were honored. The promised barricades were in place around the buildings, and more than three hundred policemen were in place behind the barricades. A few women appeared at Frantz with their signs, but patrolmen ordered them to move on immediately and they did.

Not a catcall, a boo, or a rotten egg greeted Ruby, Tessie, Gail, and Leona on their return to Frantz and McDonogh 19. They came in Ed's Cabs this year. Their paths were open and unimpeded, and their former federal protectors, unneeded now, had been replaced by local police.

Over the summer, parents of white children assigned to the four newly desegregating elementary schools had applied to transfer them to other public or to private schools, and enrollment at the six totaled only 951 in September, a loss of some 1,400. On opening day, 845 showed up for classes.

The boycott of McDonogh 19 was broken when an unidentified white boy entered the school that morning. As the afternoon session began, three more white children joined him. The three black girls who returned were joined by a black boy and a black girl, both first graders. Ruby remained the lone black child at Frantz. On opening day she was joined by sixteen white children.

At the four schools just then desegregating, the ratios of blacks to whites were daunting. At Wilson, one black girl joined 355 white children; at Lusher, two black girls joined 204 white children; at McDonogh 11, one black girl joined 174 white children; and at Judah P. Benjamin, a black girl and a black boy entered with eighty-one white children. The six desegregated schools operated at less than full capacity throughout the 1961–62 term.

After nine years of turmoil and trauma since the Bush case was taken into federal court in 1952, years of suits and countersuits, suspense, humiliation, and racial hostility, demagoguery and name-calling, arm-twisting, evasion, and artifice, a total of twelve black children had been allowed to enter a handful of elementary schools formerly reserved for whites. Schools provided for black children were more overcrowded in 1961 than they had been in 1946 when NAACP troubleshooter Dan Byrd lobbed his first petition of protest into the Orleans Parish school board offices. Citywide, by 1961–62, five thousand black children were attending school in the despised platoons. No white children were. Black New Orleanians were angry at the sluggish pace of desegregation, which they surmised was due to the onerous testing required by the state's pupil placement law as well as the highly selective standards set by local school officials. They further surmised that the delays were deliberate. At this rate, only a very few black youngsters now in public school would ever attend any of the clearly superior white schools in New Orleans.

On September 26, about three weeks after schools opened for the 1961–62 term, a contingent of irate black parents and PTA members came down from the Ninth Ward, where it had all begun, to a meeting of the Orleans Parish school board to support Dan Byrd's presentation of still another petition protesting the overcrowding of neighborhood black schools while white schools remained underpopulated. His list of Ninth Ward schools, where a total of 1,800 children still attended in platoons, included the Macarty Elementary School whose PTA had supplied the ninety-odd plaintiffs to the Bush suit, and after nine years was still choking on an unwieldy 638 youngsters on platoon.

Byrd told the board that Ninth Ward parents held "varied degrees of sentiment concerning the problem." Although most would be content with accelerated desegregation of white schools to relieve the overcrowding in black buildings, he warned that just recently he had had to dissuade one group that wanted to stage a demonstration. In view of the board's continuing tenuous relationship with the state administration, board president Riecke hoped there would be no demonstrations. He referred the parents' latest petition to the new school superintendent.

The telephone call finally came in the fall of 1961, "out of the blue sky," as Skelly Wright recalled the conversation later. Attorney General Robert Kennedy, whom Wright had not yet even met, was on the line.

"I've been holding up two nominations for the Fifth Circuit, hoping I could put you in one of them," Kennedy began. However, he added, "I've checked again with the senators and it's impossible."

"I respect your judgment," Wright replied, suppressing an impulse to ask, "Why don't you fight the bastards?" His hopes for promotion had wavered during the recent unpleasantness, but not his aim, which hadn't wavered a fraction of an inch since he took his first shot at the court of appeals in 1949.

So ended several months of speculation on whether or not Skelly Wright would be appointed to one of the two vacancies the new judgeships bill passed by Congress in early May of 1961 had allotted to the U.S. Court of Appeals for the Fifth Circuit. The nominations went instead to Atlanta lawyer Griffin Bell and Tuscaloosa lawyer Walter P. Gewin, although sitting judges Wisdom and Tuttle had lobbied zealously among Justice Department officials for Wright's appointment. They argued that if Wright were passed over, it would be regarded as punishment for his unflinching insistence on enforcing *Brown* v. *Board of Education*. Richard Rives had sung the praises of his erstwhile colleague on the numerous special three-judge courts where they'd sat together to Alabama Senator Lister Hill, and there was even gossip that Supreme Court Justice Hugo Black, then seventy-five, would resign if he could be assured Wright would be appointed to replace him. Wright had built a national reputation, and the widely circulated *New Republic* editorially urged the Kennedy administration not to cave in to pressure from southern senators opposed to Wright's promotion

> for the sake of elementary justice to an able and faithful public servant, and for the sake of the morale and continued independence of all Southern federal judges.

As expected, however, Wright's potential elevation did not play so well in Louisiana. In Baton Rouge, archsegregationist Wellborn Jack, introduced, and the state legislature passed, a resolution opposing Wright's promotion. Wright, Jack explained angrily, "had utter disregard for the sovereignty of the state of Louisiana."

The message reverberated to Washington. The young Democratic administration was unwilling to risk alienating the powerful southern bloc. That Senator Eastland, still chairman of the Senate Judiciary Committee, would oppose Wright's appointment was a foregone conclusion. In a telephone conversation with U.S. Attorney Hep Many, Eastland had once called Wright an unprintable name. When Many protested, Eastland repeated it, and Many abruptly hung up. According to Many, then Attorney General William Rogers ordered the New Orleanian to take the first plane to Washington and mend his fences. Such was Eastland's power and influence.

Louisiana Senator Allen Ellender, although he'd sponsored Wright's appointment to the U.S. Attorney's office thirty years before and professed to like the judge personally, felt that "to openly endorse him would be detrimental politically in view of the widespread criticism" of Wright. Senator Long and Wright had been close friends when the latter was practicing law in Washington and the former was a young senator, but Long had told the President in 1961 that he could ill afford to alienate Louisiana's segregationists as he prepared to run for reelection in 1962 and threatened to fight Wright's appointment on the Senate floor. According to Assistant Attorney General Burke Marshall, Wright's cause was "thoroughly aired" within the administration and the administration was "torn." Marshall urged Wright's appointment, but the Kennedys had too many other battles on their hands to spend their political capital on a circuit court appointment.

Since he knew that "federal judges are not made in heaven," Wright was not surprised that the administration "appeased" Long. He was not even "too upset with Russell; I figure he has his problems. I am just sorry they affect me." And he settled back down to the familiar routine of uncluttering his increasingly cluttered docket in New Orleans.

The judge-makers still, however, had to reckon with Wright's supporters who wanted him promoted. Then E. Barrett Prettyman of the United States Court of Appeals for the District of Columbia turned 70 and retired after fifteen years on that court.

Conditions seemed promising for Wright's promotion at last. The District of Columbia had no senators to blue-slip the nomination. Southerners who didn't want him on the Fifth Circuit could rejoice in getting him out of the South, and the Kennedys had a twofer: they could reward a devoted servant of the law and at the same time encourage Wright's colleagues on federal benches all over America to follow his example.

The next telephone call came late one Friday afternoon. Byron R. White, deputy assistant attorney general (later Supreme Court justice), was the man at the other end of the line this time. President Kennedy was anxious to announce Prettyman's replacement, and White gave Wright the weekend to decide whether he wanted the job.

Wright's son, then almost fourteen, later described his father's decision as "one of the most agonizing decisions he ever made in his life." Partly he was concerned that his leaving would be interpreted as "running away," an act of cowardice in the face of the shunning and harassment he and his family had endured over the past few years.

Partly, too, he feared that all he had done in New Orleans would be undone as soon as he turned his back. Five years before in his first written opinion in the Bush case, he had urged the "utmost patience, understanding, generosity and forbearance from all of us, whatever the race." At the same time he had forcefully declared that the "magnitude of the problem may not nullify the principle . . . that we are, all of us, free-born Americans, with a right to make our way, unfettered by sanctions imposed by man because of the work of God." There was still a good deal of unfinished business to be done in New Orleans if those words were to have a life beyond the sterile pages of the federal reports or the plaque on which Helen had had them engraved.

One thought that consoled him as he deliberated was the fact that the new judgeship bill, which mandated seventy-three new federal judgeships nationwide, included not only an expanded Fifth Circuit court, but also an enlarged district court for the Eastern District of Louisiana. The bill allotted two additional judges to the lower court Wright would be leaving.

In 1961, the two who'd been chosen appeared at least acceptable to those who would desegregate the public schools, although the fact that E. Gordon West was Senator Long's law partner and had been recommended by Long for the judgeship might have raised questions. Two years later, West was to write in a court opinion that he regarded the "now famous Brown case as one of the truly regrettable decisions of all time." In 1961, however, Burke Marshall explained, "We couldn't get anyone to say anything against him."

Bob Ainsworth, on the other hand, actually looked promising. As president pro tem of the state senate, he'd been one of the very few in that body to resist the governor's schemes to maintain segregated schools in Louisiana. After the Kennedy administration took over the government, Ainsworth had also acted as informant to the Justice Department during the war between the state legislature and the federal court, keeping the department up to date with developments in Baton Rouge. Ainsworth could, it was felt, be relied on to uphold *Brown*. Wright could leave with a clear conscience.

Which was more or less what his younger brother Jim told him when he encouraged the judge to accept the promotion. Once again Helen left the decision to her husband. "Whatever you want," she said.

What to do?

When Monday morning came, the agony of decision was over. Wright returned Byron White's call of the previous Friday:

Yes [he said] I'll go.

Attorney General Kennedy immediately notified his brother the President, and the President, although in the midst of a Latin American tour, announced it in San Juan, Puerto Rico, on December 15. There was immediate speculation in New Orleans regarding who would succeed Wright, the rumors converging on Frank Ellis, longtime local Democratic politician and Kennedy's Louisiana campaign manager in 1960.

The next several months generated their own kind of suspense as Wright tracked the progress of his nomination through the Senate. In late February he went to Washington to testify before the Senate judiciary subcommittee considering his nomination. Although it is a Washington tradition that the senators from a nominee's home state escort him or her to the hearing and introduce him or her to their colleagues, neither Ellender nor Long, in sharp contrast to the love feast they had catered in 1949 during the hearings on Wright's appointment to the district court, appeared at all. The American Bar Association gave him its highest rating—"exceptionally well qualified." The Louisiana State Bar Association neither endorsed him nor opposed him, but took no action, which, under the usual rules of interpretation, amounts to a slap in the face. Wright nonetheless was confirmed "without objection" by the full Senate on March 28, 1962.

Coincidentally, or perhaps not so coincidentally, that same day Wright announced his decision in the touchy case of *Guillory* v. *Administrators of Tulane University* that desegregated the alma mater of a good many of New Orleans's mandarins. The privately operated Tulane had long been believed to be immune to the Fourteenth Amendment's requirements, but Rosa Keller didn't think it ought to be and instigated a lawsuit to prove her point. After studying Paul Tulane's will, which had established the institution as a university for "white young persons" and listening to the hours of testimony from both sides, Wright came to agree with Keller. Questioning "whether any school or college can ever be so 'private' as to escape the reach of the Fourteenth Amendment," Wright ruled that Tulane, which began as a public institution and had a long history of public involvement in the form of tax exemptions, land revenues, and scholarship programs, indeed fell squarely under the authority of that amendment. And he prohibited the university from further rejecting applicants on the basis of race.

Wright's ruling was a stunner, but New Orleans had not heard the last of him yet. He had one more bomb, a big one, to drop.

As he and Helen went about the business of getting ready to move, selling the house on Newcomb Boulevard, and tending to the social demands of leaving—although the testimonials were fewer than they might have been under more felicitous circumstances—Wright was also attempting to cope with the black plaintiffs in the Bush case, whose impatience and restlessness over the slow progress of racial desegregation in the local public schools had sent them back into his court. This would be his final bout with the ten-year-old case.

As a warm-up, rumors had overtaken the black community that McDonogh 19, the yearlong victim of white boycott, was to be redesignated an all-black school. At A. P. Tureaud's request, Wright told the school board it could not deny Leona, Gail, and Tessie "the opportunity to continue to attend a desegregated school." If McDonogh 19 was to be reclassified, the girls would have to be reassigned to another white majority school.

Citing delays and deterrents in the procedures used by the school board to control desegregation and complaining of the continued overcrowding of the schools provided for the city's black children, Tureaud then returned to court asking for an order requiring the board to desegregate public education in New Orleans "at all grade levels in the school system without further delay." A "whole generation of Negro children," he said, was being denied its rights while officialdom twiddled its thumbs.

Sam Rosenberg blanched and wrote the superintendent of Atlanta's schools for a copy of that city's plan for desegregation. But the comfort he got was cold. Although approved by a federal court, Atlanta School Superintendent John W. Letson thought it would soon be challenged by local blacks denied transfers to all-white schools and doubted it would "withstand . . . constitutional questions that can properly be raised." In any case, Atlanta's plan, with its requirements for interviews, scholastic aptitude tests, achievement tests, and personality adjustment tests plus the usual red tape, closely resembled the regulations devised by the Orleans Parish school board.

Wright's parting shot at his native city shocked it fully as hard as his first one in 1956. It was "obvious" to him that although the school officials had testified at recent hearings that when the present building program was completed within the next two or three years, most of the platooning should be history, in fact the platooning would "continue for some years to come unless more drastic action was taken by the Board to relieve it." And he set about fashioning the "drastic" remedy he believed the situation required: desegregation on a large scale.

On April 3, days from his scheduled departure for Washington, he gave Tureaud his answer, once again ruling Louisiana's pupil placement law impermissible when used to discriminate by race, decrying the crowded conditions in local Negro schools "67 years after *Plessy* v. *Ferguson*" and crowning his opinion with an order desegregating not the third grade alone, which was the next step in the plan he had devised in May, 1960, but desegregating grades one through six citywide in September, 1962.

[A]t the present pace in New Orleans, generations of Negroes yet unborn will suffer a similar fate with respect to their rights under Brown unless desegregation and equal protection are secured for them by this court.

He sympathized with the school board's position, but, he added,

the plight of the Board cannot affect the rights of school children whose skin color is no choice of their own. These children have a right to accept the constitutional promise of equality before the law, an equality we profess to all the world.

Senator Ellender accused Wright of seeking a seat on the U.S. Supreme Court. Senator Long was outraged. Mayor Schiro called Wright's decision an "unnecessary demonstration of authority" at a time when "we were going about this job in an intelligent, sensible way." The *Times-Picayune* pointed out the "difficult changes and serious hardships" compliance with the judge's new rules would cause. It went without saying the brunt of the "hardships" to which the editors referred were to be endured by white New Orleanians. The editors had nothing to say about the "hardships" Tureaud complained of, the conditions blacks were already enduring in their overcrowded, underequipped and understaffed schools.

Sam Rosenberg applied for a new trial. Wright, however, would be long gone before it could be scheduled.

On his last day on the district court in New Orleans, his law clerk escorted Wright to the elevator. The judge turned as he stepped in, smiled, and said

Well, they'll know we've been here.

Afterword

Confirming recent rumors, President Kennedy chose Frank Burton Ellis to replace Skelly Wright on the federal district court for the Eastern District of Louisiana. Governor Davis sat smiling among the spectators in the courtroom at Ellis's swearing-in on April 16, 1962. Former Governor Kennon, Attorney General Gremillion, and Mayor Schiro were also there. The Louisiana State Bar Association sent warm greetings. John Minor Wisdom, however, dissipated any euphoria that might have clung to the newcomer, welcoming him to what the Fifth Circuit judge could "only describe as not a calm, placid and serene atmosphere. Judges, especially in the eastern district of Louisiana, are expected to be very hardy men. They must survive unexpected cold spells and freezes."

Ellis's progress from nomination to the donning of his judicial robe had been a breeze. He had met no opposition. His reputation as a "good old boy" without political enemies had preceded him to the hearing before the Senate Judiciary Subcommittee. Senator Long had proudly presented Ellis to his colleagues and given him an enthusiastic endorsement. Favorable letters and telegrams from members of the New Orleans and Louisiana bar associations had deluged the subcommittee before the hearing began. Senator Eastland presided, startling spectators after Ellis's testimony with the question:

You are not going to be another Skelly Wright, are you?

Ellis didn't answer the question then, but his behavior afterward answered it eloquently. He was not "another Skelly Wright." His personal, professional, and political history all militated against it.

The Wrights and the Ellises were longtime friends. Avid golfers, Skelly and Frank had hotly debated the pros and cons of racial segregation as they made their way along the fairways of the New Orleans Country Club. Helen Wright described the new judge as a "charming, big football type, an affable, blustering, generous man."

Ellis had in fact been captain of the LSU football team in 1929, his last year at the law school there. At fifty-four, his broad shoulders, rugged features, and erect carriage still hinted at an athletic youth.

Born in Covington, Louisiana, across the lake from New Orleans, he had been a fixture of state politics as long as anyone could remember, stumping the state for the ill-fated gubernatorial ticket of George Seth Guion and Earl Long in 1931. In 1940, he'd been elected to the state senate where he was made president pro tem, then lost his race for lieutenant governor four years later. In 1954, he'd given Allen Ellender some nervous moments during a hard-fought primary for the U.S. Senate, but the incumbent could not be unseated.

As a delegate to the Democratic National Convention in 1952 and 1956, he had stuck with the regular party candidate Adlai Stevenson despite threats of rebellion from states' rights Democrats, and he claimed credit for keeping Louisiana Democratic in 1952 despite Eisenhower's growing popularity in the South. He had not, however, been able to keep Eisenhower from taking Louisiana in 1956.

In 1960, Ellis had jumped aboard the Kennedy bandwagon early in the Massachusetts senator's presidential campaign, serving as the Democratic candidate's campaign manager in Louisiana. He had hoped for a cabinet post but had been rewarded instead with the directorship of the Office of Civil Defense Mobilization. His overzealous advocacy of the fallout shelter program—he had actually wanted to fly to Rome to discuss with the pope installing a shelter in every American church basement—irritated the President, who disposed of him by putting his agency under the Department of Defense and dispatching Ellis himself to the federal district court in New Orleans.

During the years of political adventuring, which were supplemented by various civic activities, he'd also had a lucrative law practice, and in the spring of 1962, when he took his judicial oath, he had financial as well as political standing in the community, plus the social standing afforded by a home on upper St. Charles Avenue where he lived with his wife, Alice, and their three children. His sympathies did not always coincide with those of the man from the Irish Channel, whom he'd succeeded. Ellis seemed more attuned to the protests engendered by Wright's farewell order to desegregate the city's elementary schools, and he embarked on a course of modification.

The public schools demanded immediate attention if another crisis was to be averted when they opened in September. On May 1, the new judge stayed Wright's order to desegregate the first six grades pending new hearings and his own study of the voluminous record in the decade-old case. On May 23, he permanently withdrew Wright's plan for the wholesale desegregation. He left in place his predecessor's prohibition on using the pupil placement act for the purpose of discriminating against transfer applicants on the basis of race, but he allowed the board to limit school desegregation to the first grade citywide, which would amount only to compliance with Wright's two-year-old original order with no forward movement.

A. P. Tureaud found Ellis's ruling entirely unacceptable, a giant step backward forced on an increasingly restless people, and he appealed to the Fifth Circuit. It was the fourth time the appellate court had been asked to consider *Bush*.

After some minor legal skirishing over the summer, the court of appeals announced its decision on August 6. John Minor Wisdom spoke for the court, which had diplomatically struck a compromise between Wright's order for the immediate desegregation of six grades and Ellis's order for only one. The appellate judges affirmed Ellis's opening of the first grades citywide but added the second and third grades to the options of 1962–63 and ordered a grade a year opened thereafter, a schedule that would bring the city's schools to the point Wright's stair-step plan of 1960 had anticipated. On each step the dual systems of separate geographical school districts were to be abolished.

The Orleans Parish school board was miffed, although Matt Sutherland volunteered at the regular board meeting on August 13 that the appellate court's firmness was not without provocation. "New Orleans," he explained, "is unique in that we are the only city that has not submitted a plan . . . with no plan of our own, the courts have ruled against us and gone farther with New Orleans than any other city." That night the board voted to design a program for desegregation "rather than have the city schools administered by court orders," and at a meeting a week later, made it public.

Four members of the board—Riecke, Rittiner, Shepard, and Sutherland—voted for the plan, which more or less followed the outline drawn by the Fifth Circuit judges. Emile Wagner had resigned an hour before the meeting began. "I have never," he explained, "been a party to integration. I do not intend to start now."

School desegregation progressed glacially in New Orleans, Louisiana, and in the South generally. Ten years after the U.S. Supreme Court declared racial segregation in America's public schools unconstitutional, 873 black students out of a citywide black enrollment of 64,893 were attending schools with white students in New Orleans. In the eleven states of the old Confederacy, six percent of all black students were sitting in classes with whites. Louisiana, at 0.69 percent, ranked third from the bottom, ahead only of Mississippi (0.59 percent) and Alabama (0.43 percent).

Even these small, virtually insignificant numbers had white southern populations in a tailspin. White New Orleanians found and took advantage of every avenue of escape, some more successfully than others.

The main alternative to public schools in the city, the parochial institutions, which traditionally siphoned off nearly a third of the local school population, after the years of false starts, finally desegregated in 1962, making this former option less attractive to white parents even though at the time black students made up only about 20 percent of the parochial school population. The transition was chaotic as strident opposition led by Leander Perez attempted to persuade Catholics to obstruct Archbishop Rummel's plans. But the archbishop, despite his age and failing health, stood firm this time and excommunicated Perez, who immediately accused him of trying to "frighten or terrorize" parents considering withdrawal of their children from desegregated Catholic schools.

The protests of Perez and his cohorts notwithstanding, parochial schools opened on schedule with approximately 150 black youngsters attending formerly white schools, but over the next two years, white enrollment dropped by 2,557, or a little more than 7 percent. By 1984, white enrollment had plummeted from over 33,000 in 1964–65 to just over 17,000 two decades later. At the same time, black enrollment had risen from slightly more than 9,000 in 1964–65 to 12,619 in 1984 and was approaching parity.

Two major escape routes for white New Orleanians remained open. Until the grant-in-aid program established by the state legislature was declared unconstitutional in 1967, Louisiana's private schools thrived on state money allotted to students who attended them. In 1964–65, the number reached a high of 10,777 white recipients in New Orleans alone.

The other route New Orleanians used heavily, the most popular one, was the road to the suburbs. Middle-class white families began to flee the city—not only New Orleans but other American cities; Detroit actually had a faster exit rate than New Orleans. They took with them a substantial portion of the white public school population, which had been 57 percent black when school desegregation began in November, 1960, was nearly 70 percent black a decade later, and 86 percent black in 1984. By

1993, the percentage had risen to 92 percent. Four decades after *Brown,* New Orleans's black school population was still attending all-black or virtually all-black schools, and the fleeing whites were sitting in all-white classes in nearby Jefferson and St. Tammany parishes.

What the refugees left behind were the poor, who couldn't afford to move out, and the usual coordinates of poverty: ignorance and unemployment. Drugs, violence, and hopelessness choked the social systems designed to deal with a more economically balanced population and kept the wheel of urban deterioration spinning as it had in Washington, D.C., New York, Detroit, Los Angeles, and other American cities. There were still quiet oases in New Orleans and in the other cities, too, but many of New Orleans's schools, like those in other urban areas across the country, stood on the edges of battlefields, in sight of the chalk outlines of bodies on blood-stained pavements and within earshot of gunfire.

HARRY KELLEHER described as "heartbreaking" the establishment in New Orleans of a "blackboard jungle" complete with "knives, narcotics, angel dust, rapes, assaults on teachers," all accompanied by a "lack of discipline." It was not what he had in mind when he so optimistically addressed the 1,600-plus New Orleanians in January of 1961, signaling the winding down of the school desegregation crisis. By 1993, he had come to believe that the schools had been "better before they were desegregated. . . . There was more discipline" in them then—"by far." He noted that of the 250 or so people employed in his law office—"people of all ages, some of humble origins, some of origins not so humble . . . but from the lowest to the highest, none of them send their children to public schools." He couldn't even estimate how many people in his office were commuting from north of Lake Pontchartrain, a commute that involved a twenty-eight-mile drive across the water morning and night. He knew people who drove in from communities as many as fifty miles upriver.

> Look [he said, his voice rising] your child's your most priceless possession and you know your child has to have a decent education and however committed you are to the concept of equality for all people under the law . . . you're not gonna sacrifice your child's education by sending it to an inferior school where there's no discipline, where your child's physical safety might even be at risk. . . . It's a bleak picture from where I sit.

LLOYD RITTINER ran again for the Orleans Parish school board in 1962. Local segregationists noisily opposed his reelection, as they did

Louis Riecke's the same year. He and Riecke nonetheless won, albeit narrowly. In 1969 he ran for mayor but failed to make the runoff. He returned to the school board where he remained through 1982 when he retired after twenty-five years—the longest tenure in the history of the New Orleans school system. Three years later he retired from his Rittiner Engineering Company, whose fortunes he had revived following its near-bankruptcy during the school crisis.

Was the struggle for the schools worth the personal hardship he had endured?

"Oh, yeah," he said in 1991, his six-foot frame frail and bent now. "It had to be. You can't go through life like Emile Wagner did thinking that the black man's brain is much smaller than the white man's and he shouldn't have the authority to do anything unless he's told to."

Rittiner and his wife visited their retreat in the Colorado mountains for the last time together in the summer of 1991. He died on August 5 in Colorado Springs.

SAM ROSENBERG continued on as lawyer for the Orleans Parish school board until his death in 1993 at the age of seventy-eight.

Was school desegregation worth the struggle for him, too?

"It had to be worth it," he said in 1990, "because it was unconstitutional the way they were doing it. It's unfortunate," he added, "the way it turned out and it may take another whole generation or two to have many of the whites satisfied to send their children to school with blacks." He asked that following his death, memorials be made to Dollars for Scholars in care of the Orleans Parish school board or the Jewish Endowment Foundation.

LOUIS RIECKE resigned from the school board in 1968 after two terms. He thought he had given enough time and wanted to rebuild his business, which had taken a walloping during the school crisis. He had, however, no regrets and "would have done it again." Risley Triche, one of the governor's floor leaders in the state legislature, paid Riecke what Riecke considered the ultimate compliment in a speech to the Young Men's Business Club a couple of years after the crisis ended: "I see Louis Riecke sitting out there in the audience. I want to publicly apologize for the way I treated him when he was a member of the school board. He was right and I was wrong."

MATT SUTHERLAND was less sanguine. "All we did," he said in 1992, "was drive 50 percent of the white population out. All the schools went down and we're practically back where we started." He resigned from the school board in 1966.

TED SHEPARD died in April, 1962, at the age of seventy-one.

Following his resignation from the Orleans Parish school board in

1962, EMILE WAGNER continued on as president of the Hibernia Homestead and Saving Association. As school desegregation died out as a viable political issue, Wagner's voice hushed. He died on May 12, 1971, at the age of sixty.

Long after the bitterness they saw and the hazards they endured while driving little white children to the besieged Frantz School during that turbulent winter of 1960 had faded into reminiscence, women of *SOS* maintained the bonds of comrades-in-arms.

President MARY SAND had moved to the Washington, D.C., area when her husband was transferred there, but she remained a major character in the tales the others recounted thirty years later, as they remained heroines in hers. There was a sadness in her voice when she talked about that time, grief for unfulfilled hopes. "It was worth it in the sense that it had needed to be done," she said, "a step that needed to be taken. I don't know whether we have moved as far as we hoped we would. I think that integration of the schools has been good and that's something . . . but I think that race relations, I'm not sure that we haven't regressed a little. . . . I just feel there's a moving apart." PEG MURISON, ANNE DLUGOS, and BETTY WISDOM, who stayed in New Orleans, remained firm friends.

Dlugos had "to be an optimist," she said, and described small improvements in her office: a black supervisor of a largely white work force, a white manager hosting a prenuptial party for a black employee, neither of which could have happened in the 1950s.

Even in the nineties, Peg Murison couldn't "go by that neighborhood without a little discomfort." As a matter of principle, the Murisons sent their children to the local public schools, and Peg felt the tears roll down her cheeks when she watched her daughter march with the Fortier High School band, desegregated for the first time.

The school crisis marked a "turning point" in Betty Wisdom's life, propelling her into a career of community activism: American Civil Liberties Union; League of Women Voters, where she coached potential black voters through the complexities of a registration system designed to weed them out; Urban League; VISTA. Through SOS, she said, she found her place in the community. Most important,

> It was the right thing to do. How often in life do you get a chance to do something which no matter how difficult you know is right? Not very often.

In 1991, a white-haired ROSA KELLER walked with a decided limp following a stroke but got around efficiently and continued to hold court for curious visitors in her large airy home off St. Charles Avenue. Her long bony hands lying quietly in her lap, she seemed to enjoy reminiscing about the old days when there were "things we couldn't talk about and ... people whom we couldn't associate with," then adding not without considerable pleasure that "now they're approving of the kinds of things we did."

Was it worth it?

"Absolutely."

Had the social fabric changed?

"Not a hell of a lot, but some." Social life remained segregated, but her five grandchildren went to public schools and it wouldn't occur to them to "judge people on skin color.... It's just a way of life to them, and that's from going to school for years with people. That's my hope that it will happen to everybody."

Keller collected honorary degrees and awards from various local institutions over the years since the turbulent sixties. Of all the local institutions that were now "approving of the kinds of things we did" to promote racial equality when it was unpopular, the conversion of the *Times-Picayune,* which was resisting school desegregation even before Paul Trévigne brought his suit against the New Orleans school board in 1877, must have been one of the most satisfying. In 1985, the newspaper's president and publisher Ashton Phelps, Jr., presented Keller with the coveted Loving Cup, which had been awarded to an outstanding New Orleanian every year since 1901:

> She was an integrationist [Phelps commented] before it was fashionable, when it took real courage, when caution was exercised...

Keller wept openly.

DAN BYRD, who'd started it all with his petitions to the school board back in the 1940s, believed the struggle for desegregated schools as part of the larger civil rights struggle had moved local blacks to "get full freedom," and he would "do it again" if he had to. He continued on as field secretary for the NAACP until 1978. He died in New Orleans in 1984 at the age of seventy-four.

A. P. TUREAUD died of cancer on January 22, 1972, as full of honors as he was of years. He was showered with academic tributes, had local streets and buildings, including one at LSU, named for him, and his obituary appeared on the front page of the *Times-Picayune,* which, if the paper had printed it at all a decade before, would have been buried on the back pages. There was even an editorial noting that "Mr. Tureaud was a citizen of a high order."

Tureaud had grown up in the aftermath of *Plessy* v. *Ferguson,* subject to all the social, economic, and political discriminations visited upon African-Americans during the first half of the twentieth century. He and his family had known the humiliations of the back of the bus, the top balcony at the movies, rejection at hotels and restaurants, and, worst of all, the inequities of separate education and exclusion from the political process. Thanks to his efforts, his grandchildren looked out on a very different landscape. Louisiana office seekers could no longer disregard African-American voters, and by 1972, an increasing number of those office seekers were themselves African-American. The school board could no longer thumb its nose at petitions from African-Americans. Buses, parks, playgrounds, restaurants, and other public places had been largely desegregated. Before Tureaud died in 1972, Ralph Ellison's "invisible man" had become very much visible.

Through it all, Tureaud had never been tempted to alter his approach, even as the times changed and confrontation became a popular strategy for securing racial justice. The law, despite its sluggishness, its complexities, and what often may have seemed its exclusiveness, remained for Tureaud the preferred route to equality and the first-class citizenship his hero, Rodolphe Desdunes, had so yearned for. He explained in a late-in-life interview:

> I'm more in favor of that than all this damn stuff they are carrying on in the streets. I never had to participate in one single demonstration and I've gotten all these things. All the schools that are desegregated now came as the result of litigation, not . . . demonstrations. Demonstrations haven't desegregated anything but lunch counters and we had to make it possible for them to carry those on. . . . We had to defend them in the courts.

Archbishop Philip M. Hannan, one of the celebrants at the requiem mass for Tureaud, caught the social engineer in the lawyer and emphasized it in his eulogy, fitting last words for the black Creole heir to Rodolphe Desdunes's legacy of activism:

> He knew that to defend the rights of his black fellow man was to defend the rights of every man. . . . He made his legal triumphs a victory for all society. . . . There were no vanquished—all were victors in the cause of human rights.

After temporarily desegregating then being forced to leave LSU's undergraduate college, A. P. Tureaud, Jr., earned his B.A. at Xavier University in New Orleans. Feeling a need to prove himself in competition with white students, he went north to Columbia University in New York City for his M.A. Except for one brief stint as a public school teacher in New Orleans and visits to his family afterward, he left the South, where he felt "stifled," forever. In 1960 he joined the White Plains, New York, Department of Education where he became director of special education, working largely on programs for handicapped children—"another form of civil rights," as he put it. He and his wife, another Louisiana expatriate, bought a house in a largely white section of South Salem, New York. They never had to send their two sons to racially segregated schools, they never had to "hide the brown kids" when they pulled up to a motel, and they were never relegated to the top balcony at the movies.

RUBY BRIDGES finished elementary school at Frantz. When McDonogh 19 was reclassified as an all-black school, Gail Etienne, Tessie Prevost, and Leona Tate, at the insistence of their parents and A. P. Tureaud, were transferred to T. J. Semmes, another formerly all-white school.

No boycotts attended their entrance into Semmes, but their years there were checkered with incidents, as they continued on the cutting edge of desegregation. Recesses were nightmares, scenes of frequent physical fights, and the black girls took to crouching under an overhanging tree branch to protect themselves. Prevost accused a fifth-grade teacher of holding her nose whenever the black children passed her in the hall. Etienne's parents complained to the superintendent of schools that white children were spitting on her and calling her names. Tate's mother wrote that teachers called her daughter "nigger." Their trials continued through high school, white students heckling them, singling them out as "the ones who started it all."

Prevost periodically asked her parents, "What did we do?" They tried to reassure her, noting that the white children were less at fault than their parents who'd put them up to it, but the black girl "got tired of it."

> I just didn't want to do it anymore. My stomach would start getting messed up while I was at Semmes.

Then her mother would patiently explain that Tessie wasn't doing this for herself but for other little black children who, because of Tessie's perseverance, would "be able to go to any school they want to." And Tessie would once again dig in her heels and "kind of put up with it."

All four of them graduated from high school in 1972. Etienne took secretarial courses at Southern University. Prevost, hoping to be a teacher, started at the University of Southwestern Louisiana in Lafayette.

I thought things had changed [she reminisced] but when I got to Lafayette, people were calling me nigger again.... Finally I didn't want to be a teacher anymore; I just came home.

She became a typist in the city's Department of Streets. Tate married and produced three children.

Bridges also married and produced four sons. In the 1990s, the family was living in a comfortable middle-class largely black development in New Orleans East. As she neared her forties, she seemed restless. She'd held a variety of jobs since her high school graduation but none particularly satisfying. Over the years she'd frequently asked herself why when she recalled her role in the school desegregation, and, being a religious woman, she had concluded the episode had been a necessary part of the larger plan for her life. Specifically, she decided, she had been meant for a career working with children, not perhaps unlike that of psychiatrist Coles who'd worked so closely and painstakingly with her during the hard times of her childhood.

In late 1992, a younger brother was killed in a drug-related shooting outside his apartment in a Ninth Ward housing project. He left four children, and as Ruby pitched in to help with their care following his death, she began to look more deeply into the problems of the Ninth Ward's children, of which she herself had been one all those years ago.

She dreamed up a profession for herself that she called parenting. She began volunteering at New Orleans's less affluent schools, talking with parents in seminarlike settings, the general purpose to get them involved in their children's education but often extending its reach to deal with the myriad difficulties of poverty and alienation that had come to affect much of urban America. On the advice of Coles, she established a nonprofit foundation to fund her enterprise.

In 1995, she installed herself and her program at the Frantz School, which she had desegregated singlehandedly thirty-five years before. That September Connecticut College at New London awarded both Coles and Bridges honorary degrees. At last, she said, her joy apparent in her voice as she looked at the calling she'd created for herself, she saw the "pieces of the puzzle falling together."

From the perspective of adulthood, Tessie Prevost could look back and say her personal trials at McDonogh 19 and Semmes were "worth it." Gail Etienne was less sure. Her mother, Eula, volunteered, "We don't talk about it—we just don't. But sometimes you can't help thinking about those days. The thinking isn't over yet. I wonder if it ever will be."

Ruby Bridges's feelings were ambiguous. On the one hand she was "proud" to be a part of the racial desegregation of her city. On the other hand, she felt the NAACP knew what was going to happen and failed to warn the participants. She had a lingering feeling of being used. "After that they never even looked at us. They never even cared if we finished school," and she retained "such a bitter taste" in her mouth that before allowing her own children to participate in such a program, she "would ask many questions that my parents didn't."

Her mother, Lucille Bridges, the sharecroppers' daughter from Mississippi and in 1993 the grandmother to twenty-five, said that if she "had to do it all over again," she would. "By raisin' up in the country," she added, "I was kinda hard, a hard person, hard for you to cry. I can stand a lot of things." She would give her "last penny" toward her grandchildren's education, to see them "do something for themselves."

If Leona Tate's mother, Louise Tate, had another child, she, too, would "do it all over again. We pay taxes, too," she added. "They couldn't keep us out."

All four appeared to have emerged from their experiences relatively undamaged. Etienne explained: "I think because we were so young we didn't develop a hatred and hostility against whites that older black kids going through desegregation did."

Coles had gone to New Orleans during the years of crisis expecting to find the children "developing reactions to constant threats and isolation and the struggle of meeting the social and academic challenge of the switch from Negro to white schools." Instead, he found they "had already developed ways to deal with these hurts. What I considered a stress was exactly the opposite and a challenge to them." He added:

> We tend to put a cellophane bag around kids—to be protective. What the experience with desegregation shows is that stress can be a positive thing—a creative thing.

He compared the southern children he'd studied with the children of wartime, noting that the experiences of desegregation, like those of bombings, rarely scarred children who came from a stable home with their mental and physical health intact. And he looked at the overall experience as one to provoke the reexamination of racial stereotypes transmitted by an older generation. White children sitting in classrooms with black children were forced to question the cliché of black intellectual inferiority, and black children, despite "moments of pain and anguish," were forced to challenge their parents' nostrums regarding the fear and distrust of whites inherent in the old segregation laws.

On April 18, 1984, the "New Orleans Four" and their parents were brought together with local city officials, educators, and civil rights leaders. The mayor presented the young women with certificates and they were hailed for their "extraordinary faith and courage in pursuit of equal education for all." A little child, her age in 1984 perhaps that of the "Four" in 1960, asked

What *was* segregation, anyway?

In 1968, Mack J. Spears became the first black elected to the Orleans Parish school board. In 1985, Everett J. Williams, who'd joined the local school system as a teacher in 1957 and had come up through the ranks, became the first black superintendent of the New Orleans schools since Reconstruction. He had fought the same battles New Orleans's youngsters who were on the cutting edge of desegregation fought, cringed inwardly when white colleagues looked him in the eye but refused to say "Good morning," made do with swallowing hard and gently correcting him when a colleague continued to call him a "nigra."

After he left the White House, PRESIDENT EISENHOWER wrote his memoirs. In *Mandate for Change,* his second volume, he discussed the Supreme Court and its ruling in *Brown:*

Although, as President, I never expressed either approbation or disapproval of a Court decision, in this instance there can be no question that the judgment of the Court was right.

In 1962, the political complexion of New Orleans, although slowly changing, thanks to congressional enactments, federal court rulings, and U.S. Supreme Court decisions of the previous two decades, had not yet altered enough to influence the outcome of New Orleans elections. Blacks constituted only about 15 percent of the voters in 1962, and MAYOR SCHIRO could still beat ADRIAN DUPLANTIER for the city's top office by resurrecting the state senator's opposition to the segregationists in the state legislature during the New Orleans school crisis. Schiro's charge that Duplantier was "soft on segregation" could still win elections. Governor Davis, who'd let it be known he wanted Duplantier defeated at all cost, showed up at Schiro's campaign headquarters on election night to congratulate him. Later Davis parceled out state jobs to the mayor's political supporters.

Schiro served two full terms as mayor, all that was allowed him by the City Charter, then in 1970 went back to selling insurance at his old company. He worked there steadily until 1988 when he suffered a stroke. He remained in poor health and died August 29, 1992.

Duplantier left the state senate to sit on the civil district court in New Orleans. In 1978, President Jimmy Carter appointed him to the Federal District Court for the Eastern District of Louisiana.

Constitutionally prohibited from succeeding himself, Jimmie Davis left the governor's office in 1964 with a song to the legislature and a television address to the state:

> Today, looking back, I believe the record will show that we did what had to be done, and it was done within the framework of law and order. We closed no schools. We lost no lives. We shed no blood. Let those who would find fault with our efforts compare them with some of our sister states.

He entered the governor's race for the last time in 1971, won only a humiliating 12 percent of the vote in the first primary, and retired to do what he loved best: sing country and gospel music. In 1991, when he was either 89, 90, or 91, depending upon which birthdate he was using that year, he was still performing on a circuit that ranged from Louisiana to New York. In 1994, he celebrated what he claimed was his ninety-fifth birthday with a $100-per-ticket concert at LSU, forty-five minutes of gospel, country, and a rousing rendition of "You Are My Sunshine," in which the assembled crowd joined him enthusiastically.

CHEP MORRISON left the Kennedy administration in 1963 to make his third assault on the governor's office. Campaigning—again—for economic and educational progress, he won the first primary, defeating SHELBY JACKSON, who was backed by the state's Citizens' Councils, former governor Bob Kennon, Congressman Gillis Long, and John McKeithen, Louisiana public service commissioner and former member of the state legislature.

Ernest J. Wright, a black labor leader from New Orleans, ran for lieutenant governor. Five blacks sought seats in the state legislature, and fifteen blacks sought places on the State Democratic Committee. It was too early, and they all lost, but it sent a signal through Louisiana politics that the times were beginning to change.

Racial rhetoric was muted. McKeithen came in second, but neither Morrison nor McKeithen won a majority, and a runoff was required. Adopting the strategy that had won the election for Jimmie Davis against Morrison in 1960, McKeithen became an instant political racist:

> You and I don't want a man like DeLesseps Morrison who would probably entertain Lena Horne in our governor's mansion

alternated with

Chep Morrison & the NAACP—or John McKeithen. It is up to you!

Citing primary returns, McKeithen demonstrated how Morrison had corralled the "Negro bloc vote."

Outsegged again, Morrison lost again. On his return from a vacation in Mexico, he joined a New Orleans bank. On another trip to Mexico the next year, the plane in which he and his young son were passengers crashed into a mountain. There were no survivors.

Shelby Jackson had come in fifth of five in the first primary of 1963. McKeithen gave him a state job. He died in 1972.

In 1965, the political action committee of the New Orleans NAACP branch opened a voter registration drive which that year alone increased the number of black voters by more than ten thousand. Committee Chairman WILFRED AUBERT, the same Wilfred Aubert who'd sued the Orleans Parish school board in 1948 for equal facilities in the city's black schools, believed his committee's success was due largely to the efforts of his army of young volunteers who "bird-dogged" residents (literally went into their homes and dispatched them to the registrar's office) to the encouragement offered by congressional passage of the Voting Rights Act of 1965, and to "the desire of the Negro to vote out of office the reactionary politicians who were opposed to the civil rights program."

By the time the mayoral election of 1969 rolled around, the black vote was large enough to influence it. MOON LANDRIEU had been warned that his opposition to the segregationist statutes that were speeded through the state legislature during the school crisis was political suicide; it turned out to be the politically shrewdest thing he ever did. He went from the state house of representatives to the New Orleans City Council where he again demonstrated his sensitivity to blacks' feelings when he supported the removal of the Confederate flag from the council chamber and pushed through an ordnance establishing the biracial human relations committee Mayor Morrison had promised A. L. Davis, then reneged on. Landrieu's reward was a whopping 99 percent of the black vote when he ran for mayor in 1969 on promises to pass a measure requiring open public accommodations and appointment of blacks to important positions in city government. That, combined with 40 percent of the white vote, gave Landrieu a big victory.

He kept his promises, facilitating the racial desegregation of business and professional organizations, wangled federal funds for the rehabilitation of black and other downtown neighborhoods, and assisted minority businesses. When he took office, he noted later, there was not a black "above the broom-and-mop level" in city hall. When he left eight years later, the chief administrative officer in New Orleans, among other upper-echelon officials, was black. He had tried, he said, "to put this issue behind us once and for all." New Orleans "had suffered too long."

After he left the mayor's office in 1978, Landrieu was appointed Secretary of the Department of Housing and Urban Development by President Jimmy Carter. In 1984, still stagestruck, he thought about running for president, fulfilling the youthful ambition that still nagged, but abandoned the idea. In 1992, he ran his first political race since leaving the mayor's office, was elected with 80 percent of the vote to the Court of Appeals for the state's Fourth Circuit.

Moon Landrieu was New Orleans's last white mayor. It was he who "broke the ice," prepared the political soil for the transition from patronized to patron, ruled to ruler. In 1978, the black Creole Ernest Nathan ("Dutch") Morial, heir, like his former law partner A. P. Tureaud, to the *"liberté, égalité, fraternité"* traditions of Rodolphe Desdunes, took the oath of office as New Orleans's first black mayor.

Born in 1929 in the black Creole community of the city's Seventh Ward, Morial, like Tureaud, was light-skinned enough to pass for white but from the beginning, also like Tureaud, thought and lived black. He had joined Tureaud's legal briefs supporting civil rights suits, including the Bush suit, but his preferred metier was local politics, not the courtroom. He counseled the Dryades sit-ins and the lunch counter sit-ins and was elected president of the local NAACP branch in 1963.

Morial had gone on to a long series of firsts: black assistant city attorney (1965), black state legislator since Reconstruction (1967), black juvenile court judge (1970), state Court of Appeals for the Fourth Circuit judge (1974), and then New Orleans's black mayor.

During his two terms as mayor, he tried to bring the races together, striving for an open and racially unified city in the black Creole tradition of Trévigne, Desdunes, and Tureaud. But his attempts to guide the racially divided city toward a mutually prosperous economy and ecumenical politics alienated both black and white power brokers. University of New Orleans historian Arnold R. Hirsch described him as

> less the city's first black mayor than he was probably the last of the radical creoles.

Morial died in 1989. He was succeeded by Sidney Barthelemy, also black, who served two terms. In 1994, Morial's son Marc, a state legislator, took the oath of office as New Orleans's third black mayor. One old black voter ventured the hope that the younger Morial would be a "chip off the old block."

In 1962, the legislature's joint committee on segregation had urged the use of "state authority to drive out every Negro from our white public schools and to restore educational opportunities to your white youth in our state public school system in New Orleans." In 1972, Risley Triche, one of Governor Davis's segregation stalwarts in the legislature who'd retired in 1968, was back, floor leader now for Governor Edwin W. Edwards's program to "open wide the doors of opportunity" to the poor, the elderly, and the unemployed, but especially to the "thousands of black Louisianans who have not enjoyed the full bounty of the American dream." Triche had been driven back, he said, because he

> did not want to leave my children with the legacy that their daddy was a bigot and a racist . . . I am not a bigot and a racist. I want . . . the citizenry of the state to grow out of racism and bigotry.

That very session the lawmakers repealed all the old Jim Crow laws and deleted almost all references to race and color in them. No one in the chamber gave a single racist speech against the move.

In 1967, Dutch Morial had been the first black elected to the state-house in the modern era. In 1974, there were eight blacks there.

After his defeat in the gubernatorial election of 1959–60, the feisty former state senator WILLIE RAINACH retired to his farm in northern Louisiana where he had large timber and land holdings and ran a butane business. In an interview in 1977, he indicated he had changed his mind about nothing and would have done nothing differently. He believed that "if you eliminate the militant Negro factor, we would have no problem with them." He believed he might have changed the course of race history nationally had he won the 1960 gubernatorial election in Louisiana:

> [I]t's possible in the Democratic National Convention of 1960, we could have worked out, under my leadership . . . a platform which would have brought us a change in national policy that might well have averted the whole civil rights revolution.

Four months after Rainach gave that interview, he shot himself in the head with his .38-caliber pistol. He was sixty-four.

JACK GREMILLION was reelected attorney general twice following the New Orleans school crisis. He ran again in 1972, although he'd already been convicted of perjury for lying to a federal grand jury about his financial connections and sentenced to three years in prison. Soundly defeated for reelection, he was whisked off to the federal prison at Eglin Air Force Base at Fort Washington, Florida. He served fifteen months, was paroled in April, 1974, and returned to Baton Rouge where he opened a law office. In 1991, he was still in touch with his old political cronies, including former governor Davis, and he still clung to his earlier position on the rights of the states to tend to their own affairs without federal intervention. The civil rights struggle, he charged,

> knocked out the amendment to the Constitution completely—the Tenth Amendment which says that all things not specifically granted to the federal government are reserved to the states. That's shot! That's archaic now! That's gone!

Neither advancing age nor excommunication from his church diminished LEANDER PEREZ's capacity for outrage at the forward march of racial desegregation or what he never stopped believing was a Communist conspiracy to take over the world. His immediate public reaction to the church's condemnation elicited from him his usual bravado:

> I am a lifelong Catholic and will continue to be so, regardless of Communist infiltration and the influence of the National Council of Christians and Jews upon our church leadership.

And he continued to attend services, even receive Communion by visiting churches where he was not known.

In 1963, he protested integration of the American military by persuading the Plaquemines Parish council to declare all bars and lounges off limits to personnel from the naval air station at Belle Chasse. The following year he got the council to renovate and electrify the fence around snake-and-mosquito-infested Fort St. Philip, built in the Mississippi marshes by the French in 1724. He wanted to use it as a prison for "racial agitators" who might mistakenly consider desegregating anything within his domain. He called it "preventive medicine."

In 1965, Perez appeared before the Senate Judiciary Committee to protest the voting rights act under consideration. He himself had Plaquemines Parish under control. His nephew the registrar kept no regular hours and simply slipped out the back door of the courthouse when blacks or unsympathetic white voters approached.

On January 10, 1969, Perez suffered a heart attack and died two months later. Following his wife's death two years before, he had effected a reconciliation with his church, and his funeral at Holy Name of Jesus Church on the campus of Loyola University drew one thousand mourners, including a teary George Wallace, Senators Eastland and Ellender, Mayor Schiro, Governor McKeithen, and a delegation of children from the Prytania private school carrying a heart-shaped spray of red and white carnations. Perez's was "the largest wake I have seen in my thirty-three years here," said a spokesman for Bultman Funeral Home.

Perez did not die politically intestate. Even as he was overseeing the rehabilitation of Fort St. Philip, New Orleans high school freshman David Ernest Duke, assigned to write a term paper arguing against racial integration, was spending his afterschool hours collecting material for it at the offices of the local Citizens' Council. He grew up to be a Nazi sympathizer, grand wizard of the Ku Klux Klan, and a founder of the National Association for the Advancement of White People.

Then in the 1980s he set about reinventing himself, discarding the veneer of the extremist, figuratively burning his white robe and brown shirt, changing into a three-piece suit, and in general getting himself up in the clean-cut garb of mainstream American politics. He toned down the most vicious racism for which he had become known and explained away his extremist past as the excesses of youth. He cloaked his messages of hate in the euphemisms of antiwelfare, antiaffirmative action, and anticrime rhetoric, a technique Republican presidential candidate Ronald Reagan had legitimized with his talk about states' rights and welfare queens, and his successor, George Bush, had seized on, using "quotas" as his one-word argument against affirmative action programs and Willie Horton, an escaped black convict who raped a white woman while at large, as his symbol for crime in the streets. No one misunderstood the code words, which appealed to many late-twentieth-century white people, particularly blue-collar families, who worried so much about what they might be forced to share with blacks.

In 1989, Duke ran for the state legislature from the virtually all-white New Orleans suburb of Metairie and won. The following year he took on incumbent U.S. Senator J. Bennett Johnston. Winning only 44 percent of the total vote, thanks to a heavy black turnout, Duke lost, but his share of the white vote topped 60 percent, and he was encouraged to go on.

In 1991, he ran for governor against former governor Edwin Edwards, once again pandering to white fears of a "rising massive underclass." Edwards won in a landslide, again thanks to a heavy black turnout. Duke won only 39 percent of the statewide vote this time, but 55 percent of the white vote.

Louisiana senator John B. Breaux at a postelection news conference noted that Duke had tapped into real uncertainties, dissatisfactions, and fears that disturbed a large section of the electorate and that must be addressed, although not in the style of David Duke:

[I]t's important that we enter this debate, because if we don't enter it, David Duke has the stage to himself.

As if to confirm Breaux's apprehensions, Thom Robb, grand wizard of Duke's old Klan, described a training center the organization was building in the Ozarks for whites aspiring to political office.

Louisiana has one David Duke [Robb added]. We plan to give America a thousand of them.

Three decades after D-Day, New Orleans appeared on the surface as racially integrated as any northern or western city. Its population of 496,938 was nearly three-quarters black. In July, 1983, the NAACP had held its annual convention at the posh new Rivergate Convention Center.

The forty-room motel that poultry farmer Ellis Marsalis, father of the musicians Wynton, Branford, and Ellis, Jr., had made out of his chicken barn in 1943 to house blacks unable to stay in the city's whites-only hotels had fallen into disrepair since passage of the Civil Rights Act of 1964 and the opening of public accommodations on a nondiscriminatory basis. In the 1990s, a mixed clientele in local restaurants, jazz emporiums, department stores, and hotels was taken for granted. The only colors that mattered at a Saints game at the Superdome on Sunday afternoons were the team's colors, black and gold. The cover of the Greater New Orleans telephone book for 1989–90 featured a racially mixed group of graduates posed in front of a southern colonial-style schoolhouse. The caption read: "Education—the Key to a Better Tomorrow."

All was not, however, so serene as it looked. Despite his losses, David Duke seemed to have exacerbated what kept the races apart, had kept them apart for all the years they had lived together in New Orleans, coexisting like oil and water.

During that same summer and the autumn following, the *Times-Picayune* published a long series of articles on local race relations that outlined two and one-half centuries of black and white coexistence in the city, the good times and the bad times, too. The editors called the series, appropriately, "Together Apart," and invited readers' comments, which they received by the hundreds, printing as many as space permitted. It was clear from these letters that real racial harmony, the sort that Rodolphe Desdunes and A. P. Tureaud and Ernest Morial had striven for, remained a goal for the future.

Mardi Gras, so long the white man's domain—except for the Zulu parade—had desegregated, but only under duress. On the grounds that the city's cost of $3.5 million for trash cleanup and extra police protection made the festivities a public function, black City Councilwoman Dorothy Mae Taylor introduced in 1991 an ordinance that would deny city services and parade permits to Carnival organizations that discriminated on the basis of race, gender, sexual orientation, national origin, ancestry, age, physical condition, or disability.

Over the previous decade or so, Mardi Gras had been slowly democratized, a few of the old krewes quietly liberalizing their membership to include a few token Jews and other formerly less welcome groups, although blacks remained personae non gratae. At the same time, however, new krewes had formed: women's krewes, men's krewes, men's and women's krewes, gay krewes, and Native American krewes. Some, although not all, began to admit blacks. One krewe member attributed the voluntary "opening up" of the membership partly to the economy— "krewes need members" who pay dues and spend money on costumes and such—and partly to a "natural and normal" trend following the fuller desegregation of the city. The proposal to put the trend on the law books only jumped the gun.

The reaction offered still another opportunity to bring racial animosities to the surface. Acrimony within the city council itself caused tempers to flare. Council member Jackie Clarkson predicted such an ordinance would "kill Mardi Gras."

Nine out of ten letters to the *Times-Picayune* criticized the proposal. The editors themselves called it a "grenade," adding that Carnival's "flaws need to be remedied, but we should not kill Carnival to save it." A poll taken shortly afterward showed that 60 percent of those queried—of whom three-quarters were white—opposed the ordinance. A float builder for an all-male krewe declared he was all for racial integration, but his krewe drew the line at women. "We don't want 'em, pure and simple." He liked the idea of "just a bunch of guys getting together and raising hell" and leaving the women to "pay serious attention to costumes, frills, froufrou, and sequins."

The school crisis of 1960–61 having taught the community how a political problem can drag that community to the brink of disaster, economic and social, leaders of the krewe of Rex stepped up to the challenge with soothing words to quiet the angry rhetoric. A group of business leaders agreed to form a biracial coalition to work on the city's racial problems. Soon churches were shepherding their congregations into discussions about what divided the races in New Orleans.

The krewes of Comus and Momus, whose membership was so exclusive that they kept it a closely guarded secret, had traditionally confined their membership to whites of Anglo-Saxon, Anglo-French, and

Anglo-Spanish origins, excluding not only blacks, Jews, women, and Italians, but also working-class whites of all groups. The oldest and most prestigious, these krewes had threatened to withdraw from Carnival altogether if the ordinance passed, and when it did, they did, although they continued to hold their balls.

The ordinance did not kill Carnival. The festival atmosphere continued unabated despite subterranean rumbles. The cash registers in the hotels and restaurants still rang happily, the streets filled to overflowing, and the beads and trinkets flew from the floats as usual.

There were New Orleanians who felt Carnival's expression of native ethnic culture ought to be beyond the reach of government. There were others who saw Mardi Gras's desegregation as the inevitable culmination of a process that had begun with the schools three decades before.

HERBERT CHRISTENBERRY continued on as chief judge for the federal district court in the Eastern District of Louisiana. He attracted national attention in 1965 when he cited police in Bogalusa for contempt of court because they had looked the other way while whites beat local civil rights marchers. "I'm not a swinging liberal," said this veteran of more civil rights cases than he could remember over the two decades since he'd joined fellow judges Wright and Borah in the order to desegregate LSU Law School, "but you should do everything under the law to guarantee the constitutional rights of Negroes."

A decade later, one of his last judicial acts was to set in motion the process of removing *Bush* v. *Orleans Parish School Board* from his court's docket. On his way to a judicial conference in October, 1975, he was stricken with a heart attack and died. Two years later, his successor, having heard no objections from either plaintiff or defendant, dismissed the case. It had consumed a quarter of a century. Its dismissal came a full hundred years after Paul Trévigne filed the first school desegregation suit against the city.

In 1969, it was suggested that President Richard M. Nixon appoint JOHN MINOR WISDOM, still a card-carrying Republican although long removed from politics, to the U.S. Supreme Court, but Attorney General John N. Mitchell objected strenuously:

He's a damned left-winger. He'd be as bad as Earl Warren.

In addition to his service with Wright and Christenberry on the special three-judge courts that forced New Orleans's and Louisiana's schoolhouse doors opened to blacks, Wisdom, along with his fellow Fifth Circuit judges for whom he frequently did the writing, forced open jury boxes, voter registration offices, and public accommodations that had eluded civil rights legislation. By the 1990s he and his wife, Bonnie, had moved out of the big house on First Street and into a smaller one a few streets away. He had a plastic knee and walked with a cane now, but the bright blue eyes still twinkled, and a smile creased his leathery old face as he showed off to what he liked to describe as the "red-neck" visitors to his chambers his father's diploma from Washington and Lee, signed by Robert E. Lee, president. In 1994, the old more-or-less Italian Renaissance Fifth Circuit headquarters on lower Camp Street was named the John Minor Wisdom Building.

In December of 1993, President Bill Clinton had awarded Wisdom the Presidential Medal of Freedom. Helen Wright happened to attend the White House ceremony as the guest of another honoree. Wisdom leaned over and whispered to her:

Skelly should have been here.

The U.S. Court of Appeals for the District of Columbia, abbreviated locally as the "D.C. Circuit," which SKELLY WRIGHT had joined in April of 1962, was one of the busiest courts in America. Until 1971 when Congress redesigned the entire District of Columbia court system, the D.C. Circuit served as the highest appellate court for the citizens of the federal enclave who had automobile accidents, sued their neighbors, got divorces, and committed crimes in roughly the same numbers as did the residents of other American cities. In addition, the court functioned as the home court for the federal government, the tribunal where suits by and against the regulatory agencies and other executive departments were argued and decided. It was often referred to in legal circles as the "second [to the U.S. Supreme Court] most important court." Thanks at least in part to its high visibility, two of its former members, Wiley B. Rutledge and Fred M. Vinson, had gone on to the Supreme Court.

When Wright arrived, the court was divided into two ideologically opposed blocs, their public brawling a fact of Washington legal life since the mid-fifties, their acrimony, which was rumored to have spilled over into personal relationships, apparent in the frequency of their dissents and passion of their opinions.

One bloc, led by David L. Bazelon, the court's first Jewish judge, appointed in 1949, in general followed the example set by the contemporary Supreme Court still led by Earl Warren in 1962, and, since its revolutionary decision in *Brown,* an increasingly vigorous agent for social and political change as well as a staunch supporter of individuals' civil rights and civil liberties. The other bloc, led by Warren E. Burger, stood for custom, tradition, the status quo and was characterized by its deference to governmental authority and the interests of society.

Wright eagerly joined Bazelon's bloc, assuring it of a majority. Then beginning in 1969 with Warren Burger's elevation to the high bench, all federal court appointments became more conservative. The old activist bloc on the D.C. Circuit fell apart, and Wright found himself more and more in the minority.

He grew to his full height as a judge during the quarter century he served on this court. He began writing from the gut as well as the cerebellum. He seemed less fearful of passion now, and his well-known detachment fell away when he felt strongly about an issue. His opinions grew in length and eloquence as he elaborated on some injustice he saw.

He upheld the First Amendment rights of Vietnam War protesters against government suppression, he consistently fought government personnel policies that discriminated against homosexual employees, and, despite his record as a tough federal attorney during his early years in New Orleans, he also consistently defended the constitutional rights of those charged with crimes. Continuing in the course he had set so resolutely back in New Orleans, he never hesitated to decide against racial discrimination.

By the time he got to Washington, the civil rights struggle had become a personal as well as a professional crusade for him. On a hot mid-August day in 1963, he went with his law clerk and his colleague, Judge Bazelon, to hear Martin Luther King, Jr., speak at the Washington Monument of his "dream" for America, and when five years later King was shot down on the balcony of a Memphis motel, Wright once again spoke out to chastise all those who had stood by and watched the "internal disintegration of this country." Later, he would weep unashamedly on hearing King's words reproduced on his record player.

After 1971, when Congress divested the appellate court of responsibility for strictly District of Columbia matters, and its docket increasingly consisted of challenges to lower court decisions made in connection with government departments, Wright continued to support the claims of the disaffected, from environmentalists attempting to hold the federal government to the provisions of the National Environmental Policy Act to individuals and institutions fighting for free speech against encroachment by the Federal Communications Commission.

It was an often difficult standard he strove for: to keep the scales of justice balanced, his heart and mind in sync, his compassion for the slum tenant victimized by a landlord or a consumer bilked by an "unconscionable" contract from outweighing his profound regard for the integrity of the law. Two decades after he arrived in Washington, he explained:

I want to do what's right. When I get a case, I look at it and the first thing I think of automatically is what's right, what should be done—and then you look at the law to see whether or not you can do it. That might invert the process of how you should arrive at a decision ... but in my case it developed through making decisions, which involves solving problems. . . . I am less patient than other judges with law that won't permit what I conceive to be fair. Now there's a legitimate criticism of that, because what's fair and just to X may not be fair and just to Y—in perfect good faith on both sides. But if you don't take it to extremes, I think that it's good to come out with a fair and just result and then to look for law to support it.

David Bazelon stepped down as chief judge in 1978, and Wright, next in seniority, succeeded him. On reaching age seventy in 1981, Wright relinquished his post as chief judge but continued to sit on cases. His work had begun to be recognized in academe, and he collected an armload of honorary degrees.

At some point in the early 1980s, he began to lose his car keys a little more often, then his route to National Airport or the State Department. After a period during which Helen's fears of bad news allowed her to deny her husband's deteriorating condition, doctors decided he had Alzheimer's, and in 1986, at the age of seventy-five, he resigned from the D.C. Circuit. He never wrote the autobiography he had outlined.

In the spring of 1986 he was able to join the court at its annual conference in Hot Springs, Virginia. He wasn't up to his eloquent best that day, a few words thanking his former colleagues who had just passed a resolution expressing their "admiration and respect" for him, some random thoughts on his experiences as a judge.

But he could still pull himself together enough to read the words that had guided him through more than four decades of public service. The war, a long-ago Christmas party for the blind, Willie Francis, Ruby Bridges, Martin Luther King—all of them had a place between the lines his old friend and hero Hugo Black, dead these fifteen years, had written in 1940 during the darkest days of World War II. Wright had read the same lines at the dinner in 1964 marking the twenty-fifth anniversary of Black's appointment to the Supreme Court:

Under our constitutional system, courts stand against any winds that blow as havens of refuge for those who might otherwise suffer because they are helpless, weak, out-numbered, or because they are non-conforming victims of prejudice and public excitement. . . . No higher duty, no more solemn responsibility, rests upon this Court, than that of translating into living law and maintaining this constitutional shield deliberately planned and inscribed for the benefit of every human being subject to our Constitution—of whatever race, creed or persuasion.

Wright died of prostate cancer at his home just outside Washington on August 6, 1988. He was seventy-seven.

Hugo Black had written those soaring lines into his Court's order to reverse the murder conviction, obtained on the basis of a forced confession, of Izell Chambers, one of THURGOOD MARSHALL's first Inc. Fund clients in 1940. By the time Marshall died in 1993, thanks to his own and his Inc. Fund warriors' efforts, among others', the American criminal justice system had changed so profoundly that the kind of police work that convicted Chambers was considerably less likely to happen. When it did, it was the exception. In 1940, it was the rule.

Marshall had seen his early championship in the courts of blacks' voting rights culminate in the enfranchisement of thousands upon thousands of black voters. On the fortieth anniversary of *Brown,* Marshall's biggest case, President Bill Clinton told students at Martin Luther King, Jr., Middle School in Beltsville, Maryland, not far from Baltimore where Marshall had grown up in a community of unenfranchised blacks, that he owed his election to the nation's highest office to the support of minority voters.

Progress in the desegregation of America's schools was less impressive. Marshall's euphoria of May, 1954, his conviction that equality in education was just around the corner had seemed justified at the time but was in fact short-lived. Forty Septembers in procession having passed after *Brown,* although desegregated schools were a fact of life in many places, demographics had resisted every imagined plan to achieve racial balance. Busing, "magnet" inner-city schools designed to draw white students, consolidations and closings—none of them had worked; 66 percent of the nationwide black school population remained in predominantly black schools and 66 percent of the white enrollment attended virtually all-white schools.

In Topeka, Kansas, hometown of LINDA BROWN (Linda Brown Thompson now, divorced mother of two), whose name the lead desegregation suit of 1954 carried, court battles over the numbers were continuing forty years later. Schools segregated by law in the early 1950s had been resegregated by city housing patterns by the 1990s. In 1978, the American Civil Liberties Union at the request of a group of black parents, including Thompson, reopened the *Brown* suit, arguing that the city's thirteen racially segregated schools violated *Brown.* After fifteen years of courtroom skirmishing, a lower federal court agreed, and in 1993 the city set about on a desegregation program. School Superintendent Jeffrey M. Weaver was immediately barraged with abusive letters and telephone calls.

In 1988, Thompson created, along with other members of her family, the Brown Foundation, a memorial to all the plaintiffs in the original public school desegregation suit. It raised money for scholarships and designed a multicultural curriculum for public schools. In 1994, on the fortieth anniversary of *Brown,* she sounded weary after the years of struggle:

> It's disheartening that we are still fighting. But we are dealing with human beings. As long as we are, there will always be those who feel the races should be separate.

The Supreme Court was no help now. The justices appointed to succeed those on the Warren Court who'd joined *Brown,* the last of whom, William O. Douglas, left in 1975, proved to be less sympathetic to *Brown*'s aims. Jurisprudentially, in matters of race, the 1980s and 1990s could almost have passed for the 1880s and 1890s. Joseph Bradley and Henry Billings Brown could have been sitting in their old seats.

Marshall himself was a member of the Court by then—he was appointed in 1967—but could make his voice heard only in dissent as the Court majority squelched plan after plan for school desegregation or allowed recalcitrant school boards to wriggle free of federal court jurisdiction. Liking to write dissents, he once said, became a prime consideration in his choice of law clerks.

In 1991, he summed up his final professional years to a gathering of black civil rights leaders:

> We're not gaining ground, my friends. We might be losing.

That same year, age and failing health persuaded him to retire. He died in January, 1993, at the age of eighty-five. He was given a hero's burial at Arlington National Cemetery.

At his news conference in the East Conference Room of the Supreme Court Building on the day after his retirement, he replied to reporters' questions regarding blacks' progress over the half century he'd spent as lawyer and judge:

All I know is that years ago, when I was a youngster, a Pull-man porter told me that he had been in every city in this country ... and he had never been in any city in the United States where he had to put his hand up in front of his face to find out he was a Negro. I agree with him.

"Even today?" a newsman persisted.
"I agree with him," Marshall repeated.

Abbreviations Used in Source Notes and Bibliography

ABAJ: American Bar Association Journal
APT: Alexander Pierre Tureaud
ARC: Amistad Research Center
BR: Baton Rouge
CR: Congressional Record
DAB: Dictionary of American Biography
DANB: Dictionary of American Negro Biography
DDE: Dwight D. Eisenhower Library, Abilene, Kansas
DLB: Dictionary of Louisiana Biography
DNC: Democratic National Committee
DP: Daily Picayune
FRD: Federal Rules Decisions
HLR: Harvard Law Review
HPW: Helen Patton Wright (Mrs. J. Skelly Wright)
HST: Harry S. Truman
JFK: John F. Kennedy Library, Boston, Massachusetts
JMW: John Minor Wisdom
JNE: Journal of Negro Education
JSH: Journal of Southern History
JSW: J. Skelly Wright
KKK: Ku Klux Klan
LC: Library of Congress
LH: Louisiana History
LHQ: Louisiana Historical Quarterly
LJ: Law Journal
LQ: Law Quarterly
LR: Law Review

LSU: Louisiana State University, Baton Rouge
LSUS: Louisiana State University, Shreveport
LW: Louisiana Weekly
MSRC: Moorland-Spingarn Research Center, Howard University
NA: National Archives
NAACP: National Association for the Advancement of Colored People
NO: New Orleans
NOPL: New Orleans Public Library
NR: New Republic
NYT: New York Times
OE: U.S. Office of Education
OHP: Oral History Project
OPSB: Orleans Parish school board
PPP: Public Papers of the Presidents
R&B: Records and Briefs
RG: Record Group
RRLR: Race Relations Law Reporter
SR: Saturday Review
SRC: Southern Regional Council
TM: Thurgood Marshall
TP: Times-Picayune
UNO: University of New Orleans
USCA: U.S. Code Annotated
USCRC: U.S. Civil Rights Commission
USSC: U.S. Supreme Court
WP: Washington Post
WS: Washington Star
YLJ: Yale Law Journal

SOURCES AND BIBLIOGRAPHY

I. INTERVIEWS

Elester Alexander, 5/21/91 (by Liva Baker)
St. John Barrett, 5/8/91 (by Liva Baker)
Lucille Bridges, 3/26/93 (by Liva Baker)
Daniel Ellis Byrd, n.d. (by Kim Lacy Rogers)
Elise Cain, 5/17/91 (by Liva Baker)
Robert L. Carter, 6/20/79 (by Jack Bass), 11/22/93 (by Liva Baker)
Louis Claiborne, 1/11/93 (letter to Liva Baker)
Jim Clayton, 7/20/79 (by Jack Bass)
Robert Collins, 5/23/79 (by Jack Bass), 6/8/88 (by Kim Lacy Rogers)
Dorothy R. Cowen, 7/6/90 (by Liva Baker)
Ann Dlugos, 11/11/75, 6/30/88 (by Kim Lacy Rogers), 8/8/91 (by Liva Baker)
John Doar, 3/15/95 (by Liva Baker)
Adrian Duplantier, 7/17/90 (by Liva Baker)
Lolis Elie, 11/10/78, 4/25/79, 5/22/79, 6/23/88, 7/12/88 (by Kim Lacy Rogers),
    2/26/92 (by Liva Baker)
Julian B. Feibelman, 11/7/78 (by Kim Lacy Rogers)
Jack Greenberg, 6/21/79 (by Jack Bass)
Jack P. F. Gremillion, 8/7/91 (by Liva Baker)
Jesse Grider, 5/19/92 (by Liva Baker)
Ruby Bridges Hall, 7/21/92, 3/24/93, 9/9/95 (by Liva Baker)
Robin Higginbottom Harris, 5/18/91 (by Liva Baker)
Veronica Hill, 10/7/83 (by Leatrice Roberts), 7/16/92 (by Liva Baker)
Arnold Hirsch, 7/16/92 (by Liva Baker)
D. Douglas Howard, 8/15/91 (by Liva Baker)
Frank Johnson, 10/9/79 (by Jack Bass)
Lester Kabacoff, 2/18/90 (by Liva Baker)
Harry Kelleher, 5/8/79, 6/9/88 (by Kim Lacy Rogers), 3/23/93 (by Liva Baker)
Rosa Freeman Keller, 11/9/78, 11/28/78, 5/7/79, 4/8/88, and one undated (by Kim
    Lacy Rogers), 5/15/91 (by Liva Baker)

Maurice "Moon" Landrieu, 5/22/79, 6/13/88 (by Kim Lacy Rogers), 5/21/91 (by Liva Baker)
Joseph Logsdon, 12/14/93 (by Liva Baker)
Leontine Goins Luke, 5/22/79 (by Kim Lacy Rogers)
A. Hepburn Many, 7/10/90 (by Liva Baker)
Burke Marshall, 10/19/79 (by Jack Bass), 9/18/92 (by Liva Baker)
Bill Monroe, 4/1/91 (by Liva Baker)
Sybil Morial, 2/19/92 (by Liva Baker)
Constance Baker Motley, 6/21/79 (by Jack Bass)
Peg Murison, 5/14/91 (by Liva Baker)
Elise Nichols, 9/7/91 (by Liva Baker)
Lillian Perry, 7/15/92 (by Liva Baker)
Peter Powers, 3/19/91 (by Liva Baker)
James F. Redmond, 7/3/91 (by Liva Baker)
Jackson Ricau, 11/17/78 (by Kim Lacy Rogers)
Louis G. Riecke, 8/19/82 (by Al Kennedy)
Lloyd J. Rittiner, 8/11/82 (by Al Kennedy), 5/13/91 (by Liva Baker)
Samuel I. Rosenberg, 7/12/90 (by Liva Baker)
Mary E. Sand, 7/13/91 (by Liva Baker)
Martha Scallon, 4/16/91 (by Liva Baker)
John Siegenthaler, 9/7/79 (by Jack Bass and Roy Pulver)
Claude Sitton, 1/17/79 (by Jack Bass)
Prim B. Smith, Jr., 7/16/90 (by Liva Baker)
Edgar Stern, 9/10/91 (by Liva Baker)
Matthew Sutherland, 2/21/92 (by Liva Baker)
Sarah Barth Tomlin, 8/5/90 (letter to Liva Baker)
Alexander Pierre Tureaud, n.d. (by Joseph Logsdon)
Alexander P. Tureaud, Jr., 10/6/91, 8/9/93, 3/7/95 (by Liva Baker)
Jane Tureaud, 8/15/91 (by Liva Baker)
Elbert Parr Tuttle, 3/6/79, 8/22/79 (by Jack Bass)
Harold R. Tyler, 4/9/91 (by Liva Baker)
Pam Tyler, 2/15/90 (by Liva Baker)
Caryl Vesy, 8/9/91 (by Liva Baker)
Everett J. Williams, 6/16/90 (by Al Kennedy), 9/1/94 (by Liva Baker)
Betty Wisdom, 3/23/93 (by Liva Baker)
John Minor Wisdom, 5/22/79, 9/28/79, 10/16/79 (by Jack Bass), 5/23/91, 2/25/92,
    3/24/93, 12/13/94 (by Liva Baker), n.d. (by Fred Graham)
Deborah Woodruff, 2/17/92 (by Liva Baker)
Helen Patton Wright, 4/2/90, 2/27/91, 3/23/92, 1/20/93 (by Liva Baker)
James E. Wright, Jr., 7/10/90, 1/8/92, 2/25/92, 12/15/93 (by Liva Baker)
J. Skelly Wright, 7/19/72 (by Frank T. Read), 12/9/78 (by Kim Lacy Rogers), 1/15/79,
    5/15/80 (by Jack Bass)
James S. Wright, Jr., 4/17/90 (by Liva Baker)

2. Manuscript depositories and collections

Raymond Pace Alexander, ARC
Archdiocese of New Orleans Archives
Jack Bass, Lemann Law Library, Tulane University
Harold H. Burton, LC
Daniel E. Byrd, ARC
Catholic Council on Human Relations, ARC
Eugene Davidson, MSRC
Shelby Davidson, MSRC
William C. Davis, Earl K. Long Library, UNO

Dwight D. Eisenhower Library, Abilene, Kansas
Federal Bureau of Investigation
Jack P. F. Gremillion, special collections, Hill Memorial Library, LSU
John Marshall Harlan, LC
Historic New Orleans Collection, New Orleans
Rosa F. Keller, ARC
John F. Kennedy Library, Boston
Jane T. Lemann, ARC
New Orleans Public Library, Louisiana Room
Mardi Gras, ARC
Burke Marshall, JFK
Natalie Midlo, ARC
DeLesseps S. Morrison, NOPL
National Archives
NAACP, ARC, LC, Earl K. Long Library, UNO
John P. Nelson, Jr., ARC
OPSB, Earl K. Long Library, UNO
Homer Plessy, ARC
William M. Rainach, Noel Memorial Library, LSUS
Frank T. Read and Lucy McGough, Duke University Law Library, Durham, N.C.
Kim Lacy Rogers, ARC
Charles Rousseve, ARC
Save Our Schools, ARC
Matthew R. Sutherland, Earl K. Long Library, UNO
Howard Tilton Library Archives, Tulane University
A. M. Trudeau, Jr., ARC
Alexander P. Tureaud, ARC
John Minor Wisdom, Lemann Law Library, Tulane University
Helen P. Wright, her personal collection
J. Skelly Wright, LC
Xavier University Archives

3. DOCUMENTS: HEARINGS, PROCEEDINGS, REPORTS AND OTHER RECORDS

Amistad Research Center. *Symposium on Southern Civil Rights Litigation Records for the 1960s,* December 1978, Dillard University, New Orleans.
Bicentennial Committee of the Judicial Conference of the United States. *Judges of the United States.* Washington, D.C. 1983.
Chase, Harold, with Samuel Krislov, Keith O. Boyum, and Jerry N. Clark. *Biographical Dictionary of the Federal Judiciary.* Detroit, n.d.
Compendium of the Activities of the Alcée Fortier High School of New Orleans, Louisiana: First 15 Years of Its Life, 1931–1946. n.d., no au., no pub.
Congressional Quarterly. *Guide to the U.S. Supreme Court.* Washington, D.C., 1979.
A Dictionary of Louisiana Biography. Edited by Glenn R. Conrad, New Orleans, 1988, volumes as cited.
Democratic National Committee. *Official Report of the Proceedings of the Democratic National Convention,* volumes as cited.
Landmark Briefs and Arguments of the Supreme Court of the United States, Edited by Philip B. Kurland, and Gerhard Casper, Volumes as cited.
Louisiana Advisory Committee to the United States Civil Rights Commission. *The New Orleans School Crisis.* Washington, D.C., n.d.
Louisiana Department of Justice. *Louisiana Tidelands: A Comprehensive Study.* Louisiana Department of Justice, 1957.

Louisiana Pardon Board. *Hearing, Louisiana ex. rel. Francis v. Resweber,* May 31, 1946. USSC R&B, 329 U.S. 452 (1947).

National Association for the Advancement of Colored People. *Annual Report,* volumes as cited.

———. *Teachers' Salaries in Black and White.* New York, 1942.

Official Journal of the Proceedings of the House of Representatives of the State of Louisiana, volumes as cited.

Official Journal of the Proceedings of the Senate of the State of Louisiana, volumes as cited.

Orfield, Gary. *The Growth of Segregation in American Schools: Changing Patterns of Separation and Poverty Since 1968.* A Report of the Harvard Project on School Desegregation to the National School Boards Association, December 1993.

———, and Franklin Monfort. *Racial Change and Desegregation in Large School Districts: Trends Through the 1986–87 School Year.* A Report of the Council of Urban Boards of Education and the National School Desegregation Project of the University of Chicago, n.d.

———, with Franklin Monfort and Melissa Aaron. *Status of School Desegregation 1968–1986.* A Report of the Council of Urban Boards of Education and the National School Desegregation Project of the University of Chicago, n.d.

Public Affairs Research Council of Louisiana. *Improving Quality During School Desegregation.* BR, 1969.

———. *PAR Analysis,* issues as cited.

Public Papers of the Presidents of the United States, volumes as cited.

Republican National Committee. *Official Report of the Proceedings of the Republican National Convention,* volumes as cited.

Sources and Documents of United States Constitutions. Edited by William F. Swindler, Vol. 4-A. Dobbs Ferry, N.Y., 1975.

State of Louisiana. *Acts of the Legislature,* volumes as cited.

United States Attorney General. *Annual Report,* volumes as cited.

United States Attorney's Office, Eastern District of Louisiana. *Reports on Disposition of Cases,* Record Group 60, NA.

United States Bureau of the Census. *Census of Population,* volumes as cited.

———. *Negroes in the United States.* Bulletin 18. Washington, D.C., 1904.

———. *Statistical View of the United States.* Washington, D.C., 1850.

United States Civil Rights Commission. *Federal Enforcement of School Desegregation.* Washington, D.C., September 11, 1969.

———. *Fulfilling the Letter and Spirit of the Law. Desegregation of the Nation's Public Schools,* August 1976.

United States Commissioner of Education. *Annual Report.* Washington, D.C., volumes as cited.

United States Congress. Senate. Committee on the Judiciary. *Hearings on Confirmation of Nomination of the Hon. J. Skelly Wright to be United States District Judge for the Eastern District of Louisiana,* March 1, 1950.

———. *Nomination of J. Skelly Wright (of Louisiana) to be United States Circuit Judge for the District of Columbia Circuit,* February 28, 1962.

———. 79th Congress, second session. *Title to Lands Beneath Tidal and Navigable Waters,* February 5, 6, 7, 1946.

———. 80th Congress, second session. *Title to Submerged Lands Beneath Tidal and Navigable Waters,* May 4, 5, 1948.

United States Code Annotated, editions as cited.

United Stsates Supreme Court. Records and Briefs, volumes as cited.

4. ORAL HISTORY PROJECTS

Herbert Brownell, Columbia University
Robert L. Carter, MSRC
Kenneth B. Clark, MSRC
John W. Davis, Columbia University
Lolis Elie, MSRC
Allen J. Ellender, JFK
Jack Greenberg, MSRC
Rosa F. Keller, MSRC
Anthony Lewis, JFK
Burke Marshall, JFK, MSRC
Thurgood Marshall, JFK
E. Frederic Morrow, MSRC, DDE
Constance Baker Motley, Columbia University
Leander Perez, JFK
William M. Rainach, Noel Memorial Library, LSUS
Alexander P. Tureaud, MSRC
Elbert P. Tuttle, Columbia University
J. Waties Waring, Columbia University
J. Skelly Wright, MSRC

5. VIDEOS

A House Divided: A Documentary about the Desegregation of New Orleans Through the Eyes of Those Who Remember It. Written and produced by Xavier University Drexel Center.

Carl Rowan. *Dream Makers, Dream Breakers—The World of Justice Marshall.* Broadcast on CBS, February 7, 1993.

Separate But Equal. Broadcast on ABC, April 7, 1991.

Gus Weill. *Louisiana Legends: An Interview with Judge J. Skelly Wright.* Broadcast on station WLPB, Baton Rouge.

6. UNPUBLISHED MATERIAL

Anthony, Arthé Agnes. "The Negro Creole Community." Ph.D. diss., University of California, Irvine, 1978.

Behlar, Patricia J. "J. Skelly Wright: The Career and Constitutional Approach of a Federal Judge." Ph.D. diss., LSU, 1974.

Douglas, Nils A. "Who Was Louis Martinet?" Charles Rousseve papers, ARC.

Giarrusso, Alfred Peter. "Desegregation of the Orleans Parish School System." Ph.D. diss., University of Arkansas, 1969.

Goldstein, Charles A. "The New Orleans Segregation Crisis." Paper submitted to Paul A. Freund's seminar in constitutional law, April 10, 1961. OPSB papers, UNO.

Harlan, Malvina S. "Some Memories of a Long Life." John Marshall Harlan papers, LC.

Iggers, George G., and Education Committee, NAACP, New Orleans Branch. "A Study of Some Intangibles in the New Orleans Public Schools." 1963. APT papers, ARC.

Keller, Rosa F. "Autobiography." Keller papers, ARC.

Marshall, Thurgood. "The Use of Three-Judge Court Procedure in Civil Rights Cases." Paper presented at Conference of NAACP Attorneys, June 23–25, 1949. APT papers, ARC.

McCarrick, Earlean M. "Louisiana's Official Resistance to Desegregation." Ph.D. diss., Vanderbilt University, 1964.

McDaniel, Vernon. "Developing Action Programs for Desegregation." Byrd papers, ARC.

McLain, James J. "The Economics of Mardi Gras in New Orleans." Paper presented at Eastern Economics Association meeting, session of the Association of Cultural Economics, April 27, 1978.

"Memorial Service for the Honorable J. Skelly Wright." Washington National Cathedral, Washington, D.C., August 17, 1988.

Monroe, Bill. "J. Skelly Wright: An American Judge." Remarks made at the presentation of a portrait of JSW by the NO Chapter, Federal Bar Association, to U.S. District Court for Eastern District of Louisiana, May 23, 1990.

NAACP. "Digest of Proceedings in Atlanta Conference," April 27, 1946. APT papers, ARC.

―――. "Program Book for NAACP Branches," New York, 1939. APT papers, ARC.

Norman, David L. "The Civil Rights Division of the U.S. Department of Justice, 1954–1973." Photocopy (privately owned).

Orfield, Gary Allan. "The Reconstruction of Southern Education: The Schools and the 1964 Civil Rights Act." Ph.D. diss., University of Chicago, 1968.

Read, Frank T., and Lucy McGough. "Let Them Be Judged." Original manuscript. Duke University Law Library.

Rogers, Kim Lacy. "Humanity and Desire: Civil Rights Leaders and the Desegregation of New Orleans, 1954–66." Ph.D. diss., University of Minnesota, 1982.

―――. "Lawyers' Stories: White Attorneys and the Black Civil Rights Movement." Paper presented at the Sixth International Oral History Conference, Oxford, September 11–13, 1987.

―――. "Organizational Experience and Personal Narrative: Stories of New Orleans Civil Rights Leadership." Paper to history department, Dickenson College, Carlisle, Pa., n.d.

Schwab, Thomas J. "George A. Dreyfous, An Appreciation." 1990. Privately owned.

Stowe, William McFerrin, Jr. "Willie Rainach and the Defense of Segregation in Louisiana, 1954–1959." Ph.D. diss., Texas Christian University, 1989.

"A Study of Some Intangible Inequalities in the New Orleans Public Schools." n.d. but probably 1959. APT papers, ARC.

Suitor, Mr. and Mrs. James. "This Is the Story of My Family." APT papers, ARC.

Tureaud, Alexander Pierre. "The Negro at the Louisiana Bar." JSW papers, LC.

Tyler, Pamela. "Silk Stockings and Ballot Boxes: Women of the Upper Class and New Orleans Politics, 1930–1955." Ph.D. diss., Tulane University, 1989.

Worthy, Barbara Ann. "The Travail and Triumph of a Southern Black Civil Rights Lawyer: The Legal Career of Alexander Pierre Tureaud." Ph.D. diss., Tulane University, 1984.

7. Published Material: Books, Articles

Ader, Emile B. "Why the Dixiecrats Failed." 15 *Journal of Politics* 356 (8/53).

Allen, William. *Life and Work of John McDonogh.* Metairie, La., 1983.

Allport, Gordon W. *The Nature of Prejudice.* Cambridge, Mass., 1954.

Ambrose, Stephen E. *Eisenhower the President.* New York, 1983.

"An Interview With James F. Redmond, Supt. of Schools." *Cambridge 38,* 24 (4/61).

Angelou, Maya. *I Know Why the Caged Bird Sings.* New York, 1969.

Ashmore, Harry S. "The Desegregation Decision Ten Years After." 47 *Saturday Review* 68 (5/16/64).

―――. *The Negro and the Schools.* Chapel Hill, N.C., 1954.

Attwood, William. "Fear Underlies the Conflict." 20 *Look* 27 (4/3/56).

Bailey, Thomas Pearce. *Race Orthodoxy in the South and Other Aspects of the Negro Question.* New York, 1914.

Baker, Liva. *Felix Frankfurter: A Biography.* New York, 1969.

————. "John Marshall Harlan and a Color-Blind Constitution." 1992 *Journal of Supreme Court History* 27.

————. Miranda: Crime, Law and Politics. New York, 1983.

Baker, Riley E. "Negro Voter Registration in Louisiana, 1879–1964." 4 *Louisiana Studies* 332 (1965).

Bardolph, Richard. *The Negro Vanguard.* Westport, Conn., 1959.

Barker, Lucius J. "Thurgood Marshall, the Law, and the System: Tenets of an Enduring Legacy." 44 *Stanford LR* 1237 (1992).

Barrow, Deborah J., and Thomas G. Walker. *A Court Divided: The Fifth Circuit Court of Appeals and the Politics of Reform.* New Haven, 1988.

Bartley, Ernest R. *The Tidelands Oil Controversy: A Legal and Historical Analysis.* Austin, Texas, 1953.

Bartley, Numan V. *The Rise of Massive Resistance: Race and Politics in the South During the 1950s.* Baton Rouge, 1969.

Bass, Jack. *Unlikely Heroes.* New York, 1981.

Basso, Hamilton, *The View from Pompey's Head.* Garden City, N.Y., 1954.

Bates, Daisy. *The Long Shadow of Little Rock: A Memoir.* New York, 1962.

Beecher, John. "Magnolia Ghetto." 3 *Ramparts* 45 (12/64).

Berlin, Ira. *Slaves Without Masters: The Free Negro in the Antebellum South.* New York, 1974.

Bernick, Michael S. "The Unusual Odyssey of J. Skelly Wright." 7 *Hastings Constitutional LQ* 971 (1980).

Biddle, Francis. *In Brief Authority.* Garden City, N.Y., 1962.

Biographical and Historical Memoirs of Louisiana. Volumes as cited. Baton Rouge, 1975.

Biographies of Louisiana Judges. Edited by J. Cleveland Fruge. Baton Rouge, 1971.

Bixby, David M. "The Roosevelt Court, Democratic Ideology, and Minority Rights: Another Look at *United States* v. *Classic.*" 90 *YLJ* 741 (1981).

Black, Charles L., Jr. "The Lawfulness of the Segregation Decisions." 69 *YLJ* 421 (1960).

Black, Earl. *Southern Governors and Civil Rights: Racial Segregation as a Campaign Issue in the Second Reconstruction.* Cambridge, Mass., 1976.

————, and Merle Black. *The Vital South. How Presidents Are Elected.* Cambridge, Mass., 1992.

Blassingame, John W. *Black New Orleans 1860–1880.* Chicago, 1973.

Blaustein, Albert P., and Clarence Clyde Ferguson, Jr. *Desegregation and the Law.* New York, 1962.

Blose, David T., and Ambrose Caliver. *Statistics of the Education of Negroes 1929–30 and 1931–32.* U.S. Office of Education Bulletin no. 13, 1935. Washington, D.C., 1936.

Board of Directors. *History of the Catholic Indigent Orphan Institute.* 1915.

Bond, Horace Mann. "The Extent and Character of Separate Schools in the United States." 4 *JNE* 321 (7/35).

Brady, Tom P. *Black Monday: Segregation or Amalgamation—America Has Its Choice.* Winona, Miss., 1954.

Branyan, Robert L., and Lawrence H. Larsen. *The Eisenhower Administration, 1953–1961: A Documentary History.* Vols. 1, 2. New York, 1971.

Brauer, Carl M. *John F. Kennedy and the Second Reconstruction.* New York, 1977.

Brennan, William J. "J. Skelly Wright." 102 *HLR* 361 (1988).

————. "A Tribute to Thurgood Marshall." 1992 *Journal of Supreme Court History* 1.

Brown, John R. "Hail to the Chief—Hutcheson the Judge." 38 *Texas LR* 142 (1959).

————. "In Memoriam: Judge J. Skelly Wright." 57 *George Washington LR* 1029 (1989).

Brownell, Herbert (with John P. Burke). *Advising Ike.* Lawrence, Kans., 1993.

Buggs, John. "School Desegregation, North and South." 13 *Integrated Education* 116 (5–6/1975).

Bullock, Henry Allen. *A History of Negro Education in the South From 1619 to the Present.* Cambridge, Mass., 1967.

Bunche, Ralph J. "A Critical Analysis of the Tactics and Programs of Minority Groups." 4 *JNE* 308 (7/35).

Burk, Robert Frederick. *The Eisenhower Administration and Black Civil Rights.* Knoxville, Tenn., 1984.

Burns, Ben. "'They're Not Uncle Tom's Children.'" 14 *Reporter* 21 (3/8/56).

Butler, Johnny S. "Black Education in Louisiana—A Question of Survival." 43 *JNE* 9 (winter, 1974).

Byrnes, James F. *All in One Lifetime.* New York, 1958.

Cable, George Washington. *The Negro Question.* Garden City, N.Y., 1958.

———. *The Silent South.* Montclair, N.J., 1969.

Cade, J. B. "The Education of Negroes in Louisiana." 16 *JNE* 361 (summer, 1947).

Caliver, Ambrose. *Availability of Education to Negroes in Rural Communities.* U.S. Office of Education Bulletin no. 12, 1935. Washington, D.C., 1936.

———. *Fundamentals in the Education of Negroes.* U.S. Office of Education Bulletin no. 6, 1935. Washington, D.C. 1936.

Cannon, Poppy. *Gentle Knight: My Husband, Walter White.* New York, 1956.

Capers, Gerald M. *Occupied City: New Orleans Under the Federals 1862–1865.* Lexington, Ky., 1965.

Carr, Robert K. *Federal Protection of Civil Rights: Quest for a Sword.* Ithaca, N.Y., 1947.

Carter, Hodding. "Dixiecrat Boss of the Bayous." 2 *Reporter* 10 (1/17/50).

———. "Jim Crow's Other Side." 21 *H.W. Wilson Co. Reference Shelf,* no. 3, 89. New York, 1949.

———. *The South Strikes Back.* Garden City, N.Y., 1959.

Carter, Robert L. "De Facto School Segregation: An Examination of the Legal and Constitutional Questions Presented." 16 *Western Reserve LR* 502 (5/65).

———. "Reflections on Justice Marshall." 1992 *Journal of Supreme Court History* 15.

———, and Thurgood Marshall. "The Meaning and Significance of the Supreme Court Decree." 24 *JNE* 397 (summer, 1955).

Cash, W. J. *The Mind of the South.* New York, 1941.

Cassimere, Raphael, Jr. "Equalizing Teachers' Pay in Louisiana." 15 *Integrated Education* 3 (7–8/77).

Casso, Evans J. *Francis T. Nicholls: A Biographical Tribute.* Thibodaux, La., 1987.

Cater, Douglass. "The Lessons of William Frantz and McDonogh 19." 24 *Reporter* 36 (2/16/61).

Chai, Charles Y. W. "Who Rules New Orleans? A Study of Community Power Structure." 4 *Louisiana Business Survey* 2 (10/71).

Chalmers, David M. *Hooded Americanism. The History of the Ku Klux Klan.* New York, 1981.

Chambers, Julius C. "Thurgood Marshall's Legacy." 44 *Stanford LR* 1249 (summer, 1992).

Childs, Marquis. "The Nemesis Nobody Knows." 212 *Saturday Evening Post* 23 (9/16/39).

The Choctaw Club of Louisiana. New Orleans, 1943.

The Citizens' Councils of Greater New Orleans. *The Citizens' Councils' Answers to the Questions of the Francis W. Gregory Parent-Teacher Association.* New Orleans, 6/18/60.

Claiborne, Louis. "In Memoriam: Judge J. Skelly Wright." 57 *George Washington LR* 1030 (5/89).

———. "The Noblest Roman of Them All: A Tribute to Thurgood Marshall." 1992 *Journal of Supreme Court History* 19.

Clark, Kenneth B. *Prejudice and Your Child*. Middletown, Conn., 1963.

Cohodas, Nadine. *Strom Thurmond and the Politics of Southern Change*. New York, 1993.

Coles, Robert. "As Bad as They Make It, the Stronger I'll Get." 7 *Southern Exposure* 57 (summer, 1979).

————. *Children of Crisis: A Study of Courage and Fear*. Vol. 1. Boston, 1964.

————. "The Desegregation of Southern Schools: A Psychiatric Study." In *Integration v. Segregation*, 201.

————. *Farewell to the South*. Boston, 1972.

————. "When Southern Schools Desegregate, How Do the Teachers Feel?" 47 *Saturday Review* 72 (5/16/64).

Conaway, James. *Judge. The Life and Times of Leander Perez*. New York, 1973.

Cook, James Graham. *The Segregationists*. New York, 1962.

Crain, Robert L. *The Politics of School Desegregation*. Chicago, 1968.

————, and Morton Inger. *School Desegregation in New Orleans*. Chicago, 1966.

Creole New Orleans: Race and Americanization. Edited by Arnold R. Hirsch, and Joseph Logsdon. Baton Rouge, 1992.

Cummins, Light Townsend, and Glen Jeansonne. *A Guide to the History of Louisiana*. Westport, Conn., 1982.

Curry, Leonard P. *The Free Black in Urban America, 1800–1865: The Shadow of the Dream*. Chicago, 1981.

Dabb, James McBride. *Who Speaks for the South?* New York, 1964.

Dalcher, Louisa. "A Time of Worry in 'the City Care Forgot.'" 14 *Reporter* 17 (3/8/56).

Dent, Tom. "New Orleans Versus Atlanta." 7 *Southern Exposure* 64 (spring 1979).

Desdunes, Rodolphe L. *Our People and Our History*. Baton Rouge, 1973.

Dethloff, Henry C., and Robert R. Jones. "Race Relations in Louisiana, 1877–98." 9 *LH* 301 (fall, 1968).

Devore, Donald E., and Joseph Logsdon. *Crescent City Schools*. New Orleans, 1991.

Dillard, Hardy Cross. "Freedom of Choice and Democratic Values." In *Integration v. Segregation*, 282.

Dixon, Thomas, Jr. *The Clansman*. New York, 1905.

Donovan, Robert J. *Conflict and Crisis: The Presidency of Harry S. Truman, 1945–1948*. New York, 1977.

Du Bois, W. E. B. "Does the Negro Need Separate Schools?" 4 *JNE* 328 (7/35).

Dufour, Charles L., and Leonard V. Huber. *If Ever I Cease to Love: One Hundred Years of Rex, 1872–1971*. New Orleans, 1970.

Dunbar-Nelson, Alice. "People of Color in Louisiana." 1.1 *JNE* 361 (10/16); 2.1 *JNE* 51 (1/17).

Dyer, John P. "Education in New Orleans." In *The Past as Prelude*, 116.

Dykeman, Wilma, and James Stokely. "Integration: Third and Critical Phase." *NYT*, viii, 24 (11/27/60).

Edmonson, Munro S. "Carnival in New Orleans." 4 *Caribbean Quarterly* 233 (3, 6/56).

Edwards, Newton. "A Critique: The Courts and the Negro Separate Schools." 4 *JNE* 442 (7/35).

Eisenhower, Dwight D. *The Eisenhower Diaries*. Edited by Robert H. Ferrell. New York, 1981.

————. *Mandate for Change, 1953–56*. Garden City, N.Y., 1963.

————. *The Papers of Dwight D. Eisenhower*. Vol. 13 of *NATO and the Campaign of 1952*. Baltimore, 1989.

————. *Waging Peace, 1956–61*. Garden City, N.Y., 1965.

Elie, Lolis. "Niggertown Memories." *Black River Journal* (n.d.).

Ellison, Ralph. *Invisible Man*. New York, 1972.

Elman, Philip. "The Solicitor General's Office, Justice Frankfurter and Civil Rights Litigation, 1946–1960." 10 *HLR* 817 (2/87).

Ely, Melvin Patrick. *The Adventures of Amos 'n' Andy.* New York, 1991.

Ethridge, Mark. "For a Bipartisan Domestic Policy." *NYT,* vi, 14 (11/7/48).

Everett, Donald E. "Free Persons of Color in Colonial Louisiana." 7 *LH* 21 (winter, 1966).

Everett, M. F. "Archbishop Rummell Is One of the Truly Great Leaders of Church in New Orleans History." 21 *Catholic Action of the South* 1 (5/14/53).

Fairclough, Adam. *Race and Democracy. The Civil Rights Struggle in Louisiana 1915–1972.* Athens, Ga., 1995.

Faulkner, Frances. "Too Late in a Tragic Situation." 2 *New Orleans* 18 (6/68).

Fay, Edwin Whitfield. *The History of Education in Louisiana.* Washington, D.C., 1898.

Feibelman, Julian B. *The Making of a Rabbi.* New York, 1980.

Finch, Minnie. *The NAACP: Its Fight for Justice.* Metuchen, N.J., 1981.

Fischer, Roger. "The Post–Civil War Segregation Struggle." In *The Past As Prelude,* 288.

———. "Racial Segregation in Ante-Bellum New Orleans." 74 *American Historical Review* 926 (1969).

———. *The Segregation Struggle in Louisiana, 1862–77.* Urbana, Ill., 1974.

Fiss, Owen M. *The Civil Rights Injunction.* Bloomington, Ind., 1978.

"The Five Who Sued." 47 *Saturday Review* 71 (5/16/64).

Flynn, James J. *Negroes of Achievement in Modern America.* New York, 1970.

Folsom, Fred G., Jr. "Federal Elections and the 'White Primary.'" 43 *Columbia LR* 1026 (11–12/43).

Fortier, Alceé. *A History of Louisiana.* vols as cited. Baton Rouge, 1966.

Frank, John P. "Judge Wright and the First Amendment." 7 *Hastings Constitutional LQ* 879 (spring-summer, 1980).

Frankfurter, Felix. "In Memoriam—Harold Hitz Burton." 78 *HLR* 799 (2/65).

Franklin, John Hope. *From Slavery to Freedom: A History of Negro Americans.* New York, 1980.

———. "Jim Crow Goes to School: The Genesis of Legal Segregation in Southern Schools." 58 *South Atlantic Quarterly* 225 (spring, 1959).

Freund, Paul E. "Storm Over the American Supreme Court." 21 *Modern LR* 345 (7/58).

Freyer, Tony. *The Little Rock Crisis.* Westport, Conn., 1984.

Friedman, Leon, and Fred L. Israel. *The Justices of the United States Supreme Court.* Vols. as cited. New York, 1967–78.

Fuller, Helen. "The New Confederacy." 119 *New Republic* 10 (11/1/58).

———. "New Orleans Knows Better." 140 *New Republic* 14 (2/16/59).

Galanis, Diane E. "Climbing the Mountain: Pioneer Black Lawyers Look Back." 77 *ABAJ* 60 (4/91).

Garson, Robert A. *The Democratic Party and the Politics of Sectionalism, 1941–1948.* Baton Rouge, 1974.

Gibbons, Russell W. "The South's Loneliest Lawyer." *Ave Maria* (10/19/93).

Goff, Rene M. "Problems and Emotional Difficulties of Negro Children Due to Race." 19 *JNE* 152 (spring, 1950).

Grau, Shirley Ann. "The Southern Mind: Black/White." 157 *Cosmopolitan* 34 (8/64).

Green, Constance McLaughlin. *American Cities in the Growth of the Nation.* London, 1957.

Greenberg, Jack. *Crusaders in the Courts: How a Dedicated Band of Lawyers Fought for the Civil Rights Revolution.* New York, 1994.

———. *Race Relations in American Law.* New York, 1959.

———. "Reflections on Leading Issues in Civil Rights, Then and Now." 57 *Notre Dame Lawyer* 625 (4/82).

———. "Twenty-Five Years After Brown v. Board: A Plaintiff's View." In *Schools and the Courts,* v.1, 1.

Gremillion, Jack P. F. *Louisiana Tidelands,* n.d., no place of publication.

Grey, Thomas C. "J. Skelly Wright." 7 *Hastings Constitutional LQ* 873 (spring-summer, 1980).

Gunther, John. *Inside U.S.A.* New York, 1947.

Haas, Edward F. *DeLesseps S. Morrison and the Image of Reform: New Orleans Politics, 1946–1961.* Baton Rouge, 1974.

Hacker, Andrew. *Two Nations. Black and White, Separate, Hostile, Unequal.* New York, 1992.

Hagerty, James C. *The Diary of James C. Hagerty.* Edited by Robert H. Ferrell. Bloomington, Ind., 1983.

Halberstam, David. *The Fifties.* New York, 1993.

Hall, Gwendolyn Midlo. *Africans in Colonial Louisiana. The Development of Afro-Creole Culture in the Eighteenth Century.* Baton Rouge, 1992.

———. "The Formation of Afro-Creole Culture." In *Creole New Orleans,* 58.

Hammond, Hilda Phelps. *Let Freedom Ring.* New York, 1936.

Handlin, Oscar. "Is Integration the Answer?" 213 *Atlantic Monthly* 49 (3/64).

Harder, Marvin A. "The Tidelands Controversy." 24 *The Municipal University of Wichita Bulletin* no. 20 (11/49).

Harlan, Louis R. "Desegregation in New Orleans Public Schools During Reconstruction." 67 *American Historical Review* 663 (4/62).

———. *Separate and Unequal.* New York, 1968.

Harris, T. H. *The Story of Public Education in Louisiana.* New Orleans, 1924.

Haskins, James. *The Creoles of Color of New Orleans.* New York, 1975.

Havard, William C. *The Changing Politics of the New South.* Baton Rouge, 1972.

———, Rudolf Heberle, and Perry H. Howard. *The Louisiana Elections of 1960.* Baton Rouge, 1963.

Hirsch, Arnold R. "Race and Politics in Modern New Orleans: The Mayorality of Dutch Morial." 35 *Amerikastudien* 461, April, 1990.

———. "Simply a Matter of Black and White: The Transformation of Race and Politics in Twentieth-Century New Orleans." In *Creole New Orleans,* 262.

Hobbs, E. H. "Negro Education and the Equal Protection of the Laws." 14 *Journal of Politics* 488 (8/52).

Hofstadter, Richard. "From Calhoun to the Dixiecrats." 16 *Social Research* 135 (6/49).

Holcombe, A. R. "The Separate Street-Car Law in New Orleans." 72 *Outlook* 746 (11/29/02).

Hornsby, Alton, Jr. "The City That Was Too Busy to Hate." In *Southern Businessmen and Desegregation,* 120.

Houston, Charles H. "The Need for Negro Lawyers." 4 *JNE* 49 (1/35).

"How Southern Judges Look at Segregation." *U.S. News and World Report* 48 (4/27/56).

Howard, L. Vaughan, and Robert S. Friedman. *Government in Metropolitan New Orleans.* New Orleans, 1950.

———, and David R. Deener. "Presidential Politics in Louisiana, 1952." 1 *Tulane Studies in Political Science* 3 (1954).

Hubbard, Maceo W., and Raymond Pace Alexander. "Types of Potentially Favorable Court Cases Relative to the Separate School." 4 *JNE* 375 (7/35).

Huber, Leonard V. *Landmarks of New Orleans.* New Orleans, 1984.

———. "Mardi Gras: The Golden Age." 16 *American Heritage* 16 (2/65).

———. *New Orleans: A Pictorial History.* New York, 1980.

Huckaby, Elizabeth. *Crisis at Central High: Little Rock, 1957–58.* Baton Rouge, 1980.

Hughes, Emmett John. *The Ordeal of Power: A Political Memoir of the Eisenhower Years.* New York, 1963.

Hughes, Langston. *The Ways of White Folks.* New York, 1990.

Huie, William Bradford. "What's Happened to the Emmett Till Killers?" 21 *Look* 63 (1/22/57).

Humphrey, Hubert H., ed. *Integration v. Segregation.* New York, 1964.

Hyman, Herbert, and Paul B. Sheatsley. "Attitudes Toward Desegregation." 195 *Scientific American* 35 (12/56).

Inger, Morton. "The New Orleans School Crisis of 1960." In *Southern Businessmen and Desegregation,* 82.

———. *Politics and Reality in an American City: The New Orleans School Crisis of 1960.* Chicago, 1968.

Integration v. Segregation. Edited by Hubert H. Humphrey. New York, 1964.

Jeansonne, Glen. *Leander Perez: Boss of the Delta.* Baton Rouge, 1977.

Johnson, George M., and Jane Marshall Lucas. "The Present Legal Status of the Negro Separate School." 16 *JNE* 280 (summer, 1947).

Johnson, Guy B. "Segregation vs. Integration." 60 *Crisis* 591 (12/53).

Johnson, Howard Palmer. "New Orleans Under General Butler." 24 *LHQ* 434 (4/41).

Johnson, Jerah. "Colonial New Orleans: A Fragment of the Eighteenth-Century French Ethos." In *Creole New Orleans,* 12.

Johnson, Kimberly. "A. P. Tureaud: Building Bridges and Bringing People Together." *Gumbo Magazine* 4 (4/91).

Johnston, Alva. "Louisiana Revolution." 212 *Saturday Evening Post* 16 (5/11/40).

———. "They Sent a Letter." 212 *Saturday Evening Post* 28 (6/22/40).

Jones, Thomas Jesse. *Negro Education: A Study of the Private and Higher Schools for Colored People in the United States.* Washington, D.C., 1917.

Jordan, Winthrop D. *White Over Black: American Attitudes Toward the Negro 1550–1812.* Chapel Hill, N.C., 1968.

Jupiter, Clare. "It Was Worth It." 7 *Southern Exposure* 60 (summer, 1979).

Kane, Harnett T. "Change in the Mardi Gras Spirit." *NYT,* vi, 10 (1/29/61).

———. *Deep Delta Country.* New York, 1944.

———. "Dilemma of the Crooner-Governor." *NYT,* vi, 9 (1/1/61).

———. *Louisiana Hayride: The American Rehearsal for Dictatorship 1928–1940.* Gretna, La., 1990.

———. *Pathway to the Stars.* Garden City, N. Y. , 1950.

Keenan, Charles. "Louisiana Says 'No.'" 91 *America* 439 (7/31/54).

Kendall, John Smith. *History of New Orleans.* Vols as cited. Chicago, 1922.

———. "New Orleans' 'Peculiar Institution.'" 23 *LHQ* 864 (7/40).

Key, V. O., Jr. *Southern Politics in State and Nation.* New York, 1949.

Kilpatrick, William H. "Resort to Courts by Negroes to Improve Their Schools: A Conditional Alternative." 4 *JNE* 412 (7/35).

King, Grace. *Memories of a Southern Woman of Letters.* New York, 1932.

———. *New Orleans: The Place and the People.* New York, 1968.

King, Wayne. "Bad Times on the Bayou." *NYT,* vi, 56 (6/11/89).

Kirk, Susan Lauxman, and Helen Michel Smith. *The Architecture of St. Charles Avenue.* Gretna, La., 1977.

Klein, Gerda Weissman. *A Passion for Sharing: The Life of Edith Rosenwald Stern.* Chappaqua, N.Y., 1984.

Kluger, Richard. *Simple Justice.* New York, 1976.

Knox, Ellis O. "The Origin and Development of the Negro Separate School." 16 *JNE* 269 (summer, 1947).

Kurtz, Michael L. "DeLesseps S. Morrison: Political Reformer." 17 *LH* 19 (winter, 1976).

———, and Morgan D. Peoples. *Earl K. Long: The Saga of Uncle Earl and Louisiana Politics.* Baton Rouge, 1990.

LaChance, Paul. "The American Challenge." In *Creole New Orleans,* 93.

Landry, Stuart Omer. *The Battle of Liberty Place*. New Orleans, 1955.

Lasker, Bruno. *Race Attitudes in Children*. New York, 1929.

La Violette, Forrest E. " The Negro in New Orleans." In *Studies in Minority Housing*, 110. Edited by Nathan Glazer and Davis McIntyre. Berkeley and Los Angeles, 1960.

Leflar, Robert A. "Law of the Land." In *With All Deliberate Speed*, 1.

———, and Wylie H. Davis. "Segregation in the Public Schools—1953." 67 *HLR* 377 (1/54).

Lemann, Nicholas. *The Promised Land*. New York, 1991.

———. "What Does Mardi Gras Mean?" 8 *New Orleans* 48 (2/74).

Les Cenelles. A Collection of Poems by Creole Writers of the Early Nineteenth Century. Translated by Régine Latortue and Gleason R. W. Adams. Boston, 1979.

Lesesne, Henry. "Civil Rights: What Do Southerners Think?" 21 *H. W. Wilson Co. Reference Shelf*, no. 3, 103. New York, 1949.

Lestage, H. Oscar, Jr. "The White League in Louisiana." 18 *LHQ* 619 (7/35).

Lewis, Anthony, and contributors to the *NYT. The Second American Revolution: A First-Hand Account of the Struggle for Civil Rights*. London, 1966.

Lewis, David Levering. *W. E. B. Du Bois. Biography of a Race. 1868–1919*. New York, 1993.

Lewis, Peirce F. *New Orleans: The Making of An Urban Landscape*. Cambridge, Mass., 1976.

Liebling, A. J. *The Earl of Louisiana*. Baton Rouge, 1970.

Locke, Alain. "The Dilemma of Segregation." 4 *JNE* 406 (7/35).

Lofgren, Charles A. *The Plessy Case. A Legal-Historical Interpretation*. New York, 1987.

Logan, Rayford W. *Howard University: The First Hundred Years 1867–1967*. New York, 1969.

Logsdon, Joseph, and Caryn Cossé Bell. "The Americanization of Black New Orleans 1850–1900." In *Creole New Orleans* 201.

Long, Howard Hale. "Some Psychogenic Hazards of Segregated Education of Negroes." 4 *JNE* 336 (7/35).

"Louisiana to Out-of-State Lawyers: Get Out." 157 *NR* 17 (12/24/68).

Louisiana's Black Heritage. Edited by Robert R. Macdonald, John R. Kemp, Edward F. Haas. New Orleans, 1979.

Louisiana's Legal Heritage. Edited by Edward F. Haas. Pensacola, Fla., 1983.

Lukas, J. Anthony. *Common Ground: A Turbulent Decade in the Lives of Three American Families*. New York, 1985.

Marshall, Thurgood. "An Evaluation of Recent Efforts to Achieve Racial Integration in Education Through Resort to the Courts." 21 *JNE* 216 (summer, 1952).

———, and Robert L. Carter. "The Meaning and Significance of the Supreme Court Decree." 24 *JNE* 397 (summer, 1955).

———, and Roy Wilkins. "Interpretation of Supreme Court Decisions and the NAACP Program." 62 *Crisis* 329 (6–7/55).

Martin, John Bartlow. *The Deep South Says "Never."* Westport, Conn., 1970.

Martin, Ralph G. "New Orleans Has Its Face Lifted." 116.2 *New Republic* 16 (6/2/47).

McCarrick, Earlean M. "Desegregation and the Judiciary: The Role of the Federal District Court in Educational Desegregation in Louisiana." 16 *Journal of Public Law* 107 (1957).

McCullough, David. *Truman*. New York, 1992.

McDaniel, Hilda Mulvey. "Francis Tillou Nicholls and the End of Reconstruction." 32 *LHQ* 357 (4/49).

McGill, Ralph E. *The South and the Southerner*. Boston, 1963.

McGinty, Garnie W. *Louisiana Redeemed: The Overthrow of Carpet-Bag Rule 1876–1880*. New Orleans, 1941.

McIntyre, Davis. *Residence and Race.* Berkeley, 1960.

McKay, Robert B. "The Repression of Civil Rights as an Aftermath of the School Segregation Cases." 4 *Howard LJ* 9 (1/58).

———. "'With All Deliberate Speed': Legislative Reaction and Judicial Development 1956–1957." 43 *Virginia LR* 1205 (12/57).

McKeever, Porter. *Adlai Stevenson. His Life and Legacy.* New York, 1989.

McMillen, Neil R. *The Citizens' Council: Organized Resistance to the Second Reconstruction.* Urbana, Ill., 1971.

McNeil, Genna Rae. *Groundwork: Charles Hamilton Houston and the Struggle for Civil Rights.* Philadelphia, 1983.

———. "To Meet the Group Needs: The Transformation of Howard University School of Law, 1920–1935." In *New Perspectives on Black Educational History,* 149. Vincent P. Franklin and James D. Anderson, editors. Boston, 1978.

Mecklin, John Moffatt. *Democracy and Race Friction.* Freeport, N.Y., 1970.

Meier, August, and Elliott Rudwick. "Attorneys Black and White: A Case Study of Race Relations Within the NAACP." In Meier and Rudwick, *Along the Color Line,* 128. Urbana, Ill., 1976.

Meyer, Robert E. *Names Over New Orleans Public Schools.* New Orleans, 1975.

Miller, Arthur S. *A "Capacity for Outrage."* Westport, Conn., 1984.

———. *On Courts and Democracy. The Judicial Odyssey of J. Skelly Wright.* Westport, Conn., 1984.

———, and Jeffrey H. Bowman. *Death by Installments.* New York, 1988.

Miller, Helen Hill. "Private Business and Public Education in the South." 38 *Harvard Business Review* 75 (7–8/60).

Mills, Gary B. *The Forgotten People: Cane River's Creoles of Color.* Baton Rouge, 1977.

Moley, Raymond. "Ordeal of New Orleans." *Newsweek* 110 (12/5/60).

Monroe, Bill. "J. Skelly Wright." 102 *HLR* 369 (12/88).

Morgan, Perry. "The Case for the White Southerner." In *Integration v. Segregation,* 140.

Mothner, Ira. "Exodus from New Orleans." 25 *Look* 53 (3/14/61).

Muller, Mary Lee. "New Orleans Public School Desegregation." 17 *LH* 69 (winter, 1976).

Muse, Benjamin. *Ten Years of Prelude.* New York, 1964.

Myrdal, Gunnar. *An American Dilemma.* New York, 1944.

NAACP. *Teachers' Salaries in Black and White.* New York, 1942.

Navasky, Victor S. *Kennedy Justice.* New York, 1971.

"New Orleans Experience Is New Lesson for South." 16 *New South* 3 (3/61).

"New Orleans 1960–1979." 7 *Southern Exposure* 55 (summer, 1979).

Newby, I. A. *Jim Crow's Defense: Anti-Negro Thought in America, 1900–1930.* Baton Rouge, 1965.

Newman, Roger K. *Hugo Black.* New York, 1994.

Nicholls, Francis T. "An Autobiography of Francis T. Nicholls." 17 *LHQ* 246 (4/34).

Northrup, Solomon. *Twelve Years a Slave.* Edited by Sue Eaken and Joseph Logsdon. Baton Rouge, 1968.

"Now There's a New Worry About Federal Courts." 46 *U.S. News and World Report* 88 (6/1/59).

Oberdorfer, Louis F. "In Memoriam: J. Skelly Wright." 57 *George Washington LR* 1037 (5/89).

O'Connell, Geoff. "Wisdom and Courage." 16 *New Orleans* 50 (6/82).

O'Connor, Sandra Day. "Thurgood Marshall: The Influence of a Raconteur." 44 *Stanford LR* 1216 (summer, 1992).

Olsen, Otto F. "Reflections on the Plessy v. Ferguson Decision in 1896." In *Louisiana's Legal Heritage,* 163.

————. *The Thin Disguise. Plessy v. Ferguson: A Documentary Presentation (1864–1896)*. New York, 1967.

O'Neill, Charles E. "Foreword." In Desdunes, *Our People and Our History*, ix.

Opotowsky, Stan. "The New Mob." 193 *Nation* 203 (9/30/61).

Ovington, Mary White. *The Walls Came Tumbling Down*. New York, 1947.

Owen, Lyla Hay, and Owen Murphy. *Creoles of New Orleans*. New Orleans, 1987.

Page, Thomas Nelson. *In Ole Virginia, or Marse Chan and Other Stories*. New York, 1910.

Parker, Barrington D. "In Memoriam: Judge J. Skelly Wright." 57 *George Washington LR* 1029 (5/89).

Parker, Joseph B. *The Morrison Era: Reform Politics in New Orleans*. Gretna, La., 1974.

Parker, Richard. "J. Skelly Wright." 102 *HLR* 367 (12/88).

The Past As Prelude: New Orleans 1718–1968. Hodding Carter, editor-in chief. New Orleans, n.d.

Peirce, Neal R. *The Deep South States of America*. New York, 1974.

Peltason, Jack W. *Fifty-Eight Lonely Men: Southern Federal Judges and School Desegregation*. New York, 1961.

Peterson, Gladys Tignor. "The Present Status of the Negro School as Defined by Court Decisions." 4 *JNE* 351 (7/35).

Pierce, Truman M., James B. Kincheloe, R. Edgar Moore, et al. *White and Negro Schools in the South: An Analysis of Biracial Education*. Englewood Cliffs, N.J., 1955.

Pinney, Edward L., and Robert S. Friedman. *Political Leadership and the School Desegregation Crisis in Louisiana*. New York, 1963.

Planer, Ed. "Louisiana: The Expensive Way to Fight Integration." 27 *Reporter* 37 (10/11/62).

Porter, Betty. "The History of Negro Education in Louisiana." 25 *LHQ* 728 (1942).

Prettyman, E. Barrett, Jr. "The Electric-Chair Case." In Alan Westin and C. Herman Pritchett, *The Third Branch of Government*, 84. New York, 1963.

Pugh, Robert G., Jr. "An Interview with the Honorable John Minor Wisdom." 39 *Louisiana Bar Journal* 254 (11/91).

Raines, Howell. *My Soul Is Rested*. New York, 1977.

Rankin, David C. "The Impact of the Civil War on the Free Colored Community of New Orleans." 11 *Perspectives in American History* 379 (1977–78).

————. "The Origins of Black Leadership in New Orleans During Reconstruction." 40 *JSH* 417 (11/74).

Read, Frank T. "Judicial Evolution of the Law of School Integration Since *Brown* v. *Board of Education*." 39 *Law and Contemporary Problems* 10 (winter, 1975).

————, and Lucy S. McGough. *Let Them Be Judged: The Judicial Integration of the Deep South*. Metuchen, N.J., 1978.

Reed, Germaine A. "Race Relations in Louisiana, 1864–1920." 6 *LH* 379 (fall, 1965).

Reeves, Miriam G. *The Governors of Louisiana*. Gretna, La., 1972.

Reidinger, Paul. "The Long March to Brown." 80 *ABAJ* 108 (1994).

Reinders, Robert C. "The Free Negro in the New Orleans Economy, 1850–1860." 6 *LH* 275 (summer, 1965).

"Requirement of Substantial Constitutional Question in Federal Three-Judge Court Cases." 19 *Louisiana LR* 813 (6/59).

Reston, Gail. "A Parent Talks About the Orleans Parish Public School System." 6 *New Orleans* 36 (3/72).

Rivera, Geraldo. *A Special Kind of Courage: Profiles of Young Americans*. New York, 1976.

Rivers, William L. "Segregation Costs Money." 23 *Reporter* 26 (12/8/60).

Roberts, Gregory. "Judge John Minor Wisdom." *Dixie* 8 (8/21/83).

Robertson, Minns Sledge. *Public Education in Louisiana After 1898.* Baton Rouge, 1952.
Rogers, Kim Lacy. *Righteous Lives. Narratives of the New Orleans Civil Rights Movement.* New York, 1993.
Rousseve, Charles B. *The Negro in Louisiana: Aspects of His History and His Literature.* New Orleans, 1937.
Sanders, Jared Y., Jr. "Implications of the Segregation Decision." 4 *Louisiana Bar Journal* 93 (10/56).
Sarratt, Reed. *The Ordeal of Desegregation: The First Decade.* New York, 1966.
Satter, Robert. *Doing Justice: A Trial Judge at Work.* New York, 1990.
Scheingold, Stuart A. *The Politics of Rights: Lawyers, Public Policy and Political Change.* New Haven, 1974.
Schlesinger, Arthur M., and Fred L. Israel. *History of American Presidential Elections,* iv (1940–1968). New York, 1971.
Schools and the Courts. Jack Greenberg, Thomas F. Pettigrew, Susan Greenblatt, Walter McCann, David A. Bennett, editors, vol. 1. Eugene, Oregon, 1979.
"The Shame of New Orleans." 16 *Ebony* 79 (2/61).
Sherman, George. "The Nightmare Comes to New Orleans." 23 *Reporter* 24 (12/8/60).
Sherrill, Robert. *Gothic Politics in the Deep South. Stars of the New Confederacy.* New York, 1968.
Shugg, Roger W. *Origins of Class Struggle in Louisiana.* Baton Rouge, 1939.
Smith, Lillian E. *Killers of the Dream.* New York, 1949.
———. "The Ordeal of Southern Women." 117 *Redbook* 44 (5/61).
Smith, Richard Austen. "Oil, Brimstone, and Judge Perez." 58 *Fortune* 143 (3/58).
Somers, Dale A. "Black and White in New Orleans—A Study in Urban Race Relations 1865–1900." 40 *JSH* 19 (2/74).
———. *The Rise of Sports in New Orleans, 1850–1900.* Baton Rouge, 1972.
Sorensen, Theodore C. *Kennedy.* New York, 1965.
Sosna, Morton. *In Search of the Silent South.* New York, 1977.
Southern Businessmen and Desegregation. Edited by Elizabeth Jacoway and David R. Colburn. Baton Rouge, 1982.
The South Today 100 Years After Appomattox. Edited by Willie Morris. New York, 1965.
Spain, Daphne. "Race Relations and Residential Segregation in New Orleans: Two Centuries of Paradox." 441 *Annals of the American Academy of Political and Social Science* 82 (1/79).
Spear, Allan H. *Black Chicago: The Making of a Negro Ghetto 1890–1920.* Chicago, 1967.
Spicer, George W. "The Federal Judiciary and Political Change in the South." 26 *Journal of Politics* 154 (2/64).
Stacey, Truman. "Heroes of the Law: Part One. A. P. Tureaud." 39 *Louisiana Bar Journal* 158 (9/91).
Steamer, Robert J. "The Role of the Federal District Courts in the Segregation Controversy." 22 *Journal of Politics* 417 (8/60).
Steele, Claude M. "Race and the Schooling of Black Americans." 269 *Atlantic Monthly* 68 (4/92).
Steinbeck, John. *Travels With Charlie: In Search of America.* New York, 1962.
Sterkx, Herbert E. *The Free Negro in Antebellum Louisiana.* Rutherford, N.J., 1972.
Strong, Donald S. *The 1952 Presidential Election in the South.* University, Ala., 1955.
Styron, William. *This Quiet Dust and Other Writings.* New York, 1993.
Suhor, Charles. "Coming of Age in the Ninth Ward." 6 *New Orleans* 40 (3/72).
Sullivan, Lester. "The Unknown Rodolphe Desdunes: Writings in the New Orleans *Crusader.*" 10 *Xavier Review* 1 (1990).
Tallant, Robert. *Mardi Gras.* Gretna, La., 1976.
Talmadge, Herman E. *You and Segregation.* Birmingham, Ala., 1955.

Tawes, Isabella. "The Mother Who Stood Alone." 152 *Good Housekeeping* 30 (4/61).

Taylor, Joe Gray. *Louisiana: A Bicentennial History.* New York, 1976.

———. *Louisiana Reconstructed 1863–1877.* Baton Rouge, 1974.

Taylor, Joseph T. "Desegregation in Louisiana—One Year After." 24 *JNE* 258 (summer, 1955).

———. "Desegregation in Louisiana—1956." 25 *JNE* 262 (summer, 1956).

Terkel, Studs. *Race: How Blacks and Whites Think and Feel About the American Obsession.* New York, 1992.

Thompson, Charles H. "The Availability of Education in the Negro Separate School." 16 *JNE* 263 (1947).

———. "Court Action the Only Reasonable Alternative to Remedy Immediate Abuses of the Negro Separate School." 4 *JNE* 419 (7/35).

Thompson, Daniel C. *The Negro Leadership Class.* Englewood Cliffs, N.J., 1963.

Thrasher, Thomas R. "Alabama's Bus Boycott." 14 *Reporter* 13 (3/8/56).

Tinker, Edward Larocque. *Creole City: Its Past and People.* New York, 1953.

Traub, James. "Can Separate Be Equal?" 288 *Harper's* 36 (6/94).

Treagle, Joseph G., Jr. "Early New Orleans Society: A Reappraisal." 18 *JSH* 20 (2/52).

Trillin, Calvin. *An Education in Georgia.* Athens, Georgia, 1991.

———. "State Secrets." *New Yorker* 54 (5/29/95).

———. "U.S. Journal: New Orleans Mardi Gras." *New Yorker* 138 (3/9/68).

———. "The Zulus." *New Yorker* 41 (6/20/64).

Truman, Harry S. *Memoirs of Harry S. Truman: Years of Trial and Hope.* Vol. 2. New York, 1986.

Tucker, Susan. *Telling Memories Among Southern Women.* New York, 1988.

Tulane Tidelands Institute. *Mineral and Tidelands Law.* Baton Rouge, 1963.

Turner, Arlin. *George W. Cable. A Biography.* Durham, N.C., 1956.

Tushnet, Mark. "Lawyer Thurgood Marshall." 44 *Stanford LR* 1277 (summer, 1992).

———. *Making Civil Rights Law. Thurgood Marshall and the Supreme Court, 1936–1961.* New York, 1994.

———. *The NAACP's Legal Strategy Against Segregated Education, 1925–1950.* Chapel Hill, N.C., 1987.

Tuttle, Elbert P. "Chief Judge Skelly Wright: Some Words of Appreciation." 7 *Hastings Constitutional LQ* 869 (1980).

Urban League of New Orleans. *To House a City. An Introductory Handbook on Housing in New Orleans.* New Orleans, 1967.

Velie, Lester. "Democracy in the Deep Delta." 124 *Colliers* 21 (12/24/49).

———. "Kingfish of the Dixiecrats." 124 *Colliers* 9 (12/17/49).

Vincent, Charles. *Black Legislators in Louisiana During Reconstruction.* Baton Rouge, 1976.

———. "Black Louisianans During the Civil War and Reconstruction: Aspects of Their Struggles and Achievements." In *Louisiana's Black Heritage,* 85.

———. "Negro Leadership and Programs in the Louisiana Constitutional Convention of 1868." 10 *LH* 339 (fall, 1969).

Vines, Kenneth N. "Federal District Judges and Race Relations Cases in the South." 26 *Journal of Politics* 37 (5/64).

Wade, Richard C. *Slavery in the Cities: The South 1820–1860.* New York, 1964.

Wald, Patricia M. "J. Skelly Wright." 102 *HLR* 363 (12/88).

Warren, Earl. *The Memoirs of Earl Warren.* Garden City, N.Y., 1977.

Warren, Robert Penn. *Who Speaks for the Negro?* New York, 1965.

Washington, Booker T. *Up From Slavery.* New York, 1970.

Wertham, Frederick. "Psychiatric Observations on Abolition of School Segregation." 26 *Journal of Educational Sociology* 333 (3/53).

"The White Side of the Southern Question." 31 *Nation* 126 (8/19/1880).

Who's Who in Colored Louisiana. A. E. Perkins, ed. Baton Rouge, 1930.

Wicker, Tom. *A Time to Die.* New York, 1975.

Wilkins, Roger. "The Sound of One Hand Clapping 20 Years After *Brown:* Negro Progress and Black Rage." *NYT* vi, 43 (5/12/74).

Wilkinson, J. Harvie, III. *From* Brown *to* Bakke—*The Supreme Court and School Integration 1954–1978.* New York, 1979.

Williams, Juan. "The New Segregation." *Modern Maturity* 24 (4–5/94).

Williams, W. T. B. "Court Action by Negroes to Improve Their Schools A Doubtful Remedy." 4 *JNE* 435 (7/35).

Winston, James E. "The Free Negro in New Orleans, 1803–1860." 21 *LHQ* 1075 (10/38).

Wisdom, Betty. "Letter From a New Orleans Mother." 193 *Nation* 365 (11/4/61).

Wisdom, John Minor. "The Frictionmaking Exacerbating Political Role of the Federal Courts." 21 *Southwestern LJ* 411 (summer, 1967).

———. "Random Remarks on the Role of Social Sciences on the Judicial Decision-making Process on School Desegregation Cases." 39 *Law and Contemporary Problems* 134 (winter, 1975).

With All Deliberate Speed. Don Shoemaker, ed. New York, 1957.

Wood, Joe. "Fade to Black. Once Upon a Time in Multiracial America." *Village Voice* 25 (12/6/94).

Woodson, Carter G. *The Negro in Our History.* Washington, D.C., 1931.

Woodward, C. Vann. *American Counterpoint,* New York, 1964.

———. *The Origins of the New South.* Baton Rouge, 1951.

———. *The Strange Career of Jim Crow.* New York, 1966.

Workman, William D., Jr. *The Case for the South.* New York, 1960.

———. "The Deep South." In *With All Deliberate Speed,* 88.

Wright, Helen Patton. *My Journey: Recollections of the First Seventy Years.* Chevy Chase, MD, 1995.

Wright, J. Skelly. "Color-Blind Theories and Color-Conscious Remedies." 47 *University of Chicago LR* 213 (winter, 1980).

———. "In Praise of State Courts: Confessions of a Federal Judge." 11 *Hastings Constitutional LQ* 165 (winter, 1984).

———. "Public School Desegregation: Legal Remedies for De Facto Segregation." 16 *Western Reserve LR* 478 (5/65).

———. "Thurgood Marshall: A Tribute." 40 *Maryland LR* 398 (1981).

Wright, Richard. *Black Boy.* Cleveland, 1945.

Zinn, Howard. *The Southern Mystique.* New York, 1964.

SOURCE NOTES

Pages

CHAPTER 1: "TWO, FOUR, SIX, EIGHT . . ."

1–2   During the time . . . "son of a bitch": Steinbeck, *Travels*, 219.

2   Two, four . . . verbal assaults: Ruby Bridges Hall to Liva Baker, 7/21/92; Lucille Bridges to Liva Baker; NPR "All Things Considered," 11/12/95; *TP*, 11/15/60; Steinbeck, *Travels*, 227.

2–3   The law suit . . . "states combined": *Bush* v. *OPSB*, 138 F. Supp. 336; *Louisiana Almanac*, 1988, 171; Read and McGough, *Let*, 111.

3–4   New Orleans, with . . . colorful entrepôt: Devore and Logsdon, *Crescent*, 265; *World Almanac*, 1962, 82, 1963, 670; Hall, "Formation," 59; Fuller "New Orleans," 15.

5   That same day . . . 1960 school crisis: Moon Landrieu to Liva Baker; *LW*, 11/9/60; *Manchester Guardian Weekly*, 11/17/60; Conaway, *Judge*, 113, Liebling, *Earl*, 196–97.

5–6   It was Perez . . . lawmaker wanted it: A. Hepburn Many to Liva Baker; Leontine Goins Luke to Kim Lacy Rogers; Conaway, *Judge*, 107–8; Jeansonne, *Leander*, 119, 219, 220; Read and McGough, *Let*, 120; Cook, *Segregationists*, 201; Kim Lacy Rogers, "Humanity," 85.

6–8   Down at the federal . . . *Weekly*: A. P. Tureaud, Jr., to Liva Baker, 9/29/91; HPW to Liva Baker, 2/17/91; JSW to Rosa Keller, n.d., Keller papers, ARC; *Wall Street Journal*, 11/16/60; *WP*, 11/21/60; JSW, ohp; MSRC; Monroe, "J. Skelly," 369 ff.; Brennan, "J. Skelly," 361 ff.; Wald, "J. Skelly," 363 ff.; Louis Claiborne to Liva Baker; Rosa Keller to Kim Lacy Rogers, 11/28/78.

8–9   A. P. Tureaud's full . . . "closing of the public schools": A. P. Tureaud, Jr., to Liva Baker, 10/6/91; Jane Tureaud to Liva Baker; Elise Nichols to Liva Baker; *TP*, 7/23/55; APT to TM, 7/22/60, APT papers, ARC; Junior Antoine to APT, 8/11/49, APT papers, ARC; Robert L. Carter to Daniel E. Byrd, 5/2/46, NAACP papers, LC; Worthy, "Travail," 19–20, 36 ff., 71 ff.; *Hall* v. *Nagel*; Biographical Notes, APT papers, ARC; *Louisiana ex rel. Francis* v. *Resweber*, Transcript of Board of Pardons Hearing; APT, oral history project, MSRC; Pittsburgh *Courier,* 4/11/59.

9–11   The serene mood . . . mellow veneer: Harry Kelleher to Liva Baker; Rosa Keller to Liva Baker; JMW to Liva Baker, 5/23/91; *LW,* 12/3, 10/60, 2/11/61; McGill, *South,* 283–84; Inger, *Politics,* 81–85; Kirk and Smith, *Architecture,* 12 ff.; Daniel C. Thompson, *Negro,* 104; Kim Lacy Rogers, "Humanity," 17–18.

CHAPTER 2: THE "STUBBORN" CREOLES

12–14   During one . . . white world: Donald Jones to APT, 9/24/53, APT papers, ARC; A. P. Tureaud, Jr., to Liva Baker, 10/6/91; Elise Nichols to Liva Baker; Blassingame, *Black,* 17–20; Fischer, "Racial," 935; Hall, *Africans,* 157; Logsdon and Bell, "Americanization," 201 f., 204, 236 f.; Owen and Murphy, *Creoles,* 9–11; Wood, "Fade," 26; *TP,* 8/16/93.

14–15   Eighteenth-century . . . "whole South": U.S. Bureau of the Census, *Statistical,* 1850, 80–81; Louisiana constitution of 1812; *TP,* 6/14/93; Curry, *Free,* 22–23; Fischer, "Racial," 931–33; Haskins, *Creoles,* 20–21; Jerah Johnson, "Colonial," 12–57; Logsdon and Bell, "Americanization," 204; Rankin, "Origins," 433; Sterkx, *Free,* 34.

15–16   For black Creoles . . . permanently: Blassingame, *Black,* 22, 135; Curry, *Free,* 161; Devore and Logsdon, *Crescent,* 33–34, 40, 41, 44 ff.; Porter, "History," 732–35; Rousseve, *Negro,* 42; *Who's,* 23, 24, 62.

16–17   A free black . . . disenchantment: Desdunes, *Our,* 104; Capers, *Occupied,* 215; Devore and Logsdon, *Crescent,* 42; *DANB,* 139; Dunbar-Nelson, "People," part 2, 60; Porter, "History," 733–34; Rousseve, *Negro,* 269; *Les Cenelles.*

18   Spirits soared . . . white majority: Washington, *UP,* 21; Franklin, "Jim," 229; Joe Gray Taylor, *Louisiana,* 60.

19–20   The Reconstruction . . . at the ready: Louisiana constitution of 1868; Fischer, *Segregation,* 47–52, 59, 114; Dunbar-Nelson, "People," part 2, 74.

20–21   The new constitution . . . into two peoples?: Devore and Logsdon, *Crescent,* 42; Fischer, *Segregation,* 88 ff.; *TP,* 6/15/93.

21   But the white . . . "kindle a flame": *DP,* 1/24/1870; *NO Times,* 2/17/1870; *TP,* 6/1/93; Harlan, "Desegregation," 664–65; Huber, *New,* 94.

21–22   In late November . . . a third, all black: U.S. Commissioner of Education, *Annual,* 1870, 150; *DP,* 1/24/1870; Bardolph, *Negro,* 70; Devore and Logsdon, *Crescent,* 70; Fischer, *Segregation,* 114.

22   The hard-core . . . model system: Cable, *Negro,* 9, 13; Devore and Logsdon, *Crescent,* 73, 76; Harlan, "Desegregation, 667–69, 672.

23–24   The declaration of race war . . . unsegregated basis: *TP,* 6/1/93; Devore and Logsdon, *Crescent,* 76–81; Fischer, *Segregation,* 122–23, 127–31; Harlan, "Desegregation," 672; Landry, *Battle;* Joe Gray Taylor, *Louisiana,* 281–85.

24–25   Following the close . . . became a certainty: Bardolph, *Negro,* 62–63; Blassingame, *Black,* 113; Devore and Logsdon, *Crescent,* 84–86; Fischer, *Segregation,* 137, 138, 143; Kluger, *Simple,* 60–61.

25–27   Within weeks . . . were denied again: *NO Democrat,* 6/27/1877; *DP,* 6/27/1877; Blassingame, *Black,* 76–77, 115; Desdunes, *Our,* 67, 131–33, 140; *DANB,* 16, 534, 601; Douglas, Who, n.p.; Huber, *New,* 81; McDaniel, "Francis," 357; Rankin, "Impact," 403–44.

27   A few days later . . . racially segregated schools: *NO Democrat,* 6/28/1877; Blassingame, *Black,* 115; Devore and Logsdon, *Crescent,* 87.

27   The fifty two-year-old . . . to action: *DP,* 9/27/1877; *DANB,* 601–2; Logsdon and Bell, "Americanization," 222; Vincent, *Black,* 24.

27–29   Although Trévigne . . . broke the color line: *DP,* 9/27/1877, 9/28/1877, *DP* 10/24/1877, *NO Times,* 9/27/1877, 9/28/1877.

29–30   Less than a month . . . That is all: *United States* v. *Hall; Bertonneau* v. *Board of Directors of City Schools,* 294, 296; Devore and Logsdon, *Crescent,* 56–57, 89; Friedman and Israel, *Justices,* ii, 1327; Logsdon and Bell, "Americanization," 224 ff.

30–31   The *Daily* . . . "benign neglect": *DP,* 2/21/1879; Devore and Logsdon, *Crescent,* 114, 179.

31   In 1879 . . . color line: Constitution of 1879; Dethloff, "Race," 315; Fischer, *Segregation,* 147–48; Logsdon and Bell, "Americanization," 251–53; Rankin, "Impact," 410.

32   serve on juries: *Strauder* v. *West Virginia; Neal* v. *Delaware.*

32   When C. C. . . . irrelevant: *Hall* v. *De Cuir.*

32–33   By 1883 . . . other matters: *Civil Rights Cases,* 24; Friedman and Israel, *Justices,* Vol. ii, 11.

33–34   The lone dissenter . . . condition of servitude: *Neal* v. *Delaware; Civil Rights Cases,* 62; Malvina S. Harlan, Some Memories, 2–7, John Marshall Harlan papers, LC; Matilda Gresham, *Life of Walter Quintin Gresham* (Chicago, 1919), vol. 2, 459; Friedman and Israel, *Justices,* ii, 128.

34   The Supreme Court's . . . would be required: Act 111, 1890; Report of the Proceedings of the Citizens' Committee, cover page JSW papers, LC; Reed, "Race," 383.

34–35   Once again . . . community: *DP,* 9/2/1891; *No Times Democrat,* 11/19/1892; Lofgren, *Plessy,* 28 ff.; Rankin, "Impact," 404–5.

35   Martinet . . . the board: History of the CIOI, board of directors, n.p., n.d.; Report of the Proceedings of the Citizens' Committee, 3 JSW papers, LC; New Orleans *City Directory,* 1890, 1892; Lofgren, *Plessy,* 29–32; Rankin, "Impact," 400.

35–36   Rodolphe . . . meeting: *DANB,* 174; Hirsch, "Race," 463–64; Lofgren, *Plessy,* 29 ff.; O'Neill, "Forward," xiv ff.

36–37   The first meeting . . . "fight this law": Report of the Proceedings of the Citizens' Committee, 2 ff. JSW papers, LC; *NO Times Democrat,* 11/19/1892; Lofgren, *Plessy,* 33–40; Kluger, *Simple,* 73.

37   With the assistance . . . during the argument: Brief for Plaintiff, *Plessy* v. *Ferguson;* Lofgren, *Plessy,* 30, 148, 151; Olsen, "Reflections," 177.

37–38   Henry Billings Brown . . . the same plane: *Plessy* v. *Ferguson,* 543–44, 552; *Roberts* v. *City of Boston;* Friedman and Israel, *Justices,* ii, 1154–55, 1560–61; Halberstam, *Fifties,* 415.

38–40   Brown had not used . . . by white citizens?: Brief for Plaintiff, *Plessy* v. *Ferguson,* 19; *Plessy* v. *Ferguson,* 555, 557–58, 559, 560; Blaustein, *Desegregation,* 98; Charles Evans Hughes, *The Supreme Court of the United States* (New York, 1966), 68.

41–42   Overcome by discouragement . . . not with ignominy: Report of the Proceedings of the Citizens' Committee, 7, 8, 9, 14 JSW papers, LC;; Desdunes, *Our,* 146–48; *DANB* 16, 174–75; O'Neill, "Foreward," xv–xviii; Rankin, "Impact," 405.

Chapter 3: "A Credit to His Race"

43   By the time . . . towns of the South: Bullock, *History,* 70–74; Harlan, *Separate,* 43–44.

43–44   The century turned . . . "public good": *DP,* 1/1/1900, 1/2/1900.

44   During Tureaud's . . . audiences: McGill, *South,* 117–26.

44–45   Race-hating . . . "highest negro": Bailey, *Race,* 93; Dixon, *Clansman;* Franklin, *From,* 325; Kluger, *Simple,* 84–85; Mecklin, *Democracy,* 33; Newby, *Jim,* 4, 12; LC *Gazette,* 6/10/94, 6–7.

45   The law both . . . separate classrooms: *Williams* v. *Mississippi; Cummings* v. *Richmond County Board of Education,* 545; *DeLima* v. *Bidwell; Downes* v. *Bidwell; Bailey* v. *Alabama; Berea College* v. *Kentucky.*

45–46   Louisiana's lawmakers . . . premiums than whites: Louisiana constitution of 1898, articles 248, 197; *TP,* 6/16/93; Holcombe, "Separate," 746; Kluger, *Simple,* 88.

46–48   The black Creole community . . . next twenty-five years: APT to Joseph Logsdon; A. P. Tureaud, Jr., to Liva Baker, 10/6/91; Elise Nichols to Liva Baker; Joseph Logsdon to Liva Baker, 12/14/93; Devore and Logsdon, *Crescent,* 191; Kluger, *Simple,* 100; Rankin, "Impact," 413–14.

48–50   All the way to Chicago . . . discriminated against blacks: APT to Joseph Logsdon; Franklin, *From,* 347 ff.; Lemann, *Promised,* 65; Ovington, *Walls,* 14–21; Spear, *Black,* 77–82.

50–51   Tureaud failed . . . "right the wrongs": A. P. Tureaud, Jr., to Liva Baker, 8/9/93; Joseph Logsdon to Liva Baker, 12/14/93; Jane Tureaud to Liva Baker; Elise Nichols to Liva Baker; APT to M. Hugh Thompson, 7/28/56, APT papers, ARC; *WP,* 3/7/76; *WS,* 3/7/76, Shelby Davidson obits, n.d., n.p., no publication named; APT, ohp, MSRC; Kluger, *Simple,* 123–25; Logan, *Howard,* 17 ff.; McNeil, "To Meet," 153–55; Worthy, "Travail," 16.

52   Hostility toward . . . would bring in: A. P. Tureaud, Jr., to Liva Baker, 10/6/91; Hirsch, "Simply," 265; Houston, "Need," 51; "Louisiana to Out-of-State," 18; Daniel Thompson, *Negro,* 83–84; Worthy, "Travail," 19–20.

52   Tureaud registered Republican: Hirsch, "Simply," 272–73.

52–53   In New Orleans . . . legal practice: Arnold R. Hirsch to Liva Baker; Louisiana Historical Association, *Dictionary,* 288; Hirsch, "Simply," 264; Meyer, *Names,* 44; Rousseve, *Negro,* 130–32; Worthy, "Travail," 18.

53–54   Difficult and . . . could or should do: Joseph Logsdon to Liva Baker, 12/14/93; Elise Nichols to Liva Baker; APT to "Gus," 8/8/44, APT papers, ARC; Hirsch, "Simply," 264; Houston, "Needs," 51–52; Kimberly Johnson, "A. P.," 7; Sullivan, "Unknown," 15.

54–55   Tureaud was a good-looking . . . "don't be silly": A. Hepburn Many to Liva Baker; Sybil Morial to Liva Baker; Elise Nichols to Liva Baker; A. P. Tureaud, Jr., to Liva Baker, 10/6/91; APT to James M. Nabrit, Jr., 12/4/53, APT papers, ARC; photo in Stacey, "Heroes," 158.

55–56   On his return . . . better part of a decade: Joseph Logsdon to Liva Baker, 6/11/95; William T. Andrews to APT, 3/12/28, APT to William T. Andrews, 3/15/28, APT papers, ARC; Hirsch, "Simply," 264–70; Meier and Rudwick, "Attorneys," 131, 155 ff.; Tushnet, *NAACP's,* 29–33.

56   By the early 1930s . . . teachers would require: Robert L. Carter to Jack Bass; *Scott* v. *Sandford,* 407; NAACP, Teachers, 4; Tushnet, *NAACP's,* 103.

56–59   The NAACP established . . . make us do it?: *Alston* v. *School Board of the City of Norfolk,* 112 F.d 991, 994, 995–96, 311 U.S. 393; Kluger, *Simple,* 173–217; NAACP, Teachers, 4–6, 9, 13, 14.

59   The LDF lawyers . . . to civil rights: A. P. Tureaud, Jr., to Liva Baker, 8/95; NAACP, Teachers, 7–9.

59–60   In New Orleans . . . and better schools: OPSB, salary schedule, 9/37, APR papers, ARC; Cassimere, "Equalizing," 5 ff.; Devore and Logsdon, *Crescent,* 210; Tushnet, *NAACP's,* 69; Worthy, "Travail," 37 ff.

60–61   Stirred to action . . . out of their jobs: Elise Perry to Liva Baker; Veronica Hill to Liva Baker; Thurgood Marshall to Ruth Burke, 11/22/39, NAACP papers, LC; APT, petition to OPSB, 5/9/41, APT papers, ARC; Worthy, "Travail," 38 ff.

61–62   By 1941 ... on a racial basis: APT, complaint, *McKelpin* v. *OPSB,* 5, 10–11, APT papers, ARC.

62–63   The lawyer ... both parties to the suit: Wayne Borah, court orders of 2/2/41, 7/8/41, 7/28/42, APT papers, ARC; Devore and Logsdon, *Crescent,* 211; Worthy, "Travail," 42–45.

63   "It stinks" ... August 31: Thurgood Marshall to APT, 6/19/42, APT papers, ARC; Devore and Logsdon, *Crescent,* 211–12; Cassimere, "Equalizing," 6; Worthy, "Travail," 45–46.

63–64   jubilant Tureaud ... Twelve cases altogether: APT to J. B. Cooke, 9/2/42, APT to Donald Jones, 10/17/42, Thurgood Marshall to Donald Jones, 9/9/42, APT papers, ARC; Veronica Hill to Liva Baker; APT., ohp; Hirsch, "Simply," 270; Tushnet, *NAACP's,* 98–99; Worthy, "Travail," 47–49.

64–65   By 1948 ... "forgot how it burns": Act 155, 1948, regular legislative session; Joseph Logsdon to Liva Baker, 12/14/93; photo of Tureaud, *The Claverite,* 6/40, 11; Ellison, *Invisible,* 249.

CHAPTER 4: "YA GOTTA STOP PUSHIN' THAT MULE AROUND"

66   Some years ... "way of life": Cook, *Segregationists,* 194 ff.; Jeansonne, *Leander,* 154, 174; Sarratt, *Ordeal,* 188.

66–67   Perez was the autocrat ... intruders: Carter, "Dixiecrat," 10; *Time,* 12/12/60, 21; *NYT,* 3/20/69; APT to Joseph Logsdon; Velie, "Kingfish," 9, 72; Conaway, *Judge,* 100; Sherrill, *Gothic,* 9; memorandum, Attorney General to FBI director, 2/20/61, FBI files.

67   Rumors ... figures: Glen Jeansonne to Liva Baker, 11/30/93; FBI file on Leander Perez.

68–69   One of Perez's ... got rich: Jeansonne, *Leander,* 29, 170, 225–28, 371–77.

69–70   Prior to ... local roads: Jeansonne, *Leander,* 1–2, 116–18; Liebling, *Earl,* 69; Sherrill, *Gothic,* 11–12; Richard A. Smith, *Oil,* 144; Velie, "Kingfish," 10–11, 71; *Time,* 12/12/60, 21.

70–71   The potential ... coastal waters: Ernest R. Bartley, *Tidelands,* 4, 5, 43, 44, 56–58; Joe Gray Taylor, *Louisiana: A Bicentennial,* 171–72; Garson, *Democratic,* 163–64.

71   For the century ... before the Supreme Court: HST, *Memoirs,* ii, 481–82; *PPP,* 1945, 352–54; U.S. Congress, Senate, Committee on the Judiciary, *Title to Lands ...* , 1946, 166–75, 276 ff.; Harder, "Tidelands," 14–15; 91 *CR,* 8842 ff.; Jeansonne, *Leander,* 165–66; Ernest R. Bartley, *Tidelands,* 34 ff.

72   On June 23 ... "oil": *United States* v. *California,* 38–39.

72   That business ... "Civil War": Ernest R. Bartley, *Tidelands,* 195, 254.

72   In Congress ... decision: U.S. Congress, Senate, Committee on the Judiciary, *Title to Submerged Lands ... 1948,* 500, 501, 616.

72–73   The tidelands ... they pleased: See *Missouri ex rel Gaines* v. *Canada, Powell* v. *Alabama, Brown* v. *Mississippi, Chambers* v. *Florida, Smith* v. *Allwright.*

73   "Once you get ... attention": James E. Wright, Jr., to Liva Baker, 12/15/93.

73–74   Ever since 1915 ... "time like that": See *Guinn* v. *United States, Grovey* v. *Townsend, Nixon* v. *Condon, Nixon* v. *Herndon, United States* v. *Classic, Newberry* v. *United States, Smith* v. *Allwright;* 1921 Louisiana Constitution, article viii, section 1d; TM to APT, 10/14/43, APT to TM, 10/11/43, APT to NAACP, 11/19/43, APT papers, ARC; Greenberg, *Crusaders,* 109; Key, *Southern,* 623; Kluger, *Simple,* 237.

74–75   Before the decade . . . on the books: *Hall* v. *Nagel;* Fairclough, *Race,* 111–12; Key, *Southern,* 522, 625; Anthony Lewis, *Second,* 130; Peirce, *Deep,* 21, 60; *NYT,* 7/16/48.

75–76   Harry Truman . . . growing black vote: Key, *Southern,* 330, 625; Numan V. Bartley, *Rise,* 29, n. 11; McCullough, *Truman,* 247, 588, 589.

76–77   The white South . . . campaign contributions: *PPP, HST,* 1948, 121 ff.; *TP,* 2/4/48; Garson, *Democratic,* 232.

77–78   Between February . . . optimistic: *Shelley* v. *Kramer;* Garson, *Democratic,* 241–42, 258–59; Jeansonne, *Leander,* 175–76; McCullough, *Truman,* 588; Schlesinger and Israel, *History, iv* 3103; Conaway, *Judge,* 82 ff.

78–79   It was a bitterly . . . his own nomination: Democratic National Convention, *Proceedings,* 1948, 192, 229; HST, *Memoirs,* 197; *NYT,* 7/15/48; Schlesinger and Israel, *History,* iv, 3118–19.

80–82   On July 17 . . . "Mule Around:" *NYT,* 7/18/48; Ader, "Why," 365; Jeansonne, *Leander,* 165, 177; McCullough, *Truman,* 645; Schlesinger and Israel, *History,* iv, 3118, 3170; *Time,* 10/11/48, 26; *WP,* 8/4/92.

82–83   That fall . . . won easily: Conaway, *Judge,* 86–88; Numan V. Bartley, *Rise,* 36; Garson, *Democratic,* 298; Jeansonne, *Leander,* 179 ff., 183; Key, *Southern,* 336–44; Joseph B. Parker, *Morrison,* 105; Peirce, *Deep,* 58; Phillips, "Lengthening," 14; Schlesinger and Israel, *History,* iv, 3865.

83–84   adopt a program . . . liberty: *PPP,* 1949, 5, 38; *United States* v. *New Orleans;* Ernest R. Bartley, *Tidelands,* 196; Jeansonne, *Leander,* 166, 167.

84–85   On June 5 . . . just that purpose: *United States* v. *Louisiana,* 704; *TP,* 3/18/50, 6/6,7,8/50.

85–86   As the 1950s . . . handle this problem: *LW,* 12/29/51, 3/24/51; *TP,* 6/15/50; Desdunes, *Our,* 4–5; Ernest J. Gaines, *A Gathering of Old Men* (Vintage Books, New York, 1992), 104; Garson, *Democratic,* 82–83; Gunther, *Inside,* 687; Peirce, *Deep,* 39–42.

Chapter 5: "Just Another Southern 'Boy'"

87–88   Much, much later . . . lifetime tenure: JSW to Rosa Keller, n.d., Keller papers, ARC; JSW, outline, HPW collection; BR *Sunday Advocate,* 4/16/78; *Wilson* v. *Board of Supervisors . . .* 92 F. Supp. 986; JMW to Fred Graham.

88   Never before . . . course of action required: D. D. Howard to Liva Baker; JMW to Liva Baker, 7/12/91; HPW to Liva Baker, 2/27/91; *NYT,* 12/30/90.

88–90   James Skelly Wright . . . before he became a judge: James E. Wright, Jr., to Liva Baker, 7/10/90; James S. Wright, Jr., to Liva Baker; *Choctaw,* 64; Griffin, *New,* 60; Haas, *DeLesseps,* 8, 13; *Creole New Orleans,* 96; Richard Parker, "J. Skelly," 369; Smith, *New,* 20; Tyler, "Silk," 18–19; Liebling, *Earl,* 39; Terkel, *Race,* 113.

90   An intensely practical . . . Skelly's choice: JSW to Jack Bass, 1/15/79; JSW, ohp; James E. Wright, Jr., to Liva Baker, 1/8/92, 2/25/92; James S. Wright to Liva Baker, 4/17/90; Bernick, "Unusual," 972–73; HPW to Liva Baker, 3/23/92; Chicago *Sun-Times,* 11/27/60; *Choctaw,* 64; Behlar, "J. Skelly," 4.

90–91   Nevertheless, as soon . . . at least for a time: JSW to Jack Bass, 1/15/79; JSW, ohp; D. D. Howard to Liva Baker; Bernick, "Unusual," 973; James E. Wright, Jr., to Liva Baker, 7/10/90; *Compendium . . . Fortier . . . ,* 5.

91–94   If there was any . . . everybody else took it: JSW to Rosa Keller, n.d., Keller papers, ARC; James E. Wright, Jr., to Liva Baker, 7/10/90; D. D. Howard to Liva Baker; Prim Smith to Liva Baker; JSW, ohp; JSW to Jack Bass, 1/15/79; Chicago *Sun-Times,* 11/27/60; BR *Sunday Advocate,* 4/26/78; Tucker, *Southern,* 3, 71–73.

94–96   It was in the United States attorney's . . . along the conviction route: JSW to Julio Nunez, 4/4/55; JSW papers, LC; James E. Wright, Jr., to Liva Baker, 1/8/92; JSW, ohp; Bernick, "Unusual," 973–74; *NYT,* 7/28/92; JMW to Liva Baker, 5/23/91; *Biographies of Louisiana Judges,* 198–99; "Disposition of Cases," U.S. Attorney's Office for the Eastern District of Louisiana, NA, RG 60; Arthur S. Miller, *Capacity,* 14; Monroe, "J. Skelly," 369.

96–97   As the mid-thirties . . . Louisiana scandals: Hammond, *Let,* 110–18; Alva Johnston, "Louisiana," 16, "They Sent," 28, 29; *TP,* 2/9/40; James E. Wright to Liva Baker, 12/5/93; Kane, *Louisiana,* 315; JSW, ohp; Behlar, "J. Skelly," 6–7.

97–100 Prosecuting the scandals . . . statutes were violated: James E. Wright, Jr., to Liva Baker, 1/8/92; JSW to Benno C. Schmidt, Jr., 12/9/82, JSW papers, LC; *United States* v. *Classic;* Bixby, "Roosevelt Court," 792; indictment, brief for defendants, *United States* v. *Classic,* USSC R&B; *TP,* 5/27/41, 12/20/46; *Newberry* v. *United States; 28 USCA,* 1252; Biddle, *In Brief,* 159.

100   The Court . . . five-year probations: Carr, *Federal,* 93.

CHAPTER 6: THE WAR, A LOVE STORY

101   Wright . . . submarine: JSW to Jack Bass, 1/15/79; JSW, ohp, MSRC; James S. Wright, Jr., to Liva Baker, 7/10/95; HPW to Liva Baker, 3/23/93; James E. Wright, Jr., to Liva Baker, 1/8/92; FBI file no. 77 8950, document no. 77-116, 6; *Newsday,* 11/15/60; Behlar, "J. Skelly," 8.

101   All the blacks . . . servants: JSW to Jack Bass, 1/15/79; Bernick, "Unusual," 984.

102–4   In 1942 . . . Isle of Wight: HPW to Liva Baker, 2/22/91; *NYT,* 6/16/44, 7/7/44, 8/9/44, 11/3/44, 4/27/45; Bernick, "Unusual," 974.

104–5   The end . . . election day: HPW to Liva Baker, 2/22/91, 3/23/92; *TP,* 10/6/75; *Time,* 2/4/46, 23; Bernick, "Unusual," 974.

106   I think . . . Christmas Eve: JSW to Jack Bass, 1/15/79; Bass, *Unlikely,* 112–13; Bernick, "Unusual," 974–75, 984.

107–10 In June, 1946 . . . U.S. Supreme Court: primary sources for the Willie Francis case include USSC R&B, which include the briefs submitted by Wright and the state, plus case records held in Record Group 60 at NA, which include the trial and Board of Pardons transcripts plus Wright's petition for certiorari. Secondary sources are the *St. Martinville Weekly Messenger;* Bernick, "Unusual," 975–76; Arthur S. Miller and Bowman, *Death,* and Barret Prettyman Jr., "The Electric-Chair Case." Cases cited are *Louisiana ex rel. Francis* v. *Resweber.*

111   "scared to death": HPW to Liva Baker, 3/23/93.

111   dinner party . . . Black's work: ibid; Bernick, "Unusual," 997–98.

111   Under our . . . excitement: *Chambers* v. *Florida,* 241.

111–12 Justice Jackson . . . tormented him: *TP,* 11/19/47; *Baltimore Sun,* 11/19/47; Prettyman, "Electric," 101–2; Arthur S. Miller and Bowman, *Death,* 70–74; Diary of Harold H. Burton, 11/18/47, Burton papers, LC; HPW to Liva Baker, 3/23/93.

112–14 Finally, on January 13 . . . Francises of the world: *Louisiana ex rel. Francis* v. *Resweber,* 460–65, 469, 473–74; Liva Baker, *Felix,* 282, 286; Frankfurter, "In Memoriam," 800; Oberdorfer, "In Memoriam," 1038–39; HPW, *My,* 71; JSW to C. P. Curtis, 12/29/58, JSW papers, LC.

CHAPTER 7: RUBICON

115–16 By early 1948 . . . much too early: HPW to Liva Baker, 2/27/91, 3/23/92; James E. Wright, Jr., to Liva Baker, 7/10/90; *TP,* 7/15/49, 10/6/65; JSW to Jack Bass, 1/15/79; Bernick, "Unusual," 978; JSW, ohp; Behlar, "J. Skelly," 18.

116–18   Wright's stay . . . politicizing the federal judiciary: *TP*, 1/30/40, 7/15,31/49; Behlar, "J. Skelly," 18, 20; JSW to JMW, 6/26/57, JSW papers, LC; Bass, *Unlikely*, 113–14; JSW to Jack Bass, 1/15/79; Friedman and Israel, *Justices*, iv, 2666; Bernick, "Unusual," 978, 979; BR *Sunday Advocate*, 4/16/78; Brown, "Hail," 144; JMW to Liva Baker, 5/23/91.

118   Hutcheson . . . ever write: JMW to Liva Baker, 5/23/91.

118–19   The nominations . . . untroubled future: HPW to Liva Baker, 2/27/91; JSW to George M. Fay, 10/9/51, JSW papers, LC; *NYT*, 10/16/49; *TP*, 10/27/49, 3/2/50, 10/15/50; U.S. Congress, Senate, Committee on the Judiciary, *Hearings . . . J. Skelly Wright . . .* 1950, 49 ff.

119–21   And so he *was* untroubled . . . at playing friends: HPW to Liva Baker, 2/27/91, 3/23/92, 1/20/93; Arthur S. Miller, *Capacity*, 16; JMW to Liva Baker, 5/23/91; Peter Powers to Liva Baker; Bill Monroe to Liva Baker; A. Hepburn Many to Liva Baker; Dorothy Cowen to Liva Baker; James E. Wright, Jr., to Liva Baker, 7/10/90; Monroe, "J. Skelly," 370–71; Oberdorfer, "In Memoriam," 1041; V. 87, *Federal Supplement; Crescent Towing and Salvage Company* v. *The MV 117; NYT*, 10/8/62; Prim Smith to Liva Baker; Bernick, "Unusual," 982; Satter, *Doing*, 35.

121–22   This particular occupational . . . justice before the law: Peter Powers to Liva Baker; JSW to Jack Bass, 1/15/79; 28 *USCA* 1343; Lukas, *Common*, 222.

122–23   Every court employs . . . degradation of the white race: Greenberg, *Crusaders*, 247; *Dean* v. *Thomas;* James E. Wright, Jr., to Liva Baker, 12/15/93; JSW, ohp; *TP*, 2/17/40.

123–25   His next racial . . . to admit only whites: Peltason, *Fifty-Eight*, 74, 115; JSW to Rosa Keller, n.d., Keller papers, ARC; Gus Weill, *Daily Reveille*, 9/22/53; characterization of LSU from author's reading of *Daily Reveille*, 1950–55.

125–26   Beginning in the mid-thirties . . . no less sweet: "Appendix to Petition for Writ of Certiorari to the Supreme Court of Texas," *Sweatt* v. *Painter*, ix; Charles H. Thompson, "Availability," 264–65; TM, "Evaluation," 319; *Murray* v. *Maryland;* Carl Rowan on CBS's "Dream Makers . . ."; *Missouri ex rel. Gaines* v. *Canada*.

126–29   LSU had no problem . . . at the end of the day: Worthy, "Travail," 71–75; TM to A. C. Lewis, 2/19/40, NAACP papers, LC; Kluger, *Simple*, 260 ff., 280; amicus curiae brief of the states, *Sweatt* v. *Painter*, 9, 10; see v. 339, *United States Reports; United States* v. *Louisiana; Henderson* v. *United States, Sweatt* v. *Painter*, 633, 636; *McLaurin* v. *Oklahoma State Regents*, 641, 642.

129–30   It was clear . . . not to follow them: *NYT*, 6/7/50; *TP*, n.d., n.p., APT papers, ARC; Numan V. Bartley, *Rise*, 37; Tushnet, *NAACP's*, 135.

130–31   So that when LSU . . . end of September: TM to APT, 7/12/50, APT papers, ARC; *Daily Reveille*, 11/1/50; APT, complaint in behalf of Roy Wilson, 2, APT papers, ARC; JSW to Joseph C. Hutcheson, Jr., 9/14/50, JSW papers, LC.

131–33   By the time . . . think it over and discuss it: *NYT*, 6/10/50, 9/6/50, 9/28/50, 10/23/50; *Wilson* v. *Board of Supervisors;* JSW, "Tribute," 398, 399; NO *Item*, 9/26/50; BR *State-Times*, 9/29/50; *TP*, 9/30/50.

134–35   Judge Borah came from . . . to follow the [Supreme] Court: *TP*, 10/10/50, 2/7/66, 10/6/75; *Wilson* v. *Board of Supervisors*, JSW to Kim Lacy Rogers, 12/9/78; JSW, ohp.

135–36   Then not long . . . "thought they were": JSW, ohp.

136–37   Following a daylong . . . in the federal courtroom: BR *State-Times*, 10/9/50; *Daily Reveille*, 10/10/50, 11/1/50; brief for defendant, *Board of Supervisors . . .* v. *Wilson; LW*, 1/6, 27/51; Roy S. Wilson to APT, 1/17/51, APT papers, ARC; *NYT*, 1/18/51, 5/3/51, 6/13/51, 10/17/51.

CHAPTER 8: THROWING THE BANDANAS ON THE BONFIRE

138–42   When A. P. Tureaud's . . . bring him over here: Myrdal, *American,* i, xliii; Elise
          Nichols to Liva Baker; A. P. Tureaud, Jr., to Liva Baker, 10/6/91; Urban
          League of New Orleans, *To House,* 34; Allport, *Prejudice,* 201; Daniel C.
          Thompson, *Negro,* 61; *TP,* 6/5/51, 8/19/93; Jane Tureaud to Liva Baker; Rosa
          Keller on "House Divided"; *LW,* 3/24/51, 7/21/51, 4/5/52, 1/24/53; Mary
          Sand to Liva Baker; Gloster B. Current to NAACP branches, 7/16/51, APT
          papers, ARC; *NYT,* 7/7/91, vii, 8/9/91; *Plessy* v. *Ferguson,* 544; Gunther, *Inside,*
          683.

143   By 1951 . . . twelve years of rejection: *LW,* 9/1/51; Greenberg, *Crusaders,* 246;
          Hall v. *Nagel; Tureaud* v. *Board of Supervisors* . . . 116 F. Supp 248.

143–46   In the early 1950s . . . "white man's job": TM, "Evaluation," 318 ff., Daniel C.
          Thompson, *Negro,* 96; Greenberg, *Crusaders,* 68; Appendix to Petition for Writ
          of Certiorari to the Supreme Court for the State of Texas, *Sweatt* v. *Painter,*
          xvi–xvii; Cade, "Education," 367; *WP,* 3/7/48; Richard Wright, *Black Boy,* 129;
          Maya Angelou, *I Know,* 164–78; *TP,* 5/1/60; Robert Penn Warren, *Who,* 29.

146–48   The edifice . . . "steps toward our goal": Hodding Carter, *South,* 15; 58 *Crisis,*
          1/51, 6; Du Bois, "Does the Negro," 329–30; Locke, "Dilemma," 408–11;
          Charles H. Thompson, "Court Action," 433, "Desegregation: Its Implications,"
          461; NAACP, Program Book for NAACP Branches, 9/1/39, 3, 8–9; *NAACP,*
          Digest of Proceedings; Tushnet, *NAACP's,* 111–12; Reidinger, "The Long,"
          108.

148   In New Orleans in 1946 . . . their children's schools: *NYT,* 8/16/46, 10/19/46,
          3/2/47; Kim Lacy Rogers, Humanity, 78, 79; Robert L. Carter to Liva Baker;
          Read and McGough, *Let,* 112; Daniel E. Byrd, memorandum, n.d., but proba-
          bly 3/53, APT papers, ARC; Lane and Cohen, *Gary,* 97, 100, illus.; Moore, *Citi-
          zen,* 3, 7 ff.; Greenberg, *Crusaders,* 246; Louisiana State Historical Association,
          Dictionary, 137; Hirsch, "Simply," 270.

148–50   Local school authorities . . . New Orleans's commercial section: Devore and
          Logsdon, *Crescent,* 171 ff., 179 ff.; Daniel E. Byrd to Robert L. Carter, 6/3/46,
          NAACP papers, LC; petition, Daniel E. Byrd and parents of black public school
          pupils, 5/3/46, handwritten list, n.d. n.p. untitled; Jennie Roche to Daniel E.
          Byrd, 5/9/46, 7/16/46, Daniel E. Byrd to OPSB, 7/10/46, APT papers, ARC.

150   A. P. Tureaud appeared . . . swallowed blacks' hopes: *TP,* n.d., APT papers,
          ARC, 7/26/46; Daniel E. Byrd to Jennie Roche, 8/15/46, Jennie Roche to
          Daniel E. Byrd, 8/23/46, APT papers, ARC.

150–52   A new school superintendent . . . "close the doors": Devore and Logsdon,
          Crescent, 219, 224 ff.; Lionel J. Bourgeois to APT, 9/30/46, 8/29/46, 4/13/48,
          Daniel E. Byrd to APT, 4/24/48, APT papers, ARC; Louisiana Constitution,
          1921; *LW,* 8/29/46.

152   Every city had then . . . direct legal action: Kim Lacy Rogers, "Humanity,"
          69–70; Wilfred S. Aubert, Jr., affidavit, 9/30/47, APT papers, ARC; New
          Orleans *City Directory,* 1948; *LW,* 2/16/52; Worthy, "Travail," 127.

152–54   Aubert's eagerness . . . had them in hand: Greenberg, *Race,* 237–38; Cash,
          Mind, 414–15; APT to OPSB, 5/20/48, Daniel E. Byrd to Lionel J. Bourgeois,
          4/21/48, APT papers, ARC; *TP,* 5/22/48; APT to E. R. Dudley, 5/22/48, E. R.
          Dudley to APT, 5/24/48, APT papers, ARC.

154–55   On May 30 . . . consider the board's requests: APT, complaint in civil action,
          number 2151, answer to APT's complaint in civil action number 2151, APT
          papers, ARC; *TP,* 12/22/49, 10/6/75.

156   Finally, on July 12 . . . mood had changed: *TP,* 7/15/50; Herbert Christen-
          berry, minute entry in civil action number 2151, 7/12/50.

156–58   At first, Inc. . . . fight for their rights: Kluger, *Simple,* 520; NAACP, Digest of Proceedings in Atlanta Conference, 4/27/46; Muse, *Ten,* 3–4, 7; Hodding Carter, "Jim Crow's," 100–103; TM, "Evaluation," 322; APT to J. B. Moore, 6/29/50, APT papers, ARC; *New Yorker,* 4/6/92, 23; *TP,* n.d., n.p., APT papers, ARC.

158–59   The new fighting spirit . . . number of Negroes: Trillin, *An Education,* 14; Robert L. Carter to Liva Baker; Wilkinson, *From Brown,* 73; Kluger, *Simple,* 520; NAACP, Program Book for NAACP Branches, 9/1/39, 3, APT papers, ARC; Woodward, *American,* 232.

159–61   The first suit . . . willing to spend it: Kluger, *Simple,* 4–25; Robert L. Carter to Liva Baker; Peltason, *Fifty-Eight,* 15; Greenberg, *Crusaders,* 119; Ashmore, *The Negro,* 51–52; Woodward, *Strange,* 145–46.

161–63   The trial . . . "those damned dolls": Kluger, *Simple,* 315, 321, 346 ff.; Robert L. Carter to Liva Baker; 58 *Crisis,* 1/51, 396; Clark, *Prejudice,* xx ff., 22–23, 55, 185.

163–64   Nor was the court . . . ginned that season: *Briggs* v. *Elliott,* 98 F. Supp. 529, 531–33, 535; J. Waties Waring, ohp; Kluger, *Simple,* 23–24.

164–65   J. Waties Waring . . . strangers in New York: Waring, ohp; *NYT,* 1/12/68; Kluger, *Simple,* 295 ff.; 300–301, 397–98; *Current Biography,* 1948, 656; *Wrighten* v. *Board of Trustees of University of South Carolina; Elmore* v. *Rice,* 528; *Rice* v. *Elmore,* Cohodas, *Strom,* 217; *Briggs* v. *Elliott,* 98 F. Supp. 529, 540.

166–68   Marshall and his colleagues . . . school systems into court: Kluger, *Simple,* 367, 371, 408–9, 564; Robert L. Carter, ohp; Robert L. Carter to Liva Baker; TM, "Evaluation," 324; *Brown* v. *Board of Education,* 98 F. Supp. 797, 798–800; 58 *Crisis,* 1/51, 5.

Chapter 9: Small Cracks in the Wall

169–71   Judge Christenberry's . . . urgent attention: Robert Penn Warren, *Who,* 347; JSW, stipulation in Civil Action no. 551, 4/28/52, JSW decree for permanent injunction in civil action no. 551, 4/30/52, JSW papers, LC; *Heard* v. *Ouachita Parish School Board;* Elise Nichols to Liva Baker; Worthy, "Travail," 68; Devore and Logsdon, *Crescent,* 220 ff.; *TP,* 1/13/51, 1/20/51.

171   White New Orleanians . . . no reply from the school board: *LW,* 1/13/51; Devore and Logsdon, *Crescent,* 227 ff.; Daniel E. Byrd, reports, 1950, 1951, Byrd papers, ARC.

171–73   In late 1950 . . . begin to look tempting: Read and McGough, *Let,* 112 ff.; Kim Lacy Rogers, *Righteous,* 19; *LW,* 9/2/51; Baldwin, "Hard," 63; Leontine Goins Luke to Kim Lacy Rogers; Guy B. Johnson, "Segregation," 592–93.

173   Byrd had no trouble collecting . . . indeed safe: Robert L. Carter to Liva Baker; Leontine Goins Luke to Kim Lacy Rogers; informal list of plaintiffs, APT papers, ARC; Read and McGough *Let,* 113; *Earl Benjamin Bush* v. *OPSB,* 138 F. Supp. 336 (1956).

173–75   Tureaud in the months . . . "public school systems": APT to Jackson W. Acox, 11/19/51, Biographical Notes, APT papers, ARC; Kim Lacy Rogers, 51, 61; *LW,* 2/17/51, 2/24/51, 4/28/51, 11/17/51; Inger, *Politics,* 22; Fairclough, *Race,* 240; NAACP, annual report, 1951, 1, 9; 58 *Crisis,* 8/51, 477.

175   On November 12 . . . segregation unconstitutional: NO *Item,* 11/12/51; TM, "Evaluation," 325.

175–77   On November 12, too . . . denied his petition: NO *Item,* 11/13/51; *TP,* 11/13/51; *LW,* 11/17/51; Bass, *Unlikely,* 116; Dalcher, "A Time," 17; Jorda S. Derbes to O. Perry Walker, 11/23/51, OPSB, statement, 11/26/51, APT papers, ARC.

177–78 Even while the board members ... "contained in the petition": *LW,* 2/2/52; APT to State Board of Education, 2/19/52, APT papers, ARC.

178–79 The early months ... to either race: *Davis* v. *County School Board of Prince Edward County, Va.,* 338–41.

179–82 The good news from Delaware ... would, of course, appeal: *Belton* v. *Gebhart,* 864, 865, 869–70; *Brown* v. *Board of Education,* 98 F. Supp. 797, appendix; 59 *Crisis,* 5/52, 32; Kluger, *Simple,* 434 ff.

182–83 Back in New Orleans ... customs of the community: *LW,* 8/2/52; *TP,* 6/15/52.

183–85 In Chicago that summer ... made Eisenhower President: JMW to Fred Graham; Howard and Deemer, "Presidential," 20–42; Roberts, "Judge," 8.

185–86 The platform ... in time for the November election: Republican National Committee, *Proceedings,* 1952, 321; 59 *Crisis,* 8–9/52, 412, 518–19; Howard and Deemer, "Presidential," 73 ff.; Democratic National Committee, *Proceedings,* 1952, 274.

186–87 As the summer of 1952 ... "schoolchildren of Louisiana": APT to State Board of Education, 8/14/52, Shelby M. Jackson to APT, 8/27/52, APT papers, ARC; Read and McGough, *Let,* 153.

187–88 The following day ... school board acquiesced: Kluger, *Simple,* 539; *LW,* 9/13/52; Daniel E. Byrd to TM, 4/9/53, Byrd papers, ARC; Greenberg, *Crusaders,* 247; Brown, "In Memoriam," 1029; Barrington D. Parker, "In Memoriam," 1049; *NYT,* 11/16/60; JSW to Joseph C. Hutcheson, Jr., 9/9/52, JSW papers, LC; Muller, "New," 70.

CHAPTER 10: "[W]E TOGETHER HAVE CREATED A MIRACLE"

189–91 The rally for the Republican ... not energetic applause: *NYT,* 10/11,14/52; *States-Item,* 10/11,14/52; *TP,* 10/11,14/52; JMW to Fred Graham; Schlesinger and Israel, *History,* iv, 3252.

191–92 It was the 108,000 ... talk about the future: Numan V. Bartley, *Rise,* 48 ff.; Howard and Deemer, "Presidential," 91 ff.; Schlesinger and Israel, *History,* iv, 3263; Strong, *1952,* 359 ff.

192–95 Midway ... traditions of these states: Kluger, *Simple,* 480, 525 ff., 561–62, 564 ff.; *WP,* 12/10,11,12/52; Byrnes, *All,* 412; Brief for the United States As Amicus Curiae, *Brown* v. *Board of Education,* 12/52, 28, 29; Elman, "The Solicitor," 828; *Bolling* v. *Sharpe; Nixon* v. *Herndon.*

196 As ordered ... adjustment of the child: 60 *Crisis,* 5/53, 299; Wertham, "Psychiatric," 335–37.

197 Finally on June 8 ... wholesale desegregation: *NYT,* 6/9/51; Liva Baker, *Felix,* 306–7; 60 *Crisis,* 6/53, 356, 363; 12/53, 617; Robert L. Carter, ohp; Kim Lacy Rogers, *Righteous,* 24.

198 The social revolution ... excruciating step of it: *NYT,* 9/6,28/50; APT to E. A. Johnson, 8/28/53, APT papers, ARC; 60 *Crisis,* 2/53, 111.

199–201 Tureaud was in this one ... loopholes in the procedure: A. P. Tureaud to Liva Baker, 10/6/91, 8/9/93; Elise Nichols to Liva Baker, APT to John G. Lewis, Jr., 9/15/53, John A. Hunter to A. P. Tureaud, Jr., 8/8/53, APT to Robert L. Carter, 8/17/53, APT papers, ARC; *LW,* 8/8,29/53; Kimberly Johnson, "A. P.," 5; Worthy, "Travail," 83.

201 When he finally filed ... decide A. P.'s case: JSW to Fred M. Vinson, 4/17/53, JSW papers, LC; Oberdorfer, "In Memoriam," 1041; Harold R. Tyler to Liva Baker; 4/9/91; Worthy, "Travail," 84.

201–3 The courtroom was packed ... academic term at LSU: Worthy, "Travail," 84–85; APT to Robert L. Carter, 8/28/53, APT papers, ARC; Galanis, "Climbing," 63; *TP,* 9/9/53; Kimberly Johnson, "A. P.," 5.

203   Wright made good ... in A. P.'s case: *Tureaud* v. *Board of Supervisors* ... , 116
        F. Supp. 248, 249, 251.
204–6   Within days ... alleviating their misery: A. P. Tureaud, Jr., to Liva Baker,
        8/9/93, 10/6/91; APT to Robert L. Carter, 9/14,19/53, APT to John G. Lewis,
        Jr., 9/15/53, James A. Dombrowski to A. P. Tureaud, Jr., 10/6/53, APT papers,
        ARC; *TP,* 9/17/52; *LW,* 9/19/53; Worthy, "Travail," 86; *Daily Reveille,* 9/22/53;
        Kimberly Johnson, "A. P.," 6–7; Robert Collins to Kim Lacy Rogers, 6/8/88;
        Robert L. Carter to APT, 11/4/53, APT papers, ARC; Robert L. Carter to
        Daniel E. Byrd, 1/21/54, Byrd papers, ARC; Jane Tureaud to Liva Baker.
206–7   The U.S. Court of Appeals ... enroll A. P. Tureaud, Jr.: *Board of Supervisors* ... v.
        Tureaud, 207 F. 2d 807, 810; JSW, ohp; Frank R. Mclavy to JSW, 9/19/53, JSW
        papers, LC; JSW to Frank T. Read; Bass, *Unlikely,* 69–74.
207–8   The elder Tureaud ... settled the matter: A. P. Tureaud, Jr., to Liva Baker,
        10/6/91; Robert L. Carter to Lawrence W. Brooks, 11/2/53, Lawrence W.
        Brooks to APT, 11/6/53, John A. Hunter to APT, 11/10/53, APT papers, ARC;
        Robert L. Carter to Daniel E. Byrd, 1/21/54, Byrd papers, ARC; APT to Robert
        L. Carter, 2/2/54, APT papers, ARC; *LW,* nd, APT papers, ARC; *Tureaud* v.
        Board of Supervisors ... 346 U.S. 881.
209–10 J. Waties Waring ... "not be pleasing": J. Waties Waring, ohp; Kluger, *Simple,*
        656; Leo Katcher, *Earl Warren: A Political Biography* (New York, 1967), 6; Earl
        Warren, *Memoirs,* 291; *NYT,* 12/8,9,10/53; *TP,* 12/8,9,10/53; 49a *Landmark
        Briefs and Arguments,* 447 ff.
210–12 On July 20, 1953 ... order should be enforced: Eisenhower, *Diaries,* 246 (for
        July 24, 1943); Ambrose, *Eisenhower,* ii, 142–43; James F. Byrnes to Dwight D.
        Eisenhower, 11/20/53, Dwight D. Eisenhower to James F. Byrnes, 1/21/53,
        President Administrative Series, DDE; *NYT,* 12/9/53.
212–13 That spring ... keys in his hand: Brownell, *Advising,* 174; *TP,* 6/16/93; *LW,*
        2/6/54, 4/24/54, 5/1/54, 5/8/54, 5/15/54; Kim Lacy Rogers, *Righteous,*
        39–40, "Humanity," 95 ff.; Kane, *Pathway,* 308.
213–15 On May 17, 1954 ... created a miracle: J. Waties Waring, ohp; 102 *CR* 4461;
        Brown v. *Board of Education,* 347 U.S. 483, 493, 494, 495; Kluger, *Simple,* 73;
        Cannon, *Gentle,* 249–55.

Chapter II: Rebel Yell

216–18 On the night ... "make adjustments": JMW to Liva Baker, 3/23/93; JMW to
        Fred Graham; *Marie Louise* v. *Marot,* 476; *Scott* v. *Sanford,* 591, 592; Huber,
        Landmarks, 133; Landry, *Battle,* 240; O'Connell, "Wisdom," 55; Roberts,
        "Judge," 8–9; *TP,* 5/17/54.
219–20 When they worried ... "people on this earth": Wilkinson, *From Brown,* 35 ff.,
        63; Tucker, *Southern,* 66–67; Wicker, *A Time,* 148; Atwood, "Fear," 27; Myrdal,
        American, i, 575; Lomax, "Georgia," 57; Styron, *Quiet,* 23–24; Lillian E. Smith,
        Killers, 77–79.
221   "The Court" ... head of the U.S. Supreme Court: Warren, *Memoirs,* 290; Sar-
        ratt, *Ordeal,* 249; 61 *Crisis,* 6–7/54, 347–49.
221–23 In Washington ... "to plague us": Eisenhower, *Waging,* 150, *Mandate,* 234–36;
        Branyan and Larsen, *Eisenhower,* ii, 1050; Anthony Lewis, *Second,* 12; *NYT,*
        10/14/52; Schlesinger and Israel, *History,* iv, 3263; Hagerty, *Diary,* 54; *PPP,* 1954,
        491, 1955, 7; Ambrose, *Eisenhower,* ii, 188–89; Burk, *Eisenhower,* 23; Warren,
        Memoirs, 291.
223   I know ... states' schools: Sherrill, *Gothic,* 209–10; NO *Item,* 5/18/54; Muse,
        Ten, 17.
224–25 The Louisiana legislature ... "days that lie ahead": *TP,* 5/18/54; NO *Item,*

5/18/54; *Time,* 11/12/60, 40; Samuel I. Rosenberg to clerk, U.S. Supreme Court, 5/17/54, OPSB papers, UNO; Samuel Rosenberg to Liva Baker; *LW,* 6/5/54.

225–27 Louisiana's ... local school board records: NO *Item,* 5/17/54; William M. Rainach to Hubert Humphrey, 6/28/77, Rainach papers; State of Louisiana, *Acts of the Legislature,* 1943–54, 1034–37; Fairclough, *Race,* 170, 206; 1 *RRLR,* 4/56, 239; Muse, *Ten,* 24; Sarratt, *Ordeal,* 357; Worthy, "Travail," 96, 97; Jeansonne, *Leander,* 230–33; Muller, "New," 70–71; Kim Lacy Rogers, *Righteous,* 35–36.

227–28 The committee was composed ... its leadership: Homer, Louisiana, *Guardian-Journal,* 1/15/48; Kane, "Dilemma," 30; Liebling, *Earl,* 29; William M. Rainach to Charles S. Hooks, 7/17/55, Leander Perez to William M. Rainach, 6/28/55; Rainach to Perez, 11/30/54, Rainach papers, LSUS.

228–30 They were the brainchild ... burn to the ground: Brady, *Black,* 1–90; Cook, *Segregationists,* 19 ff.; Hodding Carter, *The South,* 16–19; McMillen, *Citizens',* 19, 61–63.

230–32 It was not the climate ... in the South: Kim Lacy Rogers, "Humanity," 103; Kluger, *Simple,* 714, 720–21; DeLesseps S. Morrison to Pontchartrain Park Homes, Inc., 2/13/54, Morrison papers, NOPL; *LW,* 6/26/54, 7/10/54; Haas, *DeLesseps,* 250–51; *TP,* 8/23/54; 61 *Crisis,* 10/54, 491–93; 11/54, 522, 533; Joseph T. Taylor, "Desegregation ... One Year After," 368; Brownell, *Advising,* 196.

CHAPTER 12: "WITH ALL DELIBERATE SPEED"

233–34 Gertrude Stein ... measure of compliance: Burns, "They're," 23; Sybil Morial to Liva Baker; Sarratt, *Ordeal,* 358; Declaration of Louisiana State Conference of Branches NAACP, 5/30/54, APT to TM, 6/2/54, APT papers, ARC; Report of Program Committee, Louisiana State Conference of NAACP Branches, 1954, Byrd papers, ARC; *LW,* 7/10/54.

234–37 The U.S. Supreme Court ... boards around the state: Kluger, *Simple,* 715 ff., 726; 49a *Landmark Briefs and Arguments,* 1143, 1146, 1150, 1180, 1182, 1190; *NYT,* 3/26/55; *Brown* v. *Board of Education,* 347 U.S. 483, 496; Brownell, *Advising,* 196; Joseph T. Taylor, "Desegregation ... One Year After," 266.

237–38 Once again ... march through: *Brown* v. *Board of Education,* 349 U.S. 294, 298, 299, 300–301.

238–39 These fifty-eight ... we've got federal judges: Peltason, *Fifty-Eight,* 4 ff.; Vines, "Federal," 343 ff.; *TP,* 6/1/55.

239–40 The reactions of black ... wants to use it: 62 *Crisis,* 6–7/55, 335; NAACP, Directive to the Branches, 6/4/55, Byrd papers, ARC; TM and Robert L. Carter, "The Meaning," 397 ff.

240–41 Reflecting readers' ... trade school for New Orleans: 62 *Crisis,* 8–9/55, 424–25; Woodward, *Strange,* 152–53; NO *Item,* 6/1/55; William M. Rainach to W. E. Person, 3/16/55, William M. Rainach to Sybil Huckaby, 6/15/55, Rainach papers, LSUS; *TP,* 5/8,9,12,13,21,23,31/55, 6/1,11/55; Daniel E. Byrd to Robert S. Kennon, members of the Louisiana legislature, state board of education, LSU board of supervisors, 5/7/55, Byrd papers, ARC.

242–43 I am convinced ... "whatever the board dictates": *TP,* 6/1,8,26/55, 8/9/55; *LW,* 10/23/54, 9/3,17/55; Goldstein, "New Orleans", n. 56; Worthy, "Travail," 133.

243–45 Between the Supreme ... politely granted it: *TP,* 5/16,17/55, 6/1/55, 9/16/55; JSW to Frank T. Read; J. W. Mabry to APT 6/1/55, APT to Samuel I. Rosenberg, 5/31/55, Samuel I. Rosenberg to APT, 6/3/55, Robert L. Carter to APT,

6/11/55, APT papers, ARC; *Bush* v. *OPSB,* unsigned order, U.S. District Court for the Eastern District of Louisiana, 6/3/55.

245–46   Meanwhile, Tureaud ... Orleans, Louisiana: Clarence Scheps to William M. Rainach, 6/15/55, OPSB papers, UNO: NO *Item,* 6/27,28/55; *LW,* 7/2/55; *TP,* 6/28/55.

246–48   Six weeks after ... made it legitimate: *Briggs* v. *Elliott,* 132 F. Supp. 776, 777, 778; Peltason, *Fifty-Eight,* 23; 49 *Landmark Briefs and Arguments,* 321.

248–50   When he filed ... assessed court costs: *Bush* v. *OPSB,* brief on motion to strike "amended petition," n.d., APT papers, ARC; Samuel I. Rosenberg to Liva Baker; Read and McGough, *Let,* 116; Muller, "New," 71–72; Daniel E. Byrd to TM, 9/2/55, Byrd papers, ARC; *LW,* 9/10/55; 1 *RRLR,* 228, 1956.

250–51   Outside New Orleans ... acquit them: Cooke, *Segregationists,* 131; Terkel, *Race,* 19 ff.; Huie, "What's Happened," 63 ff.; 62 *Crisis,* 10/55, 479; *Lucy* v. *Adams.*

251   Dan Byrd reported ... school system: Byrd, memorandum to TM, 8/23/55, Byrd papers, ARC.

251–54   All of which ... "let things happen": Rosa Keller to Liva Baker; Keller, Autobiography, v. 1, 51–53, 63–68; Keller, ohp, MSRC; Rosa Keller to Kim Lacy Rogers, 4/8/88, 11/8/78, 5/7/79; Louisiana Historical Association, *Dictionary* 322; Kim Lacy Rogers, *Righteous,* 28–29, 41–45, "Humanity," 85 ff., 31 ff., 287; *LW,* 3/6/54; Fairclough, *Race,* 166, Dufour and Huber, *If Ever I,* 145, 147; *TP,* n.d., Keller papers, ARC.

254–55   Members ... anyone about it for years: *TP,* 9/13/55; Rosa Keller to Liva Baker; McMillen, *Citizens',* 64; Worthy, "Travail," 133; Daniel E. Byrd activity report, 9/55, Byrd papers, ARC; Klein, *Passion,* 189; Feibelman, *Making,* 452–53.

255–57   On December 1 ... not to order it: *TP,* 12/2,3/55; *LW,* 12/10/55; affidavits of James F. Redmond, 11/8/55, and Clarence Scheps, 1955, APT papers, ARC.

Chapter 13: Revisiting the Civil War in Legal Dress

258–59   Six inches ... opponents might be: *TP,* 2/16/56; NO *Item,* 2/25/56; King, *New,* 301 ff.; Parton, *General,* 279 ff.; Capers, *Occupied,* 61 ff.; Read and McGough, *Let,* 123; JSW to Kim Lacy Rogers; JSW, ohp; JSW to Frank T. Read.

259–62   The *Bush* decision ... paraphrase of the Supreme Court: *Bush* v. *OPSB,* 138 F. Supp. 336, 337, 339 ff., 341–42; James E. Wright, Jr., to Liva Baker 12/15/93; JSW to Kim Lacy Rogers; Dorothy Cowen to Liva Baker; JSW, ohp, 12/15/93; JSW to Jack Bass, 1/15/79; JSW, "Public School," 500; JSW to Rosa Keller, n.d., Keller papers, ARC; HPW to Liva Baker, 2/27/91; *Chambers* v. *Florida,* 241; Monroe, "In," 373–74; Blaustein, *Desegregation,* 240; Hyman and Sheatsley, "Attitudes," 35–39.

262   The time element ... damage they'd done: *Bush* v. *OPSB,* 138 F. Supp. 336; *Briggs* v. *Elliott,* 132 F. Supp. 776.

262–63   There was little uniformity ... "part of the game": *Bell* v. *Rippy,* 812; *Brown* v. *Board of Education,* 349 U.S. 294, 300; "How Southern," 48; McKay, "With All," 1208–14; Peirce, *Deep,* 62; Peltason, *Fifty-Eight,* 133; Arthur S. Miller, *Capacity,* 71–72; Read and McGough, *Let,* 78; Rodgers and Bullock, *Law,* 78; Wilkinson, *From Brown,* 80–81; JMW to Liva Baker, 2/25/92.

264–65   One of the most difficult ... in Texas: *Briggs* v. *Elliott,* 132 F. Supp. 776, 778; "Five Who," 71; "How Southern," 48; Read and McGough, *Let,* 608; Steamer, "Role," 433; Wilkinson, *From Brown,* 82.

265–66   In New Orleans ... streets of politics: *TP,* 2/16,17/56; Devore and Logsdon, *Crescent,* 238; Dalcher, "A Time," 17.

266–67   The United States Congress ... "dangerous precedent": 102 *CR* 4460–61;

Numan v. Bartley, *Rise,* 116–17, 126 ff.; Anthony Lewis, *Second,* 43; Muse, *Ten,* 63; Cohodas, *Strom,* 283 ff.

267–68   Immediately following . . . above the din: *TP,* 2/16/56; William M. Rainach to P. G. Borron, 11/26/55, Rainach papers, LSUS; *LW,* 6/9/56.

268–69   The first order . . . or constitutional law: 2 *RRLR,* 4/57, 465–98; 1 *RRLR,* 11/56, 753 ff.; Numan v. Bartley, *Rise,* 126 ff.; USCRC, *The New,* 58.

269–71   Tactically . . . agreed with him: State of Louisiana, *Acts of the Legislature,* 1956, 654, 741, 948, 15, 43, 438; 1 *RRLR,* 927, 1956; Baton Rouge *Times,* 10/11/56; *LW,* 3/3/56; Read and McGough, *Let,* 198; *Board of Supervisors . . .* v. *Tureaud,* 225 F. 2d 434, 351 U.S. 924; Jeansonne, *Leander,* 234; Worthy, "Travail," 98 ff.

271–72   Skelly Wright made . . . through the state system: *Ludley* v. *Board of Supervisors . . . , Bailey* v. *Louisiana State Board of Education, Lark* v. *Louisiana State Board of Education, Board of Supervisors . . .* v. *Ludley, Louisiana State Board of Education* v. *Lark, Louisiana State Board of Education* v. *Bailey, Lane* v. *Wilson;* 1 *RRLR,* 575, 1956; *TP,* 4/2/56; Numan V. Bartley, *Rise,* 215; Fairclough, *Race,* 194–99, 207–11; Worthy, "Travail," 105 ff.; *Wall Street Journal,* 11/16/60.

272–73   Caught between . . . for desegregation: 63 *Crisis,* 6–7/56, 356; Dorothy A. Combre to Robert L. Carter, 11/9/59, APT papers, ARC; Fairclough, *Race,* 209–10, Worthy, "Travail," 108.

273–74   Not surprisingly . . . devising the strategies: Convention of Delegates Organizing the Citizens' Councils of America, 4/7/56, Rainach papers, LSUS; Numan v. Bartley, *Rise,* 90–91; Jeansonne, *Leander,* 236.

274   On March 20 . . . were abolished: JSW to Kim Lacy Rogers, 12/9/78; McMillen, *Citizens',* 65–66; Joseph T. Taylor, "Desegregation . . . 1956," 263.

274   "the only . . . madness": JSW to J. F. X. McGoney, 2/20/56, JSW papers LC.

274–75   The eighty-year-old . . . moral prodding: *NYT,* 10/16,17,18/55; *TP,* 11/9/62; "The Morality of Segregation," written 2/11/56, sent, 2/15/56, read, 2/19/56, Catholic Council on Human Relations papers, ARC; 7 *DAB,* 668; *WP and Times Herald,* 8/6/56; Conaway, *Judge,* 108.

275–76   For the archbishop . . . at least another year: Cook, *Segregationists,* 234–35; Haas, *DeLesseps,* 254; Rosa Keller, ohp; *WP and Times Herald,* 8/6/56.

276   With the Orleans . . . 1946: *LW,* 10/6,27/56.

276–77   Nineteen-fifty-six . . . action on either side: *PPP,* 1956, 304–5; Hays, *Southern,* 13,101,123–24; McKeever, *Adlai,* 364; Schlesinger and Israel, *History,* iv, 3384 ff., 3399–400.

277–78   Only weeks . . . campaigns in 1956: *PPP,* 1956, 777–1089, 1038; *LW,* 11/3/56; Ambrose, *Eisenhower,* ii, 327–28; Brownell, *Advising,* 197–99; Schlesinger and Israel, *History,* iv, 3384–85, 3399–400, 3445.

278   On the state level . . . him in 1956: *LW,* 11/3/56; State of Louisiana, *Acts of the Legislature,* 15, 43, 438, 654, 741, 948; Fairclough, *Race,* 193; Kurtz and Peoples, *Earl,* 194–95.

278   Black voter purge: McMillen, *Citizens',* 222–25.

279   School board election: *LW,* 11/3/56; Read and McGough, *Let,* 130; Muller, "New," 74–75.

279–80   OPSB members' background: James E. Wright, Jr., to Liva Baker, 12/15/93; Lester Kabacoff to Liva Baker; Matt Sutherland to Liva Baker; Louis Riecke to Al Kennedy; Lloyd Rittiner to Al Kennedy; Kim Lacy Rogers, "Humanity," 109; *TP,* 12/26/82; *TP,* 5/13/71; Inger, *Politics,* 16, 26–27; Cook, *Segregationists,* 244 ff.

280   "stand a little" . . . "through": JSW to T. M. O'Brien, 2/28/56, JSW to J.F.X. McGoney, 2/20/56, JSW papers, LC.

CHAPTER 14: SMASHING MORE OF THE OLD FAMILY CHINA

281–83 One morning . . . pending final court action: APT, complaint, *Davis* v. *Morrison,* APT papers, ARC; 2 *RRLR,* 996–97, 1957; Fairclough, *Race,* 211–13; Kluger, *Simple,* 749–50; Kim Lacy Rogers, *Righteous,* 22, 45–46, Humanity, 135 ff.; Halberstam, *The Fifties,* 539–61; *TP,* 5/16/57.

283–84 A. P. Tureaud was spread . . . schools must desegregate: APT, memorandum, 10/19/57, APT papers, ARC; JSW to Frank T. Read; *OPSB* v. *Bush,* 242 F. 2d 156; *LW,* 3/2/57, 4/20/47; Read and McGough, manuscript of *Let,* 27a.

284–85 The three judges . . . year of precious time: Bass, *Unlikely,* 15–18, 32, 102; *OPSB* v. *Bush,* 242 F. 2d 156, 166, 354 U.S. 921; *TP,* 3/3/57; *OPSB* v. *Bush,* 252 F. 2d 253, 356 U.S. 969.

286 Wright required . . . seven appeals: *Bush* v. *OPSB,* 163 F. Supp. 701, 702; Worthy, "Travail," 138.

286–88 Late in 1956 . . . "staunch segregationist": James E. Wright, Jr., to Liva Baker, 12/15/93; JMW, "Frictionmaking," 240; William M. Rainach to Russell B. Long, 2/8/57, to F. P. Mims, 11/30/57, to Allen Ellender, 2/20/57; Long to Rainach, 2/11/57; Ellender to Rainach, 2/15/57, to H. P. Greer, 3/19/57, Rainach papers, LSUS; JMW to Fred Graham; Brownell, *Advising,* 182.

288–91 It was John . . . remained silent: JMW to Fred Graham; William M. Rainach to Allen Ellender, 4/6/57, Allen Ellender to Rainach, 4/17/57, to H. P. Greer, 3/29/57, Rainach papers, LSUS; *LW,* 5/27/57; Kim Lacy Rogers, *Righteous,* 45; Brownell, *Advising,* 182; JMW to Jack Bass; 103 *CR,* 10268; *TP,* 4/28/57, 4/30/57; Peltason, *Fifty-Eight,* 27, 28; Read and McGough, *Let,* 55–6; Sherrill, *Gothic,* 209–10; Barrow and Walker, *Court,* 41 ff.

291–92 Not three months . . . step of the way: Raines, *My,* 344; Bass, *Unlikely,* 46; 69–74; Greenberg, *Crusaders,* 248; Read and McGough, *Let,* 32, 62; *Browder* v. *Gayle;* JMW to Jack Bass.

292–93 Despite southern . . . Carolina or Louisiana: Allen Ellender to William M. Rainach, 8/31/57, Rainach papers, LSUS; 2 *RRLR,* 10, 11, 1957; *PPP,* 1957, 25; Brownell, *Advising,* 202 ff.; Eisenhower, *Waging,* 154 ff.; 64 *Crisis,* 1/57, 5.

293 In New Orleans . . . he argued: OPSB minutes, 7/57, OPSB papers, UNO.

293–95 All September . . . "recent years": Halberstam, *The Fifties,* 670 ff.; Huckaby, *Crisis;* Bates, *Long;* Helen Miller, "Private," 77–78; SRC, Little Rock Report, APT papers, ARC; Freyer, *Little,* 127.

295–96 After Little Rock . . . diehard segregationists: *SSN,* 8/58, 3; Earl Black, *Southern,* 299–301; Hodding Carter, *The South,* 101.

296 In New Orleans . . . three to one: John P. Nelson to Kim Lacy Rogers, 4/23/79, 6/22/88, 7/28/88; John P. Nelson to Jack Bass, 11/16/79; Kim Lacy Rogers, Lawyers, 15–16; *SSN,* 11/58, 6, 8; *LW,* 10/4/58; Worthy, "Travail," 196.

296–98 As if Little Rock . . . decade of litigation: William M. Rainach, election fact sheet, Rainach papers, LSUS; Fairclough, *Race,* 206–7, 219; Jeansonne, *Leander,* 230–31, 234–35; Giarrusso, Desegregation, 63–67; State of Louisiana, *Acts of the Legislature,* 1958, 831–61, 1391–92; 4 *RRLR,* 612; *Board* of *Supervisors . . .* v. *Fleming; LW,* 8/2/58, 9/13/58; *SSN,* 10/58, 15; Kurtz and Peoples, *Earl,* 299–302; Peltason, *Fifty-Eight,* 19; Read, *Let,* 200–201.

298–99 Legal efforts . . . federal district court: *Louisiana* v. *NAACP; NAACP* v. *Alabama,* 460–61; Worthy, "Travail," 109–11.

299 The courts, too . . . that fall: JSW to Lee Mortimer, 5/16/58, to Joseph C. Hutcheson, Jr., 2/1/54, JSW papers, LC; Peter Powers to Liva Baker; *LW,* 9/21/57.

299–300 The only time . . . us to desegregate: JMW to Liva Baker, 5/23/91; JMW to Jack Bass; *Dorsey* v. *State Athletic Commission; LW,* 1/18/58; *LW,* 9/21/57.

300–1   That same year . . . "act of a fanatic": *Detiege* v. *New Orleans City Park Association; Morrison* v. *Davis,* 252 F. 2d 103; JSW, ohp, MSRC; JSW to Frank T. Read; Fuller, "New," 16; Monroe, "J. Skelly," 371; Bill Monroe to Liva Baker; Oberdorfer, "In Memoriam," 1040; Kim Lacy Rogers, *Righteous,* 47; *TP,* 6/1/58; *SSN,* 7/58, 16; James S. Wright, Jr., to Liva Baker; *LW,* 6/7/58; *WS,* 5/31/58.

CHAPTER 15: "THE ONLY THING NECESSARY FOR THE TRIUMPH OF EVIL IS THAT GOOD MEN DO NOTHING"

302–5   George Washington Cable . . . counsel to the people?: Cable, *Negro,* ix, xi, 3–5, 13–14, 28–46, 132, 201; Cable, *Silent,* 1–39, 43–45; Turner, *George,* 3 ff., 12, 33 ff., 39 ff., 244, 263–72.

305–8   Three-quarters of a century . . . side of law and order: *LW,* 7/28/59, 8/1/59, 9/26/59; *SSN,* 12/59, 15; USCRC, *New,* 4; *OPSB* v. *Bush,* 268 F. 2d 78, 79; *Cooper* v. *Aaron,* 15, 17/19; Constance Baker Motley to APT, 7/1,7/59, APT papers, ARC; JSW to Thomas F. Murphy, 5/25/59, Richard T. Rives to JSW and Herbert W. Christenberry, 8/31/59, JSW papers, LC; *US News and World Report,* 6/1/59, 89; *TP,* 7/16/59.

308–9   The white parents . . . over desegregating them: *LW,* 8/1/59; Muller, "New," 75; Devore and Logsdon, *Crescent,* 240; *SSN,* 9/59, 13; 4 *RRLR,* 584, 1959; NO *States-Item,* 7/23/59; *TP,* 8/25/60.

309–10   Of all the "responsible" . . . ostrich: 66 *Crisis,* 1/59, 15–19; *SSN,* 8/59, 8; *NYT,* 7/8/59; 191 *Nation,* 12/3/60, 526.

310–11   While Montgomery's . . . forum to date: Inger, *Politics,* 25, 70 ff.; JSW to Frank T. Read; JSW to Jack Bass, 10/9/79; *TP,* 6/26/60, 9/1/60; Crain and Inger, *School,* 17; Haas, *DeLesseps,* 255 ff.

311–13   By the Fourth . . . platform shortly: *TP,* 7/5,6/57, 9/12/59; Havard, *Louisiana,* 37, 38; Liebling, *Earl,* 18–19, 45–47; Parker, *Morrison,* 116; BR *State-Times,* 7/4,6/59.

313–16   New Orleans Mayor . . . serving as governor: BR *State-Times,* 7/4,6/59; *TP,* 7/5/59, 12/2/59, 12/4/59; Haas, *DeLesseps,* 246; Havard, *Louisiana,* 39; Inger, *Politics,* 13, 14; Earl Black, *Southern,* 189–91; Liebling, *Earl,* 52; Peirce, *Deep,* 103–4; Moon Landrieu to Kim Lacy Rogers; Kane, "Dilemma," 9, 30–31.

316–18   On July 2, Willie . . . education in this state: BR *State-Times,* 7/6/59; *SSN,* 5/59, 5, 11/59, 13; Stowe, *Willie,* 271–72; Bass, *Unlikely,* 126; Havard, *Louisiana,* 117; *TP,* 12/3/59; Earl Black, *Southern,* 189–90; Liebling, *Earl,* 156–57, 201–2.

318–20   Earl Long's . . . any problem: Numan V. Bartley, *Rise,* 337; Earl Black, *Southern,* 190; Haas, *DeLesseps,* 246–49, 251–52; Kurtz and Peoples, *Earl,* 205–6, 246; Kurtz, "DeLesseps," 35; Liebling, *Earl,* 179, Lester Kabacoff to Liva Baker; *TP,* 12/4/59; *SSN,* 10/59, 11.

320   When the 840,000 . . . majority of our citizens: Havard, *Louisiana,* 42–44; *TP,* 12/7/59; Fairclough, *Race,* 231; Perry H. Howard, "Louisiana," 105–6, 559; memorandum, attorney general to FBI director, 2/20/61, FBI files.

320–24   The first gubernatorial . . . "seeing-eye dog": Jack P. F. Gremillion to Liva Baker; Conaway, *Judge,* 9, 111; Kane, "Dilemma," 30–33; Liebling, *Earl,* 204–5, 232; Earl Black, *Southern,* 215; Jeansonne, *Leander,* 235; Kim Lacy Rogers, *Righteous,* 64; Worthy, "Travail," 146 ff.; USCRC, *New,* 3–4; Havard, *Louisiana,* 51–52; *SSN,* 5/60, 14; *TP,* 5/11/59; Sherman, "Nightmare," 25.

CHAPTER 16: "GET READY FOR WAR!"

325–26   White tension . . . marketplace: *SSN,* 3/60, 1, 5/60, 14, 8/60, 7; *TP,* 6/3/60; Cohodas, *Strom,* 316; Kim Lacy Rogers, "Humanity," 177 ff., 184 ff.

326–27 Henry . . . collective psyche: *TP*, 4/30/60; *LW*, 10/6/60; Kim Lacy Rogers, *Righteous*, 67–68, "Humanity," 181; Daniel C. Thompson, *Negro*, 138–39.

327–29 Lloyd Rittiner . . . hurt this city: *NYT*, 11/15/60, 6/8/60; *SSN*, 2/60, 14; USCRC, *New*, 4, 5; Crain and Inger, *School*, 29; Inger, *Politics*, 19; Read and McGough, *Let*, 130; Kim Lacy Rogers, "Humanity," 170–71; Iggers, A study, unauthored, undated study, APT papers, ARC; *LW*, 4/30/60; *TP*, 5/4/60, 4/27/60.

329–32 At the school . . . public school desegregation: *TP*, 5/10,12/60; *SSN*, 5/60,14; JMW, "Frictionmaking," 42; JMW to Jack Bass; JSW, ohp, BR; Baton Rouge *Sunday Advocate*, 5/16/78; NO *TP/States-Item*, 7/11/84; Tuttle, "Chief," 870; 5 *RRLR*, 379, 1960.

332 Considering the options . . . more than I am: *TP*, 5/17,18,19/60, 6/23/60; *NYT*, 5/17/60; USCRC, *New*, 7; Giarrusso, "Desegregation," 101–2; Inger, "New," 86; *LW*, 5/21/60.

333–34 The Citizens' Council . . . definite possibility: *TP*, 5/18/60; McMillen, *Citizens'*, 69; *SSN*, 5/61, 9; Liebling, *Earl*, 9.

334 Working inside . . . obscurity: *SSN*, 6/60, 2; *TP*, 5/27/60, 6/1,2/60; Giarrusso, "Desegregation," 139–40; Jeansonne, *Leander*, 235; Liebling, *Earl*, 9, 36; McMillen, *Citizens'*, 318, 319; Pinney and Friedman, *Political*, 6–7.

334–35 From then on . . . details of their plans: *TP*, 5/24/60, 6/1/60, 7/6/60; Giarrusso, "Desegregation," 131; L. J. Rittiner, M. R. Sutherland, notes on conference with Davis, 7/5/60, Sutherland papers, UNO.

335–36 In rapid succession . . . trespass laws: State of Louisiana, *Acts of the Legislature*, 1960, 679, 939, 946, 948, 1072, 1075; ibid., 1956, 654; *Bush* v. *OPSB*, 163 F. Supp. 701; *OPSB* v. *Bush*, 268 F. 2d 78; *Angel* v. *Louisiana*.

336–37 Following Skelly . . . face it: *TP*, 5/9,15/60, 6/8,10,16,22,26/60; NO *States-Item*, 5/9/60; Inger, *Politics*, 76–77.

338–39 to set . . . "this matter": The Citizens' Council of Greater New Orleans, *The Citizens'*, 1; *TP*, 6/1,7/60, 8/30/60; USCRC, *New*, 19; Numan v. Bartley, *Rise*, 336; DeLesseps S. Morrison to Morris Campbell, 6/20/60, Morrison papers, NOPL; Haas, *DeLesseps*, 258.

339 The city's establishment . . . true explanation: Betty Wisdom to Liva Baker; Harry Kelleher to Liva Baker.

339–41 The first public . . . euphemism for desegregation: Ann Dlugos to Liva Baker; Peg Murison to Liva Baker; Mary Sand to Liva Baker; Rosa Keller to Kim Lacy Rogers, 5/7/79; *SSN*, 6/60, 2; USCRC, *New*, 6, 40–41; Kim Lacy Rogers, *Righteous*, 61–62, "Humanity," 165, 167.

341–42 SOS opened . . . rational discussion: Ann Dlugos to Liva Baker, to Kim Lacy Rogers, 11/11/75, 6/30/88; Betty Wisdom to Liva Baker; *TP*, 5/31/60, 6/29/60; USCRC, *New*, 40–41; Haas, *DeLesseps*, 257; Inger, *Politics*, 25, 73; Kim Lacy Rogers, "Humanity," 233.

342–43 Increasingly panicky . . . ultimately would be: Lloyd J. Rittiner to Liva Baker; OPSB, minutes, May, 1960, NAACP papers, UNO; *TP*, 6/21,23/60; *SSN*, 7/60, 7; USCRC, *New*, 7; Inger, *Politics*, 7; Jeansonne, *Leander*, 265.

343–44 Davis, however . . . "interposition fail": *LW*, 6/25/60; *NYT*, 7/20/60; *SSN*, 7/60, 7; *Bush* v. *OPSB*, 364 U.S. 803; 5 *RRLR* 655 ff.; Kim Lacy Rogers, "Humanity," 174–75.

344–45 It was not only Rittiner . . . shortly afterwards: *Bush* v. *OPSB*, 138 F. Supp. 337; *OPSB* v. *Bush*, 242 F. 2d 156; *Shuttlesworth* v. *Birmingham Board of Education*, 358 U.S. 101; *LW*, 7/23/60; *TP*, 7/7,15,16/60; USCRC, *New*, 7–8.

345–46 The state legislature . . . September 8: 5 *RRLR*, 659, 1960; *LW*, 8/6/60; *TP*, 7/6,20/60; *NYT*, 7/30/60; Kim Lacy Rogers, "Humanity," 171.

346 "there is much" . . . interposition: APT to TM, 7/22/60, APT papers, ARC.

CHAPTER 17: WAR—IN THE LEGAL SENSE

347   Struggles over ... lawyers: Robert H. Jackson, *The Struggle For Judicial Supremacy,* (New York, 1941), xi.

347–49   The NAACP ... watching its step: *NAACP* v. *Alabama; Louisiana* v. *NAACP;* Clarence Laws to branch leaders, 12/3/59, NAACP papers, UNO; *TP,* 10/25/60.

349   The intricate ... painstaking court action: *NYT,* 8/14/60; NO *States-Item,* 8/?/60, not completely dated clipping, Lemann papers, ARC.

349   Shelby ... "they are now": *SSN,* 10/59, 11; *TP,* 8/14/60; USCRC, *New,* 10; Read and McGough, *Let,* 153.

349–50   There was standing-room ... legal status: OPSB, minutes, 8/60, NAACP papers, UNO; *TP,* 8/5,10,13/60.

350   Davis assured ... "desegregating the schools": Jimmie H. Davis to DeLesseps S. Morrison, 8/15/60, Morrison papers, NOPL; 5 *RRLR,* 661, 1960; *TP,* 8/17,18/60.

350–51   Board President Rittiner's ... "hell of a fix": telegram, Lloyd J. Rittiner to Jimmie H. Davis, 8/19/60, OPSB papers, UNO; OPSB, minutes, 8/15/60, NAACP papers, UNO; *TP,* 8/10,18/60.

351   Recognizing ... worry about that: *TP,* 8/25/60; USCRC, *New,* 9.

351–52   But New Orleanians ... "hostile territory": *SSN,* 9/60, 16; USCRC, *New,* 23; Inger, *Politics,* 28; Giarrusso, "Desegregation," 122.

353   Although the white professional ... the others made: Lloyd J. Rittiner to Liva Baker; *TP,* 8/16,18,19,24,25/60; Inger, *Politics,* 29.

353–54   Unhesitatingly ... official: Robert C. Lancaster to James H. Davis et al., n.d., OPSB papers, UNO; Read and McGough, *Let,* 133–34; Kim Lacy Rogers, "Humanity," 172–74; RCP to Better Business Bureau, 8/11/60, OPSB papers, UNO; *TP,* 6/23/60.

354   There was talk ... Orleans schools: brief for plaintiff, *Williams* v. *Davis,* APT papers, ARC; Inger, *Politics,* 31; Read and McGough, *Let,* 139–41.

354–55   Recognizing ... they'd expected: *TP,* 8/20/60; *Newsweek,* 8/29/60, 30–31.

355–57   Attorney General Gremillion ... "defend" him: Jack P. F. Gremillion to Liva Baker; JSW to Jack Bass, 5/15/80; *Bush* v. *OPSB,* 187 F. Supp. 42; *OPSB* v. *Bush,* 365 U.S. 569; *TP,* 11/16/59; 8/26, 27,28/60; JSW to Frank T. Read; Liebling, *Earl,* 161–62; Read and McGough, *Let,* 135; Kim Lacy Rogers, "Humanity," 173.

357–58   Implicit ... do it, they said: JSW to Jack Bass, 5/15/80; *TP,* 8/26, 30/60; Muller, "New," 82.

358–59   They didn't ... parties to the legal suits: JSW to Jack Bass, 5/15/60; Adrian Duplantier to Liva Baker; *Shuttlesworth* v. *Birmingham Board of Education,* 358 U.S. 101; Matthew R. Sutherland to Liva Baker.

359   He conferred ... Rault's shoes: JSW to Jack Bass, 5/15/60; *NYT,* 8/30, 31/60; Lloyd J. Rittiner to Liva Baker; *TP,* 8/31/60, 9/2/60; *LW,* 9/3/60; OPSB, minutes, 9/12/60, OPSB papers, UNO.

359–60   Skelly Wright ... "offended" him: JSW to Kim Lacy Rogers; JSW to Gus Weill; Harold R. Tyler to Liva Baker, 4/9/91, 5/1/90; HPW to Liva Baker, 4/2/90; Rosa Keller to Liva Baker; *NYT,* 11/16/60; Kim Lacy Rogers, "Humanity," 228; JSW to Frank T. Read; James E. Wright, Jr., to Liva Baker, 7/10/90.

360–61   Wright wasn't at all ... relationship: JSW to Jack Bass, 5/15/80.

361–62   The way Wright ... no doubt about that: JSW to Jack Bass, 5/15/80; Ambrose, *Eisenhower,* ii, 593.

362   Except in Tyler's ... where *he* stood: Harold R. Tyler to Liva Baker, 4/9/91 and 5/1/90.

362–63   Wright proceeded ... frenzy of opposition: *NYT,* 8/30,31/60; *TP,* 9/1,13/60, 10/12/60; *LW,* 9/3/60; USCRC, *New,* 10–11; Muller, "New," 8.

363   September opened ... eligible to transfer: *LW,* 10/1/60; *NYT,* 9/4/60; *TP,* 9/2/60.

363–64 That same day ... "to Him": *TP,* 9/2,13,28/60.

364–65 Although his stamina ... Communist vultures: *TP,* 9/3/60; Conaway, *Judge,* 112–13; Jeansonne, *Leander,* 237–38.

365–66 The next day ... for admission: Kurtz and Peoples, *Earl,* 255–56; *TP,* 9/1,2,4,9/60; *NO States-Item,* 8/4/60.

CHAPTER 18: "IF THE FIGHT CAN BE KEPT IN THE COURTS, EVERYTHING WILL WORK OUT"

367   On September ... numbers: *TP,* 9/21/60; *SSN,* 10/6, 2; Devore and Logsdon, *Crescent,* 265.

367–68 Undoubtedly ... principle to work: *TP,* 8/22/60; Inger, *Politics,* 23 ff.

368–69 U.S. Attorney ... "Good day, sir": A. Hepburn Many to Liva Baker: St. John Barrett to Liva Baker; *TP,* 8/6/60.

369–70 While the majority ... living near them: James F. Redmond to OPSB, 9/26/60, APT papers, ARC; OPSB, minutes, 9/26/60, OPSB papers, UNO; *TP,* 9/13/60; *NO States-Item,* 8/4/60.

370–71 School board vice ... citywide: JSW to Jack Bass, 5/15/80; *TP,* 8/26/60; *NO States-Item,* 8/4/60; *SSN,* 10/60, 2; KKK to APT, 8/29/60, APT papers, ARC.

371   The only way ... of the first grade: State of Louisiana, *Acts of the Legislature,* regular session, 1960, 939 ff.; Read and McGough, *Let,* 136 ff.

371–72 The editors ... desegregation order: James F. Redmond to Liva Baker; Samuel I. Rosenberg to Liva Baker; *LW,* 10/22/60; *TP,* 10/11/60; Inger, *Politics,* 34–37.

372   During the time ... known at all: Fairclough, *Race,* 240; Inger, *Politics,* 36–37.

372–73 School board members ... part of a month: James F. Redmond to Liva Baker; Inger, *Politics,* 34 ff.

373–75 As New Orleanians, black ... isn't it?: Jack P. F. Gremillion to Liva Baker; *TP,* 9/4/60, 10/8/60; *SSN,* 11/60, 14; Read and McGough, *Let,* 135.

375–76 Thurgood Marshall ... "sit-ins or demonstrations": Elise Nichols to Liva Baker; *LW,* 5/17/60; *TP,* 9/11,13/60; *SSN,* 10/60, 3; Haas, *DeLesseps,* 261, 262; Daniel C. Thompson, *Negro,* 116.

376–77 The Orleans Parish school board ... for transfer: James F. Redmond to Liva Baker; OPSB, minutes, 11/10/60, 1/24/61, OPSB papers, UNO; USCRC, *New,* 11; *TP,* 10/25,28/60; Inger, *Politics,* 36; Kim Lacy Rogers, "Humanity," 197.

377–78 The board instructed ... "desegregation process": Samuel I. Rosenberg to Liva Baker; A Study of Some Intangible (1960), n.p.; *TP/States-Item,* 7/11/84; Inger, *Politics,* 38–39.

378–79 A visiting ... downtown opposition: Betty Wisdom to Liva Baker; *TP,* 11/16/60; A Study of Some Intangible (1960), 2.

379   Rising ... seemed more likely: Inger, *Politics,* 38; Suhor, "Coming," 40 ff.; Coles, *Children,* 22–23; Spain, "Race," 9.

379–80 No one ... public education: *TP,* 8/4/60.

380   While school officials ... in the making: Lester Kabacoff to Liva Baker; *SSN,* 1/60, 1; USCRC, *New,* 12; Haas, *DeLesseps,* 262; Inger, *Politics,* 41, 89.

380–81 Following a secret ... "raise hell": Adrian Duplantier to Liva Baker; *TP,* 11/1, 2, 3, 4/60.

381   Leander ... non–New Orleanians: *NYT,* 11/7/60; *TP,* 11/8/60; USCRC, *New,* 13; McCarrick, "Louisiana's," 202–3, 220.

381–83 Maurice ... in November: Moon Landrieu to Liva Baker; Moon Landrieu to Kim Lacy Rogers, 5/11/79, 6/13/88; *TP,* 12/6/59, 1/10/60; Kim Lacy Rogers, *Righteous,* 59–60.

383–84 This special ... affected his city: Moon Landrieu to Liva Baker; Moon Landrieu to Kim Lacy Rogers, 6/13/88; *TP*, 11/6/60; Kim Lacy Rogers, *Righteous*, 65; Haas, *DeLesseps*, 263–64; Inger, *Politics*, 43; Pinney and Friedman, *Political*, 10.

384–85 Chep ... in the cold: Haas, *DeLesseps*, 265; Crain and Inger, *School*, 60.

385–86 In the senate ... hardliners: Adrian Duplantier to Liva Baker; *TP*, 11/9/60; Barrow and Walker, *Court*, 139; Bass, *Unlikely*, 135; Pinney and Friedman, *Political*, 11.

386–87 All told ... battle of segregation: *State of Louisiana Acts of the Legislature*, special session, 1960, 1–48; *TP*, 11/2, 3, 4, 5, 7, 8, 9, 10, 11, 13/60; WDSU, editorial, 11/7/60; Kim Lacy Rogers, "Humanity," 201 ff.; Inger, *Politics*, 45–46.

387 Watching the show ... "day appointed": JSW to Kim Lacy Rogers, 12/9/78.

387–89 On November 8 ... home and school each day: Matthew R. Sutherland to Liva Baker; Caryl Vesy to Liva Baker; *TP*, 10/12,14/60; USCRC, *New*, 11–12; Ambrose, *Eisenhower*, i, 604–5; Muller, "New," 85.

389–90 On November 1 ... desegregation: *TP*, 11/1,4,7,9/60, 6/10/79; Inger, *Politics*, 46–47; Read and McGough, *Let*, 156.

390–91 Once the election ... up in smoke: James F. Redmond to Liva Baker; "An Interview," 25; *TP*, 10/10,22/60,11/8,11/60; Kim Lacy Rogers, "Humanity," 200.

391 He hadn't, however ... will work out: 5 *RRLR* 1001; "An Interview," 25; *NYT*, 11/12,13/60; Inger, *Politics*, 46–47; *TP*, 11/12/60.

391–92 The school board ... ongoing special session: OPSB, minutes, 11/10/60, APT papers, ARC; *TP*, 11/11,13/60; USCRC, *New*, 13; Crain and Inger, *School*, 63.

392–93 That same day ... "pray for me also": Lucille Bridges to Liva Baker; James F. Redmond, affidavit, 11/18/55, APT papers, ARC; *TP*, 11/13/60.

CHAPTER 19: THE D WORD

394–95 Monday, November ... Louisiana that did: *TP*, 11/14,15,16/60; *Time*, 11/28/60, 19; Read and McGough, *Let*, 141–42.

395–96 Local police ... whatever they asked: Jesse Grider to Liva Baker; Lucille Bridges to Liva Baker; Ruby Bridges Hall to Liva Baker, 7/21/92; *TP*, 11/15/60; Kim Lacy Rogers, "Humanity," 208.

396–97 Lucille had waited ... to William Frantz school: Lucille Bridges to Liva Baker; Ruby Bridges Hall to Liva Baker, 7/20/93, 3/24/93; Coles, *Children*, 74–75.

397–98 Jesse Grider ... feral: Jesse Grider to Liva Baker; Mary Sand to Liva Baker; "An Interview," 25, 26, 28; Sarah Tomlin to Liva Baker; *TP*, 2/28/92, 6/16/93.

398–99 Jesse Grider's eyes ... that first day: Jesse Grider to Liva Baker; JSW to Kim Lacy Rogers; JSW, ohp; *TP*, 11/16/60.

399 As originally ... her name: Read and McGough, *Let*, 146.

400 Only 105 ... that day: Mr. and Mrs. James Suitor, This Is, 1; *TP*, 11/15/60.

400 Born in Costa Rica ... walked away: Mothner, "Exodus," 55 ff.; Tawes, "The Mother," 30 ff.

400–1 Daisy Gabrielle was ... "cheerleaders": *TP*, 11/15/60; Fairclough, *Race*, 247.

401 Having prepared ... trouble: Peg Murison to Liva Baker; Mary Sand to Liva Baker; Lloyd J. Rittiner to Al Kennedy; Muller, "New," 87; Kim Lacy Rogers, "Organizational," 7; "Humanity," 212.

401–2 A few blocks away ... came the response: *NYT*, 11/16/60, 5/17/74; *TP/States-Item*, 4/19/84; Meyer, *Names*, 236; Jupiter, "It Was," 60; Lillian Smith, "Ordeal," 70; Coles, *Children*, 40.

402–3 Down at the federal ... around them: Lucille Bridges to Liva Baker; James F. Redmond to Liva Baker; Mary Sand to Liva Baker; *WP*, 11/21/60; Coles, *Children*, 194; Chicago *Sun-Times*, 11/27/60.

403   Months before . . . senate and house: Conaway, *Judge,* 107–8, 112–13.
403–4   The last-ditch . . . following morning: Moon Landrieu to Liva Baker; *Monroe Morning Herald,* 11/14/60; *TP,* 11/14/60; USCRC, *New,* 13–14; Sherman, "Nightmare," 25.
404–5   Skelly Wright . . . "risk anarchy": *Bush* v. *OPSB,* 191 F. Supp. 871, 878–79; 5 *RRLR* 1004 ff.; JSW to Kim Lacy Rogers; Behlar, "J. Skelly," 102.
405–6   Wright's boldness . . . overwhelming majorities: *TP,* 11/14,15/60; Kane, "Dilemma," 9.
406   With A. P. Tureaud . . . segregated schools: Clarence E. Laws, Report to Branches, 11/17/60, APT papers, ARC; *TP,* 11/15/60; Moley, "Ordeal," 110; Rivera, *Special,* 60.
406–7   Attorney General . . . It was theirs: James F. Redmond to Liva Baker; Lloyd J. Rittiner to Liva Baker; *TP,* 11/15/60.
407   Matt Sutherland . . . capitulate: Matthew R. Sutherland to Liva Baker *TP,* 11/15/60.
407–8   Skelly Wright . . . full confidence: Louis Claiborne to Liva Baker; JSW to Jack Bass, 5/15/80; JSW, ohp; Inger, *Politics,* 58.
408–9   As D-Day . . . lives here: DeLesseps S. Morrison, statement, 11/14/60, Morrison papers, NOPL; Louis Claiborne to Liva Baker; Coles, *Children,* 86; Dykeman, "Integration," 112–13.

Chapter 20: Courage

410–11   The Lord . . . against their sides: Prim Smith to Liva Baker; Burke Marshall to Liva Baker; Betty Wisdom to *Nation,* 353; *TP,* 11/16/60; *Ebony,* 2/61, 79; Coles, "Desegregation," 208; Kane, "Change," 56; Lillian Smith, "Ordeal," 81.
411–12   Despite the disturbing . . . fear for their lives: Lucille Bridges to Liva Baker; Ruby Bridges Hall to Liva Baker, 7/20/92; APT, ohp; *NYT,* 11/18/60; *TP,* 11/16/60; Bernick, "Unusual," 989; Coles, *Children,* 82,84–86, 376ff.; NPR, "All Things Considered," 11/12/95.
412–13   Tall—six . . . each stressful day: Coles, "as Bad"; 57 ff., Jupiter, "It Was," 60 ff.
413–14   About midmorning . . . keep a cool head: JSW to Jack Bass, 5/15/80; Sara Tomlin to Liva Baker; Joseph Giarrusso, "House Divided"; *TP,* 11/16/60; *NYT,* 11/16/60.
414–15   On Tuesday . . . now!: *TP,* 11/16/60; Read and McGough, *Let* (manuscript), 51, 56; Wichita (Kansas) *Eagle,* 11/16/60; Sherman, "Nightmare," 26.
415   Egged on . . . and the Constitution: *NYT,* 11/17/60; *TP,* 11/17/60; *Newsweek,* 11/18/60, 20; Inger, "New," 92.
415–16   On Thursday . . . protect us: Leontine Luke to Liva Baker; Leontine Luke to Kim Lacy Rogers; Clarence E. Laws, Report to Branches, 11/17/60, 4, APT papers, ARC; *TP,* 11/18/60; Coles, *Children,* 24; *A House Divided . . .*
416–18   By the end . . . one Sunday morning: Mary Sand to Liva Baker; Rosa Keller to Kim Lacy Rogers, 5/7/79; Betty Wisdom to *Nation,* 353; Steinbeck, *Travels,* 227; *TP,* 11/23,30/60, 12/4,14/60; *NYT,* 12/5/60; Back to School Trust report, n.d., 2, APT papers, ARC; *LW,* 12/17/60.
418   Construction . . . "or isn't it?": Lloyd J. Rittiner to Liva Baker; Matthew R. Sutherland to Liva Baker; *TP,* 11/19/60; Inger, *Politics,* 64; Kim Lacy Rogers, "Humanity," 231.
418–20   For their parting shot . . . standing ovation: 5 *RRLR,* 1214, 1215–16, 1223, 1230, 1960; *TP,* 11/16,17,24,29/60; Pinney and Friedman, *Political,* 15–18.
420   Skelly Wright's several . . . and McDonogh 19:5 *RRLR,* 1215, 1960; *NYT,* 11/17/60; *TP,* 11/17,18/60; Inger, *Politics,* 54.
420–21   For himself . . . be payless: James F. Redmond to Liva Baker; *TP,* 11/24/60; Coles, "Desegregation," 219; Read and McGough, *Let* (manuscript), 61.

421 Sam Rosenberg ... as the poverty: Samuel I. Rosenberg to Liva Baker; *Newsweek,* 1/16/61, 50.
422 Now that he had ... private system: 5 *RRLR,* 1224ff., 1960; *State of Louisiana Acts of the Legislature,* 1960, special session, 54–59; *TP,* 11/17/60, 12/1/60.
422 United States ... "delicacy": telegram, Jacob K. Javits to Dwight D. Eisenhower, 11/30/60; Dwight D. Eisenhower to Jacob K. Javits, 12/6/60; Eisenhower papers, DDE.
422–23 Down at the Yankee ... "J. Wrong": Adrian Duplantier to Liva Baker; Martha Scallon to Liva Baker; Samuel I. Rosenberg to Liva Baker; HPW to Liva Baker, 1/20/93; Lester Kabacoff to Liva Baker; *TP,* 11/27/60; *Time,* 12/20/60, 40.
423 At the same time ... intemperate: Elizabeth Black to HPW, 11/15/60; HPW scrapbook; J. Waties Waring to JSW, 11/25/60, JSW to J. Waties Waring, 11/30/60, JSW papers, LC; *Time,* 12/5/60, 14; boxes 12, 13, JSW papers, LC.
423–24 Closer to home ... "message?": JSW to Kim Lacy Rogers; James E. Wright, Jr., to Liva Baker, 7/10/90; HPW to Liva Baker, 4/2/90; James S. Wright, Jr., to Liva Baker.
424–25 There was relief ... "in the air": Martha Scallon to Liva Baker.
425 Wright's Irish ... he strove: Bill Monroe to Liva Baker; A. Hepburn Many to Liva Baker.
425 Establishment New ... late for that: JSW to Jack Bass, 1/15/79; JMW to Liva Baker, 5/23/91; JMW to Fred Graham; Katherine Wisdom to Jack Bass; Bass, *Unlikely,* 115.
425–26 Wright speculated ... increasingly: JSW to Jack Bass, 1/15/79; HPW to Liva Baker, 4/2/90; JSW, ohp.
426 He tried not ... his resolve: JSW to Gus Weill; James S. Wright, Jr., to Liva Baker; JSW, ohp.
426–28 As the four ... its jurisdiction: *TP,* 11/19/60, 12/1/60; Inger, *Politics,* 54.
428–29 The judges ... landslide: *Bush* v. *OPSB,* 188 F. Supp. 916, 922, 925, 926, 927, 927, 929.
429 The *Times* ... integration: *TP,* 12/1/60.
429 But in Baton ... "reason": 5 *RRLR* 1223; *TP,* 12/1/60.
429 School board members ... "without merit": *TP,* 12/1/60; *Bush* v. *OPSB,* 364 U.S. 500 (1960).
429–30 Their creative ... "former" Orleans Parish school board: *State of Louisiana, Acts of the Legislature,* first, second, and third special sessions, 1960, 1961; *Bush* v. *OPSB,* 190 F. Supp. 861, 191 F. Supp. 871; *TP,* 12/16,23,60; USCRC, *New,* 17–18; Inger, *Politics,* 63.
430–31 Local banks ... still defiant: *TP,* 12/19,22,23/60; Pinney and Friedman, *Political,* 19.
431–32 Inspired ... academic year: Mary Sand to Liva Baker; Betty Wisdom to *Nation,* 353; Plans and Program for Save Our Schools, Inc., 6 ff., SOS papers, ARC; *TP,* 12/2,10/60.
432 After police ... found work: Suitor, This Is.
432–33 The harassment ... day attained: Mothner, "Exodus," 53 ff.; Tawes, "Mother," 30 ff.; *TP,* 12/28/60.
433 The four ... "is theirs": *TP,* 12/2/60.
433–34 The city had ... of customers: *NYT,* 12/6/60; USCRC, *New,* 23–24.
434–35 The decline ... "judicial system": *TP,* 12/14,18,22,23/60.
435 Mayor Morrison ... stringent measures: DeLesseps S. Morrison to Butch L. Smart, 12/6/50, Morrison papers, NOPL; *NYT,* 12/5,6/60; *TP,* 12/30/60; Inger, *Politics,* 63; Kim Lacy Rogers, "Humanity," 225–26.
435–36 SOS member ... their souls: Betty Wisdom to *Nation,* 353.

CHAPTER 21: LET THE HEALING BEGIN

437–40   Simultaneously . . . "afford to go backward": Lester Kabacoff to Liva Baker;
Harry Kelleher to Liva Baker; Harry Kelleher to Kim Lacy Rogers, 5/8/79;
Harry Kelleher, speech draft in HPW scrapbook; Louis Riecke to Al Kennedy;
TP, 1/17,30,31/61; *SSN,* 3/61, 8; Inger, *Politics,* 35, 64–65; Kim Lacy Rogers,
"Humanity," 233–38.

440–41   Eleven weeks . . . undisclosed: Ruby Bridges Hall to Liva Baker, 7/20/92;
NAACP records, UNO; *NYT,* 5/17/74; *TP,* 1/4/61, 1/28, 31/61, 2/1/61,
4/19/83; Coles, *Children,* 92; *Time,* 2/10/61.

441–45   Ruby Bridges doggedly . . . petered out: Ruby Bridges Hall to Liva Baker,
7/20/92, 3/24/93; Coles, *Children,* 22–24, 40–67, 88–89.

445–46   As the sun . . . "spending for Carnival": Leonard Burns to Arthur Chapital,
3/13/61, NAACP papers, UNO; *LW,* 12/3/60, 2/4,11,18/61; *TP,* 2/13,15/61;
NYT, 12/16/60; Trillin, "Zulus," 41–47, 54, 94, 97, 105–6.

446–48   The gloom . . . White Citizens' Council: *TP,* 1/15/61, 2/15/61; Edmonson,
"Carnival," 233 ff.

448–50   Louisiana's lawmakers . . . effect immediately: State of Louisiana, *Acts of the
Legislature,* 1961, 83 ff.; *TP,* 2/11,19,24/61; *NYT,* 2/21/61.

450–52   St. Helena Parish . . . stand: *Hall* v. *St. Helena Parish School Board,* 649, 651,
652, 659, 660, 662; *St. Helena Parish School Board* v. *Hall,* 368 U.S. 515; John
Minor Wisdom to Liva Baker, 12/13/93; *TP,* 5/19/61, 6/1,6/61.

CHAPTER 22: LESSONS LEARNED

453–54   Shortly before . . . "than we have": JSW to Julian B. Feibelman, 8/21/61, JSW
papers, LC; *TP,* 4/19/61, 6/7/61, 8/6/61, 9/8/61, 4/5/62; *SSN,* 8/62, 15;
Time, 8/25/61, 40; Planer, "Louisiana," 37; Public Affairs Research Council,
PAR Analysis, 10/63, Table 1.

454   The state legislature . . . with trash: Transcript, hearing, 3/3/61; *NYT,*
2/25/61; *TP,* 1/22/61, 3/2/62.

454–56   For one thing . . . learned something last year: Burke Marshall to Liva Baker;
A. Hepburn Many to Liva Baker; *PPP,* 1961, 25, 124; Burke Marshall, ohp; *TP,*
2/17/61, 8/31/61.

456–57   On D-Day . . . July 17: DeLesseps S. Morrison to Robert F. Kennedy, 3/2/61,
DeLesseps S. Morrison to Leontine Luke, 3/25/61, Morrison papers, NOPL;
Arthur Chapital to Senate Foreign Relations Committee, 6/26/61, NAACP
papers, UNO; *TP,* 7/21/61, 8/6/61, 8/8/61, 8/16/61; Haas, *DeLesseps,* 283–84.

457–58   On July 20 . . . close touch with Chief Giarrusso: James F. Redmond to Liva
Baker; Louis Riecke to Al Kennedy; *TP,* 5/9/61, 8/6,8,16/61; Inger, *Politics,* 67.

458–59   Even the local . . . respect that law: JSW to Frank T. Read; telegram, Raburn
Monroe, Clifford Favrot, John Tims, Charles Keller, Jr., Darwin Fenner,
Richard Freeman, Charles Smither, Lester Kabacoff to A. L. Schlesinger,
8/9/61; memorandum, Ed Guthman to the attorney general, 8/14/61, Burke
Marshall papers, JFK; *TP,* 9/1,3/61.

459–60   Segregationists . . . "Sunshine": *TP,* 8/16/61, 9/7,27/61.

460   On August 31 . . . "public schools": NO Department of Police, Plans, Public
Schools 1961, Burke Marshall papers, JFK; *TP,* 9/1,5/61; transcript, "Our
Schools at the Crossroads," 9/6/61, SOS papers, ARC.

460–61   The buildup . . . 1961–62 term: APT to Mr. Harold, 9/6/61, APT papers, ARC;
TP, 9/8/61, 10/4/61; Giarrusso, "Desegregation," 111.

461–62   After nine years . . . new school superintendent: *LW,* 9/30/61; *TP,* 9/27/61;
Kim Lacy Rogers, "Humanity," 239–40.

462–63   The telephone call . . . Southern federal judges: JSW to Jack Bass, 1/15/79;

John Minor Wisdom to Liva Baker, 5/23/91; Elbert Tuttle to Jack Bass; Richard Rives to Lister Hill, 5/1/61, JSW papers, LC; William M. Fay to JSW, 3/31/61, JSW papers, LC; Bicentennial Committee ... *Judges,* 31, 179; *TP,* 5/5/61; *New Republic,* 6/12/61, 7; Navasky, *Kennedy,* 272–73.

463–64 The message ... docket in New Orleans: A. Hepburn Many to Liva Baker; DeLesseps S. Morrison to Robert F. Kennedy, 3/24/61, Morrison papers, NOPL; Burke Marshall to Liva Baker; JSW to Hugo L. Black, 10/9/61, JSW to Mrs. Steinman Ansberry, 6/21/61, JSW papers, LC; Bass, *Unlikely,* 133; Read and McGough, *Let,* 82.

464–65 The judge-makers ... clear conscience: *NYT,* 12/16/61; James S. Wright, Jr., to Liva Baker; Burke Marshall, ohp; *NYT,* 12/16/61; *TP,* 5/5,16,20/61; *Davis* v. *East Baton Rouge Parish School Board,* 625.

465 Which was more or less ... manager in 1960: James S. Wright, Jr., to Liva Baker; JSW to Jack Bass, 1/15/79; *TP,* 12/16/61.

465–66 The next several ... basis of race: Barrett Prettyman to JSW, 2/3/62, 2/8/62, 4/5/62; JSW to Barrett Prettyman, 12/n.d./61, 2/5/62; U.S. Congress, Senate, Committee on the Judiciary, *Nomination of J. Skelly Wright ...* ; 946 *CR* 5244; Keller, *Autobiography,* ii, 29.

466–67 As he and Helen ... Orleans Parish school board: JSW, temporary restraining order, 1/23/62, JSW papers, LC; APT, plaintiff's memorandum brief, 3/5/62, APT papers, ARC; Samuel I. Rosenberg to John W. Letson, 3/16/62, John W. Letson to Samuel I. Rosenberg, 3/22/62, OPSB papers, UNO; Read and McGough, *Let,* 159.

467–68 Wright's parting shot ... could be scheduled: JSW to G. W. Foster, Jr., 5/15/63, JSW papers, LC; *Bush* v. *OPSB,* 204 F. Supp. 568, 571, 572; *TP,* 4/4,5,6,7/61.

468 On his last day ... we've been here; John R. Martzell, "Reflections of Judge Wright," *TP,* 8/26/88.

Afterword

469–70 Confirming ... eloquently: *TP,* 2/24/62,4/17/62; Navasky, *Kennedy,* 275.

470–71 The Wrights ... modification: Martha Scallon to Liva Baker; HPW to Liva Baker, 3/23/92; *TP,* 11/5/59, 8/18/60, 2/24/61; *SSN,* 6/62, 3; Kurtz and Peoples, *Earl,* 54–55; Navasky, *Kennedy,* 273–76; Schlesinger and Israel, *History,* iv, 3445.

471 The public schools ... to be abolished: *Bush* v. *OPSB,* 308 F. 2d 491, 502–3; *TP,* 4/18,19,25/62; *SI,* 5/1/62; *SSN,* 5/62, 2, 6/62, 3; Read and McGough, *Let,* 159–60.

471 The Orleans Parish ... "start now": *TP,* 8/14/62; *SSN,* 9/62, 6–7.

472 School desegregation ... parity: *United States* v. *Jefferson,* 905; OPSB, *Facts on File,* 1964–65, 20–21, OPSB papers, UNO; *SI,* 4/16/62; *TP,* 5/26/62, 11/9/64, 7/11,18/84.

472–73 Two major ... St. Tammany parishes: OPSB, *Facts on File,* 1964–65, 20–21, OPSB papers, UNO; U.S. Bureau of the Census, *Census of Population,* 1960, v. 1, part 20, 270; *TP,* 7/11/84; Fairclough, *Race,* 461; Kim Lacy Rogers, "Humanity," 249; Orfield, *Racial,* 5.

473 Harry Kelleher ... where I sit: Harry Kelleher to Liva Baker.

473–74 Lloyd Rittiner ... Colorado Springs: Lloyd Rittiner to Liva Baker; *TP,* 12/26/82, 8/6,14/91; *SSN,* 1/64, 5.

474 Sam Rosenberg ... age of seventy-one: Sam Rosenberg to Liva Baker; Louis Riecke to Al Kennedy; Matthew R. Sutherland to Liva Baker; *TP,* 4/20/62, 10/14/93.

474–75 Following his resignation ... Not very often: Mary Sand to Liva Baker; Peg Murison to Liva Baker; Betty Wisdom to Liva Baker; Ann Dlugos to Kim Lacy Rogers, 6/30/88; *TP,* 5/13/71.

475–76 In 1991, a white-haired ... wept openly: Rosa Keller to Liva Baker; Rosa Keller to Kim Lacy Rogers, 4/8/88; *TP,* 10/7/85.

476 Dan Byrd ... age of seventy-four: Cummins and Jeansonne, *Guide,* 206–7; *TP,* 3/19/84.

476–77 A. P. Tureaud ... cause of human rights: APT, ohp, MSRC; *TP,* 1/23,25/72; NO *Clarion-Herald,* 1/27/72.

477–78 After temporarily ... at the movies: A. P. Tureaud, Jr., to Liva Baker, 10/6/91, 3/7/95.

478–81 Ruby Bridges ... "segregation, anyway?": Ruby Bridges to Liva Baker, 7/20/92, 2/18/95; Mr. and Mrs. Charles Etienne to district superintendent, 10/8/62, Mrs. L. Tate to superintendent of education, 10/6/62, APT papers, ARC; Lucille Bridges to Liva Baker; Jupiter, "It Was," 60; Coles, "Bad As," 57 ff., "Desegregation," 207; *NYT,* 5/17/74; "House Divided"; *TP,* 4/19/84; *SSN,* 10/62, 6; Elizabeth C. Rogers, personal account of the 1984 reunion, Rogers papers, UNO.

481 In 1968, Mack ... Court was right: Devore and Logsdon, *Crescent,* 270–71; Everett J. Williams to Liva Baker; Eisenhower, *Mandate,* 230.

481–82 In 1962 ... District of Louisiana: Adrian Duplantier to Liva Baker; JSW to Prim Smith, 3/2/62, JSW papers, LC; *TP,* 1/4/62, 2/22/62, 3/10,16/62, 8/30/92; Kim Lacy Rogers, "Humanity," 314.

482 Constitutionally prohibited ... enthusiastically: Jack Gremillion to Liva Baker; *TP,* 11/6/63, 9/19,28/94; Earl Black, *Southern,* 78.

482–83 Chep Morrison ... died in 1972: *TP,* 1/17/72; *SSN,* 12/63, 15–16, 2/64, 5; Earl Black, *Southern,* 76–78; Haas, *DeLesseps,* 288–89.

483–84 In 1965 ... Fourth Circuit: Wilfred Aubert, PAC Report, 12/13/65, NAACP papers, UNO; Hirsch, "Simply," 293 ff.; "A House Divided"; Kim Lacy Rogers, *Righteous,* 164, "Lawyers", 20; *TP,* 3/11/92.

484 Moon Landrieu was ... "old block": Hirsch, "Simply," 296, 304, 318 ff.; *TP,* 12/25/89; *NYT,* 3/7/94.

485 In 1962 ... eight blacks there: *SSN,* 10/62, 7; Peirce, *Deep,* 61–63.

485 After his defeat ... He was sixty-four: Rainach, ohp; *TP,* 1/27/78.

485–86 Jack Gremillion ... That's gone!: Jack Gremillion to Liva Baker; *TP,* 1/4,5/73; 4/1/74.

486–87 Neither advancing ... Funeral Home: *NYT,* 3/20/69; *WP,* 3/20/69; Gibbons, "The South's," 12; Conaway, *Judge,* 183 ff.; Jeansonne, *Leander,* 360–64; Schlesinger and Israel, *History,* iv, 3741 ff., 3865.

487–88 Perez did not die ... a thousand of them: *NYT,* 10/1,9/90, 11/10,17,18/91; *TP,* 11/18/91.

488–90 Three decades after ... three decades before: U.S. Bureau of the Census, *Census of Population, Louisiana,* 1990, 16; *NYT,* 12/7/91, 1/29/92, 2/14/93; *TP,* 7/10/83, "Mardi Gras Insert," 2/14/90, 1/20/92, 3/13/93.

490 Herbert Christenberry ... quarter of a century: orders, 8/23/75, 9/30/77, OPSB papers, UNO; *TP,* 10/6/75; *Time,* 8/6/65, 25.

490–91 In 1969 ... have been here: JMW to Liva Baker, 5/23/91; HPW to Liva Baker, 12/93; *WP,* 12/8/93; Bass, *Unlikely,* 23.

491–92 The U.S. Court of Appeals ... interests of society: *Washington Star,* 3/29/78; Liva Baker, *Miranda,* 51 ff.

492 Wright eagerly ... racial discrimination: see *Dellums* v. *Powell, Women Strike for Peace* v. *Morton, Killough* v. *United States, Hobsen* v. *Hansen.*

492   By the time . . . record player: HPW to Liva Baker, 2/27/91; Levine, "Great,"
931; Parker, "J. Skelly," 369.

492–93   After 1971 . . . law to support it: *Calvert Cliffs Coordinating Commission* v.
Atomic Energy Commission, Chisholm v. *Federal Communications Commission,
Business Executives' Move for Peace* v. *Federal Communications Commission,
Williams* v. *Walker-Thomas Furniture Company;* JSW to Jack Bass, 1/15/79.

493–94   David Bazelon . . . He was seventy-seven: HPW to Liva Baker, 2/27/91, 6/95;
119 *FRD* 461, 474; *Chambers* v. *Florida,* 241; *NYT,* 1/16/81, 5/14/86, 8/8/88;
Newman, *Hugo,* 514–15.

494–96   Hugo Black . . . Marshall repeated: *NYT,* 6/28,29/91, 1/24,30/93, 5/18/94;
WP, 6/28,29/91; Orfield, *Growth,* 7, 8; Williams, "The New," 24.

TABLE OF CASES

Index

564 • Index